VERITATEM DILEXI

I DELIGHT IN THE TRUTH

PATRONS
OF OFFERINGS TO ATHENA

This book has been made possible through the extraordinary generosity of the more than 250 people who became its patrons.

Special recognition is due to Susan L. Klaus '67 and Teresa Wallace '79 for their exceptional contributions to this effort.

Luann Wilkins Abrahams '87
Naidine Adams '81
Alexandra Q. Aldridge '57
Susan Alexander '78
Catherine Allegra '83
Barbara Allen '49
Genevieve Gish Allouche '12
Frances J. Ames '44, MA 1948
Sally A. Anson '52
Diana C. Applegate '01
Sue Auerbach '71
Cheryl Bailey '84
Anne D. Bailliere '63
Laura Bang '05
Arlene Baratz '80
Susan Barnes '76
Alexis L. Beattie '03
Lois Beekey '55
Katherine Bell '90
Sandra M. Berwind, PhD 1968
Lynne K. Beust '77
Alice Biays '59
Kimberly Blessing '97
Star Bloom '60
Karen Blumberg '95
Margaret Brandt '80
Suzanne Myers Broughton '58
Bryn Mawr Club of Boston
Ioana Butoi '05
Karen Bye '75
Erica Roggeveen Byrne '03
Terry Callaghan '82
Helen Mae Carter '85
Ann S. Carton '49
Joanna Casson '87
Raeleen Chai-Elsholz AB/MA '89
Milagros Cisneros '88
Louise Morley Cochrane '40
Frances H. Colburn '58
Jessica Bourne Collett '06
Michèle Cahen Cone '51
Alison Cook-Sather
Chaya Coppersmith '11
Lubov Coverdell '87
Nancy Craig '73
Kathryn Crecelius '73
Marilyn Reigle Crichlow '53
Tamara Crispin '85
Sheila Dickison PhD 1972
Katherine Dixon-Peugh '87
Michele D. Dominy '75
Valerie Donely '12
Betsy A. Duren '82
Melinda K. Durr '01
Judith L. Ellenbogen '62
Grace Farmer '66
Kara Faust '74

Suzanne Fedunok '67
Courtney Fennimore '99
Katharine C. Fischer '62
Dianne Coady Fisher '82
Brooke Stengel Fitzgerald '91
Ann Dennis Foley '71
Barbara Freedman '70
Helen Freeman '02
Lynn Gabriel '84
Marian Gamble '37, in memory of
Sarah Gant '81
Sara Garcia '97
Norma Garcia-Kennedy '77
Graham H. Gavert, MA 1984
Emma Geering '14
Laura Gellert '93
Gwen P. Gentile '58
Anne George-Hallgren '11
Elizabeth B. Gerlach '48
Jane L. Gerson '59
Carol Keyes Gilgen '54
Mary Kay Gilliland '78
Ellen Ginzler '65
Erin Glaser '11
Ronnie L. Goldberg '69
Margaret L. Goodman '58
Cary Berliss Goodman '80
Deborah Goodman '99
Katherine M. Gordon-Clark '56, MA 1974, PhD 1983
Leslie Anne Gossage '75
Alyse Gray '78
Lois Green '52
Rebecca Nowlin Green '93
Wendy Marcus Greenfield
Elaine Greenstone MA 1951
Janet Groff Greever '42
Priscilla C. Grew '62
Suzan S. Habachy '54
Madelyn Brown Harris '36
Nan Alderfer Harris '51
Kendra Hayde '09
Rita Rubinstein Heller '59
Angie Emery Henderson '95
Susan Kulp Herder '92
Lori Hess '87
Patricia Page Hitchcock '58
Erin Epstein Hoffmeier '02
Sally Rush Hogan
Jane McAllen Holt '43
Karen Hubler '87
John H. Humphrey PhD 1975 and Laura G. Humphrey MSS 1974
Ingrid Marian Irvin
Arlene B. Isaacson '76
Trish Richardson Jamison '52

Edie Jamison '78
Anne Jensen '78
Susan Johnson '62
Linda Rios Johnson '82
Diantha Haviland Johnson PhD 1964
Susan Jongeneel '75
Sheena Joyce '98
Catherine Hoffman Kaser '95
Marion Coen Katzive '62
Katherine S. Kellom '09
Karol Kepchar '84
Karen Ketterer '87
Cheryl M. Lee Kim '91
Gretchen Kingsley '61
Erika Klar '92
Susan L. Klaus '67
Julia Kossack '84
Jan Kristoff '93
Julia Ku '60
Jeanney Kutner '68
Jean Lacovara
Betsy Miller Landis '57
Tiffany Smith Langlas '92
Nan Lassner '71
Edith R. Lauderdale '50
Margery Peterson Lee '51
Eunice Lee '97
Maxine Lewis '58
Elisa Tractman Lewis MA 1995
Melissa Cohn Lindbeck '97
Sandra Linkletter PhD 1980
Myra Ann Rosenthal Lipman '60
Linda Butler Livesay
Norma Kent Lockwood '53
Ann Logan '76
Monique Loh '79
Andrea Lurie '68
Susan L. MacLaurin '84
Masako Maekawa MA 1960
Samuel Magdovitz
Sally Mallory '59, PhD 1963
Stephanie M. Maroney PhD 1986
Joseph Marra
Linda Matrunich '74
Patricia Paden Matsen PhD 1968
Mary Carter McConnell '75
Marsha B. McCoy '74
Sarah McGiffert '79
Eve Memmo '84
Heidi Merkel '88
Constance Murphy Miller '42
Rachel Moloshok '05
June Donzé & Briana Laraine ('07) Morgan
Barbara Morrison '62
Elizabeth Mosier '84

Yasuko Oma Moyer '79
Joan Vachule Murrin '75
Catherine Myers '55
Deborah Nedelman '69
Carol Nelson '81
Rhonda Newton '90
Dana Niblack '93
Myrtle (Mike) D. Niccolls '39
Carol Nicholson PhD 1977
Sofia Novoa Sanjurjo MSS 1980
Marghrita L. Oneil '47
Elaine Oran '66
Sydney J. Owens '64
Audrey Pappas-Wragg '83
Ruth Ann Parish '73
Ann Peters '59
Fabrizio, Minerva '12 and Diana Pinto
Italo and Maria Ginevra Saddi Pinto
Jane Phillips Power '60
Marge Pyle
Whitney Quesenbery '76
Michele Rasmussen
Esther Ratner '69
Beryl Wilkinson Rawson PhD 1961
Tammi Reichel '87
Sarah Reynolds '83
Geraldine E. Rhoads '35
Lucy Ricardo '54
Jim and Gaye Richardson
Hilary Richardson '07
Bonnie Allen Riley '38
Madhavi Rizzio '86
Barbara Paul Robinson '62
Joanna Semel Rose '52
Ariel Rosenstock '11
Steven Rothman and Janice Fisher
Gail Rudnitsky '74
Francesca Ruggiero '76
Samantha P. Salazar '11
Katie Salley '00
Cynthia Saltzman and Perry Dane
Dorothy Samuels '73
Nancy Johnson Sanquist '73
Elizabeth Schulze '79
Samara Schwartz '05
Patricia S. Schwartz '68
Mary Scott MA 1986
Aubrey Levy Sebestyen '02
Sabrina Seidner '85
Hilary Sennett '03
Carolyn Monka Serota '70
Blake Sherblom-Woodward '03
Elliott Shore PhD 1984
Mary Frances Slahetka-Rabito '81
Thalia Smith-Segal '85
Alla Smyslova PhD 2009

Nancy L. Snyder '53
Lita H. Solis-Cohen '52
Susan Speers '51
Nicole A.B. Spencer '92
Melanie Sharp Sprague '91
Heather Staines
Gillian Steinhauer '59
Chris Stepien Nevill '97
Sandol Stoddard '48
Caryn Stoess '89
Nausicaa Halkias Stoltz '80
Kathleen Lynch Strauss
Chiemi Suzuki '00
Barbara Teichert '75
Katrina Thomas '49
Adrian Tinsley '58
Barbara Trimble '60
Jane Miller Unkefer '55
Kaye Van Valkenburg '74
Joanne Vanin '69, PhD 1982
Eleni Victoria Varitimos '93
Trina Vaux
Donna L. Vogel '71
Gail Carter Volpe '74
Christie Walker '13
Teresa Wallace '79
Jennifer Wampler '95
Lisa Wardle '06
Lepska Warren '44
Elizabeth Curran Warren '49
Elizabeth Vogel Warren '72
Jean Warshaw '77
Julia D. Watkins '39
Betsy Watkins '61
Carolyn Wei '96
Joanna Weiss '96
Patricia West '79
Evelyn White MA 1956
Bina Williams '75
Brooke Williams '98
Caroline C. Willis '66
Mary Kopczynski Winkler '90
Lydia Witman '00
Bertie Dawes Wood '52
James Wright PhD 1978
Stephanie Wujcik '08
Melissa Young '80
Sally Hoover Zeckhauser '64
Un-Jin Paik Zimmerman '56, PhD 1961

PATRONS
OF OFFERINGS TO ATHENA

THIS BOOK HAS BEEN MADE POSSIBLE THROUGH THE EXTRAORDINARY GENEROSITY
OF THE MORE THAN 250 PEOPLE WHO BECAME ITS PATRONS.

SPECIAL RECOGNITION IS DUE TO SUSAN L. KLAUS '67 AND TERESA WALLACE '79
FOR THEIR EXCEPTIONAL CONTRIBUTIONS TO THIS EFFORT.

Luana Wilkins Abrahams '87
Naidine Adams '81
Alexandra O. Aldridge '57
Susan Alexander '78
Catherine Allegra '83
Barbara Allen '49
Genevieve Gish Alloudre '12
Frances J. Ames '44, MA 1948
Sally A. Anson '52
Diana C. Applegate '01
Sue Auerbach '71
Cheryl Bailey '84
Anne D. Bailliere '63
Laura Bang '05
Arlene Baratz '80
Susan Barnes '76
Alexis L. Beattie '03
Lois Becker '55
Katherine Bell '90
Sandra M. Berwind, PhD 1968
Lynne K. Beust '77
Alice Biays '59
Kimberly Blessing '97
Star Bloom '60
Karen Blumberg '95
Margaret Brandt '80
Suzanne Myers Broughton '58
Bryn Mawr Club of Boston
Ioana Butoi '05
Karen Bye '75
Erica Roggeveen Byrne '03
Terry Callaghan '82
Helen Mae Carter '85
Ann S. Carton '49
Joanna Casson '87
Radeen Chai-Elsholz AB/MA '89
Milagros Cisneros '88
Louise Morley Cochrane '40
Frances H. Colburn '58
Jessica Bourne Collett '06
Michèle Cahen Cone '51
Alison Cook-Sather
Chaya Coppersmith '11
Lubov Coverdell '87
Nancy Craig '73
Kathryn Crecelius '73
Marilyn Reigle Cridlow '53
Tamara Crispin '85
Sheila Dickison PhD 1972
Katherine Dixon-Pugh '87
Michele D. Dominy '75
Valerie Donely '12
Betsy A. Duran '82
Melinda K. Durr '01
Judith L. Ellenbogen '62
Grace Farmer '66
Kara Faust '74

Trish Richardson Jamison '52
Arlene B. Isaacson '76
Ingrid Marian Irvin
MSS 1974
John H. Humphrey PhD 1975
and Laura G. Humphrey
Karen Hubler '87
Jane McAllen Holt '43
Sally Rush Hogan
Erin Epstein Hoffmeier '02
Patricia Page Hitchcock '58
Lori Hess '87
Susan Kulp Herder '92
Angie Emery Henderson '95
Rita Rubinstein Heller '59
Kendra Hayde '09
Nan Alderfer Harris '51
Madelyn Brown Harris '36
Suzan S. Habachy '54
Priscilla C. Grew '62
Janet Groff Greever '42
Elaine Greenstone MA 1951
Wendy Marcus Greenfield
Rebecca Nowlin Green '93
Lois Green '52
Alyse Gray '78
Leslie Anne Gossage '75
MA 1974, PhD 1983
Katherine M. Gordon-Clark '56,
Maxine Lewis '58
Deborah Goodman '99
Cary Berliss Goodman '80
Margaret L. Goodman '58
Ronnie L. Goldberg '69
Erin Glaser '11
Ellen Ginzler '65
Mary Kay Gilliland '78
Jeanney Kutner '68
Carol Keyes Gilger '54
Jane L. Gerson '59
Elizabeth B. Gerlach '48
Anne George-Hallgren '11
Gwen P. Gentile '58
Laura Gellert '93
Emma Geering '14
Graham H. Gaver, MA 1984
Norma Garcia-Kennedy '77
Sara Garcia '97
Sarah Gant '81
Marian Gamble '37, in memory of
Lynn Gabriel '84
Helen Freeman '02
Barbara Freedman '70
Ann Dennis Foley '71
Brooke Stengel Fitzgerald '91
Dianne Coady Fisher '82
Katharine C. Fischer '62
Courtney Fennimore '99
Suzanne Fedunok '67

Edie Jamison '78
Anne Jensen '78
Susan Johnson '62
Linda Rios Johnson '82
Diantha Haviland Johnson
PhD 1964
Susan Jongeneel '75
Sheena Joyce '98
Catherine Hoffman Kaser '95
Marion Coen Karzive '62
Katherine S. Kellom '09
Karol Kepchar '84
Karen Kercrer '87
Cheryl M. Lee Kim '91
Gretchen Kingsley '61
Erika Klar '92
Susan L. Klaus '67
Julia Kossack '84
Jan Kristoff '93
Julia Ku '60
Carol Keyes Gilger '54
Jean Lacovara
Betsy Miller Landis '57
Tiffany Smith Langlas '92
Nan Lasner '71
Edith R. Lauderdale '50
Margery Peterson Lee '51
Eunice Lee '97
Lucy Ricardo '54
Elisa Tractman Lewis MA 1995
Melissa Cohn Lindbeck '97
Sandra Linkletter PhD 1980
Bonnie Allen Riley '38
Madhavi Rizzio '86
Barbara Paul Robinson '62
Linda Barler Livesay
Norma Kent Lockwood '53
Ann Logan '76
Monique Loh '79
Andrea Lurie '68
Susan L. MacLaurin '84
Masako Mackawa MA 1960
Samantha P. Salazar '11
Karie Salley '00
Cynthia Saltzman and Perry Dane
Sally Mallory '59, PhD 1963
Stephanie M. Maroney PhD 1986
Joseph Marza
Linda Matrunich '74
Elizabeth Schulze '79
Patricia Paden Matsen PhD 1968
Mary Carter McConnell '75
Marsha B. McCoy '74
Sarah McGiffert '79
Eve Memmo '84
Heidi Merkel '88
Constance Murphy Miller '42
Rachel Moloshok '05
June Donze & Briana Laraine
('07) Morgan
Barbara Morrison '62
Elizabeth Mosier '84

Yasuko Oma Moyer '79
Joan Vaduki Murrin '75
Catherine Myers '55
Deborah Nedelman '69
Carol Nelson '81
Rhonda Newton '90
Dana Niblack '93
Myrtle (Mike) D. Niccolls '39
Carol Nicholson PhD 1977
Sofia Novoa Sanjurjo MSS 1980
Margarita L. Oneil '47
Elaine Oran '66
Sydney J. Owens '64
Audrey Pappas-Wragg '83
Ruth Ann Parish '73
Ann Peters '59
Fabrizio, Minerva '12
and Diana Pinto
Italo and Maria Ginevra Saddi Pinto
Jane Phillips Power '60
Julia Ku '60
Jeanney Kutner '68
Marge Pyle
Whitney Quesenbery '76
Michèle Rasmussen
Esther Ramer '69
Beryl Wilkinson Rawson PhD 1961
Tammi Reichel '87
Sarah Reynolds '83
Geraldine E. Rhoads '35
Lucy Ricardo '54
Jim and Gaye Richardson
Hilary Richardson '07
Bonnie Allen Riley '38
Madhavi Rizzio '86
Barbara Paul Robinson '62
Joanna Semel Rose '52
Ariel Rosenstock '11
Steven Rothman and Janice Fisher
Gail Rudinsky '74
Francesca Ruggiero '76
Samantha P. Salazar '11
Karie Salley '00
Cynthia Saltzman and Perry Dane
Dorothy Samuels '73
Nancy Johnson Sanquist '73
Elizabeth Schulze '79
Samara Schwartz '05
Patricia S. Schwartz '68
Mary Scott MA 1986
Aubrey Levy Sebescyen '02
Sabrina Seidner '85
Hilary Sennett '03
Carolyn Monka Serota '70
Blake Sherblom-Woodward '03
Elliott Shore PhD 1984
Mary Frances Slatetka-Rabiro '81
Thalia Smith-Segal '85
Alla Smyslova PhD 2009

Nancy L. Snyder '53
Lita H. Solis-Cohen '52
Susan Speers '51
Nicole A.B. Spencer '92
Melanie Sharp Sprague '91
Heather Staines
Gillian Steinhauer '59
Chris Stepien Nevill '97
Sandal Stoddard '48
Caryn Stoess '89
Nausicaa Halkias Stoltz '80
Kathleen Lynch Strauss
Chieru Suzuki '00
Barbara Teichert '75
Karina Thomas '49
Adrian Tinsley '58
Barbara Trimble '60
Jane Miller Unkeles '55
Kaye Van Valkenburg '74
Joanne Vanin '69, PhD 1982
Eleni Victoria Varrimos '93
Trina Vaux
Donna L. Vogel '71
Gail Carter Volpe '74
Christie Walker '13
Teresa Wallace '79
Jennifer Wampler '95
Lisa Wardle '06
Lepska Warren '44
Elizabeth Curran Warren '49
Elizabeth Vogel Warren '72
Jean Warshaw '77
Julia D. Watkins '39
Betsy Watkins '61
Carolyn Wei '96
Joanna Weiss '96
Patricia West '79
Evelyn White MA 1956
Bina Williams '75
Brooke Williams '98
Caroline C. Willis '66
Mary Kopczynski Winkler '90
Lydia Witman '00
Bertie Dawes Wood '52
James Wright PhD 1978
Stephanie Wujcik '08
Melissa Young '80
Sally Hoover Zeckhauser '64
Un-Jin Paik Zimmerman '56,
PhD 1961

OFFERINGS TO ATHENA
125 YEARS AT BRYN MAWR COLLEGE
EDITED BY ANNE L. BRUDER

For Mawrters of yesterday, today, and tomorrow
Published on the occasion of the 125th anniversary of Bryn Mawr College

Front cover: M. Carey Thomas Library, southeast entrance, 2010.
Photograph by Rick Echelmeyer

Back cover: Taylor Tower, 2009. Photograph by Jim Roese

Frontispiece: Student with Athena Lemnia, Thomas Great Hall,
c. 1960s–70s *(center)*

Friends of the Bryn Mawr College Library
101 North Merion Avenue
Bryn Mawr, PA 19010
brynmawr.edu/library/fol.html

Edited by Anne L. Bruder
Designed by Tom Maciag and Rachel Shaw, Dyad Communications
Manufactured in China by Crystal World Printing

Copies of this publication may be purchased by writing to the publisher
or at amazon.com.

All rights reserved. No part of this publication may be reproduced or
transmitted in any form or by any means, electronic or mechanical,
without permission in writing from the publisher.

Every attempt has been made to find the copyright holders of works
reproduced herein. Any omission is unintentional.

Texts and illustrations courtesy of the Bryn Mawr College Archives unless
otherwise noted.

Text and compilation © 2010 Friends of the Bryn Mawr College Library

Copyright notices for individual texts and illustrations appear on page 398

Library of Congress Control Number 2010912657
ISBN 978-0-615-39868-6

CONTENTS

PREFACE BY ANNE L. BRUDER iv

FOREWORD BY PRESIDENT JANE McAULIFFE vi

Foundations: 1885–1922 1

New Directions: 1922–1942 77

Steady Aims in Changing Times: 1942–1970 127

Cooperative Developments: 1970–1978 223

Determined Leadership: 1978–1997 283

Bold Visions for Today and Tomorrow: 1997–2010 345

TRADITIONS

LANTERN NIGHT 53

MAY DAY 109

HELL WEEK 277

PARADE NIGHT 335

PREFACE

As record snows blanketed campus last winter, I divided my time between wading through Bryn Mawr's rich photography archive, perusing decades of *College News* and *Alumnae Bulletin* issues, and teaching a course to sixteen lively students on women's autobiography. It was a fortuitous marriage of occupations, examining Mawrters of the past as I engaged—and was engaged by—Mawrters of the present. Images of and texts about committed students immersed in the process of self-discovery and institutional change at the turn of the twentieth century began to take shape in these pages. At the same time, my students showed me the ways they were adapting to Bryn Mawr in the twenty-first century, even as Bryn Mawr continues to adapt itself to each successive generation of students.

Every September, in fact, Bryn Mawr defines itself anew. Customs people and traditions mistresses shepherd young women through the rhythms of the academic year, from Parade Night to May Day, from exam studying to plenary. The college's traditions continue to help define the Bryn Mawr experience, bringing forth the past as they weave together generations of students. Yet, this community on a high hill never has been a static place. In its foundational commitment to academic excellence, the college continues to embrace new scholarship, new ways of thinking, and new technologies. Each of these commitments give students a desire to continue their learning and to expand their questions long after they receive their diplomas. For 125 years, Bryn Mawr has helped turn bold visions into remarkable achievements.

Bryn Mawr, as each page of this volume illustrates, has a rich and compelling history, and more than a single story to tell about itself. There are, in fact, many Bryn Mawr histories, any number of which could, and have, sustained entire volumes. In editing this book, I had to identify an avenue through the countless narratives, some part lore and others fact, that Bryn Mawr has inspired over the past 125 years. Previous volumes have chronicled the lives of its leaders and departmental and curricular developments. An excellent collection of essays published in 1987 for the college's centennial, Patricia Hochschild Labalme's *A Century Recalled*, offered keen insights into the academic and administrative changes that enlivened Bryn Mawr during its first one hundred years. *Offerings to Athena* presents readers with a different kind of history, one that foregrounds the story of the student experience. Like the modest but ever-accumulating offerings—shiny Mardi Gras beads, fuchsia lipstick, wilting lavender, empty chardonnay bottles, stuffed owls—that even today wait at Athena's feet in Thomas Great Hall, these pages contain the colorful scraps of student life that call our attention back to the experience of living together in the shared pursuit of new ideas, fresh perspectives, and daring curiosity.

The principal editorial method that guided this project was to reproduce faithfully the writings that have animated Bryn Mawr. Unless otherwise indicated, all of the materials reproduced in this volume come from the Bryn Mawr College Archives in the Mariam Coffin Canaday Library. One hundred and twenty-five years of Bryn Mawr students wrote the majority of these texts while they bustled between Taylor and Merion, between chemistry class and field hockey practice. Other offerings, like those from the *New York Times* and the *Saturday Evening Post*, suggest that what Bryn Mawr students do—whether forging new institutional practices or performing cutting-edge plays—matters in the larger story about educational life in this country.

This volume does not attempt to modernize or standardize these texts, in style or in content, to fit current expectations or practices. This means that there is necessarily a good deal of eclecticism, perhaps even eccentricity, in composition and form. Obvious printing errors and inconsistencies within original documents, however, have been corrected silently. In order to preserve the meaning and intention of the original texts, I have not made changes in wording, though I have added missing punctuation or capitalization, or inserted brief identifications, where needed for clarity. Many of the early documents in this volume were unsigned in the original. In the case of signed student articles, however, class years, inconsistently included in the original materials, have been added to the bylines. Many of the photographs in the college's archives and reproduced here are identified in the haziest manner. Student names are often unknown and dates have, at times, been added later after a good deal of guesswork and best approximations. The captions in these pages represent what information we have about the images, although there may be incidents in which our best guesses fall short of the mark.

This book is the product of much collaboration—across time and disciplines, and among students, faculty, and staff. My work was made infinitely easier through the assistance of a group of stalwart students who meticulously transcribed their sister Mawrters' words. Undergraduates Lena Barnard, Ellie Easton, Lauren Russell, and Seth West and graduate student Angelique Wille typed scores of articles with the utmost care. Senior Taline Cox transcribed hundreds more from September 2009 to May 2010, and managed to rally my optimism about the project's eventual completion. Sarah Sheplock and Marybeth Matlack, both class of 2010, picked up missing pieces here and there.

Art History graduate student Amy Haavik-MacKinnon joined the project relatively late, yet managed to leave her careful mark on nearly all aspects of it. These students not only helped make this book possible in tangible ways, but also taught me what it means to live and learn at Bryn Mawr today.

Elliott Shore, the Constance A. Jones Director of Libraries and professor of history, along with the board of the Friends of the Bryn Mawr College Library, initiated the conversation that led to this book. My colleagues in Special Collections have often set aside their own work to answer countless questions and to help me track down missing photographs and documents time and again. Emily Croll, Cheryl Klimaszewski, Marianne Hansen, Lorett Treese, and Marianne Weldon supported this project in spirit and in deed. College staff members Emily Espenshade, Matt Gray, Tracy Kellmer, Ruth Lindeborg, Marge Pyle, and Jan Trembley helped locate recent images for the volume's final pages. Eric Pumroy, head of Special Collections and Seymour Adelman Rare Book Librarian, lent this project his fullest attention, offered me a long leash, and showed me generous amounts of patience and support. Elliott Shore nurtured this project from the beginning and championed its progress and its celebration of students. Janice Fisher offered her clear eyes and red pen in the final days of the project. Sarah Noreika, class of 2002, copyedited the text with the precision you'd expect from a Bryn Mawr graduate. Finally, I feel very fortunate to have worked closely with Tom Maciag, of Dyad Communications in Philadelphia, and his associate Rachel Shaw on the design of this book. Their remarkable work is evident on each page.

Now dive in, get lost in the past, and prepare yourselves for Bryn Mawr's next century and a quarter. May it be as productive, as thrilling, and as engaged as its last.

ANNE L. BRUDER
Editor
August 2010

FOREWORD

On the occasion of our 125th anniversary, I am delighted to offer the world-wide Bryn Mawr community this splendid new book. The College is justly proud of its academic achievements and institutional advancements, and I am confident you will celebrate the rich legacy of learning this volume records. I hope your attention will also be captured by the countless visuals and vignettes that convey the evolving narrative of this extraordinary community. In their totality, they commemorate the faculty, staff, students, alumnae/i, parents and friends whose love of Bryn Mawr and dedication to its ideals have enriched our first century and a quarter and have secured for the College a future of purpose and promise.

This book, like most books, has a history. In January 2008, during the final stage of Bryn Mawr's search for its next president, I had dinner with the senior leadership of the college. At one point, talk turned to the historic anniversary that the school would soon be celebrating. Suddenly, Elliott Shore, the Constance A. Jones Director of Libraries and professor of history, exclaimed, "We should do a book!" This launched an animated conversation that I was delighted to resume in my first months as president. During that period, Elliott began to shape the project with generous support and advice from the Friends of the Library, especially its chair, Teresa Wallace. Thanks to the Friends, we were able to recruit the good services of our wonderful editor, Anne L. Bruder, who recently earned a doctorate in English from the University of North Carolina, with a dissertation on alternative forms of women's education in late-nineteenth-century America. Elliott also set his students to work digging up new material for the class that he teaches about the College's history.

As Elliott and Anne showed me early stages of the manuscript, I shared their excitement at the range and diversity of archival material that had come to light. My attention was immediately captured by so many aspects of what you now hold in your hands. I was absorbed by the faces, the beautiful, earnest faces of our students as they gaze out at us from generations of class photos. I read with special interest the 1943 *Fortune Magazine* article about Bryn Mawr's war years, having just met alumnae at the 2010 reunion who were students during that period and who remembered all the changes—and all the continuities. I have returned again and again to the stunning photo of President Katharine McBride in animated conversation with Dr. Martin Luther King, Jr. It speaks to me of the historic stands that she took in the face of severe pressure as well as of how Bryn Mawr College strives to create an ever more diverse and inclusive community. I am sure that as you enjoy this volume you will find your own favorites, evocative texts and images that spark memories and renew your affection for this unique and cherished place.

JANE McAULIFFE
President
August 2010

Above: Students arriving on campus, c. 1940s

Foundations: 1885–1922

BRYN MAWR: A CHARACTERIZATION
HELEN THOMAS FLEXNER, *Class of 1893*

In the autumn of 1886, James Russell Lowell, in his benevolent and charming old age, traveled south from New England to give the encouragement of his presence and the inspiration of his advice to the students and faculty and trustees of Bryn Mawr College, then about to enter on the first year of its existence. He found the teaching staff and the students of the new institution a mere handling of people, sixty in all, for whom the three buildings then standing afforded ample accommodation. Mr. Henry James, in Bryn Mawr twenty years later on the same kindly errand, was met by a very different state of things. The long line of young women in caps and gowns, stretching far over the lawn as they waited for him to appear before proceeding to the assembly hall, represented only a fraction of the students and alumnae of the college, grown to the number of 1,875, while the members of the teaching staff in their gorgeous robes crowded the library reading room inside of Taylor Hall. Even with the freshmen and sophomores excluded, there was still too little space in the assembly hall for visitors, since the seven great buildings which have been added to the original three contain no auditorium, but have been put up to supply the more pressing needs of the community. The growth of the college in two decades, it will thus be seen, has been rapid; surprisingly rapid, when it is remembered that every year a large number of candidates for admission are found by the entrance examinations to fall short of the standard of excellence required and are therefore excluded. From the first the college has valued the quality of its students and alumnae far more than their numbers, and has bent all its efforts to making the education given them as good as possible and the influences surrounding them as harmonious. It was no doubt this spirit, already embodied in the courses of study announced before a single lecture had been delivered or student admitted, that interested Lowell in Bryn Mawr and has since brought to address her students a long line of distinguished men.

In the very beginning Bryn Mawr was favored by its situation, for it stands on the top and extends down the sides of a fair green hill conspicuous for its beauty among the many charming hills that form the environs of Philadelphia to the westward. The country is a fertile farming country, with many brooks running through it, many little valleys where the snow lingers un-melted in the spring time, and many rising knolls from which to get a pleasant outlook over meadows and woods. The original farm houses have now in many instances been replaced by big stone mansions and the simple country folk by denizens of the city, who have turned the countryside into a park, planting hedges of scarlet-flowering pyrus japonica, setting out fragrant magnolia trees and gorgeous rhododendrons, and training the festooning honeysuckle over many a trellis.

> IN THE VERY BEGINNING BRYN MAWR WAS FAVORED BY ITS SITUATION, FOR IT STANDS ON THE TOP AND EXTENDS DOWN THE SIDES OF A FAIR GREEN HILL CONSPICUOUS FOR ITS BEAUTY AMONG THE MANY CHARMING HILLS THAT FORM THE ENVIRONS OF PHILADELPHIA TO THE WESTWARD.

However, in certain corners, well known to the youthful pedestrian, the farmer is still to be seen driving his plough with its patient, slow-moving horses; cattle graze in the deep grass; and sheep nibble all day long under gnarled apple boughs. By good fortune one of the farms still remaining lies on the hill directly opposite the college, and a student of Wordsworth, let us say, can find an easy justification during the pauses of a recitation or lecture for watching out of Taylor Hall windows the upturning of the earth in March. To many young women who have been born and bred in cities and kept in them until June by necessity for attending school, their first spring at Bryn Mawr has proved an experience of much delight. To watch for the first time the tops of great forest trees grow green, to listen to the earliest, sweetest notes of the wood thrush, to read a romantic tale of Chaucer, the poet of spring, in a field studded over with daisies—these are indeed occupations never to be forgotten: and if by them a taste for the simple delights of the country has been cultivated, who can say they have not a serious value?

Moreover, those in authority at Bryn Mawr have not been slow to recognize the educational power of harmonious color and line. They have constructed a series of grey stone buildings in the late English Renaissance style of architecture, consecrated long ago to education by the halls of Oxford and Cambridge, and by care in their planning and placing have succeeded in producing an effect of true architectural beauty which has had, it may not be amiss to note, an immediate influence on the architecture of other American colleges. The boxlike simplicity of Dalton Hall, put up with the sole reference to the convenience of its laboratories and the economy of its constructions, and the mere serviceableness of Taylor and Merion halls are very little conspicuous, though still to be regretted. The beauty of Denbigh's long lines, Pembroke's stately towers and chimneys, and Rockefeller's ornamental gate, and above all the stately grace of the unfinished library building, are what strike the eye. The space enclosed on three sides by these buildings, to which access is gained by the archways that pierce their towers, is a green lawn planted with old apple trees, gnarled chestnuts and maples that turn golden in the autumn, and flowering shrubs of all kinds, while to the westward a view of undulating meadows fills up the picture. Here a crowd of young women, ever increasing and ever renewing itself, pass the busy hours of their student lives, and the images that meet them here are interwoven with their aspirations and thoughts, adding to them the element of beauty that has always so enchanted the human spirit.

It is not strange, then, that they should come to love with an almost pious devotion the grey stone walls that shelter them. They are familiar not only with every detail of the buildings now standing, but know also just what the plans for future buildings are, and share with the president of the college and the trustees the anxiety that each addition may be beautiful in itself and harmonious with the others, completing worthily their quadrangles. The fountain that is to stand in the center of the courtyard flanking the library, around which they will pace in thoughtful meditation or wander, it may be, idly arm in arm on a warm afternoon, has been the subject of discussion at many an informal gathering of students. With the instinctive right-mindedness of generous youth they understand that the beauty of their surroundings is a matter of vital importance in their development, and that any disfigurement of them would make the memories being stored up for the future by just so much the less precious. The following anecdote will serve to show to what lengths their interest will carry them. The question of just the curve to be taken by the stone walk leading from Taylor Hall across the lawn to the Owl gate of Rockefeller was to be decided last winter. After much consultation together they petitioned [M. Carey] Thomas, the president, asking that it might run in a certain direction, skirting but by no means disturbing a group of favorite Japanese cherry trees whose shower of pink blossoms looks so particularly pleasing in the spring time against the grey stone. And Miss Thomas was in her turn greatly displeased with the students for supposing that such a sacrifice could ever have been contemplated.

The college community is democratic and self-assertive, it will be seen. It does not hesitate to express its opinion even on subjects that might be considered beyond its sphere. For it is used to governing itself, making its own rules of conduct and imposing without fear or favor on delinquent members its own penalties for misbehavior through its association for self-government. And the salutary discipline of thus being responsible for themselves to themselves is found more than to compensate for any undue sense of self-importance and self-confidence fostered in the students by such a system.

But though it is democratic, the community is by no means undiscriminating. There are in it, at its head, three hierarchies founded on three forms of personal excellence. A girl of unusually strong character and principles is sure to be elected to the Executive Board of the Self-Government Association or to be made a Proctor with authority to keep order in her hall, and thus to exert a wide moral influence among her fellows. She is apt to take her duties very seriously, and has been known sometimes to feel that her afterlife can contain no problems more difficult to settle than some of the questions of discipline brought before her and her colleagues. The clever students in their turn form an aristocracy of intellect, setting fashions in books and ideas, and it is amusing to observe how quickly their guidance fashions prevail and how suddenly they change. One year the decorations will be pre-Raphaelite. On the walls of nearly every study will be seen the pure profiles and long lines of Burne-Jones's figures and the swelling throats and wonderful hair of Rossetti's women; while the next year Mona Lisa's mysterious personality will somehow have taken possession of the common imagination and her face will look down on many a merry party, assorting oddly with it and with the crimson Harvard flag displayed on the opposite wall. Emerson and Carlyle will be displaced from the position of honor on the bookcase shelves by Cardinal Newman and Jeremy Taylor; Thackeray will butt Hawthorne to rout, and vice versa. The third hierarchy is athletic. The student good at basketball, hockey and other sports is at Bryn Mawr as at other colleges something of an idol. It is a pretty sight to see these healthy young women playing together in the sunshine, running after their ball and tossing it down the green field with a wide sweep of vigorous young arms, and it is a small wonder that the whole college applauds. A senior class has been known to regard the loss of a college basketball championship as a calamity of almost national importance, and the personal supremacy of the class captains is naturally great.

As yet, however, there is no trace of an aristocracy of wealth or of social position at Bryn Mawr. It has happened in more than one case that a student who brought her maid with her to college found no use for her there, sent her home in six months' time, and lived the remaining three years and a half of her college course in great contentment unattended. And if a girl with very little command of money does tutoring in addition to her work it is not that she may indulge in amusements or fine clothes, after her necessary expenses are paid, but that she may buy books or have attractive pictures to hang on the walls of her study. A display of elaborate frocks is considered in the worst possible taste, and when it happens, as it sometimes has happened, that a young woman who seeks distinction by such means finds her way to Bryn Mawr, she rarely stays for more than a year in an atmosphere so unsympathetic. Moreover, the individual who attempts to discriminate in the choice of her friends along lines of external worldly importance is at once sent to Coventry as a snob, and life is made anything but pleasant for her until she evinces a change of heart.

It is interesting to fancy the effect of entering such a community on the average girl of seventeen or eighteen. Occasionally, no doubt, the discipline of standing entirely on her own merits is as severe as it is salutary. She must undergo a painful struggle before she finds her level, and is able to accept the frank impartiality of her fellow-students and professors as just rather than cruel. Her susceptibilities are often more keenly developed than those of a boy, than her brother's let us say, since from the time she was an engaging little girl with golden hair and a pink sash she has been more petted and indulged than him and more closely guarded from impersonal outside influences. In some way, no doubt, she manages to feel that she is asserting her feminine charm when, for instance, she tells her professor of philosophy that she "never had any logical power."

The quick answer, "Say rather, Miss X, that you never had a mind," gives her a not altogether agreeable shock. But even should her capabilities doom her finally to insignificance, if she not be healthy minded, she will still after the first shock is over be quite free from jealousy of the more favoured. Indeed a long observation of girls at college has taught me to know that in contradiction to the popular superstition in regard to feminine envy, they are most generous in praise of each other. They take a sincere delight in each other's good looks and also in each other's cleverness.

And it is entirely natural that this should be the case. Each individual is unceasingly busy. At twenty minutes to nine o'clock in the morning the big bell in Taylor Hall tower warns her that it is time for chapel. She snatches up her black mortarboard, pulls her gown over her shoulders and hurries out across the windy, sunlit campus, the empty green spaces of which have at the sound of the bell become suddenly astir with bright-haired figures, whose voices make a chatter like the chatter of birds. After the religious exercises with which the day begins are over, her time until luncheon is filled with recitations and lectures, interspersed with an hour or two perhaps for study in the library or her own room. She cannot afford to idle at this time and only the most beautiful day will beguile her into taking a walk or playing tennis, though if she is athletic she may have got up early to practice before chapel, tossing the ball into the basket. In the autumn or spring time she will, however, often bring her books out into the open air and sit absorbed like a girlish Buddha at the foot of a tree, unconscious of fellow Buddhas under trees all about her. Occasionally, no doubt, she will be diverted from her studies by an unusually exciting canvass for officers of the Self-Government Association, or by a vital difference of opinion on some question of morals or politics with one of her friends. Then she will wander out deep in conversation down the hill into the meadows in back of the Low Buildings, where the stream "Meander," beautiful at all seasons, winds under willow trees, and where the hourly sound of the bell swinging down to her will warn her of the passage of time; but this will not often happen. Visitors to Bryn Mawr, younger sisters and friends, have been known to complain that the college is a dreary place in the morning, when the brief intervals of bustle between the changing of the classes are succeeded by long periods of deep silence, and the slow moving shadows of the buildings and trees clearly outlined on the grass are the only things one can find to watch from the window of a deserted room. The afternoon, though no less busy, is more diversified. While many students are occupied in Dalton Hall doing laboratory work until four o'clock, others may be seen starting off immediately after lunch for a drive, or with a merry clatter of horses' hoofs for a gallop over the hills, or in short skirts for a long tramp before the daylight fails. All the tennis courts are occupied in the afternoon; the basket-ball and hockey fields are never empty and the gymnasium and swimming pool present lively scenes. Between two o'clock and seven the day's exercise must be taken, and some studying, if a student is wise, must be done. In the evening it is pleasant to sit before a bright fire with her friends and talk over the many things that cry out for discussion; she may have to learn her part for some college play soon to be acted; there are Glee Club songs to be practiced; there is class business to be attended to; and always there is the work for the next day's classes to be prepared. Four hundred and ninety-nine girls out of five hundred finally fall asleep at night without having had the time or the inclination for wistful comparisons of themselves with their companions.

The pleasure of even the dullest student in the independent use of her mind, when she attains to it, is quite touching in its intensity and is in its essence pure. I have myself seen more than one young girl's face made radiant by the realization, for instance, that she could form her own opinions of poetry and had learned, on however modest a scale, to judge of it and appreciate it for herself. And I know a Bryn Mawr student for whom the world of nature was made infinitely beautiful and mysterious by her study of the myriad forms of life that inhabit a single pool. To gaze at the great stars of Orion's sword and belt flaming low in the east over twilight fields, and to appreciate on what countless individuals, through what uncounted ages, they have shed their light, is for a moment's imagination to be freed from the limits of time and space individuality. One goes back to the narrow circumstances of one's daily life greatly the happier because of such experiences as these. For every human being the way of escape from the tyranny of circumstance is spiritual and intellectual—*internum aeternum*, as St. Augustine's famous phrase briefly puts it. Women's lives are, it is generally conceded, more restricted than men's, far narrower and more monotonous, and it would therefore seem that no more benevolent use of talent or of money could be made than the use of them to open to women the way of escape through the mind and the imagination.

> I HAVE MYSELF SEEN MORE THAN ONE YOUNG GIRL'S FACE MADE RADIANT BY THE REALIZATION, FOR INSTANCE, THAT SHE COULD FORM HER OWN OPINIONS OF POETRY AND HAD LEARNED, ON HOWEVER MODEST A SCALE, TO JUDGE OF IT AND APPRECIATE IT FOR HERSELF.

Bryn Mawr does not permit her undergraduate students to specialize beyond a certain point. All alike must devote one third of one year's work to studying some science; another third of a year's work to another science, or to a course in political economy, history law or mathematics; another third to the history of philosophy; another third to the fourth language omitted at entrance; and another third for two years to the study of English literature and of the correct writing and the correct pronunciation of the English language. In the two years that remain to her of the four years' course she may study exclusively any two allied subjects, though she may also diversify her work in certain prescribed ways; but even should she take full advantage of the permission to specialize, she will still have received a broad general foundation for her special learning. And, on the other hand, be her instincts never so catholic, she is forced to devote herself for a whole year and a third to her "major subjects," for instance, chemistry and physics, Greek and Latin, political economy and history and the like, and so is prevented from being too superficial.

Perhaps the most distinctively characteristic point shown by the above summary of requirements is the stress laid by them on English. One-sixth of a student's whole time as an undergraduate must, it has been seen, be devoted to a study of English literature and to the improvement of her power of expressing herself in English. She must study not only the construction of sentences and paragraphs and the meanings of words, she must also learn the proper enunciation of vowels and consonants and the proper accentuation of syllables in so far as they can be taught in a short time. Her attention is called to the provincialisms and inaccuracies of her individual pronunciation, and exercises are given to help her to correct her faults. The mere serious comparison of her way of speaking with that of her companions and of her teacher, an Englishman highly trained in the art of enunciation and the management of the voice, be she never so careless and indifferent, calls her attention at once to the varying beauty and harshness of various tones of voice and various enunciations. When mimicked by her teacher, her way of vocalizing a given sentence leaves her no possibility of self-delusion. She may make jokes about the matter, and often in fact does; she may practice trilling her r's, for instance, so persistently and so loudly as to be a nuisance to all her neighbors, until a skit in the college paper celebrates her willful zeal to her great delight, but she can never again be wholly careless of her speech. She will be aware that her accent is provincial, and in very many cases she will endeavor to make it less provincial and will do her part to uphold a standard of good usage.

The greatest trial of the average Bryn Mawr student in her whole college course is perhaps her French and German senior oral examinations, and the jokes she makes about it, unlike those about her speech, are too serious really to amuse her. The fair degree of fluency in reading French and German upon which the college insists before giving the degree of A.B. to its students is tested by a committee of the faculty before which the seniors are brought up one by one to translate a few passages in each language at sight. In a little quiet room, awfully quiet, sit around a long table a member of the French or German department and another member of the faculty, with the president of the college presiding. Opposite Miss Thomas is a vacant chair and in that the student must take her seat. Of her French, perhaps, she is sure, but in spite of all the stories of Paul Heyse and the plays of Hauptmann she has been hurriedly reading, her German is still very shaky, as she would say, and she feels keenly the ignomiy of stumbling through sentences that are perfectly intelligible to the three grave, attentive persons about her. From the time she is a freshman the wise student does a little reading in French and German in preparation for this inevitable moment, and she sometimes even manages to use it as an excuse for persuading her family to spend a summer in France or Germany with her, which, if not quite necessary, is distinctly pleasant. And all her life she will feel the benefit of the ability thus acquired to read easily two modern languages beside her own.

Together with the effort to prevent young students from specializing unduly, mentioned in a previous paragraph, there is also a strong effort made at Bryn Mawr to encourage a desire on their part to continue their work along definite lines and to become scholars and producers. In this the college is greatly helped by its graduate department. Its graduate students usually number from 60 to 70, of whom about ten percent come up from the undergraduate department. The fellowships and scholarships, ranging from $200 to $525 in value, are open to graduates of all colleges of good standing, and the pecuniary assistance they give enables every year thirty young women to pursue graduate work in history, philosophy, classics, archaeology, science and oriental and modern languages. Moreover, every year Bryn Mawr sends abroad to English and continental universities, by means of her European fellowships, the member of the graduating class who has received the highest average on her college course, the most able graduate student of one year's standing at the college, and the most able student of two years' standing, making three in all. Many of these European fellows return to Bryn Mawr after their year abroad to complete their training and to receive the degree of doctor of philosophy.

This body of older and more serious women living with them exerts a strong influence on the undergraduates, and many a young student has felt the inspiration of the friendship with a graduate she has thus had the opportunity to form. Fellows frequently come to Bryn Mawr from foreign countries, from England and Canada especially, and from all the colleges in the United States to which women are admitted, and their presence makes against an excess of local pride. One year, for instance, three English girls came together from Cambridge, and being possessed of a truly British frankness of speech and having the support of their numbers and personal attractiveness, they soon made the community aware of its deficiencies. There was nothing they did not object to from the college pronunciation of Latin to the use of silver knives instead of steel, to the scarcity of "puddings with eggs." The returned European fellow enlivens many an afternoon walk with accounts of the methods and manners of foreign universities. She tells how Professor Sievers in Leipzig kindly promised to "overlook her presence" at his lectures—but that was some ten years ago; or more recently of how Professor von Wölflin, of Munich University, escorted her on his arm to the first Greek lecture of the term and gave her a seat of perfect security on the platform at a little desk by the side of his own desk; she explains that she had to take a young and very pretty sister with her as chaperon to a class in Oxford, of which she was the only woman member, and she describes the great kindness of the Master of Balliol, Dr. Caird, to her and a fellow student in asking them to do special work with him in his own study. She fires the imagination of her companions by tales of excavations in Greece or of researches among the manuscripts of the Record Office at Somerset House, as the case may be. But always her influence makes for broadness and modesty. She has learned, more surely perhaps than she ever could by staying at one institution, how small a thing in the world of scholarship her own attainments are, and her comrades clearly perceive how much she in her turn is their superior. And the resolutions they mutually form to devote themselves seriously to work in philology, to problems of education and government, to writing poetry or plays or novels, to scientific investigation and the like, have already borne good fruit.

After they leave the college about one-third of the graduates of Bryn Mawr engage in paying occupations, for the most part in the occupation of teaching, though there are among them lawyers, doctors, editors, librarians, secretaries and college settlement workers. The remainder continue their studies or return home to live with their families. They scatter into nearly every state in the Union and find their way east and west across the Pacific and Atlantic oceans, settling in Japan, in China, in the Hawaiian Islands, in Russia, in Denmark, in France and in England. But, however different the futures that await them, whether they are to be court ladies in the Orient or doctors in Iowa, they carry everywhere with them the memories, the knowledge and the spiritual ambitions given them in their youth.

There is, however, more at stake here than the personal fate of a few individuals, great as is the appeal that makes to the imagination. In a country like ours, which is as yet to a large extent democratic and fluid, the dismissal of her children by an educational institution has a quite peculiar importance. The great majority of them will remain in the United States, where they are not forced by class distinctions and by absence of opportunities to fit themselves into the niches occupied by the older generation, as in more rigidly organized countries the younger generation too often must do. Obviously they will use the instruments that have been put into their hands with an effectiveness at once inspiring and terrifying to contemplate. In the comparative absence of traditional checks, and assisted by the great number of opportunities open and by our national love of quick changes (love of progress we call it), they will everywhere with surprising rapidity begin to set standards, social, intellectual and moral. They will open schools and teach in colleges and be looked up to by simple communities as exponents of culture.

This state of things imposes on our educational institutions a heavy burden of responsibility, which they can adequately meet only by maintaining the greatest singleness of purpose and by never lowering their ideals to satisfy a popular desire for quick and easy education. In the twenty years since its opening the number of students at Bryn Mawr has necessarily greatly increased and there are at the present moment 437 students within its walls, but it is the avowed intention of those who direct its policy that the college shall remain small. By upholding a standard of scholarship and of culture that is difficult and not easy to attain, she will inevitably lose many students, but she will not regret the loss. Bryn Mawr has faith to believe that as long as her grey towers stand there will never be wanting youthful enthusiasm and youthful love of learning to inhabit them. Future generations will turn to her for inspiration. Be it her part never to betray her trust.

Reprinted from the *Bryn Mawr Alumnae Quarterly*, January 1908.

Page viii: Photograph of campus showing Taylor and Merion halls, 1889

Page 3: Helen Thomas Flexner (1871–1956), class of 1893 and younger sister of M. Carey Thomas, with her husband, Simon Flexner, and sons, James (left) and William (right)

Opposite: Helen Thomas Flexner, summer 1898

FOUNDER

JOSEPH WRIGHT TAYLOR
Quaker Physician Turned College Founder
Elizabeth Cabell Dugdale MacIntosh, Class of 1956

BORN TO A FAMILY of persecuted English Quakers who had sought refuge in New Jersey in the 1690s, Joseph Wright Taylor (1810–1880) was the youngest of Sarah and Edward Taylor's seven children. He was educated in Quaker schools, learned the apothecary's trade, and privately studied medicine and attended lectures at the University of Pennsylvania School of Medicine in Philadelphia. At age twenty, he sailed to India, serving as the ship's doctor; he would later tour Europe and the continental United States. In 1835, he moved to Cincinnati, where he worked in his brother Abraham's successful tanning and leather business. Having prospered during his time in Cincinnati, in 1851 he returned to the East Coast, where he resided as a country gentleman with his only sister, Hannah, at Woodlands, his estate in Burlington County, New Jersey.

"All of his friends thought of him as a consummate gentleman, with perfect manners, carefully chosen dress, and wise though restrained speech." He was a "fusion of gentleness and strength, of caution and boldness."[1] Influenced by books, sermons, and religious conversations, Taylor developed a broad Quaker faith that influenced his own life as well as the spiritual orientation of the college he was about to found. Taylor's bold ideas and muscular vision for the college, however, were not matched by a similarly vigorous physical strength; afflicted with severe rheumatic illness at age seventeen, he suffered poor health most of his life. As the campus came into its Gothic splendor, Taylor personally supervised construction with almost daily visits, rushing from his home in New Jersey to the ferry in Camden, then traveling by horsecar to Bryn Mawr, in all types of weather conditions. This unrelenting pace resulted in severe strain on his heart, and on January 18, 1880 —five years before the first students would arrive on the campus that became Bryn Mawr College—Taylor died of heart disease at his beloved Woodlands.

1. Margaret Taylor MacIntosh, *Joseph Wright Taylor, Founder of Bryn Mawr College* (Haverford, PA: C. S. Taylor, 1936), xv, xvi.

Elizabeth MacIntosh is the great-great-great niece of Joseph Taylor. In 1960 she married Charles Archibald MacIntosh, a great-great-nephew of Taylor, and son of Margaret (née Taylor) and Archibald MacIntosh.

Above: Joseph Wright Taylor (1810–1880), founder of Bryn Mawr College, c. 1870s

Opposite: Charter of the Trustees of Bryn Mawr College, granted by the Court of Montgomery County in May 1880

A Certain Style of "Quaker Lady" Dress

IN 1877, when Joseph Wright Taylor decided to found a Quaker college for women, he had a ready group of advisors. He had pondered questions regarding the education of young men since 1854, when he joined the Board of Managers of Haverford College, founded by orthodox Quakers in 1833. Born in 1810, and trained as a doctor, Taylor prospered in his brother's tanning business in Cincinnati. A bachelor, he retired in 1851 and moved with his sister to Burlington, New Jersey, where members of his family had settled. His fortune grew with wise investments. Taylor came to know his colleagues on the Haverford board: the Baltimore banker Francis T. King and James Carey Thomas, King's physician cousin. In 1876, when Johns Hopkins, a Baltimore Quaker, left $3.5 million to found a university and an equal sum for an affiliated hospital, King and Thomas became members of his board of trustees.

In 1877, these men called a conference in Baltimore to discuss Quaker education, and Taylor attended. He asked himself an important question: Who educated Quaker women? Swarthmore College outside Philadelphia was coeducational from its beginning in 1864, but, founded by the Hicksite Quakers, it was no place for conservative Friends. A bright daughter, such as Martha Carey Thomas, one of James Carey Thomas' many children, had to venture to Cornell, a thoroughly secular university linked to the faith only by the religion of its founder, for the higher education she wanted. Joseph Taylor talked this over with Francis King and decided to found a Quaker college for women. Taylor consulted with President Thomas Chase of Haverford and with President Daniel Coit Gilman of Johns Hopkins. On one of his trips to Baltimore to see Gilman, he visited with James Thomas and talked with his Cornell daughter. She discussed her pessimistic fear that a coeducational institution would never include women on the faculty, despite their importance to women students. In 1877, Taylor made up his will, which set the outline of his future college. He named a board of trustees to gather after his death, designating Francis King president. Taylor appointed James Thomas and several of his relatives to the board: in addition to King, his cousin, there were Thomas' wife's brother, James Whitall, and another cousin, David Scull, Jr.

As president of the Johns Hopkins Hospital board, as well as a Hopkins and Haverford trustee, King naturally became Taylor's closest advisor. In addition King had a talented daughter just returned to Baltimore from the Howland Institute, a Quaker boarding school, where she had roomed with her cousin and closest friend, Martha Carey Thomas. Taylor saw his college as a female Haverford placed near his New Jersey estate. Aware of Girton at Oxford, King initially suggested that Taylor's college adjoin Haverford, repeating to Taylor the suggestion of an Oxford graduate that the two "use the same observatory, lectures, laboratory, gas, and water—but have separate courses of study, charter, endowment, and management . . . [and] divide the time of certain professors who can repeat the same lessons."[1] . . . Another advisor, later to play a very important part in the life of the college, James E. Rhoads, saw the value of propinquity to Philadelphia "where the benefit of professors and literary and scientific aids could be had, also some social influences." He wanted some separation from Haverford, where he, too, was a trustee. Rhoads did not want Taylor's college to be an annex, but fully separate, allowing "more untrammeled and vigorous growth of both Institutions."[2]

King helped Taylor select a site, a thirty-two-acre parcel in Bryn Mawr adjacent to the Pennsylvania Railroad and five miles from Haverford. King also recommended Addison Hutton, a Quaker architect who had just designed Barclay Hall at Haverford, a source of great pride to its trustees. King did not, however, approve of Hutton's Bryn Mawr residences in "very fancy style." In June 1879, in a letter to Hutton, King expressed the trustees' wishes for college buildings, hoping to tone down any excesses:

> There is a certain style of "Quaker lady" dress, which I often see in Phila, which tells the whole story—she has her satin bonnet—her silk dress—her kid gloves—her perfect slippers—but they are made to harmonize with the expression of her face which is both intellectual and holy—so may "Taylor College" look down from its beautiful site upon the passing world and we hear them say "just right."[3]

1. Francis King to Joseph W. Taylor, April 13, 1877, quoted in Margaret Taylor MacIntosh, *Joseph Wright Taylor, Founder of Bryn Mawr College* (Haverford, PA: C. S. Taylor, 1936), 184.
2. James E. Rhoads to Joseph W. Taylor, June 30, 1877, quoted in ibid., 186–87.
3. Quoted in Michelle Osborne, "The Making of the Early Bryn Mawr Campus," pt. I, *Bryn Mawr Now*, Bryn Mawr College Archives, Bryn Mawr, PA; misspelling corrected.

Reprinted with permission from Helen Lefkowitz Horowitz, *Alma Mater: Design and Experience in the Women's Colleges from Their Nineteenth-Century Beginnings to the 1930s* (New York: Knopf, 1984), 105–7.

Dr. Taylor's Will

FEBRUARY 19, 1877

I GIVE, DEVISE AND BEQUEATH all the rest, residue and remainder of my estate, real and personal, wherever found or situated to the following person—vix.: my nephew Charles S. Taylor, my friends Francis T. King, Dr. James C. Thomas of Baltimore, Dr. James E. Rhoads, James Whitall, John B. Garrett, Charles Hartshorne, Samuel Morris, David Scull, Jr., of Philadelphia City and County, William R. Thurston of New York City, and Albert K. Smiley of Providence, Rhode Island, or the survivors of them, in trust, as soon as a Corporation shall be established under the laws of Pennsylvania for a College or Institution of learning, having for its object the *advanced education of females,* as set forth below, to be under the care and management of Eleven Trustees above named, or others that they may from time to time appoint to fill vacancies in their number.

And the said Trustees of said Corporation may proceed to expend a portion of the principal in the purchase of suitable ground, chosen with care by them, and the erection thereon of substantial buildings of the most approved construction, for the comfort, advanced education and care of young women, or girls of the higher and more refined classes of society.

Said Trustees are to locate the site near to or accessible to a station on the Pennsylvania Railroad within a dozen miles of Philadelphia in Pennsylvania unless said site should have been previously obtained for said purpose, or a building procured or erected for the same.

The said Trustees shall have power from time to time to fill vacancies in their number, keeping the number at Eleven, who are to be members of the Society of Orthodox Friends of which I am a member. And it is my desire that in the selection and appointment of Trustees, great care be taken to select competent Friends of high moral and religious character, possessing enlarged and enlightened and cultivated minds, as far as may be attainable . . .

In the admission of students, other things being equal, preference is to be given to the Society of Friends; but in all cases those should be preferred who are of high moral and religious attainments and good examples and influence, and, such as are most advanced in education. But if not members of the Society of Friends all must conform to the customs and rules of the Institution and be willing to be educated as Friends, who are admitted or may be.

And I further desire that care should be taken to educate Young Women to fit them to become Teachers of a high order, and thus to extend the good influence of this Institution far and wide through them.

I would suggest for the Trustees that they consider the propriety of appointing a few wise, religious, enlightened and superior female Friends, to visit and to have the more immediate and direct care and oversight of the students, the selection of officers and the domestic arrangements of the Institution, subject to the Trustees.

I have been impressed with the need of such a place for the advanced education of our young female Friends, and to have all the advantages of a College education which are so freely offered to young men. And as at Haverford those wishing to be educated (or willing) as Friends.

At the same time to be under care and oversight and control of religious, conscientious, highly cultivated and refined Teachers and caretakers who should be concerned to guard and protect their minds and hearts from evil or injurious influences, whether as regards morals, habits, associations, or unprofitable reading.

So far as is possible the students should be deeply impressed that true refinement of mind and of manners are essential to complete the female character: and subjection to our Redeemer can alone perfect this . . .

. . . I would further add that the effects of a guarded advanced Christian education of females by expanding mental resources would strengthen character and elevate them above the foolish fashions now so prevalent and would fit for usefulness and influence. Should they become mothers, to train infant minds and give direction to character and to make home the center of interest and attraction, and thus to preserve youth from foolish follies, or haunts that lead to ruin. 19th day of Second Month—1877.

Reprinted from Margaret Taylor MacIntosh, *Joseph Wright Taylor, Founder of Bryn Mawr College* (Haverford, PA: C. S. Taylor, 1936), 207–10. Emphasis in original.

Germantown, Philadelphia
June 30, 1877

My dear Friend, Joseph W. Taylor,

It has been on my mind for some time to write thee, that on fuller information and thought, I feel as if I ought to encourage thee to carry out thy generous design for a Higher Institution of Learning for Girls. For a time I felt much discouraged about our Society, generally, but trust that the gracious Head of the Church is carrying us forward, as we are able to bear it, and that substantial unity is likely to be conserved. Probably the question of site for the proposed Institution could be better determined by more careful consideration. I should rather incline to place it near this City, where the benefit of professors and literary and scientific aids could be had, also some social influences; and yet quite apart from Haverford College as I think this would tend to the more untrammeled and vigorous growth of both Institutions.

I feel, dear friend, assured, that thou art desirous to know the mind of our Blessed and Loving Lord and Saviour, and to do it, and that He will direct thee.

With Christian love and fellowship, I am thy affectionate friend,

James E. Rhoads

Reprinted from Margaret Taylor MacIntosh, *Joseph Wright Taylor, Founder of Bryn Mawr College* (Haverford, PA: C. S. Taylor, 1936), 186–187.

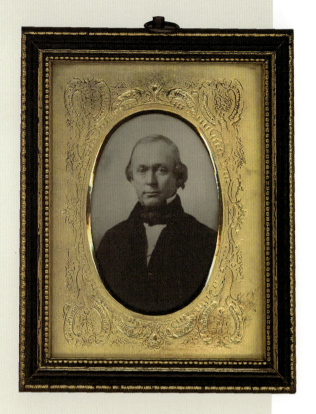

Above: Joseph Wright Taylor, c. 1860–70

Opposite: Joseph Wright Taylor's final will, 1877. Taylor bequeathed his estate to eleven trustees for the establishment of a "College or Institution of learning, having for its object the *advanced education of females*" (emphasis in original).

Next two pages: Cartes de visites of Bryn Mawr students, ranging from the class of 1889 through the class of 1905

THE TRUSTEES under the will of the Dr. Joseph W. Taylor have applied for a charter for a college for women to be called "Bryn Mawr College." The name is that of the village, railway station and post office, near which the College will stand. It is formed of two Welsh words, and seems to have been chosen by the Railway Company because the district was originally settled by Welsh (Friends), and that the site is a high and pleasing one, ideas implied in the Welsh words. The name is pronounced by the officials of the Company as if spelled Brin Maw-r. As has been previously mentioned, the plans for three buildings of the College were so far perfected during the life of Dr. Taylor that the foundations of these buildings have been laid, ready for the erection of the superstructure in the coming season . . . It is hoped that officers competent to conduct the College will also be found in the interim, so that it may open under conditions favorable for attaining the object intended.

The College will admit students irrespective of denomination, preference being given to members of the Society of Friends, except that in all cases "those of high moral and religious attainments and most advanced in education" are to be admitted.

The founder desired that "it shall be the endeavor of all connected with the Institution to instill in the minds and hearts of the students the doctrines of the New Testament as held by Friends."

Reprinted from the *Friends' Review: A Religious, Literary and Miscellaneous Journal*, April 24, 1880.

WITH THE END OF JUNE 1885, it is expected that Bryn Mawr College for Women will be nearly or quite finished, ready for the opening in the following September. The eyes of many young women throughout the land will be eagerly turned toward this event, for it is generally known that the aim of Bryn Mawr College will be higher than that of any other college for women in America.

Bryn Mawr is a fashionable suburban town, ten miles from Philadelphia, in one of the most beautiful localities of Lower Merion Township, Montgomery County. It is reached by the main line of the Pennsylvania Railroad. The College grounds includes an area of about thirty acres upon the highest hill in the vicinity, the whole region, however, being "high hills," hence the Welsh name, Bryn Mawr . . .

From the railroad station, outlined against the rich woods as a background may be seen, towering high above all surrounding objects, the magnificent granite structure known as Taylor Hall, the main building of the College. This is named after the founder of the institution, Dr. Joseph W. Taylor, of Burlington, N.J. Near by stands a picturesque villa called Merion Hall, after the township. The other completed buildings are the gymnasium, the engine-house, three professors' residences, and a residence for the president, Dr. James E. Rhoads. The grounds immediately surrounding the College are laid out in lawns, flower-gardens, and playground.

. . . No particular costume is prescribed, but every student will be expected to dress plainly. No student will be retained who does not show a disposition to make study her chief business.

Reprinted from *Arthur's Home Magazine*, June 1885.

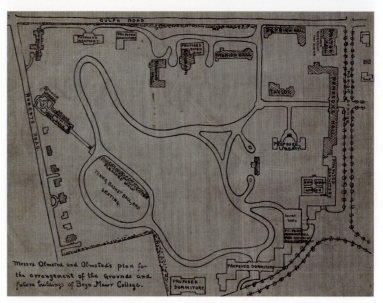

Top: Original entrance to the college, with Taylor Hall in background

Bottom: M. Carey Thomas's sketch of Frederick Law Olmsted and John C. Olmsted's plan for the grounds and future buildings of Bryn Mawr, c. 1898. Thomas decided to sketch the plan, rather than have it lithographed, to save the college money.

Opposite: Page from the record book of the college's ground purchases, 1937

FOUNDATIONS: 1885–1922

BRYN MAWR COLLEGE FOR WOMEN
Emily F. Wheeler

ALMOST EVERYONE has heard something of Bryn Mawr, the college for women, opened hardly three years ago near Philadelphia; and perhaps a few notes from a resident within its walls may be of interest to those eager for advance in the education of our girls.

The first sight of Bryn Mawr is very pleasant. The name means High Land; and tho the hill on which the building stands is bare and bleak in winter, it is attractive in the October sunshine, with the villas and gardens all about. Indeed, one's very first impression is that here is the ideal college; out of the city, and yet near enough for its advantages; in a quiet healthful place where the greatest freedom can be given, yet where no distractions interfere with work. Seeing the two pleasant halls where the girls are lodged, the well-appointed library and laboratories, the faculty, whose energy is that of youth, one feels that here is indeed a noble foundation. As one comes to know it from the inside one finds certain deficiencies in ideals and attainments; but this is only what one might expect in a young institution, and the faults, we may hope, time will correct.

What stamped it from the start as different from all its sisters, was provision for post-graduate work, and founding of fellowships. Of these there are five, Greek, English, mathematics, biology, and history. So far, with but one exception, they have been held but for one year, a time hardly long enough for definite or valuable work. All of the twelve women who have filled them have been from co-educational colleges. This would indicate that up to the present the colleges for women have not given as high training as those for both sexes. But one must remember that the women's colleges are but four against many more co-educational ones, that they are too young to have yet a large body of mature alumnae, and that their standards have, in many cases, been raised since their first graduates left them. A college for men has its standards set by comparison with older institutions. A college for women has, up to the present, been of the nature of an experiment, and its standards have risen as experience proved they might. This is an advantage of Bryn Mawr, and it has given itself the highest yet reached . . .

Bryn Mawr has profited by the experience of its elder sisters as to domestic arrangements . . . Class-rooms, the library, and laboratories are in separate buildings, and partially, at least, one throws off the school atmosphere when one steps outside of Taylor Hall. Of the residence halls it is usual to say that Merion is finer, but Radnor more home-like. Single rooms are the rule in Radnor; two bedrooms opening into a common study room in Merion. It is hard to make a school girl's bedroom attractive, but some of them are; and many of the studies are charming with draperies, pictures and pretty trifles. In each hall there is a mistress; but as there are no permissions and little responsibility her duties are light. In cases of illness a nurse from the city relieves her, and in general she is meant rather as a social head of the house. There are no study hours; no bells, except class ones; no permissions. A bell indeed rings at 10 P.M. and it is a fiction that one is expected to retire then. But the girl who chooses may get her lessons at any hour after, and promptness at breakfast is an unknown virtue in consequence . . .

The practical prohibition of music is one of the few touches which remind one that the college is a Quaker foundation. There is no organ in the fine chapel, and one must sadly accustom herself to prayers and prayer-meetings without the inspiration of song. One must get used to the same lack in the halls; and perhaps the absence of social life in them is partly due to this. Sidney Lanier has said that two material things were essential to a home—an open fire and an instrument of music. We have fire-places, but, alas! Neither fires or a piano. There is a certain truth in the saying that the piano is the great obstacle to the higher education. But as the end of culture is a symmetrical development of one's best powers, what a loss is this exclusion of music and art—a loss at once to culture and to pleasure! Again, the absence of class lines

is opposed to social life. There are pleasant circles of friends, but there is no generable sociability . . . If we were not so limited in numbers—fewer than 100—and so cut off from the world, it would not be so noticeable. But when winter comes, and the villas are closed and the city a long way off, and the one amusement is a walk, and the half-dozen practicable ones were learned by heart months ago, then, indeed, one feels a great isolation, and one plunges into work to escape homesickness.

. . . The advantages for post-graduate study are excellent, especially in philology and biology. But judging from observation and experience, the work follows too closely the line of regular undergraduate studies. It is not conducted on the seminary method of independent investigation with reports from time to time to the professor in charge. In some cases, fellows and post- and undergraduate students are in class together, and the obligation of attendance and preparation seems felt by them quite as much as by the younger ones. This is especially noticeable with the fellows, who, as women of maturity and long training, should certainly have the largest liberty. And let no one think a fellowship a place of inglorious ease. "I never worked in college as hard as here," one of them frankly says; and another adds that never in her college work did she feel such pressure on her. This is partly because the fellowships are but for a year. One is tempted to crowd too much into it. Could they be held long enough to take the doctor's degree, they would be far more desirable; and, since most of their holders are teachers, more fruitful to the cause of higher education. But half a loaf is better than none, and Bryn Mawr deserves all honor for the inauguration of this advance in college instruction. The old idea of girls' training was that mind, morals and manners were all within the teacher's province . . . The new education has changed all that, and Bryn Mawr takes frankly the ground that it is her business to provide instruction; that social life and moral development are not in her province. To leave the students as free as possible is her place . . . So too, the old idea made much of the teacher's influence and the molding of character; the new asks chiefly as to the instructor's acquirements. It all depends on the point of view, and if the sole business of a college is knowledge, then Bryn Mawr approaches the ideal type.

Reprinted from the *Independent*, June 14, 1888.

Above (left to right): View of campus with the gymnasium (built 1909), now the Marie Salant Neuberger Centennial Campus Center; and Merion and Taylor halls (built 1879–85)

FOUNDATIONS: 1885–1922

NOBEL PRIZE WINNER
Emily Greene Balch, Class of 1889
Sarah Sheplock, Class of 2010

EMILY GREENE BALCH (1867–1961), a major voice in pioneering cross-cultural studies of immigration and poverty, was a writer, academic, economist, pacifist, and Nobel Peace Prize laureate. A member of the first graduating class of Bryn Mawr, she earned a bachelor's degree in Greek and Latin, and was the first recipient of the college's European fellowship, allowing her to study economics and sociology in Paris, from 1890 to 1891. After completing her formal education at the University of Chicago and in Berlin, in 1896 Balch joined the faculty of Wellesley College, in Massachusetts, where in 1913 she was named full professor of economics and sociology. Her pacifist activities clashed with Wellesley's administration, however, and in 1918 she left the college to become an editor of the liberal magazine the *Nation*.

Committed to women's participation in bettering the world, in 1915 Balch, along with activists Jane Addams and Carrie Chapman Catt, helped found the Women's International Committee for Permanent Peace, later known as the Women's International League for Peace and Freedom (WILPF), for the promotion of peace, pacifism, and equality. She resigned as secretary of the organization in 1922, but when the league experienced financial difficulties in 1934, she resumed the position, without pay, for a year and a half. In 1946 she received the Nobel Peace Prize for her work connected to the WILPF, becoming only the third woman to win the prestigious honor. Devotion to her causes was never doubted: She donated her share of the Nobel Prize money to the league.

During her long career, Balch championed humanitarian causes through her work with the League of Nations and other international organizations.

Today, all first-year students at Bryn Mawr are required to complete one of the Emily Balch Seminars, which encourage students to approach complex issues from a variety of perspectives through intellectual inquiry and active discussion.

Above: Emily Greene Balch (1867–1961), class of 1889, c. 1905. Photograph by Harris and Ewing, Inc. (active 1905–45; Washington, DC). Courtesy of the Library of Congress, Prints and Photographs Division, LC-H25-41231-D

Right: Balch's Nobel Peace Prize medal, awarded in 1946. Bryn Mawr College Special Collections

BRYN MAWR'S FIRST PRESIDENT:
James E. Rhoads
Barbara Cary Curtis, Class of 1936

JAMES EVANS RHOADS is the only one of Bryn Mawr's five presidents about whom little has been written and, as Cornelia Meigs noted in the bibliography of *What Makes a College?* (1956), his official papers and correspondence "unfortunately have not been kept." Yet from records still available, much can be reconstructed about the life and personality of this able and dedicated Quaker physician who presided over the College's first ten years.

He was born on January 21, 1828, in Marple, Delaware County, Pennsylvania, the son of Joseph III and Hannah Evans Rhoads, devoted Quakers active in the affairs of their local meeting. Young James was sent to the Friends boarding school at Westtown, Pennsylvania, in the spring of 1843, and upon completion of the course there determined on medicine as a career. He received his medical degree from the University of Pennsylvania in 1852 and began practice in the thriving community of Germantown. He appears to have been both happy and successful in his work there, unlike Dr. Joseph W. Taylor, the founder of the College, who as a young man gave up medicine in favor of a career in business.

In 1862 James Rhoads married Margaret Ely, and two daughters and a son were born to them. Charles eventually followed in his father's footsteps, so far as devotion to Bryn Mawr was concerned, for he served on the Board of Trustees from 1907 to 1956.

Dr. James Rhoads possessed not only excellent professional training but also uncommon gifts of personal charm associated with sensitive, unobtrusive concern for the welfare of his many patients. He worked tirelessly, sometimes seeing as many as fifty people a day, yet treating each as a unique and valued individual. The Civil War and its aftermath of reconstruction left many afflicted with personal sorrows and grief. The doctor weighed in his own mind what his response should be to the issues of that troubled period. Fate suddenly intervened. Without warning the doctor awoke one morning to find himself the victim of a paralytic stroke. A long period of illness followed which he was able to overcome largely by the combination of his own inner resources, a strong constitution, and a resolute will. He accepted the fact that a resumption of his active life as a doctor was impossible. Instead he plunged into work set in motion by Friends for the relief and education of the thousands of newly freed Negroes. Hampton Institute numbers James E. Rhoads among its founders, for he felt keenly the need to educate the freedmen so that they could find a place in the changed world. Another large minority group in the United States, the American Indian, also received Dr. Rhoads' concerned attention. In company with another Quaker, Thomas Wistar, he journeyed to Indian council meetings in the Oklahoma Territory, and wrote frequent letters home, drawing on material noted in his daily journal. Some of his writing found its way to the pages of one of several Friends periodicals. Not long afterward his writing ability and his

organizational skills were enlisted in the task of editing the *Friends' Review*. He held his post from 1878 until he resigned in 1884 to become the president of Bryn Mawr College.

It was during the period of his editorship that James Rhoads first became closely associated with Joseph Wright Taylor. Both men were deeply involved in promoting higher education for young Quaker men in the Philadelphia area. At regular intervals they journeyed to Haverford College as members of its Board of Managers. Mutual respect and admiration grew steadily and it can hardly have been a surprise to Dr. Rhoads to learn that he was listed in Dr. Taylor's will as one of the eleven original trustees for the college to be established "for the higher education of females." The will was probated a few months after Dr. Taylor's death and at the organizational meeting of the board of trustees in May 1880, Dr. Rhoads accepted the position of vice president under Frances T. King.

What sort of person was this who undertook a shaping role in the creation of Bryn Mawr College? He was a man of wide vision and of great faith in human powers. The *Friends' Review*, which he had lately been editing, reflected the more liberal ideas of the Orthodox branch of the Society of Friends. His tolerance, his progressive ideas, and his own gentle reticence made public appearance in the ministry an infrequent occurrence. He never became a recognized minister in his own meeting although Friends have written that they recalled evidences of the intensity of his participation in Quaker worship. He was often observed in silent contemplation with tears in his eyes.

It takes some effort for us today to picture the life of the first college president. The days were filled with many of the challenges that recur in varying form with each college generation—faculty appointments, curricular offerings, financial organization. There were also the particular problems, ones that related to establishing a totally new institution. In close association with the young Dean of the Faculty, M. Carey Thomas, and with the support and encouragement of his hard-working associates on the Board of Trustees, Dr. Rhoads tried assiduously to carry out the intentions of the founder. It was no easy assignment, to make real that vision and to bring to fruition the hopes of many persons, both within and without the Society of Friends, for the development of a college for women dedicated to the highest standards of scholarly attainment.

Once Dr. Rhoads had assumed the presidency he began to weigh with his fellow trustees urgent considerations about the basic aims of the college, centering on the nature of the relationship of the new institution to the Society of Friends . . . In response to an inquiry, about the specific intentions of the Trustees of Bryn Mawr, James Rhoads wrote on February 20, 1885: "Two plans were open to the Trustees of Bryn Mawr: 1) Organize a Faculty of Friends chiefly. 2) To appoint as able a Faculty as practicable and give the College such Friendly influence as was possible in this course." Haverford College at that time followed the first plan and thus had appointed to its faculty almost all the available Quaker scholarly talent. A serious diminution of educational standards would have been inevitable at the very outset if the Trustees had limited themselves to appointing those who were Friends. Dr. Rhoads felt clear that undertaking the second alternative was proper. He also knew that it was likely to awaken dissent in some quarters. Nevertheless, he wrote, "We are 150 years behind other denominations in college management and college work. We have almost no first class men and women as compared with the best modern standards of attainment, who were available for Bryn Mawr." His view of the task of the new college is further shown in some of his remarks at the opening of the college when he gave his inaugural address to the first class of 35 women, "It should be clearly understood that although by the terms of Dr. Taylor's will the Trustees are to be members of the Society of Friends . . . the devise of Dr. Taylor was for a college or institution having for its object the advanced education of women. Bryn Mawr College is thus devised to the community at large, which has an interest in its advantages and a right to its benefits."

James Rhoads felt a deep responsibility for providing for the religious life of the student body. During his entire ten years on the college campus he served as lecturer in Christian ethics. He also held Wednesday-evening Friends meetings in his family home, at Carrtef on Merion Avenue, which many students voluntarily attended. He firmly opposed the formal establishment of a Friends meeting on the college grounds, preferring instead that the students attend such places of worship in the community as they desired.

After 1890, Dr. Rhoads had an unusual dual role as President both of the College and of its Board of Trustees, a situation unique to him among all those who have been President of Bryn Mawr. By the summer of 1893 he had begun to feel the strain of his many responsibilities and requested his fellow trustees to seek a new person to become head of the College. In August 1894 he happily gave over the office of the President of Bryn Mawr College to M. Carey Thomas. He and his wife continued to live on the edge of the campus in Carrtef, and Dr. Rhoads carried on his service on the Board and his course in Christian Ethics. He was, however, more worn out than anyone realized, and he died suddenly of heart failure on January 2, 1895. But Bryn Mawr was well established, and his work had been faithfully done. Under his leadership the hopes of Dr. Taylor had become a reality.

Reprinted from the *Bryn Mawr Alumnae Bulletin*, Fall 1970.

The characters of the students have been so developed by home training, and they have entered college with such well defined purposes, that there has been no necessity for any administration of discipline other than to inform them of the necessary routine of daily duties. The instructors have been well satisfied with the general interest and diligence in study they have manifested.

—*President James E. Rhoads,*
President's Report to the Board of Trustees, 1885

Opposite: James E. Rhoads (1828–1895), 1891, first president of Bryn Mawr College. Photograph by Phillips Studio (Philadelphia)

FOR EDUCATING WOMEN
The Opening of Bryn Mawr College, Founded by the Late Dr. Taylor

THE CHAPEL ROOM of Taylor Hall, the principal building of Bryn Mawr College, was packed as full as it could hold yesterday afternoon with the friends of the institution who had gathered to attend the opening exercises. In the front seats were the thirty-seven young ladies who have been entered as students at the college. On the platform Mr. Philip C. Garrett, who presided, was surrounded by such men as James Russell Lowell; Wayne MacVeagh; Rev. C. G. Ames; Hon. Horatio Gates Jones; Thomas Chase, president of Haverford College; D. C. Gilman, president of Johns Hopkins University; Dr. James E. Rhoads, president of the new college; Hon. I. Newton Evans; George W. Childs; John B. Garrett; M. Carey Thomas; Hon. William H. Smith; Dr. Wilson; Dr. Kaiser; and Francis T. White.

Mr. Garrett opened the exercise by announcing the absence of Francis T. King, president of the Board of Trustees, who was prevented from being present by sickness. He then read from the 29th chapter of 1st Chronicles, and after prayer had been offered, stated that letters of regret had been received from President Angell, of Ann Arbor; President Porter, of Yale; and Presidents Hill, Whitney and Williams; Governor Pattison; Chief Justice Smith, of New York; J. Braithewaite, of London; and others.

President James E. Rhoads was then introduced. He said: "To-day we rejoice in a preparation and a beginning. The actual life of the college has begun, and amid the rejoicings of to-day it is fit that we should remember to give due honor to Dr. Taylor, who devoted nearly his entire estate to establish it. By his death in 1880 the completion of the work devolved upon the trustees, who feel confident that they have followed out his design in husbanding the estate, so that now the fund is nearly equal to that which was originally devised. But there are yet heavy drains to be made upon it aside from defraying the mere expenses of tuition." After commenting upon the various branches

Left: Drawing of Taylor Hall bell tower, ink on paper

Bottom right: Vernon Howe Bailey (American, 1874–1953), *Taylor Hall*, c. 1906–7, charcoal on paper

Bottom left: Interior of Taylor Hall, c. 1890–1910

FOUNDATIONS: 1885–1922

> ONE OF THE MOST REMARKABLE INDICATIONS OF THE PROGRESS OF MODERN SOCIETY IS THAT WE NOW FURNISH TO YOUNG WOMEN FACILITIES FOR THAT ADVANCED EDUCATION WHICH HAS LONG BEEN ACCORDED TO YOUNG MEN.
>
> —*D.C. Gilman, president of Johns Hopkins University*

of instruction which will be taken up in the college, Dr. Rhoads said that "the duty to do well rather than to attempt to do much" has compelled the passing by of certain other branches which are by some thought indispensible.

"One of the most remarkable indications of the progress of modern society," said President D. C. Gilman, the next speaker, "is that we now furnish to young women facilities for that advanced education which has long been accorded to young men, and Bryn Mawr College, which in point of time follows Vassar and several others of their class, has a field and scope that would have been deemed unattainable a few years ago. The college which is established to-day is likely to be the leader among kindred establishments the whole world over, and it is a day therefore for congratulations, not only to those who are present, but to him who gave it all but his name, which with true modesty he withheld."

President Thomas Chase, of Haverford, being next introduced, likened Bryn Mawr College and his own to twins, and in welcoming the former to the sisterhood of colleges, said that "it is destined to shine as a star of the first magnitude." Commenting on its objects, he said that it aims to make true and whole women—not mere fractions—neither mere bookworms nor gymnasts nor cricketers, but to make them both useful, attractive and agreeable, and fitted to appear in any "sphere of life."

"It is customary," said Mr. Garrett, "on such occasions as this to conclude with an appropriate poem, but we offer something better than this in the living presence of one who is—and I say it with due deference to his presence—the greatest poet of the country—James Russell Lowell."

"It is with a certain amount of reluctance that I come forward," said Mr. Lowell, "for fear that the old instinct of lecturing may be aroused in me, and that I may detain you longer than I should. If I expound to you the reasons that brought me here I should detain you unconsciously long, for these reasons are forty years in length. Forty years ago I came in contact, in Philadelphia, with that class who call themselves Friends. The world calls them Quakers, and I know that their forbearance will permit me to call them so without offence. The blood in my veins was drawn from the veins of those who in former days persecuted the Quakers, and I was honest enough in my utterances to tell those whom I met that I thought they did right to persecute them because of their plainness. I am glad that there is now more liberality of feeling by Quakers in regard to color than there was then, though it may be that there is still some justification for persecution.

I could wish that there was still more liberality. However, remembering the uniform kindness with which I was treated by the Quakers forty years ago, I came here and I am glad to be here. I have been a trifle erratic about women's colleges, but I am inclined to take it all back. It seems to me that the object of our teaching is not to make specialists, but to make cultivated men and women. I am glad to hear that Greek is to be taught here, and still more glad to know that English is to be taught. We have inclined of late years to a certain over-accuracy. For instance a certain well-known author says, 'He turned around his head'—a feat that I'd like to see him perform. We talk about walking in the center of the street, when we should be contented to say the middle. Why the other day, when the barber cut my hair, he asked me if I parted it in the center. I told him that time, unfortunately, had made a very wide part down the center. One of the great objects of the training of the present day should be to produce men and women who know the difference between literature and printed matter."

President Rhoads brought the formal exercises to a close by inviting the party to an elegant collation in the gymnasium.

The new college was founded by Dr. Joseph W. Taylor, of Burlington, N. J., and is intended exclusively for the higher instruction of young women and for the training of teachers of a high order. The principal building is Taylor Hall, built of Port Deposit granite. It comprises the chapel, class rooms, laboratory, library and private rooms for professors. Merion Hall, the next important building, is of Fairmount stone and built for accommodation of fifty students. It contains a reception-room, a dining-room, a kitchen, a laundry, students' reading rooms and chambers for professors, students and servants. The other buildings are the gymnasium, engine-house and three cottages which were on the grounds when purchased.

Reprinted from the *North American Review*, September 25, 1885.

From the Inauguration of Bryn Mawr College, 1885

PRESIDENT RHOADS' ADDRESS is a clear account of the origination of the College in the intelligent liberality of the late Dr. Joseph W. Taylor, of the work proposed to be done by the institution, and of its curriculum. One of the most important paragraphs of the address is the following:

> As in the case of almost all our institutions of learning, Bryn Mawr was founded in motives of Christian benevolence. Dr. Taylor desired that it should ever maintain and teach an evangelical and primitive Christianity as set forth in the New Testament, and the Trustees will endeavor to carry out this trust in the spirit in which it was imposed. While seeking to uphold with reverent faithfulness the religion of Christ according to their own convictions, they will have a sacred regard to the training which students may have received at home and will respect their conscientious beliefs. In addition to attendance on such public worship as they or their parents shall select, there will be household worship in the College, and an annual course of lectures will be given on the Bible and Biblical study.

President Gilman's discourse, beginning with congratulations and some historical allusions, sets forth, in his usual happy style, the special features of the "group system" of collegiate studies; as a compromise or reconciliation between a fixed curriculum for all graduating students alike, and no curriculum whatever. Several courses or groups of studies offered, one of which must be taken as a binding choice by every candidate for academic honors. No space can be allowed here for the present writer to give the reasons which lead him to believe that this system is not the best possible improvement upon the older college curriculum; but is only a less injurious development of the now dominating idea of free choice of studies by undergraduate college students, than that which is presented by Harvard University. It may be mentioned, however, that President Eliot, of Harvard, in one of his latest utterances, objects to the group system, because it fastens upon the student, at the beginning of his college course, a combination of studies from which he cannot afterwards extricate himself, should he for any reason change his mind. To the writer of this notice, it is almost a matter of certainty that President Eliot's extreme electivism will, fifty years hence, be looked upon as hardly less preposterous as an experiment in education, than was or is the "greenback theory" of national credit finance.

President Thomas Chase's address is an appropriate and eloquent salutation, welcoming the new College to a nearer fraternity than that which neighborhood alone would call for and secure. It will not be possible for us to convey its substance by any abstract. We must, however, find room for its closing sentences, addressed to the members of the faculty of Bryn Mawr:

> Let us never forget that we have ends to pursue higher than the mere imparting of knowledge, even in those great arts and sciences which we teach. Let us not forget that all great foundations like this are set to bear a perpetual testimony to the highest and noblest ideals of life. They stand as breakwaters against the tide of material desires and ignoble aims, the love of idle wealth and sensuous ease, the Circe song. They point us to the heights of self-culture, self-knowledge, self-conquest, self-control, as well as to the shining fields of learning and science, and the winsome bowers of poetry and art. They show us a grace of being finer than ourselves; they stir us with "intimations clear of wider scope, / Hints of occasion infinite, to keep / The soul alert with noble discontent / And onward yearnings of unstilled desire."
>
> In the sure hope that this college will do its full part in the fulfillment of this great mission, I hail the promise which this day brings. All hail that long hereafter, when the name of Bryn Mawr shall be a spell to raise or quicken all noble thoughts and high aspirations, as have been the names of Bologna and Padua, of Paris and Leipzig, of Oxford and Cambridge, of Harvard and Yale!

Reprinted from the *Friends' Review: A Religious, Literary and Miscellaneous Journal*, March 18, 1886.

Opposite (clockwise from top left): Members of Bryn Mawr's first class, of 1889, photographed on campus, c. 1885; at their fiftieth reunion, 1939; on the steps of Taylor Hall, 1886

ARRIVAL

WHY I CAME TO COLLEGE
Freshman composition by Elizabeth Yarnall Maguire, Class of 1913

The main reason for my coming to college is that I did not want to stop studying when I had finished school. It seems to me that almost all of us, however, stooped we may be, must feel a certain pleasure, or at least satisfaction, in studying the lessons that are appointed us, and that we must be really interested in some of our subjects, no matter how much we grumble and groan over their difficulty. It was to go on with the subjects that interested me mightily that I came to college, instead of staying at home to study there. Since I wanted the companionship of others when I studied, I might have gone to boarding school, but I thought that the difference in the way of living necessary where you go to college would be rather good for me. College is certainly the best place to practice to be independent.

    Another, and a rather light reason for my coming to college is the fact that all athletics need not stop after the summer is over. Usually, after the vacation, there can be no more athletics for me until the next summer; and it is very pleasant to know that here at college it is possible to play tennis, for instance, far into the fall, and to always keep oneself in some sort of practice. These are the reasons, poor as they are, that made me want to come to college.

Left: Entrance examination results for Bertha Szold (Levin), class of 1895

Right: Sketch of students taking the college's entrance examination, with a "proctor snooping & gawking," c. 1909–13. Reprinted from the scrapbook of Elizabeth Yarnall Maguire, class of 1913

FOUNDATIONS: 1885–1922

ON TEA

DURING THE WINTER, before the days lengthen and tennis or a lounge under the cherry trees becomes the order of the hours between half past four and dinner, those on hospitable thoughts intent, expend their originality in the giving of "teas." We may be said to be rather addicted to "teas"—"teas" of all sorts, from the social brew at five o'clock or when work is over for the evening; or when you come in chilly from gymnasium or constitutional, or from studying in the library, to find the kettle steaming away over the alcohol lamp, and your particular corner of the divan heaped with pillows awaiting you, and three or four of your "trusty chums," as Corporal Mulvaney would say, in various comfortable attitudes on the floor, or the window-seat, or the long, soft-cushioned steamer chair, to the most formal of "teas," where salted almonds and other insignia of an advanced civilization take the place of crackers and jam and olives, the Spartan fare, which was all that the most noted of hostesses could offer her guests during the early years of the college. With advancing years there has undoubtedly crept in a certain unwonted luxury, and this is especially noticeable in the gradual complication of the pantry paraphernalia. During the first years of the college tea-making was almost a lost art. We have all heard of the student, far-famed for her hospitality, who was discovered making tea with water just as it came bubbling, but in no sense boiling, from the faucet. Now no room is complete without its dainty tea-table, and the coffee-pot and the chafing-dish have not been slow in making their appearance. More or less formality on the more important occasions is, in our opinion, by no means a bad thing; there is always a danger of our growing slipshod in minor points of etiquette, a habit of putting one's elbows on the table when they should be in position, but there is no fear of a college "tea" ever losing its individuality. A very pleasant custom has grown up of giving "teas" early in the year for the freshmen. In such comfortable fashion they become acquainted with the students, gain their first knowledge of characteristic college ways, and are often introduced to the store-house of time-honored jokes, through the medium of some memorabilia book.

Reprinted from the *Lantern*, June 1891.

```
PROFESSIONS CHOSEN BY FRESHMAN CLASS.

Intend to teach..............................33   or 26.8 %
Plan no profession...........................28   or 22.8 %
Plan some profession - not decided on........21   or 17.1 %
Intend to do social work.....................10
   "   to become doctors.....................6
   "   to do literary work...................3
   "   to do scientific research work........3
   "   to teach in colleges..................2
   "   to become lawyers.....................2
   "   to be professional musicians..........2
Intends to be a farmer.......................1
   "     to be a missionary..................1
Not stated..................................11
                                           123
```

COLLEGIANA
MVA, Class of 1893

One of the characteristics of Bryn Mawr is the absence of such clubs and societies as are found at other colleges. Here there are but two associations, the Undergraduate Association and the Reform Club. The Undergraduate Association, as its name implies, includes all undergraduate students; its object is the discussion and decision of various matters of importance and interest in college life. The Reform Club is much less formal in organization, and its membership is not limited to undergraduates. Its genesis from the prayer meetings accounts for its informal character. All students of the college and any attendants upon the prayer meetings are members; its only officers are a committee of three, elected annually by the Undergraduate Association, to invite speakers for the meetings of the club.

The founders of the club felt that the majority of the students had very few interests beyond the all-absorbing ones of college life; there were general ideas, but very little definite knowledge of the important questions and movements agitating the outside world. After consultation and discussion, it was decided to give up, once a month, the regular weekly prayer meeting, and to have in its stead a meeting, the object of which should be to give the girls a more intimate acquaintance with someone of the social movements. The first meeting was held in the fall of 1886, and others have been held with great success in almost every month of the college year since then.

Reprinted from the *Lantern*, 1891.

Above: Intended professions of the Freshman Class, 1915.

ASCENSION
Martha Carey Thomas

Left: M. Carey Thomas (1857–1935), second president of Bryn Mawr College (foreground); and Mary (Mamie) Gwinn, Bryn Mawr PhD., 1888, and professor of English (background), 1879. Photograph by D. J. Wilkes (Baltimore)

Center: M. Carey Thomas, c. 1870s. Photograph by J. H. Kent (Rochester, NY)

Right: The Friday Evening Group, so-called because its five members, all women from Baltimore, met every other Friday, to present and discuss short papers. *Clockwise from upper right*: Elizabeth (Bessie) King; Mary Elizabeth Garrett (1854–1915); Mamie Gwinn (seated center); M. Carey Thomas; and Julia Rogers, c. 1879. Photograph by N. H. Busey (Baltimore)

M. Carey Thomas
Journal
February 26, 1871

An english man Joseph Beck was here to dinner the other day & he dont believe in the Education of Women. Neither does Cousin Frank King & my such a discussion as they had. Mother of course was for. They said that they did'nt see any good of a womans learning Latin or Greek it did'nt make them any more entertaining to their husbands a woman had plenty of other things to do sewing cooking taking care of children dressing & flirtery 'what noble elevating things for a whole life time to be occupied with.' in fact they talked as if the whole end & aim of a womans life was to get married & when she attained that greatest state of earthly bliss it was her duty to amuse her husband & to learn nothing never to exercise the powers of her mind so that he might have the exquisite pleasure of knowing more than his wife of course they talked the usual cant of woman being too high too exalted to do anything & sit up in perfect ignorance with folded hands & let men worship at her shrine meaning in other words like all the rest of such high faluting stuff that woman ought to be mere dolls for men to be amused with to kiss fondle pet &, love maybe, but as for association with them on terms of equality, they would'nt think of such a thing. Now I dont mean to say that these two men believed this but these were the principles they upheld. I got perfectly enraged how unjust how narrow minded how utterly uncomprehensible to deny that women ought to be educated & worse than all to deny that they have equal powers of mind. If I ever live to grow up my one aim & consentrated purpose shall be & is to show that a woman can learn can reason can compete with men in the grand fields of literature & science & conjuncture that opens before the 19 century that a woman can be a woman & a true one with out having all their time engrossed by the dress & society that the woman who has fought all the battles of olden time over again whilest reading the spirited pages of Homer Virgil Herroditus who has sympathised in the longings after something beyond mere daily exhistance found in the works of Socrates, Plato & Eschelus who has reasoned out all the great laws which govern the universe with Newton Arago Gallileo who has mourned with Dante reasoned & speculated with Schiller Goethe & Jean Paul been carried away by Carlyle & 'mildly enchanted by Emerson' who has idealized with Milton & emerged with strengthen intelect from the intricate labyrinth of Geometry Trigonometry & Calculous is not any less like what God really intended a woman to be than the trifling ballroom butterfly than the ignorant-way doll baby which they admire.

Reprinted from the journal of M. Carey Thomas, February 26, 1871.

c/o MM Hottinguer and Co.
38 rue de Provence
Paris

8th mo 14th 1883

Confidential

Dr. J. E. Rhoads,
Germantown, Philadelphia

My dear Friend,

My old desire to see an excellent women's college in America has made the management of Bryn Mawr from the time of its first endowment a matter of great interest to me. This interest must be my excuse for writing to thee, as the newly appointed Vice President of the Board of the Bryn Mawr Trustees and Chairman of the Executive and Building Committees, in regard to Bryn Mawr and in part in regard to myself.

It is now three years and a half since I came abroad, meaning only to pursue study for its own sake. My conviction of the value of a liberal education could not but be made deeper, and my conception of what a college might become, clearer, by gradual training under German scholars, who in a certain sense aid in making the science which they teach; and I began to doubt whether it would not be a more justifiable way of life, to aid in procuring this liberal education for other women, than merely to pursue my studies quietly at home. When last ninth month I was more successful in my examination than I had before thought possible, and received the rarely awarded degree of Doctor of Philosophy, summa cum laude, I felt that I might without presumptuousness, in case no one better fit should yet have been found, offer myself as a candidate for the presidency of Bryn Mawr. I can do this with less hesitation because I am personally convinced that it is best for the president of a woman's college to be a woman; and among women I know that, thanks to my father and mother, my opportunities, not only for study, but for observation, and for comparison of methods, have been unusually good. After graduating from Howland School, I went through the Classical Course of Cornell University, taking there the degree of B.A.; I have studied for three and a half years in Germany and Switzerland, am now attending the lectures of the College de France and the Sorbonne, and am anxious to spend some little time at each of the two women's colleges at Cambridge. A man placed at the head of a woman's college feels all the circumstances by which it differs from a man's college as limitations only, a woman sees definitively the especial needs, aims, interests, opportunities and possibilities. In view of this immediate sympathy and cooperation, as well as for the sake of the power, given by recent and continuous study, to understand the needs of a new college, I have not been able to regret my comparative youth which to thee perhaps may seem a disadvantage.

However, this may be, and without further reference to any possible president-ship of mine, I should be glad if thou wouldst permit me, simply as a woman much interested in Bryn Mawr, to speak to thee of what I should desire for it, and to make a few suggestions, of which none perhaps may be at all new to thee. Only thou mightiest be interested in seeing how far my own experience as a student may have led me to the same conclusions with thyself.

Since there attends upon the opening of each new college a certain amount of public interest, which, when once disappointed, is not easily aroused again, but turns on the contrary to an enduring prejudice against the college, I am anxious that Bryn Mawr should open with a full number of competent professors, and with as high a standard as it may intend to reach or maintain—that it should not, for instance, imitate Vassar, which began with a preparatory course that was to have been dropped afterwards, but has most unfortunately been retained. On the other hand since the absence of the regularly organized preparatory schools that exist for boys, greatly embarrasses a girl who means to enter college, I consider it very important that a year, or if possible two years before the opening of Bryn Mawr, there should be sent to all Friends' schools, and published in the *Nation* and in all the leading journals, a full list, made out by the President and such professors as shall be already appointed, of the entrance requirements, and of the fellowships to be competed for—that is, if it should be decided to create fellowships as I hope it will be.

I am anxious that Bryn Mawr should not duplicate other existing colleges. Coeducation is gaining ground: Vassar, Wellesley and Smith have the start of us; in the West there are Friends' schools and colleges of a lower grade open to both sexes. Bryn Mawr, if it be not exceptional in character, can expect at most but fifty or sixty students, and these, for all post-graduate studies, will be drawn away. Moreover, the best undergraduate training can never be given by a college, which is not also able to guide advanced students. I should wish Bryn Mawr not to be a competitor amid the ranks of ordinary colleges, compelled to contend with them for its share and as it were, to go a-begging for students; but itself to give America what is lacking there—a place where elementary college work is better done than elsewhere, and at the same time a place where women may at last be able to pursue advanced studies among women.

I should thus wish Bryn Mawr, taking girls at the beginning of their college course, to give them a systematic training under professors qualified to prepare both their own graduates and those from other colleges, so that these girls may either take their place afterwards as original scholars, or carry back with them into their own homes a love and understanding of study and culture; and this end could not, I think, be better served than by establishing, in imitation of the Johns Hopkins University, at least ten fellowships, each of two or three hundred dollars, apart from board and residence. Let these be competed for by the post-graduates from other colleges, and by the future graduates of Bryn Mawr, and the successful fellows will not be the only persons

Above: M. Carey Thomas, c. 1889. Photograph by Frederick Hollyer (1837–1933; Kensington, London)

Opposite: Sketch of M. Carey Thomas, graphite on paper, c. 1890s

benefited. Their presence will assist in giving to the new college the requisite scholarly atmosphere: it will raise the standard of undergraduate work, aid in college discipline, incite the professors under whom they study to original work research, and, as at the Johns Hopkins, draw other postgraduates to the college. Each fellow might be required to prepare and deliver one course of lectures yearly; and each, as she in time accepted a position in some other school or college would carry with her the influence of Bryn Mawr, and would direct her own pupils thither. Not only this: but the fellows, especially when they had been graduates of Bryn Mawr itself, might become professors there, and thus obviate one chief difficulty when must beset the college.

I am not afraid that the character of Bryn Mawr as a Quaker institution will interfere with its excellence, even as regards the choice of instructors; for I know that, if we teach better than is taught elsewhere, we shall have students who in their turn will be better teachers than the students of other colleges can become. Therefore, to the carrying out of Dr. Taylor's plans, two things seem to me especially requisite: one, this system of fellowships; the other, that in the first choice of professors, the utmost stress shall be laid on their excellence in their own departments. That of two men equally good, a Friend would be preferred, is a matter of course, but if Bryn Mawr begins by appointing because they are Friends men inferior to the professors that could otherwise be obtained, it will hurt and not benefit the cause of education in the Society of Friends; it will make the average of education in it at least no higher than elsewhere; and the average of professional study lower, by the removal of competition. Bryn Mawr is to be a Friends' college and it is to be at the same time a good college: in order to employ Friends in it, we must educate them in it, and perhaps also out of it. We must not deceive ourselves an excellent college within the limits of any one sect or society is an exceptional thing, and must be obtained by exceptional measures. Just such professors as it requires, Bryn Mawr cannot have till its own students become its professors. For these it would be an excellent thing to institute a special kind of scholarship, open to Friends only; a kind of scholarship equivalent to the Prix de Rome or *bourse de voyage* of the French Academy of Art, and enabling the successful one among the few very advanced students allowed to compete for it, to study three years abroad. The college would have no further obligation toward these students; but it would have the choice among them: the investigations and treatises required during the three years would of course be the property of the college.

On the other hand, at the first opening of the college no professors would be chosen whose influence would be opposed to that of the Society of Friends; and those excellent professors who were not Friends in point of fact, would be accepted until they could be worthily replaced by such of their own pupils as had obtained this highest of scholarships, accomplished their years of study abroad, and plainly proved their ability in the eyes of the Faculty. The term thus set to these provisional professorships would neither be too long for the interests of the college, nor too short for the acceptance of a scholar who respects himself.

I do not know whether the treasurer of the college would find it possible to give one foreign scholarship per year; but I believe that did the college but include this in its programme, as a thing at least desirable, private liberality would come to its aid.

This scholarship should not be competed for until after the completion of two years of post-graduate study.

I am quite content that these provisional professorships (and they will doubtless be considerable in number) should be held in great part by men, although thou hast already seen from my plan as to the way in which the professorships should be refilled that I should desire a number of them ultimately to be held by graduates of Bryn Mawr. The Society of Friends has no deeper claim upon the gratitude and loyalty of its members than its steady equity and liberality toward women. In this new woman's college, which may be even better than its colleges for men, because it is more recent of foundation—which should be better because it must provide for women the ulterior training which the men of the Society of Friends can so easily obtain in any of the universities of the world, it may be proved if it gives to such of its women as are scholars not only a training but a career . . .

. . . Thou must permit me to add one word more, lest thou shouldst think some part of what I have said a little wide of the mark. I fully recognize that the majority of the girls at Bryn Mawr will not be professional scholars, and that it is not even desirable that they should become so. Nevertheless I do not wish the above solely, or even chiefly, in the interest of the post-graduates. The ordinary student never digests and appropriates more than a certain proportion of the instruction given; but I am convinced it is only from such solid and scientific instruction as is meant to pave the way for prolonged studies that there can possibly be acquired the mental discipline, and the intelligent comprehension of things, which are the best results of a briefer and more general education.

I do not at all know what are to be the accommodations provided for the students of Bryn Mawr, but I was very glad to find that at Girton College where each girl has a comfortable study with an adjoining bedroom, the Lady Principal was persuaded that this arrangement had brought a better class of girls to the college, and the professors, that the girls studied the better for it. Formerly, if I remember rightly, two girls shared one study: an arrangement which nearly all women graduates of my acquaintance have agreed with me in considering destructive of freshness of mind and faculty of self-concentration.

The system of a bedroom and a study for each girl now seems to me (and I have tried personally each arrangement) the only admissible one. To study and sleep in the same room is confessedly a most distressing nervous strain; and the most specious means of avoiding it, the common use between two girls, of a study or bedroom, is liable, not only to objection above given to the use of a common study, but to another, of yet more general nature. Those girls whom in the first part of this letter I may have seemed to thee to consider even too much—girls who by necessity or by preference and deliberate purpose mean to become scholars—will of course come wherever they are sure of finding the best instruction. On the other hand, Bryn Mawr would be glad to include among its students all the intelligent girls at least of the Society of Friends. It is well known that by a right-minded conservatism, most parents desire for their girls a far less promiscuous range of social intercourse than for their boys, and that their best hope, in sending a girl to boarding school or to college (and very often they keep her at home lest their hope should never be fulfilled), is that she may have learned a great deal, but may otherwise be precisely as though she had never left home. Now a girl at home is brought into contact only with a certain set of people, known to and chosen by her family; and if for learning's sake she be compelled for a time to forgo that society there is no reason why she should be forced into any other intimate social contact. These matters are not moral, but social and in some degree personal; so that the college cannot undertake to mediate in them by a judicious pairing of girls: the question is quite unconnected with that of study and concerns only the right of personal privacy. This is all the more important since Bryn Mawr will be apt to have for students, in addition to the children of Friends, those of thoughtful, but conservative parents of all denominations, who being afraid at once of free thought and of sectarianism, will be glad to place their daughters where, as among Friends, there is a religious influence without any excitement of proselytism.

I see that I have been drawn from detail to detail into a much longer letter than I had meant to trouble thee with. I hope thou wilt pardon it, since I am one of the many women who have desired a college education, with at least a fear of not obtaining it.

Believe me with sincere esteem,

Very truly yours,

Martha Carey Thomas

FOUNDATIONS: 1885–1922

Mary Elizabeth Garrett to M. Carey Thomas
New York, March 23, 1893

Dearest Minnie,

. . . I know there is no risk of your misunderstanding me when I tell you that what I want you to do now is to swell the interest factor. You have used all the arguments that ought to prevail and it looks as if they would not, and it seems to me too important a thing for you to hesitate about using the lower ones which may produce an effect where the others fail . . . I think you could say that you had told me of the present condition of affairs . . . or if you choose you could say you told me when I gave you $2,000 asking you to spend it on your department within the next months, as it seemed so improbable that you would be there to do it—and that I had expressed the greatest regret, that I throught no greater misfortune could befall the cause of higher education of girls and women in this country than to have the policy of Bryn Mawr changed, that of course it would be perfectly clear to every one who was interested in educational matters that your not being elected as Dr. Rhoads' successor meant a change of policy and could mean nothing else as the success under his and your policy had been so brilliant and so solid that I had hoped and intended to help the college further, this present gift only being a beginning; but that my interest would of course cease wholly and entirely when your connection with it was severed . . . Then you may say, if it seems best to be absolutely definite that I said I intended, providing you were made President, giving you to spend, at your sole discretion, for the college $5,000 next year and each succeeding year that you remained President, in the same way, $10,000 . . . Of course you see the desirability of such a proposition being regarded as absolutely confidential and I should prefer not stating the sum definitively partly because I may possibly be able to make it $10,000 next year.

Reprinted from a letter, Mary Elizabeth Garrett to M. Carey Thomas, March 23, 1893.

Above: Mary Elizabeth Garrett, c. 1900–1910. Photograph by Frederick Hollyer

Right: Page from a letter, Mary Elizabeth Garrett to the Board of Trustees of Bryn Mawr College, March 28, 1893 (transcript of letter, p. 32)

Opposite: John Singer Sargent (American, 1856–1925), *Miss Carey Thomas*, 1899, oil on canvas, 58 x 38 in. (147.3 x 96.5 cm). Bryn Mawr College. Gift of the Portrait Committee of Alumnae and Students. The Portrait Committee commissioned this portrait in 1898.

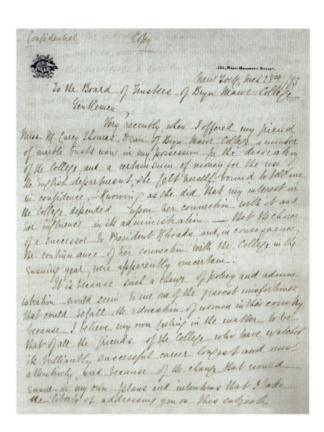

M. Carey Thomas to Mary Elizabeth Garrett
March 24, 1893, 11 A.M.

My Darling,

Your letter has completely upset me this morning coming as it has after a night in which I completely gave up and attempted to reconstruct my life. I think it needed no rewriting and how could you think—am I so unreasonable and prone to misunderstand as that it would be possible to misunderstand such a sweet and clever attempt to use Mammon for righteousness, for I really think it is righteousness. If you can afford to do it I shall be delighted to accept it and spend it as we decide, for of course if I give my own time and life I cannot think your $10,000 would be wasted or ill spent. I am however determined to save $2000 from the check and you shall not give it till we see how things turn out. I do not know but I really think that such an offer from you may have a great effect but I think it ought to be made in a letter from you independent of me or my statements of which you send me a copy. If you say it is to be entirely confidential it will surely be regarded so as the God of these trustees is their conscience. There is no reason for the least anxiety on that point. If then you are sure you can do it I shall be delighted to have this agreement also—inducement, bribe—to use too. And if you really had thought of doing it anyhow it would seem foolish not to use all legitimate means to defeat prejudice and save the College, would it not?

I will send you a copy of a letter that I think it would be most useful for you to write and you can see what you think.

Reprinted from a letter, M. Carey Thomas to Mary Elizabeth Garrett, March 24, 1893.

Confidential

New York, March 28th, 1893

To the Board of Trustees of Bryn Mawr College

Gentlemen,

    Very recently when I offered my friend Miss M. Carey Thomas, Dean of Bryn Mawr College, a number of marble busts now in my possession for the decoration of the College and a certain sum of money for the use of the English Department, she felt herself bound to tell me in confidence—Knowing as she did that my interest in the College depended upon her connection with it and her influence in its administration—that the choice of a successor to President Rhoads and, in consequence, the continuation of her connection with the College in the ensuing year were apparently uncertain.

    It is because such a change of policy and administration would seem to me one of the gravest misfortunes that could befall the education of women in this country, and because I believe my own feeling in the matter to be that of all the friends of the College who have watched its brilliantly successful career longest and most attentively, and because of the change that would ensue in my own plans and intentions that I take the liberty of addressing you in this subject.

    I am very far indeed—from meaning to assume that there is in any case any likelihood of the appointment of any other successors to President Rhoads; but it had never occurred to me that there could be any doubt in the matter, and it seems to me only just that you should be informed, at a time when you are doubtless considering all the circumstances of the College that it has always been my intention, whenever Miss M. Carey Thomas should become President of your College, to pay into her hands the sum of ten thousand dollars yearly for as long as I live and she remains President, to be used, at her discretion, for the English department in the first instance, and then for the other departments of the College but not for buildings, and furthermore, that it has always been my own intention and the intention of the other members of the Board of Managers of the Bryn Mawr School in Baltimore to aid in the establishment of other preparatory schools for Bryn Mawr College throughout the country, whenever it shall seem to us that a proper opportunity offers and that competent graduates of the College can be obtained to conduct said schools.

    The arrangements I have already made with reference to the Medical Department of the Johns Hopkins University will at present, I regret to say, prevent my guaranteeing for the use of the College more than five thousand dollars ($5,000), in the year 1893–1894, to be followed by ten thousand dollars ($10,000), yearly, in and after the year 1894–1895.

    I ought to add that I write without consultation with Miss Thomas, to whom, however, I send by the same mail a copy of this letter, and that I have never had occasion to express to her any part of my intentions in regard to Bryn Mawr College, although she must of course have been aware of the certainty of my support of any institution of which she was President.

    This letter requires no acknowledgment, and I beg that the expression of my intentions contained in it may be regarded as strictly confidential.

I am very truly and respectfully yours,

Mary E. Garrett

PRESIDENT THOMAS'S ADDRESS

I THINK I CAN BEST TELL YOU in a concrete way what has been accomplished in women's education by describing to you the condition of affairs which I found in 1884 when I returned from Germany and set about planning the academic organization of Bryn Mawr. The outlook was discouraging except for the delight women were beginning to show in going to college. No one knew at all how things were going to turn out. The present achievement was small; the students were immature and badly trained; the scientific attainments of the professors teaching in colleges for women, with a few shining exceptions, were practically nil. Women were teaching in Wellesley, Mount Holyoke and Smith without even the elementary training of a college course behind them. Men in general, including highly intelligent presidents of colleges for women as well as for men, held in good faith absurd opinions on women's education. When I protested to the president of the most advanced college for women in regard to this lack of training, he told me that I could never run Bryn Mawr if I insisted on the same scholarly attainments from women professors as from men professors. He—and I think he will forgive me for quoting his opinion in those early days because I am sure he has since changed it—and the president of perhaps the greatest university for men in the United States, both told me that there was an intuitive something in ladies of birth and position which enabled them to do without college training, and make on the whole better professors for women college students than if they had themselves been to college. Everyone I consulted prophesied disaster if we carried out our plan of appointing to our professorships young unmarried men of high scientific promise. They said: In the first place, such men will not consent to teach women in a women's college; in the second place, if they should consent, their unmarried students will distract their minds; and in the third place, if by any chance they should be able to teach coherently, then surely such will be the charm of the bachelor estate that their girl students will compete with each other for proposals out of the classroom rather than for marks in the classroom. The president of Harvard College said to me, when he visited Bryn Mawr a year after its opening and found that our students were governing themselves and going away for a night or for a week-end, as they saw fit, "If this continues, I will give you two years, and no more, in which to close Bryn Mawr College." From that day to this our students have had free and unrestricted self-government, and have proved that women of the age our mothers were when we were born are old enough to govern themselves. Student self-government is now working in eleven colleges where women study, and is, I believe, destined to spread to all other colleges for women.

And so it has been with all questions in women's college education which was an experiment only five and twenty years ago. Our highest hopes are all coming gloriously true. It is like reading the pages of one of Grimm's fairy tales. The fearsome toads of those early prophecies are turning into pearls of purest radiance before our very eyes . . .

. . . We did not know when we began whether women's health could stand the strain of college education. We were haunted in those days by the clanging chains of that gloomy little spectre, Dr. Edward Clarke's *Sex in Education*. With trepidation of spirit I made my mother read it, and was much cheered by her remark that as neither she nor any of the women she knew had ever seen girls or women of the kind described in Dr. Clark's book, we might as well act as if they didn't exist. Still, we did not know whether college might not produce a crop of just such invalids. Doctors insisted that it would; we women could not be sure until we had tried the experiment. Now we have tried it, and tried it for more than a generation, and we know that college women are not only not invalids, but that they are better physically than other women in their own class of life.

We know that girls are growing stronger and more athletic. Girls enter college each year in better physical condition. For the past four years I have myself questioned closely all our entering classes, and often their mothers as well. I find that an average of 60 per cent enter college absolutely and in every respect well, and that less than 30 per cent make, or need to make, a periodic difference in exercise or study from year's end to year's end. This result is very different from that obtained by physicians and others writing in magazines and journals. These claimants give gruesome statistics from high schools and women's colleges which they are very careful not to name. Probably they are investigating girls whose general hygienic conditions are bad. Their brothers would undoubtedly make as poor a showing as compared to Harvard or Yale men or to the boys of Groton or St. Paul's. Certainly their sisters who have not been to high school or college would be even more invalided and abnormal. Eighty per cent of the Bryn Mawr students come from private schools and from homes where their nutrition and sanitary conditions have been good. Certainly they have all been subjected to a strenuous college preparatory course. Yet their physical condition is far beyond any results I have yet seen recorded. The Bryn Mawr students are surely the more normal and vigorous type toward which girls are approaching, and their prolonged college preparation seems to have benefited, certainly not harmed them. Here, again, men studying women have confused causes and attributed to study what is simply due to malnutrition and bad sanitary conditions.

We are now living in the midst of great and, I believe on the whole, beneficent social changes, which herald the coming economic independence of women. Everything seems to indicate that women will not only make their way into all except a few of the trades and professions, but that they will be compelled by economic causes beyond their control to stay in them after marriage. Already in teaching, nursing, library work, typewriting, bookkeeping, telephoning, telegraphing, they are steadily taking possession and driving men before them.

All professional and trade training schools must admit women. It is already clear that no separate schools for women will be founded. The few university professional schools of law, medicine, theology and architecture now closed will open, probably within the next decade.

Separate professional schools are an anachronism. The expense is too vast. Indeed, women's medical schools were only brought into existence by the savage prejudices of many men physicians. They are now almost all closed.

All university graduate schools of philosophy which confer the degree of doctor of philosophy, with two comparatively unimportant exceptions, admit women. The only important graduate school which has been closed, that of the Johns Hopkins University, opened to women this autumn. Forty-one out of the 450 or so universities and colleges maintain graduate schools, and of these only twenty-seven have conferred more than ten doctor of philosophy degrees in all. Of these twenty-seven, which alone are to be seriously considered, only four, Virginia, Princeton and two of Catholic universities, exclude women. But Virginia and Princeton, taken together, have conferred only fifty-four degrees of doctor of philosophy out of 2,715—the total number of degrees conferred. Of the remaining fourteen universities, conferring less than ten degrees apiece, the four which exclude women have no organized graduate work, and have conferred only ten degrees between them.

Among these forty-one universities conferring Ph.D. degrees, there is only one women's college, Bryn Mawr. Bryn Mawr ranks fifteenth on the attendance of graduate students and nineteenth on the number of degrees conferred. It is the third largest graduate school for women east of Chicago, only Columbia and Cornell containing more graduate students. It has twice as many women as Yale.

That brings us squarely face to face with a vitally important question in women's education. Shall our colleges for women maintain graduate schools of philosophy and confer Ph.D. degrees? The experience of Bryn Mawr has shown that women will choose to pursue graduate work in such schools if they come into existence, and it has also shown that a Ph.D. from a women's college has a commercial value equal to that given by the oldest and most richly endowed men's universities. I regard the question as to all other professional schools as settled. It would be unwise and harmful to women's professional standing for women's colleges to maintain them. They must be coeducational. Is this the case also with schools of philosophy? I think not. The conditions are wholly different, from one-third to one-half of all students studying in our women's colleges expect to teach. They must be prepared by advanced work in their special subjects beyond the A.B. degree. Only one-seventh of the men and women studying in graduate schools take the doctor of philosophy degree. The remaining six-sevenths are studying for a year or more. Many more women will go on with advanced work if they can go on at the college where they have taken their undergraduate work. The experience of men's colleges has proved this. Far more women are now taking college courses in Wellesley, Smith, Vassar, Mount Holyoke, Bryn Mawr, Radcliffe and Barnard, than anywhere else in the East, and far greater than in any seven colleges in the West. In only three of the seven, Bryn Mawr, Radcliffe, and Barnard, can women really fit themselves for teaching. It is inevitable that the other four colleges for women should provide these opportunities.

But it is not only for the graduate students that the graduate school is needed. It is needed most of all for the undergraduate students. I do not believe that the best undergraduate teaching is ever given in a college where the professors do not also conduct research and investigation courses. In no other way, I believe, can a faculty of enthusiastic scholars, abreast of modern scientific methods, be maintained. Such scholars make infinitely better teachers for college students, and even for children in a kindergarten, if they were attainable. It is impossible for a teacher of any kind to know too much. Also a progressive graduate school weeds out non-productive scholars from a college as nothing else will. Already there are signs of the great colleges for women taking on this true university function. Vassar, Wellesley, Smith, and Mount

Holyoke have already created a few resident graduate scholarships and fellowships. I believe also that every women's college ought to maintain not only a graduate school of philosophy of the highest grade, but also a purely graduate school of education connected with a small practice school . . .

. . . But there is still another, and, as it seems to me, more cogent reason why our women's colleges should maintain graduate schools of philosophy. The highest service which colleges can render to their time is to discover and foster imaginative and constructive genius. Such genius unquestionably needs opportunity for its highest development. This is peculiarly the case with women students. As I watch their gallant struggle I sometimes think that the very stars in their course have conspired against them. Women scholars can assist women students as men cannot, to tide over the first discouragements of a life of intellectual renunciation. I believe that in the future many an ardent spirit will plume itself for flight into the blue empyrean in the graduate schools of women's colleges. Ability of the kind I am speaking of is very large, but for this reason it is precious beyond all other human products. If the graduate schools of women's colleges could develop one single woman of Galton's Y type—say, a Madame Curie or a Madame Kovalewsky (under happier conditions)—they would have done more for human advancement than if they had turned out thousands of ordinary college graduates.

The time has now come for those of us who are in control of women's education to bend ourselves to the task of creating academic conditions favorable for the development of this kind of creative ability. We should at once proceed to found research chairs at all our women's colleges, with three or four hours a week of research teaching, and the rest of the time free for independent investigation. We should reserve all the traveling fellowships in our gift for women who have given evidence, however slight, of power to do research work. We should bring pressure on our State universities to give such women opportunity to compete for professors' chairs. In the four women suffrage States this can be accomplished in the twinkling of an eye. It will only be necessary for women's organizations to vote for university regents with proper opinions.

Abundant opportunity for research and the endowment of professors' chairs open for competition to women scholars is the next great advance to be made in women's education—the last and greatest battle to be won.

Reprinted from the *Bryn Mawr Alumnae Quarterly*, January 1908.

Right: M. Carey Thomas, 1896

Opposite (left): Mary Elizabeth Garrett, c. 1877. Photograph by Mora Studio (New York)

Opposite (right): Mary Elizabeth Garrett, c. 1904. Photograph by Frederick Hollyer

President Thomas occupies a position at the helm of Bryn Mawr that the most capable of substitute can hardly fill. She not only controls efficiently all the machinery of the ship, but understands thoroughly the needs of her crew. Her knowledge of the course the boat must steer and her clear vision of the port towards which it heads make her an invaluable captain, one whom the whole ship welcomes back to guide it over the deeps and shoals of 1920–21.

Reprinted from the *College News*, September 28, 1920.

BEHOLD THEY ARE WOMEN!
Bryn Mawr

M. CAREY THOMAS BUILT IN STONE as effectively as she did in academic policy. She shared her era's belief in the power of the physical environment to shape communal spirit and individual character. She brought to Bryn Mawr a strong, feminist commitment to the needs of young women scholars. However inimical to Quaker traditions, she added a love of pageantry and drama. All of this is visible in the Jacobean quadrangles of Bryn Mawr. . . .

The Bryn Mawr campus remains as a monument to M. Carey Thomas' hopes for women. During her deanship and presidency the talented young Philadelphia architectural firm of Cope & Stewardson gave form to the residence, library, and laboratory of her adolescent daydream. In the two decades following Bryn Mawr's opening, building after building encircled the original Taylor Hall, creating splendid spaces for living, studying, teaching, and playing. Walter Cope —the nephew of board member Francis Cope, brother of a member of the first class, and a Friend—was the ideal designer for Bryn Mawr. While he worked as an apprentice in Addison Hutton's office, Cope had a more cosmopolitan and sophisticated sensibility. He travelled in Europe and on his return formed a partnership with John Stewardson. The two were from a similar Quaker background, and Stewardson was also related to members of the Bryn Mawr board. He had trained at the École des Beaux-Arts. With Cope as the major design partner, the firm of Cope & Stewardson gradually came to its mature style, a Jacobean Gothic that combined dignity with a festive air. Bryn Mawr offered Cope and Stewardson their first experience with college buildings. Well-publicized success led to important commissions at the University of Pennsylvania, Princeton, and Washington University in St. Louis. The firm worked in close collaboration with Carey Thomas, who always guided and, at times, fully outlined the plan. Thomas, Cope and Stewardson created a fitting setting for the realization of her girlhood dream of a life as an exemplary woman among women.

At fifteen, [M. Carey] "Rush" Thomas had envisioned surroundings that hardly suggested a woman's parlor. Her dream library had "dark crimson curtains and furniture" and "great big easy chairs," a "bright wood fire always burning" and a "great large table covered with papers." Unlike the men who planned domestic places at Smith or seminary settings at Vassar and Wellesley, Carey Thomas had no desire to adapt feminine spaces to academic uses. Rather, she wanted to appropriate the library and the laboratory of men. Though her closest relationships were with women and she became the moving force behind a women's college, Carey Thomas held no belief in a separate women's culture. The curriculum of Bryn Mawr made no genuflections to women's special nature or domestic future. She argued that courses generally deemed appropriate for women either lacked the necessary intellectual content, as did domestic science, or they equally fit men and women, as did infant psychology. The life of the mind was neuter: "Science and literature and philology are what they are and inalterable." Bryn Mawr created special opportunities for women to enter the sacred groves of scholarship, but the groves had no gender. "Given two bridge-builders, a man and a woman, given a certain bridge to be built, and given as always the un-changeable laws of mechanics . . . it is simply inconceivable that the preliminary instruction given to the two bridge-builders should differ in quantity, quality, or method of presentation because while the bridge is building one will wear knickerbockers and the other a rainy-day skirt." As the visible sign that truth had no sex, the Bryn Mawr campus gave no clue as to the gender of its student body.

Nothing about Bryn Mawr suggested a home . . . Domesticity in all its forms was anathema to Carey Thomas. After she returned from her years abroad, she had felt acutely uncomfortable in her parents' house with its informal, child-centered ways and its lack of privacy and order. The college that she envisioned had nothing of home. Unlike Mount Holyoke and Wellesley, students performed no domestic work during their four years, not even the making of their own beds. They wore a special dress on campus, the traditional mark of scholarship worn by men, the cap and gown. They enjoyed privacy unusual to young women: each student had a single room at the minimum . . . .

. . . She [Carey Thomas] insisted that female as well as male professors have full control of their time outside the classroom for the pursuit of scholarship. Following Smith's lead, Bryn Mawr installed a gentlewoman as resident mistress of Merion, in this case a Quaker lady; but in time Thomas replaced her and added to the other residence halls young Bryn Mawr graduates, increasingly outside the fold. In 1901, she renamed the mistresses "wardens," in imitation of their British counterparts. In addition, the graduate fellows, women despite the appellation, lived among the undergraduates to inspire them by their scholarly example. The students themselves regulated behavior, at least in principle. In 1892, when growth in numbers made the informal system of the first years unworkable, Bryn Mawr instituted the first plan for student self-governance in a women's college. Students held only limited power: collegians never made rules, they only enforced them. Controversy

FOUNDATIONS: 1885–1922

Left: Receipt for library tables, in the amount of $95.50, April 27, 1885

Right: List of furnishings needed for Merion Hall, 1885

Opposite: Student room in Merion Hall, Bryn Mawr's first dormitory, c. 1902

remains over their actual control even here. Carey Thomas' need to protect the college from the outside caused her to intervene to uphold conventions in which even she did not believe. For example, while she had to halt nude bathing, she confessed to Mary Garrett, "there is really no harm in it." Her love of power may have led her to create a spy system among the students, a charge her critics made. But, however limited, self-government remained an ideal and took architectural form. Cope & Stewardson designed halls for Bryn Mawr scholars as distinctive as their caps and gowns, bearing the same mark of scholarship as the traditional colleges for men . . .

. . . Bryn Mawr gave Carey Thomas a landscape in which her non-Quaker aestheticism took solid form. The initial building designed by Cope and Stewardson suggested a few signs of what followed. Radnor Hall forsook the domestic imagery of the cottage. This frankly institutional building bore some resemblance to Taylor in its verticality, but its facade of irregular stone was much cleaner. The shape of the building gave a slight feeling of enclosure over the entrance. The great octagonal room carried battlements. However, following the lead of Hutton's initial buildings, Cope & Stewardson sited Radnor in the middle of the campus. Bryn Mawr had asked Calvert Vaux, the experienced landscape architect who designed Central Park with Frederick Law Olmsted, to create a plan for the campus. He reaffirmed earlier locational decisions, though he suggested encircling the campus in trees as an arboreal barrier to the surrounding neighborhood.

The real breakthrough occurred in 1891. Cope & Stewardson designed Denbigh, the third student residence, as a long, low, elegant structure placed at the perimeter of the campus. Its irregular gray stone facade was punctuated by the bay windows of the students' sitting rooms; its roof, by their chimneys. The cornice line carried the battlements that established most clearly its English antecedents. One entered on the side, into a three-sided bay topped with battlements. Despite its decorative emphasis at the roofline, Denbigh is a calm horizontal building with clean lines and repetitions conveying order and regularity. Most important of all, its placement created courtyards between Denbigh and Dalton, the science building. With Denbigh, Bryn Mawr not only shed its Victorian skin, but bones as well; monumental masses gave way to walls that enclosed.

Cope & Stewardson reached their mature style with the building of the double dormitory Pembroke East and West. The long line of buildings of the two residence halls walled off the campus on the south. At the joining of the two residences, an arched gateway framed the carriage entrance on to the campus and created a strong perpendicular axis. This powerful square entry carried Jacobean decoration and four battlemented towers. Its impressive windows sheathed the great dining hall of the double residence. A more vital composition than Denbigh, Pembroke Hall is a courtly building, dignified yet festive. It formed a wall that defined the campus from the outside and enclosed it from the inside. With the library, it shaped handsome courtyards.

Rockefeller, the last Cope & Stewardson residence hall, continued the line of Pembroke West, turning the corner to define the southwest point of the campus. Variations in setbacks and the resulting L-shape added a needed variety to the long building. At the turn, a tall tower held a massive arch that provided a pedestrian entrance, Owl Gateway, approached by stairs. When the library was constructed, the gateway framed perfectly its delicate form.

In 1895, Frederick Law Olmsted confirmed Cope & Stewardson's basic plan. In 1893, the college had purchased land to the west of the campus. Working with his stepson, John C. Olmsted, the great landscape designer laid out athletic grounds in the informal northerly section of the campus that sloped down to Roberts Road and determined that future buildings frame the western perimeter as they had the southern. While the college never carried out the many specific plans for athletic fields and plantings, the firm set the location of new buildings and roads until 1928.

Each dormitory grouped near its entrance a drawing room, student sitting room, and dining room. The college guaranteed to each student a single room, at the minimum. But beyond this and the common rooms, students lived under quite varied conditions. They had rooms of different shapes, sizes, and locations, some with a shared or an individual study. A modest single room in an unfortunate location went as low as $100 for the year; a two-room suite or a room of unusual size cost as high as $350. In Carey Thomas' eyes, this great differential only mirrored students' experiences in other realms. Recalling her own luxurious three-room suite in Sage at Cornell, she argued that differences in housing did not affect students' judgments about each other. She dismissed the notion that students' economic backgrounds shaped college social structure because she identified with the affluent student, not the one forced to live in pinched surroundings. As time went on, Bryn Mawr attracted more wealthy students, and successive dormitories held an increased ratio of expensive rooms. Rockefeller, the most luxurious, had thirty-nine single suites, each with bedroom and sitting room. In addition, its basement had service rooms for sewing and hairdressing and a students' grocery store. Carey Thomas always hoped to attract the daughters of wealth. Bryn Mawr became increasingly successful in doing so.

Joseph Taylor intended from the beginning that his college educate "the higher and more refined classes of Society," but he expected them to be Friends. By 1897, the incoming class had only two Quakers, the same number as entering Roman Catholics, in contrast to thirty Episcopalians and twenty-four Presbyterians, a disturbing ratio to trustees committed to Joseph Taylor's vision. Little wonder that they came into conflict with Carey Thomas. They fought her on a number of grounds; but because trustees held ultimate responsibility for buildings, they took their strongest stand there. By the turn of the century, they turned against her building program. While Thomas argued strenuously that buildings provided a preferred form of investment with a high annual return, the trustees forbade further use of Taylor's endowment for buildings. Yet, while trustees created hurdles, they failed to block Carey Thomas. The attempt to stop growth merely forced her to venture outside to beg for funds. A large gift from John D. Rockefeller built a residence hall with his name and encouraged alumnae gifts for the library, Thomas' most intense fund-raising effort.

In the library, Carey Thomas found her crowning symbol of Bryn Mawr. As she planned the library, her attention to detail became obsessive, and she came into conflict not only with her trustees but with her architects.

Cope & Stewardson designed the library according to very explicit instructions from President Thomas. Its main reading room copied the dining hall of Wadham College, Oxford, while Oriel College provided the model for the entrance. Thomas wanted an enclosed cloister at its center and seminar rooms adjoining professors' offices for graduate work. The architects agreed to work within these limits and to accept her requirement that the library could not be used in their designs for other colleges. (Cope & Stewardson had repeated their Bryn Mawr residence hall successes at Princeton and at Washington University in St. Louis.) The firm created an elegant plan, perhaps unsuitable for a library—the librarian complained that the central reading room was larger than that of the British Museum—but certainly befitting the dignity that Carey Thomas demanded for Bryn Mawr.

Walter Cope died before building began. While Carey Thomas was travelling abroad, Herbert Tatnall, the chairman of the buildings and grounds committee, decided that the proposed library was thirty feet too close to Taylor Hall and detracted from its dignity. Cope's successor agreed to shift the building back. When Thomas heard, she turned livid with rage: she insisted that laymen had no right to make decisions about location and that the college should trust Cope's judgment, not some unknown with whom it had never worked. Through a barrage of long, agonized letters, she sought and gained a delay and then the restoration of Cope's plan. By 1904, Tatnall and the conservative trustees had lost on every major issue: the siting of the library was their last-ditch effort to protect the symbol of their vision of the college, Taylor Hall. A library built like a Jacobean college chapel with towers and battlements threatened to encroach upon the "Quaker lady."

M. Carey Thomas won not only on the site but also on every detail. This required both a change in architects and a messy lawsuit. In Thomas' eyes the victory justified the struggle, for it produced a library that matched her pedagogy and taste. The Johns Hopkins-influenced seminar method, where professors and students gathered around a table in the presence of books to engage in mutual research, required seminar rooms in every graduate subject. Along with their long tables surrounded by chairs or laboratory equipment, the rooms contained shelves of specialized books for graduate students' use. Senior professors' offices adjoined the seminar rooms, emphasizing by their location the importance of research and graduate teaching. Undergraduates read their books in a more splendid setting, at one of the 134 tall desks in the great and ornate reading room. This vast open space, reproducing an Oxford dining hall, with light pouring in from tall windows adorned with tracery, fit Carey Thomas' vision of the dignity of scholarship. The rectangular cloister with its handsome groined-vault passageway and courtyard arcade offered an appropriate setting for the monastic renunciation that Thomas associated with the life of the mind.

These were embattled years for M. Carey Thomas. She emerged triumphant against trustees and architects on the library, only to face, in 1916, a faculty uprising against her dictatorial rule. She could no longer count on alumnae, who felt a different stake in the college. She confronted a new generation of students, whose goals she found difficult to understand. Carey Thomas herself changed as well. She remained a brilliant feminist; but where she had once moderated her materialism and sensualism by a Quaker upbringing, she now unleashed her desires. In time her enjoyment of power became a habitual exercise. What began as leadership became autocracy. In the twentieth century, M. Carey Thomas turned formidable.

Reprinted with permission from Helen Lefkowitz Horowitz, *Alma Mater: Design and Experience in the Women's Colleges from Their Nineteenth-Century Beginnings to the 1930s* (New York: Knopf, 1984), 117–33. Notes in original not reprinted.

A QUESTION OF VOWS

Above: Clippings from various newspapers, on the issue of female college graduates and marriage, c. 1909–10

Opposite: Merion Hall, 1898

COLLEGE WOMEN DEFENDED

MISS M. CAREY THOMAS, president of Bryn Mawr College, in the course of an address delivered before the National Federation of Women's Clubs in St. Louis, contended that college women do marry, and marry wisely. If anything is proved, it is that a girl's going to college for four years does not affect her marriage any more than a man's going to college affects his marriage. The reason, then, why only about fifty per cent of college women marry is because the college women of the past have come from the classes in which only fifty per cent of women marry. College life perhaps gives to women the intelligence to select their husbands a trifle more sensibly. College women, says President Thomas, have married two-thirds more men who were college graduates than their non-collegiate sisters have, and their husbands' average yearly incomes are much higher than the incomes of the husbands of their non-collegiate sisters. President Thomas furthermore points out that there are only two classes in which as a rule all women marry—the working class, in which the woman is not an expense, but contributes her share in household labor at home, or in paid work outside the home, and the rich class, where the woman brings inherited wealth to her husband. College women, it is claimed, are at least a little stronger than other women; and although speaking generally, no modern families are large, the families of college women are a trifle larger than other women's, and the proportion of their children who survive the perils of infancy slightly greater.

Reprinted from *Zion's Herald* (Boston), June 15, 1904.

MARRIAGE PROBLEM

MISS THOMAS, the president of Bryn Mawr College, has been discussing the education of girls, and admits that only one-half of the girls who go to college ever marry. But that, she says, does not signify that college education in any respect affects the matrimonial prospects of girls, because the college girls come from a social class whereof only half the women marry. It is the intermediate class that is neither rich nor poor, the women of which do not marry unless they see in prospect a sufficient income to pay servants' wages and sustain the standard of living which servants imply. Everybody knows the matrimonial problem is somewhat perplexing to girls who are brought up to lean on cooks and housemaids, and who yet do not have fortunes of their own, but Miss Thomas' assertion that fifty per cent of such ladies never marry is pretty startling and will be not a little disconcerting to parents.

Reprinted from *Life Magazine*, June 9, 1904.

EARLY STUDENT STYLE
Caps and Gowns

A PROBLEM
Mary Bidwell Breed, Class of 1894

In cap and gown, a maiden rare,
With downcast eyes and thoughtful air,
Who wanders there so carelessly,
While academic breezes free
Caress her cheek and golden hair.

What deep reflection makes her wear
A look so far away? What care
Of Greek or Sanskrit ponders she
    In cap and gown

Is't Calculus? Or is't Voltaire—
To darken thus a brow so fair?
She gazes up; then, anxiously,
"Whom shall I ask to my next tea?"
Thus meditating walks she there,
    In cap and gown.

Reprinted from the *Lantern*, 1892.

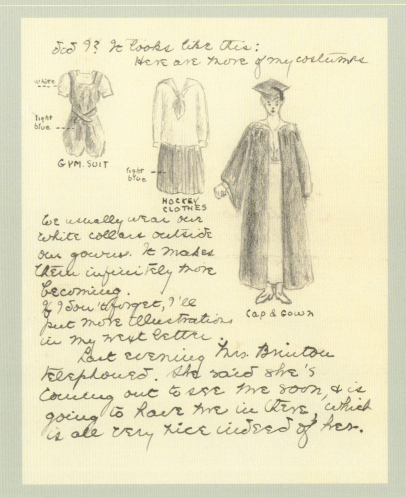

Above: Page from a letter, Natalie Gookin, class of 1920, to her mother, c. 1916–20, with sketches of some of the college's uniforms, including the cap and gown

Opposite (top): Cartes de visites of Bryn Mawr students, ranging from the class of 1889 to the class of 1901

Opposite (bottom): Students studying in caps and gowns, c. 1904

FOUNDATIONS: 1885–1922

FIRST MATH PROFESSOR AT BRYN MAWR COLLEGE
Charlotte Angas Scott
Taline Cox and Rachel Park, Class of 2010

CHARLOTTE ANGAS SCOTT (1858–1931), the second of seven children, was born and raised in England. Her father, a Nonconformist minister, recognized the dearth of secondary schools for women and provided his daughter with tutors in mathematics. In 1876 Scott received a scholarship to Cambridge University's Girton College, the first undergraduate school for women in England. Scott and her classmates faced severe restrictions while at Cambridge; for example, women were not allowed to take the university's final oral examinations. Scott, however, elected to take the exams unofficially and placed eighth overall. At the graduation ceremony, when the school's administration failed to acknowledge Scott's accomplishment, her classmates exclaimed "Scott of Girton!" when the degree for the eighth-ranking student was presented to a male classmate. After completing her doctor of science degree at the University of London, in 1885 Scott emigrated to the United States to serve as a professor in the Mathematics Department at the newly founded Bryn Mawr College, a position she held until her retirement in 1925.

Beloved by students, Scott was intolerant of students' indifference. Some historians have suggested that her influence on Bryn Mawr was "second only to that of [M. Carey] Thomas."[1] Her responsibilities and authority extended far beyond the college's realm. In addition to her research on analytic geometry, she attended international mathematics conferences and contributed to the educational standards that led to the creation of the College Entrance Examination Board. At a dinner in Scott's honor in 1922, distinguished mathematician Alfred North Whitehead proclaimed, "She is a great example of the universal brotherhood of civilization."[2] At Bryn Mawr we think of her as a great example of the universal sisterhood as well!

1. Bettye Anne Case and Anne M. Leggett, *Complexities: Women in Mathematics* (Princeton, NJ: Princeton University Press, 2005), 51.
2. Ibid., 52.

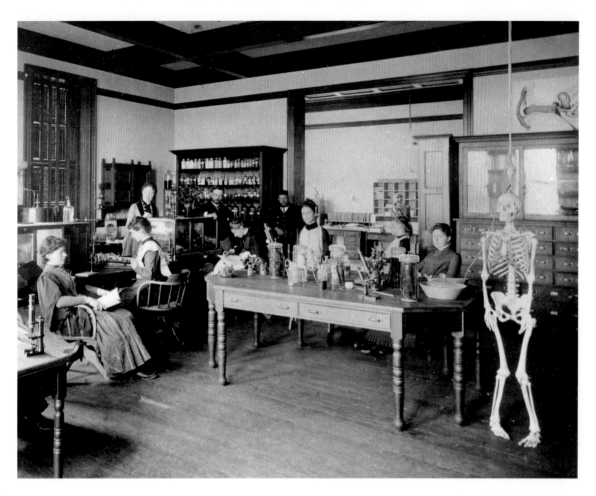

EDITORIAL
L.G., Class of 1889

IT IS IMPOSSIBLE to convey the slightest idea of the crowded state of the laboratories in Bryn Mawr College. A small frame structure consisting of two rooms serves at present as a physical laboratory and a lecture room. The chemical department occupies a portion of the third floor of the general lecture hall, while biological investigations are carried on in three rooms on the second floor. This department has been compelled to reject a large number of students applying for major and minor courses, as only twenty-nine desks can be crowded into the rooms set aside for biology. In addition to the inconvenience which it causes to the scientific department itself this lack of room seriously interferes with the work of the college, forcing the other departments to do without rooms which they sorely need. Then, too, it was the original plan that the rooms now set apart for biological work should serve as an extension to the library. Since these rooms are not available and the library has become greatly crowded, it has been necessary to use part of the main corridor for this extension. That something must be done to meet this difficulty is apparent, and it is proposed to erect

a new building in which all the scientific work shall be carried out. The plans for such a building have been drawn up and submitted to the Board of Trustees, and the only thing for which the college now waits is the money necessary to carry out this project.

Reprinted from the Lantern, *1891.*

A PLEA FOR CO-OPERATIVE STUDY

NOW THAT the examinations are over, and the marks are almost all in, the *Philistine* would like to say a word in favor of co-operative study. The students have been told that many of the faculty object to their preparing themselves for examinations by studying together, and the *Philistine* believes that there are many arguments on the side of those who employ this method. In a large class, as for example, Political Science, time cannot be spent on the discussion of every difficulty which arises in the mind of every student.

In preparation for the examination two or more students discuss and eliminate their difficulties. It is a well-established fact that the easiest and most effective way of committing to memory is by repeating aloud in order to become accustomed to the sound of the words. Poetry if not read aloud loses half of its beauty. Many a student in doing private reading lets her eyes travel over the page without attempting to take in the meaning which reading aloud would give her. Co-operative study is the one method of equalizing cleverness. The clever girl helps the dull girl, and in the very explanation of the fact which she thinks she has known so well, learns to express her ideas fittingly, while the dull girl grasps the thoughts which escaped her in the lecture room. As to the theory that students waste time in talk when studying together, all the *Philistine* has to say is that if two girls are not sufficiently in earnest to keep their minds on their work when they are together, they are just as likely to waste time when they are apart.

Reprinted from the Fortnightly Philistine, *February 18, 1898.*

Top: Students in the Taylor lab, c. 1890s
Bottom: Interior of Thomas Hall, c. 1905–10
Opposite: Charlotte Angas Scott (1858–1931), c. 1901

DULCI FISTULA
Song for the Orals

I.

In the middle Taylor office in a crimson velvet chair,
There the president is sitting, and I know she waits me there,
And with her is another talking French or talking Dutch,
And to-morrow they will seize me—yes, they'll have me in their clutch.
On the road to a degree, down here in fair B.M.C.,
Where the French and German orals soon will make an end of me.
On the road to a degree, down here in fair B.M.C.,
Where we nearly cram our heads off for that erudite A.B.

II.

When the tortuous time is over and at last we've made the leap,
Then they'll pen us up in chapel like a flock of wayward sheep,
And they'll keep us there till sunset, or till with us they are through,
While we sit and weep together—all the bluest of the blue.
Yes, the bluest of the blue, for we'll fear that we're not through,
And for that A. B. we're seeking we'll still find a lot to do.
On the road, etc.

III.

Oh, the mediaeval tortures, they were nothing in their way
To the inquisition methods in Bryn Mawr the present day,
And I'm learning here in college what all other seniors said,
When you come up for your orals, then you'll wish that you were dead.
Yes, you'll wish that you were dead,
Buried in a mossy bed,
With a little Bryn Mawr daisy nodding gently overhead
On the road, etc.

Reprinted from the *Fortnightly Philistine*, December 18, 1898.

CUI BONO?

SOMEONE SAID the other day that when she was away from Bryn Mawr, her recollection of college was hurrying, rushing from Pembroke to Taylor, from Taylor to Dalton, over exasperating curved boardwalks; always late, always vainly hurrying.

This too, as we raced along, pushing against the wind, both desirous of getting to required drill before the roll-call.

What can our contemporaries, and the coming age, for whom we are making the precedents, think of our ideals in life when we only hurry past, laden with books, and even spoiling the effect of our graceful college gowns by our ungraceful haste? And what are we hurrying for? Culture? Then let us strive to attain our beautiful ideal in a more beautiful way.

In this same breathless discussion we agreed that one of our ideals of life here in college was to sit by a study fire, in a comfortable chair, with a very good friend, or that next best of companions, a very good book; and on further comparison we found that neither of us could remember having attained this cherished ideal more than two or three times at most during the eight months of college.

One of our well-known professors was talking to his class a few days ago. "I don't suppose you have had much time to review this," he said, and there was an appreciative murmur from the class. "But," he added, "we don't aim to give you much spare time."

Is there not a mistaken idea there? It cannot do us much good to get through hasty preparation for daily recitations, and then go over the work in an equally hasty review for examinations, or, I should say, a "cram," where Chemistry, Political Science, Sudermann and Matthew Arnold are horribly, inseparably mixed. We go into an examination clinging courageously to the confused scraps of information which have seemed prominent in this hodge-podge of facts, and then the examiners send back our papers with a note on the margin to the effect that our ideas are lacking in unity!

It seems rather hard that two average girls, with no more than the average amount of work, cannot find time more than two or three times a year to sit down by their own fireside and collect their thoughts. And it seems rather pathetic, too, that amid the rushing commonplaces of our life here we have tenderly cherished this pretty idyll of peace and quiet.

It is hard! We are all attached to our rooms, especially the one we call a study—I suppose because the most obvious thing we are here for is to study. In our study we collect the things we love best, mainly books; beginning our college collection in Freshman year with *Sigurd the Wölsung*, or the Mermaid editions, of Marlowe, Matthew Arnold and Walter Pater, until in Senior year we tenderly find a place on the

Above: Clipping from the *College News*, October 14, 1915

Opposite (top): Title illustration from "Dulci Fistula," *Fortnightly Philistine*, December 18, 1898

Opposite (bottom): Drawing of student in cap and gown, ink on paper, c. 1900–1910

Next two pages: Registration photographs of students from the class of 1912

HOW DOTH THE LITTLE BUSY BEE

In the spring of 1914, Dorothy Wolf, Bryn Mawr 1912, asked the students of Bryn Mawr to keep an account of every minute of their time in order that she might use the statistics thus obtained for a thesis which she was then writing. For the purpose of making it easier for the students to keep these accounts, she had special forms printed which were filled out and collected from each student every evening. The results of her investigations are as follows:

Averages Normal Week Day.
1. Routine—Sleep—8 hours 33 minutes; meals—1 hour 20 minutes; dressing—1 hour 20 minutes.
2. Academic work—7 hours 20 minutes.
3. Athletics—55 minutes.
4. Organized student activities—1 hour 5 minutes.
5. Personal social activities—1 hour 5 minutes.
6. Personal avocations—1 hour 45 minutes.

Averages for Four Items.

	Normal week days	Slack period (after mid-years).	
	Week days	Week days Sat.	Sun.
Sleep	8.33	8.52 9.22	9.53
Exercise	0.55	0.35 0.45	0.48
Reading	0.32	0.50 1.55	1.37
Study	7.20	6.26 1.29	1.10

crowded shelves for the poetical works of Mr. Swinburne. The pictures on the study walls come to reflect, more and more, the character of its occupant; as, even without attending the college lectures, she goes through some various periods of art, generally suffering most from the Florentine Masters and the pre-Raphaelites. The plaster casts, that generally form a part of our decoration, grow from tiny three-inch medallions to tall three-foot Victories and Venuses; and in one room there is even a small collection of Venuses, varying in size, color, and beauty.

All this progress goes on, until in the fourth year at college, a study is a cozy little refuge characteristic of the tastes of its inmate and necessarily congenial to these tastes, and yet, alas, she cannot find time, more than two or three times a year, to deliberately sit herself down to enjoy the fruits of her labor.

We say, and I believe we think, the college woman is the coming woman—the woman who, when developed to her best, is to combine with the learning and solidity of the college girl of the present, the grace and charm of the modern society woman. We do not claim to have come to the fulfillment of this hope as yet, and we can hardly expect to do so until we find a cure among ourselves for the century's curse of restlessness.

Reprinted from the *Fortnightly Philistine*, January 29, 1897.

THE ORIGIN OF SELF-GOVERNMENT AT BRYN MAWR COLLEGE
Annie Crosby Emery Allinson, Class of 1892

IN JUNE 1891, just before Commencement, Miss Thomas called the students together and told them that the social life of the College could no longer be conducted without "rules." No one questioned her decision, for during that winter we had begun to feel that the Golden Age had been brought to an end by our own frailties. In the earlier years two factors had promoted freedom. The students were nearer the gods and cared more for the pleasures of Parnassus than for the fleshpots of Egypt. In addition, the size of our community—my class, at entrance brought the members up to only eighty—made it possible for us to vary work and amusement without interfering with each other. Problems of "noise" and "quiet" settled themselves. Time, however, had changed all this. With two hundred students in the halls, many wills came into conflict, and the succeeding years, which made the ivy older, brought to us the moods and humors of youth. Our premature wisdom lingered on only in an anxious feeling that we might "harm the college" and in a half-conscious appreciation of the charms of law.

Miss Thomas, therefore, met with a ready response to her general statements. But after the meeting, Miss Susan Walker (Fitzgerald) of 1893, and a few others, asking themselves whether law and liberty could not be combined, arrived at the idea of the students framing their own social code. Miss Walker, as "spokesman for this self-appointed committee," went to the Dean and gained her willing consent to the new experiment.

I had left college before Commencement and my first knowledge of the momentous events came through a letter from Miss Walker. She and her committee worked indefatigably in the summer and wrote to a large number of students in order to arouse their enthusiasm. I remember the thrill with which I enlisted in a cause whose object was government but whose slogan was freedom!

In the autumn our meetings began, and with them was ushered in the age of oratory. Although the students voted at once to accept self-government, argument and panegyric were necessary before it gained its unprecarious footing of today. My part in this early history was due to an accident of office. I happened to be president of the Undergraduate Association, and the students were too much absorbed in the issues involved in the experiment of self-government to care how the machinery was run. To save time, they appointed me president of the new association, which seemed to be superseding the old, and asked me to appoint the Executive Board, provided for in the Constitution. It had already been decided that graduate students were to be included in the association and to be subject to the same rules. To represent their body, Miss Marguerite Sweet and Miss Florence Keyes were appointed, while Miss Walker and Miss Elizabeth Winsor (Pearson), the president of the Class of 1892, represented the undergraduates. When our sense of humor suffered an eclipse, the greater detachment of the graduate members was a saving resource.

GOVERNING THEMSELVES

The Association had empowered us to draw up and present a set of resolutions. The students of Merion Hall used to say that they had never been disturbed by noise until the Executive Board held midnight sessions in my room to discuss the necessity of "quiet hours." Miss Thomas talked over the resolutions with us, but left us perfectly free to do as we chose. In later years, when, mutatis mutandis, I was an administrative officer myself among students jealously intent on governing themselves, I appreciated what it meant for her practically to entrust the reputation of the college, for which she, not we, would be held responsible, to our inexperience.

The members of the faculty did not sympathize with us, partly because faculties are usually doubtful of the expediency of vesting disciplinary power in students, and partly because they were indignant over the resolution about "social engagements" with themselves. This resolution, evoked by special circumstances, was hurried through the meeting without discussion, and I never heard any conversation about it among the students. The professors, as I later learned, knew nothing of its origin and supposed it had been a subject of general discussion. They were naturally angry that we should seem to forbid a thing which, in any general form, had never existed.

Nor did we have any support from the Alumnae, who felt that we had torn the palladium from the citadel. But alumnae, then as now, were taken lightly by undergraduates. Our real difficulty lay in defections within our own body. Some of the cleverest girls in college disapproved of the principle of self-government and began to express their opposition. One of them at a stormy meeting argued that law-making should be left to Miss Thomas and shocked our less daring intelligences by announcing, "I prefer monarchy to democracy—nor need it be a constitutional monarchy." Against philosophy like this our only weapons were an unbewildered piety and a militant faith.

The crisis came on the day, in midwinter, when the charter of our liberties, from the Trustees, was presented to the students. Skepticism showed a Gorgon face. Lethargy seemed to prevail. A supporter of the cause saved the day by an audacious experiment. Leaping to her feet, she called out, "I move that self-government be abandoned." The Chair put the question with assumed indifference. No voice answered the request for votes "in favor of the motion." To the request for opposing votes came a "No" that filled the chapel and was heard on the campus. In it was the fervor of a modern hockey "yell," and by it Self-Government was finally established. It is true that before the athletic and dramatic age, which began in 1896, we took our pleasures sadly, but I doubt if any Bryn Mawr undergraduates have been more gallantly young than we were when, with chivalric seriousness, we pledged ourselves to an idea.

Reprinted from the Bryn Mawr Alumnae Quarterly, November 1909.

Top: Meeting notice for Bryn Mawr Students' Association for Self-Government, March 31, 1896

Bottom: Card for class president Marion Reilly, class of 1901

PIGEON HOLES: SELF-GOVERNMENT

Annie Crosby Emery Allinson, Class of 1892

. . . For diversity of opinions has compelled us to inquire more deeply into the principles of self-government and to examine more closely its actual results in its influence on our characters and conduct, and in its relations to the general intellectual and social life of the College. We have found that we may assert with confidence that our Association is firmly established, because it is established not on youthful sentimentality or enthusiasm, but on sound principles of government in aims, legislation, and execution, and on earnest and successful efforts to effect the best good of Bryn Mawr.

The questions which have come before us publicly this year have concerned the "practical working" of self-government. We have been gradually making our system something more certain than "an experiment," the only term by which it could be described last year. We found that it was one thing to organize an Executive Board and Proctors, with their duties and relationship to each other defined by a few general sentences, and quite another thing to preserve without difficulties on every side a happy combination of a strong central government with individual hall rights. Accordingly, we have organized our system more minutely until it has become excellent in its simplicity, coherence and efficiency. The legislative work is confined to the general Association. The executive work is divided, according to the nature of the various matters, between the Association and the separate halls, the Association performing its share through its Executive Board; the halls performing their share through the Proctorial Boards. Yet in spite of the independent executive power lodged in the separate halls, centralization is preserved by the Executive Board, as the representative of the general Association, having the function of a board of appeal for the students and proctors, and the right to remove incompetent proctors. Various details add to the practical efficiency of the system.

Another problem has been the enforcing of our most important resolutions, those, namely, concerning quiet in the lecture halls and the halls of residence. We have realized that upon this matter depends to a large extent the possibility of good graduate and undergraduate work at Bryn Mawr, and the preservation of proper relations between the different sides of our college life. We have had to discuss the advisability of changing our former resolutions, consider carefully what class of students should set the standard for the regulation of the hours of quiet, and devise better methods for the enforcement of our decisions.

In connection with these questions arose the question of the advisability of leaving legislation on certain matters to the separate halls, instead of confining all legislation to the general Association. We decided against such a change on the ground that it would destroy the centralization of our system and decrease our power of making resolutions based on pure justice and an impersonal regard for the public good. For we realize that these principles alone must underlie general laws made by an organized body to guide the conduct of a large number of students . . .

. . . Neither last year nor this year have we in our public discussions touched on the educational power that lies in self-government. But through the experience of these two years we have grown into the knowledge that in the opportunity of working for a community that self-government affords us; in the organizing of a system of government; in the deciding for ourselves of important questions of conduct; and in our meetings, necessarily conducted according to strict parliamentary rules, and calling forth attempts, at least, at clear and logical argument or earnest and thoughtful appeal, instead of haphazard remarks and vehement personal discussion, we have the means of gaining a training which we, as women, especially need, and which will be invaluable in all future work.

Reprinted from the Lantern, *1893.*

PULITZER PRIZE WINNER
Margaret Ayer Barnes, Class of 1907
Taline Cox, Class of 2010

Above: Margaret Ayer Barnes (1886–1967), class of 1907, c. 1906

"It is the love of learning," Margaret Ayer Barnes wanted to "stress" when she reflected on her Bryn Mawr years during her fiftieth reunion in 1957. She reminded her gathered classmates that "on entering Bryn Mawr we were little more than children, but here we were awakened to the things of the mind. When that has happened you don't fall asleep again." Indeed, Barnes was decidedly awake during her long and productive life. She was born in 1886, the daughter of Benjamin Ayer, a lawyer, and Janet Hopkins Ayer, a professor in the Law School at the University of Wisconsin. She grew up in Chicago and graduated from the University School for Girls in 1904. At Bryn Mawr, she was the "go-to-girl" for almost any social activity. One classmate recalled that at the Freshman Rush Night she, "out-shouted and out-pushed all around her, friend or foe." And whenever a song or speech needed to be given or sung on behalf of the class of 1907, Barnes was called upon to do the honors. While at Bryn Mawr she studied philosophy and English. She was devoted to her academics and to the place where she began to write what one biographer called, "some of the most perceptive critiques on modern feminism." Barnes later said that, "the greatest influences in my life have been extensive reading, my college education, and love of nature, friends and family." After college, Barnes pursued a career as a writer, and in 1930, she won the Pulitzer Prize for her novel *Years of Grace*. The story chronicles the life of Jane Ward Carver, a lady who resembles Barnes in more ways than one: she hails from Chicago and takes Bryn Mawr by storm. But what makes this novel so special is the prominence not only of Bryn Mawr, but also the lively presence of Presidents M. Carey Thomas and Marion Edwards Park.

PRESIDENT OF ASSOCIATION EXPLAINS WEEK-END QUESTION
Principle of Self-Government Is Directly Involved
Katherine Gardner, Class of 1922

THE QUESTION of week-ends has come up again with a new significance. Because several students had taken frequent week-ends, which in President Thomas' opinion made them undesirable, she explained last spring a desire to limit the College to four week-ends a semester. The Undergraduates in a meeting sympathized with President Thomas' desire to keep up a high academic standard and to avoid criticism of the College for laxity of any sort, but objected to the rigidity of a rule punishing the many for the sake of the few. We left for the summer, then believing that President Thomas not only understood our point of view, but also would leave the question to the regulation of public opinion.

During the summer, however, all the students who had taken more than four week-ends, and the class of 1925, received contracts to limit themselves to four, which they had to sign before their rooms would be reserved. After the support given the spirit, if not the letter, of President Thomas' law, the students indignantly protested against the apparent disregard of their powers of self-government. The question then widens, and begins to involve the near and joy-giving principle of individual liberty.

In this light the Undergraduate Association reconsidered the subject. Inasmuch as "self-government," according to the charter, includes "the exclusive management of all matters concerning the conduct of students in their College life which do not fall under the jurisdiction of the authorities of the College, or mistresses of the halls of residence"; inasmuch as, if the matter is academic, the rule proposed is certainly not a strictly academic regulation; inasmuch as the administration based its statistics for sending out contracts on self-governing records, thereby admitting the previous jurisdiction of self-government in the matter; and inasmuch as any such regulation would transfer this jurisdiction of self-government without the assent of the governed, the Undergraduate Association passed a resolution to surrender the whole matter to self-government.

At a meeting the Self-Government Board explained the justification of taking up the matter. It emphasized that more than a question of week-ends was involved, that the principle of self-government would be infringed on, and above all, that the matter of week-ends was merely the occasion that brought up the far more important question of the power of self-government. Considering that self-government is a recognized means of expressing the will of the students in all matters concerning their College lives, the Board felt it imperative that a decision be reached between the administration and the students as to the exact powers of self-government. The Association passed a vote of confidence in their Board and upheld it in the spirit and in the spirit of its opinion.

On Sunday evening, the Board conferred with President Thomas and the dean. Although questions of jurisdiction are, by Clause 3 of the charter, to be decided by the president and dean, President Thomas felt that, in so inclusive a matter, she wished to consult the directors and faculty. In view of the fact that the contracts were sent out by the administration, they were suspended until a decision should be reached not later than November 21, when the directors meet.

On Monday the Board reported to a meeting of the Association this agreement, and, with every desire of fairness to the administration, explained their point of view.

It seems that President Thomas considers the "continuity of residence an academic matter." Similarly, she feels that proctoring, quiet hours, singing in the dining room, or going to the theater, if not regulated satisfactorily by self-government and injurious to College work, are finally under the jurisdiction of the administration. In President Thomas' opinion, the individual ethical life of each student, the good name and fame of the College, the training in independence, and the assistance given the administration in regulating College life are the objects and purposes of self-government. Whatever, in short, directly or indirectly affects academic work, whether it be for the moment in the hands of self-government or of the wardens, she feels to be within the jurisdiction of the administration.

We, on the other hand, feel that, as a self-governing body, we should have a part in making as well as in carrying out all policies regulating College life.

Reprinted from the College News, *November 2, 1921.*

SENATE DECISION ON THE CUT RULE

RESOLVED, That beginning with October 1915, attendance at classes shall be regulated by each instructor, or when desired by all its members, by each department in whatever way or ways may seem advisable by assignment of extra work, deduction of academic grade, refusal to sign course books, or by any other method including reference of students for more serious discipline to the Senate.

That it shall be made clear to the students in each class by announcement by the instructor in the beginning of each semester and otherwise that the faculty desires regular attendance at classes and to secure such attendance all students shall be definitely informed by their instructors that their recitations, answers to questions, informal quizzes, and when it seems advisable participation in class discussions will be considered in assigning final examination grades.

That in the above individual regulation of attendance each instructor or department shall be at liberty to decide what weight shall be given to illness excuses received from the Dean's office.

Resolved, That as the above individual and informal method of securing attendance at classes cannot succeed without the cordial and continuous co-operation of the undergraduates the faculty accepts the offer of the Undergraduate Association to assist the faculty in making sure that all present and future undergraduates understand the faculty's attitude toward regular attendance at classes by a means of formal announcements each semester at meetings of the Undergraduate Association and of the four College classes, and by informal individual statements made by older students to those entering the College.

Reprinted from the College News, *June 3, 1915.*

LANTERN NIGHT
A COLLEGE TRADITION

The Origin of Lantern Night
LOUISE CONGDON FRANCIS, *Class of 1900*

IT IS HARD FOR ANY ONE who sees today for the first time a Bryn Mawr Lantern Night to realize that this most beautiful and distinctive custom of giving lanterns to the Freshmen was originally closely connected with the Sophomore Play. For it is indeed a far cry from the rickety stage of the old gymnasium to the stately pageant in the library cloister.

In the autumn of 1886, when the class of 1889, who had held the campus alone for a year, wished to welcome appropriately the class of 1890, they decided to give a play. It was no elaborate affair like the Sophomore plays of today, but a farce, full of local color and college jokes, planned, written and rehearsed in a few days. At the close of the play the Sophomores gave to each Freshman a lantern, as emblematic of the bright light which would guide the inexperienced new-comer through the perilous maze of the already established college traditions.

This custom was continued without change, except that the plays became each year a little more elaborate, and each year were planned for a little further ahead, until the autumn of 1897, when the class of 1900 presented *As You Like It*. It was given under the maples in afternoon, and the presentation of lanterns in broad daylight would have been obviously inappropriate. At the time, this was considered a serious objection to presenting the play in the afternoon, but the Sophomores decided to put a brave face on the matter and choose an entirely different night for the lantern-giving. They chose the night when the freshmen first received their caps and gowns. The class of 1900 wrote a special song for the occasion, and so did that of '01; and the Freshmen were ignorant of the fact that a tradition had been broken. The experiment was a great success. The Sophomores marched from Pembroke, each carrying her own lantern and another. Near the beautiful old poplar, on the site of the present library, '00 and '01 sang to each another, and gave and received lanterns, little knowing that they were establishing a new and charming precedent. The next year '01 made a further change by singing, beside their new Lantern song, "Pallas Athene Thea." From that day to this the only radical innovation has been to change the place of the ceremony from the campus to the cloisters. There, in that lovely setting, class after class now receives the emblem and the promise of its illumination.

Reprinted from the *Bryn Mawr Alumnae Bulletin*, November 1909.

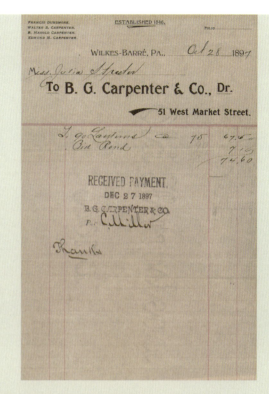

Above: Receipt from B. G. Carpenter and Co. (Wilkes-Barre, PA) for seventy-five lanterns, in the amount of $74.60, October 28, 1897

Left: Ticket for entrance to Lantern Night, October 21, 1910

Opposite: Students on Lantern Night, c. 1930s

OUTSIDERS BARRED FROM LANTERN NIGHT

AN AUDIENCE EXCLUSIVELY COLLEGIATE will see the Freshman receive their class lanterns tomorrow evening. Owing to quarantine regulations no outsiders will be admitted to the cloisters.

Unusual volume may be expected both in "Pallas Athene Thea" and "Over the Way to the Sacred Shrine" because of the comparatively small number of mutes among the Sophomores and Freshmen. 1921 has twenty voiceless members and 1922 about twenty-three.

Reprinted from the *College News*, November 7, 1918

The Music of "Pallas Athene"
BERTHA HAVEN PUTNAM, *Class of 1893*

... Our enthusiasm for Greek led us in the autumn of 1889 to arrange a Greek freshman show consisting mainly of scenes from the *Odyssey*, and inevitably therefore to conceive the ambitious plan of writing a Greek song for acknowledging the presentation to us of lanterns by the sophomores, the Class of 1892. When Madeline Abbott and I were made responsible for the task, she secured the music of a song which she had known in her Cambridge High School, and which was at once approved by our classmates. We then wrote our Greek words to fit this music, and although at the time we must have known the name of the composer, I am ashamed to say that we soon forgot it. After Madeline's early death, none of us were able to answer the many questions as to the origin of the music.

... By a fortunate chance, in preparing for our reunion, I found among my memorabilia, neglected for over half a century, two pages that had evidently been torn out of Madeline Abbott's school music book. These printed sheets ... contain on the right-hand upper corners the name N. Lincoln, and beneath, "Ode of Anacreon," and the musical notation which Mr. Lincoln had written for it:

Above: Students singing on Lantern Night, 1948
Opposite: Sheet music for "Pallas Athene," the traditional Lantern Night hymn, with words by Madeline Vaughan Abbott and Bertha Haven Putnam; class of 1893

> Θέλω λέγειν Ἀτρείδας,
> θέλω δὲ Κάδμον ᾄδειν
> ἁ βάρβιτος δὲ χορδαῖς
> ἔρωτα μοῦνον ἔχει.

Under the original Greek words Madeline had inserted in ink the words of our "Pallas Athene." The charming description of how Anacreon's lyre refused to sing of heroes and would sing only of love is replaced by our solemn invocation to the goddess of learning and our prayer that she be with us always, giving us wisdom, and that she consecrate our lanterns that they might forever illuminate our path. In later years ... this freshman response of ours to the sophomore gift of lanterns was used by sophomores in their bestowal of lanterns on the freshmen, a reversal of the original purpose of our song. Still later, by a happy accident, ... "Pallas Athene" became part of the beautiful ritual of Lantern Night, now a cherished Bryn Mawr tradition.

Reprinted from the *Bryn Mawr Alumnae Bulletin*, November 1944.

EDITORIAL

THE ESTABLISHMENT OF CUSTOMS demands the most careful consideration, and we are content to make haste very slowly in the matter. These first years have already seen a good many changes. Mistakes have been made and mistakes have been rectified, but what we, as students, need to feel with all possible keenness is that, whatever other forces may be at work to make or mar the future of Bryn Mawr, we yet have a strong power for good or ill put into our hands, and it behooves us to look to it that we make the best use of it. That Bryn Mawr has great possibilities will not be denied, but we have yet to earn the right to say that these possibilities have been realized.

Reprinted from the *Lantern*, June 1891.

FOUNDATIONS: 1885–1922

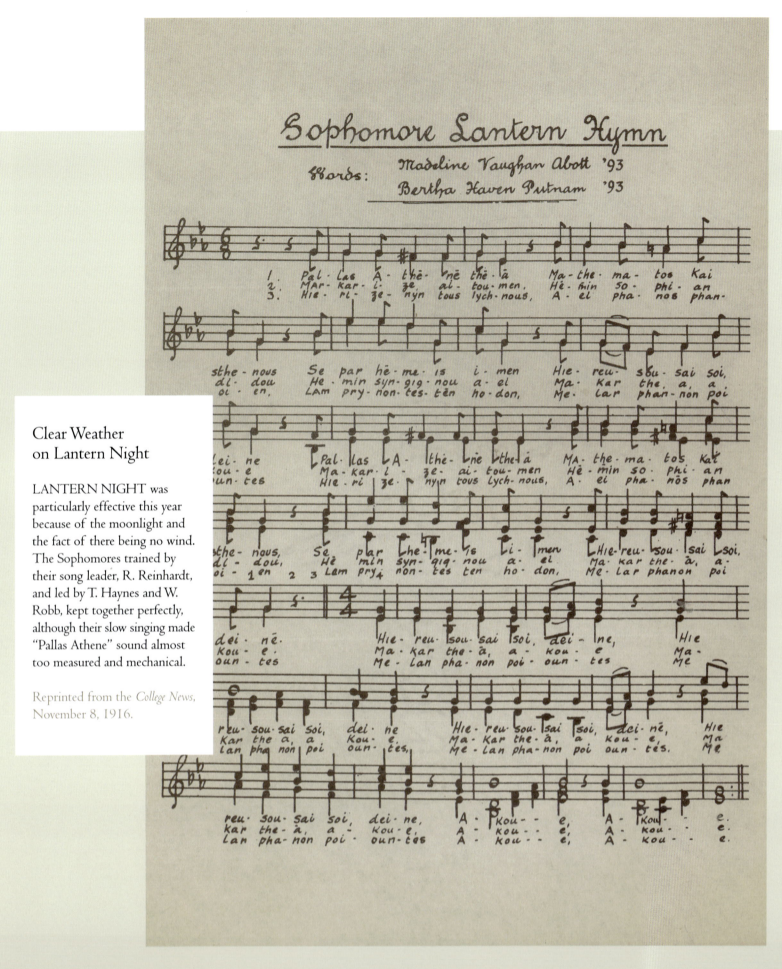

Clear Weather on Lantern Night

LANTERN NIGHT was particularly effective this year because of the moonlight and the fact of there being no wind. The Sophomores trained by their song leader, R. Reinhardt, and led by T. Haynes and W. Robb, kept together perfectly, although their slow singing made "Pallas Athene" sound almost too measured and mechanical.

Reprinted from the *College News*, November 8, 1916.

Remembering Lantern Night
Frederica de Laguna, Class of 1927

"... LANTERNS IN MY DAY were made with panes of glass in the class colors, and the shapes and numbers of windows encrypted with class numerals. We all treasured our lanterns ... In a sense the whole College student body was present at early Lantern Nights, for the lanterns bore an invitation to tea from giver to recipient; there was later singing of class songs in Pem Arch, which included those of graduated classes; and the Juniors in each dorm entertaining their Freshmen when it was Class Plays, and the handing down of most class songs by Seniors at their last Step-Singing to their Sister Class, were unifying symbolic events, and contrasted with the institutionalized rivalries between odds and evens, or between red and green on the one hand, and the blues on the other. This rivalry began at Parade Night, at the beginning of the year, when the newly arrived Freshmen had to compose words to a tune, and keep these secret, while the Sophomores undertook to discover them and parody the words. The Bryn Mawr Fire Company Band led victors and losers to the Freshmen tune down to the bonfire on the Lower Hockey Field. The Freshman Song was kept secret only in 1911, 1921, 1924, 1925, and 1945! The rule since 1916 was that the sophomores might use any ruse, except attending Freshman Class Meeting. On occasions, these attempts became rowdy, especially when gallant Juniors tried to defend their Freshmen. By 1970, the bonfires and parades were gone, due to Township Fire Regulations and the demise of the famous band.

Reprinted from the transcription of the proceedings of the Alumnae Association Symposium on Traditions, Bryn Mawr College, April 11, 1987.

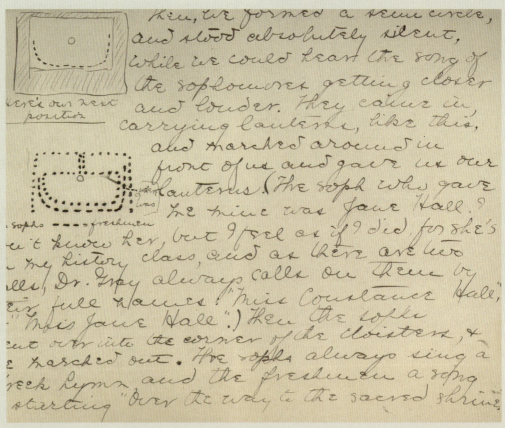

Top: Lanterns and invitations to student teas, Lantern Night, c. 2007

Bottom: Page from a letter, Natalie Gookin, class of 1920, to her mother, describing Lantern Night, November 4, 1916

PRESIDENT WILSON IN 1912 HAD MOCK LANTERN NIGHT
ALUMNAE REVIVED CEREMONY AT DENVER POLITICAL DINNER

A MOCK LANTERN NIGHT was celebrated for President Wilson by Bryn Mawr Alumnae at a political dinner given for him in Denver in 1912.

President Wilson, who started his career as an instructor in history and politics at Bryn Mawr College in 1885, was making a cross-country tour to meet Democratic leaders during his first presidential candidacy. He stopped at Denver where a political dinner was given for important local Democrats by Mrs. Richard Crawford Campbell, class of 1890, one of his history students at Bryn Mawr.

At the close of the dinner, Mrs. Campbell, as toastmistress, rose and explained that the alumnae present wished to celebrate one of the customs of their alma mater. The original idea of Lantern Night, she explained, was to quiz the entering Freshmen, and, if they showed worthiness, to give them a lantern to light them through Bryn Mawr. Mrs. Campbell said that they wished to cross-question the Governor of New Jersey, and if he came off well they would give him a lantern to light him to the White House.

"Will you faithfully promise," said one of the Bryn Mawr quizzers, "to stay in the White House if we put you there, and do no gallivanting?"

"I will," said Mr. Wilson, and so he won the lantern.

Reprinted from the *College News*, November 5, 1919.

Top: Sketch of Bryn Mawr lantern styles, c. 1906, graphite on paper

Bottom: Lois Kellogg, class of 1920, on Lantern Night, 1920

OUR FRESHMAN

DURING THE LAST FORTNIGHT two great events have occurred in the history of the Class of 1901: they have been presented their lanterns, and they have given their Freshman Play. At last they are initiated into college life and are ready to take their share in the burdens and pleasures of existence here. The *Philistine* congratulates them! The first experience in homesickness is over, the first mistakes have been made and forgotten, the first verdancy has lost its luster. They no longer write home daily, after much practice one is able to hear their cheer, and there even seems some prospect of the solving of the difficult problem: when may a freshman call an upper classman by her first name?

Clad in "our academic garb," holding firmly in their right hands the new lanterns which shed a rosy light over their paths, and in their left hands their course books, they are equipped for the four years' journey. Fight on little sisters! We understand and appreciate your struggles, for we, too, have passed over the same ground and are but a little farther on, looking back at you with interest. Remember that though we may laugh at your mistakes, and snub your budding ideas, it is all for your future good, and that there is in reality no one in college who is not ready to sing with the juniors:

"Our freshman class has come, hurrah!
We greet it with three cheers!"

Reprinted from the *Fortnightly Philistine*, November 12, 1897.

A BRYN MAWR COLLEGE FETE
Juniors and Freshmen Take Part in a Picturesque Entertainment

A picturesque entertainment was given at Bryn Mawr College on Friday evening, in the shape of an Italian carnival procession. The members of the junior class were the hosts, and the freshmen the guests, and the rest of the college community onlookers. It was a dark night, the better setting forth the gayeties of the fete. From the back of Merion Hall filled out the brilliant procession, with heralds trumpeting the advance. The two classes were in line, in the motley dress befitting the occasion. Alongside ran link bearers with flaming torches, while red lights were burned profusely everywhere. Confetti were showered on the revelers and onlookers, and the freshmen added to the life and color of the scene by shaking wands of varied hues, from the ends of which hung particolored streamers.

The paraders marched down the campus in the avenue of maples until they were at the back of the last gray hall. There the freshmen elected their Queen and crowned her, with joyful shouts. Confetti and the long white tissue-paper garlands of Paris fashion flew afresh. A French round was sung by the juniors, and then the procession passed on into the gymnasium. The floor was reserved for the two classes mainly concerned, and in the midst of the chairs of the commoners rose a dais for the Junior King and the Freshman Queen, where they sat on Morris-chair thrones. The onlookers crowded the gallery.

The opening tableau showed a Bryn Mawr student, in cap and gown, standing on a pedestal, while the representatives of other women's colleges bowed before her and an appropriate song was sung. The prettiest of the other tableaus, or little scenes, was the planting of the freshman flower. The curtain rose on a huge flower pot, filling the center of the stage, in which a little maid of 1902 was planting 1904's flower. She watered it diligently, and it grew rapidly, dropping out one long vine tendril after another, until at last the huge flower appeared and shot up with fairy rapidity, till it reached the gallery, where it burst. In doing so it let down over the flag of 1902 the pale blue one of 1904, amid the cheers of both classes.

It was by far the prettiest junior-freshman party within the memory of the campus.

Reprinted from the *New York Times*, October 16, 1900.

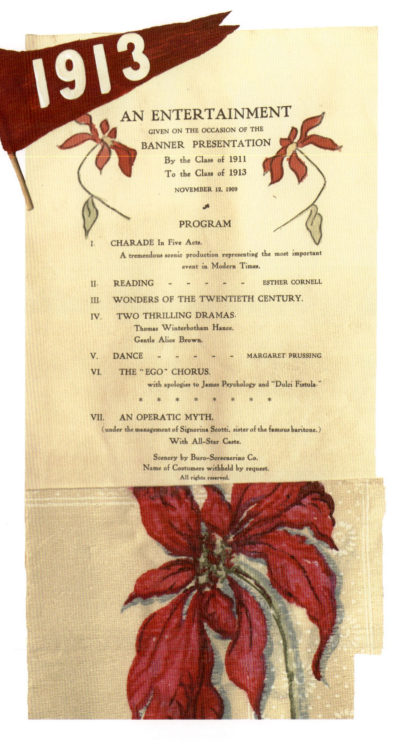

Above: Program and napkin from the Banner Presentation, November 12, 1909. Reprinted from the scrapbook of Elizabeth Yarnall Maguire, class of 1913

Left: Class Supper table card for Elizabeth Maguire, April 29, 1910. Reprinted from the scrapbook of Elizabeth Yarnall Maguire, class of 1913

FOUNDATIONS: 1885–1922

Some Decorations for Young Girls' Rooms
With apologies to the Ladies' Home Journal
CHS, Class of 1900

NOW THAT THE TIME for drawing rooms has come around again, each girl will be planning how she may beautify her apartment for next year, and may be glad of a few suggestive hints.

I am sure every girl will want to have her room entirely unique, and one way of accomplishing this is by changing the tone of the furniture. Anyone can paint her ordinary college fireplace, book-case and bureau so as to make them utterly unlike any-one else's, and the cost is very trifling. I have seen a few cans of pink paint make a college room different from any I have ever seen elsewhere.

A novel and cheap way out of papering the walls is to cut any college news items out of the daily papers, or even your own periodicals, and paste them on the walls. In time the walls will be covered, and the news items outlined in red and gold, present an interesting and attractive surface for the visitor to look at. Old quiz papers or essays may be used in the same way.

Something that I am sure no one else would have in the way of a stand for plants, is made out of an ice-cream freezer turned upside down, painted to harmonize with the room. Of course if you are skilful with your brush, it might be decorated appropriately with flowers.

Anyone who has had experience in perforating metals can make a charming hanging-lamp out of a chafing-dish and cover, and even the novice may produce surprising results in this line.

A dainty dressing-table may be constructed out of a barrel, draped prettily with cretonne. It is particularly effective if the barrel is filled with apples. Feather dusters make charming photograph holders, and add bright touches of color to the room.

Following these ideas, and others which any clever girl can originate for herself, every one may gain that desirable thing—an entirely individual room.

Reprinted from the *Fortnightly Philistine*, April 28, 1899.

Just a Dream
L. P.

Somehow you dream the queerest dreams,
When you're in bed at night,
If you have studied overmuch,
Or read a novel light.
I dreamt I saw great Taylor Tower
Take off its hat to me,
Though where it got a stovepipe hat
I'm sure I couldn't see.
I dreamt I saw the Faculty
Playing at basket-ball,
And though they thought they knew just how,
They couldn't play at all.
I dreamt I saw the swimming-pool
Filled to the top with ink,
While college maidens wrote exams
A-sitting on the brink.
I dreamt that I for breakfast had
Good coffee and thick cream—
But then, alas! I woke to find
The whole thing just a dream.

Reprinted from the
Fortnightly Philistine, March 12, 1897.

Top: Student room in Merion Hall, c. 1900–1915

Bottom: Advertisement for the *Fortnightly Philistine*, by Sylvia Scudder, class of 1899

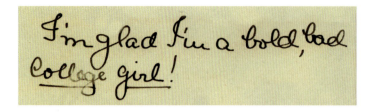

I'm glad I'm a bold, bad college girl!

Camp Asquam
Center Harbor, New Hampshire

August 23 [c. 1922]

Dear Elizabeth,

    When you look back at my name to see who is writing to you, you won't have any idea at all who I am. I am only a junior at Bryn Mawr, who would like awfully much to know you and to help you get settled at college.

    I am writing to you on behalf of the Christian Association of the college, which will also send you a handbook full of awfully valuable information about college and its ways. I strongly advise you to study it through, especially the pages about Parade Night, Freshman Rules, and Advanced Standing which sounds terribly impressive and difficult, but which isn't at all and which is awfully convenient to have.

    When you first arrive at college, you will find the members of the Membership Committee, with yellow bows pinned on them, waiting in Taylor Hall to help you register; and, by the way, you should come on October second, Monday. It really isn't so complicated a process as the Handbook intimates but it's just as well to get an early start at it.

    I'll be there too, on Monday, though I'm not on the Membership Committee, so I won't be dressed up in a yellow bow. Do come to see me as soon as you land. My room is Radnor 16. Do write and tell me yours, won't you? I'll be awfully glad to help you in any way I possibly can, by answering any questions you may have or by piloting you around campus when you get there. There are teas in Denbigh on both Monday and Tuesday afternoons to which entering Freshmen and their families are invited. If you look me up when you arrive, I'd love to go with you and introduce you to people there. I'd also love to help you pick out your courses, if I can. I don't know, of course, what sort of thing you like but I have a pretty good idea of what the different courses are like.

    But courses aren't the half of college. I know you'll love it, as we all do, whether your tastes are athletic, literary, scientific, or social. Bryn Mawr is really the most perfect place imaginable. That's not gush. I really mean it. Right now, I'm dying of home-sickness to get back. You're bound to have a wonderful time of it if you come ready to play hard at hockey and at our timeworn customs and festivities; to work a little, just enough to make life interesting; and to be wholeheartedly interested in all the rest of us and our organizations and activities.

    Please write soon for I'm waiting to hear from you.

Very Sincerely,

Katherine Van Bibber '24

Reprinted from a letter, Katherine Van Bibber, class of 1924, to incoming student "Elizabeth," August 23, 1922.

Left: Souvenir prom book, with filled-in dance cards, 1899

Right: Page from a letter, Henrietta Baldwin, class of 1921, to her mother, describing the sophomore dance, 1919

Opposite: Clipping from a letter, Anne —, class of 1905, to her mother, 1903

> Sunday morning.
>
> Dearest Mother, —
>
> I sure do feel like "the morning after the night before." The sophomore dance was a whizz. I had the time of my life! I thought a college dance with girls for escorts would be awfully tame but I certainly labored under a most false illusion. The sophomores were all dressed as sailors in "whites" and they made stunning men some of them. We had awfully clever programmes and there

PULITZER PRIZE WINNER
Marianne Moore, Class of 1909
Jen Rajchel, Class of 2011

POET AND WRITER Marianne Moore (1887–1972) was acclaimed for her "precise observation, and deliberately prosaic speech that was nonetheless highly inventive, with ornate diction and elaborate patterns."[1] Born in Kirkwood, Missouri, Moore was raised in the home of her grandfather, a Presbyterian minister. In 1905 she entered Bryn Mawr, where she was challenged intellectually, socially, and personally. After her writing was criticized for being too disconnected—a trait that later would define her modernist style—Moore decided to major in biology and to pursue her interest in writing by contributing to, and later serving as editor of, the *Tipyn O'Bob*, a student literary magazine.

She pushed the boundaries of what it meant to be a female intellectual. She debated with fellow students about the merits of suffrage; attended performances of the latest plays; and mischievously broke into Taylor Hall with Peggy James, her good friend and niece of Henry James, where they spent the night discussing poetry on the building's rooftop. When she was supposed to be studying for exams, Moore instead would write letters to classmate and future writer Marcet Haldeman. In these missives she bemoaned examination periods and homework, praised Bryn Mawr's traditions, gossiped about social happenings around campus, and extolled the friendships she had formed.

After Moore graduated from Bryn Mawr, she worked as a schoolteacher in Carlisle, Pennsylvania, before moving to New York, where her poetry caught the attention of T. S. Eliot, Ezra Pound, and William Carlos Williams, among others. From 1925 to 1929 she served as editor of the influential literary journal the *Dial*, helping to foster the careers of John Ashberry, Elizabeth Bishop, and James Merrill. Moore's *Collected Poems*[2] was awarded the Pulitzer Prize in 1951 and the National Book Award in 1952, and she was presented the prestigious Bollingen Prize for Poetry in 1951. Her ability to mix historical and current allusions, and to create a nexus of images and references has since influenced generations of poets.

Moore's spirit of independence—developed and fueled at Bryn Mawr—remained at the forefront of her personality. In a letter to fellow writer Bryher (Annie Winifred Ellerman) she reflected on her college experience: "The net of my experiences at Bryn Mawr was to make me feel that intellectual wealth can't be superimposed, that it is to be appropriated; my experience there gave me the determination to have what I want . . . the more I see of other women's colleges, the more I feel that Bryn Mawr was particularly adapted to my special requirements."[3]

As one of Bryn Mawr's most celebrated alumnae, Moore challenged convention, in poetry and in life. In doing so, she set the standards high for future Mawrters like me.

Above: Marianne Moore (1887–1972), class of 1909, at her fiftieth reunion, 1959. Photograph by Peter Dechert

Opposite: Marianne Moore (seated upper left) with students in Elizabethan costume, May Day, 1906

1. Margaret W. Ferguson, Mary Jo Salter, and Jon Stallworthy, eds., *The Norton Anthology of Poetry*, 5th ed. (New York: W. W. Norton, 2005), 1331.
2. Marianne Moore, *Collected Poems* (New York: Macmillan, 1951).
3. Marianne Moore to Bryher, August 31, 1921, in *Selected Letters*, ed. Bonnie Costello, Celeste Goodridge, and Cristanne Miller (New York: Penguin Classics, 1998), 178.

TO MY CUP-BEARER
Marianne Moore, Class of 1909

A lady or a tiger-lily,
Can you tell me which,
I see her when I wake at night,
Incanting, like a witch.
Her eye is dark, her vestment rich,
Embroidered with a silver stitch,
A lady or a tiger lily,
Slave, come tell me which?

Jen Rajchel, Class of 2011

The publication of Marianne Moore's "To My Cup-Bearer" in the April 1908 issue of the *Tipyn O'Bob*, Bryn Mawr's student literary magazine, led to her public recognition as a poet, when President M. Carey Thomas read the poem at a campus chapel talk. But what does it mean to be someone's cup-bearer? I set out to discover this as well as how the poem intersected the beginning of Moore's esteemed career and her years at Bryn Mawr.

I began by reading Moore's published correspondence and found that in a 1908 letter to friend and classmate Marcet Haldeman, Moore discussed both M. Carey Thomas's reading of her poem and the Junior-Senior Supper.[1] As a Mawrter, I have worn a black robe and sung in Greek on Lantern Night, been "helled" by a sophomore, and danced in a white dress around the maypole, but I was not aware of the Junior-Senior Supper.

With pencil and pad in hand, I made my way to Canaday Library and scoured biographies on President Thomas, but found nothing related to cup-bearing or to the Junior-Senior Supper. Then one night I happened upon a dissertation by University of Pennsylvania student Virginia Wolf Briscoe on the history of Bryn Mawr's traditions, including a ritual known as the Loving Cup. Briscoe, emphasizing the privacy of the ceremony, wrote that "although visitors had been welcome at the Junior Supper and entertainment for the seniors, when it came time for the presentation and sharing of the loving cup around the table among all the juniors and seniors, the visitors were asked to leave the room."[2] Thus, the lack of information on the Loving Cup was a result of the secrecy surrounding it.

I was intrigued and began to sleuth, poring over issues of the *Tipyn O'Bob* and Bryn Mawr histories. When I asked the college's Special Collections staff about the Loving Cup, no one knew

about it. I reviewed microfilm of M. Carey Thomas's letters, and I began to know her as more than the distant matriarch of Bryn Mawr, whose marble bust watches over me as I enter and exit the library. In reading her personal writings, I was able to trace the development of her vision for the college and her increasing sense of the campus as her home.

It occurred to me, as I looked through the lens of the microfilm reader, searching for information about a secret tradition, that because of Marianne Moore's poem I had experienced Bryn Mawr in a new and unconventional way. I had read Moore's and Thomas's letters the way I read those from a close friend. I empathized with Moore over the rigors of exams and eagerly scanned her reports of campus happenings—who bought a new hat over the weekend or which professor made interesting remarks during class. When I finished reading for the night, I would return to my dorm, just as Moore would have done. In my search for a hidden ceremony, I had discovered a past that had been unknown to me. There may no longer be formal recognition of the Loving Cup or the Junior-Senior Supper, but through her letters Moore and I had participated in a Bryn Mawr tradition that has continued throughout the school's history—the passing of knowledge and inspiration from one Mawrter to the next.

1. Marianne Moore to Marcet Haldeman, May 17, 1908, in *Selected Letters*, ed. Bonnie Costello, Celeste Goodridge, and Cristanne Miller (New York: Penguin Classics, 1998), 48.
2. Virginia Wolf Briscoe, "Bryn Mawr College Traditions: Women's Rituals as Expressive Behavior" (PhD diss., University of Pennsylvania, 1981), 500.

WORLD WAR I AT BRYN MAWR

BMC Patriotic Farm Highly Successful Venture
GIRLS RAISE AND CAN VEGETABLES

UNDER THE LEADERSHIP of four alumnae, A. Price '03, M. Nearing '09, B. Ehlers '09, and A. Hawkins '07, the 20-acre Bryn Mawr Patriotic Farm on the P. M. Sharpless estate at West Chester has flourished during the past summer. Seventy-nine other young women, chiefly Bryn Mawr alumnae and undergraduates, worked on the farm, planting and cultivating, and harvesting and canning vegetables for college consumption or immediate sale in the local market.

"It is the largest farm in the country worked by women, has the greatest acreage, and the fewest weeds," said Mr. A. D. Cromwell, the professor of agriculture at the West Chester State Normal School, who supervised the Farm. Besides the large quantities of potatoes, corn, tomatoes, peas, cabbages, kohlrabi, onions, chard, navy beans, lima beans, string beans, beets, lettuce, celery, melons, Brussels sprouts, carrots, spinach, turnips, salsify, and endives that were raised, many bushels of peaches, bought from neighboring farms, were canned. Over 8,000 cans filled by the workers in the cannery they themselves had built were sold to the college at the end of the season.

Canning, however, was not the only measure, for the "farmerettes" dried and salted beans, and put up marmalades and soup as by-products of the peach and tomato canning. Even the "split heads" of cabbage were used, as a German lady bought them to use in the making of sauerkraut.

The leisure hours of the workers were divided between Tenements A and B, as their sleeping quarters were termed; "Tillie Superford," the farm auto truck; the ice cream cone palace; and the Sharpless swimming hole. It was by "Tillie" that the girls were always recognized on their frequent trips through West Chester, and as a result of "Tillie's" popularity the Farm turned out almost as many Ford mechanics as expert canners.

Whether or not the farm was a financial success it is as yet impossible to say. Workers will go out to West Chester on Saturdays for some weeks to come, and until the last vegetables are brought in and disposed of the outcome from a pecuniary viewpoint will be uncertain.

Reprinted from the *College News*, October 3, 1917.

Clockwise from top: Student workers at the Bryn Mawr Patriotic Farm, West Chester, PA, c. 1917; workers at the Patriotic Farm, c. 1917; display of canned goods from the Patriotic Farm, c. 1917, with a poster declaring that the farm had produced 6,146 cans

"PREPARE" IN OWN WORK
Canteens and Day Nurseries Described
Industrial Service Registered

THAT EACH WOMAN should train herself very intensively for the one line of war service for which she is best fitted, Miss Simpson, the organizer of college work of the National League for Women's Service, emphasized in speaking Monday afternoon in Taylor on preparedness lines now open to college students. Mrs. Lewis Martin, chairman of the Bureau for Registration and Information of the League, speaking after Miss Simpson, urged that all students who come from Pennsylvania should send in their names as ready for industrial service, since Pennsylvania will be the first State in which the women will be fully organized.

"Pull up your petunias and roses and plant beans and potatoes," said Miss Simpson, "for one thing almost everyone can do is to join in the crusade for agricultural conservation." Women will be more efficient if they stick to the job at hand, Miss Simpson went on, whether it's on a farm or only in a back yard or a motor car. If a girl has the opportunity of keeping house this summer she can even be patriotic there by buying intelligently and economically.

. . . Social and welfare work were two kinds of service outlined by Miss Simpson, which come as new suggestions to most. Suppose a mobilization camp is pitched at the edge of one's town, then with hundreds of men having nothing to do in their recreation hours, new social conditions arise, and women can be of the utmost good in organizing "recreation groups." The same plan applies, Miss Simpson said, to towns where munitions factories will be started, bringing with them hundreds of girl employees who will need the help of organization which college students will know how to supply. Day Nurseries, relieving the soldiers' wives of the care of their children and leaving them free to earn a living, will be a very valuable kind of war service.

Canteen work is of two sorts, explained Miss Simpson, that for the troops and industrial work for the factory hands. In towns where the great munitions plants are established women will be called on to provide "lunch counters" for the workers.

Every kind of job at the "industrial front" may be obtained through the Bureau of Registration and Information in Philadelphia, Mrs. Martin explained. Already more than 150 women have, for patriotic reasons, sought and secured work at the Arsenal, she said, where uniforms, bed clothes and all sorts of equipment for the troops are being manufactured. Anyone living in Pennsylvania was urged to send in his or her name and summer address to Mrs. John C. Groom, 1426 Walnut Street, to register for industrial service, which would range in variety from sitting in an office and registering other applicants; to hunting out boarding houses for factory girls arriving for munitions factories; to meeting girls at the station.

Reprinted from the *College News*, April 18, 1917.

EVERY STUDENT TO HAVE PART
IN COLLEGE WAR SERVICE
Nine Hours a Week Quota

ALL STUDENTS of the college, as it was voted at a mass meeting last spring, will be conscripted for nine hours of work per week; four of war work, three of recreation, two of physical development.

Registration will take place during the first week of college. Everyone will be offered a choice of war work and times for doing it, which will be followed as far as possible by the Conscription Board. Conscription plans worked out by D. Peters, chairman of the Conscription Board, are:

Organization
Each hall has a captain with seven minor officers under her. The captains: Rockefeller, L. Wood '19; Pembroke West, H. Holmes '20; Pembroke East, G. Hearne '19; Denbigh, A. Moore, '19; Merion, A. Warner '19; Radnor, E. Marquand '19; Llysyfran, E. Lanier '19, form a Conscription Board to decide upon all individual cases.

The minor officers include a student in each hall for Red Cross; one for Clerical Work; one for Committees; and one for Community Center and other lines of work. Each officer will see that people in her division do not fall behind, and will answer questions concerning her line of work.

Cuts and Substitutions
Illness will be the only acceptable excuse for failure to put in the nine hours of conscripted work.

Substitution is to be limited. Thus, if a student who has signed for Tuesday night in the Red Cross room wishes to go on Wednesday, she may exchange with someone who goes on Wednesday. Her Wednesday appointment, however, may not be postponed further.

Signing Up
War Work will be signed up on the gymnasium bulletin board in the same manner and place as the required exercise. Miss Taylor will check up the lists for the Conscription Board as her share of war work.

Hockey is scheduled for three days a week and is considered as the three hours of recreation under conscription.

The two hours of physical development will be taken up in drill. Every hall forms a battalion which is subdivided into platoons and squads. A Battalion Commander is responsible for the hall; Platoon Leaders and Squad Leaders, for their divisions. The entire college, led by the Senior Commander, will drill every Tuesday at 5 o'clock on the second hockey field for half an hour.

The second half-hour period of drill commanded by the platoon and squad leaders, will be taken in two quarter of an hour periods if desired and at such times as are decided upon by the leaders.

The drills are based upon the methods in use at the United States Military Academy under Major Koehler.

Students who repeatedly fail to do the conscripted work will have their names posted on Black Lists in the gymnasium and in Taylor Hall.

Reprinted from the *College News*, October 2, 1918.

COLLEGE GOES ON RATIONS AS VOLUNTARY WAR MEASURE

Will Weigh Individual Portions

Voluntary food rations, under which every portion of food for each individual will be weighed, have been adopted by the college at the request of Mr. Morris L. Cook, Food Administrator for Pennsylvania. Aside from the actual saving of food the example of the college, Mr. Cook said, will help the work of the Administration.

A careful weighing of meat and bread and the serving of individual portions of sugar will begin as soon as possible in the halls and other college buildings.

Above: Clipping from the *College News*, March 7, 1918

Opposite: Student workers at the Bryn Mawr Patriotic Farm, c. 1917

BRYN MAWR UNDER BOMBARDMENT
Paris Workers Have Reunion
Eleanor Dulles, Class of 1917

SEVERAL BRYN MAWR graduates, taking refuge during a recent German attempt to raid Paris, planned a dinner, which was held on April 1st. About forty Bryn Mawr workers in France, whose addresses were obtainable, were sent notices.

Shells were still falling in the city when the nine who were able to be present met in a hotel in the Latin quarter to talk over the different works they were engaged in and to sing college songs. The most recent number of the *College News* was read, and there was some discussion of the Service Corps, which all at the dinner seemed to favor.

Some of the alumnae had been working at a temporary canteen for refugees passing through Paris from the present battlefield. They came to the dinner between the long shifts of the work of feeding and caring for these weary fugitives, which went on day and night in schools given over for the purpose. Of the sixty Bryn Mawr workers in France, many had recently been sent out of Paris to canteens and hospitals, and were unable to come to dinner.

Leah Cadbury '14 had just returned from Italy, where she had been working with refugees, and left immediately afterwards for a canteen at Bar-le-Duc. Shirly Putnam '09 left Paris the next day for an American hospital, where she is working for the Casualty Bureau. Margery Scattergood '17 made a flying trip to Paris from her work with the Friends at Bar-le-Duc. The others present were Alice Miller Chester '14, who is working for the Y.M.C.A.; Elizabeth Ayer '14, for the American Fund for French Wounded; and Alice Channing ex-'11, Charlotte Welles '12, Rena Bixler '14, and Eleanor Dulles '17, who are working for the Shurtleff Memorial Relief.

Reprinted from the *College News*, May 18, 1918.

EPOCH-MAKING CELEBRATION OF END OF WAR SWEEPS CAMPUS FROM THURSDAY TO MONDAY
President Thomas Says Winning of War Means A New World

OUR GREATEST REASON for rejoicing today is because of the new world that will come out of this war, said President Thomas in her brief speech from Taylor steps last Thursday. "You of the younger generation can hardly realize what it means to us who are older to see right and justice finally established after the terrible wrong and injustice of the old world in which we have lived."

Our happiness is too great for words. We can only think with profound gratitude of the gallant men—and women, too—who have made this new world possible—those who have given their lives for us, and those who are coming back to us safe.

Reprinted from the *College News*, November 14, 1918.

CLASSES GIVE WAY TO PEACE CELEBRATION
College Throngs to Philadelphia as Quarantine Is Lifted

FAVORED BY AN EXTRA HOLIDAY on Friday and a lifting of the quarantine on Philadelphia, the college's impulse to celebrate the report of peace last Thursday found full expression.

The "news" reached the campus nearly an hour before the ringing of the church bells proclaimed it to the rest of the neighborhood.

It was first announced in Rockefeller dining-room by M. Eilers '20, who had heard it by telephone from New York. From there it spread over the campus, breaking up class meetings and laboratory sessions.

Many rushed to the hockey fields, others gathered excitedly under Pembroke arch, and both throngs finally uniting on Taylor steps. National hymns and popular war songs followed incoherently. "God Save the King" was led by Miss Applebee and "La Marseillaise" sung by Mlle Lucie Mabille, French Scholar, with the college joining in the chorus. President Thomas and M. Beck, in response to loud appeals, spoke from the steps. The crowd left Taylor only to gather again around two of the Italian employees, who sang the Italian national hymn.

The climax of the campus celebration came when President Thomas told a large number waiting outside the deanery door that the faculty would follow a suggestion made by Miss Donnelly and Dr. Chew and grant a holiday the next day. Dr. David, Dr. Fenwick, Dr. Chew and Miss King spoke from the deanery porch.

A long parade, starting from Pembroke arch and marching to the Low Buildings and up Gulph Road, returned to the campus to hear Taylor bell ringing as a sign that Dr. Branson had agreed with the rest of the Health Department to raise the quarantine immediately, instead of waiting till the beginning of the week.

From 3:38 on parties left the campus to celebrate with the throngs in Philadelphia. Hockey match games, afternoon classes and all other activities were suspended. Announcements were made excusing students from conscripted war work and required exercise for the rest of the week.

The halls were dark until after midnight, and after the service the next morning the campus was again deserted until the college was reassembled Saturday night for the Banner Show.

Reprinted from the *College News*, November 14, 1918.

Influenza Outbreak

COLLEGE WELL ISOLATED: THREE SPEAKERS FAIL TO COME

Conscription Held Up Quarantine Supreme

THE COLLEGE has been violently cut off from all infusions of outside life by the influenza epidemic. Quarantine regulations exclude outsiders from the halls and forbid meetings except Sunday night chapel. All college activities are practically at a standstill.

Three speakers have been prevented from coming because of the epidemic. Dr. Wise, who was to have preached last Sunday, was detained in New York on account of his wife's illness. Dr. Wood's Bible classes have been postponed because Dr. Wood is helping to fight the influenza in Washington. Professor Baldensperger will not be able to speak next Saturday evening on account of the quarantine. Even vespers, which was to have been in the cloisters, had to be given up last Sunday on account of rain. All Varsity hockey games with the cricket clubs have been indefinitely postponed.

Conscription is held up because there is no sort of work available. The Community Center is closed. No garments can be procured for sewing and mending. Students are not allowed to enter any building off campus, hence no Red Cross work can be done.

Reprinted from the College News, *October 24, 1918.*

Anti-Flu Party: Christian Association Receives Out-of-Doors

TAKING the form of a strictly anti-flu gathering, the Christian Association Reception last Saturday was held on the lawn in front of Merion. The board and association presidents received from behind masks and extended a hearty yardstick with a warm handshake for all at the further end. They wore kilties, gowns, and strange costumes so that they would not be recognized by any chance germs.

Speeches by the presidents of all the associations were made on and in soapboxes, just as the soapbox decreed. Since all big gatherings have been prohibited, this novel entertainment with games and races was devised to take the place of a formal evening party in the gymnasium.

Reprinted from the College News, *October 10, 1918.*

Quarantine Lifted Gradually: 102 Total of Flu Cases

QUARANTINE is being lifted by degrees. The ban on Philadelphia and the village will probably be off next week, according to Dean Taft. This week parents are admitted to the halls. Students may motor to their own homes, and may visit the College Inn or Mrs. Miller's tea-house . . .

. . . The most recent infirmary reports show a total of 102 influenza cases since the beginning of the college; 57 cases were in the infirmary; 28 in the halls, and 17 at home.

Reprinted from the College News, *November 7, 1918.*

November 2, 1918

Mrs. Arthur Lyman
The Laurel School
10001 Euclid Avenue
Cleveland, Ohio

Dear Mrs. Lyman,

We realize of course the interruption to your college preparation caused by the Spanish Influenza and when we are able to find out just how many weeks have been lost I am sure that our Faculty will consider postponing the time of the entrance examinations by as many weeks as have been lost.

Under no circumstances would we, I am confident, lessen the amount of preparation required as this would mean changing the standard which Bryn Mawr College has maintained for the past thirty-two years. As you know, more students wish to enter the college every year than we can accommodate, and as long as this is the case our intention is to admit first those students who have met our requirements. If we were to allow one class insufficiently prepared to enter they would not be able to meet our standard of college work and this inability would continue throughout four years.

Very sincerely yours,

M. Carey Thomas

Reprinted from a letter, M. Carey Thomas to Mrs. Arthur Lyman, November 2, 1918.

Day Letter, Collect.

Mrs. George W. Crile
2620 Derbyshire Road
Cleveland, Ohio

Your letter just received. Influenza epidemic over. Only two convalescent students left in Infirmary. Think it entirely safe for your daughter to return. Letter follows.

M. Carey Thomas

Reprinted from a letter, M. Carey Thomas to Mrs. George W. Crile, c. 1918.

AT BRYN MAWR: PROS AND CONS
Michele Garrigan Nass, Class of 1983

BRYN MAWR'S COMMITMENT to the suffrage movement began officially in 1907, with the establishment of a branch of the College Women's Equal Suffrage Association, for the "promotion of interest in the question of woman's suffrage in Bryn Mawr College." A report from the members in the April 1908 *Alumnae Bulletin* shows their desire to show both sides of the question: "We have been given a small room in a very prominent place in the Library, [where] we have been allowed to have all the books in the stack that in any way relate to the question of women's suffrage, and we try to be liberal by collecting together the anti-suffrage as well as the suffrage pamphlets and books, and placing them in friendly proximity . . . We often find that there are no stronger arguments in favor of the suffrage for women than those very arguments advanced by the anti-suffragists against it."

When Jane Addams came to speak at the College in 1908, the chapel was overflowing—the Bryn Mawr group now numbered 110 of a college of 240 students—and "interest in the question was much renewed."

The suffrage victory in California, which passed its state suffrage amendment in 1911—the largest state yet to do so—was celebrated on campus by the stalwart believers, who waved banners and sang the campaign song:

> Everybody votes but women.
> They have lots of sense;
> When they get the ballot
> The thing will be immense.
> When they get the franchise
> Good citizens they will be,
> And if you don't believe us
> Just wait and see—
> Oh, votes for women!

The marchers were so enthusiastic that "the cold water thrown on the line as it marched through Merion Hall, famed for its anti-suffragists, did not in the least dampen the ardor of the upholders of the cause!"

Spurred on by President Thomas—"We were interested because Miss Thomas was," said Mary Case Pevear '11 in an oral history interview—the College suffragists took their interest off the campus; the *College News* describes the day of the vote on the suffrage amendment in Pennsylvania, when nine Bryn Mawrtyrs poll-watched in the Mill District of Philadelphia, handing out cards with "a plea for fair play in the question of suffrage" and a copy of the amendment for which the men were asked to vote. "Watching the polls last Tuesday was an interesting if fatiguing experience . . . [The women] were in almost every case treated with respect and friendliness, especially by members of the Reform Party. The men hanging around the polls offered the watchers chairs, and kept continually moving their chairs to keep them out of the sun, asked if their coats were not too thin, and in one case one man even came back in the afternoon and proffered an invitation to tea from his wife. Some of the men showed sympathy for the cause, taking their place beside the watchers and cheering them on with such remarks as: 'Here comes your man, nab him'; and 'Get after him like a bulldog.'"

The anti-suffragist position was expressed on campus also, though the speakers probably couldn't rival the proponents President Thomas brought: Carrie Chapman Catt, Anna Howard Shaw, Emmeline Prankhurst, Charlotte Perkins Gilman. The *College News* reported an anti-suffrage lecture, "The Economic Burden of the Double Suffrage," given by Marjorie Dorman. She declared, "Woman's service is to society, not to Government . . . As soldiers and policemen, men serve the government, establishing justice by compulsion, and they deserve the vote. But this is untrue of women . . . Feminists are the only logical suffragists, and even they in their plea for the equal division of household work are fallacious, for few homes would go on happily if the men were given a share in the domestic labor . . . Suffrage is only a doubled expense to the government, and is attended by no exceptional results. The only real way of uplift . . . is to make humanity better, and this must be by persuasion and the influence of mothers on their children."

Their fears stirred also by World War I, the "antis" predicted that the spirit of patriotism would be weakened, if not destroyed, were women to vote. Anna Howard Shaw countered this when she spoke at Bryn Mawr in 1917 on "Women Suffrage and the World War": "It is impossible to talk of women's patriotic service without speaking of woman suffrage. Our soldiers abroad are struggling for the same principle that we are. They are going to Berlin to fight for democracy. We are going to Washington for it. We will get it together . . . It is not true that all women are naturally pacifists. Women voters have nowhere weakened the Government . . . Women are ready to do their part and do it loyally."

They were given the chance, when, in 1920, the amendment was passed; the vote was won. Though the students at Bryn Mawr were too young to participate, they enthusiastically organized straw polls on campus. An account in the January 1921 *Alumnae Bulletin* tells of an early poll: "From Greek maidens in academic gowns solemnly singing to Pallas we suddenly became twentieth-century voters intent on Harding and Cox . . . With true academic independence, we voted liberally; the faculty went for Cox, the undergraduates for Harding—the romantic appeal of Debs collected twelve votes from the college. To give way to our exuberance, we rallied in the gymnasium, expending

Above: Delegation from Bryn Mawr at a women's suffrage demonstration, Washington, DC, March 3 or April 7, 1913. Courtesy of the Library of Congress, Prints and Photographs Division, Lot 5541 (G)

Opposite: Bryn Mawr suffrage pin, c. 1910

shredded paper, voice and argument in defense of miniature leaders. Work out, we read the returns on the blackboard in Taylor with stoic indifference to fact."

Many people considered the Suffrage Amendment to be only the opening battle won, with the rest of the war still to be fought. In 1923, the National Woman's Party introduced into Congress The Woman's Equal Rights Constitutional Amendment. It read, quite simply, "Men and women shall have Equal Rights throughout the United States and every place subject to its jurisdiction."

Carey Thomas, no longer President of Bryn Mawr, plunged right in. In 1925, in the *Journal of the American Association of University Women*, she wrote, prophetically: "New state laws in accordance with modern conceptions of the financial value of the wife's services in the home should, and I think would, be passed and should be made to apply equally to wives and husbands. There are already many cases of wage-earning wives supporting husbands still studying, or temporarily out of a job, or invalided, or simply idle. The entrance of women into business and professions will undoubtedly greatly increase the number of marriages between such women and purely decorative, or home-making husbands. Husbands of this kind, like women similarly constituted, are surely entitled to liberal financial compensation and support, and such compensation should be theirs by law."

She denied that a federal Equal Rights Amendment (ERA) would take away women's privileges and pointed out how difficult it would be to work state-by-state for an end to discrimination against women: "Forever behind a man in every state of the United States are the rights of man qua man with a final appeal for these rights to the Supreme Court of the United States, while forever behind woman qua woman is the medieval English common law, if she is married, holding her to be husband's chattel, bound, protected, owned and even if she is unmarried influencing every legal decision about her and controlling unjustly all her life. This is to me the compelling argument for writing an equal rights amendment to the constitution of the United States.
Only such an amendment will do away with present legal stigmas of inferiority and bondage."

Fifty years later, the ERA, still unratified, remains an issue on which Bryn Mawr women—like other women—do not agree. The unsuccessful struggle for passage came to the *Bulletin* again in 1978, when the then President of the Alumnae Association, Eliza Cope Harrison, wrote: "Up until now, Bryn Mawr's Executive Board has not taken a position on public issues, even after a strong debate during the Vietnam years. But now, when there is an issue which particularly concerns women, perhaps it is time to change. Does the Executive Board, on behalf of the Alumnae Association, have an opportunity to exert a constructive influence on the life of the nation by taking a stand for ERA?

"On the other hand, if the Board were to do this, would we be representing our whole constituency and the variety of its views? We certainly can never expect unanimity among 11,500 very independent alumnae/i—does this mean that Bryn Mawr's Alumnae Association will never, or should never, take a stand on any issue?"

Her open letter to alumnae brought a small but passionate response, running roughly two-to-one in favor of taking a stand in favor of the Amendment. "How long, oh Lord! How long will Bryn Mawr alumnae continue to inhabit intellectual towers remaining unmindful of their feminist foundations! What has happened to the spirit, vision, and courage of M. Carey Thomas?" cried Margo Vorys House '49.

Reprinted from the *Bryn Mawr Alumnae Bulletin*, Fall 1984.

Japan and Bryn Mawr
SIH

I have come to believe that schools and students and a true teacher's work are about the same everywhere in the world.
—Ume Tsuda

BRYN MAWR'S JAPANESE ALUMNAE have been setting remarkable records for successful leadership in this century's struggles to improve the status of women, especially women's right to acquire and make use of an education. Most remarkable perhaps is Bryn Mawr's role in the history these women continue to make. The story of how this came about begins before the College's founding, with the early years of our first Japanese student—Ume Tsuda, special student from 1889 to 1892.

In November 1871, just before her seventh birthday, Ume was given an audience with the Empress of Japan and there received an order from the Commissioner of Pioneering in Hokkaido to study in the United States . . . In December, she and four other young ladies, 8, 11, and two 14-year-olds, started the long voyage accompanied by the Iwakura Delegation. Two of the girls suffered from ill health and returned home very soon after arrival; the others remained for ten years. The older girls went to families in New England and, when of age, to Vassar. The youngest, Ume, stayed in Washington with Charles Lanman and his family, living at first in the Japanese Embassy where Mr. Lanman was then secretary to the delegation. Ume graduated from Archer Institute (high school) and then it was time for her to return to her homeland. Before she left, however, she had been introduced through a missionary friend of her father's to Mrs. Wistar Morris, a Philadelphia Quaker. It was Mrs. Morris who, years later, was to bring Ume to the attention of Dr. Rhoads, president of the new women's college in Bryn Mawr; and it was Mrs. Morris who, in 1893, helped Ume to realize her dream of procuring scholarships for other Japanese girls by establishing a committee that continues today.

When Ume returned to Japan in 1882, she found herself a curiosity, a stranger without one word of her native tongue. Her country was then reacting strongly against indiscriminate Westernization, including the practice of "over-educating" women. The year of her return the government had authorized a "Girls Higher School," offering a three-year course beyond primary studies and this was thought sufficient. English as a study was not approved—there was more than enough of that in the mission schools . . . Ume's first task was to remake herself into a Japanese woman—she taught herself the language, customs and habits. Of necessity, she accepted temporary jobs teaching English at the mission schools.

In 1885, the Imperial Household department established the Peeresses' School, which included English in the curriculum, and offered Ume the chance to teach English in a Japanese setting. She accepted and, except for two leaves of absence, held the position for the next fifteen years . . . The more liberal views toward women reflected by the new school further stimulated Ume's ambition to seek the college training denied her before. In any case, a leave of absence was secured, Dr. Rhoads met with Mrs. Morris, and in 1889 Ume entered Bryn Mawr as a special student with more graduate than undergraduate status.

She studied English literature, philosophy, German, and biology, and proved to have exceptional ability in science . . . During her College years, she found time for courses at Oswego Teacher's College, to visit and make future plans . . . and to join Mrs. Morris on a tour seeking scholarship money for other Japanese women. When her three-year's leave was up, she returned to her duties at the Peeresses' School.

Mrs. Morris continued the scholarship project. She became discouraged with her efforts to promote missionary zeal at Quaker meetings, so she went with her husband to Japan and brought back a student, Michi Matsuda.

With Michi as evidence, Mrs. Morris formed the Japanese Scholarship Committee—four Quakers, four Episcopalians and four Presbyterians—to fund American schooling for Japanese women recommended by Japanese educators. Michi, after two years of preparatory schooling, entered Bryn Mawr and received her B.A. in 1899. She returned to Japan and later became dean of Doshisha Girls' School. The Committee has since been responsible for 23 students, one of whom went to Swarthmore, two to Ambler Horticultural School and 19 to Bryn Mawr including, this year, Yoshimi Yamamoto in the Graduate School of Arts and Sciences. Although not a Bryn Mawr committee, many from the College appear on the roster—in the early days, to name a few, M. Carey Thomas, Abby Kirk 1892, Fanny Cochran 1902, Julia Cope Collins 1889, Mrs. Harold Pierce mother of Mary Peirce 1912.

. . . When Miss Tsuda returned to Japan, there were still only two government high schools for women. Three years later Tokyo opened the First Girls' High School; other cities soon followed this example and a law was passed requiring each prefecture to establish one or more such schools. The study of English was no longer viewed with strong disfavor. By appointment of the Educational Association in 1898, Miss Tsuda and one other Japanese woman represented Japan at the meeting of the American Association of Women's Clubs, in Denver. Before returning to Japan, she went to England and attended special lectures at Oxford, visited a Bryn Mawr alumna in Paris, and back in the United States, made serious plans with Miss Bacon for establishing her own school. Miss Bacon took the plans and the plea for funds to buy the necessary land and buildings to an interested gathering in Philadelphia.

. . . In September 1900, having rented a seven-room house, Miss Tsuda and Miss Bacon opened Joshi Eigaku Juku in Tokyo (Girls' Institute for English Studies, later renamed Tsuda College), equipped with a blackboard, Miss Tsuda's books and piano, and Miss Bacon's typewriter . . . Ten pupils had enrolled (the number doubled in the first weeks), and the faculty included the founders, Mr. H. Sakurai, and Uta Suzuki, who was to become a Japanese Committee scholar at Bryn Mawr from 1904 to 1906.

In a speech on opening day, Miss Tsuda expressed her intention to create a place for advanced study under conditions similar to those she had known in America. Her women students, she said, "would be taught to strive for the highest intellectual attainment while the utmost care would be required of them as to speech, manners and dress, nowhere to let themselves be conspicuous or to excite comment. Then they can be as intelligent as men without being criticized by anybody and so win further opportunity for themselves and other women." The plan of study paralleled the three years' course of the English departments of men's collegiate institutions. Miss Tsuda believed that "English, with all it might include of world thought and knowledge, was for Japanese women of that day the most stimulating and developing of studies." She also saw that such training would equip her students to take advantage of the changes coming in the Japanese educational system. The newly created Government high schools for girls had increased the demand for teachers; government examinations for the necessary teaching certificates were open to women . . .

By 1914, the school had 150 students, and 20 salaried teachers, and offered courses in Chinese and Japanese literature, and history, psychology and ethics, but the emphasis was still on the study of English literature and language. Tsuda graduates now became the first women to be considered qualified to teach English in middle schools for boys as well as girls.

. . . During these years, more Japanese Bryn Mawr alumnae retuned, adding their quiet voices to that of Miss Tsuda—Masa Dogura (Viscountess Uchida) in 1896, Michi Matsuda 1899 and in 1904 Michi Kawai, the Japanese Scholarship Committee's second scholar. Miss Kawai returned to teach for several years at Tsuda and became its national secretary from 1912 to 1926. In 1929, she established her own school, Keisen Junior College, and opened the first agricultural department for women. After World War II, she founded Keisen Horticultural College, with a full course offered in farm practices suitable for small farm garden plots into which private land holdings were being divided under the advice of General MacArthur. Setzue Inoue Usa, another Japanese Committee Scholar, is assistant head of this college which now has over 1,000 students and 120 faculty, men and women. In 1952, just before her death, Miss Kawai helped establish the Japanese International Christian University. After her death, Miss Kawai's friends in America founded the Michi Kawai Christian Fellowship which continues today and includes Bryn Mawr alumnae among its directors . . .

In 1946, Miss Kawai and the president of Tsuda College, Ai Hoshino '12, were appointed as the only two women to a committee of thirty Japanese which conferred with an American educational mission on changes in Japanese higher education. Recommendations presented at the 1946 meeting included the extension of women's education equal to that offered men. The proposal was accepted, and in 1948 Miss Hoshino had the satisfaction of seeing Tsuda become one of the first women's institutions to achieve university rank.

In 1960 at Bryn Mawr's Seventy-fifth Anniversary, the College awarded Miss Hoshino a citation for distinguished service. She had been president of Tsuda College from the time of Miss Tsuda's death (1929) until 1952 . . . Tsuda College continued to lead the way in women's education. In 1928, a post-graduate two-year course was added in higher mathematics, chemistry and physics . . . When university rank came in 1948, Elizabeth Gray Vining '23, then tutor of the Crown Prince, was a lecturer at the college, Rebecca Morton '25, a civilian employee of the U.S. War department, was teaching conversational English one day a week; and Esther Rhoads, principal of Friends School in Tokyo, was among the trustees . . .

Returning to the historical sequence of Bryn Mawr's Japanese alumnae, the scholar following Miss Hoshino, another Japanese Scholarship Committee student, was Makiko Hitotsuyanagi '16. She married an American, William Merrell Vories, but he took her name and moved to Japan where he founded the Omi Brotherhood. His wife served as principal of the Omi Brother schools. Just before their deaths, the Hitotsuyanagis founded a tuberculosis sanatorium in Japan.

Above: Ume Tsuda and Anna Powers, class of 1890, studying in Anna's dormitory, 1890
Opposite: Ume Tsuda (Tsuda Umeko; née Tsuda Mume) (1864–1929), c. 1881
Next two pages: Panorama of northeastern view of campus, c. 1900

Ryu Sato Oyaizu followed, getting her A.B. in 1917 and M.A. in 1918. She, too, returned to Japan, lives now in Tokyo and has tutored high school and college students in English. Fumi Uchida Kimura, the sixth to be introduced by the Scholarship Committee, graduated in 1920 and returned to teach at Tsuda College, Ochanomizu Women's University and other institutions.

That brings us to Taki Fujita '25, who is today's president of Tsuda College and who, like Miss Hoshino, was awarded a citation for distinguished service by Bryn Mawr in 1960. For twenty-five years after her graduation, Miss Fujita taught at Tsuda, becoming head of the political science department. In 1949 she was one of two Japanese women sent to the U.S. to study college administration. She enrolled at Bryn Mawr as a special student, taking Theory and Practice of Democracy and American Literature, attending other history and literature courses when she could and observing the procedures of administration throughout the College . . . Before leaving, she wrote a letter of appreciation to Miss McBride, the Trustees, Directors, Faculty and all who had helped her:

Let me tell you a few things by which I was so impressed . . . First of all, the trust you put in the student body is the most wonderful inspiration to me because the faculty-student relationship, or rather the administration versus the student relationship, is one of the most delicate problems confronting the college administration in Japan. Secondly, the spirit of cooperation and mutual help existing among the educational institutions, especially among Haverford, Swarthmore, and Bryn Mawr and also among the Seven Colleges, is beautiful and so essential . . . Japan needs this cooperation instead of rivalry, or at least we must quickly arrive to the state of the friendly rivalry among our colleges and universities . . . Thirdly, what I witnessed at the scholarship committee meeting and what I heard on May Day morning service filled me with envy as well as the determination to raise more money for scholarships for the girls of Tsuda College . . . I have come to understand why the graduates of so many colleges all over the U.S.A., as well as those of foreign countries, flock to Bryn Mawr's Graduate School.

Reprinted from the *Bryn Mawr Alumnae Bulletin,* Spring 1973.

New Directions: 1922–1942

THE IDEALS, TRADITIONS, AND AMBITIONS OF BRYN MAWR
JEANETTE EATON

College education for women is still in the experimental stage. Nobody knows just what constitutes ideal preparation for a sex whose opportunities for activity are expanding day by day. Nor is this strange. For, whereas men have been taking degrees for centuries, higher education for women has been tried for only sixty-four years.

Vassar College did not open its doors until 1865; Smith and Wellesley, not till ten years later. Bryn Mawr and Barnard, founded in the eighties, are comparatively debutantes, and Radcliffe was not an organized college until 1893. As for Mount Holyoke, a seminary since 1837, it has held college rank a bare thirty-five years. These seven colleges are the great pioneers in women's advanced education both in the United States and in Europe.

All were founded by idealists. Most of them tapped a spirit of piety which in past generations characterized every effort toward the equalization of human rights. Recently they have united in a bond of common interests. For, whatever their differences, they have a similar purpose. Furthermore, it is carried out in identical media. They are all dealing with the same dynamic generation, one which has learned to achieve its every want.

Externally these desires seem to have no relation to the ones which first set "young ladies" packing their horsehair trunks for the great adventure of going to college. For the modern girl takes that adventure for granted. Moreover, she stands in no awe either of precedent or of the faculty. She must have her say about everything—from the desserts served at dinner to the conduct of examinations.

On her demand daily compulsory chapel was abolished and smoking-lounges established. The modern girl has discarded stockings along with chaperons, and insists on inviting young men formally and informally at a rate which over the week-end gives the average campus the look of a coeducational institution. In short, she is the apostle of personal liberty.

Many an "old grad," returning after a quarter century's absence, is dazed and aghast at college girls of the present. But that individual has forgotten entirely that in her day she would have shocked even more profoundly the earnest blue-stocking of the seventies. Twenty-five years ago the era of college and class spirit was in full swing. In imitation of their brothers, girls marched a hundred strong to basket-ball games, singing the songs that Brown and Harvard had long ago discarded, and splitting their lungs at the signal of the cheer-leader.

Their dual loyalties caused them to hate all other women's colleges and to weep copiously when their "sister class" graduated. Only "grinds" won Phi Beta Kappa, and they were regarded, at best, with resolute tolerance. Indeed, the average girl of that period was a blend of hoyden and sentimentalist which was a complete guaranty against early maturity.

The type is obsolete. Today nothing is so utterly démodé as being collegiate. The dormitory is shorn of its pennants and the campus of cheering throngs. Physical training departments no longer subordinate the good of the many to the prowess of a few, and now, unhonored and unsung, everybody plays hockey and basket-ball for the fun of it. As for intercollegiate jealousies, they are yielding to mutual activities which include, also, men's colleges—debating, the National Federation of Students, the Model League of Nations, and the exchange of Glee Club concerts which represent serious artistic effort.

All such tendencies indicate increasing maturity. More impressive proof of it appears in the ardor with which girls covet the privilege of having a paper selected for publication and the opportunity of being chosen to spend the junior year at the Sorbonne. Indeed, it is in scholastic achievement where lies the truly important change in college girls. It has been little heralded.

What the public hears about is the bare-leg craze, field-day stunts, and the cigarette habit. But these things are but ephemeral symbols of modernism. The real news about college students is of a different order. As the twentieth century turned its second quarter there began to appear a phenomenon of the utmost significance. Look closely and you will see the pendulum swinging back to the earliest days of women's higher education. What we observe is the beginning of a spontaneous revival of learning.

Needless to say, this impulse has been stimulated by innovations on the part of college authorities. In the first place, standards of entrance requirements have been raised until candidates, sifted and resifted, represent American womanhood at its finest. For remember that not only mental caliber, but character, leadership, and potential capacity for growth are involved in this selective process. Secondly, the menu of studies is no longer a potpourri resulting in a mere indigestible smatter . . .

To introduce such innovations and increase individual attention given students are very expensive. It means both that faculties have to be increased and that salaries must be high enough to attract professors adequate to these demands. Because rewards are not sufficient, these colleges are always in danger of losing their best instructors. Yet the amazing thing is that charges to students have not increased in proportion to overhead . . .

It would almost seem as if a year at college with all its diverse advantages to mind and body were the one bargain left in the world. When one remembers that these institutions are doing work parallel with men's colleges, it is hard to believe how far from commensurate are their endowments. The entire group is in sore need of greater general understanding of an achievement which in so brief a period of effort is nothing short of stupendous.

Sure are the common factors of this group of seven colleges. Nevertheless, within that frame of likenesses each of them preserves an individuality absolutely distinct. Inherent differences of tradition and location, differences of academic slant, and diversity of special courses set apart each college and give it an atmosphere as unique as are the personalities of the seven presidents . . .

Of all seven colleges Bryn Mawr has changed the least. In the first place, it was not opened until the beginning of mental sophistication in the United States. Advanced education was an old story in 1885. With women making their mark in professions and businesses it was a foregone conclusion that adequate training must be provided for them. Women novelists and artists, and women scientists were rapidly pushing their way out of the old sphere of domestic limitations. True, it wasn't exactly the fashion to possess a college degree, but to do so no longer subjected a woman to comment.

In the second place, founded as it was in the Quaker tradition, Bryn Mawr was quite free both of piety and of the Puritanism which cemented the very bricks of Mount Holyoke and Wellesley. Personal liberty has always existed there. Thanks to the vision of its great leader, Miss M. Carey Thomas, the college possessed even in its early history a government by students almost as potent as it is to-day. From the first it was assumed that students came to learn as much as possible and could therefore be trusted to mind their own business.

Quite undramatically, as family customs relaxed, the change was reflected in the college. Smoking, for example, raised only the question of fire prevention. From Saturday noon on, the halls of residence hold but a handful of voluntary hermits, for week-end leaves are uncurtailed. A girl has only to report where she is going. As a consequence the student body has always consisted of mature, self-sufficient young women, and no marked transformation in type has taken place.

There is another reason why Bryn Mawr was consistently the Mecca of this once exceptional adolescent. That is the existence within its gates of a graduate school. It is readily seen that when one-fifth of the college is working for higher degrees the accent on learning is greatly stressed. Also, faculty members of high distinction are attracted and held by the opportunity to give advanced courses which offer full scope to their scholarship.

Long before other colleges began to talk about "honor girls" this type of student was to be found at Bryn Mawr. It has always been easy there for a girl to achieve individual distinction of any kind, for this is the smallest college in the group. The entire undergraduate membership of four hundred wouldn't fill freshman quarters at Smith.

With all these facts in mind, one can scarcely wonder that Bryn Mawr has had the reputation for being a bit "superior" to her sisters. In the slang of the nineties, "She was little, but oh my!" And Miss M. Carey Thomas, president for all but fifteen years of its existence, did everything possible to give this impression a factual basis. She was a woman whose tremendous force of personality and conviction swept feminism up to new heights. She accepted no limitations whatsoever for her sex, but asserted that women could attain any goal they had the courage to attempt. As an outstanding leader in women's education she determined to create a school which should be on a par with the finest institution of learning available to men.

Without doubt the model she selected was Oxford. Certainly there have always been on the faculty graduates from that cultural center. And then there was the Bryn Mawr accent carefully instilled until even girls from Salt Lake City or Dixie or Vermont struck their mothers as being completely Anglicized.

Moreover, every physical detail contributed to the same impression. Gray-stone, ivy-covered buildings all of English Gothic style, the library cloisters, smooth lawns of velvety green, arched gateways, fine old trees! Here, indeed, set down in our midst is a bit of England in a perfection of sequestered atmosphere. Here, if anywhere, can youth be imbued with the joys and rewards of the intellectual life.

Into this setting, when she was made president five years ago, stepped Miss Marion Park. Her association with the college could hardly have been closer. A graduate and postgraduate of Bryn Mawr, she had also served there as dean. On the other hand, years of foreign study, of teaching at a western college, and of acting as dean in two eastern colleges besides her own had given her wide experience and diverse contact.

Probably her main interest is scholarship. Certainly her own is proved by her possession, among other trophies, of four degrees. But her chief contribution to Bryn Mawr has been more essential to it than emphasis on intellectual acquisitions. What she has done is to humanize it, give to its atmosphere those ingredients of humility and of aspiration which are far nobler than the most justifiable arrogance.

Never was the essence of a personality more luminously revealed in manner and expression. With Miss Park it is as if such attributes as stature, feature, and coloring had been subdued the better to disclose the presence of a high-souled spirit. One can not talk with her five minutes without realizing both her force and her capacity for selfless imagination for others. There is a gaiety and sweetness about Miss Park which draws her close to youth. She knows all the girls by name. Last year when a brilliant but penniless student from the Far West was taken ill the president brought her into her own charming house for convalescence.

Due to its system of unequally priced rooms which sets a maximum annual expenditure at more than two thousand dollars, Bryn Mawr has often been accused of snobbery. For this reason it is good to sound the sturdy democracy of President Park. She is desirous of getting a larger percentage of high-school students. She believes in coeducation.

To all intercollegiate enterprises she gives eager support. In her opinion there is great educational value in the Model League of Nations, which meets every year in some college within a certain district, and students of both sexes participate. Two members from each college in the group represent a specified nation and, according to a carefully prepared agenda, discuss the very issues current at Geneva. "There is no doubt," says Miss Park, "that these meetings, together with a recent effort to stimulate undergraduates to study at Geneva in the summer, have offered great impetus to student interest in international peace."

Likewise intercollegiate debates and work for the National Federation of Students are regarded by the president as satisfying indications of a new spirit of co-operation which has drawn Bryn Mawr more closely than ever before into association with other colleges. Why, this spring Princeton students took the men's parts in a play given at Bryn Mawr and were actually entertained beforehand at a tea-dance!

It had never happened before. But such a break with Quaker traditions of sobriety seems to promise more than it does. Asked if they would repeat the experiment, the girls were casually vague. "At any rate," they asserted, "we have no intention of giving formal 'proms' here. We get enough dancing at home and at the men's colleges without going in for it ourselves. It isn't worth the bother."

Indeed, aside from teas, entertainment of the incoming freshmen, and a few special ceremonies, such as the picturesque "Lantern Night," there is only one occasion which is worth the bother. That is the superb May-Day celebration held every fourth year. In this the entire college takes part. To it flock visitors by thousands, for Shakespearian plays, Elizabethan dances, jousting-matches, and tumbling, preceded by a magnificent pageant, with everyone in costume and presented in that incomparable setting—such are the component parts of a fête—well worth, as an educational feature, the enormous amount of time and labor expended upon it.

With this exception, however, college activities are comparatively few. The Dramatic Association gives a play or two, and the Glee Club a Gilbert and Sullivan opera. The *College News* is issued weekly and the literary *Lantern* every month. The governing body and the Undergraduate Association keep their committees busy. There is always a goodly number on the tennis-courts and in the athletic field. But the casual pilgrim who sets foot within the precincts of Bryn Mawr finds that what is going on there is study.

The library with its individual stalls and reading lamps is peculiarly designed for personal seclusion. On a warm day its cloisters will show a frieze of girls conning their books with bare, brown legs dangling over the low parapet. The picture is significant. For what with the smallness of the college, where business is easily handled, and the slim program of events, it follows that here in a special way young women are engaged in mastering "learning's crabbed text."

Partly is one impressed with this because Bryn Mawr makes little attempt to include the application of theory. There is a play-writing course so popular that if the professor cuts, the girls are furious. But these plays are not performed. The music department has no major course, and gives no credit either for instrumental practice or for work in the Glee Club. Likewise, art students wishing to give tangible expression to their interest are obliged to hire their own instructors and to volunteer time in the studio, with nothing gained toward a degree.

Science lectures are, of course, supplemented by laboratory work. Students in the education department visit as observers that delightful open-air school of progressive type called "The Phebe Anna Thorne School," which tucks its pagoda-like buildings into a corner of the campus. Nevertheless it remains true that here the principle of undergraduate work is an exclusive concentration on acquiring information and on the development of processes which are purely mental.

Faithful to English tradition, Bryn Mawr stands for the humanities. Unlike others in this group, it concedes as a ticket of entrance no substitute for Latin except Greek. Furthermore, one year's college work in either of these ancient tongues is demanded for a B.A. degree. The sentence is probably endured with so good a grace because here the classics vibrate with something of the color and life of the present. This is due to the close relation between these courses and archeology.

The department, which has contributed much luster to the college, has always maintained direct contact with the American School of Classical Studies at Athens. The thrill of new discoveries which throw light on Greek and Roman civilization is felt instantaneously within the ivy-covered walls of Bryn Mawr. Graduate students and professors are always coming back from the Mediterranean ready to impart fresh zest to young tyros. This stimulus and the influence of like-trained heads of the college are potent. Thirteen per cent of 1930's senior class has chosen to major in the classics.

Modern tongues, however, are given a more generally important place on the schedule. No girl can graduate without a reading knowledge of French and German. They are taught for the most part by those born and bred in the language, and students must park all English vocables outside the classroom door. The same is true of Italian and Spanish. Fluency and proper accent are first principles, succeeded by a study of the indigenous literature and civilization. No young woman released from this environment will be able to think of Paris only in terms of couture, nor of Rome as the place where one consumes pasta and Frascati to the splash of fountains.

But Heavens above, we haven't said a word yet about the English courses! It is all the more belated because alumnae who have missed Miss Park's inoculation of modesty assure us that one who has majored in English at Bryn Mawr has a unique guaranty of erudition. An even more basic tribute, however, was offered the department by an undergraduate. "It's through our English work that we first really learn how to study," she declared. "It's a perfect blend of method, information, and a technique which makes us long to muster lucid and discriminating expression."

The compliment was returned by one of the instructors, an Englishwoman of literary forebears. Said she, "I'd rather teach American than English girls. These youngsters are rather awful, you know, as to faults. But they realize it. They don't think writing is merely a trick, and are not always laying on purple patches."

First aid in correcting this awfulness comes from every quarter. Blithely one of the history professors offered his cruel-kind process of tying up his work with English instruction. "At the third misspelled word, at the second tangled sentence, I read no further in a girl's paper. If she can't set down her information properly there's no use her knowing all the kings of France nor the dynastic ambitions of the Tudors."

Girls who don't yet know that they must think logically in order to write clearly, girls who have no passion in them for learning, are personae non gratae with Bryn Mawr professors. Some of the youngest and most austere amongst the latter say frankly that only "honor students" should come to college. But such severity is dismissed by President

> GIRLS WHO DON'T YET KNOW THAT THEY MUST THINK LOGICALLY IN ORDER TO WRITE CLEARLY, GIRLS WHO HAVE NO PASSION IN THEM FOR LEARNING, ARE PERSONAE NON GRATAE WITH BRYN MAWR PROFESSORS.

Park with a smile which gathers benignly into its curve both those autocrats and the subjects of their criticism.

"The average girl," asserts Miss Park serenely, "certainly takes away something from college which helps to lift the general intelligence, and usually she contributes something. Perhaps she is a good executive. She may be good at sports. Often a girl who responds coldly to the lure of French verbs or to physics may be awakened by music."

The music department, indeed, is an effective means of arousing the appreciation of beauty. Often as a prelude to one of the especially interesting concerts given by the Philadelphia Orchestra the class will discuss and analyze both structure and meaning of all compositions on the program. The ensuing performance, which all students may attend without formality of chaperon or special permission, is thus bound to be heard creatively. Lectures in the music-room of the beautiful Goodhart Hall are always crowded, and the head of the department said approvingly, "Often girls will spend hours playing phonograph records in order to memorize certain musical forms."

Much the same interest, moreover, is displayed in pictorial art. This department, expertly organized and adequately equipped with reproductions of a world of masterpieces, contributes that sympathetic understanding of by-gone eras which springs from a union of the mind with emotions stirred through beauty.

From a purely surface view-point, however, science work at this college has not the advantages offered elsewhere. Not here will you find the superb buildings, the elaborate modern devices, the spacious quarters, and the exhibits and collections possessed by other women's colleges. But good pedagogy, even in science, is not entirely dependent on external aids, and these last are adequate here.

Botany is not taught. Yet apparently, the work accomplished in chemistry, biology, geology, and physics is of a standard to reconcile the most ardent disciples with this lack. Bryn Mawr's long reputation for excellence in science work is amply justified by the graduate research for which it is a preparation. Theses which summarize such investigations have found their way into the most advanced scientific journals.

Nevertheless, Bryn Mawr students conform to the general rule which makes science an exceptional interest among women. Here as elsewhere they are far more apt to major in English, history, languages, or economics. True, this is one of the few colleges which seems to have mathematics on its mind. But neither in that subject nor even in psychology do many girls choose to specialize.

The cause of this selective bias probably lies deep in early educational environment. Little girls are still supposed always to prefer dolls to engines, pumps, and aeroplanes. On the other hand, in the case of psychology above all, one cannot help suspecting that the initial stages of the subject may be too abstract and technical to capture and lead on the imagination . . .

Perhaps the Bryn Mawr curriculum committee will take this matter up. That group represents the latest adventure of students who feel that they are ready for more responsibility. To educate the freshmen in rules and regulations, to judge and penalize infringements of privilege, to manage athletic and dramatic enterprises, and to engage Sunday evening speakers—all this is merely the good, familiar routine of running the college. The new interest is partly the result of a recent shock to Bryn Mawr's traditional sense of leadership.

Not Miss Park—for, after all, she was dean of Radcliffe for a year—but certainly the daughters of alumnae have been amazed to perceive that students in other colleges are putting away childish things and are taking strides which threaten to bring them abreast, if not actually ahead, of Bryn Mawr students. "Honors work," for example, is developed further in other places. So is the plan of sending specially qualified juniors to France. Realization of this astounding situation has proved a great provocation.

In her farewell article, published in the *News*, the outgoing president of the Undergraduate Association indicates what the next step in student responsibility must be. Her command is, "Take an active part in your own education. The initiative must come from you. The curriculum committee has been revised, and the faculty has shown great willingness to allow it to co-operate. You have taken the first steps. Do not let the habit of a spoon-fed education creep again. Know what you want for your education and get it!"

The challenge is definitely to the student body. The writer well knew the progressive faculty would back her up. Bryn Mawr girls are very proud of having a faculty almost evenly divided between men and women, and one possessed of an unusually large percentage of young professors. Not that students fail to discriminate between age and years. They never do. One of the juniors expressed the matter thus, "A professor isn't an old dodo just because of white hair and wrinkles. Some of our most brilliant and exciting teachers are more than old enough to have taught our mothers. A dodo is one who has such an absolutely static style of presenting a subject that you're certain in advance just what the class is going to be like. Fixed ideas, unvaried methods, even stale jokes—that's the dodo's repertoire."

Every college, of course, has its prize collection of these specimens. They irritate everybody. But they are nonetheless heart-breaking. They have given their all to the institution. Long ago they entered it with the consecration once offered to the state of marriage and have never forsworn their vow to love, honor, and obey. For this reason the problem of divorcing them is, as Miss Park says, "one of the great tragedies which face any college president." Fortunately for so sympathetic a being, her proportion of potential divorce cases is especially small.

Indeed, what with its Carola Woerishoffer Graduate School of Social Research, its non-resident lecturers, and members from across the seas, this faculty has even been free from academic narrowness. Miss Park attributes this partially to the influence of a dean who is the daughter of an ex-president of the United States. "Miss Helen Taft Manning," said she, "can always be counted on to hold before us the great issues of the day and to balance any ingrowing tendency by cosmopolitan contacts."

There is no doubt that such contacts are profoundly desired by students themselves. They reveal eagerness by a growing interest in international politics and by exchanging ideas with other colleges. They reveal it, also, in the type of speaker they invite to address, not the Liberal Club only as in former days, but the entire student body. You may be sure that some of these speakers are there to discuss religious questions.

For inarticulate as it may be and impatient of old forms and of a conventionality in conflict with modern loyalty to science and to independent thought, religious interest does exist. If girls go to chapel mainly to hear announcements of college events, they often pack the students' room to detain a great and thoughtful preacher with innumerable questions.

Still another instance of this amplitude of relationships must be cited. No smallest sketch of Bryn Mawr would be complete without a word concerning its Summer School for Women Workers in Industry. It is supported entirely by private subscriptions. For six weeks every year the college is turned over to a hundred manual workers selected by their own groups. From South, West, and East they come, these young women from mills and factories to share for once the environment of their more fortunate sisters.

They live in the halls. They go to classes every day taught by a faculty equal in every respect to the regular faculty of the college. They learn sports and take corrective exercises—alas, nearly all of them need these! Such is their joy in it all, such is their passionate thirst for learning that as one professor put it, "They are the most exhausting and the most inspiring of students!"

A single stipulation was made by the first member of the Summer School. That was that no bells should sound for dismissal of classes. "We have to answer to bells all our working lives," they said, "so couldn't we just be told when to move on?" Never was Miss M. Carey Thomas truer to her gift for spacious vision than in following her inspiration to found in 1922 this school for industrial workers. It was her last creative act before resigning the presidency.

Here indeed is outward proof of the ideal to which Bryn Mawr is dedicated. For although it is so sheltered and serene, although it is absorbed in learning for learning's sake and devoted to the highest possible development of the individual, yet the purpose of this college is quite other than a mere aggrandizement of the personal ego. Its true expression involves the spirit of noblesse oblige which is, perhaps, education's greatest contribution to a materialistic era.

Reprinted from the *Pictorial Review*, October 1929.

Page 76: Map of the Bryn Mawr campus, by J. Riegel, Jr., 1934

Page 78: Cartoon from the *College News*, June 7, 1922

Opposite top: "Footprints in the Sands of Time," a comic map illustrating daily life on campus, from the *Class Book* (1929)

Opposite bottom: Class of 1923

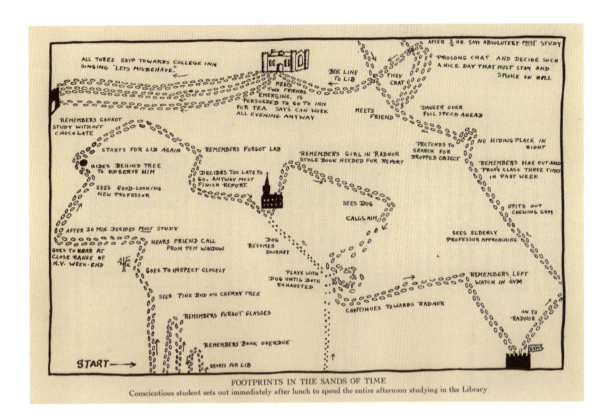

FOOTPRINTS IN THE SANDS OF TIME
Conscientious student sets out immediately after lunch to spend the entire afternoon studying in the Library

NEW DIRECTIONS: MARION EDWARDS PARK

BRYN MAWR COLLEGE CHOOSES NEW HEAD
Dr. Marion Edwards Park, Dean of Radcliffe, Elected to Succeed Dr. Thomas

PHILADELPHIA, Feb. 27—Dr. Marion Edwards Park, Dean of Radcliffe College, Cambridge, Mass., has been unanimously elected President of Bryn Mawr College by the Board of Directors, to succeed M. Carey Thomas, who retires at the end of the present academic year, and she has accepted the appointment.

Miss Park is an alumna of Bryn Mawr having graduated from that institution in 1898. She was awarded the Bryn Mawr European fellowship, the highest prize in the gift of the college, and after two years at the American School of Classical Studies in Athens, Greece, she returned to this country and became instructor in classics and acting dean of women at Colorado College, Colorado Springs. From 1918 to 1921 she was acting and associate dean of Simmons College, Boston, going to Radcliffe last October. In 1911 she was acting Dean of Bryn Mawr during the absence of Dean Marion Reilly.

Dr. Park was born in Gloversville, N.Y. Her only brother, Dr. E. A. Park is head of the new department of pediatrics at Yale.

Reprinted from the *New York Times*, February 28, 1922.

Above: Marion Edwards Park (1875–1960), 1943. Photograph by Bachrach Studios (Baltimore)

Opposite top: Invitation to President Park's inauguration, October 21, 1922

Opposite bottom: Marion Edwards Park and Rufus Matthew Jones (1863–1948) at the Bryn Mawr commencement. Jones was a Haverford professor and member of Bryn Mawr's board of trustees (1898–1936)

Wednesday Afternoon
October 18, 1922

Dear Muddie,

. . . The cap and gown came in a big box, which is handy to use. I haven't tried them on yet—I tremble to touch such badges of knowledge! This Saturday is the great inauguration of President Park and so we had to have our caps and gowns in time to walk in the procession. The governor of Pennsylvania, thirty-some college presidents, deans, representatives of academies of arts and letters and sciences, alumnae, directors—about a thousand of them will all be here. The presidents of Yale, Haverford, and Smith are going to speak. There will be a luncheon served after the ceremony but President Park said that she was sorry she couldn't invite us to that because she was afraid to add 450 hearty appetites to the number of guests already counted upon . . .

Reprinted from a letter, Elizabeth Burroughs, Class of 1926, to her mother.

THE INAUGURATION OF PRESIDENT PARK WILL BE HELD IN THE GYMNASIUM, BRYN MAWR COLLEGE, AT 11 A. M., ON SATURDAY, OCTOBER 21ST.

ADDRESSES WILL BE DELIVERED BY

PRESIDENT JAMES ROWLAND ANGELL, LITT. D., LL. D. OF YALE UNIVERSITY

PRESIDENT WILLIAM ALLAN NEILSON, PH. D., LL. D. OF SMITH COLLEGE

PRESIDENT WILLIAM WISTAR COMFORT, PH. D., LITT. D., LL. D., OF HAVERFORD COLLEGE

PROFESSOR RUFUS M. JONES, D. D., LITT. D. PRESIDENT OF THE BOARD OF TRUSTEES AND BOARD OF DIRECTORS OF BRYN MAWR COLLEGE

AND BY

PRESIDENT MARION EDWARDS PARK, PH. D.

ADMISSION TO THE GYMNASIUM WILL BE BY TICKET ONLY, AND TICKETS WILL BE SENT ON RECEIPT OF ACCEPTANCE.

REPLIES AND REQUESTS FOR TICKETS SHOULD BE ADDRESSED NOT LATER THAN OCTOBER 14TH, TO DEAN ISABEL MADDISON, OFFICE OF THE RECORDING DEAN, BRYN MAWR COLLEGE, BRYM MAWR, PENNA.

SHIFTING STANDARDS UNDER PARK

ENTRANCE REQUIREMENTS EXPLAINED BY MISS PARK

THE CHANGES in the College's entrance requirement, upon which the faculty has recently decided, were the subject of President Park's talk in Chapel last Wednesday morning.

Bryn Mawr has always stated twenty points as its requirement for entrance, she explained, but, if the points were counted as in other colleges, they would only amount to seventeen. In English, Mathematics, and Physics, Bryn Mawr gives one more point than do other colleges for examinations of equal difficulty. Besides these, however, Bryn Mawr requires two points which are actually more than those prescribed by other colleges.

Last year the Faculty Committee on Entrance Examinations worked to find some change in the requirements which would bring the College an increasingly good set of students. Now, through the elimination of examinations in two minor subjects, which after long trial have proved to be of small value as a foundation for the College curriculum, the faculty hopes to accomplish two things: first, to release time for more thorough preparation in the remaining subjects, so that no conditions need be carried over into the first year of college; and, second, to make it possible for a greater variety of good schools to prepare readily for Bryn Mawr.

Bryn Mawr will continue to accept either her own or College Board examinations, President Park went on, but on account of the reduced number of examinations they may be hereafter taken in not more than two divisions and no students with conditions will be admitted. These requirements will be optional in 1923 and obligatory in 1924, but minute arrangements have been made for students who have already offered preliminaries.

"We think these are more intelligent requirements for entrance," she concluded, "because good students in almost any kind of school can now consider coming to Bryn Mawr, unconditioned, with clear minds as regards their school work."

Reprinted from the *College News*, January 24, 1923.

THE NEW ENTRANCE REQUIREMENTS
Marion Edwards Park

THOSE BRYN MAWR ALUMNAE who have been connected with the preparatory schools, whether in the role of parent, teacher or pupil, and those who have worked at other colleges than Bryn Mawr know how hot a battle has waged around our entrance requirements. We have gallantly ranged ourselves pro or con the catalogue of the moment. We have sometimes believed the requirements were an efficient mechanism for sifting the wheat from the chaff among the applicants for the entering class and inevitably we have also sometimes doubted it, for what set of requirements could be framed in which every interested critic could always have confidence? And the College faculty has also long concerned itself in the matter and with more than academic interest for, unlike the occasional alumna, its members must live, move and have their being among the students whose admission they have regulated. Their own works do or do not praise them in the gates. A faculty is driven into a pragmatic philosophy and approves or disapproves the entrance requirements as it watches them in action.

The requirements set by Bryn Mawr have always been slightly in excess of those set by other colleges admitting by examination both in the actual number of subjects which the girl must study in her preparatory school and the actual number of examinations. Meantime during the last few years a certain routine of college preparation has become established more and more widely. For many excellent schools preparing many excellent students for Bryn Mawr this extra preparation is a matter of course. It has been another story with the school which occasionally prepares a student for Bryn Mawr and the school which sends up few students for any college examinations whatsoever. The friends of the College have been sorry to find that the intellectual and able girl from such schools almost automatically turned away from the consideration of Bryn Mawr. The difficulties not only of extra but of different preparation were made so great for her that without a superhuman effort on her own part it was not possible for her to enter the College.

The change at Bryn Mawr has been slow, but it is possible to see from the office records that with an evenly maintained number of Freshmen the number of private schools has tended to increase and the number of public schools to diminish. Variety is slowly giving way to a greater uniformity. Now even for the lover of the West and the South, the public high school and the ambitious pioneer who far from Bryn Mawr is fired by the name of the College the situation has never been really disquieting. It may still never be really disquieting, but with the practically uniform entrance requirements for all other women's colleges in the East I think the chances for Bryn Mawr with girls in all types of schools except the few preparing directly for Bryn Mawr have become less good and that this disadvantage has lost the College not only the average girl, but sometimes the rarely intelligent one. Therefore, we who have worked for many years outside the College have wondered whether the plan which Bryn Mawr was following was bringing us a permanently satisfactory result or whether it was worthwhile to lay out a new scheme and try a new entrance method.

When I came into the College at the beginning of the year I found that the Faculty Committee on Entrance Requirements had been meeting and discussing entrance requirements all the latter part of last year and it continued its work the first part of this year. Its recommendation were reported to and passed by the Faculty and finally materialized in the announcement made in January. Let me rehearse that briefly.

On the books Bryn Mawr has always offered examinations in "twenty points" of work. Actually, as any teacher who has prepared students for Bryn Mawr knows, these twenty points could be read as seventeen; that is, to certain examinations have been assigned a higher number of points at Bryn Mawr. A girl passing a College Board entrance examination in English has scored four points out of a total of twenty if she presented it at Bryn Mawr, whereas at other colleges it has counted only three out of a total of fifteen. In mathematics the combination of algebra and geometry gave a credit of four points at Bryn Mawr, three at other colleges; in physics two at Bryn Mawr and one at other colleges. Whether this way of reckoning was chosen because there was originally an intention to emphasize the time which the College wished to have given to the preparation (e.g., the four points summing up four years in each of which English occupied one-fourth of the student's time) I do not know. The facts can have been only rarely represented by the points assigned to mathematics and physics.

Of the subjects required there were two or three which were specially under fire. Over and above the required physics and the required ancient history a second science and a second history or a two-point language had to be offered. One after another the College departments concerned with science or history or language have reported to the committee that the second science, second history and two-point language were of no value in the College curriculum, that is, they formed no basis on which the College is able to build. On the other hand in the school they represented two, year-long courses, that is, half of the students' work and time for a year. It appeared that the College was demanding a serious addition to the preparation in the school for the sake of something which it then disregarded. Did not the College really prefer that the time of which it was so covetous should be spent on more fundamental subjects, subjects on which the College structure was to rise, on Latin, the second foreign language, English, mathematics, physics and ancient history? For that reason the committee recommended and the Faculty voted that these two points should be dropped out from the requirements.

Bryn Mawr has also set more examinations than the other colleges; three examinations in Latin for instance instead of the two usual elsewhere, two examinations in English instead of one. The Committee has reduced the number, first by the actual mission of two examinations (or one if the two-point language is to be offered). Secondly, in the future by the recommendation of the departments concerned there will be one English examination instead of two, two Latin examinations instead of three and one examination in the second foreign language instead of two. The total number of examinations will be nine (or eight) instead of thirteen (or twelve).

Logically then the number of divisions in which these examinations might be offered could be reduced. The value of the three divisions has always been discussed. The College has found little satisfaction in the form of examination which had to be set for young and immature students two years away from college and many schools have felt unwisdom in the early reaching down of the college requirements into the school course. The first of the three divisions will now be omitted and the nine or eight examinations divided between the last two years of the preparatory work.

And introduced side by side with these changes comes one which is almost the most important of all. Hereafter no student will be admitted with conditions. Most of us have for a long time felt that in the relation of school and college this was the only logical procedure. The student has sufficient information to build on or she has not; she is sufficiently mistress of simple methods to apply them to new problems or she is not; she is mature enough to attack more difficult problems in an independent way or she is not. The intricate Freshman year with its fifteen hours of a new type of work, with its heavy demands on her physical, mental and moral control offers no spare time to make up on the side these major handicaps. We shall hereafter allow only the applicants who present a completed school record to start on their college year.

What can we foresee as the result of such changes? Nothing very immediate, nothing very radical. The Faculty hopes that we shall find girls preparing themselves for Bryn Mawr from a gradually increasing number of schools, that we shall gradually find many more students trying the examinations, that out of these students the Entrance Committee can select those who seem best fitted for college work, those who have a sound basis of information, those who have the power of reasoning, and those who understand accuracy and proportion, who, to use a large word, appreciate truth. When we have chosen enough students to fill the vacant places in the College we then wish to start them off with no handicap in their college work, but to leave them free to make with the least possible loss of time that important and difficult transition from school work to college work, that process which is difficult even for the intelligent student.

The Committee has set for itself a hard task. It needs any information which it can reach about the students coming up from examination both from the schools which send them and from the teachers who have trained them. It hopes to get a set of students with keen brains and with a real interest in intellectual things, students who will make a successful attack on Freshman work and follow it with a more successful attack still on the problems of later years.

Reprinted from the *Bryn Mawr Alumnae Bulletin*, April 1923.

THE ORAL EXAM: SHARED STUDY AND COLLECTIVE CHEER

SENIORS ROLL HOOPS AFTER THIRD ORAL FOR FIRST TIME IN HISTORY

1920 IS THE FIRST CLASS in the history of the college to have no fourth orals. One hundred per cent passed the third French two weeks ago, and the announcement made last Saturday that 100 per cent had passed German was the signal for the unprecedented occasion of hoop rolling after the third oral. 1920 has remained true to the tradition that blue classes always roll their hoops.

Due to a rumor current on the campus for the last four days of the week that everyone had passed German, the Seniors had ordered their hoops in advance. Saturday morning they had waited three hours with their hoops for the announcement that came at noon . . . After the hoop rolling from Pembroke Arch down Senior Row, the Seniors sang on Taylor steps.

Reprinted from the *College News*, March 30, 1920.

BRYN MAWR COLLEGE

THE ORAL SONG

(Song by undergraduates, in costume)

Oh, after commencement was over,
   I waited around for the mob,
Which I had expected would gather
   To give me an elegant job.
I offered to sweep off the pavements,
   I tried to take fares on a car;
I wished they would find me employment
   In their bureau in distant Bryn Mawr!
But I knew that I had no position,—
   Though my finances grew rather tight,
That back in the year nineteen twenty
   I could read French and German at sight.

So to end all my pains I got married,
   And as I was walking the aisle,
He knew by the books that I carried
   He'd married a woman worth while.
The clergyman tied up the Gordian
   And asked me if I would obey,
So taking my little accordion,
   I sang him these words that I say:
"Yes, yes, yes, I promise to love you,
   To honour you with all my might,
Although I'm a good bit above you,
   For I read French and German at sight."

I never had need of a nursemaid,
   For baby was always quite good;
I silenced his cries with a word-list,
   As college-bred mothers all should.
I swore at the butler in German (Mein Gott!)
   In French I scolded the maid,
But they never studied at Bryn Mawr,
   So they misunderstood and they stayed.
For a time, and with tears I relate it,
   My husband shot craps every night,
But now he stays home in the evening,
   For we read French and German at sight.

Class Oral Song, 1920

Above: Lyrics for "The Oral Song," written by members of the class of 1920

Opposite: Students participating in "oral singing" with their hoops, 1915. After every member of the senior class passed the foreign-language oral examination, the students would rush to Senior Row, trundling their hoops in triumph.

"WE READ FRENCH AND GERMAN AT SIGHT"
Orals Singing Cheers Students Taking Language Examinations

Why do the Seniors work so hard when they're so young?
Why do the Seniors work so hard when they're so young?
They think it's good for morals
That they should work for orals,
That's why they all work so hard when they're so young.

"A READING KNOWLEDGE of French and German is required of all students." So reads the College Calendar. Orals and the college were born almost simultaneously. One might call them Bryn Mawr's oldest and saddest tradition. If the undergraduates who suffer over them now, however, had taken them in the years before 1917, they would count their present woes slight. In those days the French and German orals were really oral.

Candidates were locked into the chapel and there they stayed, sometimes for as long as four hours at a stretch. One by one, they were called before the examining board of three members of the faculty. An editorial published in 1895 gives a dreary account of the proceedings: "After waiting in the hall in company with some youthful marble statues you enter a dimly-lighted room and after giving a quick nod to its occupants, make for the chair that is pointed out to you. A book lies open before you. Someone says, 'begin there' pointing and saying the first word. Dimly you think it is well he spoke it for you could not have begun talking all by yourself. You catch your breath and begin to read. The words gabble along without any obvious connections. They tell you to translate and you wearily look over the page which you had read before without any comprehension—only an attempt at pronunciation. These words are strange, and after searching for the verb you suddenly find three and no subject. You drawl a few words and then stop. There is a long silence. You look at your hands clasped over the page and wonder how long it is before you can go," and so on, a whole half hour of the agony. As many as sixty percent of the Seniors used to fail the first oral, and the percentage of unfortunates in subsequent orals was usually pretty high. Every student could take as many as four German and four French orals during her Senior year. Apparently, many students used all eight opportunities.

Various customs were connected with those early orals. Flowers were sent to the Seniors who took them. Senior grades were posted on the Bulletin Board and published in the *News*. The most picturesque tradition of all was that of the hoops. Until 1919, the entire Senior class used to sit, hoops in hand, on the Senior steps, until a Sophomore runner brought them the news that the black sheep of the class had at last passed their orals. President Thomas herself, on one occasion, called the glad message down from a window in the Chapel to the hushed multitude below. Sometimes the suspense was frightful; two or three Seniors would be called back as many as four times to read again. Then when the victims at last issued forth, worn but victorious, the class in a body rushed to Senior Row and rolled hoops in wild triumph.

On three dreary occasions, in 1907, 1913, and 1919, not everyone passed her orals. Then the class glumly broke their hoops, in the traditional Hoop Massacres, to keep bad luck from passing down to succeeding Seniors. They thought they knew the reason for their misfortune in 1919. It was blamed on a Senior who had in her possession a hoop, quite intact, bearing the date of the ill-omened year, 1913. When the orals came at last to be written, in 1921, hoop-rolling and May Day were consolidated.

Reprinted from *Fifty Years of Bryn Mawr College: A Supplement of the "College News,"* October 1935.

RELAXING THE RULES: STUDENTS SHAPING CAMPUS LIFE

Opposite top: Advertisement for Maison Grayfal, a short-lived student beauty salon in Denbigh Hall

Opposite bottom: Excerpt from the Self-Government Association's rules for 1929–30, including the prohibition of students wearing men's clothing on campus

SELF-GOVERNMENT BOARD OPENS FIERY DISCUSSION

AT A MEETING of the Self-Government Association, held in the Goodhart Auditorium on Thursday afternoon, October 31, Article XXII, Section 2, was removed from the book of resolutions, with the understanding that a substitution be made at the next meeting. This article reads: "The Association does not allow its members to use fermented beverages on the campus except for medicinal purposes."

The meeting was called and presided over by O. Stokes, '30, president of the association. In receipt of a letter from Dr. Wagoner, Associate Physician of the College, the Association was forced to take some action on the specific resolution cited above. Apparently Miss Park had written to the infirmary, at the request of the Self-Government Association Board, to find out the official opinion of "fermented beverages" for medicinal purposes. The reply stated in no indefinite terms that the infirmary administration was not in favor of the last clause of the resolution, as it does not believe in the beneficial possibilities of alcohol. Consequently, it was very obvious that the resolution could not be allowed to stand as it has for so many years.

The meeting was opened by a motion to change the clause to read: "The Association does not allow its members to use fermented beverages on the campus." Then the discussion began; a good deal of it was irrelevant, and a good deal of it was non-constructive; it served chiefly to demonstrate the fact that the feeling on this subject in the college is very strong. The general tendency of the stand taken by the opposition was that alcoholic beverages had always proved to be of medicinal value, and that they were completely unwilling to pass a dictum which would prevent their usage; any ruling which would permit its use in exceptional cases would have to pass the infirmary, and would therefore be too complex an arrangement. Behind this attitude was a strong feeling against the control in the college by a student ruling of what, up to now, had been a personal privilege. It was a stand taken distinctly for liberty and the rights of the individual. Points saying that the infirmary would next attempt to limit the individual's cigarettes per diem, and her use of aspirin, all represented this line of thought.

The people who favored the motion seemed to be swayed chiefly by the letter of the infirmary. They strongly advocated Dr. Wagoner's prescription for all ailments otherwise helped with "fermented beverages," and they felt that the rule of no alcohol on the campus was a good one. It would prevent the stretching of privileges, and it would avoid much unnecessary complication.

The vote was finally taken, with a count of 70 to 74 against the motion. The next idea advanced in the form of a motion was that the troublesome clause be struck completely from the book of resolutions. This was passed with a slightly higher majority, on the understanding that a new resolution be substituted for the one which was now to be omitted from the book. Two suggestions were made for the new clause; one that it read, "The Prohibition Law of the United States will be enforced on the campus"; the other, that the clause reading, "Students staying more than twenty-five miles away from Philadelphia shall be responsible for not bringing criticism on the college for their conduct," be amended to apply to the campus and area within the twenty-five mile limit as well as that without.

It was felt that this latter would suffice to cover any cases which might occur in the misuse of alcoholic beverages.

The meeting was adjourned until further notice, when it is hoped that the old clause may be replaced by one which will answer all requirements, which will not be objectionable in the eyes of the college infirmary, and which will, nevertheless, express the will of the students of Bryn Mawr.

Reprinted from the *College News,* November 6, 1929.

MAISON GRAYFAL

A BOON TO BRYN MAWR BEAUTIES
Denbigh — Rooms 69 or 61

Soothing Shampoos	Winsome Waves .... 20¢
Long hair ...... 20¢	Tricky Trims .... 15¢
Short hair ..... 15¢	Miraculous Manicures ..... 15¢

The Maison Grayfal came into being to fill the need felt on the campus for beautification on short notice at pleasing prices. Our methods are modern, our service superior and our operators sympathetic. Sign on the appointment slip in Denbigh for an opportunity to become one of the best groomed girls in the college!

The establishment includes an unusual feature: an Experimental Clinic where you may invent your own coiffure, or have one created by our expert coiffeurs, to suit your own personality.

---

(5) No men's clothing or bathing caps may be worn uncovered by the students on campus or in public parts of the halls.

(6) Riding habits must not be worn at dinner on week-days, nor at dinner or supper on Sundays.

MISCELLANEOUS

XXIV.
Resolved: That students must not get in or out of windows. There is a fine of *Five Dollars* for any infraction of this rule.

XXV.
Resolved: That bridge may be played in the hall sitting rooms except on Sundays.

XXVI.
Resolved: That the hall victrolas shall not be played except in the following hours:
(1) Monday to Thursday inclusive, 1 to 2 P. M. and 6 to 7.30 P. M.
(2) Friday, 1 to 2 and 6 to 9 P. M.
(3) Saturday, 1 to 9 P. M.
(4) Sunday, not at all.
Special permission to play the victrola in private rooms over the week-end will be given at the discretion of Hall President.

XXVII.
Resolved: That the Executive Board shall have the power to fix penalties for infractions of rules.

BRYN MAWR WILL ALLOW STUDENTS TO SMOKE, ABOLISHING 1897 BAN BECAUSE UNWORKABLE

THE SELF-GOVERNMENT association of Bryn Mawr College, which has every undergraduate as a member and places the responsibility for the conduct of the students entirely in their own hands, has found it increasingly impossible to enforce the rule against smoking. The association, therefore, petitioned President Marion Edwards Park to permit smoking, under restrictions, for the group accustomed to it. Under an order issued by the President today, one room is set aside for that purpose in each hall of residence and on the lower athletic field when games are not in progress.

Miss Park issued the following statement in changing the rule against smoking: "The conduct of the students at Bryn Mawr has always been in the hands of the Self-Government Association, and the regulations of the association have been based on the public opinion of the moment. Such public opinion in a college democracy is controlled in larger matters by conscience and in lesser matters by convention.

As early as 1897 the regulation against smoking was made and has been in effect up to this time. A change in the attitude toward smoking by women has come in twenty-five years and is naturally reflected among college students. A regulation prohibiting smoking can no longer depend on the authority of conscience and convention, which make up public opinion, and is no longer effective."

The President also said that attempts to enforce the rule "increasingly fail" and that it "begins to affect the student relations to other regulations," and stands apart from other regulations in that "it is no longer resting solidly on intelligent public opinion."

The President of the Self-Government Association, Miss Frances Jay of New York, said: "The Self-Government Association has felt that the whole-hearted support of the student was not behind the old rule which forbade smoking in any college building, and as successful operation of the Self-Government Association depends upon its support by public opinion, the board asked President Park to consent to a change in the rule. This does not mean that all students are smokers. A questionnaire sent out showed that many supporters of the change were not themselves smokers, and that in fact less than half of the student body smokes."

Reprinted from the *New York Times*, November 24, 1925.

MENTALLY AND PHYSICALLY FIT: ATHLETICS AT BRYN MAWR

ATALANTA IN THE CLOISTERS
Class Spirit Centered in Athletic Competition

IN 1884 STRONG DOUBTS EXISTED that women could stand the rigors of the scholarly life. "Many girls become pale, some stunted in growth and nervous from bad air, confinement, wearisome study and a strained, cheerless, artificial school life." Even insanity is not to be forgotten as an "occasional result of the overtaxed brain." Therefore Bryn Mawr built a gymnasium and arranged "systematic exercise" therein. The results, even to us today, seem phenomenal: "94% of the students who had used the gymnasium have made a general gain in physical vigor during the year; 69% increased in weight; and 92% in strength of chest."

Walking and tennis supplements all of this indoor activity, and in 1892 a joint tennis match was held between Harvard Annex (Radcliffe), Girton College (England), and Bryn Mawr. After two years, however, Bryn Mawr forgot about tennis and turned to basketball.

Basketball, in 1892, set half the campus to training for the championship games in the spring. It was this that first started the cutthroat interclass rivalry in sports—a rivalry that continued for twenty-five years until the *College News* felt impelled to write: "Owing to the fact that some students feel pressed by the class captains to enter competitive athletics and feel pressed to enter more sports than they wish to in one season, a definite agreement has been entered into between the college and the students' Athletic Association." Basketball, a game played out of doors—we would hasten to explain—and between two teams of nine members apiece, became so firmly entrenched in the lives of the students that all kinds of training exercises were devised to build up the star players. They played Hare and Hounds assiduously, going so far as to get special permission for Hares to depart through the windows of Pembroke West.

Soccer became an outdoor winter sport, with the whole campus dividing itself into "Great Danes" and "French Poodles." Football also was widely played and appears to have been no new thing on the campus, for it is known that 1905 and 1906 had a great battle with any number of noted alumnae on the opposing sides . . .

"Record Marking" was an athletic pursuit which was important between 1890 and 1910, and which brought Bryn Mawr probably far more recognition than any other sport. Apparently it was held indoors at first although it resembles the track meets later held out of doors. In track and field activities, Bryn Mawr athletes were even more outstanding, and several American records were held by students. At one point Bryn Mawr was the proud possessor of a world's champion, M. Young, class of 1908, who threw the shot-put to a new women's record of thirty-three feet in one of the official meets. Track continued to be a minor sport for many years despite an abortive attempt to legislate it out of existence in 1923 when the cry of over-organization of athletics was being so loudly raised.

Athletics was so important to the college girl that in those years of frenzied activity even fire-drills called for a display of prowess. They were part and parcel of the regular athletic work and one of their most important features was climbing down from one's room on a rope, just as one would have to do in a real fire. Rope climbing and other gymnastic feats were very popular and the whole college frequently drilled together or in class groups with Indian clubs and wands. In 1898 Canon Coyle came to visit the college and the students planned a huge exhibition of their prowess along these lines but after much discussion the drill was called off because of "impropriety of costume"! A basketball game between 1899 and 1900 was held instead, the teams being chosen not because they were proficient but because their green and blue costumes provided a lovely contrast.

1902 marked the greatest change in the history of athletics at Bryn Mawr, when Miss Constance M. K. Applebee came to the college from England. She introduced water polo, cricket, and lacrosse, and established the rule that all students must be able to swim before they graduate. But most important of all she brought field hockey to America. Hockey made Varsity games the usual rather than the unusual practice in college athletics. The first outside game was played in 1904 with the Ladies of the Merion Cricket Club. By 1906 five outside games were played.

In this day and age when Bryn Mawr takes its athletics more or less for granted and the sports writers of the *College News* have to exhort the undergraduates to come out and watch Varsity games, it is hard to appreciate the excitement which attended the playing of the championship matches in any of the major sports during the decade of 1900–1910. The participants trained and practiced for weeks ahead and arrived at the field surrounded by a phalanx of loyal supporters and friends. Each individual member of a team had a trainer who not only supervised the athletic one's every waking moment during the training period, but also saw that she got enough sleep, ate heartily at meal times and not in between, and made sure that she got to practice on time. An irate captain would instantly impose a fine on her who delayed the practice and deprived her teammates of precious minutes of all-important drill! When game time came the trainers gathered together blankets and extra sweaters and towels and sponges, and hastened to the field to get everything fixed for the half-time period of rest. The athletes were stretched out on blankets and covered with warm sweaters while devoted hands mopped their fevered brows and gave them lemons to suck preparatory to further struggles on the field. Excitement was intense, and great was the moment for any class when they could see their banner proudly floating from the gymnasium as the result of a hard-fought series of championship matches.

. . . 1920 marked the next turning point in Bryn Mawr athletics. That year the Varsity hockey team met Swarthmore College in the first of a long series of games which has seen Bryn Mawr defeated only twice. At the same time baseball threatened to nose out hockey as the most popular sport, when a Bryn Mawr baseball team met and was defeated by an All-Philadelphia team.

At that point, however, there was no need to fear a baseball craze at Bryn Mawr. The sports columns of the *News* dwindled as the editorials lengthened and redoubled their protests against compulsory athletics. In the middle years of the Twenties several foreign hockey teams made tours of this country. Bryn Mawr played all of them but never succeeded in coming any closer to victory over her more experienced rivals than an 8-0 loss to the Irish in 1925. The *News* commented on this classic battle in the following succinct and revealing phrases: "Shillelagh Technique wins Hockey Game. Keening heard on campus."

Bryn Mawr still has its share of athletes who make All-Philadelphia teams and play intercollegiate tennis, but the emphasis is not athletic. There is fencing for the agile; dancing (more vigorous than it looks) for the fragile. For the rest, hockey, swimming, basketball, and tennis make up the main athletic program, intramural and intercollegiate.

Reprinted from *Fifty Years of Bryn Mawr College: A Supplement to the "College News,"* October 1935.

Above: Student calisthenics, c. 1916

Opposite: Marjorie Young, class of 1908, practicing shot put

DIRECTOR OF B. M. ATHLETICS INTRODUCES HOCKEY INTO AMERICA

(Contributed by Miss Hilda W. Smith, Acting Dean of the College)

Miss Constance Applebee, who is known to so many generations of Bryn Mawr alumnae, came from England to the United States in 1902. As head of a small private school in Devonshire, and as director of gymnastics in various Yorkshire schools, the results of her work had been so marked that her friends strongly advised her not to interrupt what promised to be an unusually brilliant career in this new field of physical education. But her interest in the development of athletics in America was so strong that after a short visit one summer to study the work of the Sargent School, she returned to the United States the following year to carry on her work. At that time field hockey for women was practically unknown in America, and Miss Applebee spent two years among the different women's colleges and schools in the East, teaching gymnastics and gradually introducing hockey among the students. A specially designed stick was made for her purposes by Spalding, and was soon copied in England, where this model is still known as the Applebee hockey stick.

In 1904 Miss Applebee came to Bryn Mawr to take charge of the out-door athletics, which at that time were not organized in connection with the gymnastic classes. Her success with the athletics was so great that in 1906 the gymnasium work also was placed under her department.

So for the past sixteen years Miss Applebee has been a familiar figure on the Bryn Mawr Campus. Not only in athletics, but also in the work of the Christian Association and the College News Board, Miss Applebee's sustained interest and enthusiasm have been an invaluable asset to the College. In 1911, during the difficult period when the Christian Union and the League for the Service of Christ were trying to unite to form a new organization it was largely due to Miss Applebee's inspiration that the plan of joining the two organizations was formulated and carried through. In all her relations with Bryn Mawr students, past and present, Miss Applebee has always stood for high standards in athletics and college activities, good sportsmanship, and the best interest of the whole college.

Above: Members of Bryn Mawr's archery team, c. 1926, *left to right:* Millicent Pierce, class of 1926; Margaret Gregson, class of 1928; Pauline McElwain, class of 1928; Mary Latnall, class unknown; and Pamela Kincaid, class of 1926

Left: Bryn Mawr's fencing team, 1909

Opposite (clockwise from top left): Student in athletic attire, inscribed in graphite on verso of photograph, "Sunny Jim"; "Director of B. M. Athletics Introduces Hockey into America," clipping from the *College News*, May 7, 1920; students practicing on the pommel horse on the gymnasium roof, c. 1920s; student fencers Alberta Sanson (*left*) and Elizabeth Winchester (*right*); member of Bryn Mawr's field hockey team, c. 1920s; Constance Applebee (1873–1981), athletic director at Bryn Mawr from 1904 to 1929, and visiting coach until 1971, demonstrating field hockey, the sport she introduced to the United States; students practicing gymnastics in front of the college's original gymnasium, now the Marie Salant Neuberger Centennial Campus Center; class of 1902 basketball team

THE CHINESE SCHOLARSHIP: EXTENDING BRYN MAWR'S REACH

A CHINESE SCHOLARSHIP

Lucy Martin Donnelly, Class of 1893, Chairman; Lillie Deming Loshe, Class of 1899, Secretary; and Marion Parris Smith, Class of 1901, Treasurer, Chinese Scholarship Committee

BRYN MAWR GRADUATES in China and Japan yearly circulate among themselves a collection of letters in which each tells something of her surroundings and her adventures —of her difficulties, her achievements and her hopes. Among the reports from Japan a peculiar interest belongs to the letters of the Japanese alumnae. They seem to give material for judging the practical results of foreign training, and they lead one into speculation as to the variety and permanence of our contacts with Eastern nations. Naturally one turns to the letters from China for further light on these questions. Surprisingly enough, one finds no letters from Chinese alumnae. The next step, of course, is to realize that we have no Chinese alumnae to write letters.

Bryn Mawr women have done and are doing much for China. One has only to recall the work of Mary James (class of 1895), Grace Hutchins (class of 1907) and Kate Scott (class of 1904) at Wuchang; of Helen Crane (class of 1909) at Foochow; and of Fanny Sinclair Woods (class of 1901), Catherine Arthurs (class of 1912) and Elizabeth Faries (class of 1912) at Canton. And there are many others. We are sending trained workers to China, but we are not bringing Chinese workers here to be trained. And however necessary foreign direction may be for the schools of China there is immediate need of well-trained Chinese women to supplement the work of foreigners. Bryn Mawr is one of the few colleges for women that is not doing something toward filling that need. It is, therefore, proposed to found a scholarship for Chinese girls with the same general purpose as the Japanese scholarship—that is, to give a carefully chosen student two preparatory years in an American school and four years of undergraduate work. In order that she may be independent of occasional and irregular help for the summer as well as for the college year it will be necessary to assure her of about one thousand dollars per year. For many reasons it seems better to try to raise a sum sufficient to bring in this yearly income so that the scholarship may be actually endowed and not left to be dependent on the perpetually renewed efforts of a committee to raise the sum needed each year—as is the case with the Japanese scholarship. Committees are being formed in the larger cities and it is hoped that, although the amount required is large, arrangements may be made to bring over the first scholar next year.

The amount required is large but it is to meet a large opportunity. Help given to China now is ten times as valuable as help given to China ten years hence. The opportunity, moreover, is not entirely one of giving to China. We hope that the coming of Chinese girls may add much to the life of Bryn Mawr. All the alumnae who have lived or travelled in China can speak not only of the needs of the Chinese and of their deserving but also of their fineness of spirit and their personal charm. The study of Chinese art and literature is becoming more and more a part of our education. Acquaintance and friendship with modern Chinese girls should give more reality to the study of their ancient arts, and should add greatly to the variety and interest of campus life. The enterprise of securing a Chinese scholarship is not merely a doing of duty. It should have something of the color of adventure, of a reaching out into new regions of interest.

Reprinted from the *Bryn Mawr Alumnae Bulletin*, April 1917.

First Chinese Scholar Enters Sooner than She Had Planned

FUNG KEI LIU '22 is the first student to enter Bryn Mawr on the Chinese Scholarship. Liu came to America from the Canton Christian College a year ago and entered the Shipley School. She expected to take two years to prepare for college, but passed all but five points last spring. Liu was at the June Conference at Silver Bay and attended the Bryn Mawr Delegation Meetings. She went from there to A. MacMaster's tutoring camp and now has passed all but two conditions.

Miss Donnelly is chairman of the Chinese Scholarship Committee and Mrs. Smith treasurer. The fund is made up from gifts from alumnae and friends of the college.

Reprinted from the *College News*, September 22, 1918.

Yuet Wah Middle School
Sai Kwah Yuen
Canton, China

March 24, 1926

My dear Miss Peirce,

Perhaps you will be interested in what I am doing. You see, I have started a school last fall. My aim is to have one from the primary up through the senior high school. I shall do this by adding one class every year. At present I have only some sixty pupils and have classes only up to the first year of junior high. Our school house is made up of three small residential flats. For assembly we have to be contented with a dark and noisy room on the ground floor. But the pupils and the staff are trying to do first rate work. Our primary children are simply bright and cunning.

. . . Small our number may be, our students come from all directions of the city. Many have to walk as long as forty minutes every morning in order to get to school. During this cold and rainy season many have to wade through water on their way. But we usually get perfect attendance. Doesn't that sound promising for such a new school?

. . . I want to keep up the good record this semester. If I could get your help it would mean everything. I trust that you will be able to respond. The world is getting smaller all the time. And the different nations often wonder how China will affect the world. Well, I am sure that depends on what kind of education the Chinese youths are getting. Will you forget the distance and the country boundary and co-operate with me in bringing up the youths with right spirit, and in cultivating the desirable kind of international good will?

It is very unfortunate to have China in this period of transition. It renders many people here unable to help in any good work. At the same time it makes people abroad hesitate in giving any money in such a place. Yet it is exactly such a time that we need more sound minded people to steer the society along in the form of quiet and solid every day work. I hope some how my present task could be maintained through this difficult period. And I hope my friends will share the same feeling with me.

Faithfully yours,

Fung Kei

Opposite above: Vaung Tsen Bang, class of 1930, Chinese Scholarship recipient

Opposite below: Fung Kei Liu, class of 1920, the first recipient of Bryn Mawr's Chinese Scholarship, with a friend's child

Yuet Wah Middle School
14B Estrada Da Victoria
Sai Kwah Yuen
Canton, China

July 28, 1928

My dear Miss Peirce,

. . . I am greatly encouraged by your last letter. You had kindly promised to work for the rent for the Lotuk buildings in Canton. As that can't be obtained and I have gotten almost as satisfactory house elsewhere, I trust that you will do the same thing for me. If you only can raise some $3,000 in addition to the $600 already promised and the $1,000 from the Shipleys which we may be able to get again, the life of the school will be ensured. And if such support can be continued for the next three years, I am sure that the school will be on its sure foundation.

While I esteem the good mission school highly, I trust that I shall be able to contribute something toward the proper kind of training for my own people which for different reasons is hard for schools started by foreign missions to accomplish. B.M.C. according to my knowledge has not yet much interest in the mission fields. At the same time, the great zeal of President Thomas for international cooperation must have burned into the hearts of many Bryn Mawrtyrs. I wonder if 500 alumnae can't be interested to contribute $10 yearly for four years in order to establish something worthwhile and original in China through one of her own people and product of B.M.C. It is rather plain now that if timely relief shouldn't come this fall term, there will be no way for the school to go on . . . I have written to President Thomas persuading her to give me a loan of $3,000. The school will need the money before the end of December. If I should get an affirmative answer immediately, everything will be heaven for me . . . How I wish I had my own money to give to this work now! Still I have great faith that you will help. I only fear that through letters I can't show you enough my sincerity. If you only could be here to see it all! What a difference it would be!

With love,

Fung Kei

BRYN MAWR SUMMER SCHOOL: TEACHING WORKERS

Working People's Education
Robert Shafer

THE BRYN MAWR COLLEGE "Summer School for Women Workers in Industry" has had a certain amount of public attention; just how much I do not know. It was started at the suggestion of President Thomas "to offer young women of character and ability a fuller special education and an opportunity to study liberal subjects." The control of the school was vested in a joint administrative committee composed of representatives of industrial workers, of the college, and of the alumnae. It was opened on June 15 of the present year, with an enrollment restricted to 82. The students were chosen from as many industries and from as many parts of the country as possible. Each had a scholarship sufficient in amount to cover actual expenses at the college. Additional expenses, railway fare, and the like, were in some cases provided for by clubs of women workers. The school was so organized that the life of its members should be approximately the same as that of usual Bryn Mawr students. Similarly the work of the school was collegiate in character. Of course the subject-matter of the teaching had to be restricted with regard to the preparation of the students, but this does not mean that the courses given were elementary. It means only that a distinction had to be drawn between subjects which require previous academic work and other subjects, equally within the province of higher education, for which adequate preparation can be got from experience of life. Such subjects were taught as modern literature, political and social history, government, and law.

This, in the briefest summary, is the character of the school. It is too early to ask about its success, though about that something could be said; but it is not too early to ask what the experiment means. Is it merely a new freak of restless philanthropy? Or is there real need for such a school?

We shall get part of the answer to these questions by realizing that the Bryn Mawr Summer School is not an isolated novelty. Workers have not only begun to feel the need of education which at present they cannot get, but they have set about supplying it for themselves.

Reprinted from *North American Review*, December 1921.

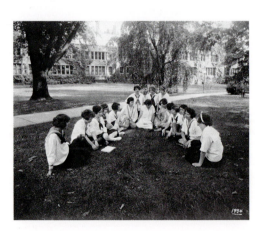

THOSE GIRLS EXPECT A LOT OF ME WHEN I GO BACK. THEY EXPECT ME TO HANG UP THE SUN FOR THEM, ARRANGE THE MOON, AND FIX ALL OF THE STARS.

—*Cora Williams, student, Bryn Mawr Summer School for Women Workers in Industry*

Reprinted from Bryn Mawr Summer School for Women Workers in Industry, *Education that Changes Lives* (Bryn Mawr, PA, 1933).

Hilda Worthington Smith, Class of 1910
Lena Barnard, Class of 2012

BORN IN NEW YORK CITY, Hilda "Jane" Worthington Smith (1888–1984) grew up a studious child and a self-proclaimed "odd sheep of the lot."[1] On her first day at Bryn Mawr, her roommate looked at her and said, "You don't look like a Hilda, you look like a Jane."[2] The name stuck for the rest of her life. As an undergraduate, she studied economics, philosophy, and psychology, and she was president of the Self-Government Association during her senior year. After earning a bachelor's degree in 1910, Smith continued her education at Bryn Mawr, graduating with a master's degree in ethics and psychology in 1911.

Smith then returned to New York where she began working with young women as a volunteer. This experience led her to enroll in the New York School of Philanthropy (now the Columbia University School of Social Work), where she completed a two-year program in social work. In 1916, she became the first director of the community center founded in Bryn Mawr by Susan Kingsbury (1870–1949), head of the college's Graduate Department of Social Economy and Social Research (later renamed the Graduate School of Social Work and Social Research). After three successful years, Smith left the center to return to her alma mater, serving as acting dean, and later dean, of Bryn Mawr from 1919 to 1922. In 1921, at President M. Carey Thomas's urging, Smith became the first director of the newly founded Bryn Mawr Summer School for Women Workers in Industry, which provided women workers a place for intellectual growth and freedom of expression during an annual summer course.[3] Smith remained the school's director until 1933 when she accepted a post in the Workers' Education section of the Federal Emergency Relief Administration, established as part of President Roosevelt's New Deal, to help unemployed teachers find employment.

In 1939, the Summer School for Women Workers was relocated to Smith's family home in Hudson Shore, New Jersey, and renamed the Hudson Shore Labor School. During its eighteen years at Bryn Mawr, the school educated more than sixteen hundred women who did not have access to traditional forms of higher learning. Many credit Smith's unique personality for the school's success and survival (the Hudson Shore school was incorporated as part of Rutgers University in 1952). Her charisma and reputation helped court and retain the school's prominent and accomplished faculty. She was beloved by students and respected by her colleagues and peers.

During her long career, Smith also directed the New Deal's Camps and Schools for Unemployed Women and lobbied for labor reform. She worked for the Office of Economic Opportunity, her last appointment, for seven years before retiring in 1972, at the age of eighty-four. In addition to her pursuits in adult and workers' education, she was a prolific poet and published two volumes of poetry, as well as an autobiography.[4] Over the course of her life, Smith worked steadily to improve the lives of others through education, the value and importance of which she had discovered at Bryn Mawr.

Top: Hilda Worthington Smith (1888–1984), class of 1910, in costume as a nurse for an undergraduate production of *Medea*, 1909

Bottom: "The Seekers," A poem by Hilda Worthington Smith. Originally published in *The Workers Look at the Stars* (Vineyard, NY: Vineyard Shore Workers School, 1927), an anthology of poetry primarily written by students of the Bryn Mawr Summer School for Women Workers in Industry

Right: Hilda Worthington Smith, c. 1929

Opposite (left): Summer school students gathered on Taylor green. Courtesy of the Library of Congress, Prints and Photographs Division, LC-F82-1796

Opposite (right): Summer School for Women Workers in Industry alumnae at a reunion, 1984. Photograph by James Stroh

1. Lyn Goldfarb and Stephen Macfarlane, introduction to *Opening Vistas in Workers' Education: An Autobiography*, by Hilda Worthington Smith (n.p.: Smith, 1978), i.
2. Smith, *Opening Vistas in Workers' Education*, 22.
3. During a temporary overlap in 1921–22, Smith served simultaneously as director of the summer school and dean of the college.
4. Smith's poetry books include *Castle of Dream* (n.p.: Smith, 1910), and *Poems* (Washington, DC: Merkle Press, 1964). Her autobiography, *Opening Vistas in Workers' Education*, was published privately in 1978.

ADDRESS BY M. CAREY THOMAS AT THE OPENING OF THE SECOND SUMMER SCHOOL FOR WOMEN WORKERS IN INDUSTRY
Bryn Mawr College, June 14, 1922

. . . ONE AFTERNOON at sunset I was sitting on my golden hilltop, rejoicing that British women had just been enfranchised and American women would soon be politically free, and wondering what would be the next great social advance, when suddenly, as in a vision, I saw that out of the hideous world war might come as a glorious aftermath international industrial justice and international peace, if your generation only had the courage to work as hard for them as my generation had worked for women's suffrage and prohibition. I also saw as part of my vision that the coming of equal opportunity for the manual workers of the world might be hastened by utilizing the deep sex sympathy that women now feel for each other before it has had time to grow less. The peculiar kind of sympathy that binds women together seems to come only to those who have not been free. It belongs to oppressed races like Jews and Armenians, to small and persecuted religious sects, to believers in unpopular reforms. It belongs at present time to all women the world over because of their age long struggle, which is not yet over, for human rights, and personal and civil liberty. Men have been engaged for centuries in bitter industrial struggles. Laboring men have been oppressed by grinding poverty and terrible working conditions. Men more fortunate financially have fought both laboring men and each other in order to secure the success and power that money brings. Men as a sex cannot be blamed for having lost this sympathy and mutual comprehension which is now for a brief moment the possession of women. Then with a glow of delight as radiant as the desert sunset I remembered the passionate interest of the Bryn Mawr College students in fairness and justice, and the intense sympathy with girls less fortunate than themselves, and I realized that the first steps on the path to sunrise might well be taken by college women who, themselves just emerging from the wilderness, know best of all women living under unfortunate conditions what it means to be denied access to things of the intellect and spirit.

When I returned to Bryn Mawr in the autumn of 1920, the Bryn Mawr Summer School for Women Workers in Industry, which I had dreamed of in the Sahara Desert, was approved by Bryn Mawr College, unanimously by the Directors and Alumnae Association and by a two-thirds vote of the Faculty. It was also unreservedly endorsed by Miss Mary Anderson, Miss Rose Schneidermann, Miss Julia O'Conner, Miss Agnes Nestor, Miss Mary Gillespie, Miss Frieda Miller, Mrs. Raymond Robbins and other women industrial leaders who sat from the first on the governing board of the School; and was later approved by the American Federation of Labor in its endorsement of workers' education, and by various unions and organizations of men workers in industry. The School opened on June 15, 1921, with 22 full time teachers and tutors and 82 students, and closed after a brilliantly successful session of eight weeks on August 10, 1921.

Reprinted from the *Bryn Mawr Alumnae Bulletin*, suppl., February 1923.

Above: Course guide for the Bryn Mawr Summer School, 1930

Opposite: Eleanor Roosevelt (1884–1962); with two Bryn Mawr Summer School students, 1925

SUMMER SCHOOL HAS OWN LANTERN NIGHT CEREMONY

PROBABLY FEW UNDERGRADUATES are aware of the existence of another Lantern Night, which is no less impressive and possibly more significant than ours, although very different. For the summer school it symbolizes the eight weeks spent at Bryn Mawr.

On the last evening, as Miss Butterworth tells us, there is a banquet in Pembroke dining room. Then, just before dark, the girls go to the Library. The guests sit on the grass between the fountain and the Library-side of the Cloister, while the girls enter singing: "With eager feet we come to thine altar, / Lanterns are lighted from every land." They wear bright-colored dresses and walk slowly, though informally, to a stone altar covered with ivy which is in the center of the Cloister lawn. They are met by a figure representing Wisdom. Then she and four handmaidens, tall girls with good voices, hold a dialogue with four others in bright tunics, who represent workers. By now it is completely dark. The handmaidens kindle their torches from Wisdom, and then fire the altar, from which the girls then light their blue lanterns. They walk out singing the school song which is to a Russian folk-tune.

There are no trained voices, but many born singers; the school has a number of Russians and Germans. They know their songs well, having sung them often at the evening gatherings in Denbigh.

The next morning they leave in buses. But, however different their future life from that of the recreation and study at Bryn Mawr, the memory of Lantern Night is inspiration in their struggle for improvement.

Reprinted from the *College News*, October 28, 1931.

TALK BY MRS. FRANKLIN D. ROOSEVELT:
Dinner, October 24, 1933

MY INTEREST in these Schools dates back to my first visit to the Bryn Mawr Summer School some years ago when my friend, Marion Dickerman, was teaching there. I sat with some of the classes and talked to many of the students, and was impressed everywhere with the quality of eagerness which comes, I suppose, to minds which are denied the opportunity of studying certain things, and when they find that opportunity within their grasp they at once respond with greater eagerness because their hunger for knowledge and their need for the special kind of knowledge they are attempting to acquire is far greater than is that of the average student.

Many of us felt the importance at that time of educating the workers of the nation. But as the years have gone on, and particularly in the last few months, we realize that the importance of education for the workers of our land is more necessary than ever before. We have talked of a new deal. We have started to achieve our aim, but only the mass of our people can successfully bring to fruition the series which have been formulated in the minds of some of our leaders. The people must understand the aims and ideals back of these series. They must do more than that. They must understand what it is in the past which has held us back, what it is in ourselves, in human nature as a whole, which must be fought down if we are successful to have a new deal. The workers of our country must know English, they must know the principles of Economics, they must know Psychology, they must know History, and they must have help in vocational courses, for some people will never again work at the thing they worked at before, and some people will need two skills in the future instead of one. All people will need one vocation at least and many avocations, for the leisure which must come with the development of the machine can only be utilized usefully and happily if people have learned avocations as well as their vocations. These are the things which the Affiliated Schools—the summer schools in the colleges at Bryn Mawr, Wisconsin, Barnard and in the South, the Vineyard Shore School at West Park, N.Y.—all of these schools have attempted to achieve these things in adult education. They are now ready to form a part of and to give assistance to a very much wider plan which must be carried on if the whole of our adult group that needs assistance in education today is to have its need met. Thomas Jefferson said, "I know of no safe depository of the ultimate powers of society but the people themselves, and if we think them not enlightened enough to exercise their control with a wholesome discretion, the remedy is not to take it from them but to inform their discretion by education. This is the true corrective of abuses of constitutional power." And because he was a great man with a very wide vision, these words are still true today. We do not wish to take the power away from the people but we do wish to give the people the tools so that they may work out their own salvation wisely and well.

Reprinted from a transcript, Bryn Mawr Summer School for Women Workers in Industry Manuscript Collection.

MASS PRODUCTION
Mary Nero, student, Bryn Mawr Summer School for Women Workers in Industry, 1938

Machines and workers;
Grating noise, steady noise.
Machines and workers;
A humming, a murmuring,
Machines and workers.

Snap machines, button machines,
Hurrying girls, stumbling girls,
Owners, managers—
Rushing the work.
Workers hurrying
To earn more pay;
Work, Work!
Clattering, grinding—
Work, machines, noise, heat,
Heat, noise, machines. Work.

Day in, day out,
Week after week,
No break, no stop—
Numbing our souls,
Drugging our minds,
Rasping our nerves.
How long can we last?
How long before our souls die?

Work, noise, machines, heat,
Heat, machines, noise, work.
Shall we die without one protest?
Have we no soul?
Do we not feel?
Do we not see?
Piles of work
Pressing down;
Waves of heat
Engulfing, drowning.

Bosses, owner
Rushing, pushing.
Roaring, deafening;
Year in, year out,
Workers' souls dying?
Dying, Dying?

Reprinted from *Shop and School: Bryn Mawr Summer School*, Summer 1938.

The Victors – Students Team

The Team
— Front — Row —
Estella Perseceta
"Dot" Stahr
Lorretta Gregoire
Ethel McGee
"Abie" Blanche Foster
"Polly" Cochran
— Back — Row —
"Skipper" — Capt.
"Burnie" Guisti
Minnie Haskins
"Hottie" Donnet
Lillian Lancto
Vera Chandler
Mildred Calkins
*Helen Sharkey

"SKIPPER"

The only team u[n]
19__ to w[in]
the annu[al]
Student–
Faculty
ball gam[e]
at the
Summer
School

The Cop
"Connie" Williams

The Drunk
"Kay" Lewis

Seen at the game

Water Boy — Doc Pill
Ann Ellor   "Polly" Cochran

BRYN MAWR'S MAIDS

A NEW REPUTATION

DO YOU KNOW WHY some maids choose Bryn Mawr above all places in which to work? This question of preference, which few people knew existed, was brought out in interviews between the heads of the Summer School and individual maids, held in an effort to classify them and discourage them from taking useless subjects. Bryn Mawr, it seems, has the reputation of giving its maids an opportunity to study so that working here will be a stepping stone to other work like nursing or stenography. The Maids' Committee wishes to stress our social responsibility toward keeping at a high level this reputation so unwittingly gained.

This year the work has been divided into three branches; the night school, the Sunday school, and the Maids' Club. Since the Maids' Committee now knows, through individual interviews, how much education each maid has had, it is hoped that the classes will tend toward some definite goal. This year the teachers will come from outside, and students will act as tutors. At the Sunday school, which met for the second time last week, there were twice as many as came to the first meeting. The Maids' Club, which is used as a nucleus for the rest of the organization, meets twice a month. At these meetings there will be sewing and a discussion of current events. A library, with a maid as librarian, is an added attraction to the club room. The maids are particularly enthusiastic about singing, and their chorus hopes to have an informal concert on the campus sometime during the spring.

> **Night School for Maids Starts**
>
> Classes in English, arithmetic, reading, writing, and psychology will be held for the Maids every Monday and Thursday evenings. D. Smith, '20, chairman of the Maid's Committee asks that everyone who would care to teach one of these subjects or either typewriting or bookkeeping will give her name to a member of the committee.

Reprinted from the *College News*, November 15, 1922.

THE COLLEGE HOUSEHOLD
Ellen Faulkner, Class of 1913, Director of Halls

WHEN MY ALUMNAE FRIENDS drop in on me at Bryn Mawr their enthusiasm at seeing me is, I am sure, stimulated by the hope that at last they are going to find out something about how the college is run. They begin to pelt me with questions about the food, the servants and the various changes on the campus. This interest seems to me a natural and indeed, a valuable one, so I am glad of an opportunity of writing to the *Bulletin* on some of the details of hall management which may be of interest to its readers.

Many an alumna when she returns to Bryn Mawr looks forward to the warm and personal welcome of an "Ella" or a "Rosa" who remembers not only her name and room but also perhaps her personal tastes and habits. Five chambermaids, with a record of almost thirty years' service, are still on duty on the campus, and twenty-nine other servants have been with us from four to fifteen years. Of our total of ninety-six only thirty-seven are new this year. Two employees are now pensioned—William Nelson, for thirty-eight years janitor in Taylor; and Joe Connelly, who claims to have helped dig the foundations of Taylor and who ended his active career as campus mailman. No automatic system of pensioning has been adopted for the college employees, but each individual case is presented to the Board of Directors and a pension proposed based on the length of service and the wages.

The last few years have been a steady improvement in our servant situation. We now rarely call on an employment bureau, but fill our vacancies with friends of maids already on the campus. In fact, during this past winter we have often had a short waiting list of those wishing to come. A fine type of colored girl has been attracted to the college by the evening classes which the students organize under the Christian Association. These classes are handicapped by the limited time which the students and maids can give, but they have proved a valuable contact and experience for both teachers and pupils, and I hope that some plan may be worked out which will put them on a permanent basis and make them more effective. Under the influence of the students and the intellectual stimulus of the Bryn Mawr atmosphere, many maids have gone back to school after a year or two with us.

Those alumnae who have difficulty in arranging their servants' schedules may be interested in the way the Pennsylvania laws regulating the hours of working women affect us as an institution. These laws require that every maid shall have twenty-four consecutive hours off each week. In order that the work may be interrupted as little as possible, the maids go off duty at ten o'clock one morning and get back at ten the next day. This means that we are always shorthanded for we have no relief maids, nor can we consider adding them to our staff because of the additional expense and the impossibility of finding room for them in our servants' quarters. The maids' quarters are on the whole better than in most institutions, but they leave something to be desired, and I hope that it may be possible some day to house them all in a building by themselves.

Reprinted from the *Bryn Mawr Alumnae Bulletin*, March 1926.

A BOLD EXPERIMENT: THE PHEBE ANNA THORNE OPEN-AIR SCHOOL

THE PHEBE ANNA THORNE SCHOOL
Mary Woodworth, Class of 1924

FOR THE LAST DECADE the undergraduates have been aware of the so-called "models." Those of us who have lived on the south side of Pembroke East sometimes complain of the babble of voices that fill a free hour of the morning. The rest of the college merely catches a glimpse of scarlet tunics darting over a hill, or comes to chapel at Christmas time to smile at the delightful manner with which the children sing their carols. Otherwise the Phebe Anna Thorne School is taken for granted.

This year as an alumna I have crossed Merion Avenue and stood inside a pagoda, and have discovered there more than strangely clad children and the babble of voices. A newcomer is first impressed by an atmosphere of informality which may be summed up as fresh air plus freedom from the usual classic schoolroom tradition. If two little Esquimaux prefer to read their part of the geography lesson on steps outside the pagoda, they are apt to feel that school is not so much a prison as report has it. They may consider it a more natural community, not where they learn what they will need when grown up, but where they have interesting things to do and to tell each other every day.

It is a community where, as is the way in life generally, privileges are earned. Regulations grow out of the needs of the group. In recitations discussions are lively, but interruptions, irrelevant comments, and noisy contributions are ruled out because they hinder the class purpose —a thorough and interested study of the topic in hand. The study hall must be a quiet place else study periods would count for nothing for the individual who, in the last analysis, is responsible for her own academic standing. Personal possessions, books, Esquimau suits, blankets, and so forth, must be kept neatly else the community suffers through confusion and disorder. All such necessary regulations are recognized and respected by this "Pagoda community." The Esquimau who has not established herself on the school list of first-class citizens knows that she may not ask the privilege of studying away from the group that is watched over by a teacher. The one who has a habit of untidiness is apt to be chosen "Pagoda girl" by her classmates and must see that desks and seats in the Pagoda are all in order at the end of the day. Each member of the small community lives out her responsibility to her group through every school day, knowing that laziness and lack of co-operation will place her on the list of third-class school citizens where she is debarred from entering into school activities, clubs, athletic teams, or dramatization, and considered incapable of living any part of her school day unsupervised. She soon finds out that freedom is worth the cost in individual effort and responsibility. The group standard becomes enviable. Her aim becomes that of maintaining the required standard in work and fulfilling her individual responsibility to the community, taking part in its government and other activities as a first-class citizen.

The work of the primary school can be admirably illustrated by this year's program. All the lessons have radiated from a visit to the grist mill at Paoli. This concrete experience has supplied the stories, poems, and facts that came formerly from the first reader. At Thanksgiving the trip inspired a charming little pageant contrasting the harvests of the Indians and Puritans.

The lower school continues the program of utilizing the play instincts of childhood for the assimilation of the necessary skills of learning; but projects are on a smaller scale. Here the curriculum is carefully planned to meet accepted school standards, but the procedure is often elastic, for the energy natural to healthy youngsters manifests itself not only in arms and legs but, best of all, in spontaneous ideas. For instance, one morning a child has thought of a new *le* and *la* game, and mademoiselle is greeted by a torrent of children excited with the suggestion. That enthusiasm cannot be met by the wet blanket, "But I had planned." The teacher is glad to change her program. Dramatization is given full rein in English, History, French, and to some degree, in Latin. Both the language and the legend pass through the active experience of each child. Often a class can be seen scattered in groups of three or four along the ledges of the pagoda arranging an act to present for the approval of the group. The acting of a story obviates the necessity for study at home. After a tale of chivalry has been read aloud, turned into three acts with several versions, and produced, no one needs to drone over a written account in a text book. Instead of home work assignments the younger girls are given opportunity to read collateral books and therefore escape the association of reading with required lessons.

Of course, in the High School years where there is intensive college preparation, homework is necessary. But the children have been found prepared to meet hard study. The classroom discussion still has interest. It is encouraging to see lively interpretation of reading and a general ease of self-expression.

Yet another feature which has impressed me is the great excellence shown in art and Dalcroze Eurhythmics. In music, also, the children are creative. A little Peggy is often asked to come forward in morning assembly; she writes an impromptu melody on the board, and then and there the school sings it. At least once each year all the unacademic branches are brought into connection with the general curriculum. Last June the occasion was a Greek Festival. Certain pupils dramatized a legend; others wrote appropriate songs and tunes; each child designed her costume, and dyed and stenciled it. The pageant really started then, in a class of English and History, and was reconsidered in art, music, and eurhythmics. One performance crystallized the various departments of study.

The success of the school, I feel, is shown in the interest of all the children in their classes. From the youngest to the oldest they are totally unconscious of what passes by on the other side of the glass walls. To be sure a squirrel or campus dog straying inside may interrupt the lesson, but he never stays for long. The good concentration does not wear down after the first two classes. By two-thirty there is still plenty of interest and spirit for any teacher to handle. All the old discipline and hard work have not been discarded in the Phebe Anna Thorne School. Here average children are merely given more liberty early to stand on their own feet. The school tries to be an attractive "prison" and it succeeds in part when a new child says, "Why, this school is fun!"

Reprinted from the Bryn Mawr Alumnae Bulletin, April 1926.

Open-Air Model School to Train Girls for College

DOWN IN PENNSYLVANIA, not far from Philadelphia, in the grounds of Bryn Mawr College for Women, stands a small building whose sides are made up principally of windows. In fine weather it is a mere pavilion. In foul weather only those windows through which the storm would beat are closed.

Fifteen ten-year-old girls, who, a few weeks ago, were started upon one of the most interesting educational experiments which the world has even known, sit within this airy structure during certain hours of every school day. On cold days they are wrapped like little Eskimos.

They are rosy-cheeked, bright-eyed, fascinating in their fine American girl childhood. Education in the open air has not been adopted in their cases as a means of healing them of ailments, but, rather, as a means of placing them beyond the reach of ailments.

At ten they have entered on a course of educational training which is planned to carry them in seven consecutive years straight to the college door and through it; and to deliver them in the halls of higher learning, mentally and physically, equipped as no group of girls ever has been, or will be, until their course in the Phebe Anna Thorne Model School is completed.

Reprinted from the New York Times, November 30, 1913.

April 5, 1927

The Deanery
Bryn Mawr
Pennsylvania

Dear President Park,

I have just written to Mrs. Francis that I do not approve of reducing tuition fees in the Thorne School for Bryn Mawr College professors' children.

The school is an independent enterprise now and has a heavy load of debt to carry. This ought to be paid off if we can or rather when we can. The number of pupils is strictly limited until we can build. I think we should fill the school with paying pupils. If we wish to help any given child, I believe we should raise scholarships in our Managing Committee. We can give or withhold the scholarship unless the child is able and industrious . . .

I approve of the increase in tuition fees. I should like, however, if you have them by you to know how our new fees compare with the Shipley School.

Yours sincerely,

M. Carey Thomas

Above and opposite: Students in the pagoda classroom of the Phebe Anna Thorne School, 1926

TENTATIVE PROGRESS: DIVERSIFYING CAMPUS

Paris, France
February 7, 1931

My dear Miss Park:

This is the first time since my graduation in 1922 that I have felt sufficiently stirred by the doings at college to write a letter about it. I have watched the progress and changes that have gone on on the campus with the greatest interest and as best I could at this distance, and on the whole have approved and applauded. Since graduating, I have made two short visits to college while it was in session, too short to give me anything but a superficial glance at the undergraduates and to admire Goodhart Hall which was only a dream in my day and ardently longed for by all of us who carried on our backs scenery from Rockefeller basement to the gymnasium.

I now read in the *Alumnae Bulletin* that the question of taking colored students into the dormitories has arisen. I feel I must oppose with all my vigor such a course of action. Perhaps the opinion of the alumnae will not be solicited but in case it is, I should like to go on record as being against it, as I shall not be there to put in my bit. I realize that the question is far too deep and intricate to deal with by letter and I shall not attempt to put down my arguments. My sentiments do not arise from any blind prejudice against the colored race. In fact I think we have shirked, so far, in dealing squarely with the negro problem in America. It is something that must be faced eventually—the sooner the better—and by the most competent and intelligent persons possible. On the other hand, I do not feel that Bryn Mawr would be serving the best interests of the negro by admitting her to the college as a resident student, nor do I think it fair to the white students already there.

Please do not put me down as a reactionary alumna. I realize, even more keenly than in my student days, that an institute of learning to be of any use, must not only be abreast of the times, but as far ahead of them as possible. There is always, however, that nice distinction between radicalism and progress.

I have been somewhat doubtful whether to write this letter to you or to the editor of the *Alumnae Bulletin*. If it is something with which she should deal, perhaps you will have the kindness to hand it over to her.

Very sincerely yours,
[An alumna, Class of 1922]

February 24, 1931

My dear Alumna:

Thank you very much for your letter, which I am sending to Miss Thompson, the editor of the *Bulletin*, along with this answer. Personally, I agree with all the premises of your letter and arrive at the opposite conclusion as to Bryn Mawr's responsibility, but officially I shall not bring up the matter of the residence of negro students this year. There is much difference of opinion, I think, in all groups connected with the college. I think perhaps no group alone should have the final decision in the matter, although it was the Directors who passed the resolution as it now stands; but I shall be unwilling to propose that a negro student should come into residence while there is strong undergraduate feeling against it, even although the feeling, as I believe it is, is actually on the part of a minority. I have special deference for undergraduate opinion because, while the undergraduates are no more interested in the college than the faculty or alumnae, they would have the practical to deal with in direct form.

Very sincerely yours,
Marion Edwards Park

CONFERENCE AT SWARTHMORE TO DISCUSS NEGRO PROBLEM
Amalgamation or Segregation to Be Discussed as Possible Solution

AN INTER-RACIAL CONFERENCE of college students will be held at the Woolman School, Swarthmore, Pennsylvania, April 11, 12, and 13, under the auspices of a committee from the Liberal Club of Bryn Mawr College, the Polity Club of Swarthmore College, and the University of Pennsylvania Forum, a group composed of white and colored students.

The purpose of the conference is to bring white and negro students together, with the hope that they may understand each other's difficulties. The committee has asked each of the colleges invited to send two delegates. If both white and colored students attend the college, it is urged that one of each be appointed in order that a broader point of view may be obtained.

The conference will have three sessions. "What is the Negro Problem?" considered in regard to the historical background of the negro, his present status, and the scientific aspect is the subject of the discussion for Friday, while on Saturday "Is racial discrimination warranted, economically, legally, or socially?" will be treated. Sunday an endeavor will be made to find the solution of the problem "Amalgamation or segregation?" while the delegates will also try to decide what they themselves can do both as citizens and students. Saturday and Sunday afternoons have been left free with the suggestion of walking in the country, while music and dancing will provide entertainment Saturday night.

Reprinted from the *College News*,
April 9, 1924.

NEW DIRECTIONS: 1922–1942

Enid Cook, Class of 1931
Anne L. Bruder

IN APRIL 1927, the board of directors voted to authorize President Marion Park "to reply to inquiries that colored students will be admitted to the college only as non-residential students."[1] The following fall Enid Cook (1907–1989), who would be the first African American student to graduate from Bryn Mawr, entered the college as a freshman. She lived in the home of a professor during her first year and thereafter with local African American families, until she completed her studies in biology and chemistry in 1931. She went on to earn a doctorate in bacteriology from the University of Chicago in 1937, where she remained as a lecturer in the department of medicine. In 1944, Cook married doctor Arcadio Rodaniche, and together they moved to Panama, where she served as the chief of the Public Health Laboratory for four years. She was a professor of microbiology at the University of Panama from 1954 to 1974, and during her career she wrote more than fifty articles in the field of arthropod-borne viruses.

As a student at Bryn Mawr, Cook was more than a budding scientist. She was also a literary humorist of sorts:

On Being a Poet

I have long been an ardent admirer of the greatest of all arts—poetry. I worshipped passionately on the lofty heights, looking down with pity and contempt upon the crude, uncultured, ignorant mob beneath who could not quote ten lines from *Hamlet* and did not even know that the name of the immortal Milton should be breathed with a thrill of awe and that the face should take on a rapt, inspired expression when mention is made of classical Melpomene.

But only recently have I discovered that I am no longer a mere humble worshipper at the feet of the great masters. I may now take my place boldly among them. I am a poet. The latent fires of poetical genius that had so long lain dormant in my breast have suddenly burst forth in glorious fire. Yesterday, as I sat reading a favorite collection of pre-Victorian verse, I found myself scribbling the following lines along the side of the page:

> When dew-pied April glimmering
> The fallen fires of leaves between,
> Sing, Oh thou Muse of ancient race,
> Contentment from the violets sweet,
> In shady dell and lamblets meek
> The all in all of God and man I glean.

Left: Enid Cook (1907–1989), class of 1931, the first African American student to graduate from Bryn Mawr

At first I could not believe that verses of such beauty and profundity of thought could have emerged from my own brain. But when, after careful search, I could find no lines exactly identical in any other poet, I was forced to conclude that I had not merely recalled them, that I had actually written them myself, that I, oh, rapture, was a poet!

Since then my whole being has become imbued with poetry. Only this morning, after I had spent the evening before reading Sara Teasdale, I awoke with these remarkable words on my lips:

> I gave all I had.
> They tested me,
> Of seeds and things unshadowy.

. . . Of course I realize that I have not yet attained the maturity of my brilliant genius. It will take many years for my art to fully develop. Yet I am delighted to see even in these earliest verses all the essentials of great poetry. Here is such depth of thought as is almost incomprehensible. The casual reader will never understand my poems. One must read them again and again carefully, thoughtfully before one can hope to grasp one-half their meaning. Here is marvelous beauty and force of expression; unique words, phrases, similes. And here most of all is that intimate personal detail, that unstinting view into the wonder of my dreams, my thoughts, and my laments, that I generously allow the world.[2]

1. Karen Tidmarsh, "History of the Status of Minority Groups in the Bryn Mawr Student Body," transcript of lecture, Fall 1988.
2. Enid Cook, "On Being a Poet," *Lantern*, June 1928.

Reprinted from the *Bryn Mawr Alumnae Bulletin*, April 1931.

MAY DAY
A COLLEGE TRADITION

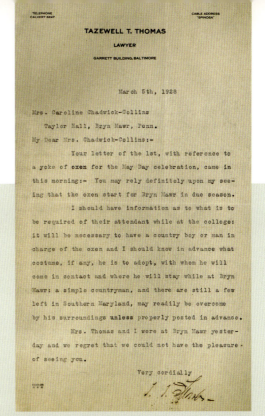

April 3, 1936

Mr. Raymond Fuller
44 South Street
Shrewsbury, Vt.

Dear Mr. Fuller:

I have told Mrs. Collins, Director of the May Day Pageant, about your oxen and have shown her the photographs since, and she thinks they are undoubtedly far more beautiful than the other oxen we have seen. We should be glad to make definite arrangements with you about them … Your price of $250 is satisfactory. In order that you may have a clear idea outlined on paper of our needs I am giving you the following:

The oxen must arrive in Bryn Mawr on Wednesday, May 6, and remain here, if needed, until 7 P.M. on Monday, May 11. If it does not rain on the dates which May Day is scheduled, May 8 and 9, the oxen can return to New England after 7 P.M. on Saturday, May 9. The transportation of the oxen and their attendants, or attendant, is to be arranged by you. You, or the person whom you designate, will have the entire charge of the oxen, including their care and feeding, from the time they leave New England until their return. The oxen attendants are to be ready by 1 o'clock P.M. for performances on the afternoons of Thursday, Friday, and Saturday, May 7, 8, 9, and at the same time on Monday, May 11, if the performance is held on that day. They will be free each day after 7:30 P.M. The driver (or drivers) is to wear during all performances blue jeans (overalls) and heavy farm shoes which he must bring with him. The college will provide a cloak for his costume. If you care to carry insurance on the oxen, that matter also must be arranged by you. The college does not demand that you carry any form of liability insurance. The food for the oxen and board and lodging of the attendant or attendants are to be provided by you. The oxen are understood to be in a condition of health to be used and in general show condition for the performances.

You were asking me about the type of yoke. I do not think it makes any difference to the May Day Director, because the yoke will be entirely covered with flowers during the Pageant. I will leave the choice to you.

I remember during our conversation you said you had seen another pair of white oxen in New England. We have had two letters from Vermont farmers which may be of interest to you. One comes from Mr. Wayland Austin, Tunbridge, Vermont. He says he has one pair of white oxen that have been shown in various fairs and are in excellent condition. We have another letter from Mr. Earl Davis, Newfane, Vermont. He says he has a pair of practically pure white oxen with one or two small black spots. If the spots are actually as small as the spots you showed me on your oxen they would make no difference to us. If they are more apparent, Mr. Davis's oxen would be out of the question.

I am giving you this information on the chance that on one of your trips to the North, you might be able to stop in and see these gentlemen and possibly discuss arrangements with them. Our preferences would be to arrange the entire business through you. In the meantime, I am asking both for more information and for photographs.

I want to put a strong emphasis on our desire for two yoke of oxen, both thoroughly broken, but we would rather have your two alone than four badly matched animals.

Sincerely yours,

Evelyn Page

Reprinted from original letter Evelyn Page to Raymond Fuller, April 3, 1936.

THE [FIRST] MAY-DAY FETE

Through Pembroke arch, beneath gay banners, came the Heralds, resplendent as to trumpets and costumes. Thousands of spectators watched the merry procession that followed the Heralds. Each Elizabethan detail, from the wooly lambs to Jack o' the Green, was complete. Queen Elizabeth sat aloft and her maids in waiting showered rose leaves upon the moving pageant beneath. The welcome sun, for whose presence we had been apprehensive, blinked at the sight.

"Bless me," he thought, "am I dreaming, or has the world rolled back three hundred years? These merry May Pole dancers are as light of foot, Maid Marian is as fair, Robin Hood as comely, the donkeys as stubborn as they were then. I'm glad I came out to-day."

So thought the privileged crowd who surrounded the green, who hastened down the Maple Avenue, who strolled across the campus to where the picturesque garb of Autolycus led them. Near Denbigh might be heard the applause due to the "Ladie of the Maise."

But how can I tell of all the sights and sounds of the most perfect production in the history of Bryn Mawr. To those of us whom kind Fate transported here it will be forever a pleasant memory. Whether it would be possible to repeat it is a problem for other classes to decide. Faithful work, conscientious rehearsals, unselfish co-operation, have been freely given by everyone concerned. To the executive and decorating committees much honor is due; no less honor to their more humble but equally zealous assistants.

Reprinted from the Fortnightly Philistine, May 4, 1900.

April 26, 1900

My dear Mrs. Hemphill,

I do not know if you have heard or read in the papers of the Mayday fête that is to be given on the College campus next Tuesday, to start a fund for the purpose of erecting a students' building.

It is to be as far as possible a revival of the old Elizabethan Mayday revels, with the Maypole dances. The dance of the Chimney sweeps, scenes from *Robin Hood*, *A Midsummer Night's Dream*, *The Winter's Tale*. Knowing that you are generally interested in such things I thought I would write to you about it.

I enclose a little circular which will perhaps explain better than I can what we are planning to do. I think it will be a very pretty scene, the Maypole dances and procession will be quite amusing I think, and we hope to give our friends a pleasant afternoon as well as to raise some money for the much needed buildup.

If you or the girls or any of your friends should care for tickets I will be very glad to send them. They cannot be procured except from the students or someone interested in the College.

Trusting you and yours are well and happy.

Very sincerely yours,

F. M. Kerr
Low Buildings
Bryn Mawr College

Accidents Do Happen in Time of Revelry
Beefeater Overcome by Weight of Costume During Court Procession
HEROINE SAVES MAYPOLE

IN SPITE OF VERY MODERN AIRPLANES above and ice cream trucks on campus roads, Bryn Mawr students successfully sustained Elizabethan atmosphere last weekend. The numerous small accidents, slips and missteps which happened during the two performances of May Day went almost unnoticed, not only by the audience, but by most of the students performing; yet since Saturday evening many incidents have come to light which seemed catastrophic at the time of occurrence. The most serious of these seems to have been the fainting of one of the beefeaters on Friday, and others range in importance from the collapse of a flowered garland on the center Maypole to the bewilderment of certain members of the audience.

On the whole, the Saturday performance seemed to run more smoothly than the Friday one. Once the huge flowered Maypole appeared to be falling off the cart as it passed the grandstands, and one of the Morris men bravely caught it, only to escape by a narrow margin being knocked under the cart by its weight. After it had been set up in the middle of the Greene, wavering precariously in its erection, one of the long streamers was discovered to have been broken. This difficulty, however, was nothing compared with that faced by three dancers from another pole whose ribbons all broke almost simultaneously as soon as the music began.

The fainting of one of the beefeaters as the court was progressing from the Greene to the scene of the Creation, caused Dr. Leary to have all of them dismissed and ordered to get out of their hot costumes, which weighed over ten pounds each. The audience must have noticed the concentric circle gesture on the part of all the dancers on the Big Greene, who with one accord wiped their hot and slippery hands on their pants with the first pause in the music.

Many students overheard strange comments and questions among the spectators, such as the query of one old lady to her companion as to whether this celebration was really given by Bryn Mawr students, or was it the exercises of Shipley School. Another member of the audience asked a student to direct her to the scene of Götterdämmerung's Needle.

One of the guards in the Dream found room to carry in her trousers a camera and films, and she also took a pillow, a thermos bottle of grape juice, a box of crackers, a towel and a handkerchief to her off-stage position in the bushes.

Reprinted from the *College News*, May 13, 1936.

FOUNDING A NEW TRADITION: THE MAY HOLE

A DANCE TO CELEBRATE WOMEN

*Kathy Roth and Emily Glick,
Both Class of 1986*

WHO ARE THOSE WOMEN who dance and run in a circle to funky music on May Day laughing in their colored dresses? They are people participating in the Mayhole dance, a rich, joyous and fun alternative celebration now in its third year. A feminist takeoff on the Maypole dance, this event is an exploration of our ability to create our own symbols and meanings and to mark with ritual something that is important to us, combining symbols of women's liberation with the May Day theme of hope for new life.

The dance begins with a group of women standing in a circle facing inward, wrapped up in white streamers. This represents the treatment of women through history, separated from each other, bound by rigid social orders, restricted in their self-expression and sexuality. Two women stand in the middle, holding hands but facing out—connected to each other while looking at the world—on a large, brightly dyed circular cloth. This is the Mayhole, its roundness symbolic of the organic, of women and their wholeness. Clothmaking and dyeing is traditionally women's work, so it calls up those themes, too. We've used different music, the first year, Central African traditional tribal music with a synthesizer backup, and the second year, Annie Lennox and Aretha Franklin's "Sisters Are Doin' It for Themselves." The only qualification for the music is that it be exciting and celebratory—and that we can dance to it.

When the dance begins, the women in the middle dance out and around the circle until they reach one woman, and release her, untying the streamers around her. That woman then dances around and unties another, who in turn frees another until all the women are unfettered and dancing. Women can free themselves, and the job is not done until all the women are free. Then everyone crosses her arms, and joins hands, facing inward, running in a circle. In one exhilarating movement, the group uncrosses their arms and faces out while still holding hands. This is a celebration of women's ability to experience their own community and then face the world, still connected and strengthened by each other. Finally the group stops and runs into the center, seizing the Mayhole and hurling it into the air, sending showers of confetti down on everybody. And the dance is over.

The response to the dance has been overwhelmingly positive. Women who participate in it have said that they really felt a sense of exultation, of liberation when they were unwrapped and then again when, holding hands, the group turns outward. Audiences, too, have always applauded and cheered at key points.

Reprinted from the *College News*, April 30, 1986.

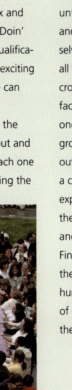

Above: Students acting in a May Day play, 1914

Left: Students gathered around the mayhole, c. 1990s. Photograph by Paola Nogueras, class of 1984

Opposite clockwise from top left: Miriam Brown Hibbitts, class of 1920, as Titania from Shakespeare's *Midsummer Night's Dream*; Lois Kellogg Jessup, class of 1920, as Robin Hood; Haroldine Humphreys Muschenheim, class of 1923, in costume for *Robin Hood*; and Jessup as Robin Hood. May Day, 1920

Page 108: May Day parade featuring white oxen provided by Raymond Fuller of Shrewsbury, Vermont, 1936

Page 109: Letter, Tazewell T. Thomas to Caroline Chadwick-Collins, March 5, 1928, regarding arrangements for May Day oxen, March 5, 1928

WOMEN'S COLLEGE CELEBRATES MAY DAY

BRYN MAWR, Pa. (AP)—The emancipated students at Bryn Mawr College, a women's college with a capital W, put down their feminist literature on May Day to don frilly white dresses and dance around five Maypoles in a ritual spanning nine decades.

"May Day is a kind of bonding for women," said Debra Thomas, college spokeswoman.

"Even the nonsense of it is something we need to preserve because we have become such a technically oriented, career oriented society that we're almost afraid of the child in ourselves anymore."

Under a bright blue sky and surrounded by the campus' medieval-style gray stone buildings, 100 women wearing white dresses and colored sashes paraded to the Maypoles behind college President Mary Pat McPherson and the senior class president, mounted on horseback.

After singing a brief English melody, the women, 20 at each pole representing the four classes and graduate school, began skipping and running in a race to be the first group to completely braid a pole with white and colored ribbons.

More than 2,000 spectators cheered and jeered, but in the end, it was the senior class, wearing light blue sashes, that won.

Some past and current students have looked upon the celebration of May Day with disdain, prompting one member of the 1953 class to comment that ending the tradition was necessary "to speed the progress of mankind."

It's also a chance for the normally sedate students, considered among the top in the country academically, to act silly before final exams. Seniors roll hoops in a race on campus, watch spoofs of Greek and Latin plays and, of course, dance around the Maypole.

"I don't think we're worried about the image it presents," said Tamara Beauboeuf, 19, of Westtown, N.Y. "We're not a finishing school, and we know that. So we don't have to worry about what people will think about 1,000 women all dressed in white. It's our day, and we deserve it."

The Maypole stems from a European custom in which a fir tree was stripped of its branches and ornamented with flowers to symbolize immortality and renewal.

Previous May Days at the college were so extravagant that planning started a year in advance and New York designers were hired to sew Elizabethan costumes. Actress Katharine Hepburn, as a student at the college in 1928, was the star of a May Day play called *The Woman in the Moon*, and that year the entire student body of 500 danced around the Maypole dressed in white.

May Day celebrations were abandoned during World War II. But since then, the college has staunchly continued the annual pageantry. Bryn Mawr is ranked by several surveys as one of the nation's top ten liberal arts colleges.

Reprinted from the *Athens Daily News* (Athens, GA), May 2, 1988.

Clockwise from top: May Day tickets, 1936; May Day ticket, 1928; Pennsylvania Railroad schedule for May Day, May 8 and 9, 1936; May Day program, May 8 and 9, 1936; May Day luncheon ticket, 1928; Elizabeth Baer, class of 1931, crowning Nancy Woodward Budlong, class of 1929, as the May Queen, May Day, 1929; students at May Day, 1988 (center)

Opposite (top): Students wearing the traditional white dresses and flower garlands, May Day, 1982

Opposite (bottom): Student dressed as a member of the Queen's Bodyguard of the Yeomen of the Guard, the British military corps created in 1485 by Henry VII for the protection of the monarchs, May Day, 1983

Next pages: Students dancing around the Maypoles, May Day, 1950

THE BOWLING GREEN: ROUND THE MAY-POLE
Christopher Morley

... Which reminds me of the pleasant paradox that Bryn Mawr College, founded by Quakers, has in its May Day revel, the prettiest paganism to be seen anywhere. It ... turns the whole college into a Merry England seminar. Was it the influence of Miss Thomas, herself so Queen Elizabeth in temperament, that started this unique pageant? It began in 1900; I myself haven't seen it since 1908 but I know by photograph and hearsay that it has grown steadily both in scholarship and sprightliness. Perhaps it's well it comes only every fourth year, for Bryn Mawr always does what she does with the brio of Pallas Athene, and a May Day annually would leave faculty, students, and alumnae little time for anything else.

"Merrily danced the Quaker's wife / And merrily danced the Quaker," says the old song. It pleases me to think of the great granddaughters of those old Philadelphia squaretoes doing their tumbling on Merion Green. "Among the pasttimes on the Green," says the program, "the tumblers perform certain pretty feats of agility ... turnings and castings, springs, gambauds, somersaults, caprettings, and flights. These gyrings and circumflexions they do with so much ease and lightness that you may guess their backs to be metalled like a lamprey that has no bone."[1] If I should happen to see, on some Long Island beach this summer, any damsel as flexible as a lamprey, I'll know (and envy) her for one of Bryn Mawr's May Day tumblers.

Bryn Mawr's May Day is indeed what the Oxford colleges call a gaudy (a rejoicing) and, true to her Minerva instinct, learning has kept pace with fun. In these 36 years she has gathered a unique library of source-material on Elizabethan pageantry, music, folk dance, and the mystery plays. Costumes have been sedulously reproduced from old prints, and when unblemished milk-white oxen proved scarce (to draw the great Maypole to the Green) they found some by broadcasting. If the Man from Stratford stopped in at Bryn Mawr on the afternoons of May 8 and 9, 1936, he would feel very much at home (except for small beer; though I see by the program that he can get tea in the garden of the Deanery). He would see the May Queen crowned; Elizabeth herself present in the person of some distinguished alumna; and then the players separating for their various doings ... And besides those lamprey tumblers there are sword and morris dances on the Green; bowling, juggling, bell ringers, madrigals, and strolling motleys and mountebanks. I don't know of any other "project" (this being the master-word of education nowadays) that brings together a whole college body, past and present, in such a unity of zeal. It is as intricate, as artfully put together, as an Elizabethan sonnet or the acrostics they loved.

There's a little known poem on this theme that has escaped research; post-Elizabethan, but still in the right spirit:

The Old Morris Dancer Saluteth Certain Virgins at Their May Day Revel

Blithe and bonny be your play,
Regimented past mischance!
Youths in ribands and array
Nymph it in the Maypole dance.

Mazed anon in gambols moe
And unpractised circumstance,
Wot you then of weal or woe:
Reckon it a Maypole dance!

---

1. The text for the May Day program appears to derive from a letter written by Robert Laneham, in or around 1575, in which he described the entertainment for the visit of Queen Elizabeth I to Kenilworth Castle, England; quoted in Joseph Strutt, *Sports and Pastimes of the People of England from the Earliest Period, including the Rural and Domestic Recreations, May Games, Mummeries, Pageants, Processions and Pompous Spectacles*, rev. ed. (London: Printed for T. T. and J. Tegg & Son, 1833), 211.—Ed.

Reprinted from the *Saturday Review of Literature*, May 2, 1936.

CAMPUS GROWTH: EXPANDING THOMAS AND BUILDING GOODHART

TO MANY COLLEGE GENERATIONS the Library, in a peculiar sense, is the college. One finds one has an infinite number of associations with it; that when one thinks of college one thinks of it—of the green under-water light striking through the windows as one came toward it in the late afternoon, of the faint musty smell of books and leather and waxed wood when one opened the heavy door, of the reading room on a week-end night when the fires were blazing and the roof was lost in shadow and the scattered reading lights made little pools of brightness here and there, and always one remembers the cloister with its water magic. More rarely one thinks of the stacks and the charm of their utter accessibility, and of the books one read when one was hunting for something quite different, of the voyages of discovery, and of the curious riches one brought back from these voyages. Everything is there, just as it was, but growing, year by year, more mellow in beauty, more rich in resources.

Reprinted from the *Bryn Mawr Alumnae Bulletin*, April 1928.

November 17, 1931

Il Nido
Route Nationale
Cap Martin Roquebrune
Alpes Maritimes, France

Dear Mrs. Wilson:

I can think of nothing that the Alumnae Association could do that would be more gratifying to me personally or more delightful than to complete the Library and give my name to the whole building. I am very glad to have the exact wording of the resolution passed by the meeting of the Association and I am very much touched by it.

All the hard work that I have done, sometimes against tremendous odds, in trying to maintain the standards of the College has been repaid over and over again by my pride in the alumnae and in their successes in the many things they are now doing. But it is a great additional happiness to be able to feel, as your resolution makes me feel, that you recognize how great was the struggle and appreciate the value of education that you have received at Bryn Mawr.

When you read the chapter in my memoirs that tells how the Library was planned, built and paid for, you will understand why I should rather have my name associated with the Library than with any other building on the campus, and how very much I care about having it completed by the alumnae.

Will you not, as you have opportunity, tell the alumnae of my gratitude and deep appreciation of the action that they have taken?

I am settled here for the next eight months in the villa of my dreams. It has a large garden overhanging the sea. My working room opens with four great windows on the sea and the mountains. There are four large balconies on the sea and all the rooms, balconies and gardens face full south. I am writing regularly four hours a day and here if ever I can write my autobiography.

I am planning to return home in October next.

With affectionate regards,

Yours sincerely,

M. Carey Thomas
President-Emeritus

The Dedication of Marjorie Walter Goodhart Hall

ON JUNE SECOND, at five o'clock, the college and the friends and neighbors of the college gathered in the great Auditorium for the first time. Mr. Meigs spoke on behalf of the architects, and figuratively turned over the keys of the building to the college. He stressed the fact that the idea of the building had been that of functional simplicity, and the exclusion of detail merely for detail's sake; everything had a purpose, and had to make that purpose clear. Miss Park, in accepting the building from the hands of the architect said, "Mr. Meigs has made it, shall we say, natural for us to cultivate here the spiritual qualities which are stirred by his particular building, by wide and quiet space, by clear entry of light, by boldness of line, by straight forward use of materials—no pretentiousness, no sentimentality, a simplicity which is never naïve, but made of an intricate variety." She then gave a brief history of the past twenty-eight years, since the first May Day was given for the benefit of a Students' Building. "To bring our long desire to fruition has needed on our part generosity and now and again sacrifice. The alumnae, fresh from giving almost single-handed, as the colleges for women must give, with only the help of their sisters, their cousins and their aunts, one and a half million dollars of the two million dollar endowment of 1920, set to work again in 1925 to build this triplicate building, and to give besides, its permanent endowment to the Department of Music . . . Their work was crowned by the eagerly proffered and generous gifts of Howard L. Goodhart with the members of his family, the husband of one of their number who had died in 1920. In memory of Marjorie Walter Goodhart this Hall in which we meet was made possible. Beyond this great initial sum the graduates and undergraduates together have given by classes and individually all the beautiful things that are in the range of our eyes—the great window, the lamps, the curtain, the carved chairs, the scarlet seats on the floor and the benches in the gallery—and all through the building, in the music room, the common room, and committee rooms, on the stage, in the same way they have turned bare walls and floors into living places."

Helen Taft Manning then spoke of Marjorie Walter Goodhart herself, of the class of 1912. She evoked her very definitely for those who had known her, and made her something more than a name for those who had not. In closing she said: "This building holds the promise that undergraduate life at Bryn Mawr may be better ordered in future years—more sanely and with more opportunity for the expression on the part of the student body of what is best in their intellectual and artistic life. It is a memorial to a girl who was herself an undergraduate here, who was gentle and loyal and had a great love of all that was true and fine. We may feel the utmost confidence that it would give her joy to know that her name is now bound up for years to come with the things which called forth her enthusiastic support during the happy years of her young womanhood."

A musical program followed the speeches of dedication. The Glee Club, led by Mr. Willoughby, sang delightfully, and then Naoum Blinder gave an interestingly varied group on the violin, and Mr. Alwyne played as one hopes to hear him play again many times in the great Hall.

Reprinted from the Bryn Mawr Alumnae Bulletin, June 1928.

Left: Postcard of Majorie Walker Goodhart Hall
Above: Goodhart Hall, built 1928
Opposite: Thomas Library, built 1904

AN INSTITUTION ONTO ITSELF: THEATER AT BRYN MAWR

BRYN MAWR IN THE LIMELIGHT
Song-and-Dance Class Shows Gave Rise to Varsity Dramatics

THERE WAS A CRY for a dramatic club as early as 1895, but for a long period class plays with a few exceptional benefit performances were almost the only type of dramatics on the campus. The custom of one class giving a play to another was introduced by the class of 1889 as soon as there was a sophomore class to act as audience. This was the first of a long series of original productions given for the entertainment of each and every class. Sophomores sported about the limited stage of the Gymnasium for the benefit of the freshmen. Freshmen returned with an entertainment for the sophomores. Then juniors gave plays or skits for the entering class and presented the freshman banner. Seniors, as soon as there were seniors, insisted on their share of the theatrical limelight and produced plays for the other undergraduates.

The first few plays given by Bryn Mawr undergraduates were of varied sorts. The Sophomore Play of '89 was Howell's farce, *The Register*, returned by the freshmen with a parody. *The Artist's Dream*, a series of tableaux, followed and the next program, a mixture of songs and dances, marked the beginning of the musical revue idea which has dominated every succeeding Freshman Show. The sophomores of 1891 introduced another new element in the setting, for their staging was as elaborate as the inadequate facilities of the Gymnasium would permit. *The Taylor Academy of Fine Arts*, the initial offering of the Class of 1892, introduced the burlesquing of Bryn Mawr "local color," a characteristic which clung to almost all succeeding Freshman Shows. The element of burlesque became so strong in all the early plays that a reaction in favor of a serious drama set in, which resulted in a cry for good plays. One incensed editor said: "To attempt Shakespeare would surely not be more ambitious than to burlesque *Paradise Lost* or the *Divine Comedy*, which is what we shall be driven to if we keep up our burlesques!"

In December, 1895, Sheridan's *The Critic* was given. Evidently everyone realized that the works of the finished masters made good productions, for after a few years undergraduate taste had become so refined that *As You Like It* was given by the sophomores. From this time on almost all plays with the exception of the Freshman Show were not original compositions. Sheridan, Goldsmith, and Shakespeare were the favored substitutes for undergraduate authors.

Banner Night shows and Junior-Senior Suppers have been varying programs ranging from carnivals to skits and burlesques to serious plays. The range of early plays may be seen from some of the titles, for *The Amazons*, *Noah's Ark*, *Alias Jimmy Valentine* have graced the boards of the Gymnasium along with *The Magic Sword*, *Everyman*, *Amor Vincit Omnia*, and even dramatizations of *David Copperfield*, *Aucassin and Nicolette*, and Anderson's fairy tales. One particular play, *The Loan of a Lyre*, almost became a tradition on campus. After its college premiere around 1900, it was twice revived but died in the final performance when the actors forgot the lines which most of the student audience could recite by heart.

Not until 1920 was there any stated order or number of plays given. In that year it was decided that each class should give three formal plays and one show during the four years of college. The Banner Show was to be the most formal of the junior plays, and the Freshman Show remained alone as the one original song and dance program

Above: Program for the graduate production of *Prunella*, 1919

Left: Cast of *The Truth about Blayds*, 1927. Katharine Hepburn (1907–2003), class of 1928, is second from right.

Opposite: Students in *The Gondoliers*, 1934

RECIPE FOR A CLASS PLAY.

50 assorted girls.

A large quantity of college jokes. They are always in season, but if fresh ones cannot be obtained the preserved will do.

½ doz. original songs, flavored with ancient airs.

2 or 3 new and pretty dances.

1 doz. characters from mythology, history and fiction. They should be carefully picked over, and all that have not striking and picturesque costumes thrown away.

Season very sparingly with plot. A few ideas may be added if liked, but be very careful not to put in too many, as too strong a flavor would ruin the dish. Mix all very thoroughly, stew three weeks, and serve piping hot. It will fall flat if allowed to cool.

E. S. W., '94.

Above (left): Members of the Glee Club in *HMS Pinafore*, 1915

Above (right): "Recipe for a Class Play," a poem by Emma S. Wines, class of 1894

Right: Cast of the Class of 1933 Freshman Show, *Palpitating Pinafores*, 1930

Opposite: Members of the Glee Club in *The Pirates of Penzance*, 1935

NEW DIRECTIONS: 1922–1942

. . . Keeping pace with the times, Bryn Mawr produced plays of real value and contemporary interest, improved technical criticism, and began the move toward thorough organization which eventually eliminated class plays in favor of the new Varsity Dramatics.

. . . During the war, feeling against the limitations of class plays grew strong on the campus, but not until 1918 was the first Varsity play produced, *The Admirable Crichton*. It was termed a "commendable performance," and the Undergraduate Association voted unanimously to continue Varsity Dramatics. The next offering was, however, three one-act plays which did not tax capacities of amateur actors so much as a long play.

This experiment apparently failed, for in 1919 class plays were reinstated, and Varsity plays excluded. For several years there were many proposals but no changes in the regime of class plays. Finally in 1925 an organized group gave a highly successful performance of *The School for Scandal* and sounded the death knell for class plays. This superior performance with charming sets and excellent acting won a retrial for Varsity Dramatics under the management of a committee of five, including a director. *Icebound*, as given by Varsity Dramatics, was a triumphant justification of the experiment. Although the next play, *Dear Brutus*, was perhaps too ambitious, the acting and staging were so excellent that class plays were permanently dropped.

Members of Players' Club, a larger organization under the auspices of Varsity Dramatics, next acted in a series of interesting and praiseworthy performances. Then Varsity Dramatics presented *The Cradle Song*, the top performance of the season. The acting, particularly that of Katharine Hepburn, was exceptional in this drama set in a convent.

The development of dramatics at Bryn Mawr was particularly aided by the building of Goodhart Hall . . . Today Varsity Dramatics has been reorganized and made an integral part of the Players' Club, and makes important decisions after discussion with the club. This new arrangement, it is hoped, will produce excellent results and will raise Bryn Mawr dramatic standards even higher than they have been before.

Reprinted from *Fifty Years of Bryn Mawr College: A Supplement to the "College News,"* October 1935.

THE GRADUATE SCHOOL: A UNIVERSITY WITHIN A COLLEGE

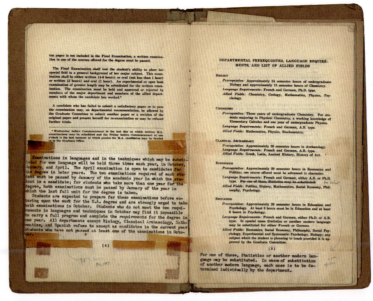

THE GRADUATE STUDENTS AND THE SELF-GOVERNMENT ASSOCIATION

THE GRADUATE STUDENTS have asked for a separate self-government organization, and at a recent meeting of the Self-Government Association the College as a whole supported them in their demand. It is of course obvious that in many important details, rules of conduct for the graduate students should differ from those for undergraduates—so obvious, indeed, that it is unnecessary to enter into the absurdities of the present arrangement where, for example, graduate students may be kept from working at night in a Philadelphia library because of chaperone rules. Such regulation could, however, be modified without any difficulty under the present system. The graduates emphasized the point that they have no real representation on the Self-Government Executive Board because their member is not elected by them but by the whole Association. We must see, though, that this is true of the Junior and Senior classes, and that, according to the graduate conception of the Executive Board as consisting of "instructed delegates," the two lower classes have no representation at all. There is of course a general desire through the College that graduates be free to govern themselves if they feel that the present system is not a true self-government—but with this general good will should go, we feel, a realization of the principle and theory of the matter. Can there be two Self-Government Associations within the same community, two sets of rules for people living in the same halls? In theory and practice, no. It has been said that common hall rules would unite the two associations wherever they came in contact. The need arises immediately for an intermediate body of some sort, and the complexity of the situation grows at a thought. And furthermore the chief reason that undergraduates and graduates should live in the same hall is that they may work a mutual influence on each other and form a harmonious diversified community. We all admit that even now the connection between the graduates and undergraduates is not as close as one should wish. How much less would it be where the two sets of people were living under different rules of conduct. The desire for a separate graduate self-government is simply an admission that the ideal of community life formerly held here, has failed.

What follows logically on this is the proposal that the graduate students be given a separate hall—a move more and more colleges are taking of late. The situation is very like that of imperial Great Britain. Ireland wants "home rule" and seems likely to get it, yet, since it is a geographical unit with England, it can never have the independent government that Canada or Australia has. An independent graduate government would only be justified when the Graduate School ceased to form a geographical unit with the rest of the College, when it came to occupy a separate hall. Let the Graduate School under the present circumstances have as much "home rule" as Ireland asks for, by making modifications of rules to suit the needs of the graduate students, without forfeiting the unity of the College under a general self-government.

Reprinted from the *Tipyn O'Bob*, May 15, 1914.

BRYN MAWR HAS ALWAYS been concerned about the Graduate School. A school of its size and importance in a college as small as Bryn Mawr is almost unique, certainly among women's colleges. There has never been any doubt of its value to the college or of the stimulus that it has given to the teaching, or of the respect that it has inspired in the academic world. And yet always there has been a feeling that it has not worked out quite as was hoped in the beginning. That association between more mature and younger students, that free interplay of minds that Miss Thomas visioned, has never been a reality. Each group has been absorbed in its own interests. With the new plan of turning Radnor into a Graduate Hall, with a Dean of Graduate students in residence, the Graduate School, no longer so closely knit with the college may, paradoxically, become more integrally a part of it.

Reprinted from the *Bryn Mawr Alumnae Bulletin*, May 1929.

Changes in the Graduate School

TWO ANNOUNCEMENTS of the greatest significance to the future of Bryn Mawr were made by Miss Park in chapel on Monday morning to the assembled graduates and undergraduates. To carry out more effectively the established policy of the college in regard to the graduate school, to establish its organization on a formal basis, and to increase its benefits both to individuals and to the college, the following steps have been taken. First, Dr. Eunice Schenck has been appointed Dean of the Graduate School, and second, it has been decided to turn Radnor into a Graduate Hall.

In preface to these announcements, Miss Park summed up the function and character of the Bryn Mawr graduate school. It is a source of great advantages and of great disadvantages to the college. The first of its disadvantages is its expense. It raises the per capita cost of each student at Bryn Mawr by one-third, and, correspondingly, owing to the policy of charging a minimum rate to graduate students, it brings in very little. Another drawback is that it lessens the thrill with which the faculty might otherwise embark on such a policy as Honors Work.

But the advantages of the Graduate School far outweigh these considerations. It provides the opportunity for advanced graduate students to study in a small residential college, where the seminars contain a very few students, and where quiet and pleasant living conditions afford the best possible atmosphere. It brings to Bryn Mawr teachers who would otherwise be most unlikely to come here. It furnishes individual attention to every student; and its foreign fellowships introduce a stimulus which is a great spur to good work.

> Miss Park and Miss Schenck
> request the pleasure of your company
> at Radnor Hall
> on Wednesday, November twentieth
> from half-past four to half-past five o'clock
> to meet the Graduate Students

Above: Invitation to a faculty and graduate-student tea, 1929

Right: Graduate school course schedule, 1907–8

Opposite: Requirements for the master's degree, as published in the graduate course guide, April 1946

For the undergraduates there are the advantages of an admirable faculty, a library adapted in scope and variety to advanced study, and opportunities for contact with more experienced scholars.

In view of these facts it has never occurred to any person concerned with the administration of the college seriously to contemplate the abandonment of the Graduate School. On the contrary, they wish as far as possible to strengthen it, and increase its potentialities for good. It is for this reason that Miss Schenck has been appointed Dean, and that Radnor will become a residential hall for graduate students.

. . . Miss Park concluded her announcement with an appeal for understanding. She said that she felt that the news just communicated was deeply important. Its object is to further the standard of the whole college by increasing the usefulness of its two great parts to themselves and to each other, and to make us content with what Bryn Mawr has done for women's education.

Reprinted from the *Bryn Mawr Alumnae Bulletin,* May 1929.

NEW DEAN AT BRYN MAWR
EUNICE SCHENCK HEADS GRADUATE SCHOOL, WHICH GETS OWN HALL

PRESIDENT MARION EDWARDS PARK of Bryn Mawr College has announced two changes in the policy of the college, first the appointment of a Dean of the Graduate School, and second, the reservation of one hall of residence, Radnor Hall, entirely for the graduate students.

Professor Eunice Morgan Schenck, head of the Department of French, has been appointed Dean of the Graduate School. Professor Schenck was born in Brooklyn, N.Y., the daughter of the late Nathaniel Pendleton Schenck of New York City. For the past three years she has directed the Graduate School, acting as the President's representative.

The reservation of one hall for the graduate students is to provide the opportunity for study in a small residential college, where the seminars contain a few students, and where quiet and pleasant living conditions afford the best possible atmosphere.

Reprinted from the *New York Times,* March 31, 1929.

BRYN MAWR FETE MARKS 50TH YEAR
Opening Two-Day Celebration, President Park Hails Founding by Equal Rights Quaker

WITH ELIZABETHAN BANNERS FLYING from the towers of Rockefeller and Pembroke Halls and animated groups of alumnae reminiscing at Owl Gate and along Senior Row, Bryn Mawr College today went back through half a century of history to pay tribute to its founders and recall the status of women's education in the 1880s.

The beginnings of Bryn Mawr, described on its opening day as a bequest "to the community at large, which has an interest in its advantages and a right to its benefits," were reviewed by President Marion Edwards Park.

She spoke tonight in Goodhart Hall at the outset of a two-day fiftieth anniversary celebration in which alumnae and undergraduates were joined by about 1,000 delegates from learned societies, colleges and universities of the East and Middle West.

Sharing the program with President Park was Cornelia Otis Skinner, '22, who presented a costume sketch of college days around 1885, written by herself. Preceding the meeting were a dinner given in Rockefeller Hall for the delegates by Dr. Park and one given for the alumnae by President-Emeritus M. Carey Thomas in the Deanery.

Miss Thomas, who has been closely associated with Bryn Mawr throughout its history, first as dean for eight years, then as president for thirty; and who, now still vivacious and keen-minded at 78, is writing her autobiography, was regarded everywhere as the central figure of the celebration. "She is Bryn Mawr," said an officer of the Alumnae Association.

The tributes to her began tonight with President Park's address and will continue tomorrow when President James B. Conant of Harvard, President Ada L. Comstock of Radcliffe and President Isaiah Bowman of Johns Hopkins speak in the morning at the chief formal meeting of the celebration.

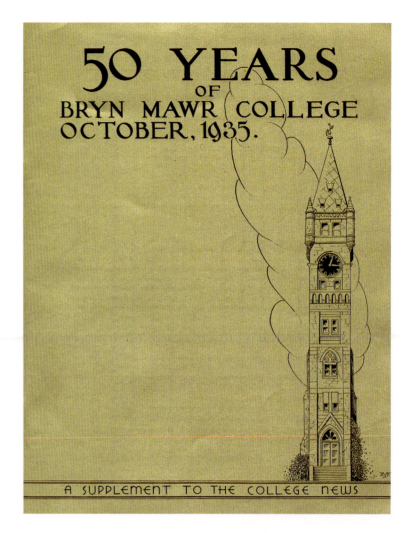

In the afternoon a $5,000 prize award named for Miss Thomas, and given at intervals to women for eminent achievement, will be presented to Dr. Florence R. Sabin of the Rockefeller Institute for Medical Research.

Miss Skinner's monologue, "A Campus Idyll," in which she appeared in a bustled plaid dress of the Eighties, described herself as worried lest the "loud" dress would "clash with the scholarly atmosphere."

She recalled the era when young women began to harbor doubts of how "Jonah could have lived so long in the whale," when they began to hunt frogs and earthworms for biology, refused to think it a sacrilege to study Greek and began swimming in natatoriums and doing calisthenics in blouses and Turkish trousers at Bryn Mawr, the "seminary of culture."

A series of tableaux which followed her monologue reproduced old pictures of college activities and were posed by undergraduates in costume.

The first was the singing of "Bryn Mawrensium," the class song of 1889. A tableau of the 1897 basketball team showed costumes in which the long skirts almost concealed the athletes' modest gaiters.

The program was concluded with a tableau of Lantern Night, the college's oldest traditional ceremony. Against a black cyclorama on a stage lighted with flickering candles in their lanterns, members of the student choir sang "Pallas Athene," the Greek lantern hymn that was first sung in 1893.

Results to date of the $1,000,000 campaign started by the Alumnae Association early this year in connection with the anniversary will be announced tomorrow. The fund has sought for the erection of a new science building and other campus improvements . . . Thirteen of the thirty-four members of the Class of 1889, the first to be graduated, had returned to their alma mater tonight to participate in the celebration. Two representatives of every graduating class since then, as well as representatives of the Graduate School will march in the academic procession preceding tomorrow morning's meeting.

Reprinted from the *New York Times*, November 2, 1935.

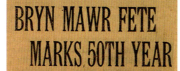

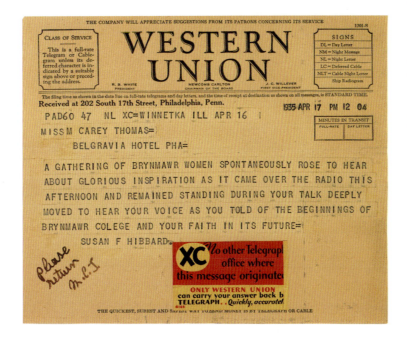

Clockwise from top: Clipping from the *New York Times*, announcing Bryn Mawr's fiftieth anniversary celebration, November 2, 1935; invitation to the fiftieth anniversary celebration, November 1 and 2, 1935; telegram, Susan Follansbee Hibbard, class of 1897, to M. Carey Thomas, regarding Thomas's national radio broadcast on the college's fiftieth reunion celebration, April 17, 1935

Opposite: Cover of the *College News* supplement, published on the occasion of Bryn Mawr's fiftieth anniversary, October 1935

Steady Aims in
Changing Times:
1942–1970

BRYN MAWR RAISES ITS TORCH:
THE GOTHIC PEACE OF BRYN MAWR'S CAMPUS REMAINS UNSHATTERED BY THE WAR

At first glance the Bryn Mawr campus looks as it has always looked. The maples stand on either side of Senior Walk and ivy softens the gray-stone Gothic walls. The bells in the tower of Taylor Hall ring the hour and students fill the corridors. Girls in skirts and sweaters and dirty saddle shoes hurry from one classroom to the next, from Taylor to Dalton, from the library down the long slope to the new science building. The College Inn is crowded and noisy at teatime, and after dinner in the smoking rooms girls still sing and play bridge and discuss plans for the weekend.

As usual, most of the social life of the college is run by the girls themselves. They all belong to Self-Government which makes and enforces the rules of college conduct. Bryn Mawr is less rigid than its conventual buildings look. Girls go off the campus for movies, dances, weekends (if they are going to be out after ten-thirty at night they must say where they are going); they smoke (in certain rooms and on certain sections of the campus); they have radios and Victrolas in their rooms. No drinking is allowed, and students cannot have cars of their own at college. Transportation difficulties have cut down somewhat on the girls' outside engagements, but they can invite men—most of them now in uniform—to the college, and wartime leniency in the rules even allows them to be married and continue in college so long as their husbands do not live near the campus. Ten of the 518 undergraduates and thirty-seven of the 118 graduate students are married.

Since the war began a few students have acted as waitresses in the Deanery, the alumnae house inherited from the late M. Carey Thomas, famous Bryn Mawr president; and all the girls make their own beds (Miss Thomas, who believed that the college's business was to train the intellect, called such tasks a waste of time). The members of the Outing Club have given up hiking and picnicking to spend weekends working on neighboring farms; the theatre workshop is closed for the winter because of lack of heat; and Big May Day, an elaborate affair that used to be held every four years, was last held in 1936. (Lantern Night and hoop rolling on Little May Day, two cherished traditions, have not been abandoned.)

> THE DETERMINED COLLEGIAN OF THE NINETEEN HUNDREDS, THE JAZZLING EXTREMISTS OF THE TWENTIES, THE DEEP AND UNTIDY INTELLECTUALS OF THE THIRTIES, HAVE ALL GIVEN PLACE TO THE STARRY-EYED BUT EARNEST AND FAR MORE POISED UNDERGRADUATE OF TODAY.
>
> —Barbara Auchincloss, "The Quizzical College Girl," New York Times, *December 7, 1941*

Wartime extracurricular activities on the campus are carried on by the War Alliance, a student organization that provides informative and morale-building lectures, arranges courses in first aid, home mechanics, typing and shorthand, and runs charity drives and war-bond sales. The girls have pledged themselves to buy $1,000 worth of war bonds each month.

The war has made some changes in the girls' choice of courses and intellectual interests. The 1942 enrollment in first-year mathematics was twice that of 1941, and the number of students in the chemistry courses jumped from seventy-eight to ninety-nine; nearly one-third of the freshman class has expressed a wish to major in the sciences. Girls have been trained to test metals at the Philadelphia Navy Yard, and students of labor conditions are helping out in the U.S. Employment Service offices.

So far, only thirteen girls have accelerated their courses to enable them to graduate in three years. New courses, added since the war began, are the theory and practice of democracy and elementary Russian. In English classes the girls prefer contemporary books on war and social problems to "literature." Professor Caroline Robbins says: "They used to discuss Auden and Spender, modern art and free love. Now they talk about sociology and labor and politics."

The Market for Students

The outward changes at Bryn Mawr are trivial, but there is one great change in the lives of college students: they are needed and wanted in the world—as they have never been before. Employers are standing, hat in hand, at the college gates, and they have good jobs at good pay to offer. These are not days when college girls have a hard time even landing jobs behind a counter; graduate students do not necessarily look forward to teaching because it is the one profession open to them; they do not even have to "choose between marriage and a career." They can have both. College-trained girls have come out of the kitchenette and schoolroom and have gone into the factory, the laboratory, and the OWI [Office of War Information].

The Bryn Mawr Bureau of Recommendations is besieged by requests from Washington bureaus and from industrial firms, banks, railroads, airlines, broadcasting companies. "WPB [War Production Board] will take anyone who ever held a drawing pen." "FBI wants a psychology major and a translator." "OWI wants them whether they have degrees or not." For the first time in history the choice of occupation belongs to the woman, particularly to the college woman, and she seems to have decided to finish her education and make the most of it. That Bryn Mawr is helping her to make the most of it is borne out by the demand for and the record of last year's graduates.

Sixty-four per cent of 1942's A.B.'s have positions, 37 per cent of them in government service and 6 per cent in war industry. Only 7 per cent are teaching. Five years ago the record of the graduates one year out of college presented a different picture. Only 36 per cent had positions and half of them were teaching. Thirty-three per cent were in graduate school, as compared to 16 per cent of last year's class.

A breakdown of the employment record of the class of '42 shows that of the twenty-three science majors, fifteen have positions, six are studying for higher degrees, and only two are without occupation. The five economics majors all have jobs, and 61 per cent of all social-science majors are working. Even the arts seem to fit the girls for the world at war: archaeologists are useful in decoding, history-of-art students make good map readers, linguists are in demand as translators. The one classical-archaeology major of last year is a Wave [Women Accepted for Volunteer Emergency Service]; the one Greek major is in government service in Washington; nine of the fourteen history-of-art majors are working—seven of them in branches of the government. The demands are persuasive, and there are many girls at Bryn Mawr who are vaguely restless, many who wonder whether or not they ought to leave college to work in war plants or government offices.

But the demands from the outside world are not merely for students and graduates to fill war jobs. They are wanted for postwar jobs, too, and those jobs require further training. The widespread belief that ex-Governor Herbert Lehman's Foreign Relief and Rehabilitation Committee was going to need young men and women for reconstruction work in Europe and Asia swept through the colleges last fall like a prairie fire, and many of the women's colleges are inaugurating training programs for the girls, who see themselves as ministering angels descending on the war-torn fields of stricken lands. The educators rub their hands with delight at the thought of participating so directly in history . . .

The Bryn Mawr Tradition

This year Bryn Mawr had to prove its liberal and intellectual belief by acting on it. The demands of war forced the choice between temporary courses in worldly skills and the long-standing liberal arts. Many of the colleges have chosen the skills; they have added courses in everything from ballistics to hangar designing (the 20,000 women students in New York City's colleges can choose among more than 900 war courses). The choice comes to the heart of [University of Chicago President Robert Maynard] Hutchins's charge that the liberal-arts colleges are "vocational training schools." He levels the charge against peacetime education, but in wartime the pressure for technical courses becomes even greater, and Chicago itself has not escaped.

Bryn Mawr had to decide whether to jettison the liberal arts in which it so firmly believes or to buttress them against pressure and preserve them for the future. Back of Bryn Mawr's decision were fifty-seven years of Bryn Mawr tradition.

The Gothic Bryn Mawr halls stand as serene on the Bryn Mawr campus as they did at the end of the last century when M. Carey Thomas built the college into a formidable tower of female learning. Students do not need to look at the Sargent portrait or the Manship bust of Miss Thomas in the library to feel what Bryn Mawr calls the

---

> A BRYN MAWR education is designed to fill two needs. The first is the need for intelligent citizens, who, apart from their special interests, will have a well-rounded knowledge of the basis of our civilization, as manifested in its languages and literature, its philosophy, its psychology, its social systems, its art and its physical dependence on the natural sciences. Graduates so educated will appreciate and encourage progress in these fields of work.
>
> The second is the need for specialists, who will make their own contributions to human knowledge. Thus, the undergraduate curriculum and—to an even greater extent—the graduate curriculum are planned to give each student intensive training in one field of knowledge.
>
> The enrollment in both graduate and undergraduate schools is limited. Admission to Bryn Mawr College is based upon the candidate's record in school and in the examinations of the College Entrance Board and upon the evidence, secured by the College, in regard to her health, character and general ability.
>
> Classes are small and admission to courses is based on the student's equipment for them, not on her status as a senior, junior, sophomore, or freshman. Opportunities are many for the student of real ability to do original and independent work under a distinguished faculty. The library is equipped to meet the research worker's needs and the residence facilities are arranged to make it as convenient as possible for the serious student both to work and to play.

"Thomist" influence upon women's education. In Miss Thomas's day the special Bryn Mawr entrance examinations were designed to be more difficult than Harvard's; the professors were the best that could be hired, and Miss Thomas did not hesitate to fire those who failed to meet her standards . . . Bryn Mawr prides itself on being free of Greek-letter societies (Miss Thomas considered an A.B. from Bryn Mawr equal to a Phi Beta Kappa from any other college) and any other form of social competition. When the college opened in 1885 there were only four women in the country holding Ph.D.'s. Bryn Mawr got them all, and even today Bryn Mawr and Radcliffe are the only women's colleges in the U.S. that prepare graduate students for Ph.D. degrees. Bryn Mawr's scholastic reputation has not perhaps so high a polish as it had at the turn of the century, but it still keeps its shine. The torch of intellectualism and liberalism is still alight, still held aloft.

Miss Thomas's successor, Marion Edwards Park, did a great deal to humanize and liberalize the college in the twenty years of her administration. The special entrance examinations were given up in favor of College Boards, and faculty and student committees were appointed to consult on curriculum and admissions. Miss Thomas had run the college by herself; Miss Park ran it with the advice of the trustees, alumnae, faculty, and students. The differences in character and precept between Miss Thomas and Miss Park still form the bases of dispute among alumnae and faculty, and any successor is in for a considerable amount of comparison. But the new president, Katharine Elizabeth McBride, who came to Bryn Mawr last fall, inherits the reversible mantle of her predecessors with full knowledge of the Bryn Mawr tradition. She brings to it a dignity and mind of her own, and the fact that she assumes the presidency at a time when war has forced unfamiliar problems on the college may save her from some of the criticisms of heroine-worshiping partisans.

Miss McBride is not actually new to Bryn Mawr; as a student (A.B. '25, M.A. '27, Ph.D. '32) and as a member of the faculty, she was directly exposed to the traditions of the school she now leads. Young and serious and intelligent, she has accepted a difficult job with justifiable faith in her own ability and judgment. Her training and practice as a psychologist, her five years of teaching at Bryn Mawr, and two years as dean of Radcliffe will have given her assurance without arrogance; she probably will never be so highhanded as Miss Thomas nor so eager to seek advice as Miss Park. Her convictions about liberal education are honest, reasoned, and conservative—and in the Bryn Mawr tradition.

The tradition touches the financial as well as the intellectual and social aspects of the college. The Trustees and Board of Directors of Bryn Mawr administer the finances, which are in excellent shape—the college has an endowment of $7,500,000, and although operating expenses have increased since the war the treasurer reported a surplus of $16,000 at the end of last year. The faculty is free to teach and speak as it likes. Faculty committees, cooperating with the president and the dean, decide all questions of curriculum, and the College Council, composed of the president and a group of faculty members and students, thrashes out problems affecting the college as a whole. Teaching schedules are light and there is time and quiet for research and writing; it is not a soft berth for teachers, but it is a safe and liberal one.

Such famed scholars as Samuel Claggett Chew (English literature), Rhys Carpenter and Mary H. Swindler (classical archaeology), and Lily Ross Taylor (Latin) have had time to add to their luster—and the luster of Bryn Mawr—by writing and lecturing outside the college, and among the new comers. Miss K. Laurence Stapleton (English) is recognized as a brilliant young teacher and educator. Members of the faculty are not constantly confined behind ivied walls—long vacations and sabbaticals provide windows to the ocean—but it is only fair to say that, perhaps inevitably in a college so devoted to learning, they are somewhat remote from the world's sorrow, sweat, and mediocrity.

Bryn Mawr vs. War

When the war forced a decision upon women's colleges, Bryn Mawr faced it with the advantages of a solid financial status and a distinguished faculty. Both helped to make the decision easier. On February 4 this year President McBride introduced what is not exactly a new program but a restatement of faith and a plan for the immediate future of Bryn Mawr's wartime students. It is an answer to immediate problems, but it also is one answer to problems of long-term liberal-arts education. And it is born of the Bryn Mawr tradition. The plan does not oust Euripides to make way for electronics, does not supplant Middle English with military theory; it is in no way revolutionary.

The pediment of the plan rests upon two pillars of belief: (1) that liberal-arts education should be maintained, and (2) that a Bryn Mawr liberal-arts education can and will fit women for responsible war jobs and, more important, for postwar jobs. It already has been proved that Bryn Mawr girls can fill responsible war jobs. But the president and faculty of Bryn Mawr are looking toward the future. They believe that when the war is over, educated, disciplined, civilized women will be needed to help in the reconstruction of the world—abroad and at home. To so educate, discipline, and civilize the students of Bryn Mawr is the purpose of the plan announced by Miss McBride.

Bryn Mawr has determined not to yield to wartime attack on the arts and humanities, not to attempt to meet all the immediate demands for technical specialties. The decision may have been "Thomist," but it came from no ivory tower. In adopting a plan that retained the existing curriculum, Bryn Mawr was acting not only in terms of its own interpretation of higher education's greatest contribution to winning the war and constructing the peace but in terms of the actual needs of various branches and bureaus of the federal government. Specifically, it was designed to anticipate the needs of the Lehman Committee, which, it was assumed, would need trained workers with a broad general education . . .

A recent announcement by the War Department and the War Manpower Commission that Bryn Mawr had been designated with many other colleges for future special training of WAACS [Women's Army Auxilary Corps] did not make clear what the college was to be asked to do (in fact Bryn Mawr did not know anything about it until the list appeared in the newspapers). College officials assume that if the program goes through it will mean taking in a small number of WAACS for training in scientific or technical work, perhaps in the special course that is already being given in the reduction of aerial photographs to maps.

Obviously, if Secretary Stimson and commissioner McNutt decreed that the liberal arts for women should be abolished during the war, Bryn Mawr would have either to close its doors or turn its whole plant over to the training of mechanics or nurses, WAACS or Waves or SPARS [of the Coast Guard]. But they have not so decreed, and there seems to be little immediate likelihood of their doing so; if government policies shift later, Bryn Mawr will shift with them. The present program was not drawn up in defiance of authority; it was, on the contrary, completed only after consultation and discussion with officials of government agencies, and before final decisions were made Bryn Mawr's dean, Christina Phelps Grant, fresh this year from Barnard, talked over the reconstruction courses with Rehabilitation Director Herbert Lehman.

The plan has allayed some of the restlessness of the girls, particularly the freshmen, who, for the first time since the war began, see their education in relation to the near future. The belief that they can have a liberal arts education and still fit themselves for useful work in the world is both comforting and stimulating—in contrast to the knowledge that many boys in college now have that their scholastic work bears little relation to the work they will be called upon to perform as drafted soldiers. There seems to be no doubt that the girls at Bryn Mawr are enthusiastic about the prospect of rebuilding the world. A recent poll, taken by the *College News*, showed them overwhelmingly in favor of cooperation fully after the war with England and China, cautiously with Russia. Their Bryn Mawr training has made them both "internationally minded" and "liberal"; they are not in favor of extremely harsh treatment of Germany, Japan, and Italy —most of them prefer "fair treatment," "policing," and "re-education."

The girls start with enthusiasm, but they are not going to find the reconstruction courses snap courses. The Bryn Mawr girls who hope to get jobs in postwar reconstruction work must learn the language, history, and economic and social backgrounds of the people they intend to succor. They must be grounded in philosophy and psychology. And under Dr. Hertha Kraus, associate professor of social economy, they must take non-credit courses in child care, feeding, transportation, communications. They must know something about such manual skills as gardening, cooking, sewing. They are to learn how to improvise shelter and sanitation, and they will have a certain amount of field work at summer training camps. Dr. Kraus, who was a field director for the American Friends Service Committee in Germany after the last war, has few illusions about postwar reconstruction; she does not intend to loose upon the devastated lands a bevy of warmhearted Florence Nightingales in Bergdorf Goodman uniforms.

In spite of the addition of the special course in photogrammetry and courses in child care and transportation taken in connection with reconstruction training, the decision has been for the liberal arts. The reconstruction courses are related to the normal Bryn Mawr curriculum; they do not supplant it. Many students will continue to major in the sciences, in philosophy, history of art, archaeology, or any other of the arts or humanities. And a girl who majors in reconstruction still will receive an education in the liberal arts; in addition to her major subject and electives she still will be required to take a year's course in English composition, science, philosophy, and either Greek, Latin, English or Biblical literature. When she graduates she will be expected to have, according to President McBride, "enough training in one major field to know its problems and techniques—and enough training beyond that field to see these problems in terms of a civilized world."

So, for the present, Bryn Mawr has answered its war problem—in the light of the Bryn Mawr tradition—and the direction of the future course has been set. But the problems of the future are still to be met by Bryn Mawr and all the other liberal-arts colleges. Bryn Mawr believes, as does President Conant of Harvard and many another, that the aftermath of war will bring greatly increased interest in the liberal arts. Bryn Mawr believes that skills and sciences—of preeminent importance now—will not be enough to solve the problems of the world; that men and women must be disciplined and educated, through the arts and humanities, to seek truth; that civilization cannot expand, or even exist, unless the generations to come understand moral values. Bryn Mawr believes that a liberal-arts education must and will provide those civilizing forces for the future.

Miss Thomas of Bryn Mawr fought and won the battle for women's right to education. She was a fiercely brilliant light in the educational gloom of the nineteenth century. Miss McBride of Bryn Mawr must bear the torch on new and wider battlefields, in a new and wider world that challenges the rights of all men to freedom.

Reprinted from *Fortune*, April 1943.

Above: Student nurses during World War II, c. 1939–45. Photograph by Clarence L. Myers (Ardmore, PA)

Page 126: Student workers at the Bryn Mawr Farm, West Chester, PA, c. 1945–46

Page 128: Admissions material promoting the purpose of a Bryn Mawr education, c. 1950–55

MISS McBRIDE

BRYN MAWR NAMES DR. McBRIDE FOURTH PRESIDENT OF THE COLLEGE
Alumna and Former Faculty Member Will Leave Deanship at Radcliffe
to Succeed Dr. Park, Retiring after 20 Years

DR. KATHARINE McBRIDE, dean of Radcliffe College, was elected president of Bryn Mawr today to succeed Dr. Marion Edwards Park, who is retiring after a tenure of twenty years. She will take office in July.

The selection of Miss McBride, who at 37 will be one of the youngest college presidents in the country, was announced by Charles J. Rhoads, president of the board of directors, who praised her as "one who is especially aware of the responsibilities of education in the colleges today."

Like the woman she succeeds, she is an alumna of Bryn Mawr and holds the degrees of Master of Arts and Doctor of Philosophy from the college.

The new president comes back to the Bryn Mawr campus after an absence of only two years. She resigned as Associate Professor of Psychology in 1940 to accept the deanship at Radcliffe.

Miss McBride was graduated cum laude in 1925. During the next ten years she was engaged in research and clinical psychology here and at Columbia University, and in several Philadelphia hospitals under a grant from the Commonwealth Fund.

She became a lecturer in the Department of Psychology at Bryn Mawr in 1935, then assistant professor and finally associate professor. She was also director of the educational service, a special educational clinic provided by Bryn Mawr for the use of the public and private schools, and served as assistant dean for a term.

In collaboration with the late Dr. Theodore Weisenberg, Miss McBride is the author of two books in the field of psychology, *Aphasia, a Clinical and Psychological Study* and *Adult Intelligence*.

The new president is a native of Philadelphia and the daughter of Mr. and Mrs. Thomas C. McBride of Germantown. She received her pre-college education here.

Although she will take office in July, Miss McBride will not be inaugurated as the fourth president in the fifty-six-year history of Bryn Mawr until after the opening of the Fall term.

President Park, in addressing the faculty and students this evening, said she was "completely happy in the choice of Miss McBride," and added: "Dean McBride has the official qualifications for which the board has been searching: High scholarship, listed not only academically, but as an independent scientist, a flair for teaching, executive experience in the dean's offices of one of the best colleges for women with its opportunity for observing the operation of a great university, and an already considerable inside knowledge of Bryn Mawr itself."

Reprinted from the *New York Times*, November 29, 1941.

Above: Katharine E. McBride (1904–1976), 1942. Photograph by Bachrach Studios (Baltimore). Courtesy of Radcliffe College Publicity Office

Opposite: Program for Katharine McBride's presidential inauguration, October 29, 1942

PRESIDENT McBRIDE'S INAUGURAL ADDRESS
Thursday, October 29, 1942

"THE CIVILIZED LIFE relies on reason as its tool: it connects the individual with the group, recognizing a perpetual and delicate balance between the two; it is sympathetic in that it does not condemn the individual to isolation or shut him up to his own resources; on the other hand it is a full life and cannot force him to submit his concerns to domination by a master or group of masters. It rests on justice and mercy for which our modern version is probably imagination about other people. It provides the means for growth into a still better form of itself."

Those qualities of a civilized world—reason and sympathy, freedom and justice, and the possibility of growth—are foundations so deeply rooted that peril does not undermine them. It mobilizes our forces—very slowly, many think—but it does not change our assumptions. We who in the nature of things must plan ahead, making plans for students just beginning their training, assume these qualities in the world for which they will work. It is not shortsighted of us to overlook alternate plans. There are none for colleges and universities—no other plans. For them all the eggs are indeed in one basket.

What is the character of the planning now going on for colleges and universities? The terms we use come easily from the war, and we ask whether our effort is toward the preservation of liberal arts colleges and graduate schools as we have known them. Partly it is, for we like this education; we have grown in it. In a very real sense we are also bound by it; taking off from the known for the unknown is as hard for the educator as it is for any man, and his flights are likely to be short affairs.

But an educational defensive has not been characteristic of colleges in the last ten months. They are clearly on the offensive; they have the vigor, sometimes even the violence, of the offensive. Like industry, they have thrown their effort into rapid production. Acceleration is widespread, though still too new to judge for its effectiveness. Like industry, they have arranged shifts which bring the kinds of production into line with the greatest needs of the war. Sections are multiplied in mathematics and science; laboratories are used beyond what was once called their capacity. This new vigor in mathematics and science is of course the bright side of the picture; the dark side is the limitation in the humanities. The darkness there is great in the men's colleges, where the humanities have often had to be compressed into brief hours not otherwise allotted or omitted entirely. It is not so great in the women's colleges. If the experience and present plans of England can be considered a guide, it is probable that women will continue to take the opportunity—and the responsibility—of college training in science or in arts. In science they will not be alone; there will be men who remain for special training, which is however differently directed from that of ordinary times. In arts the women will be almost entirely alone. As we think of that situation, the immediate responsibility of the women in arts, great as it is, is overshadowed by the further responsibility to carry on in these fields in which few others of the particular college generations are prepared to enter.

This further responsibility looks toward a post-war world, and some of the college officials have been laughed at for their concern in this direction. It was said of them last spring that they were indeed making progress, for they were ready to turn from winning the peace to winning the war. That is a sharp comment on the absurdity of overlooking present for future problems; but few of us would feel in the circumstances now prevailing that we could delay directing some of our efforts and some of our students to these future problems. Such work is a part of our educational offensive, and perhaps the most difficult part.

In the disorganization of the present we know our purposes fairly well. In the disorganization that is probably piling up ahead of us our purposes will be less clear. We must train not only the students who will be ready to deal with the technical problems of the post-war period, but students who can help define our purposes—and the understanding which is basic to such a task comes only slowly. It requires more than six-week courses or twelve-week courses. It requires still more than time; it requires new methods of teaching, with a co-ordinated approach to economic and social problems which we are only beginning to try out. Can we strike the nice balance which will give us this training without reducing too much our immediate effort? The only point of such a question is to put the problem out. It has one answer, that we must.

The colleges and universities have a third form of attack in the work of their faculties on war jobs. At no other time have such large groups of university men been on leave for war service away from the colleges, and at no other time has so much research directed toward the war been allotted to college departments and laboratories. Inside most colleges, behind the regular work of the classes, behind the pressure of substitution for men on leave, is the great pressure of research on which the course of the war may depend. With the special demands of the teaching there is again the problem of a nice balance—how much for teaching, how much for research or special studies for the war—and heavy stakes demand care in the weighing.

When we talk of an offensive education we reflect the fact that we read and think little but the war. There is always an offensive for the college or university, however. There is always an active as opposed to a passive role. That dichotomy exists, and is easy to state; it can never be held under the glass for inspection, however, for no college finds itself in a passive role. We are all active!

We are indeed active in so far as we select what directly advances our purposes. Brief statements about the purposes of a college are likely to be dogmatic to the extreme, but even at such a risk I want to talk a little about Bryn Mawr.

For KATHARINE ELIZABETH McBRIDE
President of Bryn Mawr College

Dear Katharine McBride
words have no way
of conveying to you what achievement should say,
since we have not replicas of your insight enriching our school—
of your kindled vision discerning individual promise.

What is a college?
a place where freedom is rooted in vitality,
where faith is the substance of things hoped for,
where things seen were not made with hands—
where the school's initiator being dead, yet speaketh,
where virtue trod a rough and thorny path,
finding itself and losing itself—
the student her own taskmaster,
tenacious of one hour's meaning sought
that could not be found elsewhere.

Students—foster-plants of scholarship—
at the beginning of the year,
bewildered by anxiety and opportunity
in the vibrant dried-leaf-tinctured autumn air,
pause and capitulate, compelled to ponder
intimations of divinity—
recurrent words of an unaccompanied hymn:

Ancient of Days, who sittest throned in glory.

O fosterer of promise, aware that danger is always imminent—
The free believe in Destiny, not Fate.
O fortunate Bryn Mawr with her creatively unarrogant President
unique in her exceptional unpresidential constant:

a liking for people as they are.
—MARIANNE MOORE, '09

Inconsiderable as derived from its sources, the foregoing lines attempt to thank Miss McBride for an article in the *Christian Science Monitor*, naming a number of constants which make for continuity; Mr. John W. Gardner for concepts set forth in his monographs, EXCELLENCE and SELF-RENEWAL (Harper Colophon Books); and Cornelia Meigs, '07 for WHAT MAKES A COLLEGE? (Macmillan)—March 1, 1967.

Besides the fully evident abilities which had been the basis for choosing Katharine McBride at the age of thirty-seven for this difficult place, other gifts were hers beyond what could have been reasonably asked for. She had already, as everyone knew, a high reputation for scholarly achievement. She brought brilliance of scholarship and, coupled with it, a quality of mind and spirit that were to prove an indescribably but fully tangible asset to the college which she was to serve. She brought also unflagging enterprise, a rapid and effective faculty for organization, an extraordinary and generous capacity for knowing, for liking and for understanding people, younger and older.

—Cornelia Meigs, Class of 1907, *What Makes a College? A History of Bryn Mawr* (New York: Macmillan, 1956)

Left: Katharine McBride in her office in Taylor Hall, c. 1950s

Right: "For Katharine Elizabeth McBride, President of Bryn Mawr College," poem by Marianne Moore, class of 1909, presented at a ceremony honoring McBride's twenty-fifth year as president, March 1, 1967. An excerpt from the poem is inscribed on one of the pillars of the McBride Gateway on the south side of Pembroke Arch.

Opposite: Katharine McBride, 1948. Photograph by Delar Studios (New York)

STEADY AIMS IN CHANGING TIMES: 1942–1970

First of all I should say that Bryn Mawr has been active in the selection of students, but less active in searching for them. In the matter of selection, our method for undergraduates is no longer that of a special sieve of Bryn Mawr examinations. Nevertheless we select as carefully as we can in accordance with our purposes. The emphasis in the selection rests chiefly, I think, on intelligence and seriousness of purpose. We must of course have also a basic preparation which means that the work of the college years can be entered easily. We want diversity in background and in interest and point of view, but the qualities without which our plan would fall are the intellectual power which will enable the student to undertake work in her major field and the seriousness of purposes which will make her carry that work productively. For those qualities we should be willing to search far and wide, and especially whenever we can by searching add to the diversity in the background and interest of the student body.

The admission of each season's group of students is in ordinary years our most important step. It is as I have indicated a matter of active choice. With that admission we are saying not, "You may come and try it and leave if you fail," but, "you are in our best judgment likely to succeed; when you come we shall do everything we can to ensure your success." That is a serious commitment, but it is not the only one we make to the entering student. We are to my mind committed to a plan for the College which will make for the most favorable development of the student as a person, emotionally and socially, as well as intellectually. I stress this point because of its complexity. In the first place, it is a responsibility we could never undertake if we were not most careful in our selection of candidates. Only by restricting ourselves in the beginning to fairly well-directed students of intellectual power could we set as our objective the best development of the student as a person. It cannot be too strongly emphasized that the broader the commitment to the student the more rigid the selection must be. In the second place, it is well to be certain about this broad purpose because it is a point the "progressive" educators raise. We want no less than they an education which is a development of the whole person; we are just as interested in having as graduates students who are effective individuals; but we can meet this broad purpose only by careful selection of our group. We could not bring up under one roof, so to speak, students of the kind we try to choose and students of mediocre ability and indeterminate interests; the kind of teaching and the kind of life which would make for the best development of one group would not help the other.

In relation to the instruction in the College the minds of Bryn Mawr alumnae turn first of all to members of the faculty; they are the focus, not any particular academic plan. But behind them was the plan established by President Rhoads and Dean Thomas, a plan bold in its conception and yet so considered that it stood for many years with little change. The plan embodied the "university idea," with instruction from the freshman year straight along to the doctorate and with a range of teaching in the humanities and sciences as broad as could possibly be managed. Its more particular arrangement was a group system, striking a balance between rigidly prescribed programs and free electives. Electives are chosen to greater degrees now, but the emphasis on a coherent program remains. So too does our interest in advanced work and in departments ready to teach for the doctorate as well as for the A.B.—and to my mind teaching the better for the A.B. because they are also teaching for the doctorate.

The College of the first few years had some fourteen departments. Art and archaeology, geology and pedagogy were added in the nineties [1890s]; but no further additions were made until the Department of Social Economy was organized in 1915. Music was added in 1921. The College thus has not tried to follow the university in the number of its departments; it has limited itself to those fields considered most important for most of its candidates: philosophy, history and the social sciences, most of the physical and biological sciences, literatures and languages of major influence in the Western world, art and archaeology, and finally music in so far as it could be financed—and I hope increasingly. To ourselves I suppose we rarely seem limited, but we must be just as clear about what we do not do as about what we do. We do maintain fully developed work in many fields; we do not cover all the fields of the university. We cannot, for instance, accept students who want to specialize in astronomy or botany or Far Eastern languages. We are in a better position in making these limitations than we should be in spreading our resources too thinly. At the same time the distribution of resources we make today may not be exactly what we want to make tomorrow; we must of course allow room for change.

Within our departments and sometimes beyond the fields we teach at Bryn Mawr, we have great new possibilities in our relations with Haverford and Swarthmore. When Bryn Mawr professors left for war service this fall Haverford and Swarthmore helped us with five courses, but beyond these emergency calls is the continued co-operation which will help all three of us to extend our frontiers.

After the first years there was little further action in the academic plan of the College until the twenties, when honours work was instituted by many departments for their best seniors, and when the single major took the place of the old double major. A little later President Park and Dean Manning developed for all seniors a system of reading and conferences especially directed toward an integration of work in the major field and comprehensive final examinations on it. Then the College had a schema for the more advanced work which the single major field made possible; it had a new way of helping students toward a maturity of thought which is part of the goal of undergraduate instruction. I speak of this aspect of the work with special emphasis, for it seems to me unquestionably a part of the preparation for the A.B. degree. We hear it said that first-year courses open for the student a door on a new world. Of course they do, and we should want students to push back some of these doors, but that work is not enough for students such as we try to select. Their ability must be nurtured by the very different experience of searching beyond the door, of doing the intensive work which brings a more realistic conception of the world and of the students' relation to it. We are having now a striking demonstration of the value of such advanced work; it is that more than any other single part of the training that has enabled many graduates with not more than an A.B. to take and hold war jobs of first importance.

The plan for the integration of work which carefully chosen courses and reading and conferences of the senior year make possible seems to me well established, though special aspects of it need change from time to time. Bryn Mawr is now active in developing a new kind of integration, co-ordinated teaching in related fields or newly defined fields. That plan is probably of the first interest to those who sit down to the seminar table, but its significance goes beyond any particular class. It started in 1938 in the co-ordination of teaching and research within the sciences. There courses introduced in the borderline fields, bio-physics and bio-chemistry, for example, gave students a new possibility of advanced work and a new insight into the unity of natural science. It is important to recognize first of all that these joint courses are at an advanced, sometimes a very advanced stage. They are not by any means orientation courses, so-called, in physical or biological science. They come at a time when the student, through her training in one or more sciences, is able to take an active part in the co-ordination.

In the social sciences there are also courses given by one department for the benefit of students in several. There is in addition a new approach to co-ordinated teaching, with special subjects—the eighteenth century, the theory and practice of democracy, the individual and society—chosen for joint study and presentation by a member of the faculty from each of the fields most closely involved in the problem. This plan seems to me excellent, and open to further use, but it must not hide from us the fact that we have no fully developed co-ordination in the social sciences. We have there great possibilities, even pressing needs; for co-ordinated attack in this area would strike where human understanding lags far behind and where it is now most crucial. New work

STEADY AIMS IN CHANGING TIMES: 1942–1970

136

is in immediate demand on problems the war has raised; its further progress will increase these problems. We know little about them but we do know that they cannot be solved unless we co-ordinate all our efforts, using any resources at our hand in their solution.

I have talked of Bryn Mawr—active or passive—in relation to its academic plan. There is a third part of its character I should like to consider briefly, that is, the nature of these groups which constitute the College—directors, faculty, students, alumnae. You must not suppose it is my newness to this office which makes me think they are the most active groups of this kind I have heard of anywhere. I had the same opinion earlier, as a member at one time or another of three of these groups. There are self-governing, strong, independent; and Bryn Mawr's strength comes from their qualities and their ready interest. As the tragedy of the war mounts and we as a college face new tests of our character, we are increasingly glad for the qualities of these groups. We are also finding a new factor of co-operative action among groups which have heretofore been characterized rather by their independence. The joint courses and seminars bring small groups of faculty and students together in their consideration of mutual problems; thus they add a new kind of inter-relationship to what has always been one of Bryn Mawr's strong points, the close co-operation of individual students and individual professors. Another illustration of a new kind of co-operative action—perhaps the best illustration—is the work, for division of responsibility is obvious, and so are the advantages of co-operation; but we should be alert to other ways in which we can act not as a series of interested groups but as a community.

With the war too we are seeing more clearly the importance of our relations to the community beyond College. We have often acted or wanted to act as host to that community. Some of our departments have created the more important working relation with organizations and groups beyond the College. We are not handicapped by the antagonism which has sometimes grown up in college towns, but we are far from realizing the full place of the College in the community. The war is helping us, I think, to a better understanding of that place.

It is certainly helping us to a better understanding of the place of higher education in the social structure more generally. For many students we have thought of it in terms of training toward the professions; but without fully realizing two points we now see: first, how far-reaching the group of professions is in modern life, and, second, how in a time of crisis the right hand of the professional man can be extended by the employment of assistants, who lack professional training but stand well on the systematic and intensive work which precedes the first college degree. We have needed all the training of these kinds there has been in the last years. It is in large part the force which is fighting now, and there is call for much more.

For all students we have thought of college education as a favorable source, if not the most favorable source, of cultural development. We have thought that the freedom the human spirit can attain through the liberal studies would be built into the civilization of our best conceptions. If the building has been well done that freedom should withstand the great pressures on it now. We are in the midst of the test. We cannot be serene about the outcome, but we can be resolute; and we can build for a new and stronger structure.

Reprinted from the *Bryn Mawr Alumnae Bulletin*, December 1942.

Opposite: Katharine McBride (second from left) at lunch, c. 1950s. Photograph by George M. Cushing, Jr. (Boston)

WORLD WAR II: SACRIFICE AND SERVICE

New War Major Plan Announced By Miss McBride

Preparation for Post-War Reconstruction Work Arranged

Goodhart, February 26—A new plan for Interdepartmental Majors, enabling students to prepare for work in war and post-war reconstruction, was outlined by President Katharine McBride last Friday. Under the new system, based on the best advice from heads of agencies and governmental committees, three planned majors are open to Freshmen and Sophomores. They are International Administration and Reconstruction, Community Organization and Reconstruction, and Languages for Reconstruction.

Each field includes work in social sciences and languages. The requirements are the same for all, so that the major can be changed with ease. One unit each of English Composition, Science, and Philosophy; two units of a primary language; and one of a secondary language are required, as well as two units of History, one of Geography, and one of International Relief Administration. Three new courses, Modern Greek, Economic History, and Geography, have been added to the curriculum.

There is no departmental head in the new system, but a committee consisting of the Dean ex-officio, one member each of the History, Politics, and Sociology Departments, and two from the Language Departments. This committee will serve as a consultory group for the students and will conduct the examinations. The final examination will consist of an oral and written part in the primary language; one part in either History, Sociology, or the secondary language, depending on the field; and a special report in that field. Special summer work will be required, including Typing and Accounting.

For the remaining six units, those in the field of International Administration and Reconstruction will take one unit of Statistics; a choice of Psychology, Second Year Economics, or Anthropology; Comparative Government; International Organization; one-half unit of Public Administration; and one and one-half units of History. This includes advanced work and research in special regions.

Students taking Community Organization and Reconstruction will complete their work with one unit each of Sociology, Psychology, and Statistics; and one-half unit of Community Planning and Classes and People. One unit of Advanced Sociology, The City, can be substituted for one-half unit of Labor Movements and one-half unit to be decided later. One-half unit of Community Organization taken in a Graduate seminar and another half unit decided by the Sociology Department complete the work.

Two or three units of a primary language, one or two units of a secondary language, and one unit each of Comparative Government and International Organization fill the requirements for a major in Languages and Reconstruction.

Reprinted from the *College News*, March 3, 1943.

KEEPING PERSPECTIVE

THIS YEAR we don't need to say to you, "Don't forget that there is a world beyond college." You won't have a chance to forget that there is an outside world, and that college is a part of it.

We know that you, 1946, realize the value of college in wartime, as in any time, or you wouldn't be here. We know that your attitude, your purposes in coming to college, are more realistic, more mature than those of the college student of three years ago.

Comprehension of the enduring value of the training you receive here is commendable, but it is hard to keep. Most of you have the advantage of this comprehension now. Don't lose it in the welter of Freshman English and First Year courses to which you will be subjected.

In a liberal arts college the training in method is perhaps the most useful tool that is mastered. Research technique will be of lasting utility. You come to college with consideration of the future, with an attempt to relate your education to the rest of your life. Most of you have confidence that college will, at least academically, prepare you for a world confused by war. Your faith in its preparation is well founded.

Reprinted from the *College News*, September 28, 1942.

51 BRYN MAWR UNDERGRADS START TRAINING UNDER NEW PLAN FOR NURSES' AIDES
New Program Includes Total of 111 Students Working as Nurses' Aides

THE NEW COLLEGE plan for the increase in the training of Nurses' Aides on campus went into effect last week. The primary theoretical classes were begun on February 5, with an enrollment of 51 students.

The size of the enrollment has necessitated the division of the theoretical classes on campus into two groups. Of the 51 taking the course, 30 meet on Monday and Tuesday afternoons from 1:30 to 5 P.M., and 21 on Wednesday and Thursday afternoons.

Both groups also meet at the Graduate Hospital in Philadelphia on Saturdays during the February period. Practical training will be given during March at Presbyterian, Temple University, and Philadelphia General hospitals.

Meanwhile 22 Bryn Mawr students are already working in Philadelphia area hospitals, and 14 students will complete a less intensive six-hour-a-week course in a few weeks. No college credit is given for this course.

In addition a new six-hour-a-week course is being organized by Mary K. Snyder '45, chairman of the college Red Cross Unity, and Anne Borum '46, head of the college Nurses' Aides group. To date 24 students are enrolled in this course. They will be trained at Bryn Mawr Hospital.

As the first eastern college to schedule such training for students, Bryn Mawr has made a notable contribution to the conduct of college work in these times as well as to the war effort in general. This was emphasized in a recent statement issued by the faculty committee on Nurses' Aides, which read in part: "It is in order that academic work which is done at Bryn Mawr shall continue to be done well that the Faculty recognized the absolute necessity for other work necessary for the war. To faculty and students alike, this action is a reaffirmation rather than a denial of the need for holding firmly to high intellectual standards in time of war."

Reprinted from the College News, *January 14, 1945.*

Above: Students from the Lincoln Hospital School of Nursing (Durham, NC; active 1903–71) at the Bryn Mawr Summer School of Nursing, 1942. Lincoln Hospital was founded in 1901 to serve the African American population of Durham and its surrounding area.

Opposite: Kathleen E. Hoag showing nurses' aide students how to fold a mitered corner, c. 1944–45. Left to right: Martha MacDonald, class of 1947; Elizabeth Hilbert Day, class of 1947; Jean MacAllister, class of 1948; and Julia Turner, class of 1945

THE MOMENTOUS sounds of typewriters and feverish word counting which combine to form the News Room refrain two nights out of every week was interrupted last Thursday evening by unidentified sounds from the outside. Someone looked up and vaguely suggested a blackout. Then work continued. A few minutes later the stern voice of some air-raid warden yelled threateningly "Put your lights out." A scurry. A flutter of papers. Typewriters stopped. Chairs fell. A lamp collapsed. Darkness came and the complaint outside ceased.

Suddenly a voice rose: "They can't do this to us. We are bringing out the *News*. This is a newspaper office. We have a deadline to meet. It's an outrage." But the darkness remained unbroken. Someone suggested going out and lying flat on the ground. We had visions of bodies strewn over the lawns, not looking up. We sought a bathtub to fill with water. We went outside to keep away from the windows. Finally, we saw a light in the distance and tried yelling in an authoritative voice. To our delight the light went out. We had never realized the power of the press before.

Ten minutes after the lights were again proclaimed uncensored, two reporters who had gone on an important assignment to test the food of one of the village's drug stores returned to tell the tale: they had been caught in the drug store where the lights went out promptly and a blonde at the counter went out equally promptly to the back of the store accompanied by the soda jerker. In the meantime, the owner of the store swore at the Germans and the Japanese, who made blackouts necessary, and therefore made air raid wardens necessary, and therefore had contrived to make his wife an air raid warden and consequently had prevented her from coming to meet him at the store and had so compelled him to walk all the way to the railroad station to take the train home, when he did go home, whenever that would be. The reporters sympathized and asked for cigarettes. When they were told that these could not be sold during a blackout, they ceased to sympathize.

True to their profession, the reporters, after they had futilely argued with the store owner about cigarettes, decided to stand in the doorway and see what was what. Fire engines swept past, nobody knew where or why. Blacked out trains rushed by. An Army sentry stood at the station, gun on shoulder and a fierce expression on his face that meant business of some indeterminate nature.

It was all right that time. But this can't go on. The *News* can't stop for half an hour every evening to please local authorities who want to see if their whistles are still whistling. We suggest blackout curtains, or courses in writing and reading Braille, or walling up the window completely, or maybe someone could do something about turning out the light from the full moon that ruins everything anyhow.

Barbara Kaufman, Class of 1943, *College News*, September 28, 1942.

SHORTAGE RESULTS IN GLOOMY FOOD OUTLOOK AS QUANTITY LESSENS

WHILE FUEL RATIONING will have little effect on the campus, the food situation is less optimistic.

We will keep warm this winter. While the Theatre Workshop and some of the faculty houses are heated by oil furnaces, the other buildings burn bituminous coal.

As regards food, meat rationing has not gone into official effect, but many varieties of meat are difficult or impossible to obtain. The prices of pork and beef are the same as last year, but very little is available. There is no salmon on the market, says Miss Batchellor, college dietitian, and tuna fish is 29 dollars a case, in contrast to the nine to 12 dollars of last year.

Institutions are allowed 75 per cent the amount of sugar used last year, and 50 per cent of the coffee. The local rationing board has requested students to turn in sugar ration books, and notices to that effect will be issued soon. There is little supply of tea in the country and no more is coming in. The Tetley Tea salesman now sells dehydrated soups. Prunes and raisins are virtually off the market, and Miss Batchellor has been unable to obtain currants for three years. As times goes on, it will be more and more difficult to purchase many foods at any price, and the cost of food has risen rapidly. Fewer college-sponsored refreshments insure more money for regular meals, and Miss Batchellor urges that the students cooperate and avoid waste in the dining rooms.

Reprinted from the *College News*, October 7, 1942.

FARMING

FIFTY-EIGHT STUDENTS signed up for farming on registration day. Because of poor attendance, the group has gone to work only three times, on one Friday and two Saturdays, out of three weeks. If this is indicative of campus response to war work, of which farming is now the most pressing, something must be done.

The miserable showing can perhaps be explained by considering that the hours for farming are from nine to five-thirty on Saturdays, that students must sign up by Thursday, and that having signed the weekend away, it can always rain. However, the present situation could not have arisen if volunteers had thought of these facts before, instead of after, registration. Some of them did, and credit should go to the few faithful, who have often been unable to go because of lack of cooperation from others.

The need for farmers is extremely great. For instance, at least thirty students could be used every Saturday, and ten every Friday, the farms having no other source of labor available. Instead of getting the assistance required, six is the maximum Friday turn-out, and the Saturday group, which is diminishing, at best fell below half of the necessary number. Last Saturday, two farms, badly in need of farmers, got none at all. Unless crops are harvested before winter, the food shortage will be increasingly acute. In many countries today, such a waste would be criminal.

In view of the disappointing response, arrangements have been made to limit the hours for farming to half a day on Saturday. This change goes into effect this week-end, and should make it possible for all registrants to fulfill their pledges conveniently. Compromise in the matter of war work is deplorable, but is better than nothing. All students, whether registered for farming or not, are urged to lend a helping hand.

Reprinted from the *College News*, November 8, 1944.

Above: Defense Activities chairs Jocelyn Fleming, class of 1942 *(left)*, and Elizabeth C. Nicrosi, class of 1943 *(right)*, c. 1941–42. Courtesy of the *Philadelphia Bulletin*

BRYN MAWR DECIDES TO ADOPT CO-EDUCATION
Revolutionary Decision Lauded by Students As Faculty Body Votes for Variety in Class

"BRYN MAWR has decided to cast off its outworn and discredited traditions," declared Dean Christina Ward, and she announced that Bryn Mawr would admit men next year.[1] At a special college assembly Mrs. Grant announced the revolutionary decision of the administration.

"It is not only the exigencies of the war which induced us to make this momentous change of policy," she said. "With all due respect to the founders of this institution, we feel that it would be far, far better for all concerned if the opposite sex could feel free to enter these walls," Miss McBride explained. Her announcement was greeted by hysterical applause from the ninth row in Goodhart.

Describing the long years of research that preceded the administration's sudden flip-flop, she (take your pick) said that numerous observations of the classroom behavior of students in the classrooms of all kinds of places have convinced them that they are right. It is a rather intangible thing, she asserted, but it is there nevertheless. Asked to elaborate on this matter in the discussion which followed, Dean Grant discovered that she had an important appointment.

The men will be drawn from all over, she said. "Perhaps that should be amended to wherever they can be found," she added. Since we assume that most of them will be 4-F's [unfit for service] or the equivalent, gym will not be required. The Undergraduate Association is calling a meeting to discuss the role of men in May Day.

"Housing will be a ticklish problem," said Miss Howe, director of halls. "The genders of all pronouns in the rule book must be changed," was the Self-Gov's only comment.

1. Due to overcrowding at coeducational and men's colleges after World War II, from 1944 to 1951 six men, all recently returned GIs, enrolled at Bryn Mawr. Although all six took courses, only one, Richard Logan, graduated, in 1949.—Ed.

Reprinted from the *College News*, May 19, 1943.

MANNING CORRECTS EDITORIAL: WAR JOBS NEED SOCIAL SCIENCE MAJORS

To the Editor of the *College News*:

In your editorial on New Majors in the last number of the *News* you state that until recently only the science departments have prepared girls for important war jobs. While it is true that only the science departments have given *new* courses, for this purpose it is quite wrong to suppose that the students majoring in the social sciences have not prepared themselves for jobs in Washington as important as those for which the special science courses are a preparation. As a matter of fact, the demand for well trained economics majors in the Washington departments is so great that the women's colleges cannot begin to meet it. Most of last year's economics majors were placed almost before they took their AB degrees. There is now an almost equal demand for ABs who have been trained in history, politics, or sociology. The Office of Strategic Services sent one of its research boards to all the women's colleges in February, looking for possible recruits. Incidentally, one of the qualifications for work in this office and in many other offices in Washington is a really good knowledge of German, French, or Italian. Needless to say, a knowledge of Russian has a scarcity value all its own . . .

Sincerely,

Helen Taft Manning
Class of 1915 and professor of history

Reprinted from the *College News*, March 10, 1943.

JOINING TOGETHER: EARLY TRI-COLLEGE COOPERATION

3 COLLEGES SHARE IN UNIFIED PROGRAM
Bryn Mawr, Swarthmore and Haverford Work Together without Losing Identities

DUPLICATION IS MINIMIZED
Coordination Includes Courses, Faculties and Libraries, Alumni Here Are Told

ALUMNI GROUPS of Bryn Mawr, Haverford and Swarthmore Colleges met together last night for the first time in their history to discuss a program of cooperation for the three colleges. At a dinner meeting at the Vanderbilt Hotel, Dr. John W. Nason, president of Swarthmore College, said that the time was ripe for the three colleges to work together so that each would be enriched by the mutual association without losing its identity.

Under the new program, Dr. Nason reported, "any student of any of the three colleges can now take any course he or she desires at either of the other colleges without additional expense and with full credit from his or her own institution."

"The latest result of the program," he said, "was the announcement by the three presidents that faculty appointments would be discussed and cleared before they were made." This would result in less duplication in certain departments as well as allow the colleges more latitude and a greater range of instruction, he explained.

Another benefit derived from the cooperation now in effect is to allow the three colleges to coordinate their libraries so they may broaden into fields that previously had been unattainable. Extracurricular activities also are being greatly increased.

Dr. Felix Morley, president of Haverford College, said that "this program will preserve all the advantages of autonomy while strengthening the position of each of the three colleges." Dr. Morley told of some difficulties such as the number of courses each college required of its students each semester, ranging from five in one institution to as low as two in another, but added that this was merely one of the problems to be ironed out.

Miss Katharine McBride, president-elect of Bryn Mawr, said that for the program of cooperation to be successful each college must take into consideration the individual qualities of the others that have been their strong points throughout the years. She suggested that it was necessary to preserve these particular assets while at the same time the three colleges strengthen one another by mutual assistance.

Christopher Morley, an alumnus of Haverford, was the toastmaster.

Reprinted from the *New York Times*, February 25, 1942.

Above: Bryn Mawr students biking with male companions, c. 1950s. Photograph by Hans Knopf. Published in the *Saturday Evening Post*, October 8, 1949

STATION-WAGON COLLEGE
Robert M. Yoder

QUITE A FEW of our smaller seats of learning are solving the problem of "not enough teachers, not enough courses" by a new and remarkably simple arrangement: They are sharing the professors.

For years one of the favorite studies of Bryn Mawr College girls has been Haverford College boys. The beautiful Bryn Mawr campus in the Philadelphia suburb of the same name lies only a mile out from the famous Main Line beyond Haverford. Bryn Mawr's gray Gothic halls with great scarves of ivy house about 550 girls-without-men. Haverford's dormitories house 400 men-without-girls. This being the kind of vacuum Nature abhors, traffic between the two highly esteemed colleges always has been fairly heavy.

Bryn Mawr girls rib the Haverfordians by calling them their "week-day lovers." The implication is that Haverford neighbor boys will do all right Monday through Thursday, but on weekends the girls can do better, with big-league dates from Princeton, Yale, Dartmouth or Harvard. Nevertheless, the rooms set aside at Bryn Mawr for stay-at-home dates—they are called "showcases"—are as familiar to Haverford men as their own Founders Hall, and the big dances of the year on either campus are pretty much joint affairs.

Between Haverford and Swarthmore College, eleven miles away as the crow flies between suburban homes and golf clubs, there have always been close bonds, too, though of a different sort. Neither school is big enough to cause widespread havoc in football. What damage they can inflict, they admire to inflict on each other; to nurse their wrath for this big game of the year, they would gladly lose every other game on the schedule. These are Quaker colleges, but the Quaker love of peace doesn't seem to cover this feud. Only in the last two years have the student councils worked out an uneasy truce, each side promising not to paint the other's buildings or tear down much of real value or carve an *H* or an *S* in somebody's hair with clippers.

So there have always been links of one kind or another between the three schools, ranging from a cherished mutual hatred in football season to a common interest in the two-sex system. And you might say that the three college presidents, in working out a remarkable three-college venture in co-operation, are only strengthening existing ties. Even so, "remarkable" is the appropriate word; they have attacked a remarkably difficult problem in a remarkably simple way. In times of rising costs and low receipts from endowments, when all small colleges are hard-pressed, they have found a promising way to better each of the colleges, to expand instead of retrench. They have grown bigger, so to speak, without growing larger, as they are resolved not to do. That's a neat trick if you can do it, and they can.

What they have done will disappoint all lovers of the intricate and abstruse; it's no more complicated than ordering one chocolate soda with three straws or borrowing the neighbor's silver to fill out your own for a party. Somebody tagged the result "the station-wagon college" because Bryn Mawr's two station wagons now roll down Montgomery Avenue hauling Bryn Mawr girls to class—at Haverford. That is not quite like seeing a couple of bathing beauties in the Yale crew, for Haverford has had an occasional girl student from time to time, in spite of the fact that it is a college for men. The wives of Haverfordians sometimes take a course or two, and during World War II a couple of dozen girls were trained there in the kind of relief and reconstruction the Friends traditionally carry to war-stricken countries. By the same token, men are not halted at the Bryn Mawr gates and blindfolded. There have at times been a few men around the graduate school, and like other celebrated girls' schools, this one took in a few veterans just after the war. Just the same, neither college has been much more coeducational, until this well-calculated mix-up happened, than Kappa Kappa Gamma sorority or the New York Giants.

While the Bryn Mawr girls hurry to class at Haverford, small groups of Haverfordians are making their way up to Bryn Mawr as best they can; they don't have station wagons and are not supposed to have cars. There must be a few, however, as the Bryn Mawr year-book remarked that the best argument for dropping Bryn Mawr's no car rule was the sorry state of Haverford tires. Fortunately, it's not much of a trip and will allow many a Haverford graduate to puzzle his children by telling what a hot-shot student he was at good old Bryn Mawr.

"But that's a girls' college," the tykes will say obediently.

"Sure it is, but I went to all kinds. As I once remarked to a Swarthmore professor who taught me at Haverford, why go to one college if you can go to two or three?"

That is pretty much the general idea too. Even the best of the small colleges suffer from "limited instructional resources," which is educational gobbledygook for "not enough teachers, not enough courses." Few of them—certainly not this trio—want to spread the kind of smorgasbord offered by the big private or state universities. These three would look down their noses in perfect unison at the dime-store profusion of educational odds and ends that some universities put on the counter. But they would like another course here and there, another teacher or two—providing the right card, large or small, to fill out a good hand. And the small colleges do covet the big university's ability to keep first-rate teachers contented.

What these three colleges have done, over the last eight years, is to form a loose, easy-fitting federation without giving up a nickel's worth of autonomy or character. The system involves circuit-riding teachers, commuting students and two and three-way partnerships in getting what none of the three could afford alone.

Bryn Mawr and Haverford, for example, share a teacher of drama and stagecraft. He is a Bryn Mawr faculty member, but he gives a course in the theater arts for Haverford. Bryn Mawr girls are welcome, as well they might be, for it is given in their practice theater. That is the Mrs. Otis Skinner workshop, established by Cornelia Otis Skinner.

The writer-actress-monologist was a Bryn Mawr girl; so was Emily Kimbrough, and the frightened tour of Europe related in their best-selling book and hit movie, *Our Hearts Were Young and Gay*, took off from Bryn Mawr.

This course is a somewhat confusing example of the let's-get-mixed-up-policy, because the stage is not on the Bryn Mawr grounds. It's on the campus of Baldwin, a fashionable preparatory school a block away—Miss Skinner went there too. But all you have to understand is that this is a Haverford course taught by a Bryn Mawr man for the benefit of both colleges, on the campus of neither, and you are getting the hang of this thing. Bryn Mawr girls get a course not otherwise available, Haverford gets a teacher and a stage.

In eight years—this co-operation is long out of the experimental phase—the three colleges in this pact have worked out many a two- and three-way collaboration along these lines, and with consistent success.

It began during the war, when no faculty would be on hand tomorrow. The armed forces and a dozen research agencies were stripping faculties everywhere; Bryn Mawr lost a third of its teachers. Determined to keep up their standards, the colleges began borrowing. If the army tapped a Bryn Mawr historian, a Swarthmore replacement hopped into his car and took over. Meantime a Haverford language teacher might grab a cab to fill in for a Swarthmore man called into Military Government. The habit continued into peacetime and from it developed the idea of "joint appointments," by which a good teacher might split his time between two of the colleges or all three.

"Her brother goes to Haverford."

Small colleges, however good, have trouble keeping good teachers. The big universities can outbid them on pay and have other inducements: the promise of a low teaching load, perhaps, giving an ambitious teacher time for research or writing; fine equipment maybe; or unlimited funds for research, in the case of a scientist. The small college usually must ask a teacher to give a variety of courses. A Spanish teacher may have to give a course in French. The big university can let him stick to Spanish, if that's his heart's delight.

The better the teacher, the quicker a small college is likely to lose him. They can't hope to compete against big state universities offering a full professor from $5,500 to $13,000 a year. But they'd like to keep him as long as possible—quite possibly for the best years of his career, while he's making his reputation. So all small colleges are racking their brains in search of ways to boost salaries. These joint appointments may be the answer. For the same teaching load, simply divided between two campuses, the teacher gets no more money. If it's extra work, however, say one extra course, he may get an extra $1,000 or $1,200. That's pleasant all around; the college where he teaches this additional course may be getting the skill and scholarship, part time, of a $6,000 or $7,000 man.

Neither Haverford nor Bryn Mawr could afford a full-time man to train and lead the college orchestras. But they could split one, and did. They also tried a venture in co-operative buying with Swarthmore. The Government offered a fine lot of war surplus—house-keeping equipment, furniture, and better still, good scientific apparatus, exceedingly expensive when bought on the open market. The three colleges hired an expert who knew the ropes and red tape of war surplus, and bought equipment worth many thousands dollars. Their expert's skill got them some great bargains, and the three could split his bill without feeling any pain.

Next they began to capitalize on their differences. Haverford gives first-year courses in the history of art. Now and then a student wants more. He can get it—at Bryn Mawr, where art is an old and important subject. The others get the benefit of Bryn Mawr's excellence and add a course or two at no added expense. Art is a costly subject; along with teachers you need a great deal of expensive slides, photographs and books, and the art book that doesn't cost twenty dollars ain't trying.

It's the same with astronomy. Bryn Mawr only offers one course. Here is another expensive dish. You need an observatory, for one thing, and that runs into important money. Occasionally a Bryn Mawr girl wants more astronomy than Bryn Mawr offers. She can have it, at the other colleges. A girl sprawled on the Bryn Mawr grass in jeans or shorts, with a portable radio playing in her ear, may very well be studying paleontology, crystallography, the origin of earthquakes or where to drill for oil. A little unexpectedly this girls' college is strong in geology; one reason being that many girls find good jobs in that field. Swarthmore doesn't teach geology; Haverford offers a single course. But Haverfordians can and do major in it, taking their work at Bryn Mawr. Geology is another expensive item. To set up a good department would cost Haverford or Swarthmore about $200,000 for buildings, laboratories, instruments, specimens and books, plus perhaps $12,500 a year for personnel and supplies. This way, good geology courses cost them nothing more than similar courtesies in return.

Haverford's boyish-looking president, Gilbert White—he took office at thirty-five—says the three college heads are just beginning to get the swing of this co-operation. But they worked together as smoothly as a big-league infield in their clearest triumph. That came when they presented a joint program that the Carnegie Corporation of New York found attractive enough to back with a grant of $105,000. If Russia is to be our principal rival and chief headache in the troubled future, then it may be smart to know a good deal about our Russian chums. So reasoning, the three colleges collaborated in laying out an expanded program of Russian studies which gets under way this fall. A historian in each college will offer a course in Russian history. Two portable professors appointed jointly, so they are on the faculties of all three, will teach Russian language and literature. A third joint appointee will teach Russian political institutions. Apparently a chance to help three distinguished small colleges with a single grant sounded like a bargain to those in charge of the Carnegie millions, and they underwrote the program for five years. That's what you might call ganging up on the big universities, many of which must regard the program with envy. By the combined use of six teachers, the three small colleges achieve what none could afford alone.

The student traffic is greatest on the northern leg of this triangle, between Haverford and Bryn Mawr, which are only five minutes apart by car. To reach Swarthmore is a twenty-five minute drive and a nuisance by train. Swarthmore students consequently stay on their home campus, mostly, and the teachers do the traveling. Two-way faculty appointments have worked out well and it is expected that three-way appointments will too. The only teacher who has tried it found it hard getting around, but his is an exceptional case in that he doesn't drive a car, and Swarthmore and Haverford share teachers in music and Spanish; Haverford and Bryn Mawr share them in music, drama, the history of art and orchestra work. Haverford's 1949 catalogue offered elementary or intermediate Russian and a course in Russian literature—taught at Bryn Mawr by an assistant professor appointed to both faculties. When the enlarged Russian program gets under way she'll be on the faculty of all three colleges.

"We've found," says John Nason, the former Rhodes scholar who runs Swarthmore, "that it is entirely possible to co-operate without uniformity."

He means without having uniformity or being forced into it. If other small colleges look around for partners for such a dance, that may be encouraging news. Certainly you could be excused for regarding this trio as strange bedfellows, if that's any way to talk about the alliance. You have in this cast one highly esteemed college for women, one mellow college for men. For complete dissimilarity, the third would have to be coeducational, and Swarthmore is—along with being the college famous for turning bright students loose to graze as they will.

All are residential, the great majority of the students living on the campus. All are strongly individualistic and a little aloof. Bryn Mawr's first dean, the redoubtable M. Carey Thomas, made that college the flagship of her battle for equal educational rights for women—equal, and a little better, if Miss Thomas had her way about it. For a long time the standard college entrance examinations weren't accepted there, which helped give the school a name for academic hauteur. Bryn Mawr girls note with relief that the old picture of the Bryn Mawr Type—wholesome girls from Our Better Families, with more I.Q. than maddening allure—is fading. They were pleased when the authors of *For Men Lonely*, a sort of girl-hunting guide put out by Dartmouth men, reported sighting pretty legs on the campus. Bryn Mawr girls are sophisticated, these experts concluded, but definitely female.

The college has one thoroughly feminine characteristic: It has kept observers puzzled almost since its birth. They couldn't make up their minds whether Bryn Mawr is bluestocking or downright lax. This was the first woman's college to permit smoking, and these cultivated young ladies can stay out until two A.M any night of the week and haul out at will for the weekend. When President Eliot, of Harvard, heard about all this freedom—it still startles some parents—he predicted the college wouldn't last two years. That was in 1886 and it seems not disrespectful to say that the great educator miscued. On the other hand, Bryn Mawr's unusual code kept the girls dancing with each other, a sorry sight, until the '20s; men were not allowed at the dances.

Woodrow Wilson was on the first faculty; he didn't get along well with Miss Thomas, they say. Theresa Helburn, of the Theater Guild, is a Bryn Mawr alumna; so are actress Katharine Hepburn; Alice Palache, of the Irving Trust, one of the few highly placed women bankers; and Martha Gellhorn, the correspondent. They are also proud of Dean Millicent McIntosh, of Barnard; judge Justine Wise Polier, of New York, daughter of the late Rabbi Wise; the historian Helen Maud Cam, the first woman Harvard ever invited to join its faculty; Emily Greene Balch, co-winner of the Nobel Peace prize in 1946; and Elizabeth Gray Vining, tutor to the Crown Prince of Japan.

Bryn Mawr girls study in a library copied from the dining hall in Wadham College, Oxford; the porch is patterned after Oriel College Chapel. Their lovely campus looks old, but Haverford far antedates it. Some of the Haverfordians live and go to class in Founders' Hall, which was the whole one-building works when the college opened in 1833—dormitory, classrooms, kitchen, dining room and faculty quarters. On a pleasant spring afternoon you may see a sight that tells you at once this is not the standard Old Siwash—young men in blazers and white flannels having a rousing bout of cricket. That has been a Haverford specialty from the start; the game was introduced by the English gardener imported to lay out the beautiful 216-acre "lawn," a quaint but accurate name for Haverford's great sweeps of shaded grass.

A good many times it has appeared that Haverford might run out of opponents, and the gentlemanly cries of "well tried" or "well played" might be heard no more. But there are still cricket clubs here and there, and occasionally a British battleship puts in to port with a cricket eleven hot for a pulse-stirring clash on the Haverford crease. There are recruits too; a couple of Negro colleges—Lincoln, of Oxford, Pennsylvania, and Howard, of Washington, D.C.—are going in for the game because they have West Indian students who are pretty flashy with those clublike bats.

Haverford graduated a Nobel Prize winner, the chemist Theodore Richards. Charles Rhoads, former Commissioner of Indian Affairs, is a Haverford man; so is Christopher Morley, whose novel *Kitty Foyle* told of a lass who loved a Philadelphia suburbanite above her station both socially and in a railroading sense. There is a Haverfordian in the British cabinet: Philip Noel-Baker, Secretary of State for Commonwealth Affairs.

Swarthmore, like the others, is a liberal-arts college, but has an engineering division, too, for, like the others in this *Dreibund* of individualists, it is not like the others. You will find emancipated students there who are relieved of all the customary classroom routine and left very much on their own. This is the once-revolutionary system of "reading for honors," now copied in part by perhaps 100 colleges, but for many years as distinctive and controversial as conducting classes in a blimp. Alumni feathers in the Swarthmore cap are multicolored. Pearson, '19, is Drew, the columnist; McCabe, '15, is Thomas B., chairman of the Federal Reserve Board; Bronk, '21, is Detlev, president of Johns Hopkins; Henderson, '20 is Leon, the brain truster; Michener, '27, is James, the Pulitzer-Prize winning author of *Tales of the South Pacific*.

It is a pretty improbable partnership, all things considered—three highly individualistic colleges, each doubtless convinced it lends the best voice to the trio. The alliance between Bryn Mawr and Haverford, oddly enough, is not so surprising as that between Haverford and Swarthmore. The physician-business man who founded the girl's college with part of the fortune he made in a tannery and in judicious investments—before retiring at forty—intended it for the guarded Christian education of "young female Friends." First plans were to build it right next door to Haverford, so the two Quaker institutions could share water and heating systems. High Hill, which is what Bryn Mawr means in Welsh, was chosen only to prevent the college from standing in Haverford's shadow. To the militantly feminist Miss Thomas, first dean and then president for nearly thirty years, this independence was supremely important. That forceful lady did not think highly of men, anyway, nor of marriage, either, although she once made a classic denial that tender blossoms cloistered in a college for women tended to lose their charm. Thirty-three per cent of Bryn Mawr alumnae were married, she stated, and fifty per cent had children.

Collaboration between Swarthmore and Haverford would have been unthinkable fifty years ago. Swarthmore was founded by the Hicksite Friends when feelings engendered by the Separation, the great schism of 1827, were bitter. Few remember the principles involved, but for many an angry year the devil himself hardly would have been less welcome among the good gray orthodox Quakers of Haverford than a liberal Swarthmore professor representing the dissenting Hicksites. Rival Meeting Houses stand side by side in some Quaker communities as monuments to this breach. A good many Philadelphia Friends now belong to both meetings, however, with the ancient dispute put into history's attic.

Widely different as the three colleges are, they have a good deal in common. All set the academic bar very high, all believe fiercely in the virtue of small classes under the best teachers available. They are proud schools; none of them would merge with Harvard if promised top billing in the act. They have found they can co-operate while disagreeing happily on many a point. You do need a little general compatibility and a break from geography; the co-operating colleges ought to be within easy driving distance if you can plan an interchange of students. Something of the same co-operation is developing in Massachusetts. Smith College, largest of the colleges for women; Mt. Holyoke, another of the better-known eastern girls' schools; Amherst College and the University of Massachusetts do a little borrowing of teachers and have been exploring the idea of going farther . . .

. . . All hands seem agreed that the Philadelphia coalition is working fine. No college has flunked anyone else's fair haired boy or girl, which could be embarrassing. You can conceive of a situation where a Haverford football hero might become ineligible just before the Swarthmore game because of low grades at Bryn Mawr. But it hasn't happened, and isn't likely, since all three schools go in for hand-picked students and have roughly the same grading systems. The three presidents are pleased with the scheme. They meet once every three weeks for dinner—Bryn Mawr's Katharine McBride, Nason of Swarthmore, White of Haverford —to trade news, ideas and, if somebody's money-raising campaign is lagging, sympathy. If one thinks of adding a course in thermodynamics or advanced frog-dissecting, he keeps the others informed; maybe it fits into their plans or will permit them to add something new to this stew. There is nothing in the shape of an official agreement, written or oral;

they keep this pleasantly informal. Small benefits crop up; the presidents find they can sometimes flip a coin to see which will attend a convention for all three, letting the others stay home. If they accomplish nothing else at one of their dinners, they get a lot off their minds. Miss McBride may feel like complaining that people still regard Bryn Mawr as uppity and social, although the three top girls in her class of '49 were all there on scholarships, and the daughter of a Brooklyn factory worker is running away with so many small prizes and awards that it presents her with a small income-tax problem. Nason and White may want to beef about the price of lawn mowers; Swarthmore's grounds cover 350 acres.

Their students seem to like the new arrangement. Haverford and Bryn Mawr have combined their orchestras, Haverford men take the male roles in Bryn Mawr's plays, so it's no longer necessary to pin the hero's hair up and tell her to remember to talk bass. The two colleges maintain a joint flying club and a joint literary magazine. Haverfordians haven't taken up the girls'-college thrill, hoop-rolling, and the Bryn Mawr girls don't go in for cricket. The Haverford boys do come up now and then to play a courteous game of hockey. Clearly the new system alleviates one ancient shortcoming of a women's college—no men. "How it works out academically, I wouldn't know," said one Bryn Mawr girl, "but socially, it's fine." She added that she was down on the scheme for the moment because some low Haverford man had drawn the Bryn Mawr library books she needed for a crucial paper.

Plans by which everyone gains and nobody loses are rare; this seems to be one of them. No one has put dollar-and-cents values on the collaboration, but obviously each college has more in the way of instruction and equipment than it had alone. The three have that $105,000 grant, furthermore, as a nicely concrete token that they are on the right track. It is good news from a melancholy front too; for years, word from the small colleges, to which many are devoted, has consisted of gloomy reports that costs were rising as receipts from endowments slowed to a trickle and wealthy benefactors disappeared like the passenger pigeon.

Nothing will solve that but money. Still, this plan helps; it is one of those good ideas that also work. They don't always, in this illogical world. Bryn Mawr's Miss Thomas had one that didn't. A married woman on her faculty came to the amazing seventy-four room deanery where Miss Thomas held court to describe a dilemma. She was going to have a baby; perhaps she ought to take a leave of absence. Miss Thomas had mellowed in her attitude toward marriage, and the ardent woman's-righter now felt marriage and a career might be co-ordinated. "Of course not," she said kindly. "Have it in the summer." Telling an English audience about this crisp solution, Miss Thomas paused. "She didn't," the dean said reflectively. "I forget, for the moment, the reason why."

Reprinted from the *Saturday Evening Post*, October 8, 1949.

Page 145: "Her brother goes to Haverford," cartoon by Bernice Robinson, class of 1948. Published in the *College News*, October 1, 1949

Opposite, left to right: Gilbert White (1911–2006), president of Haverford; John Nason (1905–2001), president of Swarthmore; and Katharine McBride, 1951. Photograph by Wilbur Boone (Havertown, PA)

Next page: Registration photographs of students from the class of 1951, c. 1947

POSTWAR PEACE

EDITORIAL

PERHAPS AT NO TIME IN HISTORY has education been more important. The days that lie ahead will be full of hope and promise but they will also be full of danger and stress. Women of our age who have spent the last four years in colleges and universities instead of taking an active part in war work have done so under the conviction that what is learned here can be applied to our communities and the world. We believe that through specialized studies we can perform greater services and duties to post war society. However, most of us are unsure as to what our duties are, or should be. We cannot predict with any certainty what the future will be. The majority of students on campus are mystified and even afraid as international disputes and labor strikes fill the headlines. Yet we have learned that education can be a weapon, a powerful one for good, a weapon for action which can unite a wrangling country.

Reprinted from the *College News*, February 27, 1946.

War's End Affects B.M.C. College Life

THE END OF THE WAR brings many changes to the Bryn Mawr campus. Not only are there academic changes, brought about by the return of former faculty and by new appointments, but the return to a peacetime basis enlarges extracurricular activities and in many ways will brighten the lives of Bryn Mawr students.

There has been little change in the student body except for the increase in number, and the end of the war is not expected to affect that aspect. The Cornelia Otis Skinner Workshop, located on the Baldwin Campus, will reopen this year and the Freshmen plays and all small productions will be given there instead of in Goodhart.

Concerning the food situation, Miss Batchellor told a *News* reporter that although restrictions have been cut there will be no immediate surplus of chops and steaks on campus. Meat now takes fewer points and is more available, but it is still hard to obtain good grades and cuts. Due to the harbor strikes, there is not sugar to be had; the damp weather and early frosts have played havoc with fruits and vegetables, but all restrictions have been lifted from milk, cream, and ice-cream.

Last, but by no means least, it is fervently hoped by the Bryn Mawr student body that along with the reappearance of cigarettes, Kleenex, and Hershey bars will be not only an adequate supply of, but an abundance of men.

Reprinted from the *College News*, October 10, 1945.

FORUM DISCUSSES EDUCATION'S ROLE IN ATOMIC WORLD

THE WORLD PROBLEMS OF TODAY and their relation to academic work and campus activities were treated in a round-table discussion, "The Place of Education in an Atomic World." Representing Bryn Mawr, Ann Wood '48 and Fanita Revici '48 met with other students from eleven colleges in Philadelphia and vicinity in the University of Pennsylvania Museum on Saturday.

In discussing today's trends and the question as to whether students are interested in these trends, it was generally agreed that the interest of college students needs to be aroused outside of their own fields and that they do little to obtain a world outlook. There were varied opinions as to the aim of college, including "a philosophy of life," a sense of social responsibility, and a vocation. Ann Wood claimed that liberal arts colleges give one a broad general background and the experience of getting along with people of other backgrounds.

All members of the panel seemed to agree with the current idea of teaching more of the humanities.

A cry for compulsory history and a suggestion that it be approached through today's problems arose out of the question as to whether courses and campus life equip one for the problems of today. One student declared that there was a need of correlation of subjects to immediate problems, and another suggested a course in post-war problems. One claimed that education ought to dispense with empirical traditions and direct itself toward "a brotherhood of man." It was generally agreed that the idea of racial superiority ought to be abandoned and that the quota of races, creeds, and color ought not to be regulated on campus.

The question as to whether colleges stimulate an interest in world problems was met by one student with a statement that professors tend to settle back into a pattern of merely existing and teach their students from their own texts, trying to make them think as they do.

Reprinted from the *College News*, February 20, 1946.

Peace Work

The class of 1949 is the first Freshman class in many years to be at Bryn Mawr in a world at peace. This is a challenge, not only to them, but to all of us who are undergraduates today. The war is over, but there is no reason why we should slow down the effort which last year rose to a new high, an effort to work for the community and for a cause.

The War Alliance and the Red Cross Unit have served during the war emergency; perhaps the need for them is over at Bryn Mawr. They were successful in that individual students found through them a place in which they could contribute, if only in a small way, to the war effort.

It is hard when the terrible necessity of fighting the war is over, to view the situation at hand with the knowledge that there is still much to be done, and much that can be done by Bryn Mawr in the Post-War world. The temptation to slip back into the feeling that life at college is an entity in itself will have to be faced again. It is important to be interested in the College where you spend four years; there are many opportunities for everyone to join in the extra-curricular activities. Still, the time has not yet come, nor will it come, when undergraduates can retire completely to an ivory tower of collegiate life, forgetting that we are most of all preparing to be part of the world of today, and that we will have to work now for the kind of world we want.

To the Freshmen

The Freshmen who come to Bryn Mawr this year will be coming at a time which offers many opportunities for real achievement. A chance to go to college is still a privilege though many who do go are not fully aware of this fact. But, as is true of all privileges, a college career also carries with it responsibilities which no college student should permit herself to forget.

We don't want to imply that we believe "all work and no play" should be the motto of every college student any more than of any other member of society. But we do want to point out that by virtue of her privileged position a college student today owes it to herself and to the other people in the world to train herself as far as she is able to furnish the enlightened leadership of which the world lacks sufficient quantities.

It seems, however, that qualities of mind and character such as ability in leadership can often be more successfully developed if approached indirectly. Anyone who shows a true spirity of cooperation has achieved one of the essentials of leadership. So it seems best to say to the freshmen as they begin their college career: do not try to do the things you cannot do, but leave them to those who can; and in the things you can do, try to give your very best effort to make them and yourself a success.

Above: Clipping from the editorial page, *College News*, October 1, 1945

MIDCENTURY FINANCES AND FUNDRAISING

THE FIRST STEP

THE RECENT APPROPRIATION by the Board of Directors to raise faculty salaries by $80,000 per annum is a recognition of the valuable contribution of our faculty to Bryn Mawr and to the intellectual world in general. In a wider sense it is an encouraging step toward the necessary establishment of the teacher in the position in modern society which his abilities truly merit. The Board of Directors is to be commended for its prompt action.

As undergraduates we have all realized that the teaching profession is grossly underpaid. *Crossroads*, the Drive publication, for April says, "A Bryn Mawr instructor receives less than a Civil Service P-I (the lowest professional rating) or a production worker in any one of 25 typical manufacturing industries. An assistant professor, whose salary may be from $2,300 to $3,400 a year, makes about $12 less than the average bus driver in Washington, D.C. The average weekly salary of an associate professor is about the same as that of a New York truck trailer driver."

But perhaps we are not all aware of a particular reason for increases in teaching salaries at Bryn Mawr. The college has always felt that adequate time and resources must be available to its faculty to enable them to pursue independent lines of study apart from their specific academic programs. Thus, such advances as the discovery of a new chemical compound, the writing of a new book on democracy, or the development of a philosophical theory are made possible.

This is doubly valuable. The ideas gained enrich both the material presented in our courses and the personal student-teacher contacts. But beyond this, the faculty are contributing to the progress of society as a whole.

Reprinted from the *College News*, April 23, 1947.

Top: Students in studio art class, c. 1950s. Photograph by Ben Schnall (New York)

Bottom: Students singing, c. 1950s

Opposite: Member of Bryn Mawr's diving team, 1956. Photograph by Wilbur Boone

The Drive

LAST MONDAY marked the official opening of the Alumnae Drive for faculty salaries, scholarships and academic projects through which the College hopes to raise two million dollars during the coming year. The significance of the Drive goes beyond the question of funds, however, to the problem of the importance of education itself.

This is a time when the value and purpose of liberal education is being widely discussed by most thinking people. There is a feeling that this type of education must be revised to meet the increasing pressure and challenge of current conditions, that it is, in fact, at a cross roads. Not only the form which such an education will take, but the means by which it can be made available to more and more people are at stake. Bryn Mawr and other similar institutions are faced with these increased demands, and at the same time are unable to fulfill them due to financial difficulties.

Bryn Mawr offers special advantages to faculty such as teaching in the graduate school and opportunities for individual research, to which we are indebted for the high standards of our professors. This in turn reflects upon the standing of the college so that it is essential that their work be continued and expanded both from the point of the kind of education and faculty we wish to have.

The faculty salaries established in 1920 are obviously insufficient today, so that many capable people are prevented from teaching under the present conditions. There are two alternatives open to a private institution: either to lower the standards of teaching, or to receive State aid, a dim prospect at best, but both are unsatisfactory. Unless the Drive is successful, the quality and quantity of our education will have to suffer.

None of us can deny the value of liberal education or importance of extending its influence. The campus should, therefore, cooperate as wholeheartedly as possible with the various activities and benefits which will occur in connection with the Drive throughout the coming year.

Reprinted from the *College News*, November 6, 1946.

MISS McBRIDE ANNOUNCES RISE IN TUITION AND RESIDENCE FEES
Operational Expenses Require Fee Raises in 1948–1949

Goodhart, February 9—Fifteen to twenty per cent increases in the cost of a Bryn Mawr education will go into effect for 1948–1949, announced President McBride this morning at a college assembly. Undergraduate tuition fees will be raised from $550 to $650, and residence fees (which include infirmary) from $675–$875 to $800–$1,000; graduate tuition will be raised from $300 to $400, and residence to $750.

Full tuition scholarships will be raised to meet these demands, but although some money will be added to the scholarship fund, it will be impossible to raise every scholarship proportionately.

Sources of Income

Bryn Mawr, which is privately endowed, operates on two sources of income, Miss McBride explained: that of fees, nearly $800,000, and that of the interest on the endowment, nearly $300,000. Operating expenses, currently $1,150,000, leave a $50,000 deficit this year; next year's may be $150,000. Increases were put off last year because of a $52,000 surplus accumulation from past years, plus a hope that prices would fall. However, prices rose and actual expenditures may be even higher. Extensive student cooperation, especially in meal planning, is helping hold costs; but more economies, including helping out with our own service, will be necessary.

Without the two million being raised for faculty salaries by alumnae and friends for the Drive, increases might have been larger; as it is, the entire cost of the higher scale of faculty salaries is being met by the Drive. The increases are still low in relation to the costs of operation and it should be pointed out that the $1,450–$1,650 yearly expenditures are lower than those of the other eastern women's colleges.

With the new Drive money, it is hoped that these fees will remain stable.

Reprinted from the *College News*, February 11, 1948.

REPORTING OUT:
THE HISTORY OF THE *COLLEGE NEWS*

THIRTIETH YEAR OF *COLLEGE NEWS* PUBLICATION SHOWS EDITORS THAT NO NEWS IS GOOD NEWS

IN THE OTHERWISE utilitarian habitat of the would-be journalists who comprise the staff of the *College News*, the only concession to decoration is a bronze plaque inscribed as follows: "This tablet is given by the Class of 1915 in memory of Isabel Foster, A.B. 1915, First Editor of *The College News*." To the alert editorial mind, it occurred that we, unaware, have been ignoring out thirtieth anniversary, so, belatedly, we turn to the maiden endeavors in the field of misprints and misspellings.

Organized in the summer of 1914, published first on September 30, on the opening day of the thirtieth academic year, the *News* was sent to press by three Seniors, two Juniors, a business manager, and a faculty advisor, and we wonder how they ever did it. Evidently they had their troubles, for they advertised weekly for reporters and music or theater critics, holding office hours daily for all comers in something known as the Christian Association Room. Business troubles were numerous, since undergraduates began by buying one copy of the *News* for [an entire dorm] corridor and since the price was one dollar less. This state of affairs did not persist long, however, for a few months later the *News* took over Merion for a banquet of roast beef and yellow and white ice cream for its forty "heelers." Ah, for the good old days!

Though different in size and in print, the *College News* of 1914–15 was little different from the *College News* of 1944–45 in content. It recorded a furious battle over cuts; it editorialized over the lethargic attitude of the students, the poor attendance at chapel; it received complaints for careless proofreading; it encouraged students to do their bit for the Red Cross on campus.

However, it gave a notably larger amount of space to sports, of which football was a favorite interclass game, and to the amazingly active Christian Association, to debating societies, and to alumnae and faculty notes. It published lost and found notices for two cents a word, and it waxed hysterical over "pink tea quizzes," its name for examinations all held then in the Reading Room of the Library, where you were given a pink slip and you searched for a pink desk on which was your particular exam.

And in January, the *News* editorialized "When will the college learn to take exams sensibly?" We can only reply that in thirty years we haven't.

Reprinted from the *College News*, January 10, 1945.

Above: Students typesetting an issue of the *College News*, c. 1950s. Photograph by Wilbur Boone

Left: College News staff, 1954

STEADY AIMS IN CHANGING TIMES: 1942–1970

THE UNDERGRADUATE POINT OF VIEW
Rose Hatfield, Class of 1932

WHEN I WAS ASKED TO REPRESENT THE CLASS OF 1932 on the Alumnae Council it was suggested that I discuss the *College News* as my contribution to the general topic, "The Undergraduate Point of View." I was doubly glad that the *News* was mentioned—first, because it is the only subject I really know anything about, and mainly because I believe that the *News* is more intimately concerned with the undergraduate point of view than with any other one thing. As long as I have been connected with the *News*, and probably since its first humble appearance in 1914, we amateur journalists have made it our chief occupation to take the pulse of the College regularly. The collegiate pulse is a very difficult thing to locate and even more difficult to read accurately—but we have always acted on the assumption that it exists.

Besides attempting to find out what the College thought, we have also tried to help it think and to give it every opportunity to express itself in our pages. We were especially proud of Miss Sanborn's [Lucy C. Sanborn, class of 1932] success in making a combination of these functions really vital to the undergraduate body. It was under her editorship that the present plan was adopted whereby any collegiate matters which are introduced in the editorial column of the *News* and discussed with an interest in the correspondence column are automatically brought under the consideration of the College Council, on which the editor of the *News* is privileged to sit. Several very important subjects have been taken up through the medium of the *News*, so we feel that we really do play an influential and, we hope, a beneficial part in undergraduate affairs.

The actual mechanics of the *News* is a fairly simple matter after a new editor has adjusted herself to its organization or made any necessary changes. It does require occasional prodding of board members, and the editor knows that she can plan on spending at least twelve or fifteen hours a week in routine work if nothing unexpected turns up. We have a very professional and opulent looking office in Goodhart which we share with the *Lantern*. Every Monday afternoon the Editorial and Business boards hold a joint meeting at which all the assignments for the previous week are turned in—theoretically, at least, assignments are made for the next week—and all editorials and letters are discussed. No editorials are printed without the majority consent of the joint boards—it always surprised me how often the vote was unanimous and how carefully the objections of dissenting members were considered before the final decision was made. We also tried to foresee any complications which might arise in the presentation of news, and to get the reactions of the board to the possibly dangerous material . . . Monday night is sacred to the copy editor, who is, according to the best professional etiquette, "responsible for errors in taste." That passes a great mental burden to the harassed copy editor, who is struggling to read all the copy for errors of any kind and to concoct intelligent headlines on a strictly numerical basis. I am sure, however, that the general public is unaware of this journalistic rule, for most editors-in-chief find that the blame for mistakes rarely gets to the theoretically responsible person.

All the weekly material, except for the inserts of the events of Monday evening and Tuesday, is printed on long strips of paper, or galleys, and ready for the editor-in-chief on Tuesday night. While the proof is being corrected on one set of galleys, the editor is trying to remember everything she ever learned about jigsaw puzzles in order to fit the columns into a definitely limited *News* dummy on which the advertisements have already been pasted. If the puzzle doesn't fit, the reading matter suffers, because the advertiser is a peculiarly sensitive animal who takes away his patronage if he is slighted. The editor then has to decide which item interests the greatest number least—consequently she is often accused of carelessness and favoritism. The *News* is then printed in its final form, corrected by a *News* member, and delivered—ideally without mistakes—on Wednesday night. You can see what dangers beset the *News* board at every step.

This routine goes very smoothly on the whole. The really difficult element is the choice of material, and it is here that the board must make the greatest effort to keep in touch with the undergraduate point of view. Certain things are automatically covered, such as the lectures which many students are required to attend for a course and do not want to hear.

Prominent visitors are usually interviewed; book and dramatic reviews are always included; and, of course, College activities of all sorts are reported. I believe that the readers are disappointed if they do not find those things. The editorials depend on what the board thinks the students want or should want. A regular and successful humour column arises from the presence on the board of someone with the time, the vitality and the wit to be funny every week for approximately six hundred words. Last year it was not a superhuman but a super-editorial task, so the "Pillar of Salt," which was such a sensation under Bipps Linn and Puppy McKelvey, died a much-mourned death. It is not these standbys, however, which make a newspaper, even a college weekly, interesting and necessary to its readers. Every *News* board is anxious to get one or two scoops by which it will be remembered, and a great deal of time is spent in planning ways and means to find a sensation or to create one. Fortunately, most of the ideas are still-born.

Reprinted from the *Bryn Mawr Alumnae Bulletin*, December 1932.

ACADEMIC PURSUITS OF THE 1950s

**SURVEY REVEALS HIGH STANDARDS
AT BRYN MAWR
Indicates College Trains Most Female Scholars**

IF YOU OFTEN THINK that your roommate is destined to be the Madame Curie of the second half of the twentieth century, you may not be far wrong. In the January issue of *Mademoiselle*, an advance report of an independent survey financed by the Ford Foundation Fund for the Advancement of Education reveals that Bryn Mawr produces more scholars per 1,000 students than any other women's college in the United States.

Bryn Mawr received this place of distinction with a rating which exceeds that of the second women's college by 14.9 points. Bryn Mawr also rates higher than the top men's college, which is Haverford.

It is noteworthy that the three colleges which are rated highest are Bryn Mawr, Haverford, and Swarthmore. These colleges participate with one another in a Three College Plan whereby professors and library facilities may be shared.

The survey is based on the graduates of college from 1945 to 1951. The scholars are those graduates who are most likely to make a significant contribution to the world in a scholarly field.

Although the article emphasizes the scholastic side of college life, it makes it plain that Bryn Mawr students are not exclusively brains. It does not overlook the fact that dramatic productions, parties, and other extra-curricular activities are as much a part of undergraduate life at Bryn Mawr as classes and lectures. The article points out that Bryn Mawr students use their intellects successfully on Princeton men as well as academic subjects.

Reprinted from the *College News*, January 14, 1953.

Above: Students on campus, 1952. Photograph by Sol Mednick. Published in *Holiday*, May 1952

Opposite: College News staff (clockwise from top) at a staff meeting, c. 1950s; in the newsroom, January 11, 1950 (photograph by Wilbur Boone); overseeing production, 1944 (photograph by Sarony, Inc., New York)

USUAL HYSTERIA DISPLAYED BY STUDENTS ASSEMBLED FOR PERENNIAL HYGIENE EXAM

IT IS 7:25 P.M. on Wednesday evening, April 16, 1952, when you walk into Taylor Hall. There is a crowd of girls standing around in the main hall talking, laughing. You walk into Room F and see a plentiful supply of blue books stacked on the professor's desk. A few girls are sitting at desks, dutifully keeping one seat between them. Can this be an exam? Oh, no, people are too cheerful.

Then you hear someone say, "If I don't pass this time, I don't know what I'll do. I only have one more chance."

On second thought, maybe it is an exam but it certainly isn't like the last one you took.

A girl walks up and pleads, "Tell me all that you know about mental hygiene. Please, I've got to pass."

Now, it comes back to you. Yes, you went to three lectures on hygiene. Vaguely, you remember someone mentioning an exam. So that's what it's all about.

"Please, hurry, they're going to start soon."

"I went to the lecture, but all I remember is that more hospital beds are occupied by mental patients than any other disease," you say brightly, patting yourself on the back knowing even that.

"Somebody tell me quick what Vitamin D is for!" moans another girl as she enters the room.

"I'm getting pretty tired of failing this exam. I'm going to put a statement on my paper that I'm healthy and my family is healthy, but I still get 52 on the Hygiene Test!"

Amid the giggling and talking, a small desperate voice is heard, "Please, a little quiet! This is supposed to be an exam." A peal of laughter is heard in the back of the room as someone receives the mimeographed sheet of questions. Another shriek of laughter, hysterical laughter, "An hour and a half!" The laughter ripples about the room and the exam is on; may the Juniors pass.

Reprinted from the *College News*, April 23, 1952.

A MEANS, NOT AN ENDS

EVERY YEAR, examination period and the following week bring criticism from many students, of the prevailing attitude towards grades. The competitive spirit here seems to lead to an avid interest in, and comparison of, marks.

This attitude is understandable in freshmen, as it is the result of their desire to know whether or not they will be able to "keep up" reasonably well. But far too few students, after finding out that they can get "comfortable" grades, settle down and study with the purpose of learning. Too often the goal of studying is a high average.

The students themselves must make the biggest move towards taking the emphasis off grades. We must put into practice the realization that we are here to get an education, or, as it is often phrased, to "fit ourselves for life." A practical slant may be given to this idealistic view of college: that is, that very few of our future employers, and practically none of our future friends, will ever know, or want to know, what marks we got in college. They will, however, know whether or not the subjects we studied in college were of any lasting benefit to us.

The problem which will always be raised in a discussion of grades is that of scholarship students, who make up a large part of Bryn Mawr's undergraduate body. Any student here on a scholarship feels that she must keep her grades constantly in mind. This burden might be somewhat lightened if these students could be confident that their financial need counted for far more than their numerical average.

A change in the students' attitude towards grades might be accompanied by a change in the method of grading. To use letters instead of numbers would do away with much of the petty comparison of papers and quizzes. We are aware that this suggestion will be met with a loud protest from those students with the highest averages. But everyone has asked or heard the question: How can you distinguish between an 83 and an 84 on a paper? We even venture to say that the professors would find it easier if they were not forced to make the distinction.

We have all dreamed of studying under a system where no marks were given at all. But in a college such as Bryn Mawr, this is not practical: without an extensive system of tutorials, grades of some sort are a necessary criterion of the student's work. We would like to point out only that grades are meant to be a means, not an end; they should be used as a means of telling the student how thoroughly she understands the subject, not as the ultimate goal of a course or a program of studies.

Reprinted from the *College News*, February 29, 1956.

"NEW LOOK," BRAWN AND BRAINS WELL REPRESENTED IN CLASS OF '51
Katrina Thomas, Class of 1949

BRIGHT AND EARLY Thursday morning, September 26, the Cincinnatians, the Chicagoans and all those on trains from the West (the first representatives of the class of '51) arrived in time for a breakfast of honeydew and fried eggs. But all day long they streamed in—some informally in cars with their dresses hung over their arms, some by train in their fashion plate calf-length suits and dark stockings—and all showed evidence of the higher requirements in this college boom, for Freshmen blunders, a perennial topic of conversation, were too few and far between.

'51 includes a pair of twins but no male students that we have seen: girls from China to the West Indies; the socialite who breathed ecstatically, "What, no classes on Saturday! You mean I can leave after biology Friday afternoon. Boy, wait till Jack hears that!"; and the intellectual who thought Spinoza "simply fascinating reading." In the infirmary meeting, one perturbed voice piped up: "Please, are we allowed to study while we are in the infirmary?"

Once again the Vill is being invaded. Soap dishes and waste paper baskets are becoming as scarce as hen's teeth, but Hobson's seems to be well-fortified still with easy chairs for those who arrived too late for what one Freshman elegantly calls, "the rummage sale over in Wyndham."

The wattage rule seems to have most of them baffled. "I can't have more than 60 watts in my lamp! I'll go blind!" said one pensive studier. Another, either uninformed or an ignoramus, went down to the book shop and asked Mrs. Nahm if she couldn't please buy a double socket.

The place hardest to find seems to be the gym. In directing one lost Freshman, I was asked just "how much" of a physical it was. "I've already had three or four," she explained. Later on I asked four shivering angel-robed victims sitting on a bench whether they were waiting in anticipation; the one with her teeth chattering answered: "Waiting, but not in anticipation."

Freshman Week has been cold. Although the zinnias are happily blooming in front of Denbigh and trees are still heavily green, the annual Faculty Tea held in Wyndham Garden of orange ice in ginger ale was chilly enough to congeal any Freshman who was not already frozen with fright at meeting the professors.

But the class of '51 is all too bright. Not one has asked me yet if I'm a Freshman, too!

Reprinted from the *College News*, September 29, 1947.

Above: Members of the class of 1952 arriving at the Bryn Mawr train station. Photograph by Hans Knopf. Published in *Life*, February 22, 1949

Right: Norma Aronson and Ann Morris, both class of 1957, relaxing outside, c. 1953–57

Opposite: Academic procession at Commencement, 1956

FACULTY APPROVES HONOR SYSTEM PLANS
Board of Trustees Decides May 20th

A STATEMENT of the academic honor system, drawn up under the joint efforts of student and faculty committees and approved by 94% of the student body in a vote by ballot, was submitted to the faculty at a meeting on Wednesday evening, April 28, and was approved. For the academic honor system to go into effect, however, it must be approved by a second faculty meeting in May, and subsequently passed by the Board of Trustees of the College on May 20.

The plan, if approved by the faculty and the Board of Trustees, will become a part of the Self-Government Constitution and of the faculty rules. It will in no case be possible for the system to be in effect for the examinations this spring because of the necessity for the Trustees' approval on May 20. However, if approved, it will be in operation in the coming school year, 1954–55.

It is hoped that it will in that event be possible for copies of the Constitution to be made available in the fall not only to Freshmen, but to all four classes. At that time it will also be possible to hold meetings for answering any questions which students may have concerning details of the system's operation.

Reprinted from the *College News*, May 12, 1954.

Top: Members of the undergraduate association, 1953

Bottom: Students using the card catalog in Thomas Library, c. 1950s

Opposite (clockwise from top left): Newsweek headline, October 15, 1951; students in the Thomas Library stacks, c. 1950s; class meeting, 1954

STEADY AIMS IN CHANGING TIMES: 1942–1970

EDUCATION

Dean McIntosh Proves Point: Women's Colleges Are of Age

At Bryn Mawr the intellectual process has been kept pure, undiluted by any vocational or domestic-science courses. Greek and Latin are as vital a part of the curriculum as English and mathematics—in campus festivities the girls even sing songs in Greek. Bryn Mawr's president explains that the college's high intellectual reputation stems from the fact that it has always had high expectations of what women can do. Today Bryn Mawr is high among all colleges in the proportion of graduates who take advanced degrees.

—"Tough Training Ground for Women's Minds: Bryn Mawr Sets High Goals for Its Girls," *Life*, December 24, 1956

For the period studied, 1946–51, Bryn Mawr graduates won scholarships for post-graduate study or earned doctoral degrees at a rate of 40.5 per 1,000. This was higher than the rate of any other women's college, higher than the all-female index of any co-educational college, higher than the rate of any men's college, and higher than the all-male index of all co-educational institutions, except Swarthmore and Reed colleges and the University of Chicago.

—"Bryn Mawr—A Synonym for Brainy Women: College's Record Shows Why It Leads Field," *Chicago Tribune*, June 2, 1957

"Bryn Mawr girls are the most scholarly of the students I've taught," declared Mr. Theodore von Laue, whose history teaching at Princeton, Swarthmore, and now Bryn Mawr gives him an unquestionably excellent background for a comparison.

Reprinted from the *College News*, November 5, 1952

Goodbye, Miss Taylor

LILY ROSS TAYLOR is retiring from the faculty of Bryn Mawr at the end of this year. Professor of Latin here since 1927 and Dean of the Graduate School of the College since 1942, Miss Taylor is a distinguished scholar and an authority on Roman civilization and literature, well known both through her work in this country and abroad, and her publications, the most recent of which is *Party Politics in the Age of Caesar*.

Born in Alabama, Miss Taylor received her A.B. from the University of Wisconsin in 1906, and after further study, including some abroad at the American Academy in Rome, received her Ph.D. from Bryn Mawr in 1912. Since then her work in Classical Studies has brought honors and many new opportunities for service. During World War II Miss Taylor held the position of principal social science analyst for the Office of Strategic Services. She accepted the post of Sather Professor of Classical Literature at the University of California for one semester in 1947, and two years ago received the honorary degree of Doctor of Literature from the University of Wisconsin.

Because Bryn Mawr offers its undergraduates the privilege of studying under the same professors, such as Miss Taylor, who teach in the graduate school, there is a unique opportunity for more intensive and inspiring work. Moreover, our graduate school is in itself outstanding, for Bryn Mawr is the only woman's college granting the degree of Ph.D. in all its major departments.

Miss Taylor's retirement from Bryn Mawr this year will mark a climax rather than the close of her career, for she has received a Guggenheim Fellowship and next year will act as Professor in Charge of Classical Studies at the American Academy in Rome. We say goodbye to Lily Ross Taylor with regret for the future Bryn Mawr students who will not under her surveillance learn to understand ancient peoples and appreciate an ancient literature. We know that for her "the lamp of true learning" will shine undimmed through the coming years.

Reprinted from the *College News*, May 7, 1952.

Above: Lily Ross Taylor (1886–1969), c. 1950s. Taylor, who received a doctorate from Bryn Mawr in 1912, was a professor of Latin at the college from 1927 until her appointment as dean of the Graduate School in 1942. In 1917 she became the first woman to be named a fellow of the American Academy in Rome. Photograph by Wilbur Boone

Opposite: Registration card for Jane Parry Tompkins, class of 1961

Higher Education
Jane Tompkins, Class of 1961

IT WAS IN THE SMOKERS OF DENBIGH, my dorm for three years at Bryn Mawr, that college happened for me. It was a foregone conclusion that I would go to college; the only question was where. The choice I made turned out to be a good one; at Bryn Mawr my experience of school took a definite upward turn. Right away, there are two contrasting stories. The more vivid takes place in the front smoker, one of the public reception rooms where we hung out in the daytime between classes, and where at night we drank coffee from demitasse cups and played bridge and smoked. The other story belongs to the quiet smoker at the back of the first-floor corridor where some of us studied and read and wrote papers. The two settings mirrored the division between personal life and work life, though at Bryn Mawr these two aspects of existence seemed less separate and opposed to each other than they ever would again.

My business is with the back smoker, where my work life acquired the shape it would have for a long time to come. But first I want to glance at myself and Jeannie Berkeley, sitting on the banquette of the big bay window in one of the front smokers of Denbigh, to note the softness and intensity of her eyes, brown eyes deeper than any I'd ever looked into, and to hear her throaty voice saying things so frank I was astonished a person *could* say them, as I thirstily waited for more.

Jeannie left after her sophomore year to get married, pulled away by forces whose strength I didn't understand. But not before she told me after dinner in the smoker one night what it was like having sex for the first time. Her voice was lowered, choked with emotion and conspiracy: "It hurts like hell," she said. I sat there with nothing to say, more amazed than ever.

I loved being with Jeannie, whose life, it seemed to me, went down several stories deeper than anyone else's I knew; Jeannie, who was Jewish, *named* things no one else would. She focused on personal relationships, feelings, her own and other people's. I was hurt and disappointed when she left. She was my link to something, I didn't know what, more alive and real than anything I'd yet been in contact with. When she left I had no other way of making the connection. At least not for a long time.

But the person I'm going to become is not sitting on the sofa with Jeannie. She's in the back smoker, working on a paper on the nineteenth century Shakespearean actor Tommaso Salvini. I'm a senior, I've come back from my junior year in Florence, and I feel comfortable sitting at the table under the fluorescent lights, going through my notecards, smoking, drinking coffee, getting my thoughts in order.

It suits me, this job. I do it well. The research for the paper is largely in Italian, and I like delving into books, especially if few others besides me can read them. It's like bringing back buried treasure; at the same time, I get to prove my proficiency in a foreign language. The writing is satisfying, too. I derive great satisfaction from crafting sentences that have a certain ring to them, a rhythmic rightness—if possible, a dramatic flair. I like to feel my own enthusiasm fill me up as I create a verbal picture. I enjoy the process of moving from the phase where all you've got is a collection of bits of information and few rough ideas to a smoothly polished paper, with introduction, rising action, climax, and denouement. It's hard work, I have to push and strain to do it, but I know that if I keep trying I'll get it done.

Three years before, as a freshman, I had struggled to write a paper that drew not only on Italian but French as well—at the time, I had only a few months of Italian and some high-school French to go on. I'd chosen to write on two Renaissance plays, Corneille's *Sophonisbe* and Trissino's *Sofonisba*, an Italian version of the same story, comparing them to each other in light of Aristotle's unities of time, place, and action, and with reference to Corneille's treatise, *Les Trois Unités*. The paper was for a philosophy course, so although I didn't know it, I was steering wide of the mark with my literary comparisons, but I forged ahead, overwhelmed by the difficulty of the language, the endlessness of the plays, the brute, unforgiving nature of Aristotle's dicta about tragedy, and the task of coming up with something interesting to say. Three years later, I know Italian, know how to choose a paper topic, know what my professor requires, and know that with some effort I can bring the whole thing off. Besides, it's spring, and the consciousness of sunshine and balmy air, daffodils and green grass out of doors makes the work I do inside my head, surrounded by books and papers, more intense, the cigarettes more delicious.

At Bryn Mawr I enjoyed doing scholarly work, which ranged from the technical (analyzing prosody in sonnets by Gerard Manley Hopkins and Dylan Thomas), to the archaeological (doing research on Tommaso Salvini), to the wildly exciting (finding autobiographical elements in the mystical poetry of Thomas Traherne). When I worked hard, I gained approval from my professors and felt good about myself.

Sometimes the approval came at a price. For one class we were using an anthology with a reddish brown cover, *Seventeenth Century Prose and Poetry*. The introductions to the poets in that volume—Vaughan, Donne, Herbert, Traherne, Crashaw—were the most inspiring pieces of criticism I'd ever read. I remember exactly where I was sitting in the back smoker when I encountered them. They were lyrical and impressionistic, full of passion, brimming with wonder and awe at the dazzling beauty and expressivity of the poems, The writer used words like "diamonds" and "pearls," "fountains" and "sunlight," to describe the poems; I was beside myself with happiness. But when I mentioned my enthusiasm to someone in the class, her sniggering reply warned me that it was dangerous to love this kind of prose. Soon afterward the professor dismissed the introductions as silly and effusive, not real criticism. We should ignore them. But I knew that the person who had written them had put his whole soul into those paragraphs and that it was my soul, too, because his words had expressed exactly what I felt about poetry sometimes. From then on I was careful to temper my own effusiveness. I didn't want to be associated with the names people used to describe those introductions. But the passion and exuberance I felt for literature remained nevertheless, fueling my efforts.

At Bryn Mawr the work took place in an environment that was ideally suited to me. The campus was green, secluded, and architecturally romantic. At eighteen, its cloistered atmosphere provided just what I wanted: the opportunity to be sequestered from the world for four years in order to read books, to listen to professors who were authorities on their subjects, to learn to write papers, to talk to other students, to take part in activities like singing and acting, to make friends who were similarly motivated, and to date boys from backgrounds like mine. College was a place where I could exercise my curiosity, develop my talents, and test the waters of social experience without worrying about earning a living or meeting the demands of an alien environment. It was a place where what I was good at counted, where I felt challenged but also felt safe.

Dorm life provided the right combination of society and solitude. For an only child, living with seventy-five other people with interests and values similar to mine was heaven. I never had to be alone, could always find someone to talk to, yet there was no pressure to socialize. If you liked, you could hide in your room all day. Moreover I had friends right there every day for closer companionship, and boys from Haverford and Penn who would take me out on dates. It was a tremendous relief to find I was attractive to them since I hadn't been popular in high school. My sexual ignorance, combined with the desire to please and be polite, got me into some ludicrous situations . . . .

. . . Next to dating, acting was the most exciting extracurricular activity. Probably what attracted me was the chance to feel something intensely in a safe way; you could emote onstage without owning the feelings yourself. There was not embarrassment; there were no consequences. Or maybe it was that acting provided an opportunity to practice feeling, to go through the motions of emotion without actually having any. I struggled both with having too many feelings and with the sense that in some areas where I was supposed to have them, I was completely numb. Whatever else it did, acting gave me the same thrill that I got from talking in class. While I spoke my lines, I was the sole object of attention; I existed vividly in my own and other people's eyes.

It didn't too much matter what the part was—a shepherd in a medieval mystery play, Olivia in *Twelfth Night*—I felt used by acting in a way that satisfied me deeply. My body could move, my voice could arc through its entire range, I could feel, I could think, I could respond, use my imagination, be both spontaneous and controlled—

and on top of it all I could be noticed, receive applause. Nothing else I'd ever tried did all that for me. But becoming an actress, that was another story.

When people sit around talking about what they would have done if they hadn't become what they became, I used to say that for me acting was the road not taken. But it isn't true. Yes, my mother did say to me one afternoon while I was standing by the back door in the kitchen that in order to succeed in the theater you had to sleep with the director. And yes, though I hadn't slept with anyone yet, the idea did make me afraid, since I knew that "sleeping with" someone other than your husband was supposed to be degrading for a nice girl, and I was sure I wouldn't like it. But that wasn't what made the difference.

Acting was too amorphous an occupation. I never bothered to find out what it would entail. All I knew was that you went to New York and suffered—maybe waited on tables until your break came. There was too much risk involved, too much that had to do with sex, physical attractiveness, heavy emotions, luck, and being dependent on the whims of others. As far as I knew, actresses didn't have an institution to belong to, like a school or a hospital or a church. They just floated somewhere between parts. In that intermission, I feared, one might cease to exist.

Teaching, on the other hand, was familiar. My mother, my aunt Virginia, my uncle Jim, my cousin Henry were all teachers. At home and in school, I'd been with teachers all my life. The idea that I'd become a teacher seemed to have formed under its own momentum. It felt right. My teachers at school were the people I admired most, and I looked forward to the prospect of becoming one of them. If I could become a college teacher, I would have gone further in that line than anyone in my family, and perhaps it would be pleasing to my relatives that I was following in their footsteps. Besides, teaching was simply acting in another form, wasn't it? You stood in front of a class and opened your mouth and performed.

Graduate school was the obvious choice. I could go on doing what I was already good at—writing papers, taking exams, talking in class—and there would be set tasks, and orderly progression toward a recognized goal. When I reached the goal, a Ph.D., I'd get a job. There would be no need to sleep with strange men. So in my senior year of college I applied for and won a Woodrow Wilson fellowship, which meant that I could go to any graduate school that admitted me. One bright spring afternoon, seated at a corner table in one of Denbigh's front smokers, Kathe Livezey, Clara McKee, and I decided we would go to Yale. Kathe, like me, had gotten in in English, and Clara had been admitted to the Law School. For some reason, at the time all I could think of was the number of men who'd be there. Miles of miles of men to choose from. Even the name "Yale," with its prestige, and its Ivy League sheen, had a firm masculine ring. And mixed with that was the knowledge that Yale was supposed to have the best English department in the country. We giggled in anticipation. I thought it would be just like Bryn Mawr, only better. Little did I know.

Reprinted from *A Life in School: What the Teacher Learned* (New York: Perseus Books, 1996), 66–73.

STUDENT LIFE OF THE 1950s

A LOOK AT EXTRACURRICULARS

THE *NEWS* feels that an evaluation of our extra-curricular activities is a matter of such importance that we have conducted a forum on the subject in this issue. We feel that extracurricular activities are a vital and necessary part of college life on campus. They offer students an opportunity to develop new interests or to further interests which they already have. We do not feel, however, that any student should ever be pressured into joining a club or any other organization. She should be fully informed about the organizations on campus; however, the decision to join them should be her own.

Some students who may have come from schools where they participated in many extra-curricular activities prefer not to become involved in them in college. Others feel that they would rather devote their extra time to their studies or social life. A student who joins an organization simply because she feels that she should join something because it is expected of her will never contribute much to the organization. She will simply be a name on the roll.

It is a mistake to judge the success of an organization by the number of members it has. Some campus activities will obviously appeal to a limited number of students. If the organization fulfills the needs of these students, it is doing a good job.

Perhaps one way for the campus organizations which have hall reps to retain the interest of students would be to do away with the hall rep system as it is now, as was suggested in the forum. Instead, any interested student should be eligible for the boards of these organizations. Since they are really interested, they will see that the work is done and that people hear about the organizations' activities. Under the present hall system interested people who have not been elected as hall reps feel that they are unwelcome at meetings and, therefore, do not attend.

In the forum, one student said she felt it would be a good idea to have faculty advisors for clubs. We strongly feel that one of the advantages of the present system is that there are no faculty advisors. Freedom and full responsibility are offered to every student in her extracurricular activities now.

Reprinted from the *College News*, November 16, 1955.

Left: Students posing like the Radio City Music Hall Rockettes, 1954. Photograph by Wilbur Boone

Right: Double Octet, a Bryn Mawr choral group, March 1956

What are little
Bryn Mawr girls made of?
Cigarette butts and coffee cups,
Beer and ice and all that's vice,
Oral cards and ancient bards,
Nescafe and hoops in May—
and Books!

Mold aces and haggard faces,
Blood-shot eyes and apple pies,
Seminars and local bars,
Telephone ringing and dining room singing,
Printed page and Goodhart stage—
and Books!

Lanterns green jokes obscene,
Fire drills and gargle pills,
Midnight oil and addled brains,
The Inn . . . and Sin . . .
and Books!

Caps and gowns and worried frowns,
Dirty jeans and cold baked beans,
Basket balls and Gothic halls,
Papers due and books of blue,
The lantern man and rooftop tan—
and Books!

Chewing gum and fingers numb,
Sandy salad and cuts invalid,
Payday bills and week-end frills,
Limited wattage and cheese (cottage),
College dances and complex romances—
and Books!

Argyle socks and mental blocks,
Two hour classes and bifocal glasses,
Formaldehyde and oysters fried,
The art of bull and faculty pull,
Longer for mail . . . and end of the tale—
Books!

Reprinted from a photocopy of original,
Bryn Mawr College Archives.

UNDAMPENED SPIRITS BUBBLE AT DANCE
Rioters Hover around Fire at Nero's
Anne Mazick, Class of 1955

THE RIOT moved from Rome to the gym Saturday night, as couples arrived, dripping wet, to dance to the music of Lester Lanin's band. The storm did not seem to lower the spirits of those who attended the dance. As soon as the girls doffed their rain coats and coaxed their curls back into place, they were ready for a few more hours of merry-making.

The gym was well disguised as a night scene, with dim lighting and shining stars. A globe hanging in the center of the room added sparkle to the scene by casting blue and yellow lights over the walls, floor, and ceiling.

During intermission, the entertainment represented Bryn Mawr and Harvard. Among the Octangle's selections were the usual favorites, "Let's Do It," "Who?" and "The Lady Is a Tramp." The Harvard Krokodiloes followed with "Sweet Georgia Brown" and several others, finishing with a generally well-known song about the "Harvard Man," "You can tell a Harvard man about a mile away."

At two o'clock the band played "Goodnight, Ladies," and the dancers ventured forth into the rain once more, this time to stop at Nero's, "the hottest place in town," better known as Merion Hall. Here the guests were fed with marshmallows and hot dogs, roasted in the fireplace. The Octangle gave a repeat performance, singing "Watercresses" and "Stairway to Paradise." Dr. Hugues LeBlanc, of the Philosophy Department, and Mr. José Ferrater Mora, of the Philosophy and Spanish departments, added to the Riot by participating with a few Merion residents in two skits with a Roman theme. They all donned togas for the performance.

At three thirty, a happy group of Bryn Mawr students retired to their halls, and freshmen snuggled into bed to dream sweet dreams of togas, fluorescent garters, and a spotted pony.

Reprinted from the *College News*, February 20, 1952.

> Familiar scenes for informal gatherings are found in the residence halls. These stretch along two sides of the upper campus. Alike in service and equipment, each has its own dining room, kitchen, smoking room, drawing room, library, bookshop and tea pantries. In Wyndham (the French House), the wing of Denbigh (the German House), and in East House (the Spanish House), French, German and Spanish are spoken entirely by the students.

NON-RESIDENT STUDENTS ENLARGE ACQUAINTANCESHIPS AT RHOADS TEA & LANTERN NIGHT PARTY

Emmy Cadwalader, Class of 1953

THIS LAST WEEK has been a very social one for the non-resident students. On Monday, October 15, the non-res warden, Miss Mott, who is also the warden of Rhoads South, gave a tea for the group in the Rhoads showcase. It was an excellent and much needed party, because it made it possible for all the students to get together and know one another. It has always been difficult in the past for the non-res students to function as a group, due to the fact that they are never all around at the same time. This year, thanks to a good start at this party, it is hoped that they will be able to work together more often, as the enthusiasm is definitely there.

Mrs. Paul also came, and after the discussion of many old problems that have always hindered the group, many worthwhile solutions were offered. It was also decided to redecorate the non-res room, which is in the basement of the library and is very much in need of fresh paint, curtains, more furniture that is comfortable, and a little bit of gaiety here and there. Color schemes and ideas sprang up from all over the room, and during the winter the whole group is going to work on the overhauling.

On Lantern Night the non-reses gave a party themselves for the freshmen. Many brought their parents and dates, and the common room was transformed into a gay crowd of people drinking cider and munching doughnuts. After a happy interlude from the college routine, everyone hurried off to cram just a little more for the French Oral the next morning.

Non-res parties are always amusing and entertaining, because the group is made up of so many different types. Some are married, while others have part-time jobs. If you haven't the time to take the marriage lectures, any married non-res can tell you how to cook a pea, and some can even give you needed pointers on how to bring up baby.

Reprinted from the *College News*, October 24, 1951.

Top: Clipping from a Bryn Mawr admissions brochure, c. 1950–55

Bottom: Students arriving on campus, c. 1950s

Opposite (top): Student Hula-hooping in Rhoads Hall, c. 1950s

Opposite (bottom): Students and their dates at a college formal, winter 1959

SUITE TALK

AS THE HALL DRAW approaches, the present system of assigning rooms at Bryn Mawr deserves serious reconsideration.

At present, there are three price levels for room and board. The price a student pays depends on the size and location of her room. All students receiving scholarship aid from Bryn Mawr must have a low price room. In some halls, this can severely limit her choice. For instance, there may be no possibility of her rooming with another girl, except in a very undesirable "emergency double" situation. The three price-level system causes uncalled for discrimination among students, and we believe that all rooms should be the same price.

The avowed principle of scholarship aid at Bryn Mawr is one of equality. The College awards scholarships so that students will be able to participate on an equal basis in all phases of campus life with no more than reasonable financial strain. Thus, the scholarship student will be indistinguishable from those students who are not receiving such aid. There can be no real equality as long as there are distinctions in room accommodations between scholarship and non-scholarship students.

By having three different prices for room and board, it is true that those students who can afford to pay more toward their maintenance at college will do so. Payments from individual students provide a greater percentage of the College's costs for room and board than if all rooms were the same price, since a number of students would need extra scholarship aid in order to pay the additional charge that one price for everyone would entail.

We realize that as long as the College maintains the distinction in room prices, it must require that scholarship students have low-priced rooms, since if a student can afford to pay an additional sum of money toward her room, she should invest it in her tuition, making additional scholarship money available to needy students.

We feel, however, that the principle of equality followed by Bryn Mawr in its scholarship program is more important than the money the College may gain by continuing the distinction in room prices.

Reprinted from the *College News*, May 1, 1963.

Right: "Bryn Mawr suite in Pembroke East has café curtains of muslin ($1.50 a yard), bedspreads, window-seat covers and cushions of striped denim and foam-rubber floor cushions covered in solid denim (85¢ a yard). Luggage rack ($6.50) with tray serves as table. Lanterns (left) are hung on dog leashes" (reprinted from *Life*, August 24, 1953). Courtesy of Arnold Newman Collection / Getty Images © 1953

Opposite: Bryn Mawr bobby pins, c. 1950s

PETS, NO PETTING

THERE COMES A TIME in the course of the debate of a controversial subject when it becomes necessary to take a stand. You cannot straddle a fence forever. This is no world for moral cowards! Therefore, we feel, regardless of whether or not you agree with us and despite the threat of personal injury to members of the board, that we must express ourselves on the current controversy that is tearing the campus into two warring factions. This is of course the question of keeping pets at college.

Our position is crystal clear. We are for it.

Our reasons are several. First, we believe they would prove an academic asset. They offer excellent subjects for biological and sociological study. And of course, they are useful in that they uncomplainingly listen to badly pronounced foreign languages.

We also do not agree with those who say that the animals would damage the rooms. On the contrary, by their constant prowling, they would wipe the dust off the furniture and thus spare the trouble and expense of cleaning the rooms.

In addition, they would serve a great purpose in receiving the affections of the emotionally frustrated members of this women's college. Would not the Administration prefer that we love our four-legged animal friends, and not our two-legged animal friends, in our rooms? In short, our position is: "Pets, not petting."

We also heartily disagree with those who maintain that if pets were allowed in the rooms and in the classes, the whole policy of the school would be arranged to meet their needs: that the classes and subjects would be geared to their level, that the meals would be planned solely to give them their necessary food requirements.

After all, are we men or mice? If we don't trust ourselves to run against the competition of the lower vertebrates, what chance have we in a world of equals?

But enough of words! The time has come for action!

S.P.C.A.'ers, unite!

The victory will be worth the fight!

Reprinted from the *College News*, April 1, 1954.

STEADY AIMS IN CHANGING TIMES: 1942–1970

A BREAK FROM THE BOOKS: WEEKEND PLEASURE

THE BIG WEEKEND

COLLEGE WEEKENDS are one of the most enjoyable aspects of undergraduate life. They are anticipated with a great deal of excitement and are looked back upon with pleasure; they rank among the most memorable events of one's college career. Although the last college weekend was a great success, the enjoyment of some people was marred by a few trifles. The *News* takes this opportunity to list these complaints with the hope that they will influence plans for future affairs on campus.

Taking the weekend in the order of events, many students wondered why there were not enough programs at *Othello*. Also in connection with the play, it would seem advisable for the cast to prepare to take curtain calls. It was somewhat disconcerting to see the principals almost afraid to take their bows called for by the audience and most assuredly deserved.

Once at the dance, many were sorry to see that there was so little time for actual dancing. It was felt that the entertainment, although delightful, could have been somewhat curtailed, in order not to cut into the already abbreviated time left in the evening. Also the music might have been a little more appropriate to formal dress. Charlestons and polkas are fun, but rumbas, sambas and slow rhythmic numbers could have been more abundant, since these are what people want most at a formal dance.

Looking at the weekend as a whole, the *News* feels that when a serious production of the length of *Othello* is given, it might be wiser to give the play on a separate evening, either Friday or Saturday night. As it happened, many people missed the play or half of it in order to get ready for the dance. The problem of going to *Othello* left many with the choice of having their gowns irreparably crushed by three hours of sitting down, or not dressing formally until afterwards and then finding that there was not enough time to change. In a situation like this, it seems obvious that an Undergrad Dance and a drama production are each too important in their own right to be put on a double bill. Each encroaches on the time needed by the other and both suffer as a consequence. Holding the dance on Friday night and the play on Saturday night or vice versa as is done successfully at other colleges would spread out the events to the entire weekend and allow each to be enjoyed most fully. Those who worked for and participated in the weekend are to be congratulated for producing an exceptional event, most enjoyable in spite of the minor flaws that have been mentioned.

Reprinted from the *College News*, December 5, 1951.

. . . THE TOWN OF BRYN MAWR is situated squarely athwart Philadelphia's Main Line, and one would expect to find the college of Bryn Mawr filled with chic coiffures, white tennis dresses, and talk of deb parties past and future. Instead, Bryn Mawr is perhaps the most self-consciously intellectual of all the Seven Sisters.

This intellectual aspect is fairly visible. Weekends at Bryn Mawr are oriented around concerts and plays. Foreign films are well known, well attended, and presumably well liked. Favorite hangouts are more likely to include Philadelphia coffeehouses than discotheques or bars. Foreign food is "in." Ivy League "preppies" are out-numbered among dates by the soulful, beard-and-jeans set. Indeed, at Bryn Mawr the word "Ivy" is likely to be intended as an insult. While the Bryn Mawr lass may try hard to show that she is just-one-of-the-girls, still the man prepared to discuss existentialism and Romantic poetry will get along best with her.

Part of this may be due to the fact that Bryn Mawr is married to Haverford. Well, perhaps not married, but the men's college down the road does monopolize most of Bryn Mawr's carefully rationed socializing time, a process aided by an official policy of "cooperation" between the two schools. Haverford social events are listed in the academic calendar of its "sister college." But optimists see Haverford as a source only of weekday lovers and study-daters, and visualize Penn and Princeton leading regular weekend invasions.

Invasion is easy. Almost every form of transportation existing can take you to Bryn Mawr. Cars are naturally preferred, since you'll probably want to leave again. One-third of Bryn Mawr's 750 students usually leave each weekend and, except for the two big weekends, plays and concerts are the only on-campus dating activities. Junior and Freshman Show Weekends are usually worth taking in; plan on at least taking your date out to dinner. On May Day and Lantern Night, and during Hell Week and other traditional Bryn Mawr affairs, don't bother to be present at all; you may be tolerated, but you are not particularly welcome.

Reprinted from Peter Sandman, *Where the Girls Are: A Social Guide to Women's Colleges in the East* (Princeton, NJ: The Daily Princetonian, 1964).

Allons

THE RAILROAD FARES ROSE this summer—again—but still Bryn Mawr is fortunate, say the handbooks, the Freshman Week Committee and our parents, in being located only a few miles from a major American city. Theoretically this proximity offers students easy access to all the advantages of urban culture. One of our Junior Year in Paris survivors, nonetheless, when asked to compare her experience abroad with her life here, instantly declared that the chief advantage of Paris in contrast to Philadelphia was its almost unlimited opportunity for theatre, ballet and concert attendance provided by reduced rates for students. For example, the price of a ticket to the Comédie-Française was, in American equivalent, about twenty-five cents—one could go to the Comédie three nights a week.

Here, although we are aware of all the advantages of urban culture, the big city providing all of these advantages, with the exception of the Philadelphia Orchestra, seems to be oblivious to us—a potential audience of 670, only twelve miles away. Bryn Mawr, in fact, is but one of numerous schools in the area which would conceivably accept and profit from any offer of reduced student tickets, similar to that made by the symphony. Despite the many comments we raise about our own lethargy, many of us do take joyous advantage of the Orchestra reduction, even with the sometimes difficult condition of having to subscribe to an entire series of Monday concerts. Many of us might attend a few concerts if we were able to purchase single tickets at the same rates. In addition to this, we have noted many comments to the effect that students would like to see more plays, if only the price of tickets weren't prohibitive.

Arts Council's announcement last week of a ticket agency service on campus is the best news that has yet drifted in from the more rarified world of "culture"—and should definitely serve as a needed link. Single students, quiz-and-paper-bound who are faced with the type of long-range planning necessary to take them to such an affair as the limited engagement of the Old Vic Company find themselves totally hindered by practical problems—problems which Arts Council will overcome. Now we wonder, perhaps only because we like our cake with frosting, whether in addition some financial arrangement might be perhaps made between Arts Council and the Academy

of Music box office as well as other Philadelphia theatres. The local flicks consider us a good investment, two for the price of one—any night.

Considering railroad fares which must be reckoned in the case of any theatre evening, while unchaperoned students, as most of us are, most of the time, are unable to provide themselves with any other transportation, and that opportunities do not pass unnoticed here, viz the Orchestra, investigation might be worth its time to Arts Council, Undergrad, or some other portion of the college able to speak for the whole student body.

Reprinted from the *College News*, October 15, 1958.

BMC BRAIN TRUST MEETS YALE MATES AT "MENTAL MIXER"

A CONTINGENT from "The Bryn Mawr Brain Trust" will venture to Yale this weekend for the first Mental Mixer in B.M.C.'s history.

The fourteen girls will arrive in New Haven by 2:30 P.M. at which time they will go to the home of Ellen Patterson '66, who is organizing the weekend. Ellen's father is the master of Morse College at Yale. First on the agenda is a lecture, possibly by Reverend Coffin or Bernard Ashmole, keeper emeritus of the Elgin Marbles. This will be followed by a tea given by Ellen's parents for the girls, the Yalies, and the guest lecturer. In the evening the Bryn Mawr "Brains" will be dined in the Morse Dining Hall, and then will go to a dance at the college, or as Ellen said with a smile, perhaps on a private date with some devastating Yalie met that afternoon.

The $11 train trip ticket should be just about the only expense, since the Bryn Mawrters are being put up without cost at the homes of New Haven members of the Bryn Mawr Club, who will also serve them breakfast on Sunday morning. The girls plan to return by around 4 o'clock Sunday afternoon. (Ellen has offered them a campus tour for that morning.) Social Chairman Caroline Willis has suggested that girls who find suitable companionship at Yale may remain a little longer on Sunday.

Reprinted from the *College News*, October 22, 1964.

TEA TIME

TEA POT, STERLING OR TIN-PLATE, PROVES BONANZA, BOTH ACADEMIC AND SOCIAL

AT BRYN MAWR the tea set is virtually an institution. Its long usage and manifest utility have entrenched its status as standard operating equipment and made its presence on mantle or coffee table as *de rigueur* as the Harvard pennant in a Bates bedspread ad.

Despite its ubiquity the tea set has no standard form; it may be a sterling silver heirloom, a souvenir from Chinatown, a long-discarded family samovar, or Woolworth's 79-cent special pre-college purchase. Generally considered by sub-freshmen a rather anomalous inclusion to a list of college basics, it invariably becomes, in its four years on and off the mantle, irretrievably bound up with life, both extra-curricular and academic, at Bryn Mawr.

Through long nights of two-fingered typing and take-home quizzes the contents of a tea pot (be it instant coffee or onion soup) usually proves the difference between triumphal completion of task or pre-dawn collapse. On the other hand, for a P.M. study break, a surprise birthday party, or an informal *tête-à-tête* with a favorite professor, the set and the brew it holds becomes the means of entertaining and the ostensible *raison d'être* of the party.

Happily enough, a pot of tea is an automatic excuse for a gathering and generally the inspiration for good conservation. When feelings are low there is no better balm for the spirit than a full kettle and the company it attracts; when spirits are high nothing is quite as fitting as to call in half the dorm to celebrate over tea, cookies, donuts or crackers.

By the end of this year even the most ardent supports of Coca-Cola will indubitably have become veteran tea drinkers and will have learned to wield with aplomb hot kettle, china pot and tea strainer; they will be able to detect at a sip the differences between Darjeeling and Jasmine, Lapsang Souchong and Formosa Oolong, Lipton and Salada. Lastly, and most surprising to themselves, they will find that pouring a cup of tea comes to mind immediately as standard operating procedure in the face of virtually every contingency.

Reprinted from the *College News*, October 1, 1960.

Above: Students having tea in a dorm common room, c. 1950s–60s

Opposite: Students outside Rhoads, c. 1950s–60s

BRYN MAWR IN THE *NEW YORKER*

THE BRYN MAWR TYPE IN FICTION
Katrina Thomas, Class of 1949

BEFORE WE CAME to college, anyway, we had a pre-conceived idea of the Bryn Mawr Type, and when we leave we will probably go out under Rock Arch with a model of the typical Bryn Mawr girl firmly fixed in our minds, though she may vary somewhat from the original image.

I had been warned that she was blue-stockinged and horn-rimmed, but that did not faze me as horn-rims could be very distinguished looking (inwardly I bewailed my 20/20 vision) and various colored stockings were very much in style. My conception was considerably worse. In her worst form, the Bryn Mawr Type (BMT) was an incredible specimen of over-developed brains and an under-developed body. She wore glasses, to be sure, but they were steel-rimmed, and her hair was either straight or frizzily permanented, while her back curved over the books she perpetually clutched to her flat bosom. For beauty she could only rival Lens, but she was a paragon of wisdom. She outlined, underlined, and remembered, especially she remembered. She could quote Herodotus from the Greek or from any other primary source to prove a point. The only man who had ever interested her was Zeno, or Samuel Johnson, Sir Isaac Newton, or Nebuchadnezzar, and she would probably consider me in the last analysis as not very beautiful and awfully dumb. All summer long I hoped that there would be one or two other painted hussies, flibbertigibbets like myself, with a taste for strapless evening gowns and an eye perpetually peeled for an attractive man. I should not have worried, for even the Dartmouth authors of *For Men Lonely* have found "enough feminine charm here to repel all fears of the hyper erudite" and that "although definitely on the sophisticated side, girls are girls . . . these are just a little smarter."

There are a number of male authors, who (though they have never attended Bryn Mawr) have a clear conception of the BMT, possibly inspired by some alumnae of their acquaintance. Most of us know James Thurber's cartoon, one of those amorphous representations of the battle between the sexes, which depicts a "femme fatale" kicking her heels in

THE RENASCENCE OF RUGGED INDIVIDUALISM
The Bryn Mawr Sophomore Who Wore a Town Ensemble and Correct Accessories on the Campus

the living-room. She is surrounded by a circle of entranced gentlemen while an irate wife speaks to the knot of ladies standing in a corner: "She's all I know about Bryn Mawr and she's all I have to know."

In the Pem West smoker is the Carl Rose cartoon of a scene outside the library. Taylor tower rises in the distance while a multitude of Bryn Mawr girls, in pants and long dowdy skirts with even longer-droopy slips, cluster around a chicly dressed girl in the foreground. The caption reads: "The Renascence of a Rugged Individual."

While Mr. Thurber has pictured a rugged individualist and labeled her with Bryn Mawr, Mr. Rose has the plodding Bryn Mawr students staring wide-eyed at the individualistic swan in their midst. The writers are no more in accord than these cartoonists.

Reprinted from the *College News*, December 3, 1947.

"ALACK, CAN THIS BE I?"

IT HAS BY NOW BEEN conclusively proved that the Bryn Mawr female is either extremely versatile or else completely enigmatic. During the course of the week, two national magazines which pride themselves on their ability to feel the country's pulse and to emerge with the true facts about Trends, Forces, and People have turned their medical attention to Bryn Mawr. And their diagnoses have differed to put it mildly.

From the *Saturday Evening Post* we learn that Bryn Mawr is a co-ed institution which is really a man's college, that the girls spend their daytime staring gaily out of the windows into coed-filled jalopies or lying on the grass behind Rhoads; their evenings with weekday lovers, studying their "unofficial major, each other." Against this, *Time* pictures a "highbrow Bryn Mawr, geared to the scholar's mind" and presided over by a "stately Katharine McBride." Last year, however, Mr. Luce took a different view; in *Life* he envisaged a kind of academic nuthouse in which girls died gladly, not for men, not for books, but for peacocks. And Princeton, exploding the Bryn Mawr Myth, saw a vision of a Vargas girl, barefoot in the ivied heather.

What are we—one or all of these? Our weekday lovers—Haverford or peacocks? Are we stately or rustic, scholars or gypsies?

Frankly, like Thurber's woman, we have always wanted to be inscrutable.

Reprinted from the *College News*, October 12, 1949.

Above: "Have you noticed a very festive table of Bryn Mawr alumnae?," cartoon by Helen E. Hokinson (1893–1949). Published in the *New Yorker*, January 6, 1940. Courtesy of the *New Yorker*

Opposite: "The Renascence of Rugged Individualism," cartoon by Carl Rose (1903–1971). Published in the *New Yorker*, January 25, 1936. Courtesy of the *New Yorker*

CALL ME ISHMAEL,
Or How I Feel about Being Married to a Bryn Mawr Graduate
E. B. White

THIS IS A RIDICULOUS ASSIGNMENT. The sensations of a Bryn Mawr husband are by their very nature private. Even if there were some good excuse for parading them in public, a prudent male would hesitate to make the attempt, so greatly do they differ from common sensations. But as far as that goes, a prudent male wouldn't have married a Bryn Mawr girl in the first place—rumors would have reached him of the wild fertility revels that take place on May Day, of the queer ritual of the lantern, of the disorderly rolling of hoops, and of all the other racy symbols and capers of the annual Elizabethan hoe-down. A sober male, sifting these disturbing tales of springtime debauchery, quite properly would have taken stock of the situation. A girl who has spent her senior year dancing around a Maypole and beating a hoop might easily take a lifetime to cool off. A prudent male would have boarded the first train for Poughkeepsie and sought out some simple, modest maiden with daisies in her hair.

> I ONCE HELD A LIVE HUMMINGBIRD IN MY HAND. I ONCE MARRIED A BRYN MAWR GIRL. TO A LARGE EXTENT THEY ARE TWIN EXPERIENCES. SOMETIMES I FEEL AS THOUGH I WERE A DIVER WHO HAD VENTURED A LITTLE BEYOND THE LIMITS OF SAFE TRAVEL UNDER THE SEA AND HAD ENTERED THE STRANGE ZONE WHERE ONE IS SAID TO ENJOY THE RAPTURE OF THE DEEP.

I do not, in fact, recommend that any young man enter into a marriage with a Bryn Mawr girl unless he is sure he can absorb the extra amount of emotional experience that is involved. To awake to a serene morning in a green world; to be overtaken by summer thunder while crossing a lake; to rise bodily from the earth, borne aloft by the seat of one's pants as a plane passenger is lifted from the runway—unless a man can imbibe these varied and sometimes exhausting sensations, can profit from them, can survive them, I recommend that he take the easy course and marry into Wellesley or Barnard or Smith. But if he is ready for anything, if he wants to walk straight into the jaws of Beauty, if he aspires to rise above the fruited plain and swing by his heels from the trapezes of the sky, then his course is clear and the outskirts of Philadelphia are his hunting ground.

Bryn Mawr graduates, in their appearance and their manner and their composition, are unlike all other females whose minds have been refined by contact with the classics. They have long hair that flows down over their bodies to below their waists. They rise early, to sit in the light from the east window, brushing their tresses with long, delicious strokes, and then twisting them into an intricate series of coils and loops and binding them with pins made from the shells of tortoises, or, more lately, from the plastics of DuPont. The husband's day thus begins with the promise of serenity, of order. But there is nothing static about Bryn Mawr. As the day advances, the pins grow (as though nourished by the soil of intellect), thrusting up through the warm, lovely hair like spears of crocuses through the coils of springtime. When fully ripe, the pins leap outward and upward, then fall to earth. Thus does a Bryn Mawr girl carry in her person the germinal strength

Right: Katherine Sergeant White (1892–1997), class of 1914, was a writer and the fiction editor at The New Yorker (1925–1960). Courtesy of the White Literary LLC

of a fertile world. Once a week she makes a trip to a hairdressing establishment that used to go by the name of the Frances Fox Institute for the Scientific Care of the Hair, where she is restored and cleansed by three ageless nymphs named Miss Abbott, Miss Nelson, and Miss Robinson, usually (as near as I can make out) while sitting in a booth next to the one occupied by Lillian Gish.

Bone hairpins are not the only thing that fall, or pop, from a Bryn Mawr graduate. There is a steady cascade of sensible, warm, and sometimes witty remarks, plus a miscellany of inanimate objects, small and large, bright and dull, trivial and valuable, slipping quietly from purse and lap, from hair and ears, slipping and sliding noiselessly to a lower level, where they take refuge under sofas and beds, behind draperies and pillows—pins, clips, bills, jewels, handkerchiefs, earrings, Guaranty Trust Company checks representing the toil of weeks, glasses representing the last hope of vision. A Bryn Mawr girl is like a very beautiful waterfall whose flow is the result of some natural elevation of the mind and heart. She is above paperclips, above Kleenex, above jewels, above money. She spends a large part of each day *making* money, and then comes home and rises above it, allowing it to fall gently through the cracks and chinks of an imperfect world. Yogi Berra would be the perfect husband for a Bryn Mawr girl, but I am no slouch myself; I have come a long way in the catcher's art and am still improving my game.

I have known many graduates of Bryn Mawr. They are all of the same mold. They have all accepted the same bright challenge: something is lost that has not been found, something's at stake that has not been won, something is started that has not been finished, something is dimly felt that has not been fully realized. They carry the distinguishing mark—the mark that separates them from other educated and superior women: the incredible vigor, the subtlety of mind, the warmth of spirit, the aspiration, the fidelity to past and to present—girls like Helen Crosby, Diana Forbes Lloyd, Laura Delano Houghteling, Evelyn Shaw McCutcheon, Claire Robinson, Nancy Angell Stableford, Emily Kimbrough, Elizabeth Shepley Sergeant, Sheila Atkinson, Evelyn Washburn Emery, Edwina Warren Wise, Frances Fincke Hand, Cornelia Otis Skinner. What is there about these women that make them so dangerous, so tempting? Why, it is Bryn Mawr. As they grow in years, they grow in light. As their minds and hearts expand, their deeds become more formidable, their connections more significant, their husbands more startled and delighted. I gazed on Pembroke West only once in my life, but I knew instantly that I was looking at a pile that was to touch me far more deeply than the Taj Mahal or the George Washington Bridge.

To live with a woman whose loyalty to a particular brand of cigarettes is as fierce as to a particular person or a particular scene is a sobering experience. My Bryn Mawr graduate would as soon smoke a cigarette that is not a Parliament as sign a check with an invented name. Not long ago, when a toothpaste manufacturer made the wild mistake of changing the chemical formula of his dentifrice, he soon learned the stuff Bryn Mawr is made of. My wife raised such hell that our pharmacist, in sheer self defense, ransacked the country and dredged up what appears to be a lifetime supply of the obsolete, but proper, paste.

You ask me how I feel to have undertaken this union. I feel fine. But I have not recovered from my initial surprise, nor have I found any explanation for my undeserved good fortune. I once held a live hummingbird in my hand. I once married a Bryn Mawr girl. To a large extent they are twin experiences. Sometimes I feel as though I were a diver who had ventured a little beyond the limits of safe travel under the sea and had entered the strange zone where one is said to enjoy the rapture of the deep. It was William Browne who most simply and accurately described my feelings and I shall let him have the last word:

> Briefly, everything doth lend her
> So much grace, and so approve her,
> That for everything I love her.

Reprinted from the *Bryn Mawr Alumnae Bulletin*, Summer 1956.

ILLUSTRIOUS VISITORS

BERTRAND RUSSELL REVIEWS PRINCIPLES OF INFERENCE IN LOGIC OF INDUCTION
Inferiority of Deduction Stated by Well-Known Philosopher

THE PRINCIPLES OF INFERENCE involved in inductive and probability logic were examined by Mr. Bertrand Russell, eminent philosopher and logician, in his lecture last Friday. Mr. Russell contrasted the logic of deduction, which he said consists of little more than tautologies, with the logic of induction which argues from experience. He demonstrated the inferiority of deduction by defining it as logic where the premise is true, the inference is valid, but the conclusion is only probable. This lecture, "The Limitations of Deductive Logic," is the first of a series of five which Mr. Russell will give here on the postulates of scientific method.

Inductive Inference

The modern mind wants generalizations from experience, stated Mr. Russell. Inductive logic, which revolves around the essential principle that a multitude of like instances approach certainty, formulates its generalities from particular knowledge. For scientific knowledge or even for daily existence to continue, he said, the premises made by inductive logic about such a multitude of instances must be accepted even though they can never be completely proved. Thus, from experience, one may justifiably predict that the sun will rise tomorrow.

Probability Judgments

Mr. Russell objected to the principle of inference used in probability judgments, and as an example, pointed out the limitations of a calculation of probability in a case of chance. The chance that a tossed penny will land "heads-up" is supposedly fifty-fifty but Mr. Russell refuted Reichenbach's claim that after a certain point the limits of chance continued unvaried and maintained that the probability could be accurately stated after calculations from an infinite succession of tosses.

Doubtful Judgments

Such a case of probability, stressed Mr. Russell, must be kept distinct from one of doubtful judgment, arising from distrust of either report or fact or individual impression. Thus, when Reichenbach, holding that statistics along with the rest of knowledge were only probably true, used as illustration the fact that the considered dead figuring in a mortality rate might not be actually dead, he was confusing a judgment about probability with a doubtful judgment. The probabilities about which premises are made, such as that of the penny's landing "heads-up" half the time, said Mr. Russell, must not be confused with the probabilities existent among premises due to incomplete memory or data.

Reprinted from the *College News*, October 14, 1943.

ROBERT FROST EXPRESSES OWN PHILOSOPHY THROUGH INFORMAL READINGS OF HIS POETRY

ROBERT FROST expressed his ideas through poems of "sense and nonsense" in Goodhart Auditorium Saturday night. The Nobel prize-winning poet was sponsored by the Friends of the Library.

Mr. Frost has been called the New England poet, but the subjects he discussed on Saturday night extended much beyond the thoughts of one section of the country.

Unlike most of us, Mr. Frost knew what he was thinking at any time in his career because he has it "all written down."

Thirty-five years ago Mr. Frost taught at Bryn Mawr for two years. He was secured by M. Carey Thomas to guide a club of embryo poets. He therefore started by telling the audience of his reactions to students and ideas he met on college campuses at that time.

Ideas at Bryn Mawr were "radical then." It was the poet's greatest disillusionment to discover

that "radicals were the same from Maine to California, just like the conservatives." It was then that he "stopped cheering and started jeering."

... The subjects of his poems rather than any prepared program carried Mr. Frost from one poem to the next. The mood of the evening was always informal and Mr. Frost seemed to be more a teacher than a lecturer... Applause at the end of the evening brought him back to read several additional poems.

Reprinted from the *College News*, November 17, 1954.

Above: Robert Frost with Kathleen Johnston Morrison (left), class of 1921, and Katharine McBride (right), November 1954

Pages 178–179: Registration photographs of students from the class of 1961, c. 1957

STEADY AIMS IN CHANGING TIMES: 1942–1970

NEW ENGLAND CHARACTERIZED IN POEMS OF ROBERT FROST
American Poet-Lecturer Gives Commentative Reading

"THE POET OF NEW ENGLAND," Robert Frost, reading from his poems in Taylor Hall last Saturday evening, under the auspices of the Reeling and Writhing Club, confirmed before the audience his right to his title. From "The Birches," with which the reading opened, to the final encore, Mr. Frost's poems portrayed New England life and interpreted New England characters. Unlike the poems of Siegfried Sassoon and Robert Nichols, who have given readings at Bryn Mawr in the last two years, Robert Frost's, all written before 1916, showed no influence of the war.

Contrasting the tenets of modern imagists such as Ezra Pound and Miss Lowell with his own theories, Mr. Frost said that he sought to express over and above the image, the psychological tone conveyed by the ordinary speaking voice. In this way Mr. Frost believes that clearness of image and style are achieved. "The lay of most so-called imagists is to give poems that shall convey a clear image without much attention to thought or sentiment. Such a line as 'listener to new yellow roses' does not bring any true image; it does not give one the pleasure of recognition, which is the basis for all enjoyment in art." The concluding lines of Mr. Frost's poem, "The Gum-Gatherer," show his simplicity, power and originality:

> . . . I told him this is a pleasant life
> To set your breast to the bark of tress
> That all your days are dim beneath,
> And reaching up with a little knife,
> To loose the resin and take it down
> And bring it to market when you please.

Of Mr. Frost's dramatic poems, "The Fear" was easily the most gripping and vivid, giving with intensity and insight the horror of something only half seen in the darkness of a lonely road.

"There are two kinds of style: the more bookish and the less bookish. Of all my poems," Mr. Frost remarked, "I consider 'The Cow in Apple Time' the most bookish."

> Something inspires the only cow of late
> To make no more of a wall than an open gate,
> And think no more of wall-builders than fools.
> Her face is flecked with pomace and she drools
> A cider syrup. Having tasted fruit,
> She scorns a pasture withering to the root . . .

Reprinted from the *College News*, November 3, 1920.

ELIOT CLARIFIES DUTY OF WRITER TO POET'S IDIOM

Goodhart, October 26—T. S. Eliot, as the Ann Elizabeth Sheble lecturer, drew an audience of almost 2,000 people to hear selected readings of his poems. Basing his readings on the chronological order of the poems, Mr. Eliot began with the "Preludes," which are, explained Mr. Eliot, "the least embarrassing of the earlier poems."

"La Figlia che Piange" describes Eliot's feelings about a statue which he "was told to see, searched for, but never found." Then followed "Sweeney among the Nightingales," the poet's favorite in this group. "Gerontion" was included because in a sense its rhythms and use of disconnected images prepare for *The Waste Land*. Reading the section "What the Thunder Said" from *The Waste Land*, Mr. Eliot declined to comment, for "there are so many people now who know so much more about *The Waste Land* than I do, that I have become modest."

The first and last sections of "Ash Wednesday" were read next, and an Ariel poem, "Marina," based on Shakespeare's *The Tempest*. "As relief" Mr. Eliot read two *Landscapes*: "New Hampshire" and "Virginia." "Dry Salvages," one of the *Four Quartets*, was Mr. Eliot's final reading.

Reprinted from the *College News*, October 27, 1948.

EUDORA WELTY, RECIPIENT OF L. DONNELLY AWARD, WILL FILL POSITION OF RESIDENT WRITER DURING '58

ANNOUNCEMENT WAS MADE yesterday by Miss Katharine E. McBride, President of Bryn Mawr College, of the appointment of the Mississippi author, Eudora Welty, as the Lucy Martin Donnelly Fellow for 1958–1959. The award, made for distinction in writing, carries with it a stipend of $3,000.

Miss Welty was born in Jackson, Mississippi, and has lived there most of her life. She attended the Mississippi State College for Women and took her B.A. from the University of Wisconsin. She is the author of several novels and many short stories which have appeared in magazines, such as the *Atlantic Monthly*, the *New Yorker*, and *Harper's*. Her most recent publication was *The Bride of Innisfallen* (1955), a collection of short stories.

The O. Henry Memorial prize for the short story has twice been awarded to Miss Welty. In May 1955, she received the Howells Medal of the American Academy of Arts and Letters, given every five years for the most distinguished work of American fiction published during that period, for her novel *The Ponder Heart*. This novel was later dramatized on Broadway.

The holder of the Donnelly Fellowship is expected to reside at Bryn Mawr for some part of the college year, Miss McBride said in announcing the award, but has no academic duties, making it possible to devote the entire working time to creative writing or research. Candidates must be citizens of the United States or the British Commonwealth.

Reprinted from the *College News*, May 14, 1958.

SPACE FOR DEVOTION: RELIGIOUS LIFE AT BRYN MAWR

MORE SPIRITUAL, LESS FORMAL SERVICE COULD SOLVE PROBLEM OF B.M.C. CHAPEL

To the Editor:

Of all the criticism currently to be heard on the subject of Chapel, the most frequent is that it should be held in a more appropriate place. Certainly this is true: the Music Room cannot be transformed into a place for formal worship simply by hiding the blackboard. It is not so ugly, though, and not so uncomfortable that it could not be a place of worship if the service were changed to suit the place.

The Music Room is not, I think, the real obstacle. The service itself does not fit the needs of the college. Chapel, as it exists, is not satisfactory for anyone, least of all the congregation. Those students who enjoy a formal service go to church on Sunday morning. They will not go to a formal service again on Sunday evening, especially in so incongruous a place. The people who don't go to church in the morning, will for the same reasons, not go to chapel in the evening.

Worship Service

The need is, I think, for a service without the formality of a church service. My proposition is that we change the service into a service for worship, that we subtract from the intellectual element and add to the spiritual. Instead of a service centered around the minister and his sermon, I suggest that chapel be led by a member of the Chapel Committee and that it consist of music, both by choir and congregation, prayers said by all, the reading of a passage of the Bible, and five minutes or so of quiet. Such a service would give to all the very necessary sense of spiritual relaxation which we so much need to counteract the intellectual feverishness of our week-day lives.

Speakers

I realize that the great objection to this plan is that it deprives us of so many excellent speakers; it need not. The same men could come under different—and more favorable—circumstances. As it is, they must speak within the traditional limits of the sermon; they are tired, having spoken to another congregation that morning; they have, often, a long trip home ahead of them. The discussions are limited by weariness and lack of time and our reticence when confronted with a man in robes who has just given a sermon. Why not have these speakers come during the week, when they have more time and will, surely, have larger audiences? Why not have them give talks rather than sermons, so that they will be freer to speak and we to question? Such talks and discussions would fit in with the lectures given by members of other faiths and they would supply the intellectual half of our religious life as chapel would the purely spiritual.

Most sincerely,

Geraldine A. Warburg [Class of 1949]

Reprinted from the *College News*, October 15, 1947.

INTERFAITH ASSOCIATION IS ESTABLISHED;
Fosters Religious Interest on Campus

AT THE LEGISLATURE MEETING of Wednesday, December 5, a great majority vote established the Chapel Committee as an autonomous organization on campus as of February 3, 1957. It will be called the Bryn Mawr College Interfaith Association and will be a full voting member of the college council, equal in status to the present Big Five.

The Association shall be, as its constitution declares, "interfaith and non-denominational in purpose and membership." Its purpose is to foster interest in religion; to offer opportunities for the individual student to broaden and deepen her own religious thinking; to provide an opportunity for all students to worship together; to function as a liaison between the students and the churches of the community.

The membership of this association will not be ipso facto but "shall be open to all undergraduate members of the college"; a student's personal decision of membership or non-membership shall be expressed by whether or not she chooses to vote in the annual election of the Interfaith Association president.

Sandy Grant, president of Chapel Committee, presented to the legislature the reasons for the establishment of the independent Interfaith Association, and its proposed constitution. After discussion of the idea, the motion was made by Joan Shigekawa that "upon ratification of its constitution the organization known as the Bryn Mawr College Interfaith Association will be established on campus." The motion was seconded and carried. The constitution was then discussed and ratified.

Sandy asked for independence for the Chapel Committee in order to both "clarify our present position by admitting that we already are an independent organization" and to enable the Chapel Committee to "become more outward looking and to reach more people." The structure of the present Chapel Committee confirms the first reason; the degree of interest shown in the Committee justifies the second.

The Chapel Committee has been a committee of Undergrad with a status not much different from that of the clubs. It has been a non-voting member of the Undergraduate council. However, Chapel has also had a college-elected president, something no other non-autonomous organization has, and it has an independent financial system. It does not share the Common Treasury, but is supported by a fund from the Religious Life Committee of the college trustees.

Reprinted from the *College News*, December 12, 1956.

BRYN MAWR–HAVERFORD STUDENTS FORM JEWISH DISCUSSION GROUP

FOR THOSE MANY CRITICS who claim that Bryn Mawr students lack the initiative to pursue their academic interests outside of the classroom, a weekly meeting of about ten Bryn Mawrters and Haverfordians should provide some conflicting evidence. Every Thursday evening at 7:30, these students meet in Stokes Hall to study and discuss Hebrew scripture. At the moment, they are reading the Song of Songs in Hebrew. The discussion of the text and various commentaries on it is conducted both in Hebrew and in English.

The Jewish study group developed under the guidance of Melanie Sherry, '69, and Carl Grunfeld, a Haverford junior. It not only serves intellectual interests, but also fulfills a social and religious need.

Melanie felt very strongly that there should be a Jewish organization on campus and wrote a letter to the *News* stating her opinion. Receiving a reply from Interfaith to go ahead with whatever ideas she had, Melanie joined forces with Carl to form the present group.

Present at the Thursday evening meetings to help the discussions are Professor Aryeh Kosman of the Haverford Philosophy Department and Professor Richard Bernstein, head of that department. Last year, Mr. Kosman gave a formal discussion section at Haverford on Saturday afternoons in which the book of Jonah was examined. These sessions provided the germinal idea for the developing, informal group.

All of the participants of the Jewish study group have had eight years of Hebrew at the pre-college level as well as some post-high school courses. Several have been to Israel, and one Haverford student spent his junior year there.

The group can, however, also serve a very important purpose for those who have no knowledge of the language. Melanie hopes that there will be enough interest to organize another study session in English, possibly even to establish a beginning Hebrew class at Bryn Mawr or Haverford. Furthermore, the group plans to make arrangements to facilitate the observance of Jewish holidays. The possibility of joining the Hillel organization, the National Collegiate Jewish Club, is even being considered. Whether the group joins or not, however, Melanie intends it to be an organ for publicizing Hillel activities at such neighboring campuses as Princeton and Penn.

Sometime in the beginning of December, Carl plans to hold a panel discussion at Haverford. The speaker he hopes to have is Samuel Tobias Lachs, a visiting lecturer at Haverford and Swarthmore and a well-known biblical scholar. The discussion will question the "incongruity of a Judeo-Christian Society" with Professor Kosman and Professor Gerhard Spiegler of the Haverford Religion Department participating. The discussion is open to all, and immediately following it will be an organizational meeting of the group to measure the extent of interest in its activities.

If there is sufficient enthusiasm on the two campuses, the Jewish study group hopes to have professors and rabbis in the area speak on such topics as "Jews and Existentialism" or "Jews and Greek Philosophy." Although the study sessions do require background knowledge, the panel discussions certainly do not. Melanie would appreciate all suggestions for issues to examine and speakers to address these meetings.

Reprinted from the *College News*, November 11, 1966.

INTERNATIONAL ENGAGEMENTS

INTERNATIONAL COLLEGE

BRYN MAWR has a unique reputation among small colleges for the number of foreign students it attracts. Often more than ten per cent of the undergraduate school is made up of students from abroad, and the proportion in the graduate school is much higher.

The presence of ten German experts, the new DP (displaced person) scholar, and the first Japanese scholar since pre-war days has lately drawn our attention more strongly than usual to Bryn Mawr's standing as an international college. Miss McBride has emphasized this, too, in her article which appears in the *Bulletin* this week. The number of the class of '49 who are studying abroad, and the generous allocation from the United Services Fund for the restoration of university libraries in Europe, are further signs of an interest in cross-Atlantic exchange of education and ideas which is probably stronger now at Bryn Mawr than it was before the war.

We have on this campus a remarkable chance to study Europe at home, as it were; surely no Bryn Mawr student with any spark to her mind can fail to find these opportunities exciting.

Reprinted from the *College News*, October 19, 1949.

Above: Martha Liao, class of 1970 (left), recipient of the Chinese Scholarship, with Margaret Woods Keith (right), secretary and treasurer of the Chinese Scholarship Committee, at Commencement, May 1970

BRYN MAWR'S FOREIGN STUDENTS INTERESTED IN SCIENCE, LANGUAGE
Katrina Thomas, Class of 1949

SIMILAR TO the first group of foreign undergraduates at Bryn Mawr interviewed, science and languages are the main interests of the students, who either want to travel or to take their scientific knowledge back to their native countries.

Christel Kappes, having lived in Germany with her German parents until 1936, arrived in the United States by way of a former Marine Corps troop ship from Palestine six weeks before college began. She speaks German, English and Arabic fluently and some French, and came to Bryn Mawr to study because there are no universities in Palestine, other than the Hebrew one and she cannot speak Hebrew.

Her education in Palestine was carried on in three different schools. They were: a German school in Ramallah (where she had to take all her courses in Arabic), a British school called the Jerusalem Girls' College and an American Junior College in Bayreuth. Christel plans to major in Chemistry, as she is interested in all branches of science, and hopes to return to Germany after college, although she is not sure that she wants to live there permanently.

Although Elizabeth Grey knew that she had been accepted at Bryn Mawr last spring, she could not get a seat on a plane from England until after college had started. So, she arrived here less than three weeks ago at LaGuardia Field, was dazzled briefly by the lights of New York City and rushed to Maryland to stay with her godmother for the week-end. Therefore, she has hardly been here long enough to make her mind up about anything other than to study languages so that she can travel.

D. Lynn Lewis is a citizen of both the United States and Chile. Her father is an American, now farming in Chile where Lynn was born, and her mother is English. Lynn arrived here from Santiago at the end of September, and wants to study languages, using them in some international work.

Alina Surmacka from Warsaw, Poland, is a Junior who wants to finish studying in the United States, and to do graduate work in this country in nutrition. She is a Chemistry major.

Reprinted from the *College News*, November 13, 1946.

STEADY AIMS IN CHANGING TIMES: 1942–1970

AFRICAN STUDENT CHOOSES BMC
Berna Landsman, Class of 1963

THIS YEAR for the first time Bryn Mawr's foreign scholarship program has brought to the college a student from Kenya. Wamere Mwangi, a member of the Kikuyu Tribe, the largest single tribe in Kenya, East Africa, has come as a transfer student to the sophomore class.

One of the 172 African students welcomed by a group from the African-American Students Foundation on arrival in New York in September, Wamere came on the airlift financed by the Kennedy Foundation.

How Wamere happened to come to Bryn Mawr is an interesting story, which she tells, by the way, in beautiful English. "The idea of going abroad to study first occurred to me in 1956, when I was in the 11th grade," she began. At that time she was attending the African Girls' High School of Kikuyu, and, having reached the 11th grade, had passed both the primary and intermediate examinations given at the 4th- and 8th-grade levels, respectively. Since all pre-college education is not compulsory, but is government-sponsored and privately paid for, this was quite an achievement, for the students that the few schools can accommodate ought not to be eliminated by examinations. (Many more students go to primary school, therefore, than actually finish, due not only to lack of funds but also to lack of schools.)

"At the end of the 12th grade I passed the final examinations for college entrance given by Cambridge." Passing the examinations well enough to enter college consisted of writing eight papers and receiving distinction or credit grades (A's) in at least five, one of which had to be in English. "One can pass in first, second, or third class, and only about 100, all from the first class, are admitted to college from all of East Africa." Wamere passed first of all the girls in Kenya.

"In July, 1958—our academic year runs from July to April—I entered Makerere College, the University College of East Africa (affiliated with London University), the only one in East Africa until 1956 when the Royal Technical College was opened in Nairobi." There, choosing between a program of Arts or Sciences, she took "Arts": two years each of English, geography, and history. "Towards the end of my first year, I heard of a Mrs. Thomas, an alumna of Bryn Mawr College in America, who wanted to introduce an African girl to her school. I went to see her, and I asked her how I could go there, and she told me to write to the Dean of Admissions, which I did. I explained that I was on scholarship. [College education in East Africa is paid for by the government; their system is just the opposite of ours.] I received application scholarship forms to fill out, and in May 1960, I received a letter saying I had been admitted.

"I had made sure, before I accepted," she continued, "that this school was very good. I did not want to leave my school, which I knew was good, for any American school, since I had heard that they were not all good." Bryn Mawr has a very good reputation outside the U.S.A. "I had wanted to study abroad right after high school," she explained, "but I felt it was my duty to accept the scholarship and place at Makerere because not only would I have disappointed many people, but they would have thought me silly to refuse."

Although she had decided that she wanted to come, she had no way of getting over here. "It was July 1st, school was to start again on the 7th, and I still didn't know whether I could come," she explained. "I had not told anyone at Makerere of my plans, because I was afraid they would tell the government, and I would not be able to get a passport. The Education department does not like to have the top students leave the country. But as it was, when I went for my passport, I had no trouble, because they had not heard of me." Bryn Mawr, requested by Wamere not to send for her college records, thus considered and accepted her on the basis of her high school record only, plus Wamere's description of her college courses.

"When I heard about the Kennedy Foundation airlift, I made the necessary arrangements, and all was settled," she concluded.

At Bryn Mawr, Wamere hopes to major in history, and some day to teach at her former college where there are now no African women lecturers. "My people have what you would call 'education hunger,'" she said, "and there is a great need for educated people to lead them. At the present, the Imperialists would not have us build private schools!"

Much better informed about her country's government and current political problems than the average American girl is about hers, Wamere is game for discussing just about anything. As she says, "I came to learn to live with and get to know people other than my own."

Reprinted from the *College News*, October 12, 1960.

BMC, HAVERFORD, SWARTHMORE SHARE GRANT FOR ASIAN STUDIES PROGRAM

THE FORD FOUNDATION announced this week a grant of $136,000 to Bryn Mawr, Swarthmore and Haverford Colleges for a cooperative program in Asian studies. The project has as its objective the increase of knowledge and understanding of non-Western cultures for both faculty and students and the introduction of new perspectives into the undergraduate curricula of the three colleges.

Scholars to Visit

The grant will bring two successive Asian scholars to the campuses to organize and present a seminar for faculty members. Funds will be used to make it possible for the groups of faculty to spend one-third or one-half of the year in this special joint study of Asia.

The scholars will also teach undergraduate courses and assist in increasing library materials in this field. Outside specialists will be invited as speakers to supplement the project.

Foundation Project

The grant is a part of a $376,000 program sponsored by the Ford Foundation to test approaches for developing more effective teaching about non-Western areas. The aid, formerly given solely on the graduate level, was extended to the undergraduate schools for the first time this week.

The University of Vermont, Indiana University and Denison University are also participating in the project. Unlike former aid to Yale and the University of Chicago which stressed training for specialists in the area, these grants are to expand the existing liberal arts curricula.

Reprinted from the College News, *February 25, 1959.*

FOUNDATION SENDS TWELVE OVERSEAS TO TEACH SCHOOL

TWELVE YOUNG WOMEN, June graduates of Vassar, Bryn Mawr, Smith, Mt. Holyoke, and Radcliffe Colleges, are starting teaching careers this month, not in familiar American towns, but in such distant locations as Bangkok, Istanbul, Stockholm and Northern India, it was made known here today.

These beginning teachers, pioneering in a program of international education developed by the International Schools Foundation, Inc., of New York and Washington, will spend a year as teaching "interns" in representative American-sponsored schools abroad. Their students will be American youngsters whose parents are on foreign assignment for the U.S. government and industry, as well as children of many other nationalities who also attend these schools.

Schools Involved

The program in its first year has been developed in cooperation with the Seven College Conference of women's colleges. The participating overseas schools are: the International School Bangkok, Thailand; the Robert College Community School, Istanbul, Turkey; the Brent School, Baguio, the Philippines; the Stitching International School, The Hague, Netherlands; The Woodstock School, Mussoorie, India; and Mount Hermon School, Darjeeling, West Bengal, India.

The purpose of the program, Dr. John J. Brooks, President of the International Schools Foundation, said yesterday in making the announcement, is both to give a number of carefully selected young women the broadening experience of teaching an international group of children amidst a foreign culture, and to help the schools by strengthening their faculties. The cost of bringing a teacher from the United States, he pointed out, has made it impracticable, up to now, for schools in other continents to employ teachers-in-training. One of the features of the new program is that each of the "interns" is paying for her own round-trip transportation. The schools are paying modest salaries, providing living quarters and other facilities, and assuming responsibility for supervising the work of the "interns" so that it will be of maximum benefit to them.

Great Asset

"Young teachers commencing their professional development are an important asset to schools in this country," Dr. Brooks said. "Under this new arrangement, overseas schools will no longer need to be under-privileged in this respect, and the young women themselves will be acquiring experience and knowledge which will prove invaluable to them and to the schools in which they teach when they come back to this country. Some of them, we are sure, will make a career of teaching in international schools.

"The enthusiastic response we have received from this year's seniors in this group of colleges is most promising for the future of this type of program. The screening of the candidates for these internships by our organization and by their college authorities has been intensive and thorough. We have every reason to believe that these young women will give an excellent account of themselves. They will be performing a real service for the cause of education and international understanding."

The International Schools Foundation was incorporated in 1955 and since that time has functioned as the American-based service agency for nearly 100 international and American-sponsored schools in Europe, Asia and Africa.

Reprinted from the *College News*, October 11, 1961.

Above: Participants of Bryn Mawr's Institut d'études françaises d'Avignon, 1962. The institute's intensive summer program, created in 1962 under the auspices of the college, was designed for students with serious interest in French language and culture. Courtesy of Air France Public Relations Department

Opposite (top): Chinese Scholarship recipients Pauline Chu, class of 1966 (*left*), and Linda Chang, class of 1965 (*right*), at Valley Forge National Historical Park (PA), fall 1962. Courtesy of Margaret Woods Keith

Opposite (bottom, left to right): Beatrice MacGeorge, class of 1901, with Chinese Scholarship recipients Amy Cheng, class of 1961; Shirley Seung, class of 1962; and Su Ling, MA, 1961. Courtesy of Margaret Woods Keith

RESISTING THE OATH

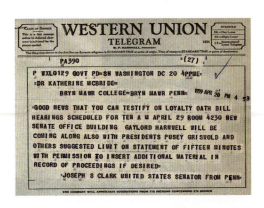

IN 1959, BRYN MAWR, like Haverford and Swarthmore, refused to take federal funds because it meant taking loyalty oaths as well. In 1968, the student newspaper reported that the FBI had investigated a black student who had gone to a conference of black students. The next time the FBI saw the student, she was in the office of a trustee who was serving as her counsel. In 1970, Bryn Mawr was the only school in Pennsylvania both to denounce and decline to sign the Pennsylvania Higher Education Assistance Act. Later declared unconstitutional, it made the reporting of disruptive students mandatory if schools were to receive state aid for scholarships and loans.

—*Catharine Stimpson, Class of 1958, "Women at Bryn Mawr," Change, April 1974.*

MISS MCBRIDE TALKS TO SENATE COMMITTEE
Discusses B.M.C. Opinion of Loyalty Oath

MISS MCBRIDE addressed a Senate Education Committee, April 28, 1959, on the subject of the National Defense Education Act. Her discussion was devoted to an explanation of Bryn Mawr's stand as regards the Mundt Loyalty Oath. This oath is required of any college applying for federal funds.

"The oath required in this section is not a test of loyalty, for the disloyal would not hesitate to take it; but it does present a danger to the freedom of thought and inquiry essential in a democratic society."

First Reason Cited
As the first of her two reasons for eliminating the oath, Miss McBride gave the opinion that "with the oath the Act is less likely to achieve its important objective of extending educational opportunity. We know that some of the most intelligent, perceptive and conscientious students and professors will not participate in programs the Act is designed to provide. They make this decision not—as I am sure the Committee knows—from any lack of loyalty.

"The principle that thought and inquiry must be free . . . has suffered both direct attack and more subtle erosion . . . I believe, as do many others, that to leave the oath in the Act would be to create a new and dangerous erosion of this bulwark of free thought and inquiry."

Distrust Implied
"The second reason for eliminating the requirement of the oath which I should like to present also has implications far beyond the particular programs the Act is designed to aid . . . The Act implies that Congress distrusts this particular group [students], and a special test of loyalty must be required of its members."

Turning to Bryn Mawr's specific position as illustrative of the difficulties faced by institutions in relation to the act, Miss McBride emphasized that "our relationship with our students is one of trust. The relationship is basic to the quality of education at the college."

Oath: Lack of Trust
"To establish a loan program, with an oath and affidavit required of each applicant, would in our opinion indicate a lack of trust of students . . . The loan fund is a fund within the institution, established nine-tenths by federal funds and one-tenth by institutional funds. The responsibility for it cannot be turned back to the federal government. The institution itself is responsible."

Bryn Mawr however did apply for aid to graduate study under the Act, limited by the same loyalty oath requirements. This McBride explained as follows: "Our basis for these two applications was that the programs involved could be more restricted, affecting certain departments only, and of course within those departments only those individuals willing to take the oath. We may have been wrong in our judgment of course, but in these two applications we put the possible benefits of the program above the handicap of the oath."

Miss McBride concluded her statement with the "strong conviction that an oath required for any part of the program is handicap to the objectives the Act is designed to accomplish and that it is a serious new danger to the freedom of thought and inquiry that we are as a nation committed to support."

Reprinted from the *College News*, May 20, 1959.

STEADY AIMS IN CHANGING TIMES: 1942–1970

JOHN F. KENNEDY
MASSACHUSETTS

COMMITTEES:
FOREIGN RELATIONS
LABOR AND PUBLIC WELFARE

United States Senate
WASHINGTON, D.C.

February 19, 1959

President Katherine McBride
Bryn Mawr College
Bryn Mawr, Pennsylvania

Dear President McBride:

Thank you very much for your very kind message regarding the bill which Senator Clark and I have introduced to delete the loyalty oath provisions from the National Defense Education Act of 1958.

Needless to say the clear and firm action taken by faculties of colleges such as Bryn Mawr has helped very substantially to create an environment in which there is a good chance for action by the Congress. Bryn Mawr deserves special thanks because it was among the very first to expose the implications of this provision to American education.

Every good wish.

Sincerely,

John F. Kennedy

JFK:mef

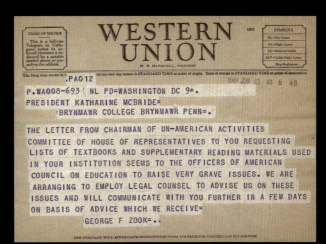

Top: Letter, Senator John F. Kennedy to Katharine McBride, February 19, 1959, thanking President McBride for Bryn Mawr's efforts in helping Congress defeat the NDEA's loyalty oath provision

Bottom: Telegram, George F. Zook (1885–1951), president of the American Council on Education, to Katharine McBride, June 10, 1949, regarding the request by the House Committee on Un-American Activities for Bryn Mawr to submit a list of textbooks and reading materials used in its courses

Opposite: Telegram, Senator Joseph S. Clark (D-PA) to Katharine McBride, April 20, 1959, confirming President McBride's scheduled testimony against the loyalty oath provision of the National Defense Education Act (NDEA) of 1958. To receive funding through the NDEA beneficiaries were

AMENDING EDUCATION ACT OF 1958

Hearings before the Subcommittee on Education of the Committee on Labor and Public Welfare, United States Senate.
Sixty-eighth Congress. First Session on S. 819
Amending Loyalty Provision of National Defense Education Act of 1958
April 29 and May 5, 1959

Testimony of Katharine E. McBride, President of Bryn Mawr College

I APPRECIATE AN OPPORTUNITY to testify in behalf of Senate Bill 819. Eliminating subsection (f) of Section 1001, Title X, would strengthen the Act. The oath required in this section is not a test of loyalty, for the disloyal would not hesitate to take it; but it does present a danger to the freedom of thought and inquiry essential in a democratic society.

I think I can show the nature of this danger by presenting briefly two of the chief reasons for eliminating the oath and then illustrating by the action Bryn Mawr took the difficulty the Act presents to members of a college or university who are trying to decide what is right.

The first reason for eliminating the oath is very direct and clear. With the oath the Act is less likely to achieve its important objective of extending educational opportunity. We know that some of the most intelligent, perceptive and conscientious students and professors will not participate in programs the Act is designed to provide. They make this decision not—and I am sure the Committee knows—from any lack of loyalty. They may indeed be adding an extra measure of loyalty when for the sake of principle they give up the personal or professional advantage that might come from participation in programs supported by the Act.

The principle that thought and inquiry must be free remains as important as it ever was. It is a bulwark of American life. It has suffered both direct attack and more subtle erosion. We must all of us, whether in the universities or out, be on our guard to see that not only the direct attack but the more subtle erosion is met. I believe, as do many others, that to leave the oath in the Act would be to create a new and dangerous erosion of the bulwark of free thought and inquiry.

The second reason for eliminating the requirement of the oath which I should like to present also has implications far beyond the particular programs the Act is designed to aid. The requirement of an oath is a disservice to all members of the educational community, in schools, colleges or universities. The Act implies that Congress distrusts this particular group, and a special test of loyalty must be required of its members. Those of us who work in educational institutions know very well that students and professors are loyal and that a special test of their loyalty is not necessary. We certainly think it is an unfortunate handicap for Congress to give those people in the country who do not know schools and colleges at first hand the idea that students and teachers are not just as loyal as themselves.

Turning now to Bryn Mawr's particular position, I want to report it in a little more detail than might be justified in the account of any one institution. I do so because it may be helpful to the Committee as an illustration of the difficulty institutions face in relation to the Act.

To establish a loan program, with an oath and affidavit required of each applicant, would in our opinion indicate a lack of trust of students. We thought that we could not isolate such a program, saying, "We do not believe that the affidavit and oath should have been required but it is a government requirement, and students may apply or not—as they individually wish." The loan fund is a fund within the institution, operated by the institution, established nine-tenths by federal funds and one-tenth by institutional funds. The responsibility for it cannot be turned back to the federal government. The institution itself is responsible.

We therefore decided not to apply for a loan under Title II, even though our failure to apply would mean a financial handicap to a certain number of students. We believed that the handicap to the whole student group through invading our justified trust would be a greater loss.

If the terms under which a grant of money is offered are not satisfactory it would seem to be simple and straightforward not to apply for the grant. But the matter of choice is not so simple. The requirement of the oath seems to us wrong not only in connection with the student loan program of Title II but in connection with the other programs of the Act as well. Yet we did apply under Titles IV and V.

Our basis for these two applications was that the programs involved could be more restricted, affecting certain departments only, and of course within those departments only those individuals willing to take the oath. We may have been wrong in our judgment of course, but in these two applications we put the possible benefits of the program above the handicap of the oath.

We should want to state with strong conviction that an oath required for any part of the program is a handicap to the objectives the Act is designed to accomplish and that it is a serious new danger to the freedom of thought and inquiry that we are as a nation committed to support.

Reprinted from a photocopy of the original transcript, Bryn Mawr College Archives.

COLLEGES OPPOSE U.S. NON-RED OATH
6 Schools Denounce Pledge as Condition for Student Loan under '58 Act

OPPOSITION AROSE in colleges yesterday to an anti-subversion provision of the National Defense Education Act of 1958. The provision requires students seeking loans to disclaim by affidavit belief in or support of groups advocating overthrow of the Government by force.

Six Eastern colleges—three in Pennsylvania and three in Maine—strongly urged repeal of this provision.

The colleges were Bryn Mawr, Haverford and Swarthmore, all Quaker institutions near Philadelphia, and Bates, Bowdoin and Colby in Maine. They held that the requirement struck at "free inquiry and association that are the heart of academic freedom," as the Bowdoin faculty put it.

Bryn Mawr and Haverford authorities were so strongly opposed that they will not participate in the program unless the requirement is removed.

Allegiance Oath Upheld

None of the colleges took exception to a companion requirement of the act that borrowers take an oath of allegiance. To require such an oath was held to be "a necessary accompaniment of citizenship" and the "right of the Government."

Under the act students may borrow a maximum of $5,000 at the rate of no more than $1,000 a year. No interest is charged until one year after the student leaves school. Then loans are repaid over ten years with interest fixed at 3 per cent.

The presidents of the Maine colleges—Charles F. Phillips of Bates, James S. Coles of Bowdoin and J. Seelye Bixler of Colby—issued the following joint statement: "The faculties and administrations of Bates, Bowdoin and Colby Colleges are in agreement that the disclaimer provision in Section 1001 (f), Title X, of the National Defense Act of 1958 constitutes a serious threat to academic freedom. They join in urging Congress to eliminate this provision of the act at the earliest opportunity."

At Haverford, Dr. Hugh Borton, the president, said the college felt that to file the disclaimer would be "tantamount to signing away one's right to freedom of thought as well as endorsing a government action which makes the individual's opportunity for education contingent upon his personal beliefs."

Haverford is making loans to its students at comparable rates to prevent hardship.

Miss Katharine E. McBride, Bryn Mawr president, said the college "would like to apply for loans and will if the act is amended." Dr. Courtney Smith, president of Swarthmore, said his school had made no final decision on whether to stay out of the program or not but he declared that "everyone here is very much opposed to filing."

Both the Association of American Colleges and the 40,000-member American Association of University Professors have taken stands against the disclaimer affidavit.

Reprinted from the *New York Times*, January 22, 1959.

Opposite: Katharine McBride with members of the field hockey team, 1951. Photograph by Wilbur Boone

STEADY AIMS IN CHANGING TIMES: 1942–1970

75

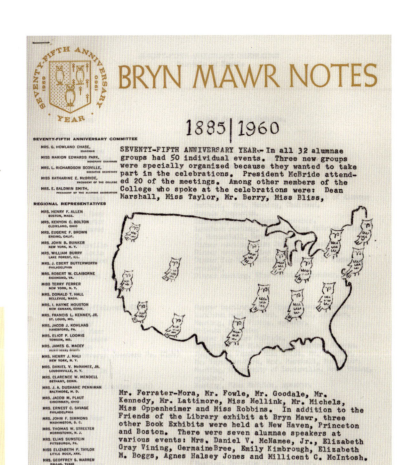

The general plan is to focus the series of meetings on the rapidly developing fields of knowledge. In so doing we should be able to consider Bryn Mawr's work and in considering our own work, reassess the state of teaching and research in those fields in which new developments are rapid, some of them sufficiently rapid to reshape the present-day world.

—Katharine E. McBride

Clockwise from top right: Announcement of nationwide alumnae events in honor of Bryn Mawr's seventy-fifth anniversary, 1960; guests at the college's seventy-fifth anniversary dinner at the Philadelphia Museum of Art, April 20, 1960 (photograph by Peter Dechert); invitation to the anniversary dinner at the art museum

Opposite: Newspaper clippings on Bryn Mawr's seventy-fifth anniversary celebrations, 1960

BUZZ IN: BRYN MAWR COMPETES IN THE COLLEGE BOWL

BRYN MAWR TO GO ON COLLEGE BOWL

ON THE SCREEN you see before you, battling to stay there next week, East Podunk University and Bryn Mawr College. This will be a tense match, with two fine groups of students, and we don't have much time so we'll start right in: You all know the rules?—General nods of assent. All right, here's our first question. What is the date of the French Revolution?—Frantic buzzing at a Bryn Mawr station, quickly echoed by Podunk U.—That question goes to Bryn Mawr. What's your answer, Miss?—Well, it's a difficult question. You could say that it began with a storming of the Bastille, and I suppose literally it did, in its violent aspect, but actually I don't think it would be unjustified to take it back as far as at least the middle of the eighteenth century. You see, it was really a revolution of the Western World, to my mind at least, and . . . —Your time is running out, Miss. I didn't get your answer. Just a date, now. Will you please state it.—Well, as I say, I hate to fix any one date; but if you insist, just arbitrarily I'd set about 1780 at the latest.—Meanwhile Podunk U. has been buzzing continuously and frantically. —Wrong. The question passes to Podunk—1879. Help! No! I mean 1789.— Right on the second try. Our next question is to give the title and author of this bit of poetry. "Water, water, everywhere, / And all the boards did shrink; / Water, water, everywhere / Nor any drop to drink." A pause, then buzz from Bryn Mawr.—All right, Bryn Mawr; have a try at the question. The author and name of the poem it comes from.—"The very deep did rot: O Christ! / That ever this should be! / Yea, slimy things did crawl with legs / Upon the slimy sea. / About, about . . .—Stop, Bryn Mawr, stop! Your time's running out. Please just answer the question.—Um, I never could get that man's name. Wasn't it Sam; Samuel, I mean. Other Bryn Mawr contestants signal wildly to coach her, meanwhile Podunk U. buzzing furiously.—I've got it! Samuel Taylor Coleridge, "The Rime of the Ancient Mariner."—Right for Bryn Mawr. You were lucky there. The time was just about to run out. Next question now; let's move along a little faster; take your time now. What is the date . . . —Outburst of buzzing from Bryn Mawr.—January fifteenth, nineteen sixty.—Bryn Mawr, if you would please let me finish reading the question. What . . . —Loud and prolonged buzzing from Bryn Mawr.—I haven't even read the question yet! Please wait until its conclusion.—A member of the Bryn Mawr contingent mysteriously hunched over and tugging at something on the desk in front of her.—I'm sorry, I can't help it. I got my knitting needle caught in the buzzer. It won't go off.—Pandemonium broke loose; one girl fainted with the strain. There was a brief intermission.

Of course we realize that a college education is more than just a knowledge of facts. Well, yes, but let's get on with the show.

Reprinted from the *College News*, January 15, 1960.

THE COLLEGE BOWL

ANNASA, KATA, KALO, KALE, IA, IA, IA, NIKE became a nationally known cheer this fall when Bryn Mawr's term in the T.V. College Bowl contest successively routed the University of California at Riverside, Notre Dame, the University of Richmond and the University of Miami. In their fifth contest, Thanksgiving weekend, they bowed to Barnard College. Coached by Dr. Robert Patten, assistant professor of English, the four girls brought back $13,000 in scholarship prize money for the College. To this, members of the Board of Directors of the College added another $3,000. The $16,000 will go into an endowment fund, the income of which will be used for freshman scholarships.

The winning team was chosen from 149 volunteers. They were Diane Ostheim, a junior from Princeton, N.J., majoring in Spanish; Captain Ashley Doherty, a freshman from Morgantown, W. Va., the College's "Betty Crocker Homemaker of Tomorrow Scholar"; and Ruth Gais and Robin Johnson, both seniors from New York City, majoring in classics (Greek and Latin) and archaeology, respectively. The two alternates were sophomores, Joanne Basin of Forest Hills, N.J.; and Mary Laura Gibbs of Huntsville, Texas.

No elaborate training program was set up and no official academic easement offered the team. The girls have their own explanation for their winning streak: they have "junky minds" that retain information whether or not it is important. They hope the scholarships will go to students with similar talents.

Reprinted from the *Bryn Mawr Alumnae Bulletin*, Winter 1968.

Opposite (top): Bryn Mawr's College Bowl team, 1967–68. Diane Ostheim, class of 1969; Ashley Doherty, class of 1971; Ruth Gais, class of 1968; and Robin Johnson, class of 1968. Photograph by Conrad Waldinger (New York)

Opposite (bottom left): Bryn Mawr's College Bowl team, 1967–68. Gais, Ostheim, Johnson, and Doherty posing with the Athena Lemnia in Thomas Great Hall

Opposite (bottom right): Bryn Mawr's College Bowl team, 1960–61, left to right: Anne Stebbins, class of 1960; Lois D. Potter, class of 1961; Sarah Bosworth, class of 1961; and Nancy Hoffman, class of 1960

EXPANSIONS: CANADAY, ERDMAN, SCIENCE

MISS McBRIDE DISCUSSES PLANS FOR SCIENCE BUILDING
Will Contain Facilities for Science Teaching, Research

PRESIDENT MCBRIDE discussed plans for the new science center on campus at today's commencement exercises. The project will cost about $1,600,000.

When completed, the center will be the first at any women's college for students in science at all levels from the first year to the Ph.D. It will occupy nearly four acres of the 70-acre campus and will bring together the college's full program of teaching and research in biology, chemistry, geology, mathematics and physics.

Planning for the center is the result of Bryn Mawr's 15 years of experience in developing a program of coordinated teaching in the sciences and mathematics. In the new layout of buildings, departments that function together will share expensive equipment necessary for interrelated work and duplication of libraries will be reduced to a minimum.

The proposed building program provides for two new units to be added to the present unit, Park Hall, built in 1938, which now houses the chemistry and geology departments. A three-story structure will be built for the biology department and another for the mathematics and physics departments.

The biology building, which will cost about $900,000, will contain laboratories and classrooms for regular work; special laboratories for teaching microbiology, biochemistry and anatomy; a lecture hall seating 125; a library; and an isotope room for storing and processing radioactive compounds.

The physics and mathematics building will have laboratories located below ground level in which the precise control of temperature and humidity necessary for modern physical research can be maintained. The plans also call for laboratories and classrooms on the upper floors, an optics laboratory, a lecture hall and a library in this unit, which will cost about $700,000.

President McBride announced preliminary gifts of $200,000 toward the center. "The building program will be accelerated," she said, "because of the crowding in all buildings in the College and because of the effort to put the teaching of science on the best possible basis in view of the demand for highly qualified personnel.

"Present shortages of scientists prepared to undertake basic research or teaching are known to be serious," President McBride went on to say, "and there is evidence that they will become more critical. Teachers of science are in such short supply that the education of future scientists is threatened."

Miss McBride also said that proportionally large numbers of Bryn Mawr students studied in science or mathematics. A recent survey showed that one quarter of all Ph.D.'s at Bryn Mawr were taken in science. A study of occupations showed that teaching was the most frequent choice of Bryn Mawr graduates holding A.B.'s, M.A.'s, or Ph.D.'s.

Reprinted from the *College News*, May 31, 1955.

Top: Mary S. Gardiner (1896–1982), professor of biology from 1928 to 1965, in the Marion Park Science Building during renovations, c. 1955–56

Bottom: Park Science Building, built 1937–38

Opposite: Clipping from the *Philadelphia Inquirer* commending Bryn Mawr's plans to improve its science facilities, June 4, 1955

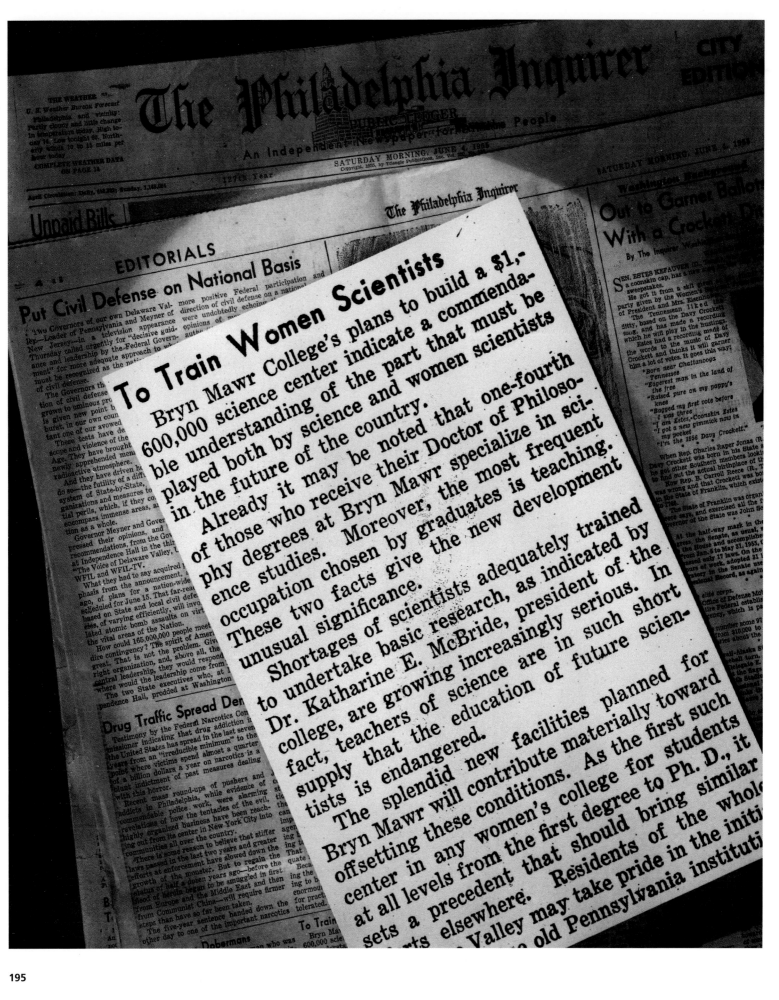

OPEN MEETING RESULTS:
REAR WING ADDITION CONSIDERED SOLUTION TO LIBRARY PROBLEM

Laura Krugman, Class of 1967

PRESIDENT MCBRIDE outlined plans presently under consideration for an addition to the library at an open meeting for students and faculty in the Common Room February 25.

The two most promising suggestions concern a new extension behind the library and an entirely separate new building.

The first idea offered for an enlargement came from Charles David, former history professor at Bryn Mawr, who wanted to build additional stacks underground. Interested in the possibility, the school called in architect Douglas Ore for consultation. He completed his study in 1958.

Mr. Ore considered a general construction plan for the campus, which includes the new physical science wing, the new dormitory, and eventually a building for the humanities as well as the library addition.

One of Mr. Ore's solutions to the library problem was filling in the Cloisters for stack space. The space would have been insufficient, and the college refused to consider the plan.

Mr. Ore contributed three additional plans. One would have destroyed the Deanery and built the core of a humanities building. This idea, however, limited space for both buildings involved.

A second suggestion would have put large stacks underground from the library to Taylor Hall. The library staff members here objected to working in artificial light in place of natural daylight.

The final, favored proposal envisioned a five-story building at the back of the library, digging into the hill. This rectangular structure, with three stories below ground, could provide space for the college's book needs for 15 to 20 years.

An important point that must be remembered, Miss McBride warned, is that the school cannot expect to raise funds for new space if all available room is not utilized.

Mr. Metcalf, a new consultant called in last summer, supported the five-story extension for the library and proposed looking further into the future's needs by considering a larger building separate from the library.

The library addition must provide space for 275,000 to 300,000 volumes. The present shortage of shelf space and facilities for processing has hampered the purchase of new books, and the library hopes to fill in the deficiency when room is available.

A faculty committee has suggested that about 20 offices be added, as well as seminar rooms for all departments requiring them to meet the needs of the enlarged graduate school and faculty . . .

Reprinted from the *College News*, February 28, 1964.

When Louis Kahn came to Bryn Mawr College as "Undergraduate Eminent Speaker" in March of 1965, he very clearly, if indirectly, brought out a basic attitude toward his work. As he talked, Kahn described his buildings as if they had lives of their own, their own needs to grow and to form themselves in certain ways. It was as if the architect were merely an instrument and guide through which they could create themselves. Although the average man does not look upon his material work as an animate companion, this attitude is hardly unique with Mr. Kahn. Many of the greatest composers, poets, sculptors, and painters have experienced an intimate, almost conversational, exchange with their creations. Perhaps best known are the feelings expressed by Michelangelo when he said that it was his duty to release a kind of being already alive within the stone per *forza di levare*—by taking away, bit by bit, the extraneous layers which covered its material form.

In Erdman, Mr. Kahn has created a building with a vivid existence of its own; and we of Bryn Mawr find ourselves in the demanding position of living intimately with a great work of art. There are many ways to learn to know it better, and surely the best is to visit it often and to experience the lively clarity and force of its projecting forms and light-filled spaces.

—Anne Coffin Hanson, Ph.D. 1962, Bryn Mawr Alumnae Bulletin, *Fall 1965*

COLD EYE CAST AT ERDMAN
N.H.

This building here I think I know
Built for the Bryn Mawr overflow
The workmen razz me stopping here
To watch their progress, one year slow.

Aesthetic mind begins to fret—
It looks like an erector set,
Within a wall, as if a moat,
To ward off Haverford, I bet.

I give my head a puzzled shake
To ask if there is some mistake.
Perhaps the boxes on the rook
Are tower suites in modern make.

The building's dusty, stark and steep.
The architecture makes me weep.
Thank God I've Rhoads in which to sleep,
Thank God I've Rhoads in which to sleep.

Reprinted from the *College News*, October 8, 1964.

Because of Erdman's unornamented elements, simple and regular geometry, and undisguised construction, the building has been described as brutal and unduly imposing. The naked forcefulness of the design may seem "brutal" to those who are unfamiliar with architectural purity and precision. However, although the building does impose itself upon those who see it, it also explains itself to those who look carefully. One usually associates the imposition of space on the consciousness with monumental buildings where the architecture is intended to lead one's thoughts toward the abstract or the spiritual. To many people a conscious awareness of space in ordinary living areas is unexpected and sometimes even disturbing. But the abstract and the spiritual are hardly foreign to academic life . . . Erdman's ability to impose itself—in a sense, its ability to express itself—is an indication of its life-like force which Kahn recognizes as the most important characteristic of a true work of art: "I believe firmly that we will become even more attuned to qualities that exist in the spaces that 'want to be'—qualities that transcend function and circumstance."

—Lynn Scholz, Class of 1966, Bryn Mawr Alumnae Bulletin, *Fall 1965*

Above: Interior of Eleanor Donnelly Erdman Hall (built 1960–65), 1965. Photograph by John Ebstel (1922–2000; Philadelphia)

Opposite (left): Mariam Coffin Canaday Library, built 1966–68

Opposite (right): Canaday Library at night, May 11, 1971. Photograph by Karl Dimler

AN EVOLVING CAMPUS: CHANGES IN RULES

SELF-GOV CLARIFIES DRESS REGULATIONS
Susan Harris, Class of 1960, President of Self-Gov

THE ADVISORY AND EXECUTIVE BOARDS of the Self-Government Association would like to remind you that the Dress Rule stating that pants or shorts must not be worn on "main roads, in the village, or on public transportation" has been clarified in the following manner:

Bryn Mawr resident students may not wear pants or shorts in the surrounding communities, on well-traveled roads, or on public transportation, or in places of public entertainment. Places of public entertainment include all public restaurants. Within private homes and academic institutions a resident student may wear pants or shorts.

The Advisory and Executive Boards ask you to be aware that you and all other Bryn Mawr students are on your honor to keep this rule. If you wish to see this rule changed, you may use parliamentary procedure to bring the rule up for campus consideration. But until the rule is altered by college vote, every student is equally responsible to keep this rule. A violation of the rule as it stands clarified will be brought before the Executive Board.

Reprinted from the *College News*, 1959.

THE UNESCORTED GIRL

IN THE VICINITY and, indeed, throughout the country, Bryn Mawr has acquired the reputation of being a women's college with "very liberal" rules. And on the basis of what we are or are not "allowed to do," we *are*, compared with other colleges, very liberal.

But we are a campus beset by dichotomies: a dichotomy between what the rules specifically contain and what may be read into them, between what we think and what we think we think. One might well say that we are liberal in action within a framework of ideological conservatism. This paradox is rooted deep in our "tradition" or "heritage." We don't have to look very far to find a parallel; the views of M. Carey Thomas are a striking example of a revolt against a tradition and yet, in some ways, a secret adherence to it.

In considering the theories behind our regulations, we were particularly intrigued with the sign-out rules. Why, we queried, does one sign out until 12:30 if one is an "unescorted girl," while, "if escorted, students may sign out until 2:00 any night of the week"? (Special dispensation, i.e., 1:30 permission, is extended to those unescorted girls who happen to frequent the opera in Philadelphia.)

Assuming that we are reasonably mature and responsible human beings, it seems illogical to draw such a distinction between "escorted" and "unescorted." An "escort" is understood to be a responsible individual who provides "adequate chaperonage" for the student. This person may be either male or female; in fact, he/she may be just about anybody who is our age or older, as long as the individual is not a resident of the Bryn Mawr campus.

The little book informs us that the reason for "adequate chaperonage" is to transfer legal responsibility for the student from the college to other responsible individuals. This is why the "chaperone" may not be a resident of the campus. The only question remaining in our minds is whether the college is *really* not legally responsible for us when we are signed out unescorted.

Assuming that the college does disclaim responsibility for us when we are signed out until 2:00, why is it willing to accept such responsibility until 12:30, or, in the event of opera attendance, till 1:30, or, returning from college vacations, till 2:00? Apparently, in the hours after 12:30, the college is willing to be responsible for us. If we are "on our own," we are not a very good risk.

If, as is more likely, the college is responsible for us, escorted or not, why do we require chaperones at all? We do not feel that either the college or the Self-Gov constitution means to suggest that non-resident students or Haverford or Penn students are more mature and responsible than we are.

Reprinted from the *College News*, March 2, 1955.

RHOADS, ERDMAN ESTABLISH RULE TO PERMIT SMOKING IN ROOMS

EMPTY SMOKERS in Rhoads and Erdman bear witness to the recent change in smoking rules affecting these two dorms. Lighting up in rooms became legal in Rhoads Tuesday night, September 28.

Erdman voted Tuesday night and Wednesday morning of last week, and with the ballots cast 2-1 in favor of smoking in the rooms, the rule went into effect Wednesday night.

Residents of these two halls voted by written ballot for the provisional change in the Self-Gov rule, which now allows smoking in students' rooms in Rhoads and Erdman. Vote was by simple majority, abstentions being counted with the plurality.

In Rhoads 95 students voted for the change, 27 voted against, and there were five abstentions.

The question of changing the smoking rule for Rhoads first came up three years ago when a petition was circulated to bring the issue before Self-Gov. This petition never acquired enough signatures to be brought up for consideration.

The following year the rule change actually came to a campus-wide vote, but while the majority of students voted for the change, the residents of Rhoads voted against it, and it was shelved once again.

The issue arose again last spring, when another petition was circulated to bring the smoking question before Self-Gov. The result of this petition was a campus-wide poll, with special ballots for residents of Rhoads and future residents of Erdman, where the low fire hazard would also make such a rule change feasible. The poll revealed that the majority of students, including Rhoads and Erdman residents, favored a change.

When the Board of Trustees met in late spring, members voted in favor of a provisional change in the smoking rules in Rhoads and Erdman, allowing students of these two halls to smoke in their rooms. Because the rule change is provisional, all residents in each of the dorms affected were required to vote for or against the change by written ballot. As long as the change remains provisional, it will have to be re-voted in each hall every fall.

No rigid rules governing the new smoking regulations have been set up, although it is likely that certain restrictions will be imposed by the fire department. The freedom to smoke applies only to students' rooms; smoking will still not be allowed in corridors, dining rooms, etc.

Reprinted from the *College News*, October 8, 1965.

ALL CONSTITUTIONAL REVISIONS PASSED IN BMC VOTING

AS A RESULT of last week's campus vote, four major constitutional changes were approved by two-thirds or more of the Bryn Mawr Self-Government Association.

On the drinking rule, 508 students voted to abolish the clause prohibiting all alcoholic beverages on campus, while 155 voted to retain the existing regulation. Subject to board approval, the final campus recommendation will permit drinking in the students' room and in one designated room in the College Inn.

The decision to give second semester freshmen 8:00 A.M. sign-outs was approved by a 509 to 174 vote. Concerning the dress regulations, 686 voted to abolish the dress rule and 109 voted to retain it.

The proposed change in parietals, allowing men in the rooms until 12:30 A.M. on Fridays and Saturdays, was approved by 532 students. The vote to retain the existing rule was 115.

These recommendations were discussed at a meeting of the student committee of the board of directors last night and will be reviewed at January's general meeting of the board. Second semester will probably be the earliest that any approved changes will become effective.

Reprinted from the News *(Bryn Mawr-Haverford), December 13, 1968.*

Above: Students in a dorm room, c. 1950s
Opposite: Students with athletic equipment, c. 1950s

ANOTHER LEAP INTO THE FUTURE

BRYN MAWR has taken another stride forward with the passage of legislation permitting men in the dorms after dinner.

The voting results in the individual halls indicate that the majority of the students support the new rule. A few objections, however, have been raised. The problem of prowlers, the resulting inconvenience to girls in the evening, and the temptation to take advantage of the new restriction—all may threaten its success.

(A more subtle criticism centers around the possibility that the more lenient rules will result in a toppling of Bryn Mawr's standards, that prospective students will be lured more by the thought of unlimited privileges than other factors.)

The new rule, however, should be regarded not as a threat to the college's standard of morality, but more properly as a practical amendment, which, in spirit and in fact, is consistent with the college's already existing rules.

Pem West, by passing a 10 P.M. limit on Friday, Saturday, and Sunday nights, and a 7:30 limit every other night, seems to have devised the most sensible solution. This way, girls have a place to take dates on Sunday nights, a date night, as well as a place to have private and leisurely coffee after week-day dinners. And girls who wish to wander around the dorm in bathrobes and curlers will still be able to do so after 7:30 during the week.

If two things are kept in mind—first, that the new rule has been passed purely in the interests of practicality, and, second, that under the honor system, all students assume individual responsibility for their actions—there should be no question of abuse of the new rule.

Regulations in other areas of the honor system (smoking, class attendance) may have seemed revolutionary, even immoral, at one time; now they merely contribute to the flexible and efficient organization of the college.

Reprinted from the *College News*, October 1, 1964.

CURRICULAR DEVELOPMENT

EVALUATION OF CURRICULUM BEGINS
Mary Kobrak, Class of 1964

BRYN MAWR'S CLASS of 1969 and its successors will benefit from an entirely renovated curriculum, adjusted more realistically to the rapid flow of events in both high school and graduate school development.

With this in mind, a faculty committee is undertaking a two-year evaluation of how a liberal arts education is to be carried out in the latter part of the twentieth century. It is imperative that this faculty study be accompanied by a more intensive concern with curriculum problems by the students.

To this effect, the Student Curriculum Committee will split up into various subcommittees to study specific problems, which are generally relevant to the overall plan of study, and then meet with its faculty counterpart to exchange ideas and present their points of view.

The Student Curriculum Committee is composed of a major from each department as well as two reps from each class, and demands close communication between students and committee members. Subcommittees will carry out surveys in their areas of interest to provide opportunities for this communication, and we hope that on a more informal level we will receive your ideas and proposals.

The topics we shall be dealing with are the following: a study of the requirements from a historical point of view, that is, why they were established and whether they still fulfill their original purpose; a consideration of interdepartmental courses, the difficulties in setting them up and their value to the students; a study of various elements within the senior year, such as honors and whether the program is presently as valuable as it can possibly be; comprehensive conferences, with regard to their stated function and whether they fulfill it. We welcome any additional suggestions.

Our activities to date have centered around two projects. The first one is gathering reading lists for all courses in the curriculum, which we will mimeograph and distribute at the end of the year, at a charge sufficient to cover costs.

We have also engaged in rewriting the course list which we mail out to freshmen during the summer. This is being done by the department reps in conjunction with the professors who teach the courses.

We have used these occasions to consult with the different faculty on departmental problems brought up at the various meetings discussing the courses in each department.

Reprinted from the *College News*, November 1, 1963.

CURRICULUM

ON THE BRYN MAWR CAMPUS, the Curriculum Committee is an important, if little publicized, influence. It acts primarily as an information center through which students can have answered any questions concerning curriculum. The committee is striving to establish a working unity between students and professors, through frequent meetings with the faculty. Also, the committee changes outdated curriculum when the need for this arises.

New courses and majors are added when there is a concrete demand for them. The most recent example of this is the addition of the music major. There has been considerable demand for establishment of such a major; plans for this have been completed this spring. Unfortunately, the music major will not be available to the class of 1954, but will go into effect for the present Sophomore class.

In a recent poll of students conducted by the committee, it was found that a majority felt that the two-oral requirement should be kept. However, students expressed a desire that Latin be included. With the addition of a Latin oral, next year's Freshman class will have more scope in choosing their languages both in preparing for college and in actual college courses.

In addition to such actual changes in curriculum, there are many lesser known functions of the committee. Among these are the class teas which are given to acquaint future majors with course requirements and other details. During Freshman Week, a tea is held for incoming Freshmen, at which members of the committee answer questions about their respective departments. In the Spring, a similar event is attended by the Sophomores.

The Curriculum Committee at Bryn Mawr is unique among most colleges. But many students show little interest in the committee and seem hardly to know of its existence. The committee and its faculty coordinators spend time and thought in sounding out students and attempting to organize curriculum changes for our benefit. If the committee is to function effectively, the students themselves must cooperate. Open meetings are announced, and suggestions and opinions are welcome at any time.

Reprinted from the *College News*, May 6, 1953.

Left and right: Students studying, February 1968

MODERN LITERATURE COURSES TO FULFILL BMC REQUIREMENT

TRADITION HAS BEEN BENT at Bryn Mawr with the changing of the literature requirement last spring for the Class of 1966 and following classes.

The requirement, formerly fulfilled only by certain courses in English, Latin, Greek, and Biblical literature, as well as by Greek I, can now be met by courses in modern literature as well.

Bryn Mawrters are now considered "literate" with English 101, and English 200 courses except Chaucer and Representative English Novelists; French 201, 202, and 300 courses; German 202 and 300 courses; and Greek 101, 201, 203 (Greek Literature in Translation), and 301. Greek I no longer fulfills the literature requirement.

Biblical Literature; Italian 201, 202, 303, and 304; Latin 101 and 201; Russian 300 courses; and Spanish 300 courses are also acceptable.

"We live in a changing, increasingly modern age," commented a junior (juniors are not affected by the change), sophomorically on the changed requirement.

Reprinted from the *College News*, October 11, 1963.

BRYN MAWR RECEIVES GRANT FOR RUSSIAN STUDIES
Three Colleges Share Carnegie Corp. Gift of $105,000

A GRANT of $105,000 for the establishment of a program of Russian studies has been made jointly to Bryn Mawr, Haverford, and Swarthmore Colleges by the Carnegie Corporation of New York. It is expected that the joint program will be inaugurated next fall when new appointments to the faculties will be made.

President McBride pointed out that "the long neglect of Russian studies has resulted in a serious situation." Despite "the importance of the Russian language, history, and culture for the world today," college students have a limited opportunity to take courses on Russia.

Reprinted from the *College News*, December 15, 1948.

TAKING A STAND: THE CIVIL RIGHTS ERA

CIVIL RIGHTS CONFERENCE ATTRACTS STUDENTS FROM TWENTY COLLEGES
Anne Lovgren, Class of 1966

OVER 150 DELEGATES from both sides of the Mason-Dixon Line are expected at Bryn Mawr and Haverford for the civil rights conference, "The Second American Revolution." Twenty colleges have already accepted invitations, and more are anticipated. In addition to these students another 50 are expected from Swarthmore and Lincoln colleges. While at the conference, the visiting students will live at Bryn Mawr and Haverford.

SNCC (Student Nonviolent Coordinating Committee) and CORE (Congress of Racial Equity) field workers who have had considerable experience in civil rights problems have also been invited to attend. The conference committee is offering financial assistance to these workers and to some southern student delegates who might not otherwise be able to attend.

The delegates and Bryn Mawr-Haverford students will attend a full two and one-half days of lectures, seminars, discussions and entertainment events.

A speaker and two discussions will highlight Friday's program. In the afternoon, the prominent Negro historian John Hope Franklin, presently Chairman of the Department of History at Brooklyn College, and Chairman-elect of the History Department at the University of Chicago, will address the conference.

In the evening, Reverend Shuttlesworth, Head of the Southern Educational Conference, will hold a discussion with either Malcolm X, a leader of the Black Muslims, or William Worthy, correspondent for the *Baltimore Afro-American*. Mr. Worthy is an advocate of a Negro labor party as a method of solving both racial and economic problems.

Mr. Worthy has agreed to speak in place of Malcolm X, in the event that the public speaking ban imposed on him by the Black Muslims has not been lifted by the time of the conference. Friday night's program will also include a debate between James Forman, Executive Secretary of SNCC, and James Kilpatrick, editor of the *Richmond Newsletter* and author of *The Case for Segregation*.

On Saturday morning a discussion will be held between Mr. Forman; Herbert Hull, Labor Secretary of the NAACP; and Bayard Rustin, leader of the March on Washington. Several members of Congress have also been invited to join in this discussion.

Saturday afternoon will be devoted to seminar discussions. Nine seminars will be held, the topics of which are Voting; Housing; Education; Violence, Non-violence and Civil Disobedience; Psychology of Prejudice; Federal Executive and State Action; Legislative and Judicial Action; Economics; and Chester, Pennsylvania—a Case Study.

Prominent persons in each of these fields have been invited to moderate and contribute to the discussion. As of now, 35 official acceptances from these persons have been received.

A maximum of twenty students may attend each seminar. Each person who registers for a seminar will receive a 40-page booklet prepared by BMC-Haverford committees containing analyses and possible solutions to the problems within each of the seminar conference topics.

Registration for the seminars will begin this week for Bryn Mawr and Haverford students.

Saturday evening will be devoted to entertainment in Goodhart Auditorium. The program will include Godfrey Chambers, star of the Living Premise (a dramatic improvisational group whose work during the last year has dealt often with the Civil Rights question).

After the entertainment at Goodhart, students will go to the dormitories for informal gatherings and discussions. The final event of the conference will be held late Sunday morning when Howard Zinn will lecture. Mr. Zinn is a former professor at Spelman College, which he was asked to leave because of his views on civil rights.

Co-chairmen Kathy Boudin and Alan Raphael have planned that Saturday's program be held at Bryn Mawr; Friday's and Sunday's at Haverford.

Reprinted from the *College News*, January 14, 1964.

Above: Program for the Second American Revolution, a civil rights conference sponsored by Bryn Mawr and Haverford colleges, February 7–9, 1964

STUDENT DEMONSTRATORS PROTEST SEGREGATION IN CAMBRIDGE IN ATTEMPT TO SECURE GREATER CIVIL LIBERTIES FOR NEGROES
Leslie Coen, Class of 1966

ABOUT 20 MILES FROM WASHINGTON, D.C., and only 150 miles from Bryn Mawr, the town of Cambridge, Maryland, still practices almost total segregation. Its bowling alleys, public swimming pool, and all but one of its restaurants do not serve to Negroes; its movie theater requires that Negroes sit in the last three rows of the balcony.

But more important than that, 40% of the Negro working force is unemployed, and Negroes make up 30% of the town's population of 15,000. Those jobs open for Negroes are usually part-time, domestic, or unskilled—the meanest, least attractive work in the town's seasonal industries.

With these poor prospects for employment after graduation, Cambridge's Negro high school offers no commercial courses. Consequently, Negroes will remain untrained for better jobs, should they come along. No Negroes attend the white high school, although the schools are officially integrated from the fourth grade through the twelfth grade. Schooling is arranged according to districts, and since the districts have been gerrymandered to create one that is exclusively Negro and four that are exclusively white, Negroes must apply for admittance to white schools. Nine applied last fall, but the three that got in could not bear the tension and harassment, and so, left after nine days.

Cambridge was offered federal aid for urban renewal last year, and turned it down, yet most streets in the Negro section have no sewers and are flooded all spring. This district is very poor, with dilapidated houses and unpaved streets. The poorest whites are much better off than all the Negroes.

Eleven girls from Bryn Mawr, I among them, went to Cambridge these last two Saturdays, to help the Negroes. The local NAACP is a conservative, unsuccessful body. Anything that has been done in the last year to advance integration has been done through CNAC—the Cambridge Non-Violent Action Committee—started by Baltimore Negroes and whites, now supported by groups from Swarthmore, Haverford, Goucher, Lehigh, and Maryland State. We worked with CNAC, whose program includes picketing, demonstrating, boycotting discriminatory businesses, and voter education and registration.

More than 60 demonstrators have been arrested so far, on arbitrary, trumped-up charges that range from "disorderly conduct" to "swearing at an officer." Thirty-two were arrested at one time for assaulting an officer. (All thirty-two "assaulted" the same officer, who was seen the next day, in perfect physical condition.) It is a non-violent group that surprises hostile policemen who threaten arrest by making no moves of resistance—they sing, and pray. They have made some progress, but it is still insignificant— a few jobs are now open; a large, integrated union of unemployed men has developed; and a voter registration drive, last year, helped defeat a strongly pro-segregation county official.

There is a lot of fear in Cambridge. Arbitrary arrests of Negroes have created a sense of hostility to the law. Negroes and whites won't go alone into each other's districts, separated, appropriately enough, by Race Street. Employed Negroes won't join CNAC for fear of losing their jobs. The unemployed have nothing to lose, and some, including many young people, have become extremely enthusiastic about CNAC. Most older Cambridge Negroes, thinking that action on their part will cause an eruption of a Mississippi-type crisis, are reluctant to move. They could easily register to vote; it seems to me that CNAC's most valuable project is making this known, in an individual, door-to-door voter-education campaign.

I went down to Cambridge certain of the need for integration, but dubious of these methods. Like most Bryn Mawrters I've talked with, I doubted the efficacy, and advisability, of having car loads of college students descend on a town, to help older, and more experienced citizens in an "internal" matter. I feared a presumptuous attitude on the part of the students, and resentment in the town. But after joining hand-in-hand with Negroes and whites in the most spirited singing that I've ever heard; after having my picket line spit on and jeered at; and especially, after helping in a perfectly integrated, crowded church kitchen, to serve hot dogs, potato salad, and Kool-Aid to what seemed like thousands of enthusiastic people, I realized that this is what must be done.

The support of the college student, both Negro and white, is needed to generate a desire for progress among Negroes who are deprived of their fundamental rights. In Cambridge, this support is given in a modest, unassuming manner. Leadership is shared among Negroes and whites, adults and students. What I was impressed with most at that hectic church supper was the perfectly relaxed atmosphere of friendship and equality, which, I believe, can be said to be typical of the whole CNAC movement. This atmosphere, certainly, must be spread through the whole nation, if integration moves made now are to have any success in the future.

Reprinted from the *College News*, May 8, 1963.

BMC JOINS OTHER COLLEGES
Encourages Negro Applicants
Edna Perkins, Class of 1966

BRYN MAWR has joined with several other colleges in the area in an attempt to increase the number of applications from Negro high school students, the Administration announced this week.

Bryn Mawr has also joined Penn, Haverford, Swarthmore, Drexel, Temple, Beaver and LaSalle to encourage applicants from the Philadelphia area. This program will be under the auspices of the National Scholarship Service and Fund for Negro Students.

The college is cooperating with the Ivy colleges, the "seven sisters," and the College Admissions Center in a program to acquaint Negro students and their advisers with the opportunities available to them. The program has recently received a grant of $38,000 from the Carnegie Corporation.

Mrs. Broughton, Director of Admissions, noted that few Negroes apply to Bryn Mawr. Some high school advisers, she says, are often surprised to learn that Bryn Mawr is willing to accept their students.

They often think of the "seven sisters" as schools for rich girls and snobs. Also, they fail to realize the availability of financial aid to qualified applicants.

Because of poor standards in high school, not many Negroes are prepared for work at Bryn Mawr. Although in these cases the Admissions Office will not expect outstanding performance on entrance exams, it will accept only those students whose high school records indicate an ability to take advantage of educational opportunities.

Mrs. Broughton believes that the current Negro movement will be important in encouraging Negroes to apply to top colleges.

Reprinted from the *College News*, March 6, 1964.

Above: Martin Luther King, Jr., who delivered the baccalaureate sermon to the graduating class of 1966, with Katharine McBride, May 29, 1966

EDITORIAL

PREJUDICE is evidenced in various forms and it is a shock to many of us when we discover one of them so close that we are obligated not to ignore it. In the recent controversy over obtaining equal privileges in the Ville for every Bryn Mawr student, regardless of color, the campus as a whole has been aroused and plans were advanced to try to change the situation. None of the plans—passive resistance, persuasion, or legal action—has been found necessary. Those who have been concerned with the problem are very appreciative that there has been a change in policy on the part of El Greco restaurant.

It is the opinion of the owner of El Greco and the Undergrad Council that all the facts in the case should be published, since widespread college discussion has given rise to some misleading rumors.

In recent years, El Greco pursued the policy of refusing service to Negroes in booths, unless they were in mixed groups, although it did serve Negroes at the counter.

This year, when a Negro student was refused service, the Presidents of Undergrad and Self-Gov contacted the restaurant owner. He felt that if he were to serve Negroes, his business might suffer. The campus was growing concerned, for it was felt that in accepting Negro and White students on an equal basis, the College had the responsibility of offering them equal opportunities in the community. At the same time, it was the opinion of the college lawyer and a lawyer in the owner's family that the restaurant's policy did not conform to Pennsylvania law.

When the restaurant owner spoke to Miss Howe and Mr. Smedley a week after seeing the student representatives, he said that he felt that the climate of opinion had changed sufficiently to enable the restaurant to alter its policy.

Realizing that there is agreement on this problem in principle, we know that it is easier for us as students to hold this view than for the owner of El Greco, as a businessman, to put it into practice; therefore we are particularly appreciative. Because of this change in policy there is one more instance in which Negroes are offered equal opportunities.

Reprinted from the *College News*, January 13, 1954.

FOUR FROM BMC ARRESTED IN CHESTER SCHOOL PICKETS
C. Brooks Robards, Class of 1964

FOUR BRYN MAWR STUDENTS, Kathy Boudin, '65, President of Alliance; Edna Perkins, '66, *College News* reporter; Dana Purvis, '67; and Barbara Ranney, '65, were arrested this morning in Chester while picketing at the Franklin Street Elementary School. The students have been picketing for several days in protest of poor conditions at the school and were arrested for blocking the doors so that no one could enter. They were first taken to the Chester Police Station where other picketers including Chester residents and students from Swarthmore and Haverford followed them, marching in front of the police station. Early this afternoon after a crowd had formed in protest of the arrests, they were moved to the Broad Meadows County Jail, which is about 10 miles outside of Chester.

When this reporter, accompanied by Clara Perkins, Edna Perkins' sister, attempted this afternoon to talk with the students being held at Broad Meadows, they were refused entrance. The guard informed us that he had been ordered to admit no one to see the students arrested for picketing and give out no information.

At the Chester Police Station, officials were uncooperative, at first refusing to give any information even to Clara Perkins as the sister of one of those arrested. After some prodding, they allowed that release had been given to the bondsman so that the picketers would probably be out on bail by tonight.

They also explained on what grounds the students had been arrested. The officer at the information desk stated that the students were arrested for "unlawful assembly and affray." He said that blocking the doors of a public school was not considered picketing, which is legal, and therefore the arrests had been made. Nearly 150 were arrested Wednesday, including 40 Swarthmore students.

The following is a report on Tuesday's picketing and an explanation of the situation in Chester: Fifteen Bryn Mawr students helped picketers of Franklin Street Elementary School in Chester to effect a 100% blockade of the school in their protest of its poor conditions. The Tuesday morning picketers included Chester residents, as well as Haverford and Swarthmore students. They were able to block all people who tried to enter the school.

Swarthmore has provided a "freedom school" for students who did not attend regular classes. The demonstrators demanded an injunction from the Board of Education to close the school.

A 67% successful boycott was achieved by picketers who demonstrated last week.

Inadequate Conditions

The elementary school was built 50 years ago, with an original capacity of 500 students. There are now 1,100 attending. Conditions are so crowded that three classes have been relegated to the boiler room of a nearby housing project. There are more than 30 students in an average class.

The school is almost entirely Negro, because of its geographical location. White schools are not as crowded, because parochial institutions are available to alleviate the condition.

The Swarthmore Political Action Club has been working in Chester for several years, trying to interest Negroes in civil rights action. Tomorrow, demonstrators will continue to block those trying to enter the school. If they are arrested, the Philadelphia NAACP has offered to provide bail.

A mass meeting was held Tuesday night from 8 to 12 to discuss the demonstration.

Reprinted from the *College News*, November 13, 1963.

FBI INVESTIGATES BRENDA JEFFERSON

ON APRIL 9TH BRENDA JEFFERSON left Bryn Mawr for a Black Students' Conference at Princeton. That same day two men showed up at Pem East looking for her. When she returned several days later, she discovered that the men were agents of the FBI and that she was being investigated.

Speaking to the men over the phone, she learned that the FBI wanted to question her about "demonstrations at national monuments and black power activities." Her immediate reaction was, "You've got to be kidding"; however, she agreed to meet with the men (although not at the site they originally proposed—the Bryn Mawr train station).

Brenda went immediately to Mrs. Pruett, assistant dean, who in turn contacted Tyson Stokes, an attorney on the Board of Trustees. When Brenda finally met the FBI agents, it was at Stokes's office in Philadelphia. (She said the agents were visibly shaken by the fact that she was equipped with legal counsel.)

The men asked her questions about alleged statements of hers concerning possible riots this summer; about activities of black radicals at Bryn Mawr and Princeton; about people who might be planning riots (Brenda: "Any introductory sociology student knows riots aren't planned"); and about "defacing national monuments." She has no explanation whatsoever about the source of the last item.

After the interview, the agents apologized for involving her in the investigation. However, Brenda says she cannot help feeling that her activities may be suspected at any time. Furthermore, she is convinced that the information the FBI had about her associations at Princeton and about statements she has made could only have come to them through someone who knew her well (say, a girl in her dorm). She concludes that "either the FBI has an undercover agent here, or else someone went running to the free phone in the dead of night" to report her. The fact that no other students at Bryn Mawr (as far as she knows) have been investigated substantiates her opinion.

Reprinted from the *College News*, April 26, 1968.

Drew Gilpin Faust, Class of 1968

Mary Zaborskis, Class of 2012

DREW GILPIN FAUST (born 1947) shook the world of higher education when she became the president of Harvard University in 2007—the first woman to hold the position since the institution's founding in 1636. Yet, she was a trailblazer long before this historic appointment.

At Bryn Mawr Faust (then known as Drewdie Gilpin) served as president of her class and of the Self-Government Association (SGA). By her own admission she resisted Bryn Mawr's four major traditions—Parade Night, Lantern Night, Hell Week, May Day—but she took her duties as class president seriously, organizing Hell Week and donning a black robe for Lantern Night.[1] As SGA president from 1967 to 1968, Faust successfully convinced Bryn Mawr's board of trustees to eliminate parietals, the rules that limited the presence of men in the residence halls and governed when students were required to return to their dorms in the evening. Faust's commitment to justice was not limited to campus matters. She participated in hunger strikes and demonstrations, including a march with Martin Luther King, Jr., in Alabama in 1965, for which she skipped midterm examinations.

Faust's political engagements went hand in hand with her studies. After graduating from Bryn Mawr with a degree in history, Faust completed her graduate studies at the University of Pennsylvania, earning a master's degree (1971) and a doctorate (1975) in American civilization. She remained at Penn as a faculty member for twenty-five years. During her tenure she served as professor of history and chair of the American Civilization Department, and directed the women's studies program. Her scholarship, which focuses on the antebellum American South and the changing roles of women during the Civil War, has received countless accolades for its contributions to the field.

In 2001 Faust left Penn to become the first dean of the Radcliffe Institute for Advanced Study—the successor to Radcliffe College—in Cambridge, Massachusetts, where her sharp leadership and organizational efforts earned her the nickname "Chainsaw Drew."[2] There she worked with Harvard's administration to increase the recruitment and promotion of women at the university.

Faust has described herself as a "rebellious daughter."[3] We have seen her "rebel" against a world in which women must continue to fight for equality. As undergraduates, we are proud of the strides Faust has made, and continues to make, for women at Harvard and beyond. She is a role model for her sisters at Bryn Mawr—past, present, and future.

Above: Catherine Drew "Drewdie" Gilpin Faust (born 1947), class of 1968, February 1968. In 2007 Faust was named the first female president of Harvard University.

1. "On Rituals: Gestures of Resistance against Time," *Bryn Mawr Alumnae Bulletin*, Fall 2001.
2. Sara Rimer, "A 'Rebellious Daughter' to Lead Harvard," *New York Times*, February 12, 2007.
3. Ibid.

Dear Fellow Students,

This year has been an unusually difficult one for Self-Gov. For the first time, Self-Gov. has confronted widespread use of drugs by Bryn Mawr students, the eight o'clock sign out, the absence of any time restrictions on women in the rooms at Haverford. We have had more individual and social honor system cases this year than Self-Gov. has had in any year since I came to Bryn Mawr. Yet, the questions with which we began this year have for the most part not been answered, but, rather, refined or restated and posed again for our successors.

We still do not have the definitive answer to the "drug problem" at Bryn Mawr, although we feel that our amendment to the Constitution concerning drugs, our subsequent reinterpretation thereof, and our drug cases, involving a total of seven students, have made an important contribution towards making clear to the student body why drugs cannot be used on the Bryn Mawr campus without posing a severe legal danger to the entire community.

We do not know the solution to the problem of cohabitation posed by the absence of hours at Haverford, but, in our effort to administer the restriction on the overnight sign out to Haverford, we have discovered, as we describe elsewhere, the difficulty of maintaining a system based on honor which contains a restriction which the student body as a whole opposes.

Rather than a specific issue such as drugs or overnights, however, the real difficulty this year has been with an attitude which seems to pervade the Bryn Mawr campus as a whole and which affects many more aspects of our lives than those directly related to the Self-Gov. system. This attitude, which seems increasingly widespread, is one of the privatism and individualism, of which the basic maxim is "live and let live." In many ways, this outlook is a valuable one, for an individual must have more knowledge of himself before he will ever be of worth to a group. Moreover, this philosophy engenders great tolerance of individual difference.

Yet Bryn Mawr's individualism is harmful as well. In its extreme form it is inimical to any kind of government. The growth of anarchistic sentiment, of the number of students at Bryn Mawr who wish to live their lives as they choose without concern for the community as a whole, poses a threat to the survival of any governmental system. The danger of exaggerated individualism exists even among those who do themselves obey the letter of the system, but will not take any responsibility for the welfare or lawlessness of their neighbors. For enforcement within the Self-Gov. system assumes that an individual who sees a violation will then speak to the violator.

Although irresponsibility seems widespread, it is not all pervasive. We have seen as well manifestations of concern for Self-Gov., such as the great responsibility with which the 8 A.M. has been used, and the enthusiasm with which hall discussion groups have for the most part been greeted.

There are other hopeful signs as well: Bryn Mawr Self-Gov. cooperates with Haverford Council this year to a greater extent than ever before. We had liaison officers from and to the council, and we met jointly with the entire council several times. This bi-college cooperation promises to continue to increase in the next years.

Self-Gov. has a number of problems with which to deal, the first of which must be to reassess its relationship with the student body. Self-Gov. depends for its existence upon the assumption by each student of a large measure of responsibility. During this time of increasing anarchism, it must, therefore, be making its actions well-considered and well-known, and encourage students to participate in their own government. We hope to have begun this re-examination with the questions we have raised before the student body concerning the reporting system, the judicial process, and punishment. The resolution of this and innumerable other problems we must leave to the new board.

The experience of a year of office has taught each member of the Self-Gov. Board a great deal. At the same time, it has often proven exhausting and disillusioning for each of us, as we have recognized that the issues which seem so important to the rest of us are often of little more than fleeting concern to the student body. When we hear Miss McBride talk of how the students learn from the process of Self-Government, we know well what she means. The Boards must now work to make both the benefits and burdens of Self-Governmental responsibility more widely shared by the student body as a whole.

Drewdie Gilpin
President of Self-Gov
March 1968

Reprinted from photocopy of original, Bryn Mawr College Archives.

BLACK STUDIES

BRYN MAWR BLACK STUDENTS SUBMIT PROPOSALS ON STUDIES TO COMMUNITY

THE BLACK STUDENTS of Bryn Mawr issued a statement this week concerning proposals for Black Studies at Bryn Mawr. The statement was addressed "to the students and faculty of Bryn Mawr and Haverford." The . . . complete text of the explanatory statement follows:

To the students and faculty of Bryn Mawr and Haverford:

We, the Black girls of Bryn Mawr, have submitted certain proposals to the Administration of the College concerning Black Studies, which we hope that they will answer to favorably and that you will support.

The issue related here is not separatist or nationalist or integrationist. It is the issue that the whole nation is being asked to face; truth, *veritatem* as it says on the seal of the college. It is not the truth when American History leaves out the part Black Americans played in building this country, or when sociology courses consistently find white writers more relevant than Black. Nor is it sufficient to add a course in Black History—or Black Economics—that becomes only a perpetuation of the lie under a new guise. Black History did not develop apart from American History. It is part and parcel of it and must be taught that way. Nor is it right that professors excuse their exclusion of Black material on the grounds that their whiteness makes it impossible to understand Blacks. It's time white Americans started trying a little harder to understand Blacks, their past and their present. These demands are not just our demands, they are also your demands because we all need all the truth we can get.

Feeling as we did about the issue, we initiated the Black Studies Committee, which consists of five Black students, two white students, and three faculty advisors, Mr. Baratz, Mrs. Dunn, and Mr. Schneider. Together with the help of other Black students and interested whites, we drew up a list of proposed courses and other ideas to begin to implement some of our fine rhetoric, and we went to see the Administration.

Miracle of Century

Since then we have met with them on the average of twice a week, and they have met to discuss us and we have met to discuss them; so far we have gotten nothing, and according to Mrs. Marshall, it will be the miracle of the twentieth century if this program (the one we have proposed) goes through this year. We have submitted careful course outlines and have prepared reading lists, suggestions for the library, and lists of possible faculty members, and we are busy working on programs to supplement the knowledge of professors in the various departments so that their work in Black Studies will be both accurate and adequate. The professors working with us have been most helpful and have spent long hours in discussions on things from getting grants from foundations to whether or not our committee should be elected.

The Black students working with the committee have tried to fulfill all that the Administration has asked of them. Yet as each assignment is fulfilled there is another added. They have done little on their part and their statements are filled with contradictions. We have little reason to expect that they will act on better faith in the future than they have in the past. They cannot even be bothered to read or keep track of the material that we have submitted to them.

It is for that reason that we as Black students have taken stand behind the committee. The Administration has made vague allegations that the committee does not represent the best Black students. We unite to say it does. We hope that our white fellow students will recognize the justness and urgency of our demands and will join with us. We have nothing to lose but our chains!

Reprinted from the News *(Bryn Mawr-Haverford), April 15, 1969.*

APTHEKER NAMED AS BMC'S DIRECTOR OF BLACK STUDIES

HERBERT APTHEKER, historian and author, has been appointed to the Bryn Mawr faculty to head a program of black studies next year.

The Aptheker appointment had been expected after he had been approved earlier in the week by the student-faculty black studies committee and by the history department.

He is currently director of the American Institute for Marxist Studies.

Aptheker is the author of several books on the history of the black man in America, and he has twice received the history award from the Association for the Study of Negro Life.

The appointment came on the exact date, April 25, that had been set by the committee as that by which they "hoped" the administration would "move on" their proposals for courses and professors in the area of black studies.

Reprinted from the News (Bryn Mawr-Haverford), April 29, 1969.

ALUMNAE COMMITTEE IN OPPOSITION TO THE APTHEKER APPOINTMENT

1830 Mariposa Avenue
Boulder, Colorado 80302

25 August 1969

Dear Parents of Bryn Mawr Students:

As concerned alumnae we feel it necessary to bring to your attention the appointment of Herbert Aptheker to the Bryn Mawr College faculty. Mr. Aptheker is to teach a course in Negro history during the 1969-70 school year.

Mr. Aptheker is a self-professed member of the Communist Party, an organization which has been cited by both the Supreme Court and the U.S. Congress as a conspiracy designed to overthrow the United States government by force and violence. He is a National Committee member of the Communist Party, U.S.A. and has served as editor of Political Affairs, the theoretical journal of the CPUSA. His daughter, Bettina, was one of the originators of the so-called Free Speech Movement at Berkeley, along with Mario Savio. His propagandist works have been published mostly by official publishers to the Communist Party. He has labored to foment civil disruption. According to a 1968 testimony of Mr. J. Edgar Hoover, FBI Director, Aptheker has stated in a public speech that "The riot in the Watts area of Los Angeles in August 1965 was a step in the right direction, but it was not nearly enough."

We feel that this appointment is a gross abdication of responsibility to all members of the Bryn Mawr College community. If you feel, as we do, that the appointment of a Communist is not in the best interests of the College, we urge you to make your dissent known immediately to members of the Bryn Mawr College administration.

Sincerely yours,

Alumnae Committee in Opposition to the Aptheker Appointment

Sheila B. Nickerson '64

(Mrs. Martinus H. Nickerson), Chairman
President, Bryn Mawr Alumnae Club of Colorado

Above: Letter, Sheila B. Nickerson, Class of 1964, president of the Bryn Mawr Alumnae Club of Colorado and chairman of the Alumnae Committee in Opposition to the Aptheker Appointment, to parents of Bryn Mawr students, August 25, 1969

Opposite: Newspaper clippings on the appointment of Herbert Aptheker (1915–2003) as Bryn Mawr's director of black studies, 1969

ONE FOOT ON CAMPUS AND ONE IN THE WORLD
Kit Bakke, Class of 1968

ARRIVING AFTER A THREE THOUSAND-MILE train trip to a campus I'd never seen, I quickly realized that I was surrounded by people who were smarter and far better prepared for Bryn Mawr's academic challenges than I was. My second surprise was discovering that most of them were intent upon immediately becoming wives and graduate students. To me, that future seemed far too personal and narrow; inappropriately ordinary for who we were and for the world we were living in.

In 1967, my junior year, the personal and the ordinary had become increasingly irrelevant. The brutal war in Vietnam and the civil rights travesties in the South exposed a democracy so flawed it made me crazy. I organized a joint Bryn Mawr-Haverford chapter of Students for a Democratic Society, and demonstrated in New York and Washington DC. My senior yearbook picture shows me in a crowd of antiwar demonstrators in New York. (Kudos to the college for including it among the other portraits of intelligent-eyed young women sitting pensively under trees or draped against picturesque stone walls.)

To protest the Vietnam War, I organized a fourteen-day orange juice–only fast that attracted the attention of the *New York Times* (article reprinted at right). My political science honors paper examined the University of Pennsylvania's campus expansion into the surrounding neighborhood, primarily comprising working-class African Americans, that resulted in homeless refugees only a few miles from the Main Line. I had one foot on campus and one in the world.

Kit Bakke is the author of *Miss Alcott's E-mail: Yours for Reforms of All Kinds* (Boston: David R. Godine, 2006).

Top: Christopher Lynn "Kit" Bakke (born 1946), class of 1968

Right: "Students Fasting over Saigon War," clipping from the *New York Times*, February 8, 1966. The fast lasted fourteen days, not eight as reported here.

Opposite: Kit Bakke, class of 1968, "Attention Must Be Paid," by Kit Bakke, class of 1968, from the *College News*, January 3, 1967.

STUDENTS FASTING OVER SAIGON WAR

100 at Philadelphia Colleges Plan 8-Day Protest

Special to The New York Times

PHILADELPHIA, Feb. 7—More than 100 students at Bryn Mawr, Swarthmore and Haverford Colleges, along with several professors, reached the midway point today in an eight-day fast in protest against United States policy in Vietnam.

On the advice of physicians before the fast began, the students are drinking orange juice to protect their health. They are continuing to attend classes and are meeting daily to discuss the Vietnam problem.

Edward Hazzard, a senior at Haverford, said the purpose of the fast was to "provide an extended period of time during which intensive discussion can go on, including study of the history and development of the war, planning of action suitable to bring the war to an end, and to changing the root conditions in America that make such wars necessary."

The colleges—all founded by the Friends, or Quakers—regard the demonstration as a matter of "individual conscience and concern" and are "not endorsing the idea of the fasting."

They have made the college health services available to the students if necessary and are providing fruit juice at meal times. They also have notified the parents of all participants.

A statement issued by the students said:

"We are suspicious of a 'peace offensive' which on the one hand ends bombing of North Vietnam, an aggressive and unjust action in the first place, and on the other hand maintains the high draft rate, increases troop and material strength in Vietnam, continues indiscriminate saturation bombing, poisoning of crops and chemical warfare against villages."

STEADY AIMS IN CHANGING TIMES: 1942–1970

Attention Must Be Paid

Bell maids, maids and porters are an often-ignored part of the Bryn Mawr community. Yet as students, we live in the same buildings with most of them and see them more often than some of our professors and certainly more often than most of the administrators.

But how much do we know about them? Not much. Perhaps the first fact a freshman realizes is that they are all black. The contrast is striking: a lily-white faculty, secretarial and administrative staff and then an all-black staff of maids and porters. It promotes a "plantation" atmosphere which is patronizing, stifling and uncomfortable.

Beginning from two admittedly superficial observations -- the fact that they are not unionized and that some seem to depend heavily on student cast-off clothing for their dependents -- the NEWS did some investigating into the living conditions of the college's 100 maids and porters.

We went to see Mr. Paul Klug, comptroller and business manager of the college, about wages and pay scales of the employees. He was dumbfounded that students were interested. The mainstream of his comments dealt with "I wear a certain hat and you wear a certain hat," the assumption being that we all have our roles to play, and worrying about the employees' conditions is not the proper role of the students. He stated that he would be jeopardizing a confidential trust to give us any information at all. He refused to give us an average salary, a minimum salary (beyond assuring us that they all made at least the minimum wage set by the federal government), the highest salary or the number of salary levels. He also refused to verify any figures we brought him from the employees themselves.

Next, we went to Miss Sarah Wright, director of halls. She flatly stated that it was college policy not to give out any figures at all. We had thought that some figures ought to be public information, such as a starting salary that would be mentioned in a want-ad, for instance. This secrecy is interesting when compared to the relative openness of faculty salaries. The American Association of University Professors has a ranking of faculty salaries at colleges and universities throughout the country, and average salaries are published in the "AAUP Bulletin."

Receiving the impression that the college was not interested in having employees' salaries a topic of community discussion, we turned to the employees themselves. Our figures are difficult to interpret, and we invite the college to interpret them for us. We do not have enough knowledge or information at this time to juggle with witholding tax, social security, amounts deducted for board and room and pensions. Therefore, we can just print raw figures. One bell maid in one of the larger dorms has worked for the college since 1938. She works seven days a week, six and a half hours a day. She gets a pay check of $156.70 each month. She has to take part-time jobs to support her sick husband at home.

A bell maid in one of the smaller dorms said that she makes $85.31 every two weeks for 70 hours of work. She reports that she was promised a $10 a month raise last spring, but that she has never gotten it. A regular maid in a smaller dorm said that she makes $82 every two weeks.

Seventy-five per cent of the employees live on campus, according to Miss Wright. We are not sure if this is the number who actually live on campus, or the number who are charged for a room and meals on campus. Several of the employees have said that they have homes and families off campus and would like to bring a sandwich from home or go home to eat and who have no need for a room, but the college insists on feeding them and then charging them for it.

Miss Wright described the living situation of the employees as "fine living." We agree that it is not as bad as living in a Harlem tenement, but we doubt the validity of "fine living." For one thing, the rooms need more light, especially in the older dorms. The walls of some need painting. The plumbing is old. Some live on the top floors, and being as old as many of them are, they would never make it out of the dorm safely in a fire. Others live in the basement, where it is either freezing cold or boiling hot. In Erdman, there is a mens' wing and a womens' wing and a married couple do not even share a room.

We would like to open a dialogue within the college community about the adequacy, let alone the "fineness" of the kind of living that can be enjoyed on $156.70 a month. Bryn Mawr College employees are part of the 30 million invisible American poor. This is not a pleasant situation. What can be done about it?

The college should be a major innovating force in the fight to improve the lives of black Americans who have been ignored for so long. One program was put into practice last spring which is a step in the right direction. The college instituted a promotion-from-within policy, giving some employees added responsibility and benefits. This is an improvement, but it is a long way from a final solution. One possibility is taking the initiative in training people for jobs on campus. Ford and other corporations have vigorous in-training programs for employees who would not otherwise be qualified for the jobs available. Why couldn't the college do this? Interest in this kind of program has been expressed by the Reverend Leon Sullivan in Philadelphia. We have been told that he offered to help the college arrange such a training program last year. Next week, the NEWS hopes to have further information on such a program.

We recognize that this is a sensitive area -- the college is under financial pressure as it is, and we do not want to see anyone fired. At present though, it is evident that the college is not taking many positive steps to provide a decent, dignified human life for its maids and porters. The promotions-from-within program is a step, but it is a small one. An imaginative discussion followed by vigorous action should now be conducted by those people who are capable of changing this disturbing situation.

RECENT REFLECTIONS
Kit Bakke, Class of 1968
January 2010

"Attention Must Be Paid" I titled a heavily black-bordered article on the front page of the *College News* in fall 1967. I was the editor, and saw no reason not to tell everyone how appalled I was at the way the college treated its all-black, nonunionized maids and porters. "The College should be a major innovating force in the fight to improve the lives of black Americans," I wrote. They were people too, and I never got used to the undeserved cosseting and care they provided us much younger students. Their seven-day-a-week work schedules, cramped attic rooms, and pathetic pay stubs were downright criminal.

Bryn Mawr, with its privilege and its rigor, provided both the foil I fought against and the ammunition I used. The college couldn't keep up with the challenges of race, poverty, and imperialism as I saw them in the fast-moving late 1960s, but it also took me more seriously than anyone, including myself, ever had before. The college's underlying lesson was that I was to *make* my life, to carefully and thoughtfully construct it, not just live it.

Bryn Mawr had the skills and the nerve to give me—a young girl who knew suffering and struggle primarily through words on paper—permission to become an adult. Bryn Mawr also gave me the analytic and synthetic tools to make decisions, follow through, test results, revise, and try again. Isn't that what being a grown-up is all about?

VIETNAM

BI-COLLEGE STUDENTS JOIN DEMONSTRATION AGAINST VIETNAM WAR

APPROXIMATELY 75 STUDENTS from Haverford and Bryn Mawr were among the 75,000 people who marched down Sixth Avenue to protest the war in Vietnam.

Two buses left Bryn Mawr at about 11:30 A.M. carrying students from Baldwin, Villanova, Penn, and Harcum, and a number of local residents in addition to students from Haverford and Bryn Mawr.

Cathy Stickney, Gail Montet, and Huck White, who organized local participation in the march, all expressed pleasure at the number of people who showed up. "It was nice to see so many people come out even in the rain," Miss Montet said. She indicated that local attendance had far surpassed the organizers' expectations.

The Haverford-Bryn Mawr group was one of the last to arrive at the parade site and marched near the end of the parade. As a result they didn't actually start the mile-and-a-half march until after 4 P.M. and didn't arrive at the site of the rally in Central Park until about 5 P.M., fully an hour after the rally began.

The local organizers felt that the march accomplished its important goals. "After the McCarthy campaign a lot of people thought the anti-war movement was dead," White said. "This proved that the movement still exists."

There was, however, some doubt as to the ultimate value of the march and rally. "There is always a question of whether a demonstration will do any good," Miss Montet said.

White echoed the view held by many of the militant demonstrators that the time is past when marches and demonstrations are likely to be a useful tool.

"I really didn't feel a spirit of unity," he said. "There were radicals and there were old McCarthyites, but they really weren't together. Maybe this will be the last big parade."

The rally was organized by the G.I.-Civilian Coalition, a Philadelphia-based organization. Many of the marchers carried signs calling for free speech for G.I.s and the release of G.I.s imprisoned for anti-war activity. One former soldier was with the Haverford-Bryn Mawr group.

Although a number of the speakers at the rally were black, the population of the marchers was overwhelmingly white and middle class. Among the speakers at the rally were Kathleen Cleaver, Yippies [members of the Youth International Party] Abbie Hoffman and Jerry Rubin, and rally organizer David Dellinger. Many of the demonstrators, especially the adults, appeared to be upset by the speeches of Hoffman and Rubin. Both speakers denounced the numerous but generally well-behaved police, as "fascist pigs."

The march was restricted to half of Sixth Avenue and was heavily policed. After groups representing the Young Americans for Freedom and the American Nazi Party were dispersed by the police at the beginning of the march, there was little heckling.

Reprinted from the *News* (Bryn Mawr-Haverford), April 8, 1969.

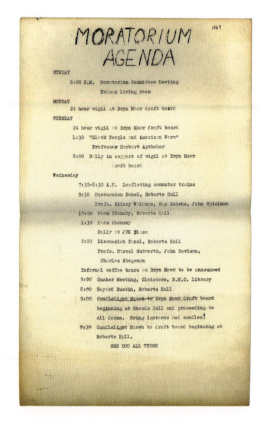

Above: Agenda for Vietnam moratorium at Bryn Mawr and Haverford colleges, 1969

Opposite: Male student playing guitar in his room in Radnor Hall, c. 1970s. The Bryn Mawr-Haverford dorm exchange permitted Haverford students to live in Bryn Mawr dorms and Bryn Mawr women to live in Haverford residences.

STEADY AIMS IN CHANGING TIMES: 1942–1970

TALKING ABOUT CHANGE: COEDUCATION

COMMUNITY ENTHUSIASTIC ABOUT COED PROPOSALS

THE PROPOSAL to give more emphasis to coeducation at Haverford made by the policy and aims committee last week has encountered enthusiastic support at both Haverford and Bryn Mawr.

Of the students and faculty that were questioned concerning the several plans, most favored a closer relationship within the Haverford-Bryn Mawr community, rather than a recruitment of girls from outside. Said sophomore William Gilchrist, "Haverford and Bryn Mawr should not be separated."

He believes the schools can be merged gradually beginning with a dorm exchange. Girls would be living at Haverford as Bryn Mawr students with the eventual goal being something in the nature of a new Haverford-Bryn Mawr College. He went on to say that there would be a problem in recruiting girls in that "it will take a while to get the quality of girls applying here that apply to Bryn Mawr."

Herb Massie, a junior, agreed that he would "much rather see us merge than each go its own way." Bryn Mawr student Debby Seltzer added that "it would benefit both schools to merge, since there is so much wasted space and time" resulting from the current relationship.

Advantages of All Girls

Another student at Bryn Mawr felt that although classes should be more mixed and that duplicate courses at the two schools should be avoided, "I don't think the two should be totally combined. There are certain advantages of an all girls school." This includes the opportunity to maintain social relations with other schools.

Faculty sentiment appears to be very similar. Said Prof. Harvey Glickman, "I don't see why both campuses can't discuss increasing moves to coeducation. A dorm exchange would be an interesting and healthy direction in which to move." Prof. Harmon Dunathan "would be against changing our special relationship with Bryn Mawr." He considers mixed classrooms to be "psychologically and aesthetically" valuable.

There are, however, some differences in opinion as to the value of coed classes. Although realizing that a men's school is "unrealistic and sheltered," Haverford freshman Dave Silverman feels that there is "definitely something superior to an all male classroom. Whereas females are more conscientious outside of class they are much quieter within." Peter Hales also related that girls rarely participated in class.

A typical Bryn Mawr reply to this was that although men were usually more dynamic in class, "most of them don't do the work."

Glickman claimed that this is often the case. Sometimes "all boy classrooms tend to degenerate into bull sessions. The girls keep the boys on their toes."

There was more optimism at Haverford than at the sister school. Sophomore Vivian Schmidt thought coeducation would be great but saw little hope of a merger. Several girls felt that the Bryn Mawr administration was already hostile to improved relations with Haverford and that a merger would be an impossibility.

Concerning a move towards coeducation at Haverford without Bryn Mawr, most girls were quite outspoken:

"I would feel so rejected."

"It would destroy a nice thing between Haverford and Bryn Mawr."

"I think it's gross. No Haverford girl would ever set foot on this campus. We'd tear them to pieces."

"I know if I were a guy I would never admit I was applying to Vassar."

"I think Bryn Mawr could use the competition."

Reprinted from the *College News*, October 25, 1968.

DORM EXCHANGE COULD REMEDY ARTIFICIAL CAMPUS SOCIAL LIFE
Jon Delano, Haverford, Class of 1971

THE BELIEF that a sexually segregated college provides the best environment for academic and social development is unsound, unreasonable, and utterly unattractive to the college student of the '70s. To believe that Haverford and Bryn Mawr can remain sexually exclusive and continue to be quality schools is to misunderstand the nature of quality education and to misjudge the desires of future college students.

Conceptions Change
Conceptions of quality education are constantly changing, but it is safe to claim that few educators believe today that the total educational experience consists of solely classroom academics. In recent years, students have come to consider the Haverford or Bryn Mawr "experience" more than just the preparation of four or five courses. Inherent in any quality education must be a social education. It is this aspect of education that we deplorably lack at our schools.

A quality college must provide opportunities for the development of a variety of relationships with both sexes in many forms and in every context. A social education is one in which the individual learns naturally to be a member of the total society. Social life at Bryn Mawr and Haverford is artificial and unrealistic. It prepares no one for a sexually integrated life; and few people intend to spend their lives at a monastery or nunnery.

More than "Dating Game"
A social education includes more than just the "dating game." The dating game on these campuses is notorious, for it is often the hunt in which the male stalks his prey via the "pig" book [freshman picture book] or the mixer; the female becomes a tactical objective. For a social education, it is tragically incomplete.

No, the social education necessary for quality education must include the development of those "natural" relationships based on interests, personality, and friendship. And it can only occur on a coeducational campus where males and females can meet outside the dating context. An experience becomes more than a game.

Quality education, then, is dependent on a union of the academic and the social. Haverford and Bryn Mawr may claim academic excellence (although even that may be challenged for not providing either the male or the female perspective) but any claim of social excellence would be laughable. The survival of these schools as quality institutions depends upon rectifying this social mediocrity; for this next decade, the colleges offering an academic but no social experience can only fail.

Coeducation Desired
A paramount desire of future college students is coeducation, as proved by 26 male schools and 36 female schools which went coed in 1968. Good students, who desire quality education of the academic and the social, will bypass the sexually segregated schools for a more natural environment.

The mass of information published by the Public Relations Office and the Admissions Office at Haverford indicates that Haverford is aware of the attractiveness of coed schools. One beige admissions pamphlet states in black, bold type: "We're an old school. Small school. Men's school. (And only a mile from Bryn Mawr.)" The Haverford "Today" booklet tries to portray our "coeducatedness" by including females in various photographs: one is a close-up of two girls in a class—no doubt in a class of 20 males.

Like What?
Another pamphlet even claims to the high school student that Haverford's relationship with Bryn Mawr is equivalent to all that is good in a coed status: "Haverford shares many social and academic programs with Bryn Mawr. Because of that relationship, Haverford has many of the advantages of a coed school without some of the disadvantages." (Like what?) This comes perilously close to misrepresenting the truth, a cheap advertising trick to attract those students desiring a coeducational environment.

Why deceive when we can establish a truly coeducational environment on the Bryn Mawr and Haverford campuses by dorm exchanges? Why not allocate various dorms at Haverford and Bryn Mawr for occupancy by the opposite sex? Such an exchange would provide many more opportunities for social contact outside the dating context—and still keep the technicality of separate male-female colleges. Obviously, this need not be a final step, but at least such a dorm exchange can be planned for the fall of '69.

Haverford and Bryn Mawr, because of their location, should have taken the lead back in the '50s to provide the coeducational environment for the quality education we all desire. They didn't. But the opportunity still exists, and further delay is unfair to present students, and damaging to the reputations of these Colleges among future students.

Reprinted from the *News*, (Bryn Mawr-Haverford) January 31, 1969.

24 MEN, 53 WOMEN CHOSEN TO PARTICIPATE IN EXCHANGE PROGRAM

PARTICIPANTS IN THE COEDUCATIONAL dorm experiment were chosen by lot last night at Bryn Mawr and on Wednesday, April 9, at Haverford.

Out of 37 applicants a total of 24 men were selected to live in Radnor next fall. Twenty-four women were selected to live in Lloyd and another 29 to live in coed Radnor out of a total of about 75 applicants. The remainder of the Lloyd suites will be filled in the usual way during the Haverford housing draw.

Radnor Choice Justified
Bill Ingram, Haverford student representative to the bi-college coeducation committee, said that Radnor had been chosen for two main reasons. First, since many current residents were already planning not to retain their present rooms only a minimum number of girls would have to be dispossessed. Second, at the time the choice was being made, it appeared that there were about 25 men interested in the exchange. Radnor is the only dormitory which would satisfactorily hold approximately 25 men and 25 women.

He indicated that by the time it became evident that more men were interested, "plans based on 24-man exchange were already far too advanced to change."

Above: Radnor Hall, built 1887

Bryn Mawr girls were able to enter the draw either individually or in pairs. Cathy Hoskins, Bryn Mawr coed committee member said, "We wanted to make sure that no one found herself in a completely hostile group."

Retain BMC Rules
All Bryn Mawr students whether living on the BMC or on the Haverford campus will continue to live by Bryn Mawr rules. Next year's Radnor residents will meet before the end of this semester to decide what parietal rules Haverford students living at Bryn Mawr will have to obey. Before the Haverford draw, Dean James Lyons emphasized that only men who were "relatively free from academic and personal problems," who could "accept and abide by Bryn Mawr's no drugs and no drinking rules," and who were "free from any undue missionary zeal to reform Bryn Mawr" should participate. He said that the men living at Bryn Mawr would have to obey the BMC rules even more conscientiously to prevent the experiment from being torpedoed by its opponents.

Reprinted from the *News* (Bryn Mawr-Haverford), April 15, 1969.

STUDENT PERSPECTIVE

Last fall, members of 1943 who, as students, had been the presidents of Undergrad, the senior class, and Self Gov, met at Bryn Mawr with their current counterparts to compare views on student life during the McBride era. Source materials included recent issues of the Bryn Mawr-Haverford *News*, 1943's Yearbooks and a tour of the campus. Post-meeting reflections appear below in the individual comments by the 1943 "students" and the collective response by this year's seniors.

Students of 1943

Sarah Matteson Mitchell, Undergrad president, biology major, now married with one child, practicing private and clinical psychiatry in Scarsdale and White Plains

It is hard to focus on change when the aging mind is so awash with the sweetness of recognition! Here we are on the same old plot with the same light on the same stone and the same tree trunks all in much the same places . . . Even the girls look very familiar—the pretty, the sloppy, the brisk, the grinding, the completed, the half-formed—all in much the same variety . . . One can't really believe how little the look of the Pem dining room has changed. I even snagged a stocking on one of the same chairs that used to bite me then. The student waitresses, the buffet serving, of course, are new . . . .

There is a distinct air of less isolation on campus. Bryn Mawr in my time could almost have been an island, connected to the mainland by the Paoli local, with perhaps a little merging out behind into the lovely Pennsylvania countryside. We seemed to have committed ourselves to four years in microcosm—one with its own special structures, values, priorities, relevances, personalities—a subculture with its own particular privileges and limitations . . . Now the prevailing student attitude seems to be that college is a place primarily for study where one happens to live for convenience's sake, but still in the world, still part of the mainstream. Greater flexibility in transferring in and out, fifth year students, coeducational and integrational developments, the media, and above all affluence—all tend to break down the walls and let the world stream in. More aware, more "relevant," more fluid, more turbulent . . .

Has anything been lost? Can Lantern Night be so stirring? Could Herben's beard be such a memorable feature? Can people know each other well? Can there be enough appreciation of individuals, enough appreciation of eccentricities? . . . When I was a Junior, I was sent to Cambridge by the *News* to interview Miss McBride following the announcement of her appointment. It was the absolute zenith of my life. Surely this special kind of parochial fervor must be fading now. Having boys around all the time on a casual day by day basis must mitigate the hysterical intensity of some of our old involvements. Imagine a Gilbert and Sullivan with an all female cast now!

Relevance is certainly the watchword. We realized, I think, that much was irrelevant. If a professor hadn't seemed to have changed his lecture notes for 40 years, we might have grumbled softly but in general accepted this as a bit of Bryn Mawr lore . . . A few interdisciplinary courses developed in our day, but they were faculty inspired. Student participation in curriculum change was undreamed of.

Oh, we were on the whole so passive and docile, so accepting of the "word." We used to complain sometimes that we were being given the answers long before we'd asked the questions. I can't believe this could be the problem today. I remember our philosophy professor in his final lecture complaining that we were a "bunch of vegetables." Would he say that now?

Harriet Case Sumerwell, senior class president, philosophy major and post-graduate psychology student, now coping in Washington, D.C., with a family of seven, four at home including seven-year-old twins

We were in the middle of a war in 1943. It was with shock that I realized we have never really been out of war during all the McBride years, that troops sent to Germany during my college years are still there, that the class of 1970 is in reality a "war class" too . . . .

For our class, the threat of war and then its actuality shaped our lives, curtailing some freedoms and expanding others. We could no longer travel abroad or even easily in this country but we developed new liaisons with institutions and people beyond our college walls. Cooperation with Haverford and Swarthmore became a necessity as professors were drawn more and more into war activities; the national government reached deep into women's colleges for trained people—faculty and students alike; job opportunities for women opened up everywhere.

There was no awkward transition period when Miss McBride returned to become president. Our Class had already encountered her wisdom and penetrating insight during our freshmen year. We already knew and loved her. She immediately led the College forward to meet the challenge of the times.

Courses were already being offered for credit which led directly into jobs with the armed services. Geology offered photogrammetry, the Navy had its own "hush-hush" course for seniors. The F.B.I. arrived on campus and fingerprinted everyone. Extra-curricular courses were instituted such as Motor and Home Mechanics. The athletic department gave credit for farm labor on Saturdays. We husked corn for neighboring dairy farms and were rewarded with pails of fresh milk and our picture in the *New York Times*.

For many students, change could not come fast enough. They chafed at the cloistered feeling of college life, impatient to be out in the "real world" where the action was. Some left to get married, others stayed but rebelled at any symbols of status quo. Senior class meetings became stormy affairs as we argued the relative merits of "keeping up the home front" versus sacrificing all to the war effort . . . Even the traditional gift of a tree to the College was vetoed because it didn't fit the austerity program. Dr. Nahm rescued us from this impasse by donating a pink dogwood from his own yard. Several of us helped him dig it up and plant it on campus.

A new student organization was created—the Alliance—to coordinate all war effort activities. I was interested to find the Alliance still flourishes, although its activities are different and its origin forgotten.

Social changes inevitably followed, bringing down the barriers between undergraduate work and marriage. Shortly thereafter, Bryn Mawr also opened its doors to returning veterans . . . .

But enough of reminiscences, what about Now? The campus leaders we met were most charming and competent. Although alert to and fully aware of campus problems, they certainly did not seem frightened or overwhelmed . . . Many traditions, of course, have changed or been eliminated, including some cherished ones such as Orals singing, maids' and porters' classes, comprehensives . . . Scholarship is still very "relevant" at Bryn Mawr. A far greater percentage of girls goes on to graduate work than in 1943. I got the impression that today's students as a whole are less impatient about the work at hand. Their scholarship seems firmly anchored in the world at large and they do not seem to feel the same need to leave college in order to begin "living." I think such a state of affairs is an outstanding achievement of Miss McBride's, especially remarkable as we read daily of riots by students who feel their college administrations are hopelessly out of touch with the needs and moods of today . . . .

Mental health care is now readily available. A crying need in our day, the demand for counseling and treatment is now met by staff psychiatrists. Best of all, students feel comfortable about using the services.

The campus itself reflects the vigorous growth—new structures inspire and delight the imagination . . . It was wonderful to discover some very important things unchanged. On the steps of the new library, my two classmates and I experienced again the same surge of exhilaration, excitement, and pride in Bryn Mawr that we used to feel upon stepping out of the old library into the cold evenings of our undergraduate days. The serenity so essential for intellectual endeavor, so unique to Bryn Mawr, has not given way to turmoil and confusion.

But most reassuring of all was the realization that we felt no generation gap in talking to leaders of 1970 . . . It was evident that we shared similar values, the same ones that Bryn Mawr has always stood for and which still prevail. And so when values remain the same there can be wonderful growth and change, but no gaps—only continuity.

Frances Matthai, Self Gov president, English major, now teaching English and Latin at the Bryn Mawr School, Baltimore

One feels that one is not coming back, but rather going ahead—that life on campus is now more of a reflection on what is going on in The World. The atmosphere is not as rarefied, the thinking not at all "removed." Why? How is it possible? It must be because under Miss McBride's leadership and guidance, the College has changed with the changing times, not echoed or followed them; the College has been the essence, a concentration of thought and action and controversy faced and lived with, and perhaps in some ways influenced.

The strongest impressions are of vitality, seriousness of purpose and sense of concern, and, as expressed by the president of Self Gov, a very mature capacity for coping with much more profound difficulties . . . How trivial and even childish seem now the details our Self Gov board worried about—whether or not it should be permissible to go to Ford's in the Village—a dimly lit bar which served mostly beer; how to collect fines when people were 20 minutes late; could actual destinations be matched with the sign-out book?

What main differences does one notice? The freedom and independence and confidence of students. The atmosphere on a Saturday morning—much more alive and stimulated by a variety of visitors, residents male and female. Is there no longer such a pattern of the weekend exodus to Philadelphia and New York? Students are asking for a Student Union Building. (Remember when an ice-cream parlor was set up in Goodhart so you could get a milkshake at 8 P.M.!) . . . The variety and depth of concerns and problems student leaders are aware of: How much can and should black students be urged to "join in" when they don't want to? Is complete social integration the best thing? The psychological aspect of the problem of drugs. And the Vietnam War—a unifying force because of the opposition to it whereas in World War II, we were unified by our desires to support the government's war efforts... Social work was the concern of a few; wasn't there a pervading atmosphere of charity? Today it is a prevailing concern, a deeply felt need shared by everyone....

"In our day" Rhoads had just been finished and was the epitome of the new—pristine and spacious and bright rooms and hallways. Now it is Erdman which practically articulates its free space and light. Perhaps Erdman is symbolic of the era—a building with a very sound framework, with solidity and permanence, light and air controlled and on a large scale. With its uncompromising walls and between the monolithic pillars, life, individually and collectively, is free to move and a change of pace is relatively unnoticed... And there is the new Alumnae house, Wyndham, the new Library, and the language complex under construction.

One tends to slip into a nostalgic reminiscence, but such indulgent personal pleasures cannot last long and soon give way to the excitement and promise of the present and the future. Perhaps this is the main thing, like seeing a child grow up, remembering how he used to be and yet never for a moment wanting him to stay that way. So the College seems to have grown indeed like an organism because Miss McBride was always not only anticipating the future but shaping it and giving students enough freedom to contribute to that change.

Students of 1970
Patricia Rosenfeld, president of Undergrad, summarizes the reflections of the three seniors. Miss Rosenfeld is a geology major with plans for graduate work in environmental earth science at Johns Hopkins. The other two seniors are Class President Janet Oppenheim, a history major and 1970–71 designate for a Woodrow Wilson National Fellowship, and Self Gov President Faith Greenfield, an English major planning to enter professional drama school and take night courses in education.

Comparing notes with our counterparts in the Class of 1943, the three of us were fascinated by both the similarities and differences in life at Bryn Mawr then and now. The similarities stem from the world situation facing both classes and also from an intangible spirit of enthusiasm to deal rationally with the college experience. We found the differences to be concentrated around the reactions to external crisis, the structure of college society, and, indeed, to the more prominent role of the student.

Both classes are wartime classes. The three alumnae spoke of their various supportive war efforts: The formation of Alliance and extension of League were two major ones, in addition to girls working and preparing to work in Washington and even volunteering for service. Today, we have mobilized against the war and for peace in a better world. While Alliance backs the various peace movements, both Alliance and League have moved into the community, supporting tutoring projects, self-help programs, etc.

Our approach to the world while in college is split in several directions. There are those who desire more realism in their education, and thus work for courses which combine teaching in ghetto schools and seminar studies. These girls are also the ones who frequently want to pattern college life after the real world. Now, for example, we have provided all forms of residence styles, including co-ed dorms, apartments, and co-operatives. Other groups include those who prefer to remain almost completely involved in their academic pursuits, deliberately uninvolved in the College and the world during their four years here. Of course, some manage to combine both activism and study. Probably these clusters existed in 1943, but in different proportions. In 1970, the silent student engrossed in her studies is most likely greatly outnumbered by those who feel the urgency to institute changes at Bryn Mawr and in the world.

Perhaps that last point underlies one of the major differences between students in 1943 and 1970. The tendency today is to desire immediate change without taking time for a thorough review of all the ramifications of that change. Students want to experiment with the curriculum, their living situations, and their social activities while lifting a majority of the restraints; the belief is that immediate innovation is worth any risk. There are, of course, those who are less rushed, who still want change, but also want to consider all aspects. Today, the central intellectual conflict is between those student combinations.

The guiding and uniting force behind the differences and similarities between the Class of '43 and that of '70, which has enabled Bryn Mawr to expand and progressively change in these years, is Miss McBride. Through her thoughtful reactions to the varied human situations ranging from her determination and keen wisdom throughout the years of World War II to her sympathetic and reasonable approach to current student problems such as Black Studies and Women's Liberation, and by keeping her door always open to those who want to come and talk with her, Miss McBride has maintained the strong spirit of Bryn Mawr.

Reprinted from the *Bryn Mawr Alumnae Bulletin,* Spring 1970.

Above: Students in an auto-mechanics class, 1946

Next two pages: Commencement, 1966. Photograph by Phil MacMullan. Published in *Newsweek*, May 31, 1966

Cooperative Developments: 1970–1978

A HIGH HILL: PRESIDENT WOFFORD'S 1970 INAUGURAL ADDRESS

Judge Spaeth, Father Hesburgh, brother and sister presidents, the faculty, students, alumnae, directors and trustees of Bryn Mawr, colleagues and friends: "No word said can make you brothers!"—so warns Archibald MacLeish:

"Brotherhood here in the strange world is the rich and/Rarest giving of life and the most valued,/Not to be had for a word or a week's wishing."

No words of mine can justify the trust you have given me. With consent withering all around us in this strange late twentieth-century world, your trust seems to me the rich and rarest gift and the most valued. I accept it gratefully and seriously. In return you have my trust, and a promise of years of work and lives lived together to fulfill the hopes of this day.

For I do trust this community—this institution forged and tempered in the double fire of Quaker concern and devoted scholarship; this original encampment of women's liberation; this College that is as old and fiercely independent as M. Carey Thomas feuding with one of the first faculty members of 1885, Woodrow Wilson; and as young and fortunately buoyant as our new dean and chief academic deputy, Mary Patterson McPherson, and a dozen of our faculty riding the rapids of the Colorado River—as old in wisdom as the third President Marion Edwards Park during the Great Depression saying at the 1933 opening convocation, "As the world careens, rights itself or sinks, so Bryn Mawr careens, rights itself or sinks," and as young in hope as this year's freshman on whose application form was this ambition: "I would like to become a Renaissance Woman."

This corporate body whose contradictions are very human but whose term, according to its charter, "is perpetual," whose name means High Hill, this College has my trust—and I hope yours. In a world of too much leveling, it will be our common trust to keep this hill high.

The period of silence was a good beginning today. I hope you will understand if there are long silences from me on many matters while I listen and learn about a formidable and fascinating list of new subjects: women, the stock market, graduate schools, and those fascinating entities that exist when two or three professors come together in the name of a common discipline, departments. And true to one definition of a university as a number of departments held together by a central heating plant, as some of you know too well, our central heating plant is breaking down.

It seems we cannot rest or rust in our tradition. We begin a process of longer range planning that will include faculty, students, alumnae, directors and trustees—all parts of the College on this hill and our College in dispersion. We must ask ourselves and think through together what we want Bryn Mawr to become in the 1970's. Since the future of Bryn Mawr is deeply involved in whether the world is careening, righting itself or sinking, we must also think of the world of the 1970's.

When I asked Bryn Mawr's beloved President Emeritus Katharine McBride for a translation of the Chinese scroll on the living room wall of our new home, Pen-y-Groes, she said the characters meant: "A small house in music and breezes is all the world." As the world goes we are a small house, but in the music made by our 1,500 students and faculty who come from all parts of the world and in the breezes of change blowing here as elsewhere—sometimes they seem like hurricanes—there is indeed all the world. And all the world is in a crisis of authority and a crisis of the intellect—of law and reason. There will be no way out unless people dare to trust their intellects in action—unless on a scale never known before reason is used with courage to right a careening world.

This will not happen everywhere or all at once but in a land where the guardians of the Republic are all the people, universal liberal education is our first and last hope for a successful self-government. It seems to me that a college like Bryn Mawr, with its strong traditions, high standards and outstanding faculty, students and alumnae, with its unique combination of undergraduate and graduate schools in a college of liberal arts, though a relatively small body of some 1,100 men and women altogether, is in a good position to discover and point

> IT SEEMS WE CANNOT REST OR RUST IN OUR TRADITION. WE BEGIN A PROCESS OF LONGER RANGE PLANNING THAT WILL INCLUDE FACULTY, STUDENTS, ALUMNAE, DIRECTORS AND TRUSTEES—ALL PARTS OF THE COLLEGE ON THIS HILL AND OUR COLLEGE IN DISPERSION. WE MUST ASK OURSELVES AND THINK THROUGH TOGETHER WHAT WE WANT BRYN MAWR TO BECOME IN THE 1970'S.

the way. I believe we are strong enough not to be blown over by these winds. Instead we must be responsible in the vigorous sense of the word—that is, to respond. For I believe that we should turn President Park's formula upside down: as small communities of men and women, especially our communities of learning, careen, right themselves, or sink, so will go America.

In American law, the common good or general reason hopefully emerges out of actual cases or controversies; very real principles are discovered and tested in very real situations; and always it is a Constitution you are expounding.

At Bryn Mawr it is a College we are expounding. For most of a century, in one controversy after another, under public fire or general apathy, in political, social or economic crisis, faculty and students have discovered and tested some very real principles of academic freedom. Out of trial and error I think we have learned that the reason for the freedom of the academy is not the unexamined liberty of students or teachers doing whatever they want to do; it is rather the public need for the Academy, by teaching and research, on campus and in the community, to discover and test the ideas that We the People require for our self-government.

Some romantics talk lightly of revolution but the real revolutionary ideas shaking the world—take Marx, Freud and Einstein—were the products of men who did the most difficult thing in this world: studied and thought, read and wrote, year upon year in the British Museum or the libraries and universities of Europe and America. It is time for the intellect of Americans to be discovered and tested, for it is the full human soul we are expounding. Our society may indeed sink in self-indulgence if the new generation of students does not begin to stretch itself to the outer limits of its intellectual capacity.

In a time when irrationality is widely celebrated, let me here confess to a continuing belief in this thing called reason. It is not so much faith in the little reason within, but faith in the larger reason that is found in greater things such as the Constitution of the United States which was

designed so that reason could rule and Bryn Mawr College which was chartered to help the rulers become reasonable. In this view of America as a learning society there is a vital and profound relationship between a College and the Constitution—between the promise and the problems of this College and the promise and problems of our whole society. So you see why I believe our charter is indeed perpetual, why we should have the courage of our contradictions, and why, especially now when reason is on trial, we should pursue with all our power the liberal education that is the precondition for and the final meaning of any human liberation.

It is time now for me to practice what I preach, by seeing how these principles are tested in three issues immediately at hand.

First, the Student Curriculum Committee of our Undergraduate College, after a year-long study, has just presented an important series of proposals for reform; and this initiative coincides with the fact that this is the year set by the faculty of arts and sciences for a major curricular review. This calls for us to ask the hardest and most important questions in a college, about the content and quality of the learning and teaching. In this complex age, with the explosion of knowledge, are we making it possible for that freshman to become a Renaissance Woman? Do modern science, technology, communications and politics indeed make possible—or impossible—a new birth of reason and law for America and the world?

If we careen, right ourselves or sink along with the world, then shouldn't the world become our great common subject—the world in all its dimensions, including our own backyard with the major questions that cut across all academic disciplines. American higher education stands indicted for its readiness to invent atomic bombs and do weapons research while neglecting questions of life and death like war, poverty, discrimination, urban breakdown, over-population and pollution. We must find the way and the will to bring these problems from the outskirts of the Academy where they appear mainly in extracurricular teach-ins or agitation, into the center of our study and research. Bryn Mawr's original and continuing emphasis on graduate studies, which account for nearly half our students, will be an important asset; indeed the experience of our Graduate School of Social Work and Social Research in placing over 100 full-time masters students in community action assignments and with its unusual Ph.D. program—this experience in combining theory and practice, in classroom and the field—should be most instructive. Our new interdepartmental course Energy Resources; Their Use and Effects on Environment should be a good step in this direction for the Undergraduate College.

In this educational search, we must not settle for chipping away at old inflexibilities or for any compromise with academic integrity in the name of relevance. Let us not take the advice of Pat Moynihan's priest who enjoined his flock to follow the straight and narrow path between right and wrong. Let us instead recall the advice of the poet who opened this college 85 years ago with a warning against "a want of thoroughness, and a disposition to value study chiefly as a means of making a livelihood." The object of education, James Russell Lowell told that first convocation in Taylor Hall, is "not to help a man as a bread-winner but rather to be the life-long sweetener of all the bread he ever earns." He added that he missed hearing in a new college like Bryn Mawr "the murmur of immortal feet" that inspired him at Oxford, but he thought we did at least "know the difference between literature and printed matter." I hope our curriculum for the future has more, not less literature; and listens more and more to the murmur of immortal feet. For the anarchy of everyone doing his thing is a far cry from the good curriculum which should be the common thing of a college. It is not a lowering of intellectual standards that we need, but a raising of them. The man or woman of a new Renaissance will need to be more intellectual in the full sense and better educated in all the liberal arts than most people have ever been. And the full use of the intellect goes beyond cleverness, even brilliance, to wisdom. We should recall the picture of J. Robert Oppenheimer, then at the top of our intellectual establishment, a man of deep social concerns, clasping his hands above his head in a victory salute, with a hundred academicians and scientists cheering, at the news that their atomic bomb had worked and wiped out 100,000 men, women and children at Hiroshima—to remind ourselves of the temptations of the technical power and the need for an education that keeps the moral questions at its core. We must be a college that keeps examining itself and the world on these fundamental issues of power and purpose.

Second, there is the matter of cooperation with other colleges and universities, and its companion question, coeducation. An angel might fear to tread in the area of women's rights now vexing the world, but there is before us the report of Haverford College's Commission on Women Students and our own study committee's report on coeducation. These reports convince me that coeducation per se is not the central question, that instead our concentration should be upon further cooperation between our colleges to improve education, not just to increase coeducation. Just as we want our curriculum to reach out to the world without lowering standards, we must seek to develop stronger and better relationships with other educational institutions without blurring our individual identities. Again we want to be open to the world, not isolated and turned in upon ourselves. Already, we have unusual reciprocal arrangements with Haverford and Swarthmore at the undergraduate level and the University of Pennsylvania for graduate work which gives students the best of several worlds. We greatly value these arrangements, and particularly the unique and promising relationship with Haverford. With this nearest neighbor and closest partner, several hundred students are enjoying the opportunity for cross-registration of classes and there is a dormitory exchange of 80 students each way.

Hoping to see us continue and extend these and other forms of cooperation, I have a proposal that springs out of our primary concern for curriculum. As we consider how the Academy can make the world's problems subjects of the best academic treatment, one of the issues before this afternoon's symposium, I suggest that our colleagues of Quaker origin commit themselves to developing substantial new ways to work together, pooling resources to deal with these problems. What the world may need most right now is the active contemplation and search for inner light of a good Quaker meeting writ large. Is it beyond our capacity to provide that?

As to coeducation, which the Haverford Commission on Women Studies is proposing on a much larger scale at Haverford—already about a third of Bryn Mawr's graduate students are men—I can only give first impressions. I suppose we should be complimented that they appear to want many more women students. In our community I have not found quite so pressing a need for more men. I hope the hundreds of men already studying or living here will take that, too, as a compliment. But I see no reason, especially in this new stage of women's liberation to abandon our special concern for women's education or to accept some unproven magic formula for the best sexual ratio. I see no compelling reason why a predominately women's college, with so many options open on its own and on nearby campuses, will not be as good in the future as it has been in the past. So I hope that the discussions of Haverford's proposals now beginning between faculty-student committees of both colleges will be an educational and not a sexual search.

The third matter involves the very existence of independent higher education in America. The immediate issue is just one sign of a larger danger ahead. Last year we were confronted with a state law which sought to impress colleges and universities into service as agents of the state—indeed as informers against students—in the enforcement of new state-imposed sanctions for a variety of non-academic offenses. Upon the recommendation of the students who were faced with loss of their scholarships and of the whole student body and faculty, the Bryn Mawr Board refused, and still refuses, to sign such an agreement. We did so and do so because the autonomy of a free college and the integrity of the student-teacher relationship are at stake. Through the magnificent response of alumnae, faculty, students and friends of the College—that same combination that has brought Bryn Mawr so far—we are going to make up the lost scholarships. We are now working with Haverford and a number of other colleges and universities in seeking federal court action to enjoin the operation of that statute. The legislature's concern about disruption is reasonable; but we believe its remedy is unconstitutional. Bomb throwers have no natural right to state scholarships—indeed they belong in jail or the hospital, but they can be dealt with by due process of law without undermining the essential freedom of the Academy.

I cannot predict the outcome of the law suit, but I think the stand we took and the price we are paying is part of what it means to keep our hill high; we are also doing our duty to the whole body of higher learning in America. For this misconceived law is just one of many bulldozers that are likely to intrude and try to level us in the year to come. Beyond this immediate case, we can predict that this is only one skirmish in a long struggle to determine whether the state will intervene in and control the internal affairs of our colleges and universities. For our own sake, for the sake of American higher education, and for the sake of the soul of this country, we need to resist all the forces that would flatten us, whether they come from Harrisburg and Washington, or from within the college community, even when they represent urgent popular passions and the latest political, social, educational and life styles.

To do this—to survive and play our part in resolving the crisis of reason and law in our national life—we will need all the support from alumnae and friends that has been given so generously over many years,

all that and more. For the first crisis facing almost every private college today is financial. The family of Bryn Mawr is already loyal and large, as this gathering shows, but it must become larger. In this sense too we must reach out to the world, to enlist collaboration of new people and new institutions, including particularly the corporations of our private sector. The program of Associated Fellows of the College, approved yesterday by our Board of Directors, can be an important step in gaining such new support. In this effort, as in improving curriculum and increasing cooperation with other colleges and universities, we must be more inventive if we are to do our duty.

With this agenda, I do not know why I should thank Judge Spaeth and the Trustees for this assignment, but I can think of no better place to be. Twenty-five years ago, at the end of World War II, I heard a former president of Amherst College, Alexander Meiklejohn, make the connection that I have made today between education and the idea of a republic. By a long route it is what has led me here. It is best expressed, for me, in the toast that a teacher, Scott Buchanan, then the dean of St. John's College in Annapolis, used to make each Christmas. With the community assembled he would drink a toast to the three republics of which the college was a part: To the America Republic, to the still unconstituted Republic of Man, and to the universal Republic of Learning.

Before this community that represents Bryn Mawr, and in the light of our history, our present cases and controversies, and our future, this is my toast.

Reprinted from the *Bryn Mawr Alumnae Bulletin*, Fall 1970.

Page 222: Student with male companion on Bryn Mawr's campus, c. 1970s

Page 224: One of the many images of owls in the Bryn Mawr College collections; pen, ink, and wash on paper

Opposite: Admissions brochure for prospective students from the middle and western United States, c. 1977–81

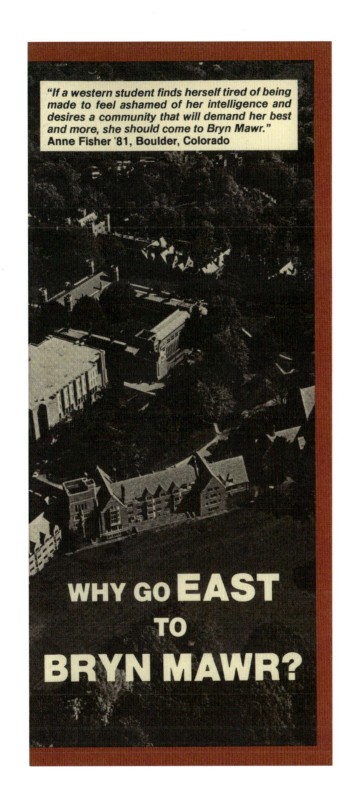

INAUGURATION OF HARRIS WOFFORD

WOFFORD'S CONVOCATION ADDRESS STRESSES WOMEN'S ROLE AT BMC

Cathy Davidson, Class of 1973

PRESIDENT HARRIS L. WOFFORD, JR., gave strong support to Bryn Mawr's tradition of special education for women in his first convocation address yesterday morning.

Wofford said, "At this time of belated and increasing concern for the rights of women, it would make no sense for one of the greatest women's colleges to lose its special concern for the education of women."

He did not exclude the possibility of admitting some men to the undergraduate college, saying, "It may be in men's interest to be a minority some of the time, as it may be in the interest of many women to be in a majority during part of their formal education."

Wofford took office this year as Bryn Mawr's fifth president in its 85-year history. His appointment to succeed the retiring president Katharine McBride was announced August 15, 1969.

Wofford also pointed out in his speech that Bryn Mawr is now the only college in Pennsylvania which has not signed the Pennsylvania Higher Education Assistance Agency (PHEAA) agreement, and has been successful in raising over $30,000 to make up for lost scholarship funds for Pennsylvania students. He said, "I think we should take pride in this particular loneliness."

Discussing the importance of maintaining standards of academic excellence, Wofford said that the Bryn Mawr curriculum must "offer the liberal arts and foster the love of wisdom every person needs, not for any one specialty but for a good life" and mark the distinction between "training and education" and "sophist and philosopher."

Citing his first law case in which he represented British bicycle makers against American manufacturers of balloon-tire bikes who wanted to impose a high tariff on the British product, Wofford said, "We won on the argument that if the American companies would get off their balloon tires and produce the good lightweight three-gear bicycle that our market needed, they could compete successfully without a tariff. If in any respects Bryn Mawr or any part of it is resting on its balloon tires we must get moving and again become inventive."

Wofford left his position as president of the State University of New York's College at Old Westbury to come to Bryn Mawr. He is a graduate of the University of Chicago and the law schools of both Yale and Howard universities.

In 1958, Wofford was counsel to the Reverend Theodore Hesburgh, president of the University of Notre Dame, on the United States Commission on Civil Rights. In 1961 and 1962, he was chairman of a sub-cabinet group on Civil Rights under President Kennedy. He later

served on the task force to set up the Peace Corps. From 1962 to 1964, he was the Peace Corps's Special Representative for Africa and director of its teaching program in Ethiopia.

During the Democratic National Convention in 1968, Wofford was arrested with other prominent liberals during a march supporting Eugene McCarthy and protesting police brutality in Chicago.

Wofford and his wife Clare have three children: Susanne, an undergraduate at Yale, and two younger sons, Daniel and David.

Reprinted from the *News* (Bryn Mawr-Haverford), September 15, 1970.

To: The Editor

Re: The appointment of Mr. Wofford as Bryn Mawr's fifth president

That Mr. Wofford is an honorable man is clear. That Mr. Wofford is an able man is clear. That Mr. Wofford is an educational innovator is splendid. That the Committee to Nominate a President failed to nominate a woman is a disgrace.

Women—whether American or Afghan—have never had the power or the dignity or the respect of men. They even lack self-respect. The letter of August 1969, says, "As to the sex of the candidate, a bare minority (of those answering a questionnaire) either found the question immaterial or preferred a man." A majority, no matter how bare, is still a majority.

However, Tractarian fulminations are not really my purpose now. What bothers me so much is simply this: that Bryn Mawr chose to reflect in its internal affairs, over which it has control, a political and social state of affairs demeaning to women, over which it may claim to have little control. It also bothers me that Bryn Mawr, searching assiduously for the "most qualified person," would find a man. What more devastating comment could be made on women's colleges: that they have refused to train even their own leaders.

I find it ironic—the Portrait of Athena as an Aunt Tom.

Catharine Stimpson, Class of 1958

Reprinted from the *Bryn Mawr Alumnae Bulletin*, Fall 1969.

"THERE IS SOME HUMOR IN IT," WOFFORD SAID WITH A SMILE WHEN ASKED ABOUT HIS POSITION AS PRESIDENT. "MOST PEOPLE SEEM TO TAKE IT ON GOOD TERMS BECAUSE IT DOES AN INTERESTING THING. IT ENHANCES THE POSITION OF A WOMAN WHO IS PRESIDENT HERE—AS I AM SURE WOMEN WILL BE PRESIDENTS HERE IN THE FUTURE—BECAUSE IT SAYS THAT THIS JOB IS FOR THE PERSON BEST QUALIFIED RATHER THAN FOR THE WOMAN BEST QUALIFIED. IT PROVIDES FOR OPEN COMPETITION ALL THE WAY."

Reprinted from the *Philadelphia Inquirer*, September 2, 1970.

THE DIRECTORS OF BRYN MAWR COLLEGE
ANNOUNCE THE APPOINTMENT OF
HARRIS LLEWELLYN WOFFORD, Jr.
WHO WILL TAKE OFFICE IN AUGUST 1970
AS THE FIFTH PRESIDENT OF THE COLLEGE
SUCCEEDING KATHARINE ELIZABETH McBRIDE

AUGUST 1969

Top: Coretta Scott King (1927–2006) with Harris Wofford at Bryn Mawr's Convocation, May 1974. Photograph by Evelyn Taylor

Bottom: Announcement of the appointment of Harris Wofford as Bryn Mawr's president, August 1969

Opposite: Harris L. Wofford, Jr. (born 1926), 1974. Photograph by Bern Schwartz (1914–1978)

BI-COLLEGE COOPERATION

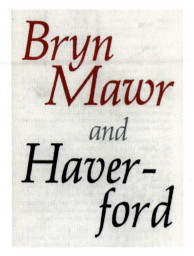

Above: Promotional brochure on Bi-College cooperation, 1973

Right: Page from a handbook for Bryn Mawr's class of 1973, describing the opportunities afforded by cooperation with Haverford

Opposite: Students and friends relaxing on campus, with a bicycle in foreground, c. 1970–75

RENEWED COOPERATION

DURING THE PAST WEEK, both College presidents have made strong verbal commitments to the importance of extending cooperation in the bi-college community. President Wofford said in an interview that he puts great weight on extending cooperation with the four-College exchange, and especially with Haverford. President Coleman said in his opening Collection speech that he looks forward to an extension of resource sharing with Bryn Mawr.

Cooperation between Bryn Mawr and Haverford should be an important issue this year, because many areas of cooperation have come to an impasse. A proposal to let Bryn Mawr students major at Haverford is presently before the faculty. Suggestions on merging many services and offices at the two schools are presently confronting the administration. And a commitment to extend the coed dorm exchange before next spring's room draw was made by many students last spring when the inequities of the situation were realized too late.

Hopefully, all segments of the community will work together on these proposals because all are very important to the lives of each one of us in the bi-college community. Decisions and compromises have been put off about as long as is feasible; this year, the issues are being brought up early enough to act on them before the year runs out once again.

Reprinted from the *News* (Bryn Mawr-Haverford), September 8, 1972.

BI-COLLEGE ENVIRONMENT CALLED MOST COED IN NATION
Nancy Herndon, Class of 1977

Two consultants hired by Bryn Mawr and Haverford to discuss the future of cooperation told members of the two administrations, along with the chairmen and some members of the boards, that the bi-College community is presently the most coeducational environment in the country.

Howard Bowen, authority on academic economics and former Chancellor of Claremont College, and Patricia Graham, who has taught at Barnard College and served as vice president of Radcliffe, met last week on campus with students as well as faculty and administrators. A separate meeting was held in New York with board members and senior administrators of both colleges.

In all conferences, Bowen emphasized the financial challenges ahead for both colleges, noting the differences in the two colleges' financial policies, and citing a need for more extensive long-range plans. Graham stressed the need for each college to define coeducation in its own terms, observing that in the number and ability of both sexes in administration, faculty, and student body, the Bryn Mawr-Haverford relationship offered a more truly equal education than any coed or single sex institution she knew, according to Cooperation Committee Co-Chairman Barbara Taft.

The only specific recommendation made by the consultants, noted Haverford President John Coleman, was the suggestion that Haverford alter its admissions to emphasize such elements as character and diversity rather than relying so heavily on Board scores and the more conventional standards. However, Coleman said, "I don't have the confidence that we would know how to deal with a substantially different student."

Reprinted from the *News* (Bryn Mawr-Haverford), September 24, 1976.

COOPERATIVE DEVELOPMENTS: 1970–1978

DENBIGH—AND MERION, TOO

IT LOOKS AT this point like close to half of each College's freshman class will sign up to live on the other campus next year. Add to them a crowd of Bryn Mawr sophomores, virtually none of whom were able to live at Haverford this year; a not-as-large but fairly substantial number of Haverford sophomores; and just average sign-ups from the junior class, and the result could well be the highest exchange sign-up by far that the bi-College community has ever seen.

It would not surprise us if the sign-up level at both campuses is close to 250. Although a certain amount of attrition always occurs, few of the freshmen who feel guaranteed of poor housing on their home campuses are likely to change their minds based on where they end up on the other campus.

Further, we believe that the majority of freshmen who sign up to exchange are not primarily motivated by the negative desire to avoid poor housing.

Most students consider it desirable to have lived on both campuses in the course of their four years. Sophomore year is an excellent year to exchange because (1) the year before the substantial major work begins offers the best opportunity to take a fair number of courses on the other campus, and (2) finding out early what both campuses are like makes it more likely students will spend their junior and senior years in the environment that is best for them.

If the level of the sign-up is indeed around 250, we would like to see the exchange level set at 220.

Lowering the quality of rooms offered to exchanging sophomores will keep the quality of upperclass rooms as high as usual without causing significantly higher attrition levels among underclass students who will do no better on their home campuses. Taking fairly unattractive sophomore housing as a given, the Colleges should at least let the sophomores be miserable on the campus of their choice.

Let's be prepared to make both Merion and Denbigh coed next year, and come closer to a coeducational environment than we have ever been before.

Reprinted from the News (Bryn Mawr-Haverford), March 3, 1978.

CONSTITUTION PASSES: SGA OPEN TO MEN
Barbara Riemer, Class of 1976

HAVERFORD MEN LIVING AT BRYN MAWR are now eligible to run for all SGA offices, due to changed eligibility regulations in the SGA constitution ratified Wednesday. The passage of what came to be called the "Equal Rights Amendment" marked a reversal from the defeat of a similar motion, 218–201, at the first plenary, held Sunday, Jan. 19.

Quorum was lost Sunday, when a number of Haverfordians and a few Mawrters walked out of the weekend plenary to protest the defeat of a motion to allow Haverford men living on the Bryn Mawr campus to run for SGA secretary.

The walk-out followed the announcement of the results of the vote and a comment from a Haverfordian in the audience to the effect that if the men on campus (whose status as members of the SGA had been ratified earlier in the evening) were not allowed equal representation, then they should not help to make up the quorum. A check to see if quorum remained after the walk-out showed that attendance fell 62 short of the required 500.

Issues Crystallize

Audience discussion both before and after the adjournment centered on the discrepancy between defining Haverfordians as SGA members but not allowing them to run for office. Resolving this discrepancy—either by excluding men from the SGA or by according them the rights of all other members—soon became the major issues of the reconvened plenary.

The second plenary opened with a proposal to hold a revote on the definition of SGA membership. A statement from Rockefeller (which was adopted at a dorm meeting) proposing that Haverford men living on-campus be bound by the same regulations applying to guests as stated under the Honor Code, rather than by SGA regulations, followed on the heels of the proposal.

A revote was called, but the mood of the majority was apparently unswayed as 442 of the 558 voters opted for retaining the definition of membership as written.

A Clear Mandate

The expected motion to permit any member of SGA—Mawrter or Haverfordian—to run for office followed directly after results of the membership vote were announced, and was carried by a clear-cut voice count.

In the spirit of eliminating restrictions on eligibility for office, a motion to allow SGA members of any class to run for all offices—with the exception of student members of the Admissions Committee, class Honor Board representatives and class presidents—was passed on its second voting, 269–262.

The principle of the "Equal Rights Amendment" was extended to eliminate the two male jurors previously required on the Social Honor Board when trying a Haverfordian. The only change proposed for the Honor Code—the creation of a statement of confidentiality confirming the students' right to privacy—was passed easily. Liquor regulations now extant were questioned, but the majority resolved not to vote upon the restriction.

Reprinted from the News (Bryn Mawr-Haverford), January 24, 1974.

> IT WAS DISCONCERTING TO HEAR GUYS SINGING NEXT DOOR IN THE SHOWER BUT I GOT USED TO IT. MY FATHER WON'T GO TO THE BATHROOM WHEN HE COMES HERE THOUGH.
>
> —*Salli Madden, Class of 1978*

ABOLISH RETENTION

A REFERENDUM ON ABOLISHING dorm and room retention at Bryn Mawr will be voted on Tuesday night at hall meetings. It is none too soon for this issue to be acted upon—to the contrary, it is almost too late if any viable change in the dorm space allotment is to be made this year.

The referendum is a direct result of students' inability last spring to effect coed dorm expansion. All attempts at change became futile in the face of existing retention rules. Students agreed that their hands were tied until a campus-wide vote on retention could be taken in the fall. Until retention rules are abolished, it is virtually impossible to convert any further women's dorms into coed ones which freezes the amount of students that can be involved in the dorm exchange.

The issue has become an even more important one this fall in light of the plight of freshman dorm housing. Upperclassmen are occupying huge single rooms, while freshmen are crowded into triples. It is granted that the large size of this year's freshman class accounted for the overcrowding, however it is very probable that future freshman classes will maintain the numbers of this year's class, according to Carl Blumenthal, chairman of the residence committee.

The original concept behind dorm and room retention was to allow continuity in the community from year to year. A good concept, perhaps, in 1908 when there were student government resolutions to forbid young ladies to eat in town with males, and required them to be in by nine at night. But Bryn Mawr is no longer a bastion of learning isolated from most of the real world, it is part of a world that has changed radically over the past twenty years.

And similarly, Bryn Mawr must also change with its growing and changing needs. A retention system prohibits any flexibility in dorm arrangements. As long as it remains in effect, there can be no expansion of the coed dorm exchange, no equalization of freshmen housing arrangements, and no co-ops. Without retention, an infinite number of housing arrangements can be coordinated. For instance, certain dorms can be allotted as coed each year depending on the number of people who indicate interest. With all the dorms at the residence committee's disposal, they could use larger or smaller dorms each year as coed dorms depending on rise or decrease of interest.

Upperclassmen would still receive priority once they drew into a dorm, so it is doubtful that this change would seriously affect the quality of upperclassmen living arrangements. And since it would become more difficult to store things in closets, which has annually proved to be risky storage at best, this would force the community to make better security arrangements.

For any institution to survive, it must be flexible enough to change with the times. Our time is overdue.

Reprinted from the *News* (Bryn Mawr-Haverford), October 6, 1972.

ROOM DRAW PROPOSAL: NO LIMIT ON COED DORMS

Mike Rosenfeld, Haverford, Class of 1978; and Nancy Herndon, Class of 1977

THE BRYN MAWR Residence Committee and SGA Executive Council have unanimously approved support of a room draw proposal in which the number of Bryn Mawr students wishing to live in coed dorms will directly determine the number of coed dorms on campus.

There will be no artificial ceiling set on the number of coed dorms, or on the number of students living in coed dorms. Under the new proposal, students must sign up to live in one of three dorm situations: single sex, coed at Bryn Mawr, or coed at Haverford.

Any student switching from one dorm category to another will be penalized by having her priority number lowered. The penalty for switching between coed and single sex dorms at Bryn Mawr would be minimal—perhaps five places, according to Residence Committee Chairman Lucy Hunt—but a whopping 50 places for dropping out of the Haverford exchange.

It is possible that more than the five present coed dorms will be coed under the new proposal, but according to Hunt this is unlikely. "We don't feel the mood of the student body would cause it to happen," Hunt stated.

In the past, the number of coed dorms at Bryn Mawr has been based in part on the number of students signing up to live at Haverford, but the Residence Committee no longer sees this as a reputable reflection of the number of students wishing to live in a coed environment at Bryn Mawr. The proposed penalty will hopefully make the student sign up an accurate indication of student preference.

The proposal will now go to students and then the deans for approval. The referendum of a few weeks ago on limiting dorm exchanges was invalid, Hunt said, because the options listed on the ballots were not sufficiently explained.

Reprinted from the *News* (Bryn Mawr-Haverford), November 21, 1975.

BLUE BUS RESOLUTION
Statement from the Blue Bus Committee

IN CONJUNCTION with the new blue bus schedule, Students Council and SGA have unanimously passed the following resolution:

In order to abide by normal school-bus safety procedure, the number of passengers on the blue bus shall be limited to 60, i.e., no more than 12 standees. In order for this regulation to be effectively instituted, the bi-College community must be willing to do the following:

- Self-enforce the limit. It is unfair to place Tex or any other bus driver in the position of closing someone off the bus. Translated that means don't hassle him—wait for the next bus or find another means of transportation.
- Some students must take the bus on those runs which will arrive at the other campus long before their class is to begin. Since the new MWF morning schedule precludes the possibility of double runs any passengers in excess of 60 will be forced to miss the bus, and thus possibly a class or appointment. In particular, this affects anyone getting out of class who has another class at the other campus within the next half hour. In the spirit of cooperation we must be willing to help each other out.

Although we realize there will be inconveniences, we believe the goal of a safe bus to be the primary and only reasonable one.

Reprinted from the *News* (Bryn Mawr-Haverford), October 16, 1975.

Left: Students on the Blue Bus, which travels between Bryn Mawr and Haverford colleges, 1983

WOFFORD OPPOSES HAVERFORD COEDUCATION
Harris L. Wofford, Jr.

TAKING SERIOUSLY Mr. Coleman's assurance last spring that he would not raise the issue of coeducation again, we have proceeded with cooperation in recruiting and admissions, in curricular planning and appointments, and in exploring joint financial and administrative services. We have been doing this on the assumption that Haverford would not become another nearby competing coeducational college. We consider the continued development of a two-college community comprising a men's college and a women's undergraduate college in full cooperation to be the more interesting, more innovative, more challenging and more promising course.

The time and energy taken by the question of coeducation in the last few years has diverted us from the curricular planning and other joint efforts necessary to realize the full potential of these two colleges. We greatly regret that this may now happen again.

The possibility of Haverford recruiting and admitting its own women students puts in jeopardy some of the present programs of cooperation and most future prospects. For example, cooperation in recruiting and admissions will be pointless if we are seeking students from the same pool of applicants. Since the number of applicants we get each year is substantially less than Haverford gets and our joint recruiting is only beginning to bear fruit, Haverford's immediate concern about admissions seems premature. Nor do we understand why competing with Bryn Mawr for women students must be an "essential ingredient" for the proposed expansion. Such competition will certainly not promote expansion.

There are important problems in our cooperation that do need to be solved, particularly finding appropriate ways for freshmen and sophomores to enjoy the benefits of the two-college community sooner and on a larger scale. The solution to that problem will be very difficult, if not impossible, if Haverford is instead faced with the many different problems of integrating its proposed women students into a largely male institution, and with the problems of substantially expanded classes.

We much prefer the vision of the two-college community in which men at Haverford enjoy the rare experience of living and studying in a predominantly women's institution, and Bryn Mawr women have the experience of similar participation in a men's college. The Discussion Paper expresses the wish to cooperate with Bryn Mawr while Haverford becomes fully coeducational with its own women. We are convinced that in any true sense we cannot have both, and that many women and men students would benefit by the two-college arrangement instead of the conventional coeducation available elsewhere. We believe that continuing the course we have followed so far would be a much greater contribution to American education.

From the fall of 1965 when there were just over 200 cross-registrations on both campuses to today when the total is more than 1,000; from 1969 when the dormitory exchange began with 25 students from each college to the present 115, we have come a long way. About 230, or 25%, of our undergraduates, now live in coeducational halls, and more and more departments are joining in academic collaboration. Louis Green's recent report on the state of inter-college cooperation indicates progress on so many fronts. I would expect the upward trends to continue and cooperation to increase in many areas—if Haverford does not turn to another course.

Though we would disagree with Haverford's decision to follow the customary path now being taken by most men's colleges, we would respect its right to do so. If indeed this becomes Haverford's course, we would seek to continue cooperation within the limits necessarily imposed. What course Bryn Mawr would choose as an alternative to the full two-college community I cannot say, but we would then proceed to consider that matter.

Reprinted from the *News* (Bryn Mawr-Haverford), November 3, 1972.

COED CONTROVERSY

HAVERFORD REJECTS COEDUCATION NOW; BACKS COOPERATION

HAVERFORD, PA., Jan. 14—Haverford College, a men's liberal arts school in Eastern Pennsylvania, has decided to work toward coeducation through cooperation with nearby Bryn Mawr College, a women's school, rather than becoming independently coeducational.

Haverford's board of managers concluded last night that "the impact of coeducation on Bryn Mawr would be sufficiently negative to threaten relations between the two schools," but it left open the possibility that coeducation may be desirable in the future.

Currently, students may take courses and live on either campus. Some departments have federated, and all extracurricular activities are jointly funded and operated.

The board also moved to expand the number of students from 725 toward a "tentative maximum" of 1,000 adding no more than 50 students each year.

These decisions were compromises forced by sharp splits within the board and among faculty, students and administration at Haverford and Bryn Mawr. The chairman of the board, John White, made it clear at the meeting yesterday that the issues had not yet been resolved. The board could reverse itself at any time.

Haverford's president, John R. Coleman, had urged the board to make Haverford bigger and admit women. An increase in size, he said, is necessary to correct a yearly deficit of over $200,000.

But the Bryn Mawr community is almost unanimous in rejecting these proposals. They believe the existence of two strong schools sharing resources to be wiser in a time of fiscal and educational uncertainties than by becoming independent of each other. They also conceded that a coed Haverford would seriously damage their own admissions figures.

Reprinted from the *New York Times*, January 15, 1974.

Above: Students and friends conversing on the lawn at Bryn Mawr, c. 1970s

Opposite: Cartoon from the *News* (Bryn Mawr-Haverford), October 16, 1975

COOPERATIVE DEVELOPMENTS: 1970–1978

TO BRYN MAWR

CHIN UP, OLD GIRL. It is time to face facts. Haverford will be going coed. If not within the next three years, certainly within the next five. Don't cry. You're a big girl now. You can take it. He is not going to be completely out of your life, after all. But your relationship will certainly be altered drastically, and you will not be the lovers you once were.

Now is not the time to throw yourself at him, hoping he will stay with you a little longer.

Now is not the time to propose this marriage contract you have drawn up in a last ditch hope to save your relationship, in which you agree to change your name, and share your children. This is not the basis on which to begin a marriage. Nor will the marriage last. The end is in sight.

It is time you realized that a woman does not need to live with a man in order to survive. Sometimes it is better to be friends. Hopefully, you will remain friends with him for some time.

No longer will you be able to look in the mirror and say, "I am attractive because I have a boyfriend." You must look deeper into yourself, in your womanhood that makes you attractive and strong. This is part of growing up. After 90 years, isn't it about time?

You must offer to us, your daughters, what we could not find in someone who was not so dedicated to our welfare as women. Some of these things you already have: a faculty that is approximately half female—an astounding figure compared to nationwide statistics for Colleges—a wealth of successful, exciting alumnae to come back and give us courage. From these two groups we can draw our role models. What else could make you attractive to a young woman scholar?

A dedication to her needs as a woman: an emphasis on Bryn Mawr's femaleness, on the high record of achievements of your alumnae, and a commitment to feminism. You need feminist authors, artists, and musicians in residence. You need a women's studies concentration. You need to attract young women on these grounds, rather than on the incentive "look at how many coed dorms we have." And young women need this kind of education, even those who come for the coed dorms, because they have all been socialized in a sexist society.

Was it not for you she spoke, when a famous lesbian/feminist college president, said, "Only our failures only marry"? Shall you, our mother, present us with so poor an example to follow that you become one of these failures?

Reprinted from the *News* (Bryn Mawr-Haverford), October 15, 1976.

But Bryn Mawr is no longer a bastion of learning isolated from most of the real world, it is part of a world that has changed radically over the past twenty years.

—"Abolish Retention," News *(Bryn Mawr-Haverford), October 6, 1972.*

BMC URGES BI-COLLEGE CONFEDERATION
Nancy Harrison and Brenda Wright, both Class of 1979

THE BRYN MAWR Board of Trustees last weekend approved with only one dissenting vote a statement proposing a confederated Bryn Mawr and Haverford to the Haverford Board of Managers. The statement includes proposals for a joint degree, a common name for the two Colleges, a joint recruiting effort, and admission of upper class transfers of either sex to both Colleges.

The proposal states in its introduction that its provisions are contingent upon Haverford continuing to admit only men, and Bryn Mawr only women, as freshmen.

It further notes that the idea of admitting transfers of either sex to both Colleges is included only because of Haverford President John Coleman's conviction that Haverford's expansion and coeducational goals require the admission of women from outside Bryn Mawr. "We think that of the possible ways of doing this, the transfer option will do the least damage to cooperation," the proposal states.

Common Name
The proposal recommends that the two Colleges share a common name, and institute a joint Council of Managers and Trustees which will report to the Boards of each College and to a Joint Faculty Council composed of members from both faculties and administrations. It proposes that the existing cross-registration and major requirements policies continue as they now exist for courses taken at either undergraduate or graduate Colleges.

The proposal allows both Colleges to accept transfers of either sex, but specifies that Haverford only admit male freshmen and Bryn Mawr only female freshmen. It recommends a joint recruiting and admissions effort aimed toward achieving the admissions goals of each College, and suggests that measures be taken to equalize cross-registration imbalances. The main points of the proposal are to be followed for a trial period of four years.

The initial Bryn Mawr reaction to the proposal appeared to be favorable. "Bryn Mawr's overt attitude toward cooperation with Haverford and commitment to the bi-College community is incredibly strengthened by this proposal," said SGA President Cynthia Grund, adding that she strongly supports the proposal.

"Total Support"
Sociology Prof. Eugene Schneider told the *News* that he and the entire Bryn Mawr sociology department are "100 percent in support" of the proposal, and that he has the impression that a majority of the department chairmen also favor it.

Bryn Mawr Board Member Barbara Taft noted that while presentation of the proposal was advanced a few months because of Haverford's decision to consider coeducation, Bryn Mawr has been moving toward a more cooperative stance since 1973.

Although the Haverford Board of Managers is scheduled to make its decision on admitting women Dec. 10, Bryn Mawr Dean Mary Pat McPherson stated that she expects the Bryn Mawr proposal to be carefully considered by Haverford. "I think it's too important a question not to be given the time needed," she said.

Commenting on the possibility that Haverford might have to postpone its decision in order to consider the proposal, she stated, "It's their timetable, not ours." Chairman of the Bryn Mawr Board of Trustees Judge Edmund Spaeth noted, however, that the proposal "is not offered as an attempt to slow anyone down."

According to President Coleman, any decision to go coed must be made by December if women are to be admitted to next fall's freshman class.

Needn't Change
McPherson described the proposal as "a vision that must be worked out in detail by the two Colleges," noting that it "wouldn't be appropriate" for one college alone to spell out specific provisions for consideration.

The Bryn Mawr faculty will discuss the proposal Wednesday, and vote on it at some unspecified time. "We'll have to see if they [the faculty] are even interested in it," said McPherson, adding that while the proposal has "potential" for moving the two institutions closer together, "without vigorous support from either side, it needn't change things at all." However, if the faculty does adopt the proposal, she said, they will support it, in which case "lots could happen."

History department Chairman Arthur Dudden said his reaction to the proposal was "favorable," adding "in principle and in spirit I wish it well." Maria Crawford, geology department chairman, termed it "a positive proposal on cooperation."

"It's a real initiative to address areas of Haverford's concerns—I hope they give it serious consideration," she said.

Five Years Sooner
Schneider commented that members of the sociology department are "convinced of the need for it [the proposal] and have been for a long time," adding that he wished the proposal had come five years sooner.

He stated that the crucial point of the proposal is its specification that Haverford not admit freshmen women, which he said would greatly increase cooperation. He commented that the proposal would make Haverford's enrollment easier and also increase the coed environment because it would allow more women to cross-major.

"We would be crazy to destroy the present situation," Schneider said, noting that he considers it vital that the proposal be passed by the faculty.

Some faculty members expressed reservations about the idea of admitting male transfers. Crawford commented that the transfer provision would have to be the "most seriously considered" of the items in the proposal, adding however that she did not think the provision was "central to the spirit of the proposal, which is the future of cooperation with Haverford."

Bryn Mawr President Harris Wofford explained that the wording of the statement leaves open the male transfer question, which he termed "the main issue on campus." "We have not tried to decide whether Bryn Mawr will admit male transfers," he said.

Wofford also mentioned that a discussion on accepting male students might be "tied up with the idea of a joint A.B./M.A.," suggesting that men could perhaps be admitted as undergraduates with the provision that they be seeking a graduate degree from Bryn Mawr as well. Wofford added that he and McPherson would personally "favor the transfer option."

One Name
The common name for the two Colleges suggested in the proposal is intended as a way of describing the cooperative relationship, but not of impairing the autonomy of the individual Colleges, McPherson commented. While she referred to the common name as a tool for a federated admissions effort, McPherson noted that she did not expect the two Colleges to share a catalog and listing in Barron's guide to colleges, although these details might be worked out in future negotiations with Haverford.

Neither the Joint Council of Managers and Trustees nor the Joint Faculty Council suggested in the proposal would have the power to supersede that of the existing Boards and faculties, McPherson stated, but would exist in an advisory capacity.

While the Faculty Council would decide the requirements of a joint degree, she said, the home faculties would have the final vote on accepting these requirements.

Under the provisions of the proposal, the Joint Council of Managers and Trustees and the Joint Faculty Council would not include student representation. McPherson noted that students already serve on the existing committees to which the new committees would report.

Taft explained that "the feeling is that students are already cooperating in every aspect" of cooperation, but Wofford commented that the issue of student representation would be looked into, and that "certainly students should be a significant element."

SGA President Grund stated that she felt student input "must be built into the proposal."

Majoring Options
McPherson noted that the only way for students to major at the other College under the proposal is through transferring to that institution or receiving a joint degree, except where the departments are federated. She commented that she expected departmental cooperation to increase under the proposal because of the Joint Faculty Committee and of the provisions made for an equalized workload between the two faculties.

The proposal holds the door open for more departmental cooperation, but does not guarantee it, she explained, adding that it "opens up new paths for students to move between the two institutions."

Wofford commented on the implications of the proposal for Bryn Mawr's status as a single-sex institution by noting, "That's not an accurate description now. We haven't called ourselves a women's college for a long time." "I don't think that Bryn Mawr has ever been concerned with the education of women in isolation," McPherson observed. Board Chairman Spaeth also spoke to this issue, stating, "Bryn Mawr's mission is to give the finest possible education it can to its students," adding that this mission is not necessarily restricted to women students and pointing out that Bryn Mawr's graduate schools admit men.

Willing to Experiment

Grund commented at last Sunday's SGA meeting that the proposal showed that Bryn Mawr opinion had "really turned around from the hard line of being a women's college, to a willingness to make an educational experiment."

Several Haverford students attending the meeting, where the proposal was first presented to students, questioned whether the statement's provisions would allow Haverford to meet its admissions needs, and asked that this issue be emphasized in discussions on the proposal at Bryn Mawr. "You've got to show them [Haverford] that even if this does show a new unity, how can you prove this will attract students," one Haverfordian stated.

It was also suggested that Haverford students consider the possible effects of Haverford's admitting women on the future of bi-College cooperation. "The risk of it dying will be high," one student declared. "Let that be put to Haverford students."

Helping Haverford

McPherson said she believes the proposal will be able to help Haverford achieve its enrollment goals, and that she thinks Bryn Mawr Admissions Director Elizabeth Vermey agrees. Wofford commented, "The main hope [of the proposal] is that all the steps taken together will increase the appeal of the community so that Haverford can meet its enrollment needs."

McPherson was unable to predict if specific items in the proposal might still be implemented if Haverford decided to admit women as freshmen. Wofford stated that, although "nobody's talking about ending cross-registration," a Haverford decision to go coed would probably cause Bryn Mawr to put more energy into "things that don't relate to Haverford."

"We will all profess an interest in cooperation, but factors will be pushing us elsewhere," he continued.

McPherson has mentioned that if Haverford decided to admit women, Bryn Mawr would have to consider coeducation for itself within five years. She commented, however, that the idea of "two conventional institutions competing for students" would be "much less interesting" than Bryn Mawr and Haverford's cooperational relationship.

Reprinted from the *News* (Bryn Mawr-Haverford), October 8, 1976.

Previous page: Student with male companion on the steps behind Rockefeller Hall, c. 1976–79

Opposite: Coffee hour in Thomas Great Hall, November 1976

HAVERFORD GO COED? BRYN MAWR BRISTLES
Ben A. Franklin

HAVERFORD, Pa., Oct. 20—Resembling a family fight that the neighbors can hear, the Quakers at Haverford College are almost at the point of having a crockery-throwing set-to with the Quakers down the road at Bryn Mawr College over a proposal by Haverford to go coeducational.

In the tree-shrouded fieldstone halls of Haverford, a small, 143-year-old, respected school for men on Philadelphia's Main Line, the debate has been long and heavy going. Today, a report released by a Haverford committee said that not to go coeducational would be "prima facie, unjust."

In addition, Haverford is hungry for bright students who can pay the $6,000 yearly tuition. There will be budget cuts, the report said, unless able female recruits can be found to expand the enrollment from 750 to 1,000 as planned.

The Haverford board of managers is scheduled to reach a decision on coeducation Dec. 10.

Bryn Mawr Feels Threatened

The school, which has a politically liberal, liberal arts tradition—its president joins a garbage truck crew in his spare time to "relearn what it is like to be at the bottom" and its vice president has been arrested several times at Quaker peace vigils—has abandoned proposals to go coeducational twice before in the face of stern disapproval from Bryn Mawr and its 1,000 women students.

The women's school views the proposal as a competitive threat in the race for top women students and as injurious to its happy relationship of "cooperation."

There is a Bryn Mawr counterproposal with Haverford advocating more intercampus cooperation. Possibilities include degrees that are granted jointly and the admission of women to Haverford as transfer students, but not as freshmen.

For a decade, Bryn Mawr and Haverford have met the demands of their once sexually segregated students for greater and greater social and academic integration by steadily expanding a system of "community."

"The Best of Both Worlds" has been one of Bryn Mawr's special recruitment appeals. To bright young women—a pool that is shrinking for the same reason as is Haverford's pool of men, the declining birth rate—Bryn Mawr can say, "To share in a coeducational experience you don't have to go to Harvard or Yale."

At Bryn Mawr, young women can choose, from year to year, to stay on their own campus, or they can study and live at the Haverford campus. Students at each college commute daily to the other for courses.

Like "a Marriage Fight"

According to Elizabeth B. Vermey, Bryn Mawr's director of admissions, "Haverford regards us as a mistress and it wants its own wife, its own women. We are not now in that kind of legal or conventional relationship."

Asked why the idea seems to be generating such passion and anxiety at Bryn Mawr, Aryeh Kosman, the bearded Haverford philosophy professor who was chairman of the committee that issued today's report, said: "It's like walking in on a marriage fight—there are hidden agendas."

"It is easier for a Bryn Mawr student to have a loyalty to Haverford than the other way around," said Harris L. Wofford, Jr., who is only the second male president of the women's college since it was founded in 1885. "Haverford has a great sense of its own community, whereas we have a tradition of individuality. We have accepted the idea of dual loyalty, but it is harder for them."

The Kosman committee includes Haverford's president, John R. Coleman, an economist whose administration has long favored coeducation.

It is one of the "family fight" aspects of the dispute that three of the 40 or so members of Haverford's policy-setting board of managers also are members of Bryn Mawr's board of trustees. One, in fact, is the Bryn Mawr board chairman and others are Bryn Mawr administrators or the husbands of Bryn Mawr graduates still active in campus activities.

"We think that if Haverford goes coed, with roughly half its expanded enrollment women, we will then have a college community here of perhaps 1,500 students, only 500 or 600 of whom are men," said Mr. Wofford. "We think the present balance is better."

Reprinted from the *New York Times*, October 21, 1976.

PRESIDENT OF HAVERFORD RESIGNS IN CONTROVERSY WITH BRYN MAWR

HAVERFORD, Pa., Jan. 18—John R. Coleman, president of Haverford College, announced his resignation today, calling it the culmination of a long dispute with neighboring Bryn Mawr College over the admission of women students to this small Quaker institution for men.

His decision to leave Haverford on June 30, at the end of 10 years as its president, followed what many in the two-college community on Philadelphia's Main Line took to be a rebuff to Mr. Coleman by the Haverford board of managers on his long-standing proposal to make the 143-year-old men's college fully coeducational.

Bryn Mawr, an all-women's college a mile away, had resisted the Coleman plan that was viewed to be direct competition for bright, well-to-do women applicants and a threat to a major Bryn Mawr recruiting appeal. This stressed that Bryn Mawr's close cooperation and student exchange with Haverford in the upper three classes offered its students "the best of both possible worlds"—a choice of single-sex education on the Bryn Mawr campus or optional coeducation, including dormitory exchange, at Haverford.

The two campuses are connected by shuttle buses and most student activities are conducted jointly.

Under Mr. Coleman's plan, rejected by the Haverford board last month, freshman women would have been admitted directly to Haverford and would have had access later to courses and dormitories at Bryn Mawr if they chose to use the inter-campus system of cooperation.

Bryn Mawr officials said that this would alter the "two-college community" from one that is now roughly half men and half women to one that might be two-thirds or three-quarters women. Under a compromise approved by the Haverford board last month, women will be admitted, but only as transfer students in the upper classes.

The board's deliberations were believed to have been influenced by members of Bryn Mawr's board who also serve on the Haverford board. In an interview recently, Mr. Coleman called that "a conflict of interest situation."

The 55-year-old Canadian-born educator and labor economist was also chairman of the Federal Reserve Bank in Philadelphia until his term expired Jan. 1. But he had found time in recent years to pursue experiences in what he called the "world of work," hiring on anonymously for weeks-long stints as a ditch digger, a garbage truck helper and a short-order cook in various areas of the country. This unorthodoxy, and his encouragement of students to do the same, was not popular with some Bryn Mawr administrators.

Mr. Coleman, who became a Quaker 18 months ago, announced his resignation this morning at a meeting of Haverford students and faculty.

Reprinted from the *New York Times*, January 19, 1977.

Left: Coffee hour in Thomas Great Hall, c. 1970s

Opposite: Promotional brochure for college applicants, c. 1970

POLL ON COEDUCATION REVEALS BMC PREFERS STATUS QUO

Nancy Herndon, Class of 1977

NEARLY THREE-FOURTHS of the Bryn Mawr students participating in a poll conducted last week by the SGA indicated that they viewed social and academic cooperation as important to their satisfaction with life at Bryn Mawr.

A majority also indicated that they would be "less satisfied" with both these areas of cooperation if Haverford admitted an equal number of women and men students.

The poll, supervised by Rhoads Dorm President Fred Marx and Curriculum Committee Chairman Dori Heinrich, questioned 666 Bryn Mawr students, comprised of about 84 percent of the Bryn Mawr campus, 64 percent of the Bryn Mawr students living at Haverford, and about 10 percent of the non-resident population.

Eighty-five percent of these students indicated that they thought the "general Bryn Mawr College atmosphere" would be harmed if Haverford were to admit an equal number of women and men. Under these conditions, 76 percent said that they would be less satisfied with social cooperation; 55 percent said they would be less satisfied with academic cooperation; and 62 percent would be less satisfied with activities cooperation.

However, 71 percent of the students polled indicated that their decision on whether or not to cross-register would not be affected if Haverford went coed.

When questioned about making a decision to live at Haverford, assuming the room draw policies remain the same, 39 percent of the students indicated that a Haverford decision to become fully coed would have no effect on their decision. Thirty percent said that they "might not" live at Haverford, and 21 percent said they would not anyway, according to Marx.

While 72 percent of students polled said they would not transfer to Haverford if it went coed, 26 percent—173 students—indicated that they might transfer at least under certain conditions. Five percent said that they definitely would transfer, 14 percent said they might transfer, and seven percent said they would transfer only if cooperation is maintained.

Students were not given the opportunity of indicating specifically that they might transfer only if cooperation was not maintained, or that they might transfer to another school besides Haverford.

Status Quo Supported

Fifty-six percent of the students ranked the option of retaining status quo cooperation with single-sex Haverford first out of six possible options listed. The option of Bryn Mawr and Haverford accepting the Bryn Mawr Board proposal was ranked first by 34 percent. Marx noted that three of the options listed were ambiguous because they did not specify whether or not Haverford is assumed to be coed or single-sex in their description of a possible future for Bryn Mawr.

Marx added that the figures seem to indicate, however, that Bryn Mawr students would prefer an option that allows them to cooperate with rather than withdraw from Haverford, coed or not.

The poll results compiled by Marx revealed that although only 55 percent of the students said they would be less satisfied with academic cooperation if Haverford were fully coed, and 40 percent said they anticipated no effect on academic cooperation caused by such a situation, 66 percent indicated that they thought "the atmosphere in Bryn Mawr classes" would be harmed if Haverford were fully coed.

Marx stated that the questions producing these results were not clear and ought perhaps to have been asked differently. He commented, however, "If you ask a question directly, people may respond the way they think they should respond instead of saying what they think."

He noted that the interchangeable use of the terms "coed," "admitting females," and "admitting an equal number of women and men," in other questions might also have been ambiguous.

If Haverford accepted "a small number of female students," over half the Bryn Mawr students polled said that their satisfaction with academic and activities cooperation would not be affected. Fifty-five percent of them indicated that they would be less satisfied with social cooperation in such a case; 40 percent said they thought their satisfaction with social cooperation would not be affected.

The poll was given to each student individually. Sixty to 100 percent of each dorm was polled. Of the 666 people polled, about 17 percent are seniors, 24 percent are juniors, 28 percent are sophomores, and 30 percent are freshmen. The students polled were also classified by majors, with 28 percent social science majors, 23 percent natural science majors, and 29 percent humanities majors.

Importance of Cooperation

In a breakdown of the question of how important cooperation is to the satisfaction of Bryn Mawr students with their life at the College, 60 percent of those in single-sex dorms rated it as important, as opposed to 84 percent of those in coed dorms; and 78 percent of the social science majors, 69 percent of the natural science majors, and 73 percent of the humanities majors also rated cooperation as important.

Marx presented the results of the poll to the Bryn Mawr faculty last Wednesday night.

Reprinted from the News *(Bryn Mawr-Haverford), November 12, 1976.*

FEMINIST CONSCIOUSNESS

FROM SEPARATISM TO FEMINISM
Kathleen Murphy, Class of 1977

BRYN MAWR COLLEGE is coming from a strong tradition of feminism. That tradition can be destroyed through student apathy; it is up to us to keep our strongest and most valuable tradition alive.

The national feminist movement, of which Bryn Mawr and all women's colleges are a part, stands for more than bra-burning; every thinking person knows this. What is not so often apparent, however, is that the success of feminist-directed social change depends on freeing *all* people from sexist stereotypes. It means that men must change their ideas about themselves, and that women must change their attitudes towards men. Bryn Mawr has a unique opportunity to foster these changes and to provide an atmosphere in which a humanist attitude can grow. The combination of Bryn Mawr's feminism with Haverford's Quaker philosophy is more dynamic than many Mawrters or Fords may realize. It is one of the finest opportunities presented by our system of cooperation. But unless Mawrters or Fords *do* engage in intellectual, emotional, and basic social exchange, a valuable opportunity for individual and social growth is lost.

The above ideology has direct practical implications for the dorm exchange, SGA membership, the *News*, the Women's Alliance, as well as the futures of Bryn Mawr, Haverford, and cooperation itself. The idea of cooperation is based on a compromise between coeducation and sexual separatism. To see the other sex as an equal partner in humanity, it is necessary to work with and be involved with them on levels other than the purely social. Hence we have introduced coed dorms, classrooms, media, and student governments. However, women seeking to remove themselves from a two-sex society in order to identify and evaluate the repressive and the nourishing aspects of living with men need to have that option respected. Hence we have retained single-sex dorms, separate institutions, and most important, the Women's Alliance. The system as it now exists is working. It is up to those who care about their school to keep that system working, through active participation in the community.

Reprinted from the *News* (Bryn Mawr-Haverford), February 7, 1975.

BMC EXPLORES FEMINIST ROLE
Deidre Berger, Class of 1975

"IS BRYN MAWR A COLLEGE attended by women, or a women's college?" That was the main question that Bryn Mawrters struggled to define at the sessions on Educational Goals of a Women's College at the recent Colloquium.

The first problem in the discussion was that Bryn Mawr presently has no specific commitment to being a women's institution, yet it does not admit men to its undergraduate school. What then justifies its being a non-coed institution?

Prevailing sentiments ran strongly in favor of Bryn Mawr remaining a women's college—if it becomes a feminist institution. "A women's college has a responsibility to give its students a sense of what women are and what 'culture' women have and don't have," said one student. Other advantages of a women's college that were cited included less discrimination, more general respect, and a chance to know the female mind. Many people also felt that the atmosphere created is a good one because you realize that there is nothing wrong with being a bright woman, and there is no need to hide it . . .

Women's studies were very intently discussed, but without a general consensus. Many people felt that an entire women's studies department needs to be created, because if it is not available here, where would it be? Many others were worried that there is not a lot of academic value to women's courses, and felt that it is much more important to integrate women's studies into the curriculum. One professor felt that one area to be explored was the contribution women can make to knowledge. In an institution such as Bryn Mawr, we can explore what *is* academic about feminism . . .

Many women indicated their unhappiness with the present lack of preparation they are being given for the world after graduation. There was general assent with students' opinion that the predominant attitude here is that preparation for the real world is non-academic. There seems to be an attitude of prejudice against women preparing for professions, or anything beyond graduate, medical, or law school. Liberal arts should not exclude the business world, and we must prepare women to do other things . . .

During this reevaluation of Bryn Mawr as a feminist institution, it was noted that the faculty, and especially department heads, are very male dominated. One professor brought up the point that there is a dearth of women professors now because so many women of our parents' generation threw away their education in favor of suburbia. She feels that the pool has been steadily increasing in recent years. There was overwhelming agreement, indicated on questionnaires, that if an equally qualified man or woman were applying for a position at Bryn Mawr, the woman should get the position.

Reprinted from the *News* (Bryn Mawr-Haverford), March 31, 1972.

INSTITUTIONAL COMMITMENT FOR WOMEN

WEDNESDAY NIGHT'S MEETING discussing Bryn Mawr as a feminist institution has some valuable lessons to teach the College. Of the almost 200 women crowded into the Erdman living room, most were discontent. That such a significant number of students are so upset should convince even the most conservative people that the school must take immediate steps to reform its attitudes towards women. The spirit of community at the meeting was rare and beautiful, but it must be followed by action.

The speakers and audience had several complaints. Many argued that the College treats women as inferiors. They cited the 3.2 ratio of men to women on the faculty, the high number (75%) of women lecturers, and the small number (30%) of women professors. Several departments, they noted, have no women at all or only employ them in low-ranking jobs.

Other speakers attacked the formal structure of the classroom, and called for more discussions and fewer lectures; women should develop more intellectual self-confidence. Still others asserted that the infirmary's birth control policy treats students as children. They questioned whether the placement service was equipped to find women interesting jobs, and to help them handle offers of typing jobs.

One of the most important accusations made at the meeting concerned women's studies courses. Only Lila Karp's sociology course and, next semester, Mary Maples Dunn's history of women course presently are scheduled.

Women repeatedly stated that Bryn Mawr failed to instill in them a consciousness of the problems they would face as women when they graduated. Bryn Mawr creates a false sense of security by telling its students that they are better than other women; in reality, all women face the same discrimination.

It is clear that Bryn Mawr must make a firmer institutional commitment to bettering the status of women. As Kate Stimson so accurately pointed out, such a move would be important to both the outside world and to Bryn Mawr students in that they are fully the equal of any man. But what forms should this institutional commitment take?

Stimson and Elaine Showalter supplied some answers when they discussed women's activities at Barnard and at Douglass College. Women's centers there work on a full range of activities, from child-care to counseling. Centers also catalyze legal actions, and publish literature about the movement. The schools themselves offer varied courses on women.

It is, first of all, obvious that courses on women can be instituted without detracting from the academic quality of the College. Lila Karp's suggestion for a course refuting Freud's ideas about women is interesting; so might be courses on the general psychology of women, the biology of women, or paintings of women.

It is also clear that Bryn Mawr must sponsor activities aimed at discussing and improving the status of women. Bryn Mawr can and should encourage the development of a women's center, and should publish studies on the current situation of women, much as the Seven Sisters' placement offices publish a guide to job opportunities for women. The school should encourage student project courses. And it goes without saying that the school should give more than high priority to the hiring and promotion of women faculty. And, of course, students should be treated as adults by all offices of the College, including the infirmary.

Students must play an active part in determining their own destiny. They must ask hard questions of the institution and demand long-run changes, not just temporary or superficial ones, and they must ask for a permanent share of the power of running their own institution.

Lastly, the College and its students should explore several crucial questions. Why are women alienated from each other, and are therefore prevented from uniting to help themselves? What are the changing needs of women, and is the College adapting to those needs? How does Bryn Mawr's relationship with Haverford play a part in women's struggle for equality? And what does it imply about women's present feelings about themselves?

The open meeting Wednesday night raised many interesting issues, but those issues must be translated into action. As President Harris Wofford so aptly said, the meeting "did a good job of raising the heat, and now we will have to transform it into light."

Reprinted from the *News* (Bryn Mawr-Haverford), November 20, 1971.

Above: Student on campus, fall 1976.
Photograph by Karl Dimler

Opposite: Students at coffee hour in
Thomas Great Hall, November 1976

FEMINISM: A SPECTRUM OF VIEWS

Deborah Frishman, Class of 1976; Nan Herbert, Class of 1977; Roberta Paley, Class of 1976; Celia Pedersen, Class of 1977; Margaret Turner, Class of 1978; and Sharon Witherspoon, Class of 1978

IN LAST WEEK'S *NEWS*, the word "feminist" was thrown around indiscriminately and irresponsibly as it was throughout the week of Plenary. The *News* editorial spoke of the "need for clarification of issues"; we wish to address ourselves to this need.

First of all, we object to the use of "feminist" as a label applied to anti-male or Bryn Mawr isolationist sentiments. Just as the expression "male-chauvinist" is inappropriate when universally applied to groups of men with diverse opinions, so it is equally inappropriate and harmful to characterize as "feminist" one point of view or another in the debate over male representation in SGA. Such labeling can easily lead to misplaced hostilities towards feminism, as well as to misconceptions about the real issues at hand. As an example, the editorial seems to imply that the ideals of the "feminist community" are inherently in conflict with those of bi-College cooperation. Does the continued support for bi-College cooperation imply that we must redefine our "fast-disappearing ideals"?

The issues need to be clarified further, and a distinction must be made between those concerns that are institutional in character and those that are specifically feminist. People opposed to the eligibility of Haverford students to hold Bryn Mawr offices may or may not be committed feminists. While feminism may be a strong factor inclining an individual towards either side of the debate, the fact remains that opposition to the new eligibility rulings and the specific issue of feminism are by no means synonymous.

We see two central concerns at stake: (1) Bryn Mawr's autonomy as an institution versus merged identity with Haverford; and (2) a female apprehension of male dominance (as a reaction to traditional societal patterns) versus a wish to avoid "reverse sexism" in an exclusion of males from Bryn Mawr community government.

A committed feminist could take any of these points of view. We, as members of the Bryn Mawr community, hold a wide spectrum of opinions on this issue, as well as on others. There are valid arguments on all sides of the SGA debate; the important thing is to avoid the inaccurate equation of any single point of view with feminism.

Feminism encompasses widely varying, and often opposing social and political philosophies. The National Organization for Women, which is committed to reform within the existing social structure, contrasts sharply with Radical Women, which espouses revolutionary alternative lifestyles. Both are feminist institutions.

These examples should illustrate the great diversity of both beliefs and interests represented by the feminist movement.

Clearly, then, the words "feminist" and "feminism" do not connote a specific set of beliefs. In the discussion of these issues immediately confronting Bryn Mawr, the avoidance of facile generalization is imperative.

Reprinted from the *News* (Bryn Mawr-Haverford), January 31, 1975.

A FEMINIST CURRICULUM

BRYN MAWR'S ROLE as a vanguard in women's education is in no way proven by its still half-hearted attempts to provide a heightened consciousness of feminism in its curriculum.

The impending departure of Lila Karp as visiting lecturer in sociology at the end of this semester points up the glaring deficiencies in the College's women's studies program. Among these shortcomings is the continuing practice of appointing a "feminist-in-residence" who may serve a year or so before a new guest feminist is appointed. Not only does the deficiency manifest itself in the present lack of courses on women, but the fact that this professor is neither full-time nor permanent makes the professor and women's studies much less integral parts of the College.

Karp may have left her Bryn Mawr positions at the end of this year anyway, but her particular circumstances are less important than the institution's apparent willingness to continue this policy in its next women's studies appointee. In all, some four hours of class time per week is being devoted to women in sociology and history this semester. Prof. Mary Dunn's history of women course drew such a response that rather stifling prerequisites had to be established to keep the enrollment at a reasonable level. Clearly, this is a most abysmal situation for "the most frankly academic of the Seven Sisters" (as Bryn Mawr is described by Cass and Birnbaum[1]), even if one ignores the political ramifications of women's studies.

It is not just the social sciences that can use a greater dose of women-centered study. Imaginative and relevant courses in disciplines from philosophy to art history to biology can focus on women.

If, as was claimed last fall during the Haverford coeducation controversy, a case can be made for an all-women's college, Bryn Mawr should begin to prove it can fill this need. Institutional commitment for women begins in the curriculum; a full-time interdepartmental professor of women's studies, plus courses taught within departments by present faculty members is an imperative first step.

1. James Cass and Max Birnbaum, *Comparative Guide to American Colleges* (New York: Harper & Row, 1972).—Ed.

Reprinted from the *News* (Bryn Mawr-Haverford), February 18, 1972.

BMC FINE ARTS PROFESSOR SUPPORTS COMMITMENT TO FEMINIST ART
Catherine Pages, Class of 1978

MIRIAM SCHAPIRO describes herself as the "Juanita Appleseed of consciousness raising" on the art lecture circuit. She has spent the last six years enjoying her "network" approach to feminism, making a point of meeting as many women as possible wherever her activities take her.

This semester, she commutes from New York two days every week to teach fine arts in the Arnecliffe studio at Bryn Mawr.

Schapiro's self-proclaimed commitment to feminist art involved dramatic change in the style and focus of her painting. Her previous work had been what she describes as "clearly ambitious" geometric abstractions.

In 1972, she, a partner, and 21 students received funding from the California Institute of the Arts for a project called "Womanhouse": the transformation of a building in downtown Hollywood into an expression of "female fantasy." One of Schapiro's contributions was a dollhouse, an initial step in her exploration of the meaning of objects traditionally associated with womanhood.

Feminist Gallery

The "Womanhouse" project was a decided success; the result was the creation of "Womanspace," the first feminist cooperative gallery on the West Coast.

"Women . . . are formed around a central core, and have a secret place which can be entered and is a passageway from which life emerges." This concept, presented in a 1973 issue of the "Womanspace Journal," has served as a point of departure for refinements and exploration of Schapiro's concerns about women as artists and people.

She now works with collages, her most recent work including her "Connection Pieces": collages fabricated from handkerchiefs and aprons. She has also produced a "Collaboration Series," reproductions of paintings by prominent women artists incorporated in her own work.

Schapiro's interest in the medium of collage dominates her teaching in Arnecliffe. Although she has done most of her teaching in professional schools, she finds the liberal arts environment at Bryn Mawr conducive to an attitude she feels is essential to artistic work.

"Art is about information, systems of organization; art only flourishes in an analytical framework. The artist must be both relaxed and intellectual. He or she must work in an atmosphere of sensitivity and order."

SoHo Visit

Next weekend Schapiro's afternoon classes will visit her New York studio, in SoHo, in order to get an idea of what is happening in contemporary art. She finds her students surprisingly ignorant of the work of today's artists.

Schapiro said she feels this exposure will be useful to the students. "If you've never tasted citrus fruit, biting a lemon can be an informative first step."

Schapiro feels her teaching reflects the positive feeling she has about everything she does. "I'm made very anxious about ritualized teaching in the fine arts. I feel that students best absorb teaching in a relaxed situation."

Similarly, she says, her collages of traditionally feminine objects and images are stripped of the repressive connotations they evoke in feminist circles. Her work is an attempt to rediscover their positive values, rather than an expression of disillusionment with a stereotype.

Schapiro is currently preparing a show for the Artspace Gallery, on the West Coast, as well as contributing to "Heresies," an artist-writer collective in New York. Next year she plans to resume her "network" peregrinations, continuing to explore what she calls "the woman's sensibility."

Reprinted from the *News* (Bryn Mawr-Haverford), March 4, 1977.

Opposite: Student on campus, fall 1976. Photograph by Karl Dimler

---

200 ATTEND FIRST MILLETT CLASS; SHE CALLS LIBERATION "ONE IDEA"

"YOU HAVE TO DO EVERYTHING. Work from every single side at once," commented Kate Millett on women's liberation.

"I belong to everything," she said. "Factions don't matter; women's liberation is based on one idea."

The New York sculptor, teacher, and author of the book *Sexual Politics* is currently teaching a sociology course at Bryn Mawr. The first session, held last Wednesday afternoon in Taylor, was attended by nearly 200 students, 20 of them men.

The course will be offered once a week in two sections. To meet the demand of the 160 people who appeared just to sit in on the course, she will deliver one public lecture a month, on the theory that "a little of that goes a long way for some people."

Millett was asked by the Women's Studies Committee to teach the course. "They called me last year and said the students were sitting in," she said. "I came to the campus and met a lot of people. I got to like a lot of them, and besides, how can you turn students down?"

She is especially interested in Bryn Mawr as a women's college because "it's the only institution we have." Because she will be staying overnight Wednesdays in Wyndham, Millett will be able to attend the Women's Studies Committee meetings and confer with students.

Millett's primary target at the present is the national news media. "*Time* magazine kind of blows up a balloon and paints someone's face on it. I never gave them permission to put my face on the cover. They treated my family very badly," she continued, "calling them and saying I had given permission for an interview."

The press, she believes, has misrepresented her by making her a heroine of the movement: "Women's lib is not about that kind of thing." Her fame has "happened very fast," and is "lovely. I just wrote my doctoral thesis, and all this happened," she said.

Reprinted from the *News* (Bryn Mawr-Haverford), September 18, 1970.

NEW ALLIANCES

STUDENTS EXPRESS DIFFERING ATTITUDES ON GAYS
Jon Price, Haverford, Class of 1978

THE FOLLOWING is an in-depth analysis of attitudes which both gay and straight members of the bi-College community have expressed about gays.

> I don't think that anyone could be a really good friend of mine if they were gay. I don't know—I would be forced to think about it. It would concern me . . . I can't say I'm comfortable with it.
> —*a Haverford student*

> The practical way to look at it is just that . . . people are people. It [being gay] is a part of someone just like whether he likes to take showers in the morning or evening.
> —*a Bryn Mawr student*

Early this semester, a foreign student who had not been in America for long became curious when she saw a sign posted by the Bryn Mawr-Haverford Gay People's Alliance (GPA) announcing their Thursday night meetings in the College Inn. She was a little embarrassed, but asked, "Does that mean they're queers?" It was explained that queers is a derogatory term for homosexuals, that "gay" is as acceptable a term as "black" or "Catholic," but she interrupted, "Oh, they're women, too?"

Yes, women are gay as well as men, and this is one of the common misconceptions about gays that induced a small group of bi-College students last September to establish the Bryn Mawr-Haverford Gay People's Alliance. Their purpose was four-fold: to provide for gay individuals a community from which they could receive moral support and not feel isolated because of their sexuality; to dispel what they felt to be common societal prejudices against gays by educating the bi-College community about homosexuality; to raise the consciousness of the bi-College community about the oppressions of gay people and to combat those oppressions; and to provide a social opportunity for gays to meet other gays.

The founders of GPA were concerned that gay people were separated from society and from each other by widely-believed myths; for example, that gays pervert the people with whom they interact and that "all gays are so intensely sexual that they can't keep their hands off of each other," in the words of GPA president Gail Schauer. In addition gays are often denied jobs because of their sexuality and a gay couple often has trouble renting an apartment together.

But perhaps the most compelling need which GPA founders wanted to meet was to make it easier for gays to "come out," to be open about their sexuality and comfortable among everyone. GPA members argue that homosexuality is a natural thing, contrary to what they see as the long-time beliefs that there is something wrong with homosexuality, that it is a symptom of social illness, and that it is not anything innate to a person but a condition to be cured.

GPA founders resented the fact that gays have to overcome emotional problems created by fears about their own sexuality. "It takes an awful lot of energy to be in the closet," said Schauer, explaining that much personal time and energy is "wasted" covering up tracks, lying, worrying that someone might know. "The problem was how everyone was going to look at me," said one GPA member of his coming-out. "I had no one to talk to."

One might find it surprising that so many gay members of GPA are perfectly comfortable with their gayness and worry more about other people's attitudes than their own identities. Most gay members of GPA have already come out to many people and are concerned more with gay political and social issues than with any problems relating to accepting their sexuality. One GPA member commented, "Coming out was my problem, not being gay," and now that he has come out, he says, "the people who can't handle it, it's their problem."

Members of GPA stress that the organization was not established solely for gays and that participation in the organization or attendance at meetings is not construed to suggest anything about one's sexual preference. They feel that coming out should be as much a concern for a straight person as it is for a gay. "We're trying to present an image of gay people as we are—accept us as who we are. Why should we have to come out at all?" asked one GPA member.

Ironically, the attitude which one GPA member described as "why should other people feel threatened if they are secure in their own orientation" has been a problem as well as a strength for the group. Many newcomers who are unsure about their own sexuality or are simply curious about gay issues are sometimes alienated at meetings. The group, numbering about thirty members, is tightly-knit and, as one GPA member said, the gay members are pretty much at the same stage of coming out.

When a new person comes to a meeting, he or she could be gay, but it is not necessarily so. If that person is in fact gay and attended the meeting because he/she was afraid to come out, that person must take the lead in saying anything about him/herself, which is a difficult thing to do when a group of gay people and "straight liberals" do not seem to be providing any help or personal support. "The group is nervous with new people," Schauer said, adding that all GPA can do is to provide a "model for coming out."

Another GPA member elaborated, "Our role is to be visible . . . you can't seek out individuals." To this end, GPA, riding on the success of last year's dance, is planning a dance for each semester of the year. They plan to bring in Lee Lehman, director of the National Gay Student Center, on Nov. 11, and another speaker is planned for next semester.

GPA has office hours in Jones basement and holds regular Thursday night meetings at 8:30 in the College Inn. In addition, posters have been put up on both campuses with the promise to be put up twice as big if torn down. These posters have cards with the names of people to contact for information and advice.

Although GPA's conscious efforts to be noticed have attracted attention on gays and gay issues, and although the group's efforts have succeeded to some extent—one Haverfordian commented that coming to Haverford "has raised my consciousness about it [being gay]"—many people in the bi-College community think that GPA's efforts are counterproductive.

"I think there's a problem with the consciousness-raising program," one student remarked. "I wonder what's being achieved; I don't know if it's making their life any easier. They want to be accepted as equals and gay—a mass media campaign is maybe highlighting the distinction between gays and straights."

Others are uncomfortable about the whole issue and feel put upon: "I do treat them differently; that's why I don't want to know who's gay in the community. Just as it's hard for them to come out, it's hard for people to know that they come out."

Whatever the case, it is certainly safe to say that few people are indifferent to gay issues. GPA is hoping that people can and will be considered as real people, and that they can live happy and comfortable lives.

Reprinted from the *News* (Bryn Mawr-Haverford), November 5, 1976.

GAY DAY: A STATISTICAL ANALYSIS
Mona Cardell, Class of 1978

DID YOU WEAR BLUE JEANS last Friday? Lots of people didn't, probably because last Friday had been proclaimed Gay Day, the day on which gay people were supposed to wear blue jeans. Our observers were out on Gay Day, as they had been on previous Fridays, counting the number of people wearing blue jeans. Observations were made each Friday at lunch—at Haverford, in the Dining Center from 11:25 to 12:25; and at Bryn Mawr, in Erdman Dining Room, from 11:30 to 1:30. We noted a statistically significant decline in the proportion of people wearing blue jeans on Gay Day. (Control samples were taken on Friday, March 25, and Friday, April 1. We used April 1 as the control date in our statistical analysis, because it was comparable in temperature to Gay Day.) On Gay Day, only 33.8% of the 625 people who passed our checkers were in blue jeans (cutoffs and overalls included). In comparison, 50.4% of the 690 people who passed our checkers on April 1 were wearing blue jeans. Both men and women were significantly affected by our experimental stimulation. On April 1, 55.7% of the men and 43.7% of the women in our samples were in blue jeans; on Gay Day, only 37.7% of the men and 27.6% of the women were wearing blue jeans.

Statistical analyses were performed on data from all of our subgroups of subjects: men, women, people at Bryn Mawr, people at Haverford, men at Bryn Mawr, men at Haverford, women at Bryn Mawr, and women at Haverford. All subgroups except one showed very significant declines in percentage wearing blue jeans on Gay Day. One subgroup, women at Haverford, showed a non-significant trend toward decline. (The non-significance of the results of this subgroup may be attributed to the relatively small number of habitual jeans-wearers in the subgroup of women at Haverford lunch; many of the women who eat lunch at Haverford are faculty or staff.)

So what do the statistics mean? There are at least two alternative explanations that could account for the decrease in jeans-wearing on Gay Day. One explanation is that people were afraid that if they wore jeans others would label them as homosexual. Another explanation is that people were simply following what they thought the "rules" were: since our publicity told people to wear blue jeans if they were gay, perhaps heterosexual people thought they weren't supposed to wear blue jeans. There may be other explanations also; probably the effectiveness of our experiment was due to a combination of contributing factors.

What factors influenced your choice of clothing last Friday? Whether you wore jeans or not, how did you feel about the experience? If you'd have a chance to let us at GPA know how you felt, please stop into our office in the basement of Jones, or send comments by campus mail to Gay People's Alliance, Haverford. The members of GPA look forward to hearing your reactions.

Reprinted from the *News* (Bryn Mawr-Haverford), April 22, 1977.

SEXISM

THIS WEEK'S ARTS PAGE REVIEW of the Bryn Mawr Junior Show provides us with a good opportunity to state what probably should never have to be said at all: sexism, like racism, is a sick and destructive attitude in individuals and a cruel and oppressive force in society.

Sexism, as the Junior Show amply illustrated, is not confined to male disrespect and scorn for women. It is also commonly expressed in the ridicule heaped upon the male and female homosexuals in our community, students who are often so feared and fearful that they cannot reveal their true feelings even to close friends without danger of complete rejection.

Just as the *News* has opened its columns to women for the expression of their feelings with regard to sexual oppression, we now offer space to any homosexuals who would like, with or without anonymity, to express their experiences and attitudes to the community at large.

Reprinted from the *News* (Bryn Mawr-Haverford), October 30, 1970.

GAY PEOPLE'S ALLIANCE ORGANIZES, ATTEMPTS TO OVERCOME IMPRESSION
Trayton Davis, Haverford, Class of 1977

THE BRYN MAWR-HAVERFORD GAY PEOPLE'S ALLIANCE (GPA) held their third meeting last Thursday. Although still in the organizational stages, the group is well on its way to becoming an established part of bi-College life.

According to Marjorie Patterson, a graduate student in the Bryn Mawr School of Social Work and a moving force behind the group, approximately 20 people attended the first two business meetings. Patterson was "very pleased with the turnout, because it's a difficult thing to do."

"Attendance at the meetings or affiliation with GPA is in no way a statement of sexual orientation or preference," she continued.

The participants so far are about evenly split between men and women, and are predominantly undergraduates. Patterson also indicated that members of the faculty and staff will be visiting the group from time to time. In addition, several people who have not been attending the meetings have told Patterson they were interested in the group.

Activities
The group intends to have various activities grow out of the weekly business meetings, including social events and various consciousness-raising activities. GPA has scheduled an on-campus appearance of Tom Wilson and Joan DeForest, representatives of Philadelphia's Eromin Center. Eromin, a professionally run clinic for erotic minorities, has an entirely homosexual staff, including a psychiatrist, physician and paramedical personnel. The presentation will be open to the entire community.

The group has set up multi-purpose bulletin boards at both colleges, where matters of interest and resources available to the gay community will be posted regularly. GPA is also subscribing to several periodicals.

Another function of the bulletin boards will be to reach gays anonymously; the group is concerned with providing its resources to gays who are not willing or ready to take the semi-public step of attending the meetings.

A system involving index cards that is available at the bulletin boards will be the basis of the anonymous contact. Counseling and other resources will be made available in this fashion.

Privacy Worries
Patterson is concerned that some gays may be worried that involvement in the group may lead to infringements of their privacy. Any political activity or public action that involves an implicit statement of sexual preferences can be handled by a nucleus "of a few people who are no longer anonymous." There will be "no effort on our part" to force anyone to come out, Patterson said.

It is only "when the atmosphere in the outside world is such that one can't relate that experience anyplace that (sexual preference) becomes an issue," Patterson said. Much of the repressive atmosphere towards gays in the heterosexual world is reflected in the fact that homosexuals are continually forced to justify their sexuality in public, a painful process usually not required of heterosexuals, she said.

Peer Group
Patterson sees the group as having a viable function as a peer group, a focusing point for dialogue between gays. She feels that giving gays a forum where they can relate their experiences to each other fills a social void for the gay who can't normally discuss his or her Saturday night activities at Sunday brunch. "I don't think anyone at either college would argue the benefits of a peer group at college," she said.

Oppression of gays in the bi-College community is covert, according to Patterson, who adds that "judging by the fear level . . . it's quite ostensible." Oppression that is not overt is the hardest to deal with. "X," a Haverford student who is active in GPA and considers himself a bi-sexual, says that oppression of gays at Haverford has nothing to do with the outside world. "It's all of us," he said. "Haverford is a growing experience in every form of the word, except as far as sex goes. There is no way for people [here] to grow up sexually in a community."

Oppression
"Lots of people share my viewpoint," "X" continued, "but you can still feel the oppression. People here are afraid of it; they don't understand. Most liberal modern students have experienced feelings along that [the gay] line. I don't see any other reason for people to be so uptight about it."

"X" said that a valuable function of GPA is "forcing people here to confront an issue that they have refused to confront before."

Patterson says that heterosexuals who feel challenged by gay liberation are unsure of their own sexuality, in a sense that is essentially "questioning whether or not their sexuality should take precedence over someone else's."

Heterosexuals have expressed such feelings before at Haverford, as when "A," a gay student said in the *News*, Nov. 13, 1970: "I'm convinced that the College isn't ready for a public clique of gays—it would threaten the masculinity of the whole campus." GPA hopes to provide a rallying point for a fight against what they see as reactions, whether covert or overt, of a threatened heterosexual majority who have kept most gay social life off campus, or firmly locked in the closet on campus.

Attitude Statement
Patterson gave the *News* a statement of GPA's attitude towards sexuality: We believe that homosexual and heterosexual are not mutually exclusive terms. Each represents an end on the spectrum of human sexuality. Every person has the capacity for same-sex affection, and we hope by presenting the various aspects of the homosexual end of the spectrum to present people here with the other side of the picture . . .

GPA hopes to "free up people from having to deposit themselves at any one place on the spectrum and stay there," she said.

"X" echoes this concern, saying, "Neither side is something I want to jump into. I'd feel like I'd be cutting myself off from experiences. [It's] really uncomfortable being in the middle; you just can't seem to put your foot down somewhere." Patterson adds that "sex role transcendence is an important step towards human liberation."

Reprinted from the *News* (Bryn Mawr-Haverford), October 3, 1975.

STUDENTS OF THE 1970s

Below: Members of the class of 1975 on the steps of Taylor (left); students processing in the rain during Commencement, 1978 (right)

MAGIC MOUNTAIN MALAISE

THE HUMIDITY HANGS HEAVY of late, and has settled like a stifling blanket over the shrouded towers of ivy and isolation. The drawbridge was lowered, and the castle's occupants unenthusiastically trodded across. Some made the crossing safely, while others were unpreventably sucked into whirlpools of the deceptively calm waters surrounding the fortress.

The more sure-footed and nimble-footed inhabitants winded their way without mishap into the empty island, and provided the oil to set the well-poised machinery back into gear for another eight months. But all was not well . . . the gears were grinding into action, but very painfully and reluctantly.

Freshman week unwound smoothly until boredom set in. Upperclassmen arrived, but without much energy or excitement. At Convocation, both Bryn Mawr President Harris Wofford and Dean Mary Patterson McPherson cited reports that characterized the students of the '70s as fatigued, uncertain, confused, and lacking in optimism and self-confidence. Both expressed the hope that these reports would be proven false, but so far their fears seem to have been true harbingers of the year.

Very rarely have so many students been so indecisive about course registration. The amount of students who would like to leave, or accelerate their graduation is increasing. A feeling of depression pervades the hallowed halls, perhaps because the sluggish air has seemed to drug the natives with liberal doses of lethargy, limpness, and fatigue.

Almost all activities have gotten off to little or no start. The film series nearly wasn't; Colloquium referendum tabulations are at the same non-existent state as they were last spring because no one felt like doing any work over the summer; the coed dorm expansion issue that split the campus last spring seems to have been but a bad dream dutifully erased in all minds; and while stored reserves of energy were mustered to finish course evaluations, they have caused nary a ripple in the community. Appointments are made and not kept, meetings are announced and not attended, commitments made but not met.

Political activism has virtually disappeared . . . everyone wants to be the uninvolved third party. News passes by as if it is spun of trivial threads of life, broken too easily to be bothered with. The tragedy of the murder of eleven athletes at an international festival designed to promote peace and understanding among all nations was hardly felt; after all, it was not a tragedy proven by the centuries, something that could be studied again and again like a Greek tragedy, or a Shakespeare masterpiece.

Who knows what is to account for the malaise of the '70s? Its source is elusive, yet its force is omnipresent. We have a choice ahead of us. We can wear the mantle of malaise, restless disquiet, though unable to shake off the aura of vague discomfort. Or we can wait for a catastrophic event to shake us out of our Castorp-like stupor on our magic mountain.

Reprinted from the *News* (Bryn Mawr-Haverford), September 22, 1972.

THERE'S NO BRYN MAWR ACCENT
Harold J. Wiegand

ERNEST HEMINGWAY was an expert on bullfighting, lion hunting and deep-sea fishing.

He had another specialty: he was convinced he could tell a Bryn Mawr girl by the way she talked.

This peculiar notion has mystified students and graduates of the Main Line college ever since, because no one besides Hemingway has ever agreed that there is such a thing as a Bryn Mawr "accent."

There was a time when it was thought that nearly all Bryn Mawr girls talked like Katharine Hepburn, or the other way around. This is something like saying that everybody at West Philadelphia High School for Girls talked like Jeanette MacDonald, because she had attended classes there.

Bryn Mawr students may wear the same kind of clothes and hair do's, but they do not all speak with the same voice. You can talk to any group on their way to class, or playing hockey, or dancing around the May Pole, and you will find as many variations of speech as the places they come from.

A girl from the Midwest will say "wahter" instead of "wawter"; the Southerner will give a good imitation of Scarlett O'Hara; the Bostonian will broaden her "A's"; and the girl from Brooklyn will lapse once in awhile into Brooklynese.

Hemingway apparently got involved in the accent thing when he discovered that his first wife, Hadley, had spent a year at Bryn Mawr. She had a certain way of talking, and he decided that this must be the way all Bryn Mawr girls talked.

So when the woman who was to be his third wife walked into Sloppy Joe's, where he was having a solitary drink one afternoon, there was no doubt in his mind, when he heard her speak, that she was a Bryn Mawr girl.

Her name was Martha Gellhorn, and she had in fact attended Bryn Mawr. She and her mother were vacationing in Key West, and they had looked into the bar with the peculiar name out of curiosity.

Her "recognizable Bryn Mawr accent," as he described it later, intrigued Hemingway as a reminder of Hadley, and he eventually married her.

It is strange that it evidently never occurred to him that both his first and third wife came from St. Louis, and that what he thought was their Bryn Mawr way of talking was probably no more than a Missouri twang. If they both spoke in a certain way, so did Harry S. Truman.

Ernest Hemingway did not have the delicate ear for variations in speech that John O'Hara possessed. The Pottsville expatriate could ride a crowded elevator in the Bellevue Stratford and know at once from their conversations where his fellow-passengers came from. This one from South Philadelphia, that one from Manayunk. This couple from Scranton, the other from Richmond.

He had developed this talent back home in the coal region, where it seemed important to know whether a new acquaintance was from Shenandoah or Frackville.

Stereotypes abound everywhere. There is an old superstition that all women on the Main Line dress alike, talk alike and look alike—an impression gained, no doubt, from a ride on the Paoli Local or any matinee day at the Academy of Music.

It is not true. There is as much nonconformity on the Main Line—or almost, anyway—as anywhere else. There is said to be a Villanova matron who still rides side-saddle at the Radnor Hunt.

Reprinted from the *Philadelphia Inquirer*, September 3, 1974.

Top: Students relaxing outside, c. 1970s

Bottom: Student on the phone, c. 1975–80

Opposite: *The Other Side*, an alternative introduction to college life, published by the Bryn Mawr-Haverford Social Action Caucus, 1979

"BRYN MAWR WALK" GOES WAY OF HIGH HEELS

Jill Gerston

IN THE MOVIE *OBSESSION*, Cliff Robertson characterized the "Bryn Mawr walk" as a "kinda glide." For the girls on campus, trudging and strolling to class, that view is about 20 years behind the times.

Halfway through the new movie *Obsession*, there is a scene in which Cliff Robertson tells Genevieve Bujold that she looks exactly like his dead wife except for one difference: She doesn't have a Bryn Mawr walk.

"A Bryn Mawr walk is a kind of glide, you know?" he explains with much difficulty. "You see, those girls used to wear those long polo coats in those old days, the long raincoats . . . they'd kinda glide. Like you're late for class. They'd move fast, ya know and just kinda glide . . ."

Well, maybe that's what they did in the early '50's when women trooped to class in polo coats and taffeta petticoats and perfected their posture through horseback riding, tea-pouring and curtseying at coming-out parties.

But today things are different, what with the popularity of Levis and clogs and the demise of formal teas and debutante balls.

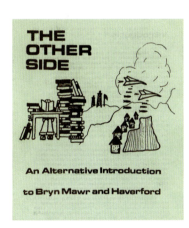

There wasn't a glide in sight the other day when a reporter and a photographer roamed through the leafy, tree-shaded campus in search of a Bryn Mawr walk.

Students ran, sauntered, trudged, shuffled, pedaled, plodded and strolled, but no one glided. Indeed, if there was one trait they all had in common it was the "student slouch," the hunched-over posture that comes from lugging around Horst Janson's *History of Art* and Paul Samuelson's *Economics*.

How do Bryn Mawr women feel about this recent bit of Hollywood stereotyping? Do they think that their walk is any different from that of their sisters at Wellesley and Vassar or, for that matter, UCLA and University of Iowa?

Those were among the questions asked at random of about two dozen Bryn Mawr students as they walked across campus on a recent weekday afternoon.

To a student, they were all amused that Hollywood had chosen to enshrine their walk on the silver screen.

And while each student had his or her own interpretation of a Bryn Mawr walk, nearly all of those interviewed agreed that it definitely was not a glide.

"It's more of a predatory stomp," said Pomphylia Baker, a sophomore from Los Angeles, with a broad grin. "And as for gliding when you're late for class, forget it. You run—or you don't go."

Kristin Rose, a senior, denied there was such a thing as a Bryn Mawr walk but added there was a Bryn Mawr behind—"which is really just ordinary student spread."

Wayne Winn, a student from nearby Haverford College who was chatting with Bryn Mawr senior Joy Afuso, said while he couldn't define "the walk" he could differentiate between a Bryn Mawr walk and a Harcum walk.

"Bryn Mawr women have a sort of slouch," he said, hunching his shoulders and striding forward in long, loping steps to illustrate his point. "But Harcum girls have a more pronounced, sexy sort of walk that you can, well, just spot right away."

Spotting a Bryn Mawr walk is impossible, said a rather breathless Wendy Brennan after she had dashed down the steps of Taylor Hall.

"You can't type a Bryn Mawr woman because of their damned cussed individualism—that's what *The Yale Insider Guide to College* said and it's true," said Ms. Brennan, a freshman from New York City. "There's no special walk or Bryn Mawr 'type'—the people here are all different. They're all individuals."

Still, a number of students, like Libby White, said they could understand why Hollywood chose Bryn Mawr to represent the well-bred, well-schooled daughter of the Main Line establishment.

"Bryn Mawr has a reputation of being sort of snobbish and prudish," said Ms. White, who was wearing a blue jogging outfit and was rushing off to archery class. "So you can see how they'd describe a Bryn Mawr girl's walk as being sort of straight and smooth and gliding.

"But of course, that sort of stereotyping just isn't true," she added very quickly. "It's so friendly here—no one is snobby or put on."

Judith Shapiro, a young anthropology professor at the college, said that the Bryn Mawr walk represented "an earlier, upper-class phase of Bryn Mawr that doesn't really hold true today.

"That ethereal glide that's described in the movie couldn't possibly be done today," added Dr. Shapiro, who was sleekly turned out in black pants, black sweater and black gaucho hat. "It went with a different style of dress, when long full skirts and heels and stockings were in fashion. No one goes around like that today."

While all the women interviewed tossed off the Bryn Mawr walk as just a funny piece of Hollywood fluff, Phillip Kaplan, a Haverford senior, seemed rather angry about the incident.

"I think the whole thing is sexist," he said very seriously while he ate lunch on the outdoor terrace of the Campus Inn. "You hear about the Bryn Mawr accent and the Bryn Mawr walk, but people here aren't any different than anywhere else. I resent classifying Bryn Mawr women as having a particular affectation. They're all individuals."

Reprinted from the *Philadelphia Inquirer*, October 3, 1976.

CAMPUS LIFE IN THE 1970s

TRUSTEES GRANT BMC STUDENTS COMPLETE AUTONOMY IN NEW SGA

BRYN MAWR'S new Student Government Association (SGA) was approved and granted complete autonomy by the Board of Trustees at a meeting Tuesday. The constitution of the new organization, which will encompass all duties, responsibilities and activities formerly handled by the Self Gov and Undergrad, had been approved the previous week in a campus-wide vote.

The new agreement stipulates that the Board's recommendation on proposed SGA legislation should be considered before campus balloting, but that the results of the voting would not be subject to Board approval. Under the old agreement, derived from the original Self Gov charter of 1892, all major Self Gov and Undergrad actions required Board approval . . .

The proposed regulations provide for a completely revised statement on the use of alcohol, which would remind students of the State laws and of the possible dangerous results of the consumption of alcohol. The revised resolution specifically prohibits the serving of alcohol at public college functions. It specifically holds responsible any student involved in offense to other SGA members, destruction of property, smoking in prohibited areas, or the presence of unescorted guests in the halls, when such an offense occurs after alcohol has been served.

The Board approved a proposed resolution making permanent the elimination of specific hours for guests in student rooms. Rules pertaining to the escorting of non-residents in the halls would be retained.

The structure of the Honor Board is clarified under the new resolutions, with the institution of the "rotating member" system.

At the beginning of the academic year, the names of ten members from each class would be drawn at random, to serve on the Honor Board. As a case arises, two from among each class's group of ten would be asked to sit on the jury, one as a member, the other as her alternate. The student being tried would have the right to disqualify any member of the jury without providing a reason, and any potential member could decline her seat.

Structural changes in the Academic Honor Board were also proposed. The Academic Honor Board would be altered to consist of five students. Each year two students, a junior and a sophomore, would be elected for a two-year term, the first year of which they would serve on both the Social and the Academic Honor boards, the second only on the academic. A senior member would also be elected, to act as counselor and not as a voting member of the board. The chairman of the Academic Honor Board is elected separately under the constitution.

The student being tried would have the right to appeal to the president of the College for a retrial. The president formerly chaired the board.

The standards of the academic Honor System would remain unchanged under the new resolutions.

Reprinted from the *News* (Bryn Mawr-Haverford), March 12, 1971.

BOARD OF DIRECTORS APPROVES THOMAS AS STUDENT CENTER
Marsha Guzy, Class of 1976

THOMAS READING ROOM has officially become Bryn Mawr's student activities center. Yesterday, the Board of Directors' Committee on Student Affairs approved plans for the room's use, releasing the $2,000 promised by the administration last spring pending submission of the plans. Immediately after vacation, an open student-faculty committee will begin work on the room.

The floor plan and plans for the room's activities were formulated by the Student Center Steering Committee that met last Wednesday. The committee is composed of students Sue Herman, Melissa Colbert and Mary Workman, and faculty members Eugene Schneider and Charles Frye. Workman submitted the proposals to President Harris Wofford Tuesday, and she and Herman presented them to the Board committee.

Coffee, a lounge and student services are the three main aims of the Center, each to be represented by a separate area. The entire room will be carpeted and refreshments will be on a round table in the room's center. Bulletin boards will separate the three sections, act as a sound barrier, and enable regular campus communication. It is hoped the lounge area will also serve as a gallery for art exhibits. The student services area will be a volunteer center for any who wish to donate time and information to the college community.

Physical needs are the most pressing matters now. "We will need everyone's time and energy to track down the best resources for furniture, carpets, plants, art works and bulletin boards," according to the Steering Committee proposal. Workman has spoken to Sarah Wright, Director of Halls, and found that there is no furniture lying in any attics.

There is a possibility of obtaining rugs from Wyndham, and Workman will speak to Thomas Trucks to formulate a lighting system. Though funds are not expected immediately for the lighting, the Center will be open during the day as soon as possible. The Board has been considering funding the lighting.

Reprinted from the *News* (Bryn Mawr-Haverford), October 20, 1972.

COMMUNITY—A LOSS?
Christina Del Piero, Class of 1979

STUDENTS, FACULTY AND ADMINISTRATORS have been recently involved in discussions of "community" at Bryn Mawr; the community, however, has shrunk to exclude one segment that used to play a large part in campus life. When Jacob Roselle, the hall manager in Haffner and Rockefeller, started working here thirty five years ago, members of the staff worked much more closely with students than they do now.

"I think it was better when there was more closeness in the college because we knew about more problems than we do now," Mr. Roselle explained. "A girl would go to her chambermaid, her porter or her waitress and talk about problems. With all those people to help, she felt wanted."

In the 1940's, when Mr. Roselle began working in Pembroke as a porter, most students stayed in the same room for four years. Employees knew the students in their residence hall and took care of their rooms for them. Porters hung draperies, sent packages and took shoes to the shoemaker to be repaired. They also built fires in the public rooms and, on special occasions, in students' rooms. "If one of the girls went out and forgot to make her bed, you'd make it for her," said Mr. Roselle. "It was like a family, very close."

Many factors have contributed to the change in atmosphere at Bryn Mawr over the past few decades. For example, only porters and hall managers used to have room keys. When a student went to class, she left her room open. This led students to make their rooms as neat as possible. Because dining was more formal and waitresses served the meals, students saw these employees and other dorm residents every day and came to know them well. In addition, social activities included a wider range of community members than most do today.

Every year, until recently, the maids and porters put on plays directed by the students. "We had no trouble in getting participation," Mr. Roselle said. Later, he explained, everyone was too busy to continue the old traditions. Students had little time to direct the plays, and the staff began working longer hours.

"Now everyone is going, going all the time," Mr. Roselle commented. "They don't play cards any more. They don't use the smokers like anything any more. Back then, I didn't go into a smoker where there was not someone playing cards or studying." Students used to play cards in their spare time, he said. "If they didn't have a partner, they'd ask me. Every Wednesday night in Wyndham there was a card game . . . Students came to play with us."

Individuals would also invite their professors to outdoor teas. Every year students would invite the faculty to a large tea on the lawn in front of Pembroke.

Although it may seem to today's students that those of the past were waited on hand and foot, Mr. Roselle would welcome the closeness such a relationship brought.

Freshmen Stage Moan

Thirty-five to forty freshman gathered on Merion Green Sunday night to usher in a new tradition, the Freshman Moan. The Moan originated at a discussion of traditions in a Freshman Class meeting.

"It resembled primal scream therapy and I am now able to face exam week with an open mind and a closed mouth," commented Anne Fabiny, a Merion freshman who participated in the Moan. It will be a tradition, she estimates, as long as demand remains high.

Not only did Bryn Mawr employees perform more services for students, but the students also shared more with members of the staff. Most employees felt that they were appreciated. As an example, Mr. Roselle spoke of a habit he had of meeting the students and saying good morning. "At the end," he continued, "one left me a note that said, 'your good mornings really helped me through these four years.'

"Back then, a girl would come to Bryn Mawr just to study. They didn't do much else except the different plays," Mr. Roselle recalled. He feels that now there is not much time due to opportunities provided by cooperation with Haverford, participation in college government and outside jobs.

Although he believes that things must change with the times and that life cannot return to the style of the past, Mr. Roselle offered the following suggestion as to how Bryn Mawr students can regain some of the community feeling that has been lost:

> If a student would check into her surroundings—into those connected with the college—and put herself out to see and talk to people around her, I think she'd get more of a feeling of understanding employees and other students. We have girls here who don't even know the employees who work on campus. I think any girl living in a dormitory should know the maids, bells girl, porter and hall manager working there. It makes things more closely knitted when you know who is making things work. Students should speak with those who are trying to give them the best they have. Only a few seem to appreciate it.

Reprinted from the *College News*, December 12, 1978.

Above: Clipping from the *College News*, December 12, 1978

Opposite: Elizabeth Whitten and Cathy Lawrence, both class of 1977, posing as statues on Thomas Library, April Fool's Day, c. 1974–77

Clockwise from top left: Pages in a Denbigh backsmoker diary (a shared student journal kept in a dorm's smoking lounge), with entries dated November 24–26, 1977; 1974 song book; students in Erdman dining hall, 1972; student eating, 1979

Opposite (top): Students at a barbecue, c. 1970s

Opposite (bottom): Students in their dorm, 1979. Photograph by Martin Natvig

COOPERATIVE DEVELOPMENTS: 1970–1978

STUDENTS CONFRONT DIRECTORS ON WAR
Chuck Durante, Haverford, Class of 1973

EIGHT BRYN MAWR and Haverford students picketed yesterday in front of Wyndham awaiting the arrival of the Bryn Mawr Board of Directors.

The students were protesting Bryn Mawr's investments in Honeywell, a company which makes computers and other electronic devices used in the current United States air war in Vietnam.

The number swelled to 15 by the time the demonstration broke up at 3:30. The group had spoken to Judge Edmund Spaeth, chairman of the board, and President Harris Wofford. Wofford told the group that an "ethical investor proposal" similar to that adopted by the Yale Board a year ago may be set up. There has been a student-faculty-administration group working toward this goal during the past year.

Wofford mentioned that the College has had a policy of not investing in such companies as Dow Chemical and Lockheed. He added that the College is in the process of selling its Honeywell holdings.

The board did not actually pass through the picket line. When Spaeth and Wofford came out of Wyndham to speak with the demonstrators, it was the first time that they had seen either of the two. Demonstrators had been in the area since 1 P.M.

Eric Sterling, one of the demonstrators, said that friendly conversations were held with a number of those going into the board meeting, including Dean Mary Patterson McPherson. Sterling stressed the cordial nature of the confrontation, and was optimistic that the Board would see the demonstrators' concerns. Among those whom they met and spoke to were Profs. Frederic Cunningham, Richard DuBoff, and Anne Mendelson, all of whom gave their support to the position of the students.

In addition, the students met with J. Edgar Rhoads, former head of the board who also supported the concerns of the students, according to Sterling. The Bryn Mawr faculty the night before had given its support to a "sense of the faculty" resolution calling on the College to divest itself of holdings in such companies as Honeywell. The one-sentence resolution was passed at the end of the meeting.

Wednesday night, President Harris Wofford told the *News*, "I have always favored that position." He had been asked to report on this issue by the board, and he is expected to ask for a divestiture of such stockholdings when he makes that report.

Reprinted from the *News* (Bryn Mawr-Haverford), April 21, 1972.

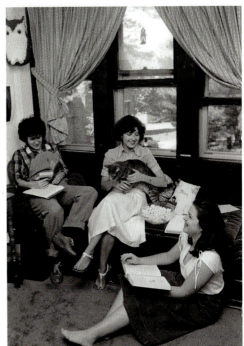

TEN YEARS AFTER
Student Protest Movement Has Petered Out
Howard Kee

Howard Kee is the Rufus Jones Professor of History of Religion and Philosophy Emeritus at Bryn Mawr.

TEN YEARS BEFORE we arrived in Berkeley to begin our sabbatical stay here—that is, in early September 1964—the Free Speech Movement began. Its repercussions and its imitations were to be felt on campuses throughout the land and in Washington itself.

In early December of that year, Mario Savio was throttled by a strong-arm policeman, and in a single day 814 were arrested. The issue was an important one for academic freedom and for civil liberties, and the students won that battle when the faculty voted seven to one in support of freedom of speech on the campus and against regulation of political activities by students off campus. By exactly ten years ago today (March 3), however, the affections of the students for the excitement of protest per se had mounted in inverse proportion to the substance of the issues in behalf of which the protests were staged. Accordingly, exactly one decade ago the Dirty Word Movement was launched, with the puerile aim of freedom to display four-letter words in public.

In the intervening years the student protest movement throughout the nation has achieved its most mature and effective peak in the anti-war demonstrations in 1971. What does the place where the student protest movement began look like today?

Above and opposite: Students in the cloisters, c. 1970s

Where Are They Now?
The sidewalks once lined with tables for distributing leaflets and collecting signature on petitions are now covered with mid-to late-twentyish men and women selling belts and handcrafted jewelry. Many of the peddlers have offspring on their backs. Here and there among the craft tables are seemingly able-bodied beggars, with their broad-brimmed hats lying among the butts and candy wrappers, with a couple of decoy dollars plainly visible in each hand. The Bancroft Strip itself has been redesigned in part as a kind of student shopping mall, though many of the shops are empty. The sidewalks on Bancroft echo to the shouts of the Hare Krishna devotees or the clangor of an African band rather than to political harangues. Just prior to the November election a mass rally was called to protest our continuing involvement in Southeast Asia. Plans went well, but no one except the organizers showed up. The more conservative candidate for governor of California, Houston Flournoy, drew a respectable crowd a few days later, on the other hand.

The present mood of Berkeley is perhaps best epitomized in a graffito inscribed by spray paint on the wall of an abandoned gas station on Telegraph Avenue, still the center of student life. It reads: "Love without Reserve. Enjoy without Restraint. Live with No Dead Moments." The fraternities seem to be booming, and groupiness is definitely in. The lifestyle seems to be not so much free of restraint as compulsive. "Do your own thing" manifests itself in rigid patterns of conformity. Nonchalance is carefully cultivated. Spontaneity is studied. Leisure and relaxation are tightly structured and rigidly channeled: weekends one must go to the ski slopes, or in warmer weather to surf. There is some laughter but no joy.

The most pathetic results of the Berkeley style in the mid-seventies are evident among the geriatric set who are still aping the hippies, tottering about in long dresses or baggy bell-bottoms. Spaced-out dropouts wander along Telegraph mumbling to themselves. Here and there a furtive, filthy scavenger-student rummages through the trash cans in search of a few crumbs of potato chips. The more affluent dash about in their Porsches and Triumphs; one learns to assume that Berkeley drivers will ignore stop signs, will turn without signaling, will stop without warning in the middle of a block. And the pedestrian learns that some drivers will obey the California law giving the pedestrian the right of way at cross walks— and some will not. Victory belongs to the wary and the agile.

Students seem on the whole to be serious about their studies. There are, of course, exotic "free university" type courses offered under various auspices. For example, "Eleusis," sponsored by the New, Reformed, Orthodox Order of the Golden Dawn . . . "governed (sort of) by a Confederation of Craft covens," offers such rare items as Psychic Massage, Esoteric Divination, Witch Doctoring ("acupuncture through zap!"), and a special course in Witchcraft for Gay People. But there is little indication that the students are crowding into these non-curricular classes. On the campus the libraries are crowded.

As a visiting scholar, I have found nearly everything I have needed by way of books and journals, and the colleagues have been cordial, stimulating and helpful. My research could scarcely have been carried out in a more productive and gratifying way anywhere.

Yet there is an air of unreality about the whole enterprise. Although the temperature has hovered in the 35 to 50 range most of the past two rainy months, the publicity books all say that California is sunny and warm, so people dress and deport themselves accordingly. There has been a steady string of earthquakes this fall and winter, some of them quite sharp, but construction continues on housing projects that are located either directly on the San Andreas Fault or in filled areas overlooking the bay that would be flooded in the event of a major seismic shift. Streets sink, the shoulders of main roads slither off down the sides of hills after the soaking of the winter rains, but no one seems to notice.

Reprinted from the News (Bryn Mawr-Haverford), March 21, 1975.

BMC, HC STUDENTS DEMONSTRATE AGAINST NUCLEAR ARMS SPENDING
Steve Aseltine Ross, Haverford, Class of 1976

BI-COLLEGE STUDENTS are joining Philadelphians Organized for Nuclear Disarmament (POND) in a demonstration against military spending on nuclear arms at 12:15 P.M. today in downtown Philadelphia. The demonstration was planned to coincide with today's deadline for filing income tax returns.

POND's primary focus is on tax resistance as a means of expressing dissatisfaction with United States military expenditures, according to Haverford senior Doug Holtzman. POND encourages individuals to withhold any amount from $1 to all of their income tax as a gesture of protest.

Today's major event will be a demonstration inside the Internal Revenue Service (IRS) office at 6th and Arch streets. This demonstration will include several skits of "guerilla theater" as a symbolic act of civil disobedience.

"Guerilla Theater"
Today will be the first time "guerilla theater" has been performed inside the IRS office rather than out on the street. "Guerilla theater," or "street theater," consists of informal dramatic productions, sometimes in whiteface, intended to increase public awareness of issues central to POND. One of the skits will be a reenactment of the Boston Tea Party, drawing parallels between citizen reaction to "unfair taxation" then and now.

POND demonstrations have been held almost every week this semester. They always end at the IRS office with some type of minor and non-violent, but technically illegal, action. These gestures of civil disobedience have included carrying tables covered with "alternative tax information" into the IRS building and stamping slogans on IRS pamphlets.

No Arrests
Members of the Social Action Caucus (SAC) have been working with POND all year. Wendy Martin reported that "we've developed a good rapport with the security people at the IRS offices" and that no POND demonstration has yet resulted in arrests. However, she admitted, "there is always that possibility."

Sue Hibbard, another SAC member, said, "Sometimes we've expected to get arrested, but the police don't seem to want to arrest us."

Holtzman expressed dismay that past POND demonstrations had not been as effective as had been hoped, partly due to a lack of press coverage. Martin agreed, but expected today's demonstration to be a "much bigger thing" than usual and anticipated "a substantial amount of press coverage."

Reprinted from the News (Bryn Mawr-Haverford), April 15, 1977.

IN THE CLASSROOM

Being proud of Bryn Mawr doesn't make me some kind of rare animal. Those who feel as I do (and we're not such a small minority) aren't the kind to make a lot of noise. True pride runs deep, not loudly and fanatically. Perhaps some do need to redefine Bryn Mawr's meaning in their lives—and leave if necessary. For many of us, however, Bryn Mawr is not an institution of outmoded academic concepts and comic traditions, but a living body of highly intelligent and deeply committed people. If M. Carey Thomas were merely a comic figure, would we bother to quote her at all?

—*Barbara Miller, Class of 1975*

BMC OFFERS NEW COURSES IN LAW, SOCIAL JUSTICE
Julie Caroff, Class of 1978

COURSES IN A NEW BRYN MAWR master's degree program of law and social justice will be available to bi-College undergraduates. Public law is to be the focus of the new program, formally under the auspices of the Grad School of Social Work and Social Research.

The curriculum is in response to the growing demand for legal knowledge in the field of social work. The program will give students a working background in law as it pertains to the field of social research, according to President Harris Wofford. Last spring, a committee headed by Judge Edmund Spaeth recommended the program because law "offers a critical perspective, potentially valuable skill, and leverage to shape public policy."

Allowing selected undergraduates to participate in the program would add to Bryn Mawr's existing law-oriented courses. The committee felt, however, that there is no special need for a pre-law program at Bryn Mawr. They recognized in the report "that pre-law courses are neither required for law school nor often recommended for would-be law students."

"The advantages for undergraduates are by-products of the master's program," Wofford added.

The program would lead to an advanced degree to be used in such areas as: social welfare, community action and development, and legislative research and drafting. Possible employment opportunities include paralegal counseling, probation workers, clients' rights advocates, and consumers' legal rights advocates.

The holder of such a degree would not be able to practice law. However, the committee felt that "law is too important to be left to lawyers." The graduate would function as a mediator between lawyers and social workers in order to promote social justice by bringing the fields together.

Reprinted from the *News* (Bryn Mawr-Haverford), November 8, 1974.

GRADE INFLATION HITS BRYN MAWR
Jeff Bendix, Haverford, Class of 1976

LIKE EVERYTHING ELSE THESE DAYS, college grades have been hit by inflation.

Across the country educators are becoming worried over the rise in the numbers of A's being given out and the corresponding drop in the numbers of C's, D's, and F's.

Grade inflation has not bypassed the bi-College community. At Bryn Mawr, for example, the percentage of C grades dropped from 18.8 in second semester of 1973–74 to 11.1 a year later. Similarly, D grades dropped from 4.4 percent to 1.1 percent of all grades given out.

On the other hand, the percentage of A's went from 35.5% to 41.4% in the same time period. As Dean Mary Pat McPherson commented, "That's a pretty big percentage of A's."

Cum Laudes

The general rise in grade point averages was also reflected in the number of Bryn Mawr students graduating with distinction. Fifty-two percent of the class of '75 graduated cum laude, 13.4 percent graduated magna cum laude, and 3.5 percent graduated summa cum laude, for a total of 69.1 percent. That total was up from 61.6 percent the previous year.

Despite these statistics, Bryn Mawr students applying to graduate schools may suffer in competition with students from less prestigious colleges where grades are even more inflated. However, McPherson feels that this is a disadvantage only in the first round of the selection process, when a student may be rejected by a computer for having a grade point average below the standards of the school. After that, any deficiency in actual grades is compensated by Bryn Mawr's reputation among graduate schools, she said, emphasizing that institutions such as Yale and Princeton are in the same situation during both rounds.

Mawrters are getting into graduate school though it's not necessarily the one of their choice.

All medical school applicants from the class of '75 were accepted somewhere, and 65% of all Bryn Mawr students go on to graduate school, according to McPherson. "I think people get in where they want to go, for the most part," she said.

Theories Why

Union College's student-run newspaper *Concordiensis* recently listed a few of the numerous theories that have been advanced to explain the proliferation of higher grades around the country. One is that today's college students are more qualified academically than ever before. According to the *Concordiensis*, however, this theory is contradicted by a general decline in SAT scores.

Another explanation is that the economic situation has made colleges and universities resort to grade inflation to keep enrollment figures as high as possible. In addition, educators are having growing doubts about the validity of the grading system itself, and whether it can effectively evaluate a student's performance.

Reprinted from the *News* (Bryn Mawr-Haverford), September 19, 1975.

BRYN MAWR FACULTY APPROVES CHANGE TO LETTER GRADING
Cathy Davidson, Class of 1973

THE BRYN MAWR FACULTY of arts and sciences has approved a change in the grading system which will replace percentages with a five-category literal system consisting of A, B, C, D, and F.

The faculty also approved several other grading changes, including the institution of a credit/no credit option, and the elimination of the audit, of cumulative averages, and of class rankings for all students registered after Sept. 1971. However, averages and ranks will continue to be supplied for students who graduated or withdrew from the college before that time.

Above: Student typing at her desk, 1975. Photograph by George Krause

Opposite: Students in class, c. 1970s

Next page: Members of the class of 1972

Dean Patricia Pruett, chairman of the faculty-student Curriculum Committee which proposed changing the grading system last spring, said she thought, "it's going to be helpful for those of our students who are applying to graduate and professional schools. I don't think it's going to hurt anybody who's applying for jobs, either."

Beginning this semester, a student may take one course per semester under the credit/no credit option, which is similar to the pass/fail system used by many other schools. The student will be required to complete all class work on schedule, and her professor will not be told that the she is taking the course under the new system. He will submit a regular grade to the recorder, but the grade of credit or no credit is all that will appear on the student's transcript.

Courses taken under this option may be used to complete distribution requirements and freshman composition. The recorder will keep the professor's original grade on file, and this will replace credit/no credit should the student decide to use the course as part of her major work plan.

Courses taken at Haverford or Swarthmore will go on a student's transcript in the system used at the school where the course was taken. Haverford and Swarthmore students who take a course at Bryn Mawr will use the letter grade.

The executive committee of the Undergraduate Council will continue to work on other aspects of the grading change this fall, such as redefining College distinctions, distinguished work in the major subject, and a satisfactory general record, and designing a conversion scale for external use.

Reprinted from the *News* (Bryn Mawr-Haverford), September 10, 1971.

INTERNATIONAL EXPANSION

BRYN MAWR EXPANDS INTERNATIONAL PROGRAMS
Tara Steck, Class of 1977

IN THE PAST FEW YEARS Bryn Mawr has received over $100,000 in funds to be utilized as loans and grants for new programs in international research, study, and projects.

One of these is the International Initiatives Fund, established by an anonymous expendable donation of $50,000. Part of this money has been set aside to set up a loan fund to aid a student who wants to study overseas on a project-type basis and whose project cannot be funded by any other programs available.

The first loan was given to a member of the Class of 1974 for postgraduate study and archaeological field work in Egypt. These loans are available to undergraduates as well as graduates at low interest rates.

African Grant

A $50,000 anonymous endowment established the African Commonwealth Scholarship which is being used to support further work and to increase Bryn Mawr's involvement with Africa. These are grants which are open to students from any department with a plan to study or teach in Africa. Three of its first recipients have just completed work in Ethiopia, Gambia, Uganda, Zambia, and Kenya.

Another new internationally oriented program is a $40,000 Japanese Fund for Educational Exchange with Bryn Mawr, funded by donations from a Bryn Mawr alumna in Japan. For the first award, they would like a Bryn Mawr graduate student to come and work in Japan. These fellowships are limited to graduate students.

Long-established programs include the Chinese Scholarship Fund, the Marguerite N. Farley Scholarships, and the Thomas Raeburn White Scholarships. The first is an endowment fund implemented many years ago by a group of alumnae and friends of the College. Since 1917 thirty-six students have received this grant.

The Farley Scholarships also support a number of foreign students, over 136 since 1956. This endowment totals $331,000.

Summer Study

For summer study abroad there are the Thomas Raeburn White Scholarships. A $25,000 fund has been given, the income of which is to be used for prizes to undergraduates who plan to study foreign languages abroad during the summer under the auspices of an approved program.

These loan and scholarship funds are one facet of the many which comprise the gamut of international programs at Bryn Mawr.

Others include archaeological digs presently in progress in Murlo, Italy, and in Lycia, Turkey. Faculty members have recently been doing research in areas stretching from Iran to New Guinea.

Not to be forgotten are Bryn Mawr's two summer institutes for advanced language and cultural studies at Avignon and Madrid. Bryn Mawr also maintains longstanding ties with the American Academy in Rome and the American School of Classical Studies in Athens.

Input

The input, however, is just as important, if not more noticeable, than the output. Thirteen percent of Bryn Mawr's alumnae are from foreign countries. Many were supported by special scholarship funds; the Chinese Scholarship, the Marguerite N. Farley Scholarships, and the independent Philadelphia Japanese Scholarship Committee alone have sent 192 foreign students to Bryn Mawr since the turn of the century. In 1973–74 there were 66 foreign students in Bryn Mawr's three schools.

A large proportion of Bryn Mawr's regular faculty have come from foreign countries. The College is doing even more, though, to bring in international personalities to teach by seeking overseas replacements for members of the faculty on sabbatical. Since 1970 Bryn Mawr has had twelve visiting professors or lecturers from Australia, Britain, Denmark, France, Israel, Spain, Sweden, and Switzerland who have taught in no less than twelve different departments.

Old Idea

Additional plans are being considered to further Bryn Mawr's role of an educator in "world citizenship," the need for which was voiced as far back as the late nineteenth century by M. Carey Thomas, who spoke of "providing the kind of education required for citizenship and leadership in an interdependent world." In her *Declaration of Interdependence*, she voiced the need for us "to initiate whenever possible, and to cooperate with other nations, in the interchange of professors, teachers, and students; to found, and whenever possible to assist in the foundation of traveling fellowships for study in other countries; and in general to endeavor to train the young people of the United States in world citizenship."

In this spirit Thomas convinced the Board of Directors to establish the European Fellowship as the first award Bryn Mawr would bestow upon a student. This is still Bryn Mawr's highest academic award. Funds were set aside to enable a graduating senior to study in Europe.

Now, President Wofford is actively soliciting money from major foundations, because, he said, "overcoming national provincialism is one of the key functions of education." At Bryn Mawr, "the main effort now is to bring the programs into focus."

Reprinted from the *News* (Bryn Mawr-Haverford), October 11, 1974.

Opposite: Brochure for the Friends of International Programs of Bryn Mawr College, c. 1970s

BMC SEEKS STUDENTS IN MIDDLE EAST, ASIA

Esther Von Laue, Class of 1979

WITH THE $21 MILLION Campaign over, some members of the Bryn Mawr administration are turning their attention to foreign student recruitment, according to Admissions Director Elizabeth Vermey.

Vermey has made five trips to the Middle East in the past year and a half. Two of these trips, including one last November, were to attend the Near East–South Asia Conference of secondary schools, where Vermey was able to publicize Bryn Mawr to a large number of schools in Greece, India, Saudi Arabia, Kuwait, Afghanistan, Pakistan, Nepal, Israel and Iran.

Vermey is concentrating on the Middle East and Malaysia because there is a shortage of universities in those places. European students have little incentive to come to Bryn Mawr as the European universities are comparable in quality and cost much less, according to Vermey.

Vermey envisions Bryn Mawr's playing the same role in the Middle East as it has in Japan, where there are currently 70 Bryn Mawr alumnae. A Bryn Mawr graduate is the first female member of the Japanese legislature; and another alumna was the founder and first president of Tsuda College, and all subsequent presidents have been Bryn Mawr graduates. It is Vermey's hope that Bryn Mawr can train some of the women who are going to be influential in the development of the Middle East and Malaysia.

There are 16 foreign students in the freshman class, a number which has been increasing every year over the past several years, according to Vermey. Vermey would like to bring the number up to an average of 25, or 10 percent of each class.

One hindrance to increased foreign enrollment is the lack of scholarships available. There are only three scholarships now, and a new Middle Eastern scholarship is slowly being built up. Vermey reported that eighty percent of foreign students need large amounts of financial aid. Although the lack of scholarships limits students from most Middle East countries, Vermey hopes that the oil-rich countries of Saudi Arabia and Iran will provide a larger number of Bryn Mawr students.

Reprinted from the News *(Bryn Mawr-Haverford), January 28, 1977.*

"In an increasingly interdependent world in which concern for the higher education and professional advancement of women is rising everywhere, Bryn Mawr accepts a special responsibility."

"The Friends of International Programs of Bryn Mawr College is an organization of alumnae and friends who have joined together to assist the President in promoting the international activities of the College."

A WIDER WORLD FOR WOMEN

INTERNATIONAL BRYN MAWR

JUNIOR YEAR ABROAD OPTION LIMITED ONLY BY IMAGINATION
Miriam Ehtesham, Class of 1976

BRYN MAWR STUDENTS who have always wanted to study abroad are provided with ample opportunities to do so through any one of the many Junior Year Abroad (JYA) programs in which BMC students can participate. There are almost unlimited possibilities for overseas studies through the programs open to Bryn Mawr students, for a Bryn Mawr sophomore may apply for admission into any approved JYA program of studies sponsored by an American college. Suggestions, help and credit are given by the College—all that is required of the student is a working knowledge of a European tongue (in most cases) and the desire to broaden her outlook on her major subject by overseas study.

These facts were revealed in an interview with Dean Patricia Pruett and Dean Jo-Anne Thomas, two of the people responsible for guiding students interested in JYA or other foreign studies. Dean Thomas, who is Dean of the Class of '75, is at present heading the Bryn Mawr program. She defines her role as principally one of an advisor, and is in charge of assisting interested students in applying for admission into the various programs.

The deans explained that there are two different categories under which it is possible for a Bryn Mawr student to study abroad for a semester or a year. One of these is through a leave of absence. A student on a leave of absence may study in any program that she wishes to follow, and is independent of any set system of studies and unlimited in the country she may visit. However, full credit work done on such a leave is not guaranteed, and a student must petition the Transfer Credit Committee for such credit upon her return.

The second way in which a Bryn Mawr student may study overseas is through a Junior Year Abroad program sponsored by an American college which has been approved by the Curriculum Committee and the department in which the student is majoring. A student who follows this system will receive full credit for the work she does during her year overseas, or at least a predetermined credit according to the program which she decides to follow. The American colleges and universities which have programs open to BMC students have contacts established with their overseas counterparts; an interested student must get accepted into the program, but does not have to go through the red tape involved in applying directly to the European school.

Financially, JYA differs somewhat from a year abroad taken on a leave of absence. A scholarship student who takes an approved Junior Year Abroad will receive the same financial aid from the College as she did while studying at Bryn Mawr. But a student taking a year or semester on a leave of absence will not continue to receive such aid. However, any financial aid received by a BMC student before her leave of absence will be continued after her return. This system, though, may soon undergo amendment, according to Thomas and Pruett.

There are almost an unlimited number of U.S. colleges which will accept BMC students for a Junior Year Abroad program. Among these are Sarah Lawrence, Vanderbilt, Smith, Drew, Tufts, Stanford, Johns Hopkins, Brandeis, and the American Colleges of the Midwest. The countries one can visit under the JYA programs of these institutions include France, Spain, Germany, England, Israel, and Russia. Programs that have never been tried by any Bryn Mawr student may be presented to the Curriculum Committee for JYA approval.

One popular misconception concerning study overseas is that it is an opportunity open only to language majors. Dean Thomas emphasized that the approval of the department under which the individual student's major falls is the most important factor in determining whether or not overseas study would be beneficial to the student and whether or not any JYA program for that student would be approved.

The dean said that there are a large number of BMC students who study abroad who are not language majors—majors from the departments of Political Science, Philosophy, the Classics and Classical Studies, History of Art, English, and even Biology have taken a Junior Year Abroad or leave of absence for overseas studies in the past and are continuing to do so. Some of the BMC departments are interested in certain of the JYA programs for their majors to participate in but not others.

There are currently 13 BMC students on JYA programs and 14 students on leaves of absence, figures which are considerably lower than those of previous years. The deans added that this smaller number of absences from the junior class had been a contributing factor to the overcrowding on the Bryn Mawr campus this year. Although at the beginning of the year a large interest was shown in overseas study for next year by the sophomore class, this interest has waned and the number of students currently interested and making plans for overseas study is about 40.

The Junior Year Abroad programs, according to Thomas and Pruett, add something to the College as well as to the individual participant, for each returning senior brings something back with her, perhaps a new outlook on her education through exposure to change.

Reprinted from the *News* (Bryn Mawr-Haverford), November 3, 1972.

SISTERHOOD WORKS FOR INSTITUTIONAL CHANGE

SISTERHOOD'S ALL-BLACK MAGAZINE *RĀ*, TO BE PUBLISHED NEXT FALL
David Wessel, Haverford, Class of 1975

THE BRYN MAWR SISTERHOOD is working on the publication of an all-black literary magazine called *Rā*. The magazine, named after the Egyptian fire god, is expected to publish its first issue early next fall.

Rikki Lights, editor, said, "It will be our cultural connection with the world outside the academic community." The Sisterhood is contacting outside poets, perhaps Gwendolyn Brooks or John Williams, for contributions. Lights commented, "We see a need for a separate magazine because there is no such black cultural program at Bryn Mawr College and this might be a start." The magazine will be shared with black people inside and outside of the academic community.

Rā will be distributed to other campuses including the University of Pennsylvania and Southern schools such as Morehouse, Spelman, and the University of Kentucky. The two issues each year will also be mailed to subscribers. Lights said that the information of *Rā* "is a step towards defining what culture is, what revolution is. We have to redefine everything."

Rā is part of the entire cultural program being planned by the Sisterhood for next year with headquarters in Perry House, now to be called the House of Rā.

A poetry forum, to benefit *Rā*, is being planned which would include 15 to 20 black poets. A lecture on jazz, in conjunction with a course on jazz to be offered at Haverford next year, is also in the works. It would be given by Harrison Ridley from Philadelphia, the owner of 30,000 albums of black jazz dating from 1910. Tom Weatherly, author of *Thumbprint*, is also being invited to speak.

Although all members of the Sisterhood will produce *Rā*, Bonita Dixon will design the cover, Rhea Graham will coordinate layout, and Claudia Colbert and Anne Staveren will coordinate business.

Lights added, "An expression of blackness by black people couldn't possibly be achieved by *Works and Days*," which has a mostly white staff who "must judge black literary work in order to create an issue on black people. This is something which they are not equipped to do." *Rā* will also include works by younger poets, such as an 11-year-old from South Carolina, and may include works by American Indians, Puerto Ricans, and Chicanos.

The idea for a literary magazine "came about through my own experiences as a writer," said Lights. She started to write poetry last year and has had several readings including one in North Philadelphia with Gwendolyn Brooks, arranged by James Spady of the Black History Museum Committee and another at the Penn Coffee Shop.

Reprinted from the *News* (Bryn Mawr-Haverford), March 24, 1972.

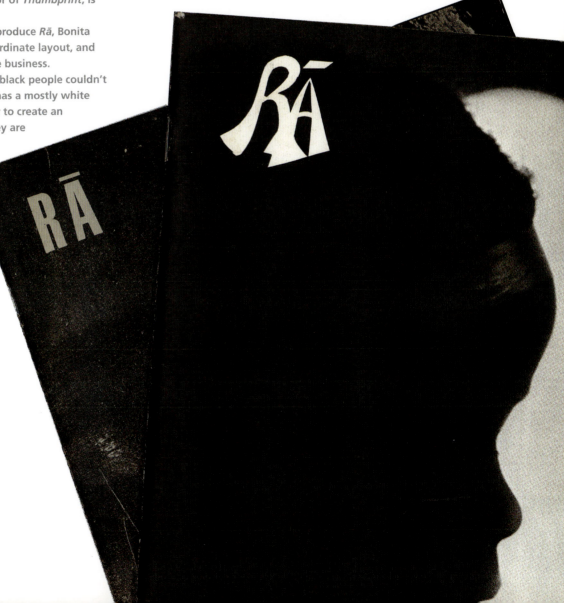

Right: Rā, a literary magazine published by the Bryn Mawr Sisterhood. Only two issues were produced, both in 1973

Opposite: Class of 1977 Commencement

BLACK STUDENTS LEAGUE ACTION HAS PRECEDENT: BRYN MAWR SIT-IN IN 1970

A sit-in by 35 black students that received the support of 45 white Bryn Mawr students March 13, 1970, resulted in President Katharine McBride's agreeing to a list of 10 demands presented to her by the blacks.

Among the reforms were the establishment of a black cultural center, hiring of black faculty, and augmenting of black enrollment by an intensive recruiting program.

A summer program was also among the demands. Established by Bryn Mawr the following summer, it will continue this year, as funds have been received by the College within the last two weeks for that purpose. "We were committed to the program for this summer, but we weren't yet sure that funds would come in," said Dean Mary Patterson McPherson.

The demands for black faculty included expansion of the sociology department to four members, with the fourth to be black. That demand was met the following autumn, with the appointment of Professor Robert Washington, who teaches three courses this year.

A black appointment was to be made in the English department during spring of 1970, but the candidate refused Bryn Mawr's offer to take another position.

A demand for the rehiring of Herbert Aptheker as lecturer in Afro-American history was met, and his duties have since been expanded to three courses per year. Professor Kathryn Morgan was appointed this year to teach to two courses in Afro-American history.

A black house, the third demand, was established by the fall of 1970, with the Board of Directors having budgeted some funds to begin the library and social center at the house, located at Roberts and New Gulph roads.

The recruiting and acceptance increase of blacks that was demanded at the sit-in has begun to be implemented, according to McPherson, through the work of black undergraduates with the admissions department,

and a black staff member has been added to the office's staff. In addition, Patchie Poindexter '70 has been recruiting for the Seven Sister Colleges in more remote areas, doing an "excellent job," according to McPherson.

Beginning in the fall of 1970, students have been allowed to take African languages offered at the University of Pennsylvania to fulfill language requirements, and to apply for transportation funds to take such courses. McPherson says, however, that no one has asked for such credit or funds.

For this reason, the promise made after the sit-in that by 1971 an African language course would be offered at Bryn Mawr has never been followed through upon. "We'd have to have a lot of interest before we try to duplicate what is offered at the University of Pennsylvania," said McPherson.

The eighth demand called for black employment in professional areas to be increased by September of 1970. McPherson cited some seven members of the faculty and administration who are black. She added that the history department has been authorized to conduct a search for a full-time faculty member in the African and Afro-American history fields.

The ninth demand was met several weeks after the sit-in, when McBride issued a College-wide memorandum with respect to maids and porters at Bryn Mawr.

The final demands, for the "total educational structure of the College to be revamped in line with the recommendations" of the colloquium held that spring on April 2, has never seen definite action. Published results of surveys taken at the colloquium did not make clear that there was a general desire for educational policy change or that new approaches to black studies would be implemented.

Reprinted from the *News* (Bryn Mawr-Haverford), February 25, 1972.

COLLEGE RACISM WORRIES BLACK STUDENTS

Margie Starrels, Class of 1977, and
David Behrman, Haverford, Class of 1977

"THE CAMPUS OF BRYN MAWR does not fulfill the needs of Black students," said Jill Dockett, co-president of the Bryn Mawr Sisterhood, when explaining the need for an organization on campus devoted to Black culture.

Glenn Alveranga, a member of the five-man steering committee of Haverford's Black Students' League (BSL), cited several major functions of the organization. It acts as an "organization to provide security for Black students when Haverford is too much to deal with," he said, and to "provide a method for dealing with racism at Haverford."

Racism on campus is a major concern of the two groups. Members of both organizations cited examples of what they consider to be racism— "very, very subtle racism," according to Dockett, who termed it "covert."

"Intellectual Racism"
. . . Joanne Yancey, the second co-president of Sisterhood, told the *News* that racism appears in the form of cultural bias in course material. She observed that Black history and culture are ignored in most courses.

Of particular concern to Yancey are the history and English departments. She specifically criticized the Western Civilization course, saying that it gives an impression of "whites having done everything in Western society." Dockett echoed the thought, saying, "You're required to read that the white man was the best in the world."

Dockett sees the racism in social terms. "White students have this stereotype of a Black student," she said, as loud, constantly partying, and staying up late.

Elaborating on what she called covert racism, she said that "practically every Black person here has come across those false smiles."

Both organizations claim that there is little they can do by themselves to eliminate the racism they see on campus. Yancey said that the Sisterhood does not see itself as a group for educating white students.

"People have to want to know what's going on," said Yancey. "We can't get rid of it."

. . . Last weekend, BSL and Sisterhood sponsored Black Weekend, which offered a variety of Black cultural events on both campuses. Several Black prospective students attended.

Reprinted from the *News* (Bryn Mawr-Haverford), May 11, 1975.

We the undersigned Black women of Bryn Mawr College find it impossible to tolerate the present conditions of this campus, and therefore voice our dissatisfaction in the following demands:

1. We demand the fourth appointment in Sociology as promised by September, 1970. This appointment should be a Black professor.

2. We demand the appointment of a Black professor in English and the reappointment of Mr. Herbert Aptheker in History.

3. We demand an active search for Black professors to fill vacancies in other departments--Biology, Psychology, and Economics.

4. We demand an African American house. This house will be a cultural center, housing the Black Library, and a meeting place for business and social functions. We suggest the present Spanish House for this purpose.

5. We demand Bryn Mawr's support in (facilities and faculty) a Summer Pre-Enrollment Program starting summer 1970. We also demand that Bryn Mawr should supply funds in the event that outside funds are not sufficient.

6. We demand that there be a diligent effort to increase the Black enrollment and to provide funding for intensive recruitment program to find qualified applicants.

7. We demand that African languages and literature satisfy major requirements (language, literature, and/or major) and that transportation allowances be provided for these courses and other courses that have to be taken outside of the Bryn Mawr, Haverford, Swarthmore community. We demand that these languages be introduced into the Bryn Mawr curriculum by September 1971.

8. We demand increased Black employment i.e. Black secretaries, librarians, bookshop clerks, etc. We want a progress report on May 1, 1970.

9. We demand the address of the maids and porters by respectful titles i.e. Mr., Mrs., Miss. We want this done by Administrative memorandum.

10. We demand the total revamping of the educational structure of Bryn Mawr College through student and faculty participation in college decisions.

Above: List of demands submitted by Bryn Mawr's African American student population to President Katharine McBride, 1970

Opposite: Black at Bryn Mawr, an informational brochure for prospective students,

SISTERHOOD CALLS FOR BLACK DEAN, EXPANSION COMMITMENT AT CONVOCATION

THE BRYN MAWR SISTERHOOD spoke to the college at Sunday's Convocation. Representative Rikki Lights spoke and several Sisterhood proposals were included in the summary of the major proposals resulting from the Colloquium which was handed to all who entered.

Speaking about racism and blackness, Lights told the Goodhart gathering, "Blackness through black women exists on this campus. Ignorance considers it invalid. Ignorance and malevolence will not allow it to be recognized or taught. Blackness is not a fad; it is a reality."

The Sisterhood proposal explained the origin of the organization. It was "founded due to the existence of overt and covert racism on this campus. The Sisterhood has served as a vehicle for expressing the unique cultural needs of black women."

Stating that the academic and counseling system at Bryn Mawr is not responsive to the cultural needs of black students, the Sisterhood proposed that a dean be hired to serve black students exclusively. That dean would counsel black students in academic and social matters, financial aid, career planning and placement, and referrals to psychological counseling services.

Black Admissions Dean

In order to recruit more black students, the Sisterhood called for a full-time black dean of admissions and a written commitment to an expansion of the black population to 10% of the student body. The dean would not be subordinate to the present dean of admissions, but would be on an equal administrative level with her. The Sisterhood also demanded that they be consulted in the selection of all personnel hired to meet the needs of black students.

Asking for a written pledge to eliminate all forms of racism, oppression, and cultural ethnocentrism through institutional changes, the Sisterhood said that minority individuals must be allowed to "function as a group." They do not want to be "forced into roles that represent personal opinion only." In addition, commitment to cultural diversity, similar to the one at Haverford, should be endorsed by the administration, said the Sisterhood. Each aspect of governance must include the Sisterhood representative and at least one dorm must have a black warden.

All Black Contributions

"Because the College, as it is presently constituted, ignores the black contribution, it is absolutely necessary that all courses thoroughly integrate the contribution of peoples of African descent," wrote the Sisterhood. Such an integration would require a task force to implement this proposal. The group also demanded the development and establishment of an African Studies major, including all aspects of past and present African civilization and people of African descent, and an Afro-American interdepartmental area of concentration, similar to Hispanic Studies.

The last proposal asked the library to acquire by September, "germinal works of black thought in all disciplines." The Sisterhood promised to submit a list of works to the library. In order to enlarge educational resources, they also requested an exchange program for black students enabling them to study elsewhere.

The document concluded, "Finally, because we are the daughter of a proud and great people, the righteousness of self-respect requires that we request these vital changes in Bryn Mawr College."

Reprinted from the *News* (Bryn Mawr-Haverford), April 14, 1972.

BMC RESPONDS TO SISTERHOOD PROPOSAL:
Admissions Staff, Wardens Included
Dorothy "Dorry" Martin, Class of 1974

LAST SPRING, THE SISTERHOOD of BMC gave the administration a list of proposals. They were presented shortly after the Colloquium proposals. Since then, members of the Sisterhood have met with President Wofford, Dean McPherson, and Director of Admissions Elizabeth Vermey to discuss action on them.

At this time, with one exception, none of the proposals has been completely accepted and implemented,

The list of proposals (now posted in Haffner) is divided into three sections. The first concerns the needs of blacks after they have become students at Bryn Mawr. It asks for a dean who would exclusively handle the academic and social counseling of blacks. This dean would also be responsible for the financial aid, career planning, and placement of blacks.

According to Claudia Colbert, who participated in the talks with Wofford, McPherson, and Vermey, no such dean will be appointed. Colbert said the administration refused on the grounds that one person could not understand all the problems encountered by students during four years at college.

The second section of the paper calls for an increase in the black population of Bryn Mawr. The specific requests include: a full-time director of admissions who would spend all her time recruiting blacks from "unconventional" schools; and a written commitment from the college to expand the black population to 10% of the student body.

In response to the second request, Elizabeth Vermey said that admitting given percentages of students was too limiting and would not be done.

Concerning the first request, Bryn Mawr has hired Carolyn Dent, a black associate director of admissions. The admissions office also has a new part-time black recruiter, Brenda Lucas Hazzard, who will look for applicants in predominantly black public schools in New York City. Dent's position, however, is not exactly what the Sisterhood's proposals specified. Dent is one of the regular admissions staff, and must handle standard admissions duties as well as recruitment of blacks. She expects that her time will be divided about equally between the two.

Colbert felt that the job required full-time black recruitment and said that other schools had admissions officers for this purpose. She also contrasted the progress made by Wellesley in expanding the black student body with the decreasing numbers and percentages of blacks accepted at Bryn Mawr.

(Over the past three years, there has been a decrease in the number of black students applying, being accepted, and coming to Bryn Mawr once accepted.)

Vermey said that hiring a full-time black recruiter seems "too separatist, too segregationalist." She said that the admissions office is exploring a substantial number of avenues to find black students in "unconventional" schools as well as in conventional ones. Among these avenues are memberships in College Bound, a New York-based group, and in SEARCH, a branch of the College Entrance Examination Board. The second group supplies names of blacks with test scores above the college's cut-off point. Bryn Mawr has used these services in past years.

Vermey suggested that one possible explanation for the greater success of Wellesley in expanding the black student population was a greater willingness on Wellesley's part to "take risks" in their admissions. She indicated that Bryn Mawr would not accept students who would not have a good chance of finishing.

The last section of the proposals expresses a need for cultural diversity at Bryn Mawr. It asks for a written commitment from the college to eliminate "racism, oppression (intentional and unintentional) and cultural ethno-centrism" in both the academic and social spheres. It suggested the selection of a black warden for at least one dorm as a concrete gesture to this end. (Bryn Mawr does have a black couple as wardens this year. They are the Humphreys in Merion Hall.)

Bryn Mawr has not, however, issued a statement such as Haverford's, committing the college to cultural diversity. The closest thing has been a letter from President Wofford to the Sisterhood expressing hope for mutual cooperation this year.

Commenting about student requests in general as well as the Sisterhood requests in particular, senior Ann Whatley said, "The administration is willing to give a lot of aesthetic appreciation to your suggestions, but not much action."

Reprinted from the *News* (Bryn Mawr-Haverford), October 13, 1972.

Opposite: Students sharing a communal meal in Perry House, c. 1970s. Photograph by Katrina Thomas, class of 1949

CHANGES IN THE GRADUATE SCHOOL

MINORITY STUDIES GROW AT SOCIAL WORK SCHOOL
Marlene Goodhart, Class of 1978

THE GRADUATE SCHOOL of Social Work and Social Research is expanding the content of minority issues in its curriculum. This expansion is occurring because "a gap existed in the education of social workers regarding Blacks, Puerto Ricans, and other minorities," said Thelma Jacks, a student at the school, during Convocation, Jan. 14.

The need for an increase in minority studies was recognized by faculty in touch with social work programs, students working part-time in the community, and the school itself.

The plan to enrich minority studies has three parts: an increase in course material concerning minorities, the creation of a data bank, and invitations for guest lecturers to come to the school. The Ad Hoc Committee of the Curriculum Committee is now working on these proposals.

Improving Old Courses

Course selection this year offers a few courses dealing specifically with minorities, such as Institutional Racism. Bernard Ross, dean of the school, said that the primary objective is to improve all the courses by making course material more relevant to minority issues, rather than just creating new courses dealing only with minorities.

Whether a minority course will be a requirement or not is under discussion. Ross said that to date the school's philosophy has been to require minimal prerequisite courses. Hopefully, the student will recognize the need for a minority course and elect to take it on his or her own, Ross commented.

The data bank will be a compendium of minority studies and information. The bank is being created so the students and instructors will have a current source of knowledge. Ross cited good cooperation from the Bryn Mawr College Library in purchasing books and other information about minorities. The data bank should be ready for use by the end of the current academic year.

The Committee has not yet decided who the guest lecturers will be, but costs must be kept at a minimum, Ross noted. Lecturers will be social researchers, both from within the community and outside it. The lecturers from the community will relate life histories, showing examples of discrimination. Students will thus be able to gain firsthand knowledge and understanding of discrimination.

Minority issues within the school are also being considered. The College is committed to affirmative action in hiring minority teachers. There are now some part-time and some full-time minority teachers in the School of Social Work and Social Research.

Minority students are also being recruited. The minority enrollment has increased from six percent during the 1968–1969 academic year to twenty-five percent during the 1974–1975 academic year. There are about 160 students enrolled at the School of Social Work and Social Research.

Reprinted from the *News* (Bryn Mawr-Haverford), January 24, 1975.

GRAD SCHOOL, "BORN WITH" UNDERGRAD, REPORTS AN INCREASE IN APPLICATIONS
Cathy Davidson, Class of 1973

ALTHOUGH MANY GRAD SCHOOLS are cutting back on admissions and report that their applications are also down, "neither of these things is true at Bryn Mawr," according to Elizabeth Read Foster, dean of the Graduate School of Arts and Sciences.

Foster said that, in fact, applications to the grad school have increased, enabling a more selective admissions policy. Enrollment has remained even at about 450; of these, about 40% are on scholarship.

The graduate and undergraduate schools "were born and grew together," Foster commented. Bryn Mawr was the first [women's collge to offer graduate study] for women in the U.S.; men were not admitted until the 1930s. The greatest growth has taken place within the last five years, after the Board of Directors voted to increase the size of the school because of a national shortage of teachers. "It was a deliberate choice on their part," said Foster.

Proud of Smallness

The department of education and child development is one of the fastest growing in the school. The French, history of art, and philosophy departments are also relatively large. The school is small, however, and is proud of its smallness. "You need all kinds of grad schools," Foster said. "You need a great variety of educational patterns to teach different kinds of students."

Students are allowed to take courses at the University of Pennsylvania for credit, in order to offset the limited curriculum of a small school. Many graduate students also take advanced undergraduate courses, with the understanding that they must do extra work in order to receive graduate credit.

Part-Time Students

Unlike most graduate schools, Bryn Mawr encourages part-time students and offers them financial aid if they need it. "We have always encouraged part-time students," Foster affirmed, "as part of our special obligation to women." Many of the part-time students are local teachers or married women with families.

The major emphasis of the School is still on full-time students. "You have to keep a balance. You can't have a grad school that's all part-time," Foster commented. One of the largest problems facing these students is finding housing in the area. Only sixty students live in on-campus housing, and the rest face a tremendous problem in finding housing that they can afford which is also convenient to the campus. Foster said that there will probably be no new building, but there was a possibility that an existing building could be converted to use by grad students.

Communication

Communication among the students is another large problem. This will be partly solved by the new grad student lounge in the old periodical room of the M. Carey Thomas Library, which will provide a place for the students to gather, and will also have a mailbox for every grad student. Although undergraduates seem interested in increasing cooperation with the graduate school, the graduate students are less eager for any such arrangement. "We're concerned with more tangible things such as facilities and housing," said Myrl Hermann, chairman of the Graduate Council.

Foster attributed the reluctance to their desire to keep the seminars small, and said that the graduate students seem most content with the kind of cooperation which goes on in the science departments, where graduate and undergraduate students share the same labs. "This is probably the most successful cooperation that we have," she added.

Reprinted from the *News* (Bryn Mawr-Haverford), October 17, 1970.

Opposite: Students in dormitory living room, c. 1970s. Photograph by Katrina Thomas

SOCIAL WORK SCHOOL BEGINS ITS FIRST YEAR OF AUTONOMY

Peter Goldberger, Haverford, Class of 1971

THE DESIGNATION THIS AUGUST of Bryn Mawr's former graduate department of social work and social research as an independent graduate school within the College has "clarified much more than it has changed," according to the new dean of the School, Professor Bernard Ross.

"We've been functioning in most ways as an independent school for years," Ross explained.

In effect, he said, the change will mean more autonomy in admissions, a separate budget allowing him to "plan and project developments," and more direct access to the College administration and faculty.

125 Students

The social work school has 125 students in its pre-professional Master of Social Service degree program, which requires two or three days each week of field work; and 27 in varying stages of obtaining a Ph.D., a scholarship and research degree. About 40% of the social work students are men and about 20% are black.

Students enter the school intending to study either casework services or community organization and planning. In the second and final year of the M.S.S. program they must specialize in one of four tracks developed this year: social service delivery, social service management, community development, or social planning.

Two Groups

Although Ross stated that the school was "trying to break down" the traditional division of the discipline, the students commonly see themselves divided into two distinct groups, with about two-thirds in casework, and the rest in social planning and community organization.

Ross said that the social work school has both a "reputation of being concerned with social policy" and a "strong tradition of psychiatric casework" emphasis.

> In Celebration of
> The Sixtieth Anniversary of
> The Graduate School of Social Work and Social Research
> Bryn Mawr College
> Anthony Lewis
> New York Times Columnist and Author of *Gideon's Trumpet*
> will speak on
> Power, Protest and Responsibility
> Friday, November Fourteenth at eight-thirty p.m.
> Goodhart Hall
>
> Reception following
> The Great Hall, Thomas

Militants

Some activist students see a trend toward community organization by more militant students, but Ross said, "I haven't seen the evidence yet of that much social consciousness among students. A very small number of articulate and concerned people are going into community organization."

Alan Stillman, president of the social work students' association, guessed that the number of students with an activist orientation might be as high as one-third of the enrollment.

Stillman said that many students this year were interested in increasing their roles in the new school's decision-making process. Presently there are non-voting student representatives on faculty committees, and there have been joint student-faculty task forces in the past in such areas as admissions.

According to Ross, a "very small group of students" wants a vote on the committees, but many more want "a voice to affect their destiny and the destiny of the school."

The social work school is "medium-sized," Ross said, compared to other such schools, with 18 full-time faculty, six visiting or part-time lecturers, and three field work consultants.

First Program

Bryn Mawr's department of social work and social research was the first graduate program of social work education in the country. The department opened in 1915 with eight graduate students. Its plan of field work, and its inclusion of work in labor and industrial relations and community organization are unique among programs in other early schools of social work.

The school continues today to make unusual field work placements, including two this year with Philadelphia city councilmen, several in health services, and one with the Haverford Center for Nonviolent Conflict Resolution.

Before being named dean of the newly autonomous school, Ross had been director of the graduate department for two years. He joined the faculty in 1958, after teaching at the Michigan State University School of Social Work.

During the 1940s, Ross served as regional director for the 11 western states of President Roosevelt's Committee on Fair Employment Practices, and then as regional race relations adviser for the Federal Public Housing Authority.

Reprinted from the *News* (Bryn Mawr-Haverford), October 17, 1970.

Above: Announcement for a lecture and reception in honor of the sixtieth anniversary of the Graduate School of Social Work and Social Research, 1975

Opposite: Graduate School of Social Work and Social Research students, 1985

BRYN MAWR GRAD STUDENTS SEEK GREATER RECOGNITION
Alice Taylor, Class of 1976

AT BRYN MAWR there's a student government with $259 in its treasury. With no representation on the council that decides its academic regulations. And a hall president with no higher body to report to.

This may sound like one of the "no plenary, no SGA" scenarios so prevalent in early January, but these are actually some of the realities facing the Graduate Students Council (GSC) of the Bryn Mawr Graduate School of Arts and Sciences.

The Graduate Student Council is funded by the vending machines in Thomas. It is meant to include a student representative from each graduate department, but the history department has not sent one. The Graduate Center Hall President has no formal connection with the Graduate Students Council.

No Contacts

Theoni Trangas, GSC president, is trying to involve the students of the Graduate School of Arts and Sciences in the decisions that determine the direction of their educations.

"We would like to know what's happening in the school," she says. When she was elected last spring she had sat on GSC but had had very little information about its previous activities. Contact with the graduate students in Arts and Sciences is through their departments. As in the case of the history department, sometimes this system does not succeed in reaching everyone. The Graduate School of Social Work and Social Research is a separate body, as is the undergraduate College. Trangas tried to reach SGA president Sue Herman to discuss general problems in the respective student governments, but her messages were not answered.

Trangas characterized the work of GSC last semester as an attempt "to reach both ends"—the administration and the students. There is presently no established channel for the GSC to reach either the administration or the students of the Graduate School of Arts and Sciences.

Departmental Input

Formal input to the administration is minimal. "Our fate is decided by the Graduate Council," admitted Trangas, who added that there are no students in that body and none on its subcommittees. Phyllis Bober, dean of the Graduate School of Arts and Sciences, has been "exceedingly cooperative" with GSC, Trangas said, but Bober is not in a position to grant them extended powers—since control of the Graduate School rests in the individual departments. GSC is hoping that students will be able to increase their contributions to deciding matters within their own departments.

GSC recently sent a letter to each department chairman asking for more say for graduate students in department decisions. According to Trangas, some departments, like anthropology, now include graduate students in important discussions such as appointments. This is something she would like to see more frequently. "We want some say about what we are learning and how we are learning it," said Trangas, and added that graduate students should "demand, if necessary, that they are asked" about department decisions.

Reaching the graduate students can be just as much of a problem as reaching the administration. One of the goals of GSC has been to involve more graduate students in college government, to develop "more interest in Bryn Mawr as such," but complicating matters is the fact that only a small percentage of graduate students live on campus, said Trangas. Many have families and think of their education as a "part-time" occupation. Often, she adds, "Your commitment is to your field, not even to your department."

Isolation is one of the primary problems facing GSC. History of Art representative Mary Pardo noted one effect of the separation of graduate students from each other and from the rest of the College: "It's like we have no status in the College," she said.

In an effort to bring a sense of community to graduate students, GSC is sponsoring a series of "Polylogues" featuring graduate students talking about their work for a general audience. There have been three successful Polylogues and another is planned for early March.

There are also many practical everyday problems facing GSC now. Graduate council is reviewing the Graduate School grading system. Inadequate graduate students' living conditions are also of major concern to the GSC. The room draw for on-campus residences is now being discussed, and GSC is taking a poll on residents' opinions of how the draw should be run and whether they consider the housing adequate. The GSC is also trying to maintain a current list of lodgings outside the College. Trangas expressed a hope to "make the students realize that their fate depends on these decisions." She wants to interest more graduate students in political action here.

Reprinted from the *News* (Bryn Mawr-Haverford), February 14, 1975.

RETAIN THE GRADUATE PROGRAM AT BRYN MAWR
Phyllis Pray Bober, Dean of the Graduate School of Arts and Sciences

DISCUSSION AT LAST MONTH'S COLLEGE COUNCIL, SGA's review of the Healy committee's preliminary recommendations, and various letters to the *News* indicate that undergraduates have very limited understanding of the extent to which they benefit from the Graduate School of Arts and Sciences at Bryn Mawr (and I do not refer simply to the resources of Canaday Library). It seems important at this time to give a little background history, to make a few observations about the current situation of the College, and to express my strongly held conviction concerning our readiness for the future.

Miss Vermey's research in statistics of admissions and the reasons applicants gave for choosing Bryn Mawr among other options reveal an overwhelming priority given to academic excellence. The particular variety of educational challenge which Bryn Mawr offers its undergraduates is the direct result of M. Carey Thomas' insistence from the outset that there should be at least one graduate student, a Fellow, in every subject taught (the new College conferred its first Ph.D. in 1888, a year before the first class graduated).

To her mind, the participation of these fellows would insure that professors continued to expand the boundaries of their disciplines instead of resting on their research laurels. At the same time the graduate fellows would serve as inspiring role models to those "young ladies" she expected to rival the finest products of the top men's universities.

You who are undergraduates today may be dubious about the value of graduate students as role models, but there is no question about your gain from a tradition that sees faculty in the vanguard of their fields of study, teaching at every level from the freshman through the Ph.D. You are introduced to the full meaning of a discipline—its critical lessons—instead of just its subject matter.

Don't let anyone convince you that there is an inherent conflict between teaching and research; for either to be superior, each must reinforce the other. Miss Thomas' vision has made Bryn Mawr "the leading academic institution for women in the United States . . . the hardest girls' college" (Yale Daily News, *The Insiders' Guide to the Colleges,* 2nd ed., 1971), where a "phenomenal" number go on to advanced study . . .

Graduate students also benefit at Bryn Mawr because the mature scholars who guide them are less tempted to dig "slit-trenches" in their specialties when undergraduate teaching is the chief focus. Other advantages for our students are the opportunity to engage in independent work and the emphasis placed on method—the two most serious lacks in their education as voiced by Ph.D. candidates elsewhere in a nationwide evaluation survey.

In this day and age there are other reasons for maintaining and strengthening Bryn Mawr's graduate schools. Given the bewildering range of choices facing college-bound students—and the intense competition for them that is predicted for the future—it becomes increasingly important for institutions of higher learning to define their individual differences, to discriminate their missions one from the other. Bryn Mawr has a great advantage in this respect: we are unique. We are the only liberal arts college for women with a full range of Ph.D. programs. And the tutorial, personalized nature of the education they provide cannot be matched elsewhere.

What this means in terms of quality for even our smallest departments is reflected in a list of the institutions granted funds by the Mrs. Giles Whiting Foundation for dissertation fellowships in the humanities (which might be likened to pre-doctoral Guggenheims): Columbia, Harvard, Princeton, Stanford and Yale universities—and Bryn Mawr College.

Reprinted from the *News* (Bryn Mawr-Haverford), December 9, 1977.

Above: Brochure for the symposium in honor of the sixtieth anniversary of the Graduate School of Social Work and Social Research, held November 14 and 15, 1975

HELL WEEK
A COLLEGE TRADITION

Hell Week's Shrouded Origins

SO HELL WEEK IS OVER NOW and you don't know what to do with your life. Whether you're a freshman, a sophomore, a junior, or a senior, your life has been ruled by "The Schedule" for the last week, and now it's time to make decisions for yourself again. Just remember: the road to Hell is paved with good intentions.

The question has been circulating: how long has Hell Week been going on? The earliest suggestion of a Hell Week such as ours being celebrated at Bryn Mawr is from an article in the *College News* in 1943. However, a woman at a certain supply store us Traditions Mistresses use said that her mother was in the Bryn Mawr Class of 1946, and therefore was helled in that infamous year 1943. Her mother assured us that Hell Week had been going on for some time before that and was definitely not a new tradition.

Hell Week developed out of two other Traditions at Bryn Mawr: Freshman Show and Class Animal. We still have a Freshman Show every year (even though a lot of you might not have been aware of that), but the Tradition of Class Animal has unfortunately fallen by the Traditions wayside, along with other things such as Junior Show and Class Dinners. In the olden days, every class would choose a class animal, and, much like today's Parade Night Song, would try to conceal the identity of this animal from the sophomores. The Class Animal was presented every year at the Freshman Show, with this catch: it had to be presented for real, in person. The freshmen were supposed to keep some sort of representation of the animal (alive, stuffed, drawn, whatever) on campus for a day or two for the sophomores to find. The sophomores' efforts to find this animal and to keep freshmen from getting to rehearsal for the Freshman Show proved to be the base upon which the Tradition of Hell Week came to be developed. As time went by, Hell Week detached itself from the Freshman Show and overtook it in importance. It is not known exactly when Hell Week was first celebrated as its own Tradition, but we do know it has been going on for over 50 years.

T-shirts should be in momentarily—we're very sorry about the delay. Did any frosh happen to do a Hell Week T-shirt design? We're serious—we'll do them if you guys will buy them.

On another subject, ever find yourself thinking back to songs at step sings and wishing you could hear "What I Did for Lab" or "Colossal Pain," without having to wait all the way to the next Step Sing? Well, we have a project in the works right now that will enable BMC students and alums to hear all those favorite songs 24 hours a day. In conjunction with the Alumnae Office, we are organizing a professional recording of a Step Sing. We need 40 BMC voices willing to put in ample rehearsal and studio time. If you are interested, please audition for us. Signs will be posted soon with more information. Hopefully, the song tape will be ready for sale by May Day. Speaking of that glorious festival, start thinking of fun, exciting activities which you or your club would like to sponsor, and get in touch with us!

Reprinted from the *College News*, February 7, 1991.

Above and opposite: Students handing down a "guilty" verdict (detail) and judges from the senior class (detail), at the Hell Week trial in Erdman, February 21, 1985. Photographs by Karin Schwartz, class of 1986

CORRESPONDENTS UPHOLD HELL WEEK FUN AND SPIRIT
Jane Miller, Class of 1955, and Barbara Floyd, Class of 1954

LOOKING BACK on the last few weeks there seems to be some question as to the relative merits of Hell Week. As two students who have seen both sides of Hell Week (one of us able to view it also as an onlooker), we would like to defend one of Bryn Mawr's most enjoyable traditions. There has been much criticism of uniting Hell Week with Freshman Show. However this time of year is the best for both the Freshmen and the Sophomores. The Freshmen have begun to feel really at home and by this time know most of the upperclassmen as well as those in their own class. Usually done in the spirit of fun, Hell Week does bring the Freshmen and Sophomores closer together. You will also find that the Sophomores take into account the amount of time each Freshman is putting into Freshman Show and act accordingly.

We do think that a greater attempt should be made to keep Hell Week out of the classroom. But as for Hell Week destroying the sophisticated and intellectual myth of Bryn Mawr we say, "Hooray." The majority of the college enjoys a good time as much as anyone can and as long as Hell Week is carried on in the spirit of good fun it should stay . . . We know the spirit of Hell Week is one of friendly rivalry backed by understanding and goodwill on the part of the Sophomores, and we are sorry that any Freshmen feel there are clashes of personality—it is never so intended. Hell Week to us is a necessary and wonderful part of Bryn Mawr.

Reprinted from the *College News*, March 3, 1953.

Committee Revises Hell Week, Welcomes Students' Comments

AFTER TWO CONSECUTIVE Monday evening meetings, freshman and sophomore representatives from each hall have considered criticisms and suggestions on Hell Week, and have proposed certain revisions which will be presented to Undergrad. The group agrees that the Hell Week tradition is essentially worthwhile, but that its purpose needs more careful definition and its structure, closer coordination.

The purpose of the suggested changes is to remove the elements of fear and persecution from Hell Week, thereby making it a period of creative competition between the freshman and sophomore classes. Hopefully, such an image would encourage all freshmen to participate and would avoid individual incidents of persecution.

The central committee, begun this year, would be enlarged and strengthened by including one sophomore representative from each hall, plus the sophomore class president, vice president and traditions chairman. Sophomores from each hall would submit statements of the Hell Week themes to the committee before the semester break in order to avoid theme duplication and to make certain that themes are in the realm of the fantasy. In addition, the committee would encourage sophomore participation, the degree of which determines the success or failure of Hell Week in any hall.

It was decided that a positive approach should be taken by sophomores, juniors and seniors in their Hell Week tales, which form the basis of freshman preconception of the activities involved. Rather than stressing punishment and persecution, they would better stress wit, creativity and competition.

Concrete rule proposals include:

- Hell Week would begin Thursday evening by delaying freshman show rehearsal that night. Activities, by being shorter, would reach their peak Friday rather than Thursday, and would prevent the common Friday afternoon letdown.
- Thursday evening sophomores would present their introductory skit, hand out costumes and make assignments for Friday. Friday morning freshmen would be in costume and would present their songs at lunch. The afternoon would be spent preparing skits and retaliation, though the freshmen who need to sleep or study would be able to do so by signing up for a location in the library, in their rooms, or with other freshmen. At 4:00 all skits and activities would be performed, followed by the trial.
- The demerit system would not be used, as some freshmen felt it became too personal.
- Punishments and activities would be assigned to groups of at least two people, or individually only with great care, to protect those who are naturally more quiet or retiring.
- The sympathetic sophomore would contact each freshman in her hall on Thursday and Friday briefly. Complaints could be easily aired by this means and freshmen would appreciate the concern shown. The hall president, not directly involved in Hell Week, could speak to the freshmen as a group, inviting them to see her with complaints.
- All freshmen would be blindfolded during the same hours Friday—lunch to 7:00.
- Friday night's bedtime would be set officially at 12:30 for all freshmen, with no group activity (i.e., retaliation) allowed between that hour and 8:00 Saturday morning. They would be told that for purposes of health, they would need a full night's sleep, with the show and punishments ahead.
- Individual freshmen would still be allowed to abstain from Hell Week activities but would know this through personal contact, not official notification.

Reprinted from the *College News*, March 5, 1965.

Above: Students handing down a "guilty" verdict, at the Hell Week trial in Erdman, February 21, 1985. Photograph by Karin Schwartz

Opposite: Judges from the senior class, at the Hell Week trial in Erdman, February 21, 1985. Photograph by Karin Schwartz

Next page: Hell Week ephemera, 1957 (background)

Happier and Healthier Hell Week Evolves from Stress of Last Year
SARI HORWITZ, *Class of 1979*

LESS HARSH HELL WEEK RULES made this year's Week more successful than that of last year, Sophomore Class President Alex Bowie stated at a recent meeting of dorm Hell Week chairmen.

"We were so much happier with Hell Week this year. People were sensitive and Hell Week was more humane," Bowie said.

Rules Relaxed

As a result of controversy over the harshness of last year's Hell Week, a group of students from the Class of '79 wrote a list of Hell Week rules to be followed this year.

The rules established, among other things, the right of individual freshmen to abstain from Hell Week activities, and provided for Hell Week tasks to be assigned to groups of at least two people.

"The stress of last year was alleviated," remarked Haffner Hell Week Chairman Lisa Gaston. "Everyone thought of it as a fun time to relax and be crazy."

Varied Tasks

The only complaint voiced at the meeting was that there was no uniform program for all freshmen. Erdman freshmen had no Hell Week tasks, while in other dorms freshmen were given humorous tasks, or asked to dress up in costumes or perform skits for upperclassmen.

The general feeling of the Hell Week chairmen was that people who were unhappy about Hell Week last year ran it this time in a manner that would have been comfortable to them as freshmen, Bowie said.

Pembroke West Chairman Allison Hess, however, questioned the entire validity of Hell Week. "There is nothing funny about the whole thing," she commented.

A freshman at the meeting responded by saying, "Nobody should take Hell Week too seriously and lose her sense of humor. Hell Week brought us all together in a very special way."

Reprinted from the *News* (Bryn Mawr-Haverford), February 18, 1977.

HELL WEEK RULES

- Punishments and activities will be assigned to groups of at least two people.
- There will be no transfer participation.
- Individual freshmen will be allowed to abstain from Hell Week.
- Each dorm will maintain a sympathetic upperclassmen to whom all grievances may be brought by freshmen. Freshmen may also seek out the sophomore class president with complaints.
- The sophomore class president will check with the Hell Week chairman in each dorm to be sure all rules are followed.
- There will be a midnight curfew for freshmen Saturday night.
- There will be individual dorm parties Friday afternoon or evening.
- There will be no midnight calisthenics.

Reprinted from the *News* (Bryn Mawr-Haverford), February 4, 1977.

HELL WEEK: IS IT UN-BRYN MAWR?
Emily Bass, Class of 1995

ALL RIGHT, BEFORE I SAY ANYTHING ELSE let me say that I am glad that I had the Hell Week experience. This may be all that I can commit to, but the infamous tradition, from beginning to end, has definitely made people on this campus, including myself, think about their environment. And that in itself is a good thing.

The first draft of this article was a livid composition begun last Friday at six in the morning to the tune of broomsticks beating on trash can lids. The second draft was the product of the sweet relief associated with the painless resolution of my task of collecting fifty signatures in support of a New Kids on the Block fan club (dressed as Donnie Wahlberg, of course). It was also inspired by an appreciation of the re-union of our community and of the real warmth coming from upperclasswomen in our dorm.

In what is turning out to be the third draft, I can still say that my taskmistress was a sweetheart (she's not making me write this), and that my experiences were not embittering. But this did not stop me from realizing that Hell Week works because of the tension it creates. It is a dangerous thing to try to manipulate divisiveness, especially under the guise of a tradition with long-standing normative roles dictated by class standing. The long-awaited end should not have to function as an apology from the upperclasswomen.

One of the most common things I have heard people say about Hell Week was that at some point during the tradition it was decided that the whole concept was very "un-Bryn Mawr," suggesting some ideal which, along with relations between the classes, was betrayed. Whatever this quality is, it goes beyond Bryn Mawr's identity as an academic community and a women's college, for these are not and cannot be our sole distinctions. In other academic communities, Greek-related traditions are not considered out of character; other women's colleges have sororities.

There is undoubtedly a special quality to Bryn Mawr's environment that draws students here which contributes to our unique and supportive community. On the other hand, this ideal seems to be vaguely defined and perhaps most revealing in its absence, as during Hell Week. Yet, I wonder what right we have to single out Hell Week, an ultimately well-intentioned tradition, as "un-Bryn Mawr," when there are more glaring examples of un-BMC-ness fully incorporated into our everyday lives.

As a self-sufficient community of women, we have this incredible opportunity to create a feminist space for ourselves. Feminist in the sense that the flaws, marginalizations, and oppressions of society (racism, sexism, homophobia) should have no place here except as we identify and address them. Feminist in the sense that we are all women interested in controlling and directing our own lives.

We are also a community of students attending an institution which offers academic excellence in a tradition dominated by the legacy of Dead White Men. We do not have a Women's Studies major, or enough existing courses for the students willing to study diversity without a requirement. The persistence of these issues characterizes Bryn Mawr much better than do the problems associated with Hell Week. Or rather, they may be all indications of the same basic problem, with Hell Week operating as a prime example rather than a contradiction of the norm.

This is not for those students who object to Hell Week. For those of us with no serious quarrels, there are a number of other problems looming on this campus which seem to run counter to what we are all about on a much larger scale. Eating disorders are "un-Bryn Mawr." An unsafe campus is "un-Bryn Mawr." These conditions persist for more than a few days out of the year. Without slighting the large number of women who are concerned and active, it seems that without concrete change the only thing that Hell Week is incongruent with is our ideal. The feelings of betrayal associated with this tradition might be avoided by forming a clear idea of what Bryn Mawr is, what we want it to be, and what forms of our traditions can work within this framework.

Besides reclaiming and redefining history, language, empowerment, we can put a little of our energy into reclaiming other traditions. The danger is the degree to which the borrowed tradition remains intact within our community, and the degree to which we do or do not control other aspects of our time here.

Reprinted from the *College News*, February 13, 1992.

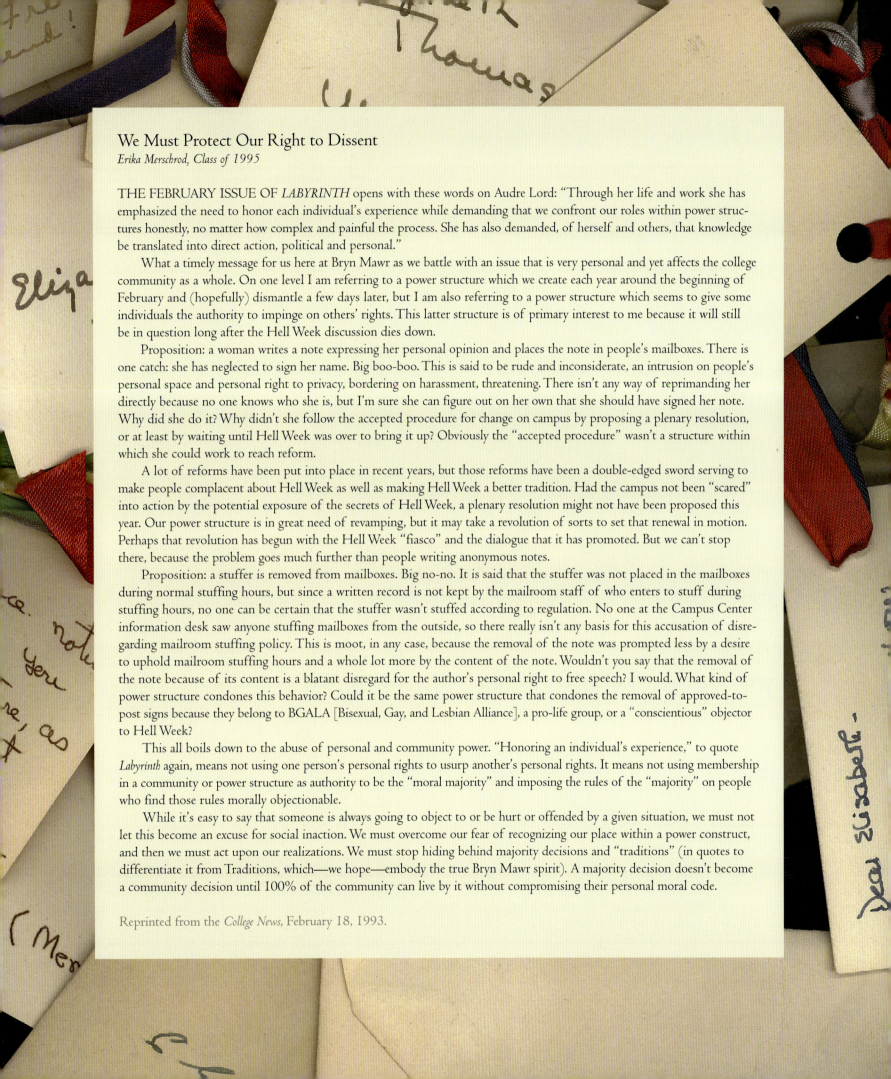

We Must Protect Our Right to Dissent
Erika Merschrod, Class of 1995

THE FEBRUARY ISSUE OF *LABYRINTH* opens with these words on Audre Lord: "Through her life and work she has emphasized the need to honor each individual's experience while demanding that we confront our roles within power structures honestly, no matter how complex and painful the process. She has also demanded, of herself and others, that knowledge be translated into direct action, political and personal."

What a timely message for us here at Bryn Mawr as we battle with an issue that is very personal and yet affects the college community as a whole. On one level I am referring to a power structure which we create each year around the beginning of February and (hopefully) dismantle a few days later, but I am also referring to a power structure which seems to give some individuals the authority to impinge on others' rights. This latter structure is of primary interest to me because it will still be in question long after the Hell Week discussion dies down.

Proposition: a woman writes a note expressing her personal opinion and places the note in people's mailboxes. There is one catch: she has neglected to sign her name. Big boo-boo. This is said to be rude and inconsiderate, an intrusion on people's personal space and personal right to privacy, bordering on harassment, threatening. There isn't any way of reprimanding her directly because no one knows who she is, but I'm sure she can figure out on her own that she should have signed her note. Why did she do it? Why didn't she follow the accepted procedure for change on campus by proposing a plenary resolution, or at least by waiting until Hell Week was over to bring it up? Obviously the "accepted procedure" wasn't a structure within which she could work to reach reform.

A lot of reforms have been put into place in recent years, but those reforms have been a double-edged sword serving to make people complacent about Hell Week as well as making Hell Week a better tradition. Had the campus not been "scared" into action by the potential exposure of the secrets of Hell Week, a plenary resolution might not have been proposed this year. Our power structure is in great need of revamping, but it may take a revolution of sorts to set that renewal in motion. Perhaps that revolution has begun with the Hell Week "fiasco" and the dialogue that it has promoted. But we can't stop there, because the problem goes much further than people writing anonymous notes.

Proposition: a stuffer is removed from mailboxes. Big no-no. It is said that the stuffer was not placed in the mailboxes during normal stuffing hours, but since a written record is not kept by the mailroom staff of who enters to stuff during stuffing hours, no one can be certain that the stuffer wasn't stuffed according to regulation. No one at the Campus Center information desk saw anyone stuffing mailboxes from the outside, so there really isn't any basis for this accusation of disregarding mailroom stuffing policy. This is moot, in any case, because the removal of the note was prompted less by a desire to uphold mailroom stuffing hours and a whole lot more by the content of the note. Wouldn't you say that the removal of the note because of its content is a blatant disregard for the author's personal right to free speech? I would. What kind of power structure condones this behavior? Could it be the same power structure that condones the removal of approved-to-post signs because they belong to BGALA [Bisexual, Gay, and Lesbian Alliance], a pro-life group, or a "conscientious" objector to Hell Week?

This all boils down to the abuse of personal and community power. "Honoring an individual's experience," to quote *Labyrinth* again, means not using one person's personal rights to usurp another's personal rights. It means not using membership in a community or power structure as authority to be the "moral majority" and imposing the rules of the "majority" on people who find those rules morally objectionable.

While it's easy to say that someone is always going to object to or be hurt or offended by a given situation, we must not let this become an excuse for social inaction. We must overcome our fear of recognizing our place within a power construct, and then we must act upon our realizations. We must stop hiding behind majority decisions and "traditions" (in quotes to differentiate it from Traditions, which—we hope—embody the true Bryn Mawr spirit). A majority decision doesn't become a community decision until 100% of the community can live by it without compromising their personal moral code.

Reprinted from the *College News*, February 18, 1993.

Determined Leadership:
1978–1997

THE AGENDA FOR THE FUTURE

LETTER FROM THE PRESIDENT
April 14, 1995

Friends,

With the publication of the *Agenda for the Future*, we bring to a close an important stage in the College's on-going planning endeavors. We began this process over a year and a half ago under the leadership of Judith Shapiro and a steering committee composed of faculty, staff, administrators, and students, and the Provost of Haverford. They organized nine separate Task Force teams composed of representatives from all campus-based constituencies and including the President of the Alumnae Association. Those teams then began a campus-wide conversation about planning for the future of the College. Unlike recent planning efforts that focused on the College's financial situation or on its fund-raising needs and goals, this initiative was designed to explore and evaluate nearly all aspects of the College's identity and functions. In a difficult time for higher education, perhaps particularly for the selective, high-cost, independent liberal arts college, it seemed wise to attempt an assessment of the current state of the College and to engage the community in the development of a plan or plans to move the College strongly into a next century, hence, the *Agenda for the Future*.

. . . Apparent in each of the Task Force reports is the deep commitment of the faculty, staff, administrators, and students to the sort of educational institution that Bryn Mawr is and should attempt to remain: a college with a special commitment to the education of able undergraduate women and to graduate men and women in the College's two graduate schools; a college composed of a faculty devoted to fine teaching and first-rate scholarship; and a college composed of staff members and administrators whose desire for professional growth contributes to the enhancement of the College's educational enterprise. Apparent too in the reports is the commitment of faculty, staff, administrators, and students to strengthen the sense of community within the College and to act on their responsibilities to the wider community beyond the College. These are essential ingredients for the continued success of our educational mission as a small liberal arts college.

> "THE SHADOW SIDE OF OUR 'CULTURE OF EXCELLENCE' IS AN EQUALLY VIGOROUS CULTURE OF COMPLAINT," SAID THE MEMBERS OF THIS TASK FORCE. STUDENTS ARE BASICALLY OVERWORKED AND OVER STRESSED, AND MANY FEEL THAT ACADEMIC STANDARDS ARE NOT JUST DIFFICULT BUT UNATTAINABLE.

. . . Throughout the reports there is a yearning for a kind of community that existed more easily when the College was a smaller, less complex institution. And there is also a recognition running through many of the Task Force reports that we—faculty, staff, administrators, and students—are among the privileged few in our increasingly distressed society. There is an acknowledgment that with the privileges of our positions and our educations there should be a more articulated sense of service to those in less fortunate circumstances in society. These are among the newer notes struck, and we need to pay attention to them because they so clearly speak to our time and place.

Finding ways to promote more harmonious interaction among the various constituencies of the College should take a higher priority for all of us. And the appropriate representative bodies need to initiate a careful evaluation of whether service activities within the wider community should receive higher institutional recognition—be it credit for student work or some part of the assessment of faculty, staff, and administrators' service.

Out of one of the last major planning efforts of the College, the initiative to secure financial equilibrium, came an important recommendation to involve faculty members more formally in the setting of academic priorities. Out of the current planning effort, I think there is a recognition that our decision-making and communication could be further strengthened by formalizing the ways in which students, faculty, staff, and administrators who carry special responsibilities within the College come together to inform each other and to think about the College's next best steps . . .

My thanks,

Mary Patterson McPherson
President of the College

Reprinted from Bryn Mawr College, *Agenda for the Future*, April 1995.

SETTING THE AGENDA FOR THE FUTURE
The Task Forces and the College-Wide Discussion
Robert J. Dostal, Provost and Chair of the Steering Committee

THOUGH THE TASK FORCES were asked to address different aspects and functions of the institution, two common themes and concerns run through the reports like threads that bind the many voices, concerns, and suggestions into a loose-knit unity: community and outreach.

Throughout the reports and the discussions surrounding them I find a deep concern for "community"—an aspiration that this be a more welcoming and inclusive place. This community concern is, of course, a reflection of our often fragmented and somewhat fractious personal lives which this institution cannot make whole. Yet the Task Force reports make a number of helpful and challenging suggestions in this regard. One dimension of this aspiration toward community concerns the way the various constituencies of the College interact—students, faculty, and staff. In particular, students would like more interaction outside class with the faculty. And staff would like to see better recognized their contribution to the central enterprise of the institution, teaching and learning. More appropriate places and occasions in which we come together are sought. Another dimension of this communal aspiration concerns the relationship of the families of Bryn Mawr students, faculty, and staff to the institution.

The other common theme, "outreach," presents a number of aspects. The Task Forces recommend that the College's curriculum provide more opportunities for service learning and fieldwork. The theory of the classroom should better connect with the world of practical experience. This need may be felt the strongest in the social sciences where important efforts are being made in this regard. The reports similarly recommend that the College community, students, faculty, administrators, and staff, seek and find more opportunities for extracurricular service to the surrounding communities. Another area of outreach concerns connecting students with the post-graduate world through advising, internships, externships. And, finally, in this regard the reports suggest that the institution could do better staying connected to its alumnae/i. The alumnae/i might both better serve the institution and the current students, and the College might better be of service to the alumnae/i.

The common threads of "community" and "outreach" tend in opposing directions—inner and outer directed. Clearly we have to find a place of balance sustained by the pull in the two directions. The reports are replete with similar tensions, contradictory tendencies and varying perceptions of the institution from faculty, students and staff. This is indicative of the strengths and weakness of this planning process as we have structured it. The reports provide more evaluation and diagnosis than they do a plan. What we have been conducting has been more a conversation about what we are about and how we are carrying out the task than it has been a planning effort. The broad representation and participation invited complaints and constructive criticism. It also exhibited the enormous good will of faculty, students, and staff, and has revealed some of the great characteristics and strengths of the institution: that we perceive ourselves as a community and not simply as a workplace, that the constituencies wish to be more involved with one another, and that all are vitally connected with the short- and long-term future of the institution. The planning process addressed the breadth and complexity of the institution but it has not been able to address sufficiently the depth of many of the most important issues. Nonetheless, a number of important issues have been "moved along" by the process. Importantly, a wider and more appropriate context for coming to terms with the issues has been established. It must also be said that the reports provide us with an impressive list of suggestions and recommendations—many of which have already become mandates of various College committees and offices.

. . . The institution's identity is, of course, a complex and manifold one. We do many things; most important, we maintain two graduate schools and an undergraduate college. But at the core of this enterprise is the undergraduate liberal arts college. And though we have two graduate schools, we should not understand ourselves as a mini-university. Teaching must have a very high priority here. And the faculty must continue to find a way that the tension between their teaching and their research be a fruitful one. We will continue to have a higher teaching load than research universities. And we will continue not to rely on graduate students for teachers. If this is to work well for faculty and students, we need a faculty that does not stay exclusively within their individual research specialties or even the department. The conversation with colleagues and students in and out of the classroom requires a broader view and, needless to say, a deep love of learning. It goes without saying that we need to continue to attract a student body prepared for and interested in a liberal arts education.

My conversations with faculty, students, and staff have reconfirmed the importance of and institutional consensus on the central defining feature of the undergraduate college: that Bryn Mawr is a college for women. This premise of the planning procedure has found consistent and repeated reaffirmation. Furthermore, I have found the planning conversations, formal and informal, renewing the College's long-time commitment to maintaining and supporting a diverse student body, faculty, and staff. Similarly reaffirmed has been the international character of our student body and curriculum.

This commitment to an excellent liberal arts education for women which is diverse and international provided the background for the planning and self-evaluative process. The conversations and reports continue to grapple with the many ambitions of the College—the great number of departments and programs, undergraduate and graduate. A persisting difficult question asks whether our reach exceeds our grasp. Here I should note the fundamental significance of our close relationship with Haverford College which in many quite different ways helps us define what we do and who we are. It not only complements and supplements what we do but provides institutional and individual conversational partnership for the ongoing task of self-definition. Our planning procedure suggests that Swarthmore College should become a greater participant in our joint enterprise.

Inasmuch as the institution's identity is complex, manifold, and historical, it is ineluctably contestable. The institution, like the liberally educated and self-reflective individuals we trust we graduate, must continue the discussion with itself about itself. The various planning initiatives inaugurated by this planning for an agenda must now be followed up.

SUMMARIES OF TASK FORCE REPORTS

A Faculty of Teacher-Scholars

This Task Force report makes it clear that Bryn Mawr's faculty is highly involved with and committed to the College. Faculty invest a great deal of time, effort, and emotion in their work. Many faculty are delighted to be at the College and identify with the College's mission as a liberal arts institution especially concerned with women. Faculty members generally appreciate the flexibility which is often possible at Bryn Mawr, and the ways in which research and teaching opportunities can evolve over time as professional interests shift.

A number of concerns in the Task Force's conversations pointed to the inherent tension, sometimes "creative," sometimes not, between the College's twin historical goals of offering a liberal arts education, which aims at the encouragement of the arts and habits of living thoughtfully, and offering the specialized education of the scholarly disciplines, which aims at the excellence of scholarship as an end worthy in itself. These twin goals, often complementary but at times incompatible, require of the faculty a commitment to both teaching and scholarly research. Maintaining these two goals, as Bryn Mawr has done throughout its history, has been understood by most of the faculty and academic administrators to be not only possible but desirable—certainly far preferable to pursuing one of the goals at the expense of or in isolation from the other.

It is clear from the Task Force report, however, that the creative tension between teaching and research needs monitoring so that it remains in a healthy, mutually informing and mutually supportive balance and does not become an unmanageable opposition.

The College needs to promote a continuing conversation about its special mission as a liberal arts college so that faculty members feel that their efforts to combine high-quality scholarship with first-rate teaching are encouraged, supported, and recognized as central to the educational purposes of the College . . .

The Undergraduate Experience

This Task Force reports wide endorsement of the College's identity as a community of high achieving students who not only take their academic work very seriously but get genuinely excited about ideas and value the life of the mind. Applicants choosing to matriculate, seniors speaking about their undergraduate experiences in exit interviews, and alumnae all endorse the College's commitment to educational excellence.

But the Task Force also reports that while students choose to come to the College because of its academic excellence, they also feel overworked and overstressed by their academic pursuits—so much so, that a "culture of complaint" exists side-by-side with a "culture of excellence."

Students who speak supportively about the College's academic mission tell us that while they highly value the opportunity to work closely with faculty committed to fostering habits of inquiry, self-reflection, and judgment that long outlast the information they acquire and the grades they receive, they are often discouraged by an impossibly high standard of academic achievement, which leaves them feeling unable to relax and guilty about taking time for other College activities.

... In seeking to explain why Bryn Mawr's tradition of academic excellence is at once a badge of pride, a source of frustration, and a focus of complaint for undergraduates, the Task Force proposed several reasons they believe might account for what they were hearing.

Students in the '90s come to College with experiences, expectations, and preparations very different from earlier generations of students. And this makes for a more difficult process of adjustment to the academic expectation we place upon them.

Students entering the College in 1994 have read less than previous generations and have had more experience with media such as TV, video, and film. This may make it difficult for students to manage the considerable amount of reading and writing expected of them at Bryn Mawr. Today's students also work more than their predecessors did to contribute to their college expenses.

In addition, students have phones in their rooms, often TV and VCRs, and a great deal of self-reported time is spent on e-mail and other computer activities, all new distractions taking student time that earlier might have been spent on academic work.

Although the College's academic support services have been considerably strengthened over the past decade in response to the needs of entering students, the Task Force concluded that faculty members need to help students learn to be more productive by making academic expectations more explicit.

> INASMUCH AS THE INSTITUTION'S IDENTITY IS COMPLEX, MANIFOLD, AND HISTORICAL, IT IS INELUCTABLY CONTESTABLE. THE INSTITUTION, LIKE THE LIBERALLY EDUCATED AND SELF-REFLECTIVE INDIVIDUAL WE TRUST WE GRADUATE, MUST CONTINUE THE DISCUSSION WITH ITSELF ABOUT ITSELF. THE VARIOUS PLANNING INITIATIVES INAUGURATED BY THIS PLANNING FOR AN AGENDA MUST NOW BE FOLLOWED UP.

A major focus of this Task Force became the undergraduate curriculum, particularly the experience of the first two years before a student elects a major. If students perceive the general requirements as hurdles to be gotten over with as little strain or engagement as possible, this attitude will certainly preclude the rigorous and exciting introduction to new approaches, methodologies, and fields which these requirements are supposed to afford.

The College will certainly not be meeting its aims as an educational institution if our students understand the academic side of College life to be an unremitting, hard, unpleasant, and endless experience. This suggests that the curriculum review currently underway is of special importance . . .

Graduate Education

Given the size of the Undergraduate College, the presence of two graduate schools at Bryn Mawr is unusual, but, as this Task Force reports, the presence of the graduate schools is seen by some as a natural complement to the undergraduate enterprise. Not surprisingly, the Task Force found divergent views in conversations about the mission and place of graduate education in an institution devoted in large part to undergraduate education.

A large number of faculty members referred to the satisfaction they receive from teaching and mentoring graduate students as among the greatest provided by their professional lives. Collaboration with graduate students was seen as enhancing the quality and quantity of the faculty's research. Some faculty members said the presence of graduate programs was a key factor in their accepting job offers from Bryn Mawr. Many felt the commitment to graduate education testifies to the College's deep commitment to scholarly research.

Though faculty agreed that the original reason for including graduate work at Bryn Mawr—giving women the opportunity to pursue graduate education which was not available in other institutions in the country—no longer applied, some pointed out that we still serve a population, predominately women, who wish to go to graduate school part-time. For many women and men, the small size of Bryn Mawr's classes and research groups, the accessibility of faculty members, and the faculty's serious commitment, in the case of the Graduate School of Arts and Sciences, to undergraduate teaching remain appealing.

Some faculty point out that the interaction between undergraduates and graduate students in research groups, as TAs (teaching assistants), and in the College's counseling programs is valuable to both groups of students.

Other faculty express uncertainties and concerns about the mission and role for graduate education at Bryn Mawr in the mid-1990s. Some departments and the Graduate School of Social Work and Social Research, they note, have national and international reputations while others serve a largely local population. Some faculty worried about the disparity, which can only grow as new faculty come into the College, between those faculty with graduate students and those without. They were concerned that such a situation could result in a two-tiered and less cohesive faculty in the College.

Even though the College now provides a greater level of support than in the past, funding for graduate students and the institution's ability to provide adequate support for them and their needs while at the College were of concern to most faculty members questioned.

The faculty and administrators in the two graduate schools expressed an interest in increased collaboration between the two in those areas where curricular enhancement could be achieved.

Staff Development

The Task Force found that, although many staff members at all levels had worked for some time at the institution and felt deep loyalty to it, they were concerned about practices in a number of areas. This Task Force report accordingly focuses on issues related to: staff recruitment, retention, and job mobility; the current system of incentives and rewards for staff; and priorities in the area of staff development.

Across departments, many staff feel they are trying to address increased job responsibilities with no increase in personnel. Many employees find the evaluation process flawed. There is a feeling that the evaluation system leads to strain within offices and seems in the end to make no difference to compensation. Supervisors agreed they could benefit from more training in evaluating. And there was support for a system whereby the evaluators would be evaluated by their employees.

Concerns were raised about a lack of communication within the institution. Some people felt there was a lack of clarity about the expectations for performance. Staff also expressed a wish that there be better communication between staff members and the faculty. Some staff are concerned that the faculty have access to benefits not available to staff (particularly, tuition benefits for children) and, further, that the faculty fail to acknowledge the presence or the importance of the staff's contribution to the work of the College.

Concern was also expressed about a wide-spread impression of rather low morale among workers that seem to follow from the above noted conditions.

The Task Force report makes clear, however, that these concerns originate in the staff's desire to perform their role in the College's mission, to continue to grow professionally, and to have their work recognized as essential to the functioning and future of the College.

The College as a Community

This Task Force considered how effectively Bryn Mawr was functioning as a community, reviewing whether the different constituencies of the College felt a sense of belonging and a shared commitment to the institution. Some members of the College with whom the Task Force spoke felt the College has lost some of its cohesion as the College has grown in scale and complexity. And there is concern that Bryn Mawr is a hierarchical community without adequate procedure for redress and collective action.

The Task Force found a high level of concern for the quality of life at the College. For faculty these concerns focused on the balance of service commitments against expectations for publishing and teaching; comparatively low salaries; day care and recognition of family demands—particularly the desire to slow the tenure clock for child-birth/family responsibilities. Staff shared similar concerns relating to family responsibilities; they were concerned, as well, with being respected for their role in the College. Students reported feeling that their nonacademic work was not adequately recognized, and graduate students expressed a desire to be more involved in the activities of the College. All constituent groups reported a desire to be more actively involved in the decision-making procedures of the College. To facilitate this increased level of involvement, as well as address a range of other concerns, the Task Force believes that the College needs to improve the system and spaces for communication. The information to be communicated should take in not only events, activities, and announcements but also opportunities for jobs, professional development, and service activities; forums should be established for discussion of general and particular issues; and the general happenings that are part of the life-blood of any community should become part of the information system uniting all members of the community.

Philadelphia and the Region
The College has a long tradition of education for citizenship which must continue to develop. Many students come to the college with excellent service-learning and volunteer experience which they wish to continue.

The College community includes many faculty, staff, and students who are very connected to community efforts in and around the city of Philadelphia, and several programs in the Graduate School of Social Work and Social Research and Arts and Sciences routinely engage students and faculty in important outreach efforts and are committed to in-service learning. The Task Force found that the College has a long and distinguished list of outstanding efforts in and contributions to the region.

The Task Force believes that the College needs to structure these efforts more effectively and to engage in long-range planning aimed at reorganizing and increasing the College's involvement with its surrounding communities. The Task Force feels that the College should be reaching out in a more organized way to its communities and should also continue to present itself as an intellectual and cultural resource to its neighbors.

Bryn Mawr in Dispersion
The Task force recognized the many ways the College needs to keep in touch and to support adequately its various external constituencies, alumnae/i of its Undergraduate College, its two graduate schools, and its special program graduates, and the parents of all of these.

Support for those working for the College in Admissions, Career Development, Resources, the Alumnae Association, and the President's and the Dean's offices should be provided in an efficient way so as not to waste the time of loyal but busy members of the College family. More involvement of parents is recommended as well as a greater engagement with alumnae/i of our own geographical region.

The College should provide the appropriate technology to support its programs. It should also continually review its own publications to see that they represent the College accurately and efficaciously.

The College should think of its role with its alumnae/i, parents, and friends as lifelong. The College should be in a position to be of use to its constituencies in different ways appropriate to their different needs over their life spans.

The Task Force believes that it would be highly desirable to sustain the development of a distinct administrative structure at Bryn Mawr to provide information, communication, and support for community service activities . . . Strengthening the commitment to community service creates valuable connections for Bryn Mawr students to communities outside the College, builds crucial bridges for the College to those communities, sends an important message about the College's desire and efforts to contribute to the communities, and responds to a growing concern for service in students.

The Task Force proposes several curricular changes to integrate fieldwork experience and methods with classroom approaches to learning. This, the Task Force believes, will make the College and its students more visible throughout the region and beyond. Such heightened visibility can lead to real opportunities for the institution and for the individual students. These efforts, the Task Force concludes, can work at international as well as at local levels, with the College's alumnae/i as well as with constituencies not a part of the College.

Recruitment and Retention
The Task Force found wide-spread agreement that Bryn Mawr has a distinctive identity and purpose. Students and alumnae/i tend to describe the College as a place for particularly able young women and "not for everyone." There is concern that the image of the College or its tacit messages may lead students to misapprehend the College's commitment to academic excellence as prohibitive of nonacademic interests and pursuits. The Task Force recommends that the College look

carefully at the unintended messages and try to assert a healthier balance between academic and nonacademic pursuits.

The Task Force also recommends that the College, while adhering to the planning parameter of the continued admission of only women to the Undergraduate College, continue in the future, as it has in the past, to consider the wisdom of a move to coeducation, if for no other reason than to be clear about the College's mission and direction.

The Task Force explored a range of issues related to its main charge: the curricular concerns of transfer students; the advantages and limitations of the organization of the College into an undergraduate college, two graduate schools, and the division of general studies; the role of technology in the recruitment process and its attractions for retaining students. And the Task Force proposed strategies for enhancing the College's recruiting efforts by focusing on geographic areas which show promise for providing the quality of student we are interested in.

Facilities, Technology, and the Organization of Work Facilities

The charm of Bryn Mawr's facilities is a major asset to the College. Their upkeep and the meshing of old spaces with new ways of working are major challenges facing the College. In its conversations, the Task Force found a common concern for the relatively little communication about this important aspect of the College's operation. The Task Force suggested that better communications could help to focus the constituencies' attentions on what will surely become an accelerating concern for the College as new technologies make their impact on work and on building use. The Task Force felt, too, that more extensive communications could boost morale and better coordinate the efforts for faculty, staff, and students in their classroom work and in integrating technology in both the classroom and in the College's other services . . .

Technology

The Task force reports that the College has made good progress in adopting new technologies, but the Task Force feels that the College, in order to remain competitive with other institutions and to prepare students for an increasingly technological future, needs a more comprehensive approach to planning and budgeting for these technologies and for integrating them into the work life and academic enterprise of the College community. The Task Force also urged that the decision-making that constitutes this approach needs to be more public and formal. The Task force believes that initiatives to expand technology will require the College to address issues of productivity, the reorganization of work procedures, the low student-to-faculty ratio, and the number of educational programs the College offers. The Task Force reminds the College that new funds and an increased budget will be needed to support a technologically competent and adequately sized support staff and a program to acquire and to replace equipment.

Work

The Task Force reports that faculty and staff take pride in doing much with little. But there is widely voiced concern that this will lead to stress. There is a need, therefore, to examine what is expected and to eliminate those expectations and tasks that are least critical to the College's mission.

There is concern, too, as noted by other Task Forces, that departmental supervisors and managers are not as competent in both supervisory and technological skills as they should be. There seems to be a need, therefore, for wide-ranging, comprehensive, and compulsory training in both functional and technical capabilities.

In a similar vein, the Task Force believes that the College's commitment to improved productivity and enhanced quality of work requires a commitment to a policy promoting the professional development (particularly in technological proficiencies) of staff. Such a policy would more adequately recognize staff desires for professional growth and more effectively integrate such efforts with the College's educational operations . . .

The Task Force explored a range of issues related to outsourcing of College work, to the optimal use of technology for teaching and learning, and to the manner in which technological changes could be implemented and supported.

Reprinted from Bryn Mawr College, *Agenda for the Future*, April 1995.

Page 282: Student in a T-shirt commemorating Haverfest (Haverford's annual end-of-the-school-year campus party), relaxing outside, c. 1988

Page 284: Students on campus, October 1984

Opposite: M. Carey Thomas by Paul Manship (American, 1885–1966; 1923, marble, 16¾ x 20 1¼ x 11 inches), adorned with headphones, in Thomas Great Hall, c. 1980s.

McPHERSON INAUGURATION

Now for the second time in the College's history a Bryn Mawr dean without a Bryn Mawr A.B. succeeds a male president. From many points of view there could be no better omen for the coming administration, since Miss Thomas' strengths and achievements are legendary. But we all should perhaps take warning from this coincidence, remembering that at least one result of her administration was the Great Faculty Revolt of 1915. It is perhaps a good thing that since that revolt relieved the presidency of some of its power, no successor of Miss Thomas can ever hope to kick up quite so much dust.

—Mary Patterson McPherson, inaugural address, September 7, 1978

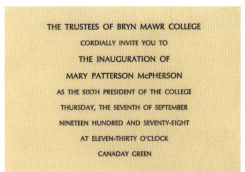

Mary Patterson McPherson has often made a difference at Bryn Mawr by doing things differently.

   Beginning with her approach to her position.
   After all, how many college presidents have strong-armed an adolescent extortionist in New York; been bitten by a distraught student; enjoyed hot tubs, white-water rafting and hiking in Death Valley; and been pulled from a quicksand-like bog in England, while managing to sit on more boards of directors than many captains of industry?
   And are on a nickname basis with faculty and students?

Steve Goldstein, "The President of Bryn Mawr Has Shucked the Old-School Approach," *Philadelphia Inquirer*, November 3, 1992.

AS A FURTHER COMMITMENT TO THE COMMUNITY, I TAKE MOST SERIOUSLY THE NEED TO ADDRESS THE ECONOMIC NEEDS OF THE COLLEGE'S VARIOUS CONSTITUENCIES, NECESSARILY IN THE CONTEXT OF THE BOARD'S MANDATE THAT THE COLLEGE'S BUDGET BE IN BALANCE BY 1982. TO SUCCEED, HOWEVER, WILL TAKE THE UNDERSTANDING AND THOUGHTFUL ACTION OF EVERY MEMBER OF THIS COMMUNITY. LET US WORK TOGETHER FOR THE FUTURE OF THIS COLLEGE, STRIVING FOR THE COURAGE AND WISDOM THAT WILL BE REQUIRED.

—*Mary Patterson McPherson, inaugural address, September 7, 1978*

THE CULT OF "MARY PAT"
Rachel Soltis and Megan Munson, both Class of 1998

MARY PATTERSON MCPHERSON, Bryn Mawr's president, has had a tremendous impact on our college as an institution and on the student body. Whether students like her or are intimidated by her, whether they are in awe of her or disapprove of her, as Kelly Mack '99 said, "Everyone has an opinion on Mary Pat."

Our president has, over the many years she has been president, become so enmeshed in the culture of Bryn Mawr that she has come to represent its essence. The question that must be asked is: how has this happened?

President McPherson has an extensive history within women's colleges; she attended Smith as an undergraduate, Bryn Mawr as a grad student, and she was a dean at Bryn Mawr before becoming president. Thus, she is familiar with the type of culture that develops in an all-women environment, and she knows how to act within it. Also, she has been at Bryn Mawr for so long that, through familiarity, she has come to be associated with the college; she seems as lasting as Taylor Hall. No students and few professors were here when President McPherson was not. She has become almost an icon, as professors and upperclasswomen have passed down stories about her to incoming students.

Also, the simple fact that she is a woman in a position of authority adds to her persona. Women in such visible positions of power are rare, and so we cling to the few examples we can find. As Bryn Mawr is a women's college, it is more likely that a woman be its president than at a co-ed school. But it is nevertheless very important that this is so. In a sense, we—also products of a women's community—can see her as one of us.

In addition to her real authority, President McPherson's appearance adds to her aura. One sophomore, when asked about the president, responded immediately, "She's . . . the tallest woman I've ever seen." Another sophomore likened her to George Washington, "powerful and unapproachable." As a woman in a position of power, physical presence is crucial, regardless of height, and President McPherson carries herself well.

Though some students are daunted by the thought of any interaction with President McPherson, most feel a certain familiarity. In conversation, students refer to her as "Mary Pat"—a very informal nickname which (rumor has it), she doesn't care for and won't tolerate from anyone other than students. We marvel that we have a president who is willing to dance to the well-oiled 50s tunes of the Razorbacks at a BMCDS (Bryn Mawr College Dining Service) special dinner, who will meet with undergraduates to discuss forming a crew team, and who invites new students into her home for tea and dessert. Melissa Miscevic '99 commented that she'd "never been in a school before where you can go up to the president of the college and . . . have a discussion with her about Oreo cookie pie."

Nevertheless, not all Mary Pat stories are complimentary, and some students don't buy into the culture of Mary Pat-worship. Some don't believe in worshipping anyone at a distance. Others actively disapprove of her. One junior told me, "I think she's very fake," and added that she believed the president did not always use her power appropriately. Another student, a freshman, disagreed; she reasoned that we tend to hear only rumors of how she acts in official situations, and thus we can't make any really informed conclusions.

And she is right; we really can't make any informed conclusions. Although most of us are familiar with the President McPherson we see walking by on campus or giving a speech at May Day, few of us know her at all in her official presidential capacity; in fact, most of us aren't even sure what she is supposed to do. Instead we are creating the persona of a president to fulfill our expectations of and needs for a women's college that is supposed to create strong women. We selectively pass on stories; we elaborate on rumors. In a sense, the Mary Pat we think we know is simply an image. By interacting with the students on a regular basis, she provides us with the raw data to interpret and convert this image, but we ultimately are its creators.

Reprinted from the *College News*, October 8, 1996.

IMPRESSIONS OF BRYN MAWR
Richmond Lattimore

A mining town in Wales.
A gray rock in the wind.
A difficult flower in the crack of the rock.
The rigor, time, toil and patient
imagination of science,
wissenschaft, that is, which is all of the
learned studies.
The honorable estate of being a woman.
Contempt for fads and facility.
The fascination of facts and figures.
The problem puzzled out in private agony,
then shared.
The mind the soul and the body.
Austere but willing to be sometimes silly.
Nerves, nerves sometimes in the spells of
hysteria any college has to go through.
Yet still
not modeled on but model.
Tradition and innovation.
The great names of the past and
the young promise.
In black and white, beauty on the grass.
Fresh lawns and cool towers not of ivory.

Read on the occasion of Mary Patterson McPherson's inauguration, September 7, 1978. Lattimore was the Paul Shorey Professor of Greek at Bryn Mawr.—Ed.

Top: Mary Patterson McPherson delivering May Day greetings, c. 1980–82

Bottom: Telegram, Constance M. K. Applebee (1873–1981) to Mary Patterson McPherson, September 5, 1978, wishing the new president "a long and happy administration"

Opposite (top left): Invitation to the inauguration of Mary Patterson McPherson, September 7, 1978

Opposite (bottom left and right): Mary Patterson McPherson (born 1935), c. 1970s–80s

FEMINISM AND SEXUALITY: CHANGING THE CONVERSATION

OPINION

TO AN AUDIENCE that braved the elements of winter, President Mary Patterson McPherson gave her clearest and most openly feminist speech in a year. Miss McPherson gave the type of talk that we have been longing to hear. She answered questions that have been thrown around campus for the last few years such as "What is the purpose of Bryn Mawr?" and "What is the relevance of a women's college to modern society?" In one section of her speech McPherson confessed that "in my darker moments I think that, in many ways, women are less well off now than they were twenty years ago. They have been given a place, to be sure, in many formerly male preserves, but it is conveniently just that, 'a place,' and the reason for their inclusion in these institutions was too often inspired by financial concern." On the question of the relevance on women's colleges to modern society, McPherson said, "You remember that Miss Thomas said that Bryn Mawr should be a college for women as long as that is necessary. We have asked ourselves about that necessity several times in the past and probably will ask it several times in the future. Once, fifty years ago, we determined it was no longer necessary to exclude men from the graduate schools, and we have never argued that men should not a have a strong role in our Board, or in our faculty, or in our administration." Regarding women at Haverford, McPherson said, "I suggest that Haverford too knows that it will need to redefine its purpose if it wants to include Haverford women as full partners at every level of its endeavor."

Reprinted from the *College News*, February 2, 1982.

SISTERHOOD SHOULD TRANSCEND SCHISMS IN BI-CO COMMUNITY
Pam Mery, Haverford, Class of 1992

I'VE BEEN PONDERING this article for months, wanting to write it, sitting down at the computer to write, and never quite getting it down. I realized last night that one reason I am so hesitant is because I know that there are more important issues. However, I think that this is important, too, perhaps not in and of itself, but in what it says about Bryn Mawr, and Haverford, in general.

What have I been pondering? What it means to be a Haverford woman, particularly a Haverford woman living (and majoring) at Bryn Mawr. Personally, it's great! I have all sorts of amazing friends and interesting experiences. My world gets to be larger. The best of both colleges is available to me because I am familiar with both. As a category, though, it sucks. I am invisible. Let me explain:

Haverford hates distinctions. Haverford is so quick to erase categories of people, to say we're all part of one big community, I feel like I have to scream to exist as a woman. This situation makes confronting sexism twice as hard, and tiring. Haverford men don't expect Ford (women) feminists to speak up. I guess they feel betrayed by their "sisters."

So, then Bryn Mawr. I feel invisible here, too. Bryn Mawr is so possessive of the word "woman" that there seem only so many labels to dole out and Haverford females just don't qualify. We are not women. Certainly we aren't men. I suppose we're just neuter. I once heard a Bryn Mawr lesbian state that she would NEVER date a Haverford "woman." She didn't realize I am from Haverford.

Then there are the few of us Haverford women living at Bryn Mawr. We're okay; we are unqualified women. We get the title. But then, it is assumed that we are "converts" of a sort. Interestingly, of the six of Haverford women living at Bryn Mawr whom I know, none was included in the *Bi-Co News* article about "Haverford students" living at Bryn Mawr. Only once throughout an almost full-page article was it stated that the article only related to Ford men living at Bryn Mawr. That statement was in the title, and no rationale within the article was made. From reading the article one could actually assume that there is no such animal as a Haverford woman living at Bryn Mawr.

I've lost track of how often I've been asked which college I prefer. I refuse to swear allegiance. I won't / wouldn't swear allegiance to any school. My allegiance is to women, and to people. The question is part of my life, though, and I ask it of myself frequently. It's interesting to compare, but usually in the form of which dining center or which library I prefer. I don't frame my life by the question of where I "belong." I don't choose one college; I select aspects of each. When other people ask me which college I prefer I want to answer, "I am the same person no matter which I choose to say." What doesn't frame my life shouldn't frame others' opinions of me.

So how should we women get along? Are Haverford women really unfeminist? I can tell you that I'm feminist (I won't give you my definition here), and my role models were all powerful Ford women. Do Haverford women compete with Bryn Mawr women for men? Well, I never have fought over a man. I know straight women from Haverford who could claim the same thing. So we can get along, but again, how? I'd like to see support and cooperation happen at a categorical level, beyond just the personal level. Women, whether we are Bryn Mawr or Haverford students, should aid each other because we are women—not just on a friend-to-friend level . . .

We need female unity. Why? Haverford has been co-ed only ten years, as of this year. I don't know what those first seven years were like, but I know that during that first year four brave and strong women fought the system. One of those women that first year was gang raped outside Barclay. She reported the rape, she was not taken seriously, the men got a slap on the wrist. She eventually had to leave the college, to save her personal sanity.

I ask you Bryn Mawr women, WHERE WAS YOUR RIGHTEOUS FEMALE OUTRAGE? This woman was unapologetically gang raped six miles from this very campus. A fellow student. If I have to swear allegiance to this college that is Bryn Mawr to feel protected and supported as a woman what other conditions do you demand? If this college supports women it should be unqualified. If there are qualifications (and I would submit that there are more qualifications than merely being a matriculated Bryn Mawr student) they should be rigorously questioned and thrown out.

Fight the patriarchy. Let's do it together.

Reprinted from the *College News*, November 15, 1990.

OUT OF THE DARK: DISCUSSING SEXUALITY
Karen Tidmarsh, Dean of Freshmen

THE BELATED RECOGNITION of the epidemic of adolescent pregnancy in this country has caused a reexamination of the whole issue of what ought to be taught about sexuality in the elementary and secondary schools. That issue is obviously complicated since there are such wide differences of opinion in our society over how much children and adolescents may know and whether any of it should be learned in the schools. Add to that the current schisms in our society over issues such as homosexuality, sexual harassment, abortion, and pornography, and it is not surprising that schools have found it easier to lie low and to say that sex education is the parents' prerogative and responsibility.

Bryn Mawr and other colleges have also found it hard in the past decade to decide what, if anything, they ought to be doing in the way of sex education for their students. By the late seventies the only remaining vestige of the once-mandatory Hygiene Lectures were talks on birth control. That had seemed a responsible and necessary minimum in the sixties, but ten years later students objected to it and voted with their feet. They argued rightly that many of them were not sexually active and disliked the implication that they were or ought to be; most of those who were already heterosexually active were practicing birth control and didn't need a lecture presenting facts and statistics that they already knew; such a lecture ignored the needs and existence of homosexual students; and those who had questions about birth control would be better advised to discuss their own needs and preferences individually with a doctor or one of the nurse-midwives on the staff of our Infirmary. For a little while, student resistance to the birth control lecture was interpreted to mean that they really did not want or need to hear about sexuality in college—or at any rate not from the College.

That assumption was quickly undermined, however, as upperclassmen came to the Dean's office to express concern about how little was being done to help freshmen cope with the wide variety of sexual attitudes, experiences, and behaviors which they encountered in the halls. Some eighteen-year-olds were prepared for it, and used to an equally diverse and open high school scene, but many were not. Since few, if any, formal social restrictions govern life in the halls in 1986, the students were essentially on their own to come to terms with a potentially confusing situation.

Even with the reassurance that students did want the "right kind" of sexuality program, it wasn't easy to determine what that would be. Over the past couple of years, we have tried to develop one that will meet several goals. One is simply to reassure students that it is legitimate to be confused by the range of values and behaviors they are facing and that they aren't alone in their confusion. Another is to make it clear that there are adults on campus who are sympathetic, objective, and informed to whom students can turn when they have questions. And a third is to get them talking and thinking about the need to be at once faithful to their own needs and values and tolerant of those of others. For the past two years, a program led by Jean-Marie Barch, a consulting psychologist on the Bryn Mawr counseling staff, and Lindsey Will, a nurse-midwife who sees students in the Infirmary, has focused on such topics as date rape, the physiology of sexual response, and differences in sexual needs, identity, and activity. The program does not attempt to cover all possible areas of concern, but it has had a quite favorable response and seems to be on the right track.

One point that became clear as we redefined the freshmen sexuality program was that since college students, like everyone else, are ready for information and advice on sexuality at very different times, there needs to be more than just a program for freshmen. A second program that would go considerably beyond the broad, general issues appropriate to present to a whole class ought to be available for those students who want it later on.

That recognition led to the development of a Human Sexuality seminar offered for the first time last fall to all interested undergraduates on a voluntary, non-credit basis. The seminar was led by John Scholl, Ed.D., and Leslie McCook, A.C.S.W. (Academy of Certified Social Workers) of Whitemarsh Associates. They have led courses on sexuality and on relationships at Swarthmore College for about seven years, and came to Bryn Mawr with high recommendations and very useful experience with a group of students similar to Bryn Mawr's. (As John and Leslie put it, "bright students who want to intellectualize everything—including sex.") While they had never worked with an all-female group before, they were interested in the possibility. (John Scholl expressed some appropriate intimidation at representing the entire male sex in such an experiment, but accepted the challenge.) Their method at Swarthmore had been to find two student coordinators who then helped select about a dozen student facilitators who could lead small group discussions. I approached a number of students last spring about the possibility of such a course and asked a group of them to meet with John and Leslie to exchange ideas about it. The meeting was very successful—the students were pleased that such a course was being planned and liked the sound of John and Leslie's method. They, in turn, liked the students, and by the end of that meeting we had two excellent coordinators—Kim Grahl '86 and Irene Lambrou '86—and a core group of "facilitators."

The course attracted thirty-five participants this fall and was led by John and Leslie. Ten student "facilitators" spent a full day in training before the seminar began, and then met with John and Leslie for a half hour preceding and following each session to discuss problems that might or did arise in the small group discussions. At the first meeting of the seminar, John and Leslie introduced the course and discussed their own sexual development—thus providing models of mature and candid expression of feelings related to sexuality. Individuals' feelings and the importance of communicating them were, in fact, the focus of the seminar. In addition to their own presentations to the whole group, John and Leslie used explicit educational films and the small group discussions to help participants define and discuss their feelings. The films, produced by a progressive congregation that acknowledges the need for educational materials concerning sexuality, present real people involved in actual relationships. While they are explicit, they are not pornographic, and are frequently used by medical schools in training their students; they not only provide topics for discussion but they also serve to help student participants to the point where they overcome uneasiness in discussing sexuality.

At the final session of the seminar the students were asked to complete written evaluations. Of the respondents, thirty said that they would recommend the course to a friend. Some of the specific comments were interesting, and suggested that the seminar had been very successful for students with quite a variety of needs. Some had wanted to develop a vocabulary for their sexual feelings, others hoped to gain confidence about their own sexuality or their morality. Many cited a desire to bring sex "out of the dark" and to be able to compare ideas with peers that they couldn't discuss with their friends. One hoped "to be more honest with myself (I was) and with my boyfriend (I was) and with my family (I wasn't)." Despite the wide range and lofty nature of expectations, when the students were asked to rate the seminar on a scale from one (not helpful) to seven (very helpful), the mean response was five. For a typically critical Bryn Mawr audience, that seems very positive, and suggests that this program, like the freshmen one, should continue—at least until the students make it clear that a new direction is needed.

Reprinted from *Bryn Mawr Now*, Winter/Spring 1986. Karen Tidmarsh became dean of the undergraduate college in 1990, a position she held until 2010.—Ed.

BRYN MAWR PUTS WOMEN IN THEIR PLACE: TRADITION AND INTELLECT THRIVE TOGETHER
Connie Leslie

Notes from a women's room wall:

> Feminism is not a sexual choice or preference. It is a political framework for exploring the oppression of women.

> To love men does not mean to be submissive.

> Ladies, know thy enemy . . . we must understand men—they have the power.

Just because their college prides itself on intellectual rigor—and the buildings that are listed in the National Historic Register—does not mean that Bryn Mawr students abjure graffiti. But clearly, this is not "Mary loves John" country, here in Philadelphia's Main Line suburbs. When Mawrtyrs (as they call themselves) are moved to scribble, says Claudia Callaway, president of the student Self-Government Association, "it always turns out to be about God and sex, the two great mysteries of everyone's life."

The opposite sex may be a bit more mysterious at Bryn Mawr than at many other schools, since it is now, as it has ever been, a liberal-arts college for women only. Founded in 1885 by Joseph Wright Taylor, to give females the same high-quality education that males could obtain, Bryn Mawr was also the first women's college to offer graduate degrees to women.

Not that Bryn Mawr is cloistered; Haverford, a Quaker college for men that went coed in 1980, is only a mile away, and in recent years students from the two have shared classes and even dorms. For men who venture over to Bryn Mawr, being a minority can be an enlightening experience. "Feminism is the structure of a lot of activity here," says Haverford sophomore Greg Mohr, the only man out of 22 in his Spanish class at Bryn Mawr last year. "The men here have a higher social consciousness —the ones at Haverford who are afraid don't come over here."

Indeed, Bryn Mawr appears to revel in a bluestocking image, which is why president Mary Patterson McPherson's comment at last year's centennial celebration caused such a ruckus. She actually hinted that she would not be surprised if Bryn Mawr "within the decade" decided to admit men to its tiny (1,070 students) undergraduate body.

Though there has since been no formal consideration of the matter, McPherson sticks by her sentiment. "Women's colleges were founded in protest because women were not given equal access and open opportunity educationally," she now says. "When one comes to the point institutionally of believing that the reasons that one was founded have largely disappeared or become less important, then does one take the next step for one's institution?"

There are pressing reasons why even Bryn Mawr is at least entertaining the notion of going coed in its second century as, most recently, Goucher has done. Like all colleges, it is battling for a share of a shrinking pool of high-school students of either sex. Bryn Mawr's reservoir is shallower still: only 2 percent of all female college students attended women's colleges last year, and even the most favorable recent research indicates that only 11 percent of all 17-year-olds would consider attending single-sex schools.

Encouraging uptick: Yet lately, signs of a single-sex countertrend have sprouted. Several recent studies have supported the belief that women's colleges serve a special purpose, instilling confidence as well as competence in their graduates. "You need a place that says to you that the male way isn't necessarily the best way," says senior Marcy Epstein. One survey by the Women's College Coalition found that 81 percent of graduates from member schools went on to grad school; nearly half work in male-dominated fields such as medicine and business, and their median salaries are considerably higher than those for all women with college degrees. Perhaps as a result of such data, women's colleges are seeing an encouraging uptick in applications.

Bryn Mawr demonstrates its commitment to women's rights in myriad ways. Graduates looking for jobs can find mentors through Bryn Mawr's Alumnae Career Network and Externship Program. On campus not only the president but also the chief financial officer is female; so is more than half the faculty, and women chair 14 of the departments while men chair 12. "I'm never going to have the chance again to be in an environment where women play the whole range of roles," says Laurie Fenlason, editor of Bryn Mawr's feminist newspaper, the *College News*.

The college grants students a great deal of autonomy. At the end of each semester undergraduates may set their own exam schedules. Students sit on the board of trustees and on all college-wide committees—which can be a double-edged sword. When minority students protested two years ago that there were not enough minority teachers, "we got a commitment from the administration that they would hire five more minority candidates," says Dominique Parker, former co-president of The Sisterhood, Bryn Mawr's black student organization. "But they also put me on the search committee. It's a lot more complicated than we thought."

Among a number of outstanding curricular offerings, Bryn Mawr boasts the only undergraduate department of classical and Near Eastern archeology; students can "dig" in Greece, Turkey and Italy. Although

English is the most popular major, fully 30 percent major in the sciences. Bryn Mawr also features career-oriented classes. The International Economic Relations program, for instance, combines advanced studies in languages with economics. Students spend summers studying in Russia, France, Spain, Germany or Italy in hopes of landing jobs in international finance, diplomacy or law.

Vocal radicals: This urbanity is reflected in the student body, which last year came from all 50 states and 37 foreign countries. On the other hand, there were only 35 blacks and 18 Hispanics. One highly visible group is the lesbians, who maintain a small but active presence, sponsoring "women only" concerts, forums and other programs without seeming to stir the controversy that has erupted at some women's colleges. A few students, though, complain that the radical feminists are carpingly vocal. "If you take any position in the newspapers like pro-life that is not the dominant view of the people who edit it, you get attacked endlessly," says one student. "I feel really intimidated."

The tension of learning can be unnerving at Bryn Mawr—"It can be so gloomy and so serious," says one senior—but its setting represents almost an ideal of higher education. The school sprawls across 125 acres of hills lush with grass and trees. The dorms range from romantic Victorian Gothic towers to the sleek plate glass and slate of Erdman Hall, architect Louis Kahn's renowned interpretation of a modern castle. Many rooms have fireplaces, window seats and stained-glass windows.

And Bryn Mawr treasures tradition. On "Lantern Night" each October, students dress in black academic robes and assemble in the courtyard of Thomas Hall. While singing ancient Greek anthems by candlelight, sophomores present each freshman with "the lamp of learning"—a lantern painted in the class color. On May Day students dress in white, and a team of four white oxen carts a flower-bedecked Elizabethan Maypole to Merion Square for Maypole dancing. And sophomores are expected to stage teas throughout the year to introduce freshmen to the upper classes. To watch such activity is to find it difficult to believe that Bryn Mawr's status as a single-sex font of excellence is an endangered tradition.

Reprinted from *Newsweek*, September 1986.

Above: Student and friend in the cloisters, c. 1980s

ALL-WOMEN BRYN MAWR COLLEGE DEFIES TREND
Saundra Keyes

WHY, IN AN ERA when women have breached the fortresses of virtually every male-dominated institution in America, would students choose to attend a women's college?

That's not really the first question high school seniors consider when they apply to a place like Bryn Mawr College, said the institution's president, Mary Patterson McPherson.

"We are selected most often by people not because we're a women's college, but because of our high academic standards and no-nonsense curriculum," said McPherson, who was in Nashville this weekend for a regional meeting of Bryn Mawr alumnae.

"Our applicants don't usually start out saying, 'I want to go to a women's college.' They start out investigating good liberal arts institutions and then, after they narrow their lists down, they confront the question of Bryn Mawr as a women's institution."

McPherson said visitors to her campus in Pennsylvania probably would initially have no sense of being at a single-sex institution, since men have been admitted to Bryn Mawr's graduate programs for more than 50 years and since undergraduates from nearby Haverford College, a men's school, are permitted to study and live on the campus.

On the other hand, she added, "M. Carey Thomas, the second president of Bryn Mawr, said, 'It should be a women's college as long as that's necessary.'

"We've asked ourselves several times if that is still necessary. We continue to say, 'Yes, there is indeed a place for a first-class institution run by women for women.'"

That is partly because of the role models provided by Bryn Mawr's 45% female faculty and the predominance of women administrators and trustees, McPherson said.

Too, she said, because the college's undergraduate student body is entirely female, women receive more intellectual encouragement than they might get from professors at coed institutions.

"Professors tend to want to devote most of their time to people they think will carry on the torch," McPherson said.

"In coeducational institutions, too often they say of even the brightest woman student, 'She's just a woman and will get married and have kids and not do anything,' so they concentrate on the male students."

At Bryn Mawr, McPherson said, "We're doing a better job for young women.

"Why should you pay $10,000 a year to go to college and have to fight for everything you get there?" she said. "You should be a full partner in the enterprise."

A 1981 study of more than 70 of the nation's 117 women's colleges suggests her comments are based on more than the natural enthusiasm of an institution's president.

The study, financially supported by the Ford Foundation, found that women's colleges "are producing achievers out of proportion to their size" and attracting increasing numbers of applicants.

It repeated the finding of several earlier studies that graduates of women's colleges are about twice as likely as their counterparts from coeducational schools to achieve prominence sufficient to win listings in *Who's Who in America*.

The study also found women at single-sex colleges more likely than their counterparts to major in fields such as chemistry, physics or economics that traditionally have been dominated by men.

Contrary to stereotypes which depict the schools as shelters from the "real world," the study found that women's colleges encourage their students to take leadership roles, develop self-confidence, and succeed in their post-graduate endeavors.

At Bryn Mawr, like many selective private colleges, that cost of those advantages does not come cheap.

McPherson said, however, that Bryn Mawr retains a relatively diverse population despite its $9,950 yearly tab.

Reprinted from the *Tennessean* (Nashville), January 31, 1982.

BRYN MAWR IS NOT A WOMEN'S COLLEGE IN THE STRICT SENSE. I CAME HERE BECAUSE I THOUGHT I WOULD BE IN PREDOMINANTLY FEMALE CLASSES IN WHICH I COULD LEARN TO SEE OTHER WOMEN, IF NOT MYSELF, AS LEADERS. ALTHOUGH PEOPLE DO NOT THINK WHAT THEY SEE AFFECTS THEM, IT REALLY DOES. SEEING HAVERFORDIANS TALKING . . . SUGGESTS THAT MEN ARE THE ONES WHO WILL STAND UP FOR WHAT THEY THINK. I DO NOT THINK WE ARE A WOMEN'S COLLEGE. ANY COLLEGE WHICH HAS A JOINT PROSPECTUS WILL TEND TO PRODUCE BI-COLLEGE, HENCE COED, CREATURES. I DON'T THINK YOU CAN BE COED AND SINGLE-SEX SIMULTANEOUSLY.

—*Bryn Mawr Student, Class of 1982, reprinted from the* College News, *April 1, 1982*

Left: Action figure of Lady Jaye, aka Staff Sergeant Alison R. Hart-Burnett, a character from the *G.I. Joe: A Real American Hero* comic book and television series of the 1980s. According to *G.I. Joe* lore, Lady Jaye is a Bryn Mawr graduate. Figurine made by Hasbro © 1983

Opposite (top): Students in class, c. 1980s. Photograph by Katrina Thomas, Class of 1949

Opposite (bottom): Students in front of Rockefeller Arch, February 1985

CHANGES IN COOPERATION

MAJORITY POLLED FAVORS CONTINUING OF COOPERATION
Keith Belton, Haverford, Class of 1983

EIGHTY-ONE PERCENT of the bi-College community believes that cooperation between the two Colleges should continue as it is now, the recent *News* poll on cooperation/coeducation shows. The survey of Bryn Mawr and Haverford students received 1,166 responses to a poll conducted October 13, 1981.

In addition, only eight percent believes that cooperation between the two schools should be changed from its present form, while 11 percent said that they were unsure.

A full two-thirds of the community indicated that they felt cooperation to be essential to their social life, while only a third disagreed. Haverford men and Bryn Mawrters answered affirmatively, 74 and 68 percent, respectively. Haverford women deviated from this trend significantly, as only 28 percent said that cooperation was essential to their social life.

Students at Bryn Mawr were overwhelmingly in favor of keeping Bryn Mawr an all-women's college. A resounding 75 percent indicated that they wished Bryn Mawr to continue to admit women only. Only 10 percent of the Mawrters responding said they wished to see their school admit men, and 15 percent were undecided. Among classes at Bryn Mawr, however, the percentage of students wishing to see the school admit men increased sharply from underclassmen to seniors.

About three-quarters of the students at both schools said they felt academic cooperation was an equal trade-off. Sixteen percent of the Bryn Mawr students polled said they believed Haverfordians gained more, as compared to only 6 percent of the Mawrters thinking cooperation favored them. Haverfordians responded in a similar manner, as 10 percent said they thought Bryn Mawrters gained more, as compared to only 6 percent believing they themselves benefitted more from cooperation. The poll also showed that only 10 percent of both Haverford and Bryn Mawr students either already do or intend to major at the other school.

Nearly half of the Bryn Mawrters said "yes" to the question asking if they thought Haverford should have continued to admit only men as freshmen. A quarter of them said no, and a full third said they were undecided about the issue. Three-quarters of the men polled said that they believed Haverford had made the right decision to admit freshwomen.

The academic excellence of the two Colleges was clearly the primary factor in students' decisions to matriculate at either school. A full eighty percent of the community said this reason was the most outstanding, while ten percent said that they came because the schools were the best ones they could get into. Five percent said that the size of the Colleges was the reason for their matriculations.

Reprinted from the News *(Bryn Mawr-Haverford), November 6, 1981.*

I was glad to see it. And there were other Bryn Mawr women (and maybe Haverford men and women) who are Haverford majors, enrolled in Haverford courses, members of bi-college organizations, and otherwise supporters of "cooperation" who were glad to see it. For these women, the banner over Merion Green with its terse message "End Cooperation" had very little to do with cooperation per se but presented in arresting form, after all this time, the feminist dissatisfaction with Bryn Mawr.

Eliza Dixon, Class of 1982, and Wendell Carter, Haverford, Class of 1983, reprinted from the *College News*, September 1981

Above: Student boarding the Blue Bus, which travels between Bryn Mawr and Haverford colleges, April 1983

BANNER AT LABOR DAY PICNIC SPARKS CONTROVERSY
Anne Shaughnessy, Class of 1982

AT THE PICNIC held on Merion Green of Monday, September 7, a banner which read, "Welcome Class of '85 / Centennial Goal: End Cooperation," was hung from the windows of two Merion residents' rooms. A group of students entered the rooms and removed the banner; this was greeted by applause and cheers from some of the picnickers below.

The plan to hang the banner began after Parade Night, according to Sharon Gerstel, one of the students who displayed the sign. "We felt that Bryn Mawr was being desecrated and that traditions were being destroyed," she explained.

The purpose of the banner was "to make known the views" of some Bryn Mawr students on cooperation. "Despite the 'best of both worlds' propaganda, no provisions are made for the woman who came here for Bryn Mawr, the women's college," asserted Lisa Schiffren. "As students with a significant view, we are tired of not being listened to," she said.

The students involved in planning the banner felt that the picnic itself was a political statement. They saw the fact that Haverfordians were invited as an action on the part of the Bryn Mawr administration which indicated approval of cooperation.

"We did not intend this as a gratuitous discourtesy. We especially did not intend to offend Haverford women," said Lisa Schiffren.

While the banner was hanging, a group of students entered Merion. One of them was a Resident Advisor (RA), who asked a member of the Bryn Mawr security force to unlock the rooms where the banner was displayed. The students then entered the rooms and removed the sign.

"When I first saw the sign, I was very hurt. People all around me were very hurt and very worried," said one of the students who removed the sign. Another student explained, "Speed was needed, because it was an antagonistic sign. The longer it was up, the more damage it would do."

According to Dean Vanin, neither the RA nor the security guard had authority to have the rooms unlocked. "No one has the right to open another student's room," she said, except in cases where the safety or health of the student is at risk. Vanin stated that the Dean's office is "deliberating whether any action should be taken or not" regarding the RA. Vanin also said that she had discussed the role of security officers with Security Head Vincent DeCerchio.

When asked her personal opinion about the banner, Dean Vanin termed it "unfortunate," but added, "those students have a right to their opinion."

Reprinted from the *College News*, September 1981.

MISCALCULATIONS
"A Ford Speaks"

When I was but a freshman, my
    Imagination ran
With this oft-whispered lullaby:
    "Three girls for every man!"

That year, I didn't realize
    The ratio's limitations.
Adult-er, now, I rhapsodize
    With brand-new calculations.

This three-to-one of which they speak—
    Pernicious fallacy!
Observe: my friend's a loser geek,
    So I absorb *his* three!

I now have six, but Alan woos
    A Mawrter girl, so he
Donates the two he doesn't use.
    There are now *eight* for me!

And then there's Mark, who on the Kinsey
    Scale scored up a seven.
And he, with just a spark of whimsey
    Leaves me with—*eleven*!

And then—Oh, wow—Mark's lover!
    Three
Big cheers! God save the Queen!
The sum of girls to cover me
    With kisses is *fourteen*!

And Chris, an intellectual,
    Writes his papers by the ream.
I'm sure he is asexual.
    Hey, I've got *seventeen*!

And then there's John, who has a nose
    The size of a potato
Because his chances decompose,
    I've *twenty* ripe tomatoes!

My roommate has a girl at home
    So he ignores his three
And that would leave—Ah, oats unsown!
    Twenty-three girls for me!

A harem! I've a harem! My
    Allotment's twenty-three!
My former life was barren! I
    Now have a barony!

THE MAWRTYR'S REPLY

I saw your calculations, 'Ford.
    If you do not revise,
We'll wrap your privates up in cord
    And cut you down in size.

You think you are entitled to
    A herd of twenty-three?
Well, five are Lesbians, so you
    Have eighteen left. Hee hee!

Of those eighteen, at least six are
    Bisexual, so they've
A choice superior by far.
    You're down to twelve, my knave!

And of those twelve, chop off a few—
    In fact, I'd say, count four—
Who'd rather study than date you.
    You're down to eight, señor!

And of those eight, I'd say that four
    Have long-distance romances.
They'll tell you quick where to stuff your
    Incompetent advances.

The four who're left are hot and single.
    Still your lines will fail.
'Cause three of them don't choose to mingle,
    Or depend on males.

Well, that leaves one, but what if she
    Has one small grain of TASTE?
Oh, Heavens! Such catastrophe!
    I guess you'll just be chaste!

If you suppose we Mawrters yearn
    For wham-bam-thank-you-ma'am, sir,
You've got an awful lot to learn.
    Buzz off. Go date your hamster.

Reprinted from Robin Bernstein, Class of 1991, *College News*, October 13, 1988.

ASSESSING FINANCIAL STABILITY: THE CAMBRIDGE REPORT

SUMMARY OF "CAMBRIDGE REPORT"
September 7, 1986

A BASIC PREMISE of the Cambridge Associates' study is that chronic financial instability will undermine the quality of an institution and jeopardize its future. The four conditions necessary for financial equilibrium are:
- Endowment spending at or below the level that will preserve purchasing power of the endowment
- Renewal and replacement of physical assets that will preserve those assets in perpetuity
- Annual balanced budgets
- Balanced growth in income and expense

The Cambridge Associates concluded that Bryn Mawr does not meet these conditions satisfactorily at present, and that continuation of current operating policies will lead to a steady deterioration of the College's financial condition.

Recent financial history of Bryn Mawr College:
- The operating budget has been in balance, but the balance has been achieved at the expense of the long-term value of the endowment and by deferring much major maintenance.
- While the nominal value of the endowment has more than doubled over the last 15 years, the real value has declined by 16%. Gifts and additions to the endowment prevented a further decline, but they have not kept pace with the rate of spending from the endowment and withdrawals from the quasi endowment.
- Bryn Mawr has increased its scale of operations over the past 15 years. Hence, an endowment which has decreased in value is supporting a more complex and broader educational operation than existed in 1970.

Bryn Mawr College must address four questions:
- How to correct a structural imbalance between expenses and income
- How to bring long term growth in expenses into line with growth in income
- How to maintain the recent growth in quasi endowment
- How to prevent an eventual cash shortage

If the institution continues to operate as it does now, by fiscal 1991 it will have exhausted its quasi endowment funds by using them to balance budgets.

Reasons for Bryn Mawr's financial difficulties:
- For a college of its size, Bryn Mawr is engaged in a very broad educational enterprise encompassing undergraduate liberal arts education, graduate education in the Arts and Sciences, and graduate professional education in Social Work. The enrollment size is not sufficient to support the range and scale of the educational programs.
- Because of the small size of the undergraduate college, the undergraduate academic programs are expensive to support. The financial situation is exacerbated further by the fact that the undergraduate programs must to some extent subsidize the graduate schools.
- The number of eighteen year olds is declining and Bryn Mawr has access to only half of this market each year. The competition for those students is intense, thus increasing the demand for financial aid.
- There is insufficient financial support for the faculty from student sources (enrollment) and from external grants. Therefore, the support must come from the endowment. The capacity of Bryn Mawr's endowment to support its faculty is not as strong as that of many institutions in the comparison group. (Swarthmore and Amherst have almost twice the amount of endowment per faculty FTE [full-time equivalent]).

Alternatives for establishing financial equilibrium:
- No single change in Bryn Mawr's operations will sufficiently alter the balance between income and expenses to allow the College to reach and maintain financial equilibrium.

Alternatives that the Cambridge Associates' study explored for their financial impact include:
- Reduction in the size of the faculty and staff
- Increased real growth in undergraduate tuition and fees (without compensating increases in financial aid)
- Increased undergraduate enrollment
- Major increases in unrestricted annual giving
- Capital campaign for the endowment
- Reduction in graduate programs

In summary, it is clear that Bryn Mawr finds itself committed to a set of priorities competing for financial resources. It wants at once to provide an intensive liberal arts education to its undergraduate women, and to maintain graduate programs in Arts and Sciences and Social Work which are not normally self supporting. It seeks to maintain its selectivity and will not compromise the quality of its students, faculty, and programs. It is strongly committed to diversity, need-blind admission, and financial support of those who cannot afford the high cost of a Bryn Mawr education.

Bryn Mawr cannot continue to do everything it now does without seriously compromising the ability of the College to maintain its future integrity (fiscal and programmatic). The task ahead is to choose carefully those priorities which will protect the College's place among the very best institutions in the country.

Reprinted from a photocopy of original, Bryn Mawr College Archives.

Opposite: Students drinking coffee, c. 1980s

COMMUNITY DISCUSSES CAMBRIDGE REPORT OPTIONS

Ann L. M. Smith, Haverford, Class of 1985

BRYN MAWR ADMINISTRATORS, faculty, staff and students were asked to give their reactions to the six possible actions that may be implemented to reduce College expenses and that were pointed out by the Cambridge Report.

The six actions the report mentioned are:
- Reduction of faculty and staff
- A real increase in tuition without a compensatory increase in financial aid
- An increase in enrollment
- An increase in unrestricted annual giving
- A capital campaign to increase the endowment
- A reduction of Bryn Mawr's graduate programs

The report states that implementing only one of these measures would not reverse the College's financial decline.

Reduction of faculty and staff

Concerning faculty and staff reductions, several officers pointed out that staff reductions are nothing new. In administrative services, which oversees Bryn Mawr's housekeeping, food service, copy center, mailroom, summer conferences and purchasing, Director Gail Finan pointed out that Housekeeping has reduced its staff from 51 to 49 in the past four years at the same time as the College has opened a new gym, the Campus Center, and most recently, the Computer Center. Further "staff cuts may happen and they may not," Finan said. "I haven't been told that I have to cut X number of bodies."

Faculty cuts are difficult, said Mabel Lang, Bryn Mawr Greek professor and Secretary to the General Faculty, because "the faculty is no longer used to being examined, but is used to examining others." What appears clear is that the faculty does not want a repetition of the way in which cuts took place after the release of the Healy financial report ten years ago. In that case, faculty had maximum say and involvement in determining which faculty stayed and which were let go, explained Maria Luisa Crawford, Bryn Mawr geology professor and faculty rep to the Board of Trustees. The "faculty hated pick[ing] on colleagues. Likewise last year, with graduate recommendations, the faculty disliked the other extreme of having too little say in the process." Crawford felt that "when one is going to cut, the faculty are not going to like it."

Arthur Dudden, Bryn Mawr history professor, called the Cambridge reevaluation "the latest in a series." "Most would agree that [cuts in the past] have harmed the College's capacity to teach as it said it was." Dudden also felt that it was "too much to expect the faculty to be constructive [in suggesting faculty cuts], as essentially one is asking which one of your colleagues you can spare which makes vulnerable the untenured among your faculty who are the ones needed to make this place lively," Dudden said.

Dudden feels Bryn Mawr should create a new, undergraduate-focused teaching faculty. Bryn Mawr doesn't do as well as other schools which have been committed to undergraduate teaching throughout their history, Dudden commented, because it has one foot in graduate school programs. With its graduate programs, Bryn Mawr has been more committed to "premium scholarship" than "glamorous teaching" found in undergraduate institutions, Dudden said. Dudden sees a danger in not being able to "revitalize by hiring young people."

A real increase in tuition without an increase in financial aid

Claudia Callaway, president of the Self-Government Association (SGA), said that she "doesn't feel that marked tuition increase is the issue. With a tuition increase above the rate of inflation, I think the demographics of the school would be changed so much that that's not what anybody wants."

The issue of increased tuition without increases in amounts of financial aid affects graduate schools and programs also. Crawford explained that it's a fact of life that at most institutions graduate students are offered financial aid. Because aid is a "requisite for attracting students," Crawford noted that all departments have had or will have to cut back on the number of students in their graduate programs.

The geology department, she noted, has cut back on its number of teaching assistants but has creatively managed through sources of funds to keep the same number of graduate students, Crawford said.

Ruth Mayden, Dean of the Bryn Mawr School of Social Work, noted that the school is trying to increase grants to offset costs.

Dudden noted that due to a lack of major funding for graduate students in the history department, the department is "virtually out of business at the graduate level."

The history department is a Class II department for graduate programs which means that it has a graduate program but receives no major funding to attract more graduate students. The geology department is a Class I department which means that it competes for graduate funding with other Natural Sciences and Social Sciences and Humanities. "Unless students can pay their own ways," Dudden said, "the graduate program is on the shelf."

Bryn Mawr senior Elizabeth Rader commented that Bryn Mawr should enroll "students who pay full tuition and have a financial aid program based on merit." Rader felt that people will come to Bryn Mawr if they feel that it's the best school, even if they have to pay a little more."

Increase in enrollment

Freshman Tina Tong said that she does not feel that "increasing the student body is a good idea." Tong would rather see coeducation implemented. Other students feel as senior Polly Stephens, who offered a common adage, "Better dead than coed." Many students do not see coeducation as either a financially economical plan or a viable option given the long-term responses the report requires.

Deirdre O'Halloran, a Bryn Mawr sophomore said she'd "feel saddened if Bryn Mawr went co-ed in response to a financial report." Stephens said she would like Bryn Mawr to hold out on coeducation as long as possible.

Senior Jennifer Hill reiterated Stephens, saying that she thought coeducation should be the very last alternative.

Some felt Bryn Mawr is not at present financially very efficient. Rader commented that Bryn Mawr is "spending money in the wrong directions—on cushy things. For example, "We don't need 'Bryn Mawr' printed on napkins," she said. Sophomore Kim Pidcoke commented on the inefficiency of Bryn Mawr's dining services, "we need one centralized place," she said. Rader noted that "going coed isn't a panacea." Pidcoke concurred, "We have Haverford if we want coed, Bryn Mawr should definitely not go coed." "The idea of a women's college is important," Pidcoke added.

Faculty differed on the issue of coeducation and increased enrollment. Dudden said "If [the fact that] we are a single-sex institution is an illusion, does this mean we are denying ourselves access to the fullest population pool? I'm not sure coeducation gives financial stability," Dudden said. "The question also is, is there a better number of students to solvency," Dudden noted.

Crawford said that there would be no problem in the geology department if the college gets larger, but she is personally ambivalent about coeducation—she doesn't think it would work.

Lang said "most women feel that they've seen the way Bryn Mawr students have grown in this environment. The topic of [coeducation] comes up so often that I can't believe it'll be decided now." "Its chances of paying off financially are obscure," Lang added.

Director of Bryn Mawr's Alumnae Association Jane Unkefer commented that it's time for coeducation; if Bryn Mawr's mission is fulfilled as a women's college, "not everybody will be happy—but they'll accept that."

Unrestricted annual giving
Director of Resources Donna Wiley explained that Bryn Mawr will be seeking "higher proportions of unrestricted funds" from Bryn Mawr alumnae and from corporations. "We will discourage extraneous funds" for specific projects, Wiley said. "The emphasis will be on our annual fund, an efficient currently unrestricted fund."

Unkefer stated that "increasing levels of giving is not a solution" to Bryn Mawr's financial stability. She noted that Bryn Mawr alumnae are a very small constituency (10–11,000). She said that the office will "try to find people we haven't got tied to the College," but she noted that "there's not much that we can do but spread the word and keep Bryn Mawr in everybody's hearts." Unkefer pointed out that alumnae are very willing to give unrestricted money to the College and mentioned that currently there is the highest per capita annual gift average of $16,054.

Both Unkefer and Wiley said that in some ways Bryn Mawr has never been in a better financial position—new buildings, endowment. "We need to keep it that way," Wiley said.

Capital Campaign
Wiley said that Bryn Mawr does not plan another campaign in response to the Cambridge Report, but will campaign among small groups and will run another major campaign in 1990, as previously planned.

Wiley noted that people want to know now where the $50,000,000 that was raised in Bryn Mawr's Centennial Campaign went. Wiley explained that money went to building construction, the endowment and increased faculty salaries. "We have larger endowment goals," Wiley said. But in general Bryn Mawr plans to maintain its fundraising level, using challenge grants to meet goals, Wiley said.

Unkefer said that the alumnae knew that "50 million was not enough money." But Unkefer cautioned, "We can't keep looking to the endowment" for financial stability.

Lang mentioned that "those who say we should raise more money don't realize how hard it is to raise money, and how much we do raise. It is short sighted to look at the gym and campus center as frills." Lang said, "When one is competing with the Harvards of the world we need to have as many extras as necessary."

Reduction of Bryn Mawr's graduate programs
There were differing opinions concerning the future of Bryn Mawr graduate programs. In general most felt that some graduate programs are important and should be maintained.

Crawford said, "Deep down I feel that Bryn Mawr is a first-rate undergraduate college, and there are consequences for that. But, I believe it's a better undergraduate college because its graduate schools condition the faculty."

Dean of the Bryn Mawr School of Social Work and Social Research (SSWSR) Ruth Mayden commented that "it is not a thinkable alternative [for the School of Social Work] to shut down." A more viable alternative is a change in the degree of dependency of the school on Bryn Mawr's general budget. "We are being asked to generate more of our own income," Mayden said. Mayden feels that SSWSR will be able to do this through grants and certain graduate agencies. Mayden noted that the School of Social Work is "fully absorbed in the cost-cutting process and has been looking at other institutions' programs to see what they are doing. Bryn Mawr is not alone in this process."

Crawford would be "distressed if we lost the Bryn Mawr geology graduate program—we'd have to do many things differently," she said. Crawford pointed out that graduate programs are different in the sciences than in humanities. "In the sciences we have group-oriented research. The graduate program is an integral part of what the department does," Crawford said.

Dudden commented on the ramifications of the dwindling graduate program in history. "What this will do is wipe out the program at the time when demand for new professors will reappear because of population demographics. The [history graduate program] pipeline is empty," Dudden said. Dean of the Graduate School of Arts and Sciences Catherine Lafarge noted that "certain areas [of graduate study] have not done well. If [departments] haven't drawn new students to campus we will have to cut them. Do we want to tamper with strong schools in the area—like the Bryn Mawr School of Social Work? We have to answer that in terms of cost. There will be more deep cuts in graduate programs."

Sophomore Rosa Lewis said that "graduate programs don't affect us whether they're here or not. I'd say cut [them]." Tong and Stephens disagreed, saying that graduate programs are important to Bryn Mawr, particularly as Stephens said "if they can support themselves."

Reprinted from the *News* (Bryn Mawr-Haverford), October 31, 1986.

In a financial sense, Bryn Mawr has been squeezed—tightly. The evidence of this is everywhere. Departments have not replaced retiring, or departing, faculty. The Growth and Structure of Cities Program, once prominently advertised in admissions materials, now consists of one permanent faculty member. The English Department made its Senior Thesis optional this year, citing an inability to handle the workload of both advising students and grading their papers. Student/faculty ratios have increased. Course offerings have decreased. Financial Aid has a waiting list for admitted students who are ranked on the aid list based on their admissions rankings. Even the budget for the daily "Coffee Hour" (which used to be a daily "Donut Hour") has been slashed for next year. Clearly, Bryn Mawr does not have a lot of money.

—Rachel Winston, Class of 1990, "Assessing the Past Five Years Brings Insight on BMC's Shifting Priorities," *College News*, May 13, 1991.

DIVESTMENT: STUDENTS FIGHT FOR CHANGE

DIVEST NOW!

HAVERFORD AND BRYN MAWR are Quaker-founded colleges with traditions of adhering to high moral standards. South Africa is a country where the majority of its citizens can't cross the street without a pass because their skin is the wrong color.

Haverford and Bryn Mawr earn several students' tuitions worth of money from South Africa every year.

Let's practice what we preach. And get out of South Africa. Now.

The Sullivan Principles are a nice idea. The Sullivan Principles are also a halfway measure. South Africa is an extreme situation where the Sullivan Principles aren't working.

Sure, we can say that divestment will only hurt blacks, who have suffered enough already. Or we can say that less than one percent of the U.S. labor force in South Africa is black and that only dramatic change can help them—because they've suffered enough already.

Haverford is currently investing in (among others): IBM, General Motors, General Electric, Boeing and Westinghouse. Bryn Mawr still holds stocks in several other companies in South Africa.

IBM's computers help maintain South Africa's pass system. General Motors sells trucks to the South African police to stop civil disturbances. Boeing sells transport planes to the South African army. Westinghouse sells nuclear technology to the South African government.

In South Africa, violence is escalating daily. Blacks are getting shot. Blacks are being transported. Blacks are being jailed. Blacks are getting desperate. How much longer before South Africa erupts in revolution? The time for pacification, for halfway measures is over. We have to demonstrate strong disapproval of the apartheid system.

At Columbia University, students have done just that. They have made a strong statement against apartheid. They wound up on the front page of the *New York Times*. They made people think about apartheid.

In the Bi-College community, we're still making money on it.

Reprinted from the *News* (Bryn Mawr-Haverford), April 26, 1985.

ANTI-APARTHEID PLANS
Mary Catherine Roper, Class of 1987

BRYN MAWR and Haverford students are planning many events to express their opposition to apartheid, South Africa's system of racial segregation. The bi-college Anti-Apartheid Group will be co-ordinating most of the actions planned for the semester.

Education is one of the Group's chief concerns, and a variety of events are planned to bring the issue of apartheid to the attention of the members of the bi-college community. There will be a weekly newsletter which will present facts and analysis about how it affects the United States. There are also many films planned for the semester, which will be publicized as they occur.

The trustees meet Saturday, Mar. 1. What will you do about **DIVESTMENT?**

In addition to these regular events, there are several larger actions being planned, according to Gina Dorcely. Dorcely is a member of the Bryn Mawr class of 1987 who is currently on leave and working for the American Friends Service Committee in Philadelphia, coordinating student activism on South African issues at several colleges, including Bryn Mawr. Dorcely said there are tentative plans for a group of speakers for Wednesday the 25th which would include Dennis Brutus, an African poet who is teaching a course at Swarthmore this semester.

The group also is planning a rally in early October, intended to complement the National Anti-Apartheid Protest Day on October 11, sponsored by the American Committee on Africa and various campus anti-apartheid groups around the nation. Since Bryn Mawr and Haverford begin their fall break on the 11th it would not be feasible to plan any action for that day. Dorcely expects a large rally and expressed her personal hope that this action would not emulate what she termed the Bryn Mawr tradition of "polite protest."

The largest and probably most important educational event planned will be a weekend-long symposium to be held late in the semester. This program of speakers and workshops will be designed to give members of the bi-college community an opportunity for extended exposure to the issues of divestment and ending South African apartheid. The symposium will be similar to an event held at Swarthmore College last spring. Students, faculty, administrators, and trustees will be invited to attend.

The symposium will also address the important issue of divestment. It is specifically planned to include the administrations of the two colleges and the trustees, as part of the continuing pressure by the Anti-Apartheid Group and others for complete divestment by Bryn Mawr and Haverford colleges. The Anti-Apartheid Group has formed committees to work specifically on the issue of divestment, which will act throughout the semester to accumulate information on Bryn Mawr's and Haverford's investment policies and to pressure the trustees to act.

There will also be many activities designed for the benefit of the students involved in the movement. The Group is planning intensive educational workshops for its members and will send delegates to the National Student Conference on South Africa, to be held at Hunter College in November. The Conference will provide opportunities for education and for formation of strategies, and access to a support network, according to Dorcely.

Reprinted from the *College News*, September 25, 1985.

Above: Student poster, 1986. Many students protested the college's plan to divest from five of twenty-one companies involved in South Africa; students had called for total divestment.

Opposite: Memorandum, Mary Patterson McPherson to the Bryn Mawr College community, March 3, 1986, regarding the board's policies on divestment

PROTESTERS DEMAND DIVESTMENT
Annie Avery, Class of 1986

OVER A TWO-DAY PERIOD from Thursday evening to Saturday afternoon of last week, Bryn Mawr students slept overnight in Wyndham, displaying signs, and singing protest songs in support of divestment. They gathered to show the Trustees, who were meeting on Thursday, Friday, and Saturday, their belief that divestment is a "moral issue" and that Bryn Mawr should sell its shares in companies which do business in South Africa. It was the latest in a series of pro-divestment demonstrations and actions which have been escalating throughout the semester.

According to Lori-Christina Webb, a senior and a member of the Sisterhood, an organization of black Bryn Mawrtyrs that came to a consensus early in the semester that Bryn Mawr's holdings with companies that do business in South Africa is the most pressing issue facing them. They decided to withdraw from the Social Honor Code in protest because "we feel a commitment to the larger black community." Webb stressed that as . . . the Sisterhood includes both black Americans and black international students, "the issue is one that addresses all of us."

The Sisterhood and the Anti-Apartheid Group placed signs reading "Blacks Only" and "Whites Only" all over campus. Sisterhood member Binaifer Nowrojee, '86, explained that the signs were "an awareness-raising campaign. They caused attention and engaged different sectors of the community." Nowrojee and Sisterhood co-president Dominique Parker, '86, were continually replacing them, especially in Taylor, Thomas, and Canaday.

Members of the Sisterhood met with the Trustees last Friday afternoon. At that meeting, the officers of the Sisterhood laid out their criteria for rejecting the Sullivan Principles, to which the Bryn Mawr Board chooses to adhere, as a means of change. Nowrojee pointed out that since companies such as General Motors and IBM sell equipment and provide assistance to the South African government, the American companies in South Africa "cannot be a means of peaceful change." Senior Becky Young, who was active in organizing last weekend's demonstrations in Wyndham, believes that "it is naive to think that the corporations in South Africa can affect the situation in that country and it is also naive to believe that withdrawing the relatively small amount of money which Bryn Mawr has invested in those companies will have much effect on them. What is important is the symbolism of the gesture." Webb pointed out that Bryn Mawr can set an example for other colleges because "our name carries a whole lot of weight—we have influence here at home."

President McPherson stressed that the Board does not disagree with these points. The Board's problem, she adds, is that they "want to conduct business with the banks and companies as responsibly as possible. The Board has just sent out letters to those banks and companies asking some very hard questions, and the Board members feel that they owe them a chance to respond. The Board will not act until it gets some response from the letters." She believes that it is very important for students and Board members to "continue listening to each other, and not allow the present level of discourse to disintegrate."

In her statement to the Trustees during their meeting on Saturday, Nowrojee said that "the way minority and international students are recruited by Bryn Mawr is in direct contradiction to the way we are treated here." She feels that the decision not to divest is a political stand as clearly as the decision to divest would be, and not divesting says to her that the College does not mind continuing to support a government which is oppressive to blacks.

In response, McPherson pointed out that the Board has not made the decision not to divest but rather has kept that possibility open. Their decision to use an ongoing process of reevaluation, which they are currently carrying out by corresponding with every bank and company, "does not show that they are insensitive to the position of black Americans. They appreciate that position."

McPherson added, "If I were a student, I would be doing exactly what those students are doing. But I am in a different position with different responsibilities and I think the Trustees have to feel that way too."

The students who are pro-divestment feel that since the Trustees' actions reflect on them as Bryn Mawr students, they are being forced to cooperate with apartheid. They say that they will not stop demonstrating and organizing until the Board has divested.

Reprinted from the *College News*, December 12, 1985.

BRYN MAWR COLLEGE
BRYN MAWR, PENNSYLVANIA 19010

OFFICE OF THE PRESIDENT

TO: The Members of the Bryn Mawr College Community
FROM: Mary Patterson McPherson
RE: Board of Trustees Policies on Divestment
DATE: March 3, 1986

On Saturday, March 1, the Bryn Mawr Board of Trustees, continuing its process of reviewing its investment policies with regard to those companies doing business in South Africa, approved the prompt sale of stocks in five companies that did not appear to be attempting actively to oppose institutionalized racism in South Africa. It further confirmed its intention to continue to hold stocks in sixteen companies in the portfolio that appear to be engaged in active opposition to South African government policies of apartheid.

The group of five companies from which we are divesting will receive letters indicating the reasons for Bryn Mawr's decision; the second group of companies will receive letters indicating our support as stockholders for their present unusual activities.

The Board will continue to monitor the progress of individual companies within the portfolio, and as part of the process, in December 1986, will decide whether its support of the active companies is proving effective in bringing about the dismantling of the "three pillars" of apartheid (the influx control laws, the group areas act, and the denial of universal franchise). If in December 1986 the Board finds no evidence that apartheid is being effectively dismantled, it will plan an orderly process of divestment in order to meet its goal stated this past October -- that it divest all holdings in South Africa by the end of May 1987 should apartheid not be effectively dismantled. In addition the Board is considering urging companies to disinvest (that is, to leave South Africa) if their current efforts should prove to be in vain.

Furthermore, the Board wishes to invite interested members of the Bryn Mawr College community to join with it in an organized effort of this and other colleges and universities to urge Congress and the President to take leadership with regard to South African affairs much as they have recently managed in Haiti and the Philippines.

Finally, the Board wishes me to express its thanks to members of the faculty and student body for their individual and collective expressions of opinion and the numerous ideas for useful activity that emerged from the various discussions this weekend. The Board's Committee on Investment Responsibility will continue to meet with interested members of the college community.

Discussions on Divestment
Caryn Libman, Class of 1987

This past weekend was the first meeting of the Board of Trustees in the present academic year. By far the most significant and controversial discussions of this meeting were centered around whether or not the Board of Trustees should divest from companies in South Africa, in which Bryn Mawr College has about 4 million dollars invested.

On Thursday, October 3, the Investment Responsibility Committee of the Board of Trustees scheduled a meeting to which 10 students were invited to attend as representatives of the student body. It is this committee's responsibility to research the companies and institutions in which Bryn Mawr College has investments and to review whether these investments are in keeping with Bryn Mawr's moral beliefs and social concerns.

This meeting was planned as a forum for students to express their opinions on divestment. Over 75 students protested outside Wyndham before the meeting and entered the room at the beginning of the meeting. Many of these students participated in the ensuing discussion.

Senior Binaifer Nowrojee, a Kenyan, stated to the Trustees that the problems in South Africa are "a lot closer to home for me than for you." She went on to emphasize the relative ineffectiveness of the Sullivan Principles, calling them a means by which to "pacify conscience." Senior Beth Ogilvie argued with President McPherson's assertion that through demanding compliance with the Sullivan Principles the College hopes to be "a burr under the saddle" of corporations in South Africa, and to bring about change in that way. Ogilvie asserted that considering the relatively small amount of money that Bryn Mawr has invested in companies which do business in South Africa, "You have to decide whether you can be more effective by staying in and bothering them, or making the strong statement of divesting completely." Senior Becky Young added that Bryn Mawr should make the decision that will have the most impact on the problem, arguing for divestment because "our scope of influence can be larger in the effect it will have on other institutions if we divest" and because it's the way we can "retain our own moral dignity."

Reprinted from the *College News*, October 9, 1985.

BOARD APPROVES MCPHERSON'S DIVESTMENT PLAN
Annie Avery, Class of 1986

IN THEIR MEETING ON SATURDAY, the Trustees discussed long-term planning for the sciences, voted to raise tuition, and voted to divest from five companies which have holdings in South Africa.

. . . In the general meeting on Saturday morning, when the Trustees voted, there was prolonged discussion of divestment. Some Trustees do not believe that divesting is the most effective way the College has of using its influence to effect change in South Africa. Alternative forms of action mentioned included pressuring members of Congress to withdraw the U.S. Government's political support of the Botha regime. Some Trustees believe that divesting could be inconsistent with their role as Trustees, which is to ensure the financial health of the College and see that the money which is given to the College for education is used as effectively as possible for that purpose.

The Board voted to pass a resolution proposed by President McPherson calling for "prompt" divestment from five companies and asking that the remaining seventeen companies show how they are pressuring the white minority government to end the system of apartheid.

The five companies from which Bryn Mawr divested are Air Products, American Brands, Ashland Oil, Crown Cork and Seal, and Goodyear Tire. All five failed to respond to the letter that members of the Board sent inquiring about their efforts toward ending apartheid. Three became signatories of the Sullivan Principles only recently, and two have low ratings.

Reprinted from the *College News*, March 6, 1986.

BOARD DIVESTS 5, STUDENTS PROTEST
Kip Voytek, Haverford, Class of 1987

Bryn Mawr's Board of Trustees March 1 approved the plan originally proposed by President Mary Patterson McPherson to divest from five of 21 companies doing business in South Africa, while students called for total divestment in nearby Taylor Hall.

Two hundred students took over Taylor to show support for divestment, and the institution of a diversity requirement, and to commemorate the end of black history month.

Trustees departed from their Saturday meeting via Wyndham's windows when students blockaded the lobby in protest of the stock holdings.

The takeover began at 6 A.M. Friday when 30 students entered Taylor, set up tables to barricade entrances on the second floor, and put up signs outside the building announcing the protest and explaining its purpose.

The Coalition for Divestment, an umbrella group working for divestment, organized the takeover, which was covered by the Associated Press, United Press International, local newspapers, and channels 3, 10, and 29 in Philadelphia.

The takeover included readings from students' poetry describing their personal experiences with racism. Students also spoke out.

The protest activities had been scheduled to last until 6 P.M. Friday; nevertheless approximately 30 students spent the night in Taylor, during which time they planned activities for the trustee meeting the next day.

While the students in Taylor made plans for a Saturday protest in Wyndham, about 100 students continued the demonstration in the Campus Center with a candlelight vigil at the entrance through which all of the trustees had to pass to get to a reception. After the reception, the students, still holding their candles, followed the trustees to Wyndham.

Fifty students lay down at 12:15 on Saturday in the Wyndham lobby outside the trustees' meeting room. According to participants, the purpose of the move was to force some trustees to talk to the students. While most of the trustees crawled out the windows to catch their respective trains and planes, seven did remain to speak with students.

"It really seemed like they were listening to us," said Gina Srinivasan. "I really got the feeling they wanted to start a dialogue."

Despite the trustees' decision to divest from only five companies, many students still felt that the actions that weekend had been successful.

Srinivasan thought that the actions were important in mobilizing students who would have otherwise been inactive. "There's always been a few people active with a core group, but it takes something blatant like a takeover to get more people active," she said.

Lisa Schiff said she "didn't think Bryn Mawr students had any guts" before the takeover, but ended up "being impressed by their organization and their positive attitude. It made me change my mind about activism and divestment among Bryn Mawr students."

Reprinted from the *News* (Bryn Mawr-Haverford), March 21, 1986.

DIVESTMENT COMPLETED
Thomas Hartmann, Haverford, Class of 1988

ON MAY 31, Bryn Mawr and Haverford both completed divestment of their assets from companies with direct investments in South Africa.

Haverford Vice President for Finance and Administration Richard Wynn and Bryn Mawr Treasurer Margaret Healy were both unable to assess the consequences of the action because financial information for the applicable months has not yet been gathered.

"It's too early to assess," said Wynn. "There is no immediate negative or positive impact."

"Two months is entirely too early to give any assessment," said Healy. She said three years is a more acceptable amount of time after which the performance of investments can be judged.

By the end of May, Haverford's two money managers completed reinvestment of $55 million of the college's endowment.

. . . Bryn Mawr's two money managers, J. W. Bristol and Geewax, Terker, invest $21 million and $24 million, respectively. Healy said the two companies reflect the same two investment philosophies that Haverford's money managers do.

"Given their druthers, they wouldn't have pulled out," Healy said. She said, however, that neither of the managers refused to divest, and that the college expects both to maintain good returns.

Bryn Mawr also had $14 million invested in a mutual fund at the time of the divestment decision. Rather than persuade the mutual fund, Guardian Mutual Fund, to divest, Bryn Mawr removed the money from the fund and reinvested it with its two money managers, Assistant Treasurer Suzanne Spain said.

She said that Bryn Mawr's Trustees, when approving the divestment decision last December, anticipated no more than a percentage point difference between pre-divestment and post-divestment return rates.

"We're willing to accept that," Spain said of a possible percentage point difference in return on investments. "If it suddenly became five percent, I think we would have to re-examine our decision," she said.

Wynn said that Haverford's board "did not feel we would do significantly less well than the market" when the decision was made. However, he said, "it was prepared to."

"Things in South Africa are worse than ever. But from an investment standpoint, the problem is largely solving itself," Wynn said.

Reprinted from the *News* (Bryn Mawr-Haverford), September 4, 1987.

SHRINKING THE GRADUATE SCHOOL

To: Members of the Faculty of Arts and Sciences

From: Mary Patterson McPherson

June 4, 1985

THE REVIEW OF GRADUATE PROGRAMS in Arts and Sciences was initially prompted by two considerations. Given the national demographic situation for graduate education, some of our programs appeared to be in danger of attracting too few full-time students of quality either to provide a viable advanced learning experience or to enable a sensible allocation of faculty time for graduate education. Changing national support patterns for graduate students and their consequent expectations for both aid and resources meant that our financial aid offers, spread too thinly across the existing programs, were proving noncompetitive, which threatened the quality of all of our program areas.

The review helped us to understand better our graduate situation, and as we now must determine a course of action for the next few years for the College as a whole, several considerations prompted a decision to focus and consolidate our Arts and Sciences graduate effort. Our new dean should be free to move on to the important tasks of presenting to the public a realistic graduate program, appropriately supported, and of seeking additional funding to bring a manageable number of stipends up to competitive levels.

Several departmental reports and the current dean's experience suggest that a number of our graduate students each year have become either disillusioned or frustrated by the limited offerings in some areas and/or by the lack of a critical mass of peers with whom to work. One cannot look to the federal government at this point for the infusion of funds needed to support adequately the nation's graduate enterprises. And Bryn Mawr is not in a position to fall back, during these lean years, on strategies available to larger universities to help tide them over until the nation realizes, as it inevitably must, that we have a general crisis in graduate education. That crisis will become fully apparent in the mid-1990's when we will face the retirement of large numbers of faculty members appointed in the 1950's and 60's and a simultaneous increase in the college-bound population, but meanwhile Bryn Mawr must adopt its own strategy which can carry us through to the national response which may then aid us.

In considering how to address the hard question of appropriate resource allocation for an interim structure, I have read all departmental reports, spoken with departments and chairmen, considered existing reports from outside visiting committees where available, reviewed criteria with the Graduate Council and the continuing faculty members on the committee on Graduate Awards, and listened carefully to the discussions in the Arts and Sciences faculty meeting on May 17th.

I have also attempted to take into account in my own thinking a variety of factors, which vary in their applicability to individual departmental situations:

- The number of applications and the yield rates and yield profiles of programs over a period of time
- The success of a department in attracting at least a small group of able full-time students which can help give balance and solidity to a program and aid the interactions and experiences of part-time students
- The possibilities for and/or actual interactions with allied departments at the graduate program level
- The service value of a program to the instructional needs and programs of the Undergraduate College
- The faculty composition and consequent coverage of needed areas in a graduate program as assessed by each department, and the feasibility or non-feasibility of remedying coverage deficiencies
- The commitment of department members to fostering and sustaining their programs: active interest in attracting students; appropriate support for them as people having chosen a risky professional route; a concern for opening professional opportunities; and finally working with them at securing employment
- A consideration of the different needs, where they exist, of the undergraduate and graduate programs

In order to move us ahead and give us a chance to resolve some of our problems, it seems vital to adopt a plan which will concentrate our efforts but at the same time provide as many graduate options as possible. With this in mind, I have concluded that we must control the number and extent of free-standing graduate programs while also encouraging the greatest possible participation of all faculty members in the graduate enterprise. Cooperative, interdepartmental initiatives at the graduate level are interesting to many members of the faculty, and in some cases altering our graduate program structures could be attractive and beneficial to students as well as more directly take advantage of faculty interests and talent. It is therefore my hope that many members of the faculty, whatever the status of their own graduate programs, will wish now to engage in some rethinking of our offerings. It is also my hope that all members of the faculty will continue, as in the past, to support excellence at the graduate level at Bryn Mawr.

Until the newly appointed Task Force on Graduate Financial Aid has completed its work, some questions concerning our capabilities cannot be answered. However, we must begin by controlling 1986–87 admissions. The situation in each curricular division can then be re-evaluated in early 1986, by which time the Task Force will have reported and we may also have a clearer picture of some trends and possibilities not yet fully explored. The funding scheme sketched here represents, I believe, the minimum retrenchment dictated by Bryn Mawr's present circumstances and the graduate situation nationwide. The additional information we should have by early 1986 may give us some flexibility in determining the outlines of our graduate structure for the ensuing three years. In early 1989 we would then wish to review again the entire graduate situation. It is in my view unlikely, however, that an institution of our size will be able in the future to provide the base necessary to support a return to the original number of autonomous graduate programs.

The 1985–86 catalogue, and therefore 1986–87 admissions, will need to reflect the following plan:

Comprehensive Funding and Admissions
- Departments which will receive aid (fellowships, scholarships, tuition awards as approved by the Committee on Graduate Awards; and TA's and GA's [teaching and graduate assistants, respectively] as approved by the Academic Deputy and the Graduate Dean of Arts and Sciences) for new as well as continuing Ph.D. students: Anthropology, Archaeology, Greek-Latin, English, History of Art, Human Development, Russian.
- Departments which will receive aid, for new as well as continuing Ph.D. students, primarily in the form of TA support (numbers related to the instructional needs of the Undergraduate College) and RA (research assistant) support (dependent upon faculty grants); upon occasion a department in this group may also wish to propose a student for a one-year fellowship: Biology, Chemistry, Geology, Physics, Psychology.

Limited Funding and Admissions
Departments which will be assured annually, effective for new students as of the 1986–97 year, one TA or GA (as approved by the Academic Deputy and the Graduate Dean of Arts and Sciences) plus no fewer than 6 units of tuition support (as approved by the committee on Graduate Awards); the units may be used either to make up a single scholarship or to support several part-time students. (If approved by the Academic Deputy, Mathematics may instead have two TA's.) These departments will normally admit students working toward the M.A., but may on occasion admit a Ph.D. student for whom an essentially tutorial experience is judged by the department, the dean, and when necessary a designated committee of the Graduate Council, to be educationally appropriate. (Students admitted before 1985 or for the 1985–86 year will have available the full range of aid.) These departments are: French, History, Philosophy, Sociology, Spanish, Mathematics.

No Further General Admissions
Economics, German, Political Science, Music (Any remaining degree candidates in these departments may apply to the Committee on Graduate Awards for aid.)

It should be recognized that the departmental groupings reflect only current realities; some traditionally excellent graduate programs, either because of dwindling applicant pools or the quality or composition of the pool, or because of coverage problems, no longer seem fully viable in a period of financial constraint. Many leading research universities across the country have had to make similar decisions in the past five years and Bryn Mawr is not in a position to constitute an exception. Moreover, such decisions have been made administratively, after consultation with appropriate bodies of the faculty and Board of Trustees, since the issues are primarily those of resource allocation.

It is my hope that faculty members will take an active part in considering, with the new Dean and Graduate Council, a restructuring effort of the sort suggested earlier in this document which could lead to broad faculty participation in a more focused and manageable graduate enterprise.

Reprinted from a memorandum, Bryn Mawr College Archives.

GRAD SCHOOL CURTAILED
Penny Chang, Class of 1985

SIX DEPARTMENTS AT BRYN MAWR will no longer accept doctoral candidates, except in exceptional cases, and three departments will accept no graduate students at all, if the proposal written by President Mary Patterson McPherson goes into effect, following a review of the Graduate School of Arts and Sciences (GSAS) this year.

The general arts and sciences faculty discussed the draft this morning at its final meeting in May.

The decision to curtail Bryn Mawr's graduate program is a response principally to falling numbers of applicants to graduate school over the past 15 years and keen competition between graduate schools for available students, said Barbara Kreutz, dean of the GSAS.

Beginning next year, the departments of French, history, philosophy, sociology, Spanish and mathematics will offer master's degrees only.

An "occasional" exception may be made to accept a doctoral candidate "for whom an essentially tutorial experience was judged by the department and the Graduate Council to be educationally appropriate," according to the proposal by President Mary Patterson McPherson, for the next three years.

Each of those departments will receive financial aid funding for the equivalent of only two new full-time graduate students a year.

Students of those departments who are currently enrolled in Ph.D. programs will continue to receive full support toward completing their degrees, according to the proposal.

The German department will no longer offer any graduate degrees, along with the philosophy and economics departments, who announced their sole concentration on a growing undergraduate enrollment earlier.

Kreutz said the decision of which departments to cut was based on a variety of factors, including the number of graduate students in the department, range of fields covered by the faculty and the number of applications received.

For instance, she said, although the philosophy department has ten students currently taking graduate courses, only one student entered the department this year. Another consideration, she said, is the lack of an ancient philosophy expert, which she said has caused graduate students to leave in the past.

Right: Students gathered near Pembroke Arch, February 1985

The College cannot afford to hire a new professor in that department, she said.

The drop in graduate school applicants is a reaction to a lack of jobs for professors, Kreutz said.

She said universities greatly expanded in the 1960s, when much federal money was available for education. Since then, hiring by universities has slowed considerably. As a result, many students are not staying in academia, but heading for professional schools—business, law—where more jobs are available.

Larger institutions cope with that economic pressure with the fees from their large undergraduate student body, by using graduate students to teach lower-level undergraduate courses, and by obtaining grants for their professional schools from corporations, McPherson said.

She predicted the situation will change in the 1990s, when large numbers of professors who were hired in the 1960s begin to retire. Then the job market for professors will open up and graduate school enrollments will rise.

Kreutz said she thinks 1980 was the bottom of the enrollment drop, and that she has seen slight improvement since then.

The departments of anthropology, archaeology, English, Greek, history of art, human development and Russian will continue to admit M.A. and Ph.D. candidates with full financial support.

The science departments, except mathematics, will admit both kinds of candidates with aid packages that include working as teaching assistants in undergraduate courses.

Reprinted from the *News* (Bryn Mawr-Haverford), May 17, 1985.

DETERMINED LEADERSHIP: 1978–1997

GRAD STUDENTS LAMENT CUTS IN ANTHRO, FRENCH AND ENGLISH DEPTS

Margaret Jewett, Class of 1988

AS MANY OF BRYN MAWR'S graduate programs are no longer admitting new students, with the plan to end the programs after students currently enrolled have finished their work here, several graduate students shared their feelings about how they and their departments will be affected by the graduate cuts.

Michelle Friedman, a second-year student in English, says that when cuts to the English department were announced last year, "We felt betrayed—there was a sense of loss. It really affected our work last year." Although Bryn Mawr has promised to continue offering graduate courses and financial aid to graduate students enrolled in the affected programs until they have finished their degrees, the proposed cuts are already affecting many students in subtler ways. Friedman says that although there is generally a good relationship between students and professors in the English department, now "there is a rift between the graduate students and professors. No one talks about [the proposed cuts]."

Kusimba Makokha, a first-year graduate student in anthropology, noted that because the college will continue to offer graduate students the same programs and aid they had when entering, "we are not affected as individuals, but as a department we are." Next year, there will be four remaining graduate students in anthropology. Makokha says that this year different students can bring opinions to graduate seminars from many areas of expertise. With fewer students in the seminars next year, he feels that it may be difficult for remaining students to get as much out of the material in class discussion.

Jackie McDonald, a second-year graduate student in French, feels that her department has unique strengths that she would not be able to find in another program. She especially appreciates the combination of quality teaching and a small department. She says, "Every class I've taken here has been worthwhile. The faculty is comparable to the faculty at any large university—Stanford or Yale wouldn't have anything over the Bryn Mawr Graduate School." In addition, the department's smaller size allows close relationships to form between students and professors. "The professors really care," she says. "They want our input." McDonald receives no financial aid from Bryn Mawr, but she says cheerfully, "The program is well worth taking out those loans."

Friedman feels that Bryn Mawr's graduate program in English is also unique. She notes that Bryn Mawr is the only women's college awarding the Ph.D. in English, and that professors here are especially amenable to a feminist point of view in the discussion of literature. The department's small size means that professors get to know the students personally and that "there is no cut throat competition" among the students. Friedman stresses that cooperation with the University of Pennsylvania is possible at both the graduate and undergraduate levels, while such cooperation is a rarity among graduate programs. Friedman is impressed with the quality of both the professors and students she works with here, and finds it interesting that several graduate students in English are in their late 20s and 30s, and that four students entering this year already have their M.A. degrees. She feels that these students have obviously been able to compare these programs with programs at other institutions, and that their choice to come here shows that Bryn Mawr's English program is among the best.

Makokha, an exchange student from Kenya, says that Bryn Mawr is known in Kenya as one of the best colleges in the United States. Bryn Mawr's anthropology program was recommended to him by Richard Leakey, one of the most famous researchers in the field. Makokha cites the department's exchange program with African students and its initiation of studies of the Northwestern United States as some of its unique characteristics. He says that Bryn Mawr's anthropology department is certainly "one of the best ten in the nation."

Makokha believes that undergraduates and professors will miss the presence of graduate students. He says, "Without graduate students, there will be less motivation for undergraduates." He also believes that graduate students are now helpful to professors, because graduate students bring new ideas to the department from other institutions and are more likely than undergraduates to question a professor's standpoint and thus to help the professor strengthen it.

McDonald agrees that "undergraduates will feel the effects" when French graduate students have gone. Friedman says that English students now teach "each other—professors would miss that." Senior English major Patty Keleman says that now there is "an amazing rapport developed" between graduate and undergraduate English students, and that graduate students contribute much to class discussion. She also notes that being in class with graduate students "helps you have more of a concept of what graduate school is—I would be more likely to go now that I've seen what they do."

Many students have wondered how the graduate programs could be costing Bryn Mawr so much that they would need to be cut. Both Friedman and McDonald have noticed that not all graduate programs here are funded by the college, while full tuition and a stipend are the norm at other institutions. Since the departments are fairly small, professors do not have to offer very many graduate courses each semester. "What do we cost?" asks Friedman.

Makokha is comforted by the thought that Bryn Mawr is not the only institution with financial troubles, and thus these troubles are not an indication of any decreasing quality at Bryn Mawr. "Cambridge and Oxford are having the same problems," he says. "It's a universal trend." He feels that Bryn Mawr now has a unique academic atmosphere for a college of its size and that somehow even with the impending cuts, "One hopes that this atmosphere will go on and on."

Reprinted from the *College News*, November 4, 1985.

ATHLETICS AND BRYN MAWR WELLNESS: A RENEWED EMPHASIS

APPLEBEE TO WELLNESS: ATHLETICS AT 100
Noreen O'Connor, Class of 1986

THE FITNESS-CONSCIOUS 1970S AND 80S may have given birth to the Wellness Program, but health concerns have been as important as competition all through the history of the Bryn Mawr physical education department.

The driving force in the early years of the College was Constance M. K. Applebee, an Englishwoman who introduced field hockey to the United States and firmly believed that a fit mind, soul, and body all were integral to health.

M. Carey Thomas held the opinion that physical exercise was just as important as intellectual ability in women, and she made mandatory four hours of physical education per week. Basketball, the first team sport played at Bryn Mawr; tennis; walking; and skating were popular activities.

Cutthroat interclass rivalry in sports marked the mania for baseball as early as 1892. Teams in soccer were called the "Great Danes" and the "French Poodles."

Applebee came to the United States in 1901 to teach field hockey at Harvard Summer School; a year later, Thomas invited her to Bryn Mawr and in 1904, Applebee became the director of athletics.

The first year she was director, between 50 and 60 students presented doctors' notes excusing them from exercise. "I thought we should hire someone to give them corrective work and if they were still too unfit they could lie on the gymnasium roof for half an hour," Applebee once said.

Another often-quoted remark of Applebee's was her comment to Thomas: "You want all these students to go out and do something in the world, to get the vote. What's the good of their having the vote if they're too ill to use it?"

The early years of the century were marked by great enthusiasm for sports, due to Applebee's inspiration. Often 12 teams would practice in one season. Applebee taught sportsmanship, above all.

In a 1977 interview, Applebee stated her "holistic" approach to sports: "They had to have the physical side of it, which was also the health side of it so you didn't injure yourself. You had to have the mental side of it . . . and you saw the great power of the strategy of games. And you had to have the spiritual side which meant you loved your neighbor as yourself but you didn't let them have the ball."

Applebee was involved in the life of the College even beyond athletics. She was the first "censor" of the *College News*, and she was also an advisor to the Christian Association. In 1922 she founded the United States Field Hockey Association.

In 1929 she left the director's post to devote more time to her field hockey camp and to touring and teaching, but she returned to Bryn Mawr often—sometimes on a weekly basis—until 1967. She died in 1981 at the age of 107.

From 1929 to 1947 Josephine Petts was the director of athletics.

After that, Irene Clayton headed the physical education department until 1969.

In 1969, Ann Lee Delano became the director. She recalls the impact of Title IX, which required that men's and women's sports programs receive equal funding. "Suddenly students came in wanting to do more" in athletics, because they were "getting more in high school and expected it in college," she said.

Delano, who is still active in the department, finds the students at Bryn Mawr "very bright and great fun." During her time as physical education director, Haverford men were allowed to take Bryn Mawr physical education classes, which was "sort of new."

Social dance, self-defense, and gymnastics teams started up at this time also.

In 1980 Jenepher Shillingford, the present athletic director, took over the post. A joint venture among the physical education department, Health Services (a department which Applebee founded in 1912), and Food Service created the Wellness program.

The program, established with a $75,000 grant from the Elizabeth S. Hooper Foundation, focuses on the areas of stress management, nutrition and weight control, fitness, and drug and alcohol abuse. Lectures, classes, and activities for faculty and staff have been included.

Reprinted from the *News* (Bryn Mawr-Haverford), May 3, 1985.

BRYN MAWR'S "WELLNESS" APPROACH TO PHYS. ED.
Frederick C. Klein

ONE OF THE MOST VIVID memories of my first semester at the University of Illinois is a course I took in wrestling. I didn't want to take it—I had to. Every freshman and sophomore was required to enroll in what the university called "physical education," and since freshmen registered last we were stuck with the sweaty stuff.

The course was taught at 1 P.M. twice a week. I soon learned that wrestling was bad for my digestion, so I had to skip lunch. My next class was at 2 P.M. in a building about a mile from the gym. That meant no shower, which put a cramp in my social life on the days involved.

For reasons still not clear to me, my assigned partner in the class (we tried holds on one another) was a muscular youth who outweighed me by at least 20 pounds. I spent the better part of the class with my head in his armpit. Don't ask where I spent the worse part.

My campus sources tell me that things have changed on the physical education front since my college days, and that the news is mostly bad. For budgetary and other reasons, a good many schools have chosen to throw out the baby with the bath water by abolishing the P.E. requirement and casting adrift in matters of physical fitness the multitude of students who don't measure up to varsity team standards.

But there is good news, too, and from an unlooked for source: Bryn Mawr College. Utilizing a couple of fortuitous grants, the upper-crust women's school near Philadelphia this year began linking traditional P.E. fare with programs stressing "lifetime" sports, nutrition and relaxation techniques, and putting the whole thing into a package it labels "Wellness."

"Too many colleges segregate athletics from the rest of their curricula and limit participation to the most talented," says Jenepher Shillingford, Bryn Mawr's director of physical education. "We want to do just the opposite—get as many people as possible involved in fitness. We want our girls to leave here with the idea that good health is as worth working for as anything else in life."

If numbers are any guide, Bryn Mawr is succeeding very well in this. The college's enrollment totals 1,150 and P.E. is required only for first- and second-year students, but 1,240 persons are signed up for P.E. classes this term. The "extras" include members of the faculty and staff and students from nearby and mostly male Haverford College, which has a course-exchange program with Bryn Mawr. (Lucky guys.)

"Wellness" at Bryn Mawr encompasses such women's sports standbys as swimming, basketball, gymnastics and field hockey. Indeed, some 200 women—almost 20% of the student body—participate in at least one of the eight varsity teams the school fields. That total is swelled by the fact that Bryn Mawr never "cuts" from a varsity squad a student who follows its training regimen.

But there are new wrinkles, including courses in jogging, bicycling and aerobic dancing, the last of which has emerged as the most popular offering in the program. In addition, old-line courses have been spruced up to make them more palatable. Swimming, for instance, isn't just laps these days, it's also scuba diving, water polo, water volleyball and balloon races.

The program extends to the college's dining halls, where posters promoting nutrition abound, dishes are labeled for calories and students can get their diets evaluated by computer for vitamin content. The P.E. staff chips in with frequent appeals for proper eating. "The problem with some of our kids isn't overeating; it's fad diets that lack important nutrients," notes Leigh Donato, the school's wellness coordinator. "We find ourselves pushing meat a lot."

Another part of the program is "stress management," something the school considers vital at a time when the anxieties and pressures of fast-track colleges like Bryn Mawr approach those of the adult world. December—when exams hit—appropriately has been designed as "Stress Month" for special attention to the subject. Although the P.E. folks at Bryn Mawr believe that working up a good sweat regularly is the best relaxer, they also are providing advice in such esoteric methods as yoga and transcendental meditation. Relatedly, the post-exam month of January, when some of the heat is off, has been set aside as Alcohol/Smoking Cessation Month.

Bryn Mawr students say that everything isn't always hunky-dory under the wellness regime. Just as in the bad old days, gym classes still get scheduled right after lunch and there isn't always time for a shower before the next class.

Yet the verdict seems favorable. Elizabeth Ameisen signed up for jogging, and notes delightedly that she can run a mile without stopping now, compared to "about 10 feet" in September when the class started. And Debi Nathanson allows that while she's "not really worked up" over wellness, she has cut down on her smoking and even drinks a glass of milk once in awhile. "That's not bad, considering," she says. "I know my parents are pleased."

Reprinted from the *Wall Street Journal*, November 30, 1982.

Above: Student playing field hockey, c. 1980s

Opposite: Student fencing, 1982

BRYN MAWR'S WELLNESS PROGRAM HAS REACHED STATE OF GOOD HEALTH

Jonathan Kane, Haverford, Class of 1987

THE WELLNESS PROGRAM has fast become a major factor in Bryn Mawr's athletic department. In only two years, the program, run by basketball and lacrosse coach Leigh Donato, has grown from being a series of lectures about physical fitness and health maintenance to an active program serving the bi-College community.

Currently, the Wellness program is divided into two sections: a goal-setting course under the guidance of Donato and trainer John Kalohn, and a Special Events Series operated by Training Intern Cindy Hooper. The course on goal-setting is taken for physical education credit and is the fundamental idea behind the program.

Before any goals are set, the student takes a pretest which has five steps: a cardio-vascular assessment, done by using a stationary bicycle; a nutritional assessment to determine any diet problems; an activities analysis to find possible improvements with one's daily routine; a wellness inventory which is a set of questions dealing with lifestyle; and a physical to get a complete picture of one's current physical condition for later comparison.

After the pretest, the student has a conference with the instructor to decide what the primary area of concern should be. Once this is determined, a program is designed to improve that area. After the program is made, students set their own goals and then begin the program in hopes of attaining those goals. As part of the process, the student is usually asked to take two half-semester courses that complement this particular program. These physical education courses are often the type that a student can use even after graduating from college.

Throughout the course, the students monitor their physical state and work toward their goals accordingly. Once every two weeks, meetings are scheduled with the instructor to discuss the individual's progress. These meetings can motivate the students to strive harder to reach their goals, or they can be a reassurance that everything is on schedule.

The other part of the Wellness program is the Special Events Series. It offers events to the bi-College community such as the up-coming cardio-pulmonary resuscitation (CPR) training courses, bike-hikes, and ski trips. This year's events should help publicize the Wellness program, and allow more people the opportunity to hear about and become interested in the program.

According to Donato, a big factor in attracting more participants will be the Bern Schwartz Gymnasium. The new facility presents an immense improvement over last year, when the course was centered in the old gym. Conferences with individual participants can be held in the private conference rooms and the testing can be done in the training room. Donato hopes to open the training room during second semester to allow students to use the equipment for self-testing even if they do not enroll in the course. These clinic hours should facilitate students' desires to improve their overall fitness without officially entering the Wellness program.

Donato stresses the emphasis on self-responsibility. The goals that one sets can only be attained through self-motivation. With minimal guidance, one should be able to improve overall fitness as well as improve in specific areas, she says. Since the course is limited to 40 students, guidance is on an individual basis.

The other factor that Donato stresses is that the Wellness program brings in other areas of College life to students' physical education. The health service becomes a large part of teaching students about physical fitness. For example, the health service runs a special event for learning how to relax and handle the stress of finals week.

Food service also makes a contribution, because a large part of complete awareness is nutrition. Only when one knows what and how to eat can a total fitness program be effective. The students involved get to see food service staff in a different manner, not just as the people who put cafeteria food on plates.

Because of the cooperation with food and health services, as well as the necessary cooperation of the entire athletic department, Donato feels that the Wellness program has a unifying effect. "There are activities for everyone," she says and these activities come from the entire Physical Education department. By using all that the athletic, food, and health services have to offer, students can reach their goals. Even when students cannot attain their goals, they still increase their awareness of their physical state as well as learn how to maintain good physical condition. This information is designed to help the students in College, and the Wellness program is very useful to its participants for their future.

Reprinted from the *College News* (Bryn Mawr-Haverford), November 4, 1983.

Above: Bryn Mawr's gymnastics team, 1980–81. left to right: Carie Bargman, class of 1983; Debra L. Stetter, class of 1984; Erica Turner, class of 1983; Julia Ann Yang, class of 1983; Julia Tuchler, class of 1984; Linda Britto, class of 1984; Maura C. Cooper, class of 1983; Karen Avagliano, class of 1983; Linda Castner, coach. Kneeling in front: Suzanne M. Schoch, class of 1982, team captain (left); Letitia Pfeiffer, class of 1982. Not pictured: Ann Korn, class of 1982; Carolyn G. Friedman, class of 1984

Opposite: Members of the field hockey team listening to their coach, October 3, 1982. Photograph by Stuart Math

"YES, VIRGINIA, THERE ARE ATHLETES AT BRYN MAWR"—REFLECTIONS OF A JOCK
Rachel Baker, Class of 1986

HELEN COLLINS was my admissions tour guide when I was a prospective visiting Bryn Mawr. You remember her . . . She's the legendary Bryn Mawr swimmer who went to Swimming Nationals in three events, training in the old pool.

Well, Helen did an amazing job convincing me that there were some very serious athletes at Bryn Mawr, and after scrutinizing ten other colleges I chose to come here where I could make the most of my academic and athletic propensities.

Well, I must admit that I was a little shocked when I saw the old gym for my second time during customs week. There really were gargoyles spouting into the tiny pool in the basement of the "castle." But I quickly adjusted to the life of a jock at a college where the athletics department's motto was "Bryn Mawr Athletics: A Contradiction in Terms?"

We had no fields for lacrosse my first two years here. So, freshman year we drove over to Haverford twice a week at 7:30 in the morning for preseason practice.

Sophomore year I got cocky and moved to HCA (Haverford College Apartments) with two friends thinking that we would only have a short walk up to the Field House for preseason. Of course, they finished the Bryn Mawr gym in time for lacrosse, and we had to go from HCA back to Bryn Mawr at 7:30 in the morning all January and February.

There are some advantages of having no fields, however. We traveled all over the East Coast for our games. Other people would sleep and read but I had my forehead pressed against the window—I was busy "seeing the East Coast" courtesy of Bryn Mawr tours.

Sophomore year our home field was at Haverford while the new fields at Bryn Mawr were being planted. The morning of the Haverford/Bryn Mawr lacrosse game there were posters reading "Mangle the Mawrters" on one side of the Dining Center and "Fry the Fords" on the other side. Bi-College cooperation? Or schizophrenia?

Of course, the most complicated aspect of a Bryn Mawr athlete's life is managing to stay in college. I mean, we jocks don't get a lot of respect here.

When I had to leave philosophy early to get to away games, Professor Carol L. Berstein would seize the opportunity to demonstrate problems of freedom and justice in class. "Well, Rachel—I don't have to let you leave for this game, do I?" And as I fidgeted nervously, he would pose the questions, "Is Rachel free to leave? Is this just?"

Well, now we have a beautiful new gym and lush playing fields. It's great having a full-size gym for indoor lacrosse practice but I'll never understand how they managed to design the interior to be the precise shade of buff yellow as a lacrosse ball.

Imagine 40 women in there hurling passes at each other and each time the ball gets airborne it disappears like a golf ball on televised golf tournaments. You are left staring at a buff ceiling trying to pinpoint the trajectory of the buff ball when it hits you right between the eyes.

We have fans now, too . . . President McPherson has been a faithful cheerleader since we got our fields. She came to the Swarthmore game and was heard screaming "Kill Her! Kill HER!" as a Bryn Mawr defender valiantly guarded the goal.

Moments later the Swarthmore player was lying on the ground with a large lump on her head where she had been hit by a defender's stick. President McPherson was trying to make her six-foot frame blend into the scenery (a tree, a lamp post perhaps) lest she be accused of inciting violence.

Now there are some of you who think it's dumb to be a jock at Bryn Mawr. Granted, we spend ten times as much on laundry trying to clean our practice clothes. So, we have to wear hideous green and yellow uniforms that look like we're advertising the "great LYMON taste of 7UP." But we get the last word . . . who's trying to fulfill their gym requirements?!

Reprinted from the *News* (Bryn Mawr-Haverford), May 16, 1986.

FINALLY: VARSITY SOCCER
Hadyn Kemal, Class of 1989

THIS YEAR BRYN MAWR is fielding a new varsity team. After four years of hard work and endless legislation Bryn Mawr College at last has a varsity-level soccer team. Ann Hitchcock and Rachel Baker deserve special credit, having pushed for a varsity team since their freshmen years. Although there was always consistent interest among the students, Hitchcock and Baker led the crusade.

In the fall of 1982 Bryn Mawr and Haverford fielded a bi-College recreational club soccer team. Practices were held every Saturday morning at 9:00 A.M. A coach was not employed and the students involved received no P.E. credit. The team had six games that year, mostly with local club teams or high schools. Because the team had no home field, all the games were away. One of the college games, against Swarthmore, ended in a lopsided defeat for the fledgling team.

At the end of the season Hitchcock and Baker began a series of meetings with Mrs. Shillingford in an effort to upgrade the team to varsity level. In 1983, a graduate student was hired to coach the team, and practices were held twice a week at Haverford. The athletics department gave participants one P.E. credit for their efforts, and they were allowed to speak at the sports banquet. Finally at the next season's opening, the team boasted twenty-five full-time players. When they again faced Swarthmore, the game ended in a close defeat.

In 1984, the team split, giving Bryn Mawr and Haverford their own club teams. A full-time coach, John Amorin, was hired, and players were given full athletic credit. Bryn Mawr's administration continued to deny its team varsity status on the grounds that the College still didn't have its own field and that funding was insufficient. Hitchcock and Baker continued to meet with Mrs. Shillingford and wrote countless letters to the trustees, the budget committee, etc. That year the team was given a full schedule. They defeated Haverford and tied Swarthmore in double over-time.

At the end of July 1985, they were finally up-graded to the varsity level. An experienced full-time coach was hired and pre-season practices were held. The team has faced four opponents so far this year, boasting three victories and one close defeat. Their first home game against Beaver College was played Thursday, September 19th, on Bryn Mawr's new soccer field. The team's captains, Hitchcock, Baker and Carolyn Buser, hope that by next year there may be a Junior Varsity team and an even fuller game schedule.

Reprinted from the *College News*, October 9, 1985.

Top: Member of the soccer team stretching on the sideline, c. 1985–90. Soccer became a varsity sport at Bryn Mawr in 1985.

Bottom: Bryn Mawr's track team, 1987

Clockwise from top left: Lacrosse players at practice, 1983; gymnastics team members at practice, 1982; swimmers taking their marks, 1982; student athlete on the field, 1982

INVESTING CLUB: STUDENTS COMMAND ATTENTION AND REAL ASSETS

STUDENTS TEACH A LESSON IN INVESTING

BRYN MAWR—On the long list of things people perpetually do wrong, investing in the stock market ranks supreme. But for the past year, a group of students at Bryn Mawr College had lessons to teach: The rate of return on their stock portfolio outperformed that of the college's. "It was a great learning experience," says Margot Jeffroy, a graduating senior and treasurer of the college's Student Investment Committee, an investment club which got its initial $100,000 to invest from an anonymous donor. "When I first joined the group, I knew nothing about investing. But after a while, we all began to learn the nuances of the market." The portfolio, now valued at $134,000, was up 27% from May 1983. The college's portfolio had a return of 20%.

Reprinted from *USA Today*, May 25–28, 1984.

STOP-LOSS ORDERS HELP BRYN MAWR

AT FIRST, Mercedes Meyer laughed off word of the crash. The head of the Bryn Mawr Student Investing Committee was in the dining hall when a friend asked: "The stock market can't go down 500 points in one day, can it?"

"I thought, 'Very funny,'" recalls Meyer, a law school-bound chemistry major from Long Island. But in the aftermath, "We looked at each other and said, 'Okay, we lost a lot. But we learned.'"

One lesson: stop-loss orders—standing orders with a broker to sell a stock when it drops below a set price. The technique got the group out of 13 of its 20 stocks after the crash, preserving still-hefty profits for all but three.

Bryn Mawr's investing group began 13 years ago with a $100,000 gift from an anonymous alumna. Part of each year's profits goes to the school's general endowment, but the fund remains separate and investments may carry over from year to year, allowing a long-term strategy.

The 20-member group consistently has outperformed the S&P 500 index. Now, heavy with cash, the group is eyeing stocks to buy when their prices slump. No 1. Pick: Merck ($158½ Thursday) below $150.

Reprinted from *USA Today*, January 4, 1988.

THE BRYN MAWR COLLEGE FUND IS FOR STUDENTS TO INVEST

Charles V. Zehren

IT WAS ONLY 8 A.M. on Oct. 20, but eight desperate undergraduates already were huddled in a Bryn Mawr College dormitory cafeteria to contemplate disaster.

Roughly $34,000 had disappeared overnight, and although all of them had a good idea of where it went, no one knew whether they would ever get it back. To make matters worse, the missing money didn't belong to them in the first place.

So went the first portfolio-strategy meeting of the Bryn Mawr College Student Investment Committee after the Dow Jones industrial average's 508-point collapse on Black Monday.

The committee has more to worry about than trying to learn from its mistakes. That's because the members and their predecessors have been investing real money since 1974, when an anonymous donor awarded the women's college $100,000 for students to invest any way saw fit.

"The donor thought women often ended up with a certain amount of money, either made or inherited, had no sense of how to handle it, and were put at the mercy of others with more experience," said Bryn Mawr President Mary Patterson McPherson.

Although the donor "wasn't uptight about them blowing the whole $100,000 the first year," McPherson said she was somewhat nervous. But in the last 13 years, the committee has realized its benefactor's great expectations.

Despite their recent crash course in negative market psychology—as well as an ill-fated dip into sugar futures during the late 1970s—the Bryn Mawr students have not only survived but prospered.

As of Nov. 18, the fund was valued at $137,611.28, off from a high of about $227,000 in March. And given returns on investment of 24 percent and 22 percent for the 1985 and 1986 school years, respectively, the club has become a model for other college-investment groups.

But unlike the members of most of the thousands of other private-investment clubs throughout the United States, the students at Bryn Mawr don't pocket the proceeds.

"There's an element of pride involved," said committee director Elizabeth Trabulsi, a senior, citing the competition among clubs over the years to best one another's rates of return.

More significant, the committee over the years has donated about $70,000 of its winnings to the college. This included a $35,000 check from cash reserves signed over in June for scholarships, a career-development program, an AIDS awareness project and campus repairs.

"The gifts help worthy programs, students are learning how to handle money responsibly and take risks. They are gaining experience that liberal arts colleges don't regularly offer as part of their curriculum," said Suzanne Spain, the college's assistant treasurer.

Today, the committee—which now numbers about 40, including four elected directors—touts itself as the most successful undergraduate club in the nation.

Any Bryn Mawr student can join, and students from its Main Line neighbor, Haverford College, were admitted in 1986. Although Haverford students are full voting members, Bryn Mawr prohibits Haverford students from holding office.

"The Bryn Mawr crowd is very sharp, very intelligent," said the committee's stockbroker, Vincent Celii of Donaldson, Lufkin & Jenrette in New York.

"I make suggestions, but they have the final say," Celii said. "I treat them just like I would the account of a high net-worth individual investor . . . It's fun, but they take it very seriously."

This year's committee has adopted a relatively conservative strategy, playing widely traded stocks in a variety of industries. About 15 stocks are in the portfolio at any time and are generally valued at $10,000 to $15,000 each.

At weekly meetings, members of the club review the portfolio's performance and chart its future course. Members complete research assignments covering individual stocks and industries, and discuss their findings before investment decisions are put to a vote.

"We don't try to influence the way the student committee invests its money," said Spain.

On the face of it, that might be just as well.

The college's own $98.1 million endowment posted a total return of 9.76 percent for its fiscal year ending May 31, far below that of the student committee.

But Spain attributed the lower rate of return to the college's adoption of rules barring investment in stocks of companies that do business in South Africa. As a result, the school's portfolio managers bailed out of many then-high-flying blue chips. The student committee does not maintain a "South Africa-free" portfolio.

Many of the investment club's senior strategists were oblivious to the bloodletting on Black Monday until after the market closed because they were holed up in campus libraries, chemistry labs and classrooms.

According to Celii, though, there was a silver lining—albeit a thin one—surrounding that dark cloud.

"The committee wound up hanging on to their blue chips, which were the first to rebound." As a result, when the club eventually did sell some of its portfolio, prices were up from their lows. "They ended up outperforming the overall market by a little," he said.

Still, "our initial reaction that morning was, 'Let's sell everything,'" Trabulsi said.

After a quick check of the markets in London and Tokyo, however, cooler heads prevailed.

"We figured all the damage was done, and we should stay in there," she said. The members apparently were right. Their portfolio is down 21 percent from the market's August high, while the Dow is off 27 percent.

Reprinted from the *Philadelphia Inquirer*, November 27, 1987.

Above: Students in their dorm, 1986

Opposite: Students on campus, April 1978. Photograph by Katrina Thomas

CENTENNIAL

CENTURY TWO BEGINS
Mary Patterson McPherson

OUR ORGY of Centennial celebrations has made this a very special year. Stimulating, satisfying programs have brought to the College many well-known and valued colleagues, inspired new contacts, and made new friends for Bryn Mawr. We enjoyed symposia, lectures, and workshops arranged by many departments, looking at such issues as population control, the poetry of Bryn Mawr's own Marianne Moore and Hilda Doolittle, the latest work in neuroscience and in gender studies, the Trojan War revisited. We reveled in the artistic programming which brought to the College poet Seamus Heaney, pianist Kathy Selby '83, the Dance Theater of Harlem, a student performance of *Lysistrata*, and a three-college choral concert. Robert Lifton spoke on politics in the late eighties, and Gloria Steinem on women and equity as part of the Graduate School of Social Work's 70th anniversary celebration; Svetlana Alpers, art historian from Berkeley, gave the Flexner lectures on Rembrandt—almost indigestibly rich fare but wonderful for all of us.

The Centennial celebrations, permitting us a period of remembering, reflecting, and enjoying, however, followed upon an intense six-year period devoted to assuring that the College move into its second hundred years and then into the

21st century with a talented, appropriately prepared faculty to meet the needs of both today and tomorrow, with the brightest and most diverse student body we can attract, and with the facilities that will help us to do our jobs well both inside and outside the formal classroom. In other words, we have spent our time looking and planning ahead.

The Centennial Campaign, producing $50 million—well beyond its $41 million goal—has made it possible to realize much of the planning.

You need only to look about you in Goodhart, now the home of our developing program in the Arts; walk through the new Katharine McBride Gateway at Pembroke Arch, or Glenmede, the new graduate residence on Morris Avenue; take a swim in the new pool in our splendid Bern Schwartz Gymnasium; peek into the Campus Center, located in the imaginatively renovated old gymnasium; wander through renovated Thomas, Radnor, Denbigh, Pembroke West, the Ely House, the third floor of Taylor, the Career Planning Office, the Departments of Anthropology and Psychology in Dalton, or Biology in the Science Building; or peer into that huge hole into which Denbigh and Dalton appear to be almost toppling, imagining our new Computer Center, to sense the commitment we have all made to providing suitable facilities for the work and living of the College and its denizens. These improvements have been made possible through the generosity of a number of alumnae and the Pew Memorial Trusts.

Curricular review and planning in all three of the College's schools and the introduction over the past four years of approximately 25 new members to the faculty—many young and bringing with them different training and fresh perspectives which invigorate departments and programs—have moved us in some

interesting and important directions. Starting with this past year's Freshman class, all students must take mathematics, a requirement adopted in the hope that our students will not be stymied or held back by a lack of confidence in dealing with quantitative materials. Students and faculty alike are working interdisciplinarily as interests in comparative literature, gender studies, and area studies are encouraged, and the lines that once divided the sciences are obviously blurring with interesting consequences for faculty members and students.

Old and new programs that take us out and about have enriched us—students will study this summer in Bryn Mawr-sponsored programs in France, Spain, Italy, Russia, Germany, and in new excavations in Nemea, Greece, and Karluk, Alaska. And our Peace Studies Fact Finding Missions, a Bryn Mawr-sponsored aspect of our Bryn Mawr-Haverford Peace Studies Program, have taken students from the two colleges last year to London, Bonn, and Ottawa, this past January to Nicaragua and Costa Rica, and we were to have left in May for Kenya and South Africa, but owing to student unrest over South African investments in this country and general student unrest in South Africa itself, we are still trying to secure visas. Two anthropology students have left for Kenya on a new exchange program developed with Richard Leakey, which will involve our students working in his new field school at Koobi Fora and his students working in our anthropology graduate program next fall. In July, two undergraduates represented Bryn Mawr at the UN Decade for Women meeting in Nairobi.

New programs here permit us to consider the effects of television on American politics, education, and culture, and bring persons in management positions in a variety of fields to campus to talk with students and faculty members. Increasingly sophisticated work is being done on the computer; new work in intensive language instruction, involving the use of the computer and video equipment, will move students ahead much more rapidly to work of a satisfying nature. The effort will be much strengthened by our planned addition of a state-of-the-art language laboratory to be housed in the old Denbigh dining room.

We have been enriched as well by programs which permit us to bring to the campus young scholars for a year or two to teach and/or do research in fields we do not represent. Most recently, we have enjoyed the participation of two young women, one a specialist in communication through film, the other a Chinese cultural expert.

DETERMINED LEADERSHIP: 1978–1997

Clockwise from top left: Invitation to the Centennial Campaign Celebration Dinner, May 25, 1982; Mary Patterson McPherson (left) and Barbara Auchincloss Thacher, class of 1940 (right), at the Turn-of-the-Century Picnic, part of Bryn Mawr's centennial celebrations, June 2, 1984; and guests in costume at the picnic

Opposite: Sallie Robinson and Barbara Trinker singing at the 1904 vs. 1905 hockey game, part of Bryn Mawr's centennial celebrations, October 1984. Photograph by Polly L. Stephens, class of 1987

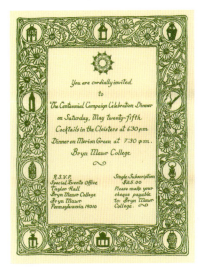

The most recent of these awards came to us out of the blue as Bryn Mawr was chosen as one of ten institutions—all the others major research universities—to receive the first Getty Fellows in History of Art broadly defined. It was fun to note that of the 20 Getty Fellows chosen this year, one came to Bryn Mawr and two others were Bryn Mawr alumnae; one chose to go to Harvard, the other to Columbia.

The students are a marvelous and distinctive lot. They come from all 50 states, Puerto Rico, the District of Columbia, and 54 foreign countries. Although they are indeed the victims of financial pressure—coping with family sacrifice and their own debt level—and are therefore earlier more practical about life's choices, I find them a remarkable, intelligent, socially concerned, politically aware group of women. This generation also has a sense of humor, as would have been evident to you on May Day, or at Commencement weekend, when I awoke Saturday morning to find the lawn of Pen-y-Groes covered with pink plastic flamingos and a large sign which said: "New Century, New Bird."

Education today is a fascinating yet fragile business. We have a Secretary of Education in Washington who does not seem to understand that this country has from its beginnings given education a different mandate and defined the responsibilities of a citizen differently from those societies we or our ancestors rebelled against and left. We have asked of our educational system that it educate young people to be leaders of the polity in every sense—people of individual integrity, citizens effective in word and deed. Such education is vital for the success of America's social and political institutions, given our revolutionary commitment to eschew reliance on any social class or established church for the development of the character and skills public life demands. The health of both the independent institutions and our great public systems

is vital to the strength of our economy and the actual defense of our democracy. I believe that college and university presidents and Boards of Trustees understand fully that all sectors of our economy will have to readjust and cooperate to address the country's fiscal excesses. Education does not believe it should be in some privileged position in relation to the needs of the poor, the elderly, a sensible defense structure, or a knowledgeable bureaucracy. But to suggest to the public that this is a time to curtail student access to education, to make the teaching profession even more unattractive than it is already, or to cripple basic research, is truly not to understand the way to defend this nation and keep it economically and politically strong.

Here we have a special mission—and that is to be sure that an especially talented group of young women learn that they can use their abilities fully to make a difference. Society, simply put, cannot afford to permit its able women to achieve less than their full potential, and we bear a responsibility here to see that these able women become firm and secure in that purpose.

Reprinted from the Bryn Mawr Alumnae Bulletin, *Summer 1985.*

Weecha Crawford, Class of 1960
Vanessa Van Essen, Class of 1997

Above: Maria Luisa "Weecha" Crawford (born 1939), class of 1960 and professor emeritus of geology, in the field, c. 1990s

CRAWFORD HITS PAY DIRT
BMC Geology Professor Wins MacArthur Fellowship

BRYN MAWR COLLEGE GEOLOGY Professor Maria Luisa "Weecha" Crawford, class of 1960, recently won a $320,000 MacArthur fellowship. The money will be awarded over the next five years and is hers to use as she chooses.

"Most of the money will go towards research I'm conducting in southeast Alaska," Crawford said. "My husband and I spend about two months each summer there, and undergraduate and graduate students from Bryn Mawr are involved in the research."

The Crawfords study the origin of the Coast Mountains, which extend from Vancouver, British Columbia, to Juneau, Alaska. Through the study of the different geological processes the mountains went through in formation, geologists gain information about younger mountain ranges.

Crawford's work has impacted the fields of metamorphic petrology and geologic terrains, which have to do with the reconstruction of past geologic processes and how they affect the earth's crust.

The MacArthur Foundation awarded between $150,000 and $375,000 to gifted individuals this year.

The purpose of these awards is to free recipients from financial concerns so that they can use their creativity to contribute to society.

People cannot apply for MacArthur fellowships; they must be nominated by an anonymous committee. The whole process of nomination and awarding is secretive. There are 100 nominators around the country who change each year. These people are chosen by the MacArthur Foundation.

Crawford has won other awards, including a National Science Foundation research grant and an Outstanding Educator Award from the Association for Women Geoscientists Foundation in 1988.

Crawford became interested in geology when she was an undergraduate student at Bryn Mawr.

Before graduating in 1960 as a geology major, she won the Hoop Race down Senior Row on May Day. Bryn Mawr legend has it that the winner of the Hoop Race will be the first member of that class to get a Ph.D. After this illustrious victory, Crawford went on to graduate school at the University of California, Berkeley.

Seven people in the area have been honored with fellowships this year. The recipients were not only found in academic areas. Scientists, a public broadcaster, and a gospel singer were all named fellows along with Crawford.

"It's a diverse group of people that are awarded the MacArthur fellowships," Crawford said. "You can't put them all into a box."

Crawford will lead an expedition to Antarctica in January with several Bryn Mawr alumnae and President Mary Patterson McPherson.

Reprinted from the *News* (Bryn Mawr-Haverford), September 17, 1993.

ATHENA'S THEFT AND REPAIR: A PRANK GONE AWRY

Above: Athena Lemnia (late 19th- to early 20th-century plaster cast after marble copies of the original 5th-century B.C. bronze sculpture attributed to Phidias, c. 490–430 B.C.) in Thomas Great Hall, c. 1960s. From c. 1906 until its theft in 1996 by Haverford students, the statue stood in Thomas. After the damage that resulted from the theft was repaired, the statue was installed in a niche in the Rhys Carpenter Library.

Page 325 (left): Head of Athena Lemnia ("Athena II"), in a visor, 2009. Copy of the late 19th–early 20th-century plaster cast, made by Jan Trembley (class of 1975), 1997; papier-mâché, plaster gauze, fiberglass resin, and foam peanuts. After the 1996 abduction of Athena (illus. this page, above) from Thomas Great Hall by Haverford students, the statue was deemed too fragile to withstand further damage. To ensure students could continue to leave offerings for Athena, Trembley created this replica, which to this day stands, adorned with gifts, in Thomas Great Hall.

Page 325 (right): Athena Lemnia ("Athena II"), with offerings from students, in Thomas Great Hall, 2009

GODDESS LEAVES CAMPUS IN THE BACK OF A PICKUP

BRYN MAWR, PA.—In a prank of Olympian proportions, Haverford College students made off with one of Bryn Mawr College's most revered statues.

Five male Haverford students kidnapped the 200-pound statue of Athena, throwing her into a truck and hiding her in a Haverford dormitory. In the process, Athena lost an arm and her head.

Since Bryn Mawr's founding in 1885, students at the women's college have gone to the statue of Athena to bring them good luck. Bryn Mawr students saw the pranksters putting Athena in the truck. The men will have to pay $6,000 to repair the statue.

But that didn't end the controversy, which has taken on a playful tone. In an act of "revenge," Bryn Mawr's president, Mary Patterson McPherson, issued a memo on Haverford stationery, announcing her selection as the college's interim president, to replace Tom Kessinger, who will step down in July. Bryn Mawr students have erected an effigy of Mr. Kessinger in the place of Athena.

Reprinted from the *Chronicle of Higher Education*, May 24, 1996.

OFFERINGS IMMORTALIZED IN ARCHIVES
Julia Alexander, Class of 1996

HEY! DID YOU KNOW you can go and visit the college archives any time you want to, between nine and four, I think, and they have to let you in? Cool, huh? Among the many fascinating things you can find in the archives (like copies of old yearbooks and handbooks) are the gifts that have been given to Athena since the Archives began collecting them in the late 70's.

In the box, collected on January 14, 1991, there were:
- 1 dry twig
- 1 copy of excerpts from *The Praise of Folly* by Erasmus, with several sections highlighted
- 1 blue pencil with "Happy Hanukkah" written on it
- 1 large negative of some body part (skin, I think), in a frame that reads: "Thanks for the negative reinforcement!" with a black thread attached with which to hang it
- 2 pennies
- 1 Jack London stamp
- 1 small, smooth white stone
- 1 red garter edged with black lace and a red bow
- 1 chain of different colored paper stars
- 1 envelope made out of paper with yellow daffodils; inside, there is a photo of an older couple and a lot of writing about someone's grandfather

I don't know what to say about all of this, so I'll leave you to draw your own conclusions. Just remember the next time you leave something for Athena, that you will be forever immortalized in the archives!

Reprinted from the *College News*, September 20, 1994.

To: Carol W. Campbell
Curator of the College's Collections
Bryn Mawr College

From: Virginia N. Naudé, Norton Art Conservation;
John Phillips, Phillips Casting, Inc.

Sculpture examined May 1, 1996:
    Title: *Athena Lemnia*
    Material: plaster, painted black
    Date: c. 1900
    Height on record, with raised left arm: 7' 6"

Background:
Information from BMC states that the original bronze statue by Pheidias, 5th c. B.C., was displayed on the Athenian Acropolis. The image is known from a Roman marble copy of which the head is in the Museo Civico in Bologna and the body in the Albertinum in Dresden. The absence of a right arm reflects the actual condition of the stone. The plaster cast composite copy has been in Thomas Library since the building opened in 1905.

Present Condition of Sculpture:
The sculpture was damaged as the result of a prank, April 21, 1996. It was examined on May 1, 1996, in a room in the basement of Merion Hall in the Public Safety Department. Snapshots taken during the inspection are attached to this report.

Breaks and Fragments:
Eight fragments from the heroic-scale standing figure have broken off and been saved. They are sufficiently stable for reattachment. Powder and smaller fragments were not saved. The head is in one piece with two square steel rods embedded in the solid plaster neck, projecting outwards and curved away from each other. There is a vertical fold fragment from the front drapery, and a large part of the left arm which includes the hand and elbow and five smaller fragments which appear to be associated with the arm. The left hand is missing all four fingers. Fragments of the former third and fourth fingers are attached at the end of armature wires. The first and second fingers are missing.

Cracks:
The standing figure is cracked all around just below knee level. The join moves but is held in place, presumably from original jute reinforcement and perhaps also from armature.

    The figure is probably hollow-cast and weighted at the bottom with armature and auxiliary plaster. There is a crescent-shaped crack below the neck break at the front, and a crack at the top of the left shoulder, traveling through the top of the cut-off. The latter is stable but there is a fragment loose at the back along the crack line.

Left Arm Attachment:
A steel pin with a forked end projects from the left arm cut-off. The pin is shaped at its blunt end to fit into a rectangular steel sleeve embedded in the cut-off area. The mechanism for releasing the hardware supporting the left arm appears to be two steel pins that drop vertically into holes at the top of the arm. One pin was loose and could be removed during the examination, but the tenon did not release.

Treatment Requirements:
- Stabilize cracks and loose fragments on sculptural elements
- Reattach separated fragments
- Fill voids. There will be several options for levels of compensation, including modeling of missing fingers on the left hand. Ethical and aesthetic considerations of the options should be discussed by the curator and conservator.
- Cosmetic work on presentation surface; nature and extent of work to be discussed

Options and Estimated Costs for Casting at Phillips Casting, Inc.:
90 East Church Lane, Germantown, Philadelphia, PA 19144
To make a mold on the surface, prepared to approximate contour and texture by the conservator but without its final presentation finish, to apply and remove a release agent: $7,000. The mold will be serviceable for approximately 8 years. From the rubber mold any number of any selection of the following can be cast:
- Fgr 95 Hydrocal gypsum cement with fiberglass and stainless steel armature. Lightweight, harder and consequently more durable than the present plaster cast, fireproof. Fingers and folds vulnerable and subject to cracking. Cost for each cast: $4,000.
- Epoxy cast (plastic) with stainless steel armature. Lightweight, very strong, not fireproof. Fingers and folds subject to cracking. Cost for each cast: $10,000.
- Bronze, strongest and most durable option. Cost for each cast: $19,500.

Recommendations:
Decisions about conservation and casting options should be made at the same time for aesthetic and budget reasons. A secure, reversible system of affixing the sculpture to its base should be designed and built into both a conservation and a recasting project. To preserve the appearance of the conserved original cast and any new casts, a routine of monthly dusting by custodial staff, trained by a conservator, should be established as well as a provision for superficial wet cleaning, and perhaps touch-up waxing, by a conservator every two or three years.

Reprinted from the examination report, May 5, 1996.

ATHENA OR A RIVAL'S PRESIDENT, BRYN MAWR HAS ITS LUCKY CHARM
Karen W. Arenson

BRYN MAWR, Pa.—For more than a century, Athena stood in a corner of Thomas Great Hall on the campus of Bryn Mawr. Generations of Bryn Mawr women have turned to the seven-and-one-half-foot statue for luck, bringing poetry, term papers, jewelry, twigs and other offerings to lay at its feet.

Then last month, in the dead of night, five male students from neighboring Haverford College shoved the statue, a plaster replica of a fifth-century B.C. work from the Acropolis, into the back of a white Ford Escort station wagon and took it to their campus a mile away.

Their action set off a chain of events that would reach the highest levels of the two campuses. Haverford's president would be mounted in effigy on Bryn Mawr's campus, and Bryn Mawr's president would frighten Haverford into thinking she might become its temporary president.

Although the two colleges, which are outside Philadelphia, have a history of pranks, Athena's disappearance might have been a mystery but for Danika Haueisen, a Bryn Mawr junior history and political science major from Hudson, Ohio. Ms. Haueisen, who had just come back from a sailing meet, saw the men leaving with Athena's feet sticking out of their tailgate. She grabbed some friends and followed them to Haverford, where they caught up to the statue and its kidnappers.

The statue was in sad shape: the head and outstretched arm had broken off and there were hairline cracks around the lower torso. Realizing that Athena was too delicate to move, the Bryn Mawr students settled for the head.

By 2 A.M., the Haverford men had been rounded up and made to return the statue, escorted by Bryn Mawr security officers.

Bryn Mawr, a women's college that takes its traditions seriously, is still weighing how to fix Athena and is considering making a hardier model of fiberglass. It has not been decided whether the Haverford students, who said they meant no harm, will be billed for repairs to the statue.

With exams approaching, the next order of business at Bryn Mawr was deciding on a temporary replacement for the college's good luck icon. Bryn Mawr's president, Mary Pat McPherson, two other officials and a student newspaper editor put their heads together.

They settled on Haverford's president, Tom Kessinger. Now Athena's pedestal holds a six-foot foam effigy robed in a toga, sandals on his feet, rhinestones in his beard. Around his neck is a sign saying he is shouldering the burden until Athena returns.

Next came a further bit of revenge. Using Mr. Kessinger's stationery and signature, Ms. McPherson sent out a memorandum to all Haverford students and faculty saying that she would become interim president after Mr. Kessinger left in July. "We have made a choice which might at first surprise—even shock—you," the memorandum said, "but upon reflection we know you will all agree that Mary Patterson McPherson is in fact the most obvious choice to see our institution through this difficult transitional year."

Mr. Kessinger, who is becoming the general manager of the Aga Khan Trust for Culture in Geneva, later noted that the timing was perfect. His own trustees were scheduled to meet a few days later to approve an interim president. "Three quarters of the campus went for it," he said of the phony memorandum. "I looked at it and said, 'This is her work.'"

He quickly sent Ms. McPherson a note saying he was running short of official stationery but understood that she had a good supply. "Could you send some over?" he asked.

Reprinted from the *New York Times*, May 15, 1996.

Athena is back at Bryn Mawr, confined to a storage room to await restoration. It's the second time she has had her head knocked off; the first time was also during an abduction.

The timing is unfortunate for Bryn Mawr students, who traditionally shower Athena with food, flowers, jewelry, notes and poems, all designed to help them through exams. By the end of exam week, Athena is usually covered with such gifts.

"The real concern is how are our students going to get through finals without Athena," said Bryn Mawr spokeswoman Debra Thomas. "The proposals have ranged from having Haverfordians come and stand in Great Hall so students can make offerings, to having a substitute Athena.

"I suggested we have a hologram."

It appears, though, that the Bryn Mawr women are going to have to get through the semester without help from Mount Olympus."

Reprinted from Ralph Vigoda, "Athena Lost Her Head in a Statue Theft Prank," *Philadelphia Inquirer*, April 25, 1996.

CAMPUS LIFE IN THE 1980s AND 1990s

DISPUTING THE IDEA THAT WOMEN JUST AREN'T FUNNY

BRYN MAWR, Pa.—Women just aren't as funny as men, a former editor of the *Harvard Lampoon* once told Karen Tolchin.

Viewing that statement as a ticklish matter that demanded a response, last week Ms. Tolchin issued the *Howl*, Bryn Mawr's first humor magazine in 87 years.

"Humor isn't very high on the list of priorities at Bryn Mawr," said Ms. Tolchin, a sophomore English major from Bethesda, Md., and the editor in chief. "That's one of the things we're looking to change. We need to be Renaissance women, and part of that is taking ourselves less seriously."

Not only themselves, but resident dorm roaches, male pick-up lines, long-distance parental interrogations, the politic way to act politically correct and other aspects of life at Bryn Mawr.

"Slapstick to Subtle"

The *Howl*—the name refers to the mascot of the women's college, the owl—has essays, poetry, photographs and cartoons. "It is something that we really need here," said Alix Cohen, a senior Russian major from Baltimore.

Andrea Bial, a sophomore sociology major from Wilmette, Ill., said: "It has lots of different kinds of humor, from the slapstick to the subtle. But I don't know why we get such a bum rap for not being funny. Most of the people I know here are funny. We just don't get printed up."

It took Ms. Tolchin and 30 editors and writers more than a year to get the magazine off the ground. Bryn Mawr's first such venture, the *Fortnightly Philistine*, thrived between 1895 and 1903. Although there have been other publications that included humor, the *Howl* is the first since then dedicated to lightheartedness.

It is an annual publication, but Ms. Tolchin said she hoped to publish twice a year.

"There is a very negative stereotype still floating around in the world—that of the humorless woman," she said. "That stereotype is something we'd like to chip away at."

Reprinted from the *New York Times*, April 8, 1990.

Above: Student reading during coffee hour in Thomas Great Hall, November 1982

Left: Cover of the *Howl*, Bryn Mawr's humor magazine, c. 1990

Opposite: Students at coffee hour in Thomas Great Hall, 1983

DETERMINED LEADERSHIP: 1978–1997

PAYING FOR DONUTS: FINANCIAL CONCERNS MEAN SACRIFICING A LITTLE
Tamara Beauboeuf, Class of 1990

SOME BRYN MAWR STUDENTS feel that an important social tradition has been sacrificed by the College's decision to charge for the donuts at Coffee Hours this year.

Bryn Mawr decided to charge students and faculty members for the donuts served at Coffee Hour in an effort to raise revenues and cut expenses in light of the College's financial situation, according to Director of Student Services Chuck Heyduk. Although many students understand the reasons for this change, they feel that Coffee Hour is no longer the social time it once was.

"No one eats donuts [now]," commented Sophomore Laura van Straaten. "People can't bring themselves to pay for them." The cost is $.35 per donut or three for $1. When asked to compare the atmosphere to last year's she said, "It seems last year people hung out more. Now it's more like people run in and go. Last year I would go and meet people there, and I think other people did as well."

However, she defended the College's decision, saying that it is "more important for Bryn Mawr to recover what money it lost or needs. [Coffee Hour is] a luxury, and in crisis you give up certain things."

Haverford Junior Scott Curlee described last year's Coffee Hour as being "a convenience that was very appropriate to student life . . . I think a lot of people were mainly drawn there because of the [free] food."

He added, "[now] I don't sit around so long; it's so much easier to pick up a cup of coffee and walk out . . . [Last year] people tried to work it into their schedules more . . . Now it doesn't have quite the same attraction, and I haven't seen the great hordes there that used to be shuffling in," he said.

He added, "But I can see how it would cost a fortune with people walking out and eating lots of donuts." He added that the prospect of free donuts at Coffee Hour would "probably bring me back."

Sophomore Alecia Domer is one of 13 people who signed a petition in Thomas Great Hall at the start of the semester which said, "In the beginning there were doughnuts. Now we are left with holes. Bring back a BMC tradition."

Opposing comments written on the petition stated that financial aid and more courses are more important than Coffee Hour, that graduate students receive funding below the national average at Bryn Mawr, that the money could be used to hire more staff, and finally that students are actually doing themselves a favor by not eating "fatty, sugary, empty calories that create more tiredness and depression."

While respecting the arguments against free donuts, Domer also stressed that Coffee Hour is "a tradition, and [that] social life has to enter into college life. Some students want to have a balance."

She suggested that the cost of running a free Coffee Hour be calculated and that students then be permitted to vote whether or not they would want the extra cost to be added to room and board tuition. She feels that if there were a specific fund paid to Coffee Hour and if the cost to students were less than $20, enough students would be willing to pay it.

Beth Habansky, a senior, thinks that the atmosphere of the café may also be a cause for the lack of crowds at Coffee Hour: "I find myself going to the café more" where the atmosphere is more social, nearer to that which Coffee Hour used to have, and where people don't run in and out as much.

She also feels that there don't seem to be as many faculty members there as in previous years, and that what interaction there is between students and faculty is not as casual as it once was.

Professor of Greek Gregory Dickerson has also noticed a "dramatic" drop in attendance. "I understand the financial situation and the pressing needs the college has; however, I miss it. It's one of the few places as a faculty member that you get to see people you're not teaching."

He said in former years he would see colleagues and students there and thought it was a "nice situation," noting that this year his contact with them has dropped 75 percent. With so few people, "you don't stay around so long," he explained.

He feels the incentive for faculty to attend, to mingle with colleagues and students, is gone, adding, "Why not pour yourself a cup of coffee [in your office]? I'm just sort of sad; maybe it's inevitable. If it takes the donuts [to bring faculty and students together], maybe we could have them once a week."

Professor of Greek Richard Hamilton wondered if the cutback is a "false savings," if more students were attending breakfast. According to Director of Dining Services Joe Giamboi, there has been an increase of "only 20 or 30 more students, which is not really significant."

He added, although "it's been a savings, we haven't broken even." Giamboi approximated that six dozen donuts are sold a day. But, "it's not a money-making situation for us; it hasn't covered the cost."

Although they haven't experienced the Coffee Hour of former years, some freshmen feel that it's not the gathering time they had heard about. "I was told that it was a lot of fun and a nice time to congregate . . . I think it's a good idea, but there's not that many faculty there," observed Freshman Kate McNulty. She said that when she has attended Coffee Hour, she socialized with "maybe one or two people."

Sonia Chattha, also a freshman, commented, "It's nice to go there and know they'll [the donuts] be there. It's not as stressful as going to the dining hall and waiting in line. I think it's really mellow, but I don't know about the faculty-student interaction."

"It's more of a coffee hour than a coffee and donut hour, but I'd rather pay $.35 for a donut than have them raise tuition or do away with need-blind admissions. They're trying to keep the tradition alive the best way they can," said Freshman Stacey Lewis.

Reprinted from the *News* (Bryn Mawr-Haverford), October 23, 1987.

BRYN MAWR COLLEGE ENDS ITS DAILY PERK
Walter F. Naedele

BRYN MAWR COLLEGE paid for Coffee Hour yesterday morning.

Isn't that precious.

Students who missed it will have to wait until the one day in April when it will be offered again.

Some traditions survive.

Some traditions die.

Some just wither away.

At Bryn Mawr, students and administrators say, Coffee Hour is either slowly withering or barely surviving.

But it sure isn't what it used to be: a daily event.

Since about 1970, Coffee Hour has been the occasion where students and faculty could happen upon each other casually and discuss face-to-face what the rest of a hurried day might not allow.

Up until the 1986–87 school year, the college offered free doughnuts and coffee between 10 and 11 A.M., five days a week, in the enormous former reading room of Thomas Library, a building whose cathedral ceiling and cathedral windows enhanced the sense of tradition.

For the four school years after 1986–87, the college offered free coffee . . . but buy-your-own doughnuts.

Since the fall, the college has offered dime-a-cup—well OK, OK, free if you bring your own mug—and free doughnuts . . . but . . . only . . . one . . . day . . . every . . . month.

And because the Thomas Library building is being renovated, the once-every-day-but-now-only-once-a-month tradition has been taking place in the uncathedral-like atmosphere of the lounge of the building known as the Campus Center.

Why less and less?

"It was about $25,000-a-year worth of free doughnuts" in the last school year, Bryn Mawr spokeswoman Debra Thomas said.

"We can't afford it," said Gail Finan, director of administrative services. If that daily tradition of free coffee and doughnuts were reinstituted, Finan said, "it would be much higher than $25,000."

The current annual cost of tuition, room and board and fees for a full-time Bryn Mawr undergraduate is $21,450.

Finan graduated from Cornell, not Bryn Mawr.

"We didn't have the wonderful nice traditions that Bryn Mawr has," she said, "or had."

So yesterday, students wandered into the Coffee Hour, sampled the earthly delights of the seven plates of pastry and the urns of coffee and sat themselves amid the monastic quiet that lay gently on the eight couches of the lounge.

Quiet?

"So, he goes, like, he says, 'I like your shoes . . . ' and I was, like, pretending I was secure and he wasn't going to, like, shoot me."

Well, relatively quiet.

"I tried to rally for having Coffee Hour every day, last spring," said Kalyani Broderick, 21, standing near the piano in the lounge.

A senior from San Francisco majoring in feminist and gender studies, Broderick said that Coffee Hour had been such a Bryn Mawr tradition that she had used it as an enticement in talking to high school students curious about attending the college.

"There were definitely faculty members there every day," Broderick said. "A lot of times, I would meet my major adviser and it would be the only time I could see her."

Fewer faculty drop by now, Finan said, because faculty offices were close to the library reading room but are far from the Campus Center lounge.

Fewer students drop by, she said, standing in the lounge: "I don't think they know about it very well. If they did know, you'd see more people here."

Fewer Coffee Hours.

Fewer students and fewer faculty at the fewer Coffee Hours.

Watch a tradition wither.

Bryn Mawr used to have a tradition of afternoon teas. Bryn Mawr also used to have a tradition of after-dinner coffee hours in the dorms.

Dead. Both now dead.

They used real silver pots and cutlery at the afternoon teas, Finan said. It was part of the job of housekeeping staff "to polish that silver and keep it shiny."

"When it started to stop was in the mid-'60s," she said, smiling, the mere mention of the counterculture decade explaining the moral wound delivered to that tradition. When teas began and finally died, she said, is lost to memory.

Caroline Rittenhouse, college archivist, recalled the other tradition of after-dinner coffee hours.

"It used to be—in the '50s, when each dorm had its own dining room that after-dinner coffee was served from a great urn."

And, said Rittenhouse, who was a Bryn Mawr student then, that was the time for the leisurely conversation that the hurried day had not afforded.

"It was about 1970s or so," Rittenhouse said, "that the dorms ceased each to have a dining room," and the evening coffee hours died.

So now, all that is left is the morning Coffee Hour—what is left of the Coffee Hour.

Reprinted from the *Philadelphia Inquirer*, March 19, 1992.

Left: Students at coffee hour in Thomas Great Hall, November 1982

Opposite (left and right): Students conversing in a dorm, 1983; students congregated in a dorm room, 1982. Photograph by Stuart Math

BMC SOCIAL LIFE DECLINE MOURNED
Cheryl Kramer, Class of 1991

AH, THE BRYN MAWR COLLEGE PARTY SCENE. "What party scene?" quipped Bryn Mawr freshman Su Kao, laughing at her own joke. But this is no laughing matter. Since the adoption of the new alcohol policy, the social scene at Bryn Mawr has slowed down to a snail's pace, and it is just now beginning to pick up speed.

"It's become apparent that large, dry parties aren't working," asserted former Social Committee Head and Junior Laurie Saroff. They have had "poor attendance" and are a waste of money, she said.

One freshman concurred. "Campus Center parties are generally boring. It's sad but true—parties are better when alcohol is provided."

To where, then, is the search for an alcoholic party leading the party-goers? Recently, there has been an increase in the number of medium-sized parties held in conjunction with "private parties" (or booze for bucks in the basement). Many of these have been successful because they combine a festive atmosphere with the opportunity to drink. It was reported that an "invite" party at Brecon last weekend held upwards of 100 festive people.

Another option in use for those who wish to drink is the tried but true "getting drunk with friends before the party." But this plan does have its drawbacks, according to Bryn Mawr Sophomore Theresa Gordon. She explained that it is not nearly as much fun showing up at a party where everyone is at a different degree of sobriety. "A drunk person and a sober person just can't have a meaningful conversation . . . it's more fun having a few drinks with few friends."

According to one Bryn Mawr senior, small gatherings, with or without alcohol, have been the norm for upperclassmen who "haven't been part of the party scene since [their] sophomore year." More and more underclassmen are catching on. But does that mean the imminent extinction of the large party as we know it?

Doubtful. Bryn Mawr Freshman Meredith Jones has her answer. "Most of the parties I go to are at Haverford," she said with a bi-co gleam in her eye.

Bryn Mawr Junior Lisa Orlandini, the newly appointed Social Committee Head, recognizes this shift. Orlandini, along with Saroff, Self-Government Association President and Sophomore Jaye Fox, and Student Services Coordinator Chuck Heyduk, heads the list of minds at work to restore a successful social life on the Bryn Mawr campus.

Among the ideas this group has come up with include possible plans for a game room with video games and pool tables, a movie series to be shown cheaply in the campus center, the return of Thursday night dorm teas to replace the unsuccessful Dorm Discretionary Fund program, and a possible outdoor festival in the spring complete with bands and good food.

These ideas are expensive, however. Even the additional funds allotted by the administration for post-alcohol policy depression are not enough to pay for them. Heyduk, acknowledging that his suggestion is unpopular, said that more money should be raised through an increase in SGA fees. Even more strongly, Heyduk stressed the need for more effort and enthusiasm from the students to invigorate the social scene.

Small Parties Fund Head Dee Warner suggested using the funds that are made available. Armed with these suggestions, a willing party-goer should be able to hunt out a party suited to her or to hold a successful bash of her own!

Reprinted from the *News* (Bryn Mawr-Haverford), March 3, 1989.

Left: Students and friends gathered in a dorm common area, c. 1980s

Below: Students sitting in a hallway in Erdman, October 1984

SERVICE TRIES TO MATCH DATES
Emily Love, Haverford, Class of 1985

BY STARTING a Haverford/Bryn Mawr Dating Service, two Haverford seniors, Andy Horwitz and Andrew Smolar, hope to improve what they see as the bi-College community's "waning social life."

The students have not attempted to institute a computer dating service in the community. Rather, their service tries to match people for an evening, based solely on general interests, they said.

"We have gotten a fair number of responses," said Horwitz. He hoped that the turnout, which was fairly evenly divided between males and females, would stimulate others to fill out the application. "Once they see people are using it, they'll be more encouraged to try it," he said.

The two received $55 out of the $100 they requested from the budget committee to print letters and pamphlets on places to go on dates in the Philadelphia area, they said. They are applying for grievance because this sum "doesn't even cover the printing costs of what we've already done," said Horwitz.

Student reaction to the plan was varied. While some students interviewed were violently opposed to the idea, saying that it did not fit into the community, others thought that the service was a good idea, with the potential to improve the social life of the college.

One student's dissatisfaction with the service was shown in a statement sent to Horwitz and Smolar anonymously through campus mail. Horwitz remembered it verbatim "because it hurt. It said, 'You two, whoever you are, must be the two most repulsive individuals in this so-called community,'" he said.

One sophomore woman who supported the service expressed hope that it would work and aid the social life. "This campus is very shy on the whole, myself included, and I'm hoping that this will combat that problem," she said.

Added a male senior, "I think it's a very good idea, especially if it would pick up the social life around here."

Most students spoken to were indifferent, saying there was nothing wrong with the idea but they would probably not participate. One junior male commented, "If you're willing to participate and there's a need, what the hell."

One objection to the new service is that it takes away the mystery behind meeting new people, as one sophomore woman said. "I realize that the social life does leave something to be desired at the moment, but there's nothing worse than an unnatural social life. Life is at its best when it's unpredictable."

Responded Smolar, "All we're doing is the following: 'A wants to meet B, so here's the phone number.' None of the fun and mystery of meeting someone new is being tampered with."

One male sophomore raised the issue that Haverford and Bryn Mawr encourage people to do things in groups, rather than twos. Horwitz disagreed. "I don't really see that as true. What that would be saying is that the Haverford and Bryn Mawr ideal is in opposition to people really developing a strong relationship."

Smolar and Horwitz see negative student attitudes as their biggest problem, but they think that, given the chance to explain their idea, they can overcome this problem. "Most of the criticism we face is about dating in general, about putting yourself on the line," said Horwitz. Added Smolar, "After five minutes we've been able to convince most people that it's a good idea."

"I've thought about the stigma that a dating service has, that only 'losers' who cannot otherwise get a date use it, and I don't understand it," said Horwitz. "Does going to a party mean that you can't get friends any other way? I think that if Andrew or I could speak to everyone about their questions or concerns we could convince them that even if the service isn't for them, it is a viable alternative for other people in the community."

Reprinted from the *News* (Bryn Mawr-Haverford), October 8, 1982.

AN ACTIVE SOCIAL LIFE IS YOURS FOR THE MAKING

Beth Green, Class of 1983

SOCIAL LIFE IS ONE of the most talked about subjects in the bi-College community. Opinion varies, however, concerning what makes up a person's social life, what options are available at Haverford and Bryn Mawr and what the quality of social life is.

Impressions depend on a student's expectations of a college social life. In an informal survey, one Haverford freshman said that he had expected to meet many people and to socialize informally with them. A Haverford junior commented, "Social life here is fine. Outside of college no one is going to play activities director."

A Bryn Mawr junior noted, "The social life here is basically what you make of it. You can have one or you cannot have one. Social life to me does not particularly mean partying. You can just go out with your friends. You have the four College system. I've been to Penn and Swarthmore. You do have a choice and it's basically what you do with that choice."

Taking advantage

While those questioned generally agreed that social life was what the individual made it, there was a feeling that many people didn't try to take advantage of activities. One Bryn Mawr junior said, "People in this community study intensely and then grumble about having no social release. They sit around on a Friday or Saturday night instead of calling a few friends. There is a lot to do. It would merely take a few phone calls."

Many do take advantage of the social activities offered throughout the bi-College community. Elon Spar, one of the coordinators of Haverford's film series, estimated that an average Wednesday crowd totals 350–400 students and that an average Saturday crowd totals 800 students. "Many people live for the films," he said.

Aside from the movies and parties Spar did not believe that there were many "big events." He thought that after the Roberts renovation there will be opportunities to host more events, such as concerts and plays. Commenting on social life in general, Spar said that "social life here is impromptu." "One good aspect," he continued, "is that there is no social pressure. No one is forced to go to big parties."

Social Committee organizes

Large parties at Bryn Mawr are funded, in part, by the Social Committee, directed this year by Catherine Searle and Christine Wu. Made up of representatives from each dorm, the committee in the past has been responsible for such events as Casino Night and the Winter Formal. Continuing the tradition of a formal dance is uncertain because of low attendance last year. This year's plans do include a Christmas party and a closed, "interdorm" party.

Small parties at Bryn Mawr are funded, in part, by Self-Government Association (SGA) funds. Many of the students living at Bryn Mawr take advantage of the small party fund. Last semester, 29 checks were written by SGA Treasurer Jim Tanner. Tanner believes that the fund aids social life at the College by making it "affordable for someone to throw their own party."

One dimension

On-campus "rounding out" is possible at both schools. At Bryn Mawr, both Afterwords and 'Forewards provide the bi-College community with places to "hang out." Occupying the former Denbigh dining room, Afterwords, now open seven nights a week, averages 150 people on week nights with 200 people stopping by on the weekends. 'Forewards, opened for just six mornings a week, is a bagel and fresh fruit alternative to breakfast and/or coffee hour. Both are café-style operations.

Small scale social life

Lynn Gordon, student manager of both Afterwords and 'Forewards, believes that both provide a place to socialize. Gordon said, "Social life on a small scale is fine. People do have a small circle of friends. What has lacked in the past has been a place. Afterwords and 'Forewards provide the place. They are a centralized meeting ground for socializing." Gordon thinks that the back room addition of Backwords, a planned penny arcade and ice cream parlor, will help even more to further social life at both schools.

Reprinted from the *News* (Bryn Mawr-Haverford), November 6, 1981.

"SO MANY FREAKS . . . "?
The Truth About the "Backsmoker" Community

Shannon Cochran, Class of 1998;
Jessie Bennett, Class of 1998;
and Christy Kissileff, Class of 1996

WE'RE HAVING A GREAT DEAL of trouble writing this article. We know it's about identity, and think it might be about politics—it's about who we are, anyway, and what people think about us. Beyond that, though, we get into trouble. We are only three people, but we are attempting to represent the entire backsmoker community—a problematic label that has never really been defined. And as to what people think of us—well, how can we know that for sure? The three of us have always been inclined to believe that most of Bryn Mawr doesn't know who we are at all, and wouldn't care if they did. But recently we've heard (secondhand) some rumors about ourselves that would be enormously flattering if they didn't reflect disturbing misconceptions. The fact that no one is hunting us down and burning us at the stake makes it safe for us to laugh at the utter absurdity of the things that are being said, but it would be truly sinister if these rumors reflected the serious views of larger, more influential groups. Apparently, there is some interest in us and what we do.

We're back, then, to Who We Are. The present backsmoker community centers around Erdman Backsmoker, although in the recent past there have been backsmoker cultures in Denbigh and Brecon. We're not sure precisely how old it is, although we think it's been around for at least ten years. These days, it encompasses some fifteen people, including a few alums who remain involved, but it has been much larger in the past. The history of the smokers creates something of a problem in self-definition, because, although there are continuous traditions, student turnover obviously causes constant change in the nature of the community. So what we are, and the public perception of what we are, are hard to separate from what we have been. Also, we are not one, unified group; there are several distinct circles of friends who share the smoker, linked only by a few common traits and interests.

Those traits and interests? When we threw out words, we ended up with *fantasy/sci-fi*, *pagan*, *queer*, *punk*, *feminist*, and *leftist*. Obviously, not all of these labels apply to each of us . . . but that's the flavor. We're (some of) the ones who wear cloaks and goth-y black around campus. We're the ones who howl at every full moon. We're mostly responsible for the Robin Hood May Day plays, and, until recently, the King Arthur May Day plays as well. We host High Table (a celebration in Denbigh backsmoker which is open to all but especially geared toward returning smokerite alums) once every semester. We keep *Elsinore*, the ongoing interactive fantasy novel residing in Erdman backsmoker (by the way, we're always happy to have new writers . . .), as well as the Erdman backsmoker diary (a collective dorm diary), and the Doublestar Library, the collection of fantasy and science fiction also kept in Erdman (check them out!). We run pagan rituals and vampire roleplaying games. We don't, contrary to rumor, drug people, drink blood, feed off hate, sacrifice squirrels (or anything else, except for the occasional *Wall Street Journal*), worship Satan, or plot harm to anyone. A lot of these ideas probably stem from misinformation concerning neo-paganism, the nature-based spirituality that some of us practice. Judith Leone has written an article for the *Bi-Co News* that explains this religion in much greater detail.

The one word that lies at the heart of the issue, the touchstone of the relationship between the backsmoker community and much of the rest of the campus, is "freak." This word is used both as an insult by others, as in "They're all f——ing freaks" (actually said to one of us) or "too many freaks on this campus" (written on the comment board in the Campus Center), and as a term of pride in one's individuality, contrasting the "freak" smokerites with the "normie" mainstreamers. Shannon feels that both usages are objectionable: She thinks everybody is, at some level, deeply weird. Jessie, however, sees labels such as "freak" and "normal" as purely matters of definition (by self or others) and alliance with or separation from perceived "camps," not declarations of intrinsic nature. Therefore, although relishing the self-descriptive "freaks," she feels that the terms have no innate negative or positive charge.

It is easy to get lost in the world of Bryn Mawr identity politics, the baffling attempt to codify the myriad complex wholes of the Bryn Mawr student body. Often, one can get so bogged down that it becomes difficult even to classify one's self. The gist of the matter for Christy is to plumb all the depths of who she is and "out" them to her heart's content. She believes that college might be the only chance she will get to be so wildly and fully herself, and, although her antics might shock the innocent passer-by, she does nothing out of malice. With apologies to any to whom this does not apply, this seems to be an approximate description of most of the present smokerites.

Reprinted from the *College News*, March 5, 1996.

PAGAN TRADITIONS ARE INCREASING AMONG STUDENTS

BRYN MAWR, Pa.—It is exam time at Bryn Mawr College, and in the seasonal tradition, votive offerings have increased at the feet of a plaster statue of Athena, the ancient Greek goddess of wisdom.

"Everybody does this to bring good luck in exams," said Emily Cotlier, a sophomore from Woodbridge, Conn., who added that the tradition dates to at least the 1940's. "They leave a lock of their hair or a half-eaten doughnut—whatever."

Athena is not the only recipient of student devotions. A large bust of Juno, the Roman goddess of light and women, stands outside the campus library and has student adherents. The wife of Jupiter, the god of the sky and weather, Juno is believed to have a strong control over the climate.

Gifts to these goddesses are signs of a growing interest in pagan traditions at Bryn Mawr. Neo-paganism, a nonstructured religion that revives pre-Judeo-Christian practices, has a significant following at the college.

"A Hodgepodge"

Some students said there are 30 neo-pagans at Bryn Mawr, though there might be more who practice secretly.

Neo-pagans, who say they have been on campus since at least the early 1980's, described the nature-oriented religion as self-defined. "Though it's a polyglot spirituality," said Melissa Demian, a sophomore anthropology major from Brookline, Mass., "the best part is what a hodgepodge it is. You can choose to practice and believe in whatever aspects strike you as true." One common thread, she said, is a belief in a pantheon of gods and goddesses.

Most campus neo-pagans say they come from families that are nominally religious, but have found that neo-paganism speaks to them more than mainstream religions do. They say their families are not always aware of their beliefs.

Bryn Mawr's administration is treating neo-paganism the same as other religions. After a cross of talcum powder was made outside the room where neo-pagans were celebrating the Celtic New Year on Oct. 31, President Mary Patterson McPherson and two other campus officials sent a letter to all students condemning the harassment and reminding them that "the college's policy on nondiscrimination on the basis of religion extends its protections to all."

Another pagan tradition revived recently, but not necessarily associated with neo-pagans, is howling at the moon to release tension. Starting last year, students and occasionally professors have congregated at the so-called moon bench on the green in the center of the campus and released angst-ridden shrieks that echo throughout Bryn Mawr. The 40 or so people who participate howl early and respect campus quiet hours.

Reprinted from the *New York Times*, December 16, 1990.

WITCHCRAFT SURVIVES
April Robb, Class of 1989

WITCHCRAFT has been recorded in Bryn Mawr's history for several decades, and the tradition is still carried on.

"Wicca" is an ancient European religion of witchcraft which pre-dates Christianity. According to two witches at Bryn Mawr, it primarily draws women who have rejected other religions, especially the three monotheistic ones, because of anthropocentric (male-centered) perspectives.

Wendy Strandtmann, a Bryn Mawr sophomore who is involved with witchcraft here, "learned about it through feminism" because "along with the rise for women's political needs, there was a rise in spiritual needs, as well."

Strandtmann said she, along with many of the other witches in the bi-College community, belongs to the sect of Wicca which acknowledges both gods and goddesses.

Annemarie Schuetz, another sophomore involved in the sect, agreed: "the most important tenet for us is the equality of power between men and women."

Traditionally, 13 witches join together to form a coven. Six men and seven women are included. One man plays the part of high priest, while one woman fills the role of high priestess.

This organization exemplifies Strandtmann and Schuetz's belief that men and women should have equal status within the religion.

Strandtmann emphasized the "need to have power with, and not over" the opposite sex. She does not, however, deny the difference between male and female, contending that she "feel[s] different energies from men and women, but feel[s] both as strengths."

Strandtmann and Schuetz's group worships three gods and three goddesses. The gods are related to different seasons, while the goddesses represent separate phases of the moons.

For many witches at Bryn Mawr, worship also includes paying tribute to the statue of Athena in Thomas Great Hall. Students leave gifts and libations for her. Witches worship the deities according to their personal preferences. Strandtmann, for instance, "like[s] to go out on a new or full moon and try to feel one with the earth."

Wicca has its own network of holidays. There are eight major ones within each year, including spring equinox, autumn equinox and Candlemas.

Strandtmann believes that there is "widespread interest in [the religion and its practices] at Bryn Mawr, but relatively few constant practitioners."

Both she and Schuetz surmised that this is due to a fear of harassment by fellow students. They explained that in past years, witches have suffered because of their peers' misconceptions of what they actually do.

Schuetz and Strandtmann have encountered students who believe that the practices of Bryn Mawr witches include the slaughtering of animals and the cursing of fellow students. Wicca is not associated with Satanism and does not share its rituals.

"One of the most important things about this religion," concludes Strandtmann, "is a love for life, a feeling part of the life of the planet."

Reprinted from the *News* (Bryn Mawr-Haverford), November 15, 1985.

Opposite: Page from a Denbigh backsmoker diary, dated April 1981

PARADE NIGHT
A COLLEGE TRADITION

TUESDAY BEGINS TRADITIONAL GAME AT BRYN MAWR
Slightly Singed Senior Tells of Parade Night

Dear Freshmen:

Next Tuesday, September 30, is Parade Night, your first introduction to that all too well-known phrase "Bryn Mawr tradition." 1952's yearbook dubbed Parade Night, "Ring around the Fire." The event is, as a matter of fact, a distant relative of "Ring-around-the-Rosie." The principal difference is that it is a "grown-ups'" game, played by very much grown-up Bryn Mawr freshmen and sophomores. The object of this game is for you to compose a song (preferably with a tune that fits the somewhat limited repertoire of the Fireman's Band—"Farmer in the Dell," "For He's a Jolly Good Fellow," etc.)—and keep the song a secret from your opponents, the sophomores. They will try diligently to steal the song and write a parody of it. On Tuesday night, at Pem arch, you, surrounded by be-robed, be-capped, and (of course) dignified juniors and seniors, will parade to the field behind Rhoads, where a large bonfire, surrounded by the nasty ol' sophomores, will be waiting for you. As the procession from Pem travels to the fire, the freshmen are to sing their song with as much spirit as they can

muster (this is a test of whether or not you are a spirited class). Then, if you have been clever, the sophomores will concede victory to you in song, but if they have been cleverer, they will try to out-sing you with their parody. In any case, much singing and noise will probably ensue, and (again depending on the spirit of your class) a small brawl. Step singing ends the evening on a quieter, more musical note. Good luck, Freshmen! Keep your song hidden well, watch out for sophomoric spies, and don't burn your toes!

Sincerely,

A Slightly Singed Senior

Reprinted from the *College News*, September 28, 1952.

Top: Students in the cloisters during Parade Night, 2009. Photograph by Jan Trembley, class of 1975

Bottom: Students with their lanterns, Parade Night, 2009. Photograph by Jan Trembley

Opposite: Parade Night poster, c. 2009

RAIDERS OF THE LOST ARCHIVES: 100 YEARS OF STEP SINGS
Stephanie Olen and Elhanna Porter, both Class of 2007

SOPHIAS PHILAI PAROMEN . . . So begins the start of the step sing, the cornerstone of Bryn Mawr tradition. But since this year's first step sing didn't quite go off without a hitch, writers Olen and Porter, fearless Raiders of the Lost Archives, thought they'd delve into the musical history of the step sing. This week's column is in honor of the freshman class who, aside from being thoroughly uneducated on proper step sings, conveniently pester their customs people into making sure that certain articles get written on time.

Fall 1908. The newly arrived freshmen are paraded from Pem Arch down to the Hockey Fields. A roaring bonfire awaits them. The freshmen create a circle around the fire and the sophomores form another around the new frosh. As soon as one's arrived, the freshmen burst out into their class song:

Come march and sing, of 1908
These happy days to celebrate.
We'll sing the praises of Bryn Mawr,
And make the song ring clear and far.
As birds in air, we're gay and free.
And yet thy willing slaves are we.
Long may we serve thee loyally,
Long may we serve thee loyally!
Though now thy stately towers we see,
Yet in the future, memory
Will call to mind those happy days
When as a class we sang thy praise
Then may it be that truly we
May say in all fidelity,
Bryn Mawr we've served thee loyally,
Bryn Mawr we've served thee loyally!

They had written and learned the song in complete secrecy. Keeping it hidden from the sophomores who, somewhat more intensely than today, had been shadowing the freshmen, hiding in their closets and under their beds. Anything to steal the song's melody and parody it! After the freshmen finished singing, the sophomores would break into their parody song. If the sophomores failed to steal the melody, the students would erupt into applause and so began the first step sing of the year. This would hardly be the only step sing of 1908, however. One hundred years ago, step sings were held every clear night in autumn and spring, led by the seniors, as they are now, on the steps of Taylor. The sophomores, their sister class, sat across from them on Thomas green. The juniors sat at their left, and their sister class, the freshmen, sat across from the juniors at the seniors' right. The songs mistresses stood in their billowing black robes, ready to lead their individual classes in song.

Well into the 1950's step sings were still held on almost every clear night in the fall and spring (suddenly our three a year don't look like so much, do they?). At the turn of the century, Mawrtyrs sang Greek hymns ("Pallas Athena" started out as a class song) and traditional college cheer songs. Towards the middle of the century, the songs, like the women themselves, were still very traditional; "White Carol Bells" and "New England on a Summer's Day" were two favorites. The 1970s brought forth the classic "Cocaine Bill," a tune that included such memorable lyrics as: "This is the story of a Bryn Mawr wench / Who began to study her French; / That's why she started in to sniff cocaine, / In to [*students sniff loudly*] cocaine." And "Casanova from Villanova / Gave her a shot that bowled her over: / Ah, Bebe have a little—on me, / Have a little—on me." Wow, those 70s sure were wild, weren't they? The 80s, though, were truly a renaissance of song; they saw the penning of such classics as "If I Only Had Some Grain," "What I Did for Lab," and "Academic Life."

Well, it's a beautiful fall afternoon, and we raiders are finding that the outside is singing an irresistible siren's song of its own. Before we leave you, though, we'd like to give a cheer to school spirit, bat robes, lanterns, drunken seniors, confused freshmen, and off-key singing. So until next time loyal readers, when we bring you another thrilling installment of Raiders of the Lost Archives!

Reprinted from the College News, *September 15, 2004.*

Above: Step sing with seniors on the steps of Taylor Hall, May 1997

Top right: Parade Night T-shirt design, 1990

Opposite: Page from Traditions Mistress's notebook with Parade Night pointers, signed by Robyn Ruffer, class of 1990, and dated September 22, 1988

DETERMINED LEADERSHIP: 1978–1997

Robyn Ruffer

9-22-88) Parade Night —

I think parade night was meant to be a little sloppy. It's a chance for everyone to practice and for the freshmen to see what a step sing is.

A few pointers:
1) Let the freshmen practice 1 to 1½ hours before the event starts in Pem Dance Studio.
2) The other songsmistresses will organize their classes.
3) Buy candy for the juniors to throw to the freshmen, their sister class.
4) It's held on Denbigh Green with the seniors' backs to Denbigh, facing Taylor.

[diagram: Frosh / Sophs | Seniors / Juniors]

Use as much of the Green as you want. There's no need for people to be squished.

★ 5) Have the freshmen sing their Parade Night song while they walk through the classes!
6) At the end of the step sing, while everyone else is singing "Good Night" the freshmen leave by walking toward the Computer Center, through the other classes.

McBRIDE PROGRAM

BMC ADMITS OLDER WOMEN
Laura Miller, Class of 1988

THE KATHARINE E. McBRIDE SCHOLAR PROGRAM is a recently established program for older women who wish to earn bachelor's degrees. Applications will be available by Feb. 15, and the first admitted students will enter the program in the fall semester of 1986. The program has been developed by its future director, Ann Salyard, Dean Pruitt of the Division of Special Studies, and the 11-member Division of Special Studies council made up of faculty and administration. The aim of this program is to give women over the age of 25 an opportunity to successfully matriculate into Bryn Mawr's undergraduate program.

According to Ann Salyard, assistant director of the Division of Special Studies, there are many women who, although already successful with current occupations and achievements, feel that earning a degree is still important to them. Although these women are competent and gifted, entering a full-time college program after a ten- or twenty-year absence from the academic world can be intimidating. The program, typically completed in two years, is basically a preparation for admission to Bryn Mawr as a full-time bachelor's degree candidate.

Because a woman applying to the McBride scholar program will be very different from a traditional seventeen- or eighteen-year-old applying to undergraduate school, Salyard recognizes that the criteria for admission must be different as well. According to Salyard, high school transcripts and even current SAT scores may have little relevance as a measure of a thirty-year-old woman's academic abilities. Instead, the admissions committee for the McBride scholar program acknowledges that life experience and actual "doing" is as valuable as high SAT scores. They will ask applicants for credentials that will demonstrate an ability to do Bryn Mawr work. Reports on major community projects, examples of freelance writing, art portfolios, or demonstrations of organizational skills through business achievements are examples of credentials looked for. Above all, Salyard would like a Katharine McBride scholar to be "a strongly motivated woman who wants to earn a degree at a highly selective women's liberal arts college."

Once admitted to the program, the McBride scholar is given a structured series of entry-level courses. The program is designed to allow the students to take light course loads at flexible times. Salyard says that the reasoning behind this is to give these women time to adjust their lives to balancing academic work with jobs and family. For this reason, three courses are the maximum load allowed a semester, and many will take only one or two. Each McBride scholar is required to take a special section of English 015/016, Math 002, and a choice of laboratory sciences, foreign languages, and humanities. The special section of English 015/016 is taught by Jo Ellen Parker, and will be attended only by McBride Scholars. Although taught with the same expectations as other freshman English sections, the material will be directed toward specific interests of more mature women. This class will also be part of a support network for women, giving them an opportunity to meet each other and to share common experiences. There will also be seminars and workshops to help smooth what could be a difficult transition into academic life. According to Salyard, many women are intimidated by the thought of a full-time program at an institution like Bryn Mawr. The structure of the McBride program is designed to build confidence by starting slowly, while simultaneously giving the student time to adjust career and home life to academic work.

After completing 6 to 8 courses, typically accomplished in 2 years, the McBride scholar is ready to apply to the undergraduate school through the regular admissions process. Although not a degree candidate while in the McBride program, the student can transfer all credits earned once accepted as a full-time Bryn Mawr undergraduate. The McBride scholar now has a record of 6 to 8 courses to show to the admissions office, which will work with the Division of Special Studies on the admissions process. Once admitted, the McBride scholar will have 6 to 8 credits toward an A.B., and hopefully all the tools to succeed in a rigorous liberal arts program. Ann Salyard feels the Katharine E. McBride scholar program is extremely valuable because "there are many talented and intelligent women who, unable to complete college at an earlier time, are, as adults, now in a position to do so. This program will make a Bryn Mawr degree accessible to women, regardless of age and formal traditional academic credentials. In addition, the program will be valuable to Bryn Mawr itself, by adding to the campus community a group of students who will bring rich life experience to their academic work."

Reprinted from the *College News*, February 5, 1986.

FIRST McBRIDE SCHOLARS TO GRADUATE THIS SPRING
Simona Goi, Class of 1991

NINA SPRECHER, Charlotte Espy, and Eleanore Fields will be the first McBride scholars to graduate from Bryn Mawr this spring. Together with approximately 45 other women, they have taken part in the Katharine E. McBride program, offered through the Division of Special Studies, which is designed to allow qualified women who are beyond the traditional college age to work toward a degree from Bryn Mawr.

"Part of both the difficulty and the excellence of this program is the fact that it is not in the evening, it is not in the summer, and thus it offers exactly the same kind of experience that traditional students have," Dean of Special Studies Jean Wu said. "It integrates women into the life of the college, and while they gain an experience they had never had, they also bring the contribution of real life experience and wisdom. It is a wonderful relationship."

...The most difficult aspect of the program for these women is to finance it, Wu said, especially because they have to face many other responsibilities, such as a family or a job. "This is an easily forgotten population," Wu added, "since most institutions focus on the 18- to 22-year-olds. We always have to work hard to find money to support the program."

Despite some of the problems with the program, the three McBride scholars graduating in May strongly support it, and all feel they have gained almost indescribable satisfaction from their experiences at Bryn Mawr.

Sprecher said that this was definitely an incredible experience that changed her life 100 percent. "I acquired self-esteem, and I feel like there is nothing I can't do at this point.

"What an extraordinarily rare privilege to go through college with my children," Sprecher continued enthusiastically. She became a McBride scholar as her son was a freshman at Brown, and she had the opportunity to share with him and with her daughter every aspect of the college experience, from writing papers to spending spring break on the beach.

Sprecher, who is a Growth and Structure of Cities major, began studying architecture as a member of the Fairmount Park House Guide program. She immediately loved this subject, she said, and when she found out that Bryn Mawr offered the cities program she thought it would be perfect.

Sprecher has a very positive impression of the McBride experience. "I came in at the beginning, I saw the seeds planted and I knew the program needed time to grow," she explained. "It has been a bumpy road, but overall it is a good program."

According to Sprecher, the McBride program essentially needs more publicity, and the presence of a McBride representative at the trustees meeting would definitely help. "As a broad statement we could say that everything traditional undergraduates do we should be able to do also," she added, "and we need to be known to do this."

Sprecher finds that McBride scholars are capable of bringing a great contribution to the community, not only in terms of

> "Finally, it's my turn and I want the best education I can have."

different experiences, but also in terms of concrete help to younger students to enter the professional world.

"As I was writing my thesis, I noticed that I was able to get in and out of critical offices and to obtain interviews easily," she said. "Because of my age I am taken more seriously and I have better contacts than traditional undergraduates, and I could be of help to my classmates. As they are graduating and looking for jobs, I could refer them and recommend them."

On the other hand, Sprecher is enthusiastic about the diversity of the Bryn Mawr community, and she feels that this has helped her to acquire a global perspective.

This view is also shared by Eleanore Fields, a political science major, concentrating in international relations and comparative politics, who feels that diversity at Bryn Mawr is one of the best things about the institution. "It really opened up my mind, and now I want to have a global view," said Fields.

After graduating she is interested in working for a company that is involved in international relations.

Fields said she came to Bryn Mawr primarily for its reputation for excellent education. "Also I was looking for an academic challenge, and I got what I expected," she added.

As she came in she did not feel adequately prepared, she said, and the first courses were very hard for her.

However, Fields believes that she would not change anything in the program from the academic point of view, because, for her, academics are what make Bryn Mawr so good. She thinks, though, that women need to be told all the facts about the program so that they can be prepared to meet the challenge.

Fields would also like to see more direct support from the administration and more space for McBride scholars in the activities of the community, like the student papers for instance, so that they can be a broader representation of the student body.

Charlotte Espy enjoyed meeting the younger students on an equal level, and she defines her experience at Bryn Mawr as a McBride scholar as very exciting, even if very different. She felt that at the beginning the program was a little disorganized, but she is aware that it has been undergoing a lot of changes, and that Wu is working on reestablishing it.

Espy feels that all the McBride scholar women are exceptional and very capable people. She said she thinks it was an experience just to meet people like them, especially because they were united by a stronger sense of camaraderie than traditional students.

Reprinted from the News *(Bryn Mawr-Haverford), April 20, 1990.*

SO WHAT IS A McBRIDE, ANYWAY?
Mary Green, Class of 1994

WE HAVE COME HERE from many walks of life. We have come for many reasons, and in this respect, McBrides are no different from the regular, traditional-age students. We, too, are seeking quality educations; and we too are interested in carving out futures for ourselves, like many other students at Bryn Mawr. When we first arrived, many of us were excited at the same. Some of us are filled with certainty, confidence, and serious expectations, while others of us are doubtful, lack confidence, and are filled with trepidation. We all hope we have made the right decision in coming to Bryn Mawr. Sometimes it takes a while to find out.

It is not easy to be a McBride scholar, but nobody has said it would be; they say instead that it is do-able. We are told that Bryn Mawr has such a high success rate with students because the expectation is that they will succeed. The reason that students do succeed is because of all the resources at their command and their willingness to make use of what is available. It is challenge, they say, but like other students, we welcome the challenge. That challenge begins in our first class, on the first day, with the first professor we meet. But that is just the first academic challenge, which is not necessarily the first challenge we confront in coming to Bryn Mawr.

Some of us have shared-family obligations, by which I mean that our education necessarily involves a partner and children. Some of us are single parents which again involves some other person in our education. Some of us have ourselves only; so our responsibilities vary as do our support networks. Those of us without family obligations and without a ready-made support system must build our own. The source is often other McBrides, who meet each other first in the McBride section of English 015/016.

We all start out with the same dean, Jean Wu, who must juggle the needs of the first-year McBrides, as well as the veteran McBrides who are still only provisionally matriculated. There are differences between the two groups of McBrides.

First-year McBrides have a rigorous schedule. Their day (I call it that because it is the one day that all the first-year McBrides are on campus) looks like this: Tuesday, 11:00–12:20, Math Workshop; 2–4, English 015/016; 4:30–6:00, McBride Seminar; I know that may not seem like a whole lot of classes, but Tuesdays are a long day for many McBrides, who, as commuters, cannot come for the math workshop and then go to a room of their own to relax or study. Many simply hang out in the campus center or go to the McBride Lounge or the library. But most of them are here from 11:00 A.M. to at least 6:00 P.M. These hours do not reflect their traveling time to and from Bryn Mawr. Some take public transportation, some drive, some come from as far away as Harrisburg. In addition to the first-year Tuesday schedule, some first-year students take additional classes because the program is designed to be self-paced. Additional classes are necessary for those of us who need to take student loans in order to pay for our education. And there are quite a few of us. Juggling time, however, is a part of the challenge that is Bryn Mawr.

. . . I understand that many students are curious and want to know more. We do have a newsletter that is published two or three times a year and I invite the student body to read it and ask us questions. We welcome you, as you have all welcomed us.

Reprinted from the *College News*, April 1, 1993.

---

single
coupled
mothers
daughters
grandmothers
chefs
sheriffs
preschool teachers
actresses
childcare workers
carpenters
homemakers
artists
financial consultants
nurses
computer technicians
bankers
community activists
electricians
secretaries
horticulturalists
musicians
beauticians
medical technologists
poets
journalists
novelists

PRESIDENT CLINTON AT BRYN MAWR

CLINTON VISITS CAMPUS

TELEVISION VIEWERS OF C-SPAN and national network news got an eyeful of the College under brilliant skies on December 13.

In return for casting a decisive vote on the President's budget package last August, U.S. Rep. Marjorie Margolies-Mezvinsky (D-PA) asked him to participate in a conference on cutting federal entitlements programs, a move that she and many in her conservative district favor.

Bryn Mawr was chosen to host the day-long event from over 40 area institutions considered for their locations and facilities. Although the conference was organized by Margolies-Mezvinsky and the Congressional Institute for the Future (CIF, a Washington, D.C.-based bi-partisan non-profit organization), a committee of bi-college staff, faculty and students spent six weeks planning for the event. Some 500 bi-college volunteers helped accommodate the 2,500 participants. Kathryn Roth '86, one of two lead advance staffers for the President at the White House, coordinated his participation, and Julie Demeo '92, who works for the Department of Agriculture, took a special assignment as assistant press liaison for the White House. The conference was funded through CIF; the College provided the gymnasium seating and the lunch for the President and the Congresswoman's guests in Thomas.

An editorial in the *Main Line Times* noted that "some may have taken issue with some of the information or participants in the conference itself. No one who attended and surely none who were involved can take issue with the professional, patient, considerate and well-organized people of Bryn Mawr College who made it happen. The volunteers were in themselves a tribute to the institution and the community. Administrators, students, faculty, staff and alumnae/i were ready to tackle any and all jobs once the word got out that the conference would take place at Bryn Mawr."

Although serious discussions of issues, not personalities, drew the thousands attending the conference, hundreds of students and area residents gathered in a fenced-off area in front of Thomas well before Clinton began his walk from the Bern-Schwartz Gymnasium to the luncheon in the Great Hall. (Students raised periodic cheers of "Anassa Kata" while waiting, including one that ended, "Where's Hillary?") Clinton slowly made his way around the perimeter of the enclosure, shaking hands with every person he could reach, and made a short address to the crowd before going in to eat. Another thrill for many was the sight of two Sikorsky and two Boeing CH-46 Sea Knight helicopters landing on the soccer fields. William H. Taft is the only other president to have visited the campus while in office, and he came up alone from Washington by train.

Top: President Clinton speaking on campus, December 13, 1993. Photograph by S. Lyons

Bottom: President Clinton with members of the Bryn Mawr community, December 13, 1993

The conference featured panels on health care, jobs and welfare, retirement programs and steps for the future. Clinton chaired the panel on health care; during his keynote address, he argued that controlling health-care costs instead of cutting benefits was the most effective way to control the federal deficit. Speakers and moderators included House Speaker Tom Foley (D-WA); Sens. John C. Danforth (R-MO), Harris Wofford (D-PA and Bryn Mawr president emeritus) and Bob Kerrey (D-NE); former U.S. Sens. Warren B. Rudman and Paul Tsongas; former New Jersey Gov. Thomas Kean; Office of Management and Budget Director Leon E. Panetta; Secretary of Health and Human Services Donna Shalala; Laura D'Andrea Tyson, chair of the President's Council of Economic Advisors; Patricia Ireland, president of the National Organization for Women; and Jonathan Karl, co-founder of Third Millennium, a political action group for people in their 20s who are angry about the $4 trillion national debt. Alumnae speakers were Office of Management and Budget Deputy Director Alice Mitchell Rivlin '52, and Dean of the School of Social Work and Social Research Ruth Mayden, M.S.S. '70.

College President Mary Patterson McPherson, Ph.D. '69, told the audience, "It seems important to note that this public, bipartisan discussion is taking place on a college campus ... Educational institutions ... encourage the rational consideration of the complex and difficult issues facing our society. We thrive on a rich mix of views and plan for our students to consider a variety of positions, to base their opinions on fact, and to develop a set of beliefs on which they can act." Noting that the day's program would be like a college seminar, she made the participants honorary students of Bryn Mawr College.

One of the many gifts for Clinton collected in a big box by Secret Service agents ended up on the presidential torso several weeks later. While golfing in Hilton Head, N.C., in early January, Clinton was photographed wearing a long-sleeved red jersey that reads "Bryn Mawr College Physics Department, 1985–1994, 109 Years of Women in Classically Forbidden Regions." A bemused White House reporter writing for the *New York Times* wondered "exactly which constituency (or gift-giver) Mr. Clinton was trying to appease" by wearing the shirt. The slogan, created by Ursula Adrienne Allen, '94, refers not only to women breaking out of traditional roles, but to the distinction between classical and quantum mechanics—a distinction explained in full in an amusing follow-up story in the *Philadelphia Inquirer*.

Reprinted from the *Bryn Mawr Alumnae Bulletin*, Winter 1994.

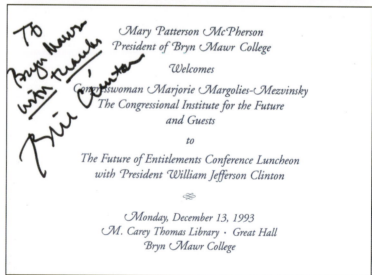

Top: President Clinton (center) with Mary Patterson McPherson (left), Alice Rivlin (second from right), and others, December 13, 1993. Photograph by S. Lyons.

Bottom: Invitation signed by President Clinton, to the Future of Entitlements Conference luncheon, signed by President Clinton, December 13, 1993

DETERMINED LEADERSHIP: 1978–1997

Bold Visions
for Today and Tomorrow:
1997—2010

THE WORK OF THE TASK FORCE ON BALANCING MISSION AND RESOURCES

One

The principal challenge facing the Task Force on Balancing Mission and Resources is that of building—within a context of shared governance—a process for making difficult institutional decisions and acting upon them. Functioning, as its members have, through newly conceived structures and re-imagined working relationships, its practice is by definition emergent: it progresses along non-linear paths; it introduces correctives; it acknowledges missteps. We began almost two years ago by carefully sketching the outline of an annual structural gap (approximately six million dollars) between Bryn Mawr's existing funding levels and those appropriate to our aspirations. We examined possible econ-omies and potential sources of new revenue. While we were working, the College both successfully completed an ambitious fundraising campaign and significantly advanced its ability to manage enrollment and endowment. Between 2006 and 2008, we thus reduced the gap by over two million dollars. The model before you today presents multiple paths to reducing that gap even further; it takes it, over the course of five years, to less than 20% of its original size.

A College budget is a puzzle made up of many pieces and, as you can see, we have examined a good number of them. However, we have spent much of our time in the past year and a half on a single piece—Bryn Mawr's commitment to graduate education. This is the topic that rises to the surface every time we face a budget crunch. It is, after all, a commitment that genuinely renders us unique among our peers, an instance in which we choose to define ourselves as a radically different form of liberal arts college. It is also a commitment that in most contexts—and at every level of our organization—prompts fervent disagreement: it silences those opposed to Bryn Mawr graduate study who fear alienating their colleagues, and it produces flurries of alumnae/i letters and emails. There is no small eagerness for this debate of a quarter century (or more) to come to an end. Indeed, a decade ago, our Middle States Team observed divisiveness within our faculty rooted in our graduate history and warned: "If continued unchecked, the division is bound to weaken the institution, erode its fine reputation, and drain the productive energy of its members." Lack of resolution, too, has a cost. And though consensus cannot be achieved (intelligent, thoughtful and impassioned colleagues continue to hold valid positions on both sides), we have through this process found at the very least both a majority view and a will to listen to one another. In addition, thanks to the labors of two extremely hardworking subcommittees, we have meaningful data on both quality and cost (including opportunity cost) that can inform reasoned decisions going forward. We also have, I believe, a still keener sense of common academic values that run just below the surface of our disagreements—a shared sense that Bryn Mawr's center is positioned (as it has been historically) on a vital, rigorous undergraduate mission that is both demanding and exciting enough to engage young women who share the intense intellectual commitment, the purposeful vision of their lives, and the desire to make a meaningful contribution to the world that ultimately make them "characteristic" Bryn Mawrters. Any resolutions regarding the future of graduate education at Bryn Mawr, the Task Force therefore concluded, must serve to advance in significant ways our core mission: undergraduate education.

Two

Our excellent reputation, both national and international, is in large part driven by a history of academic pre-eminence earned to a significant degree by our historic engagement in graduate study. Our driving conviction, be it based in fact or enabling fiction, is that we take scholarly and academic achievement more seriously than our peers. This was M. Carey Thomas' vision; it is the bedrock of our reputation; it is who we are. Graduate and professional programs contribute to fostering both "intense intellectual commitment" and a sense of making a "meaningful contribution to the world" at an institutional level; in this context, the Task Force believes they can do more. Many of us brought a healthy skepticism to the Bryn Mawr scene: we wondered if our graduate programs were the vestigial traces of an era long past, and, in the absence of thorough and systematic data, we worried about cost and quality.

We have within the past six months undergone significant peer reviews of both graduate schools: the first by an ad hoc committee of highly respected graduate deans and academic officers, and the second by a re-accreditation team appointed by the national social work accrediting agency. Peer review is a defining principle of the academy. Presses, editorial boards, foundations, granting agencies, colleges and universities all depend upon it as the gatekeeper of publication, promotion and tenure. Bryn Mawr relies upon it internally, in the forms of the Committee on Academic Priorities and the Committee on Appointments, to advise the President and the Board on who joins and who continues on our faculty. We insist upon the regular peer review of our departments and programs. I believe that, within this context, it is our responsibility to take very seriously what our peer reviewers have said. Granted, not every detail of their reports will prove correct, but their overarching assessments should strongly influence our decisions.

What is striking about both of these reports (and the second exists only in the form of an exit interview at this stage) is their enthusiastic endorsement of who we are and what we do (with, of course, recommended changes) as well as their excitement about our potential. Our social work reviewers deemed the GSSWSR [Graduate School of Social Work and Social Research] a "gem" that truly occupies a special position in quality social work education; our Arts and Sciences reviewers saw in us a unique opportunity to "do graduate education right." They also gave us three options going forward: (1) eliminate all graduate programs, (2) maintain the status quo, or (3) proceed differently. Both the Task Force and I have chosen the path to which they obviously would lead us, i.e., to "proceed differently" in every graduate and professional program that goes forward. What our reviewers saw in us was the exciting possibilities that our small size presents to serve both our graduate students and our undergraduates by fostering a richer intellectual and social community.

The Task Force's proposed principles and practices advance at least two categories of change that are real and substantive and that would refocus the operations of all graduate programs. First, these measures seek to take maximum advantage of our distinctive small liberal arts setting by fostering both vertical and horizontal integration. Our small size should make us collaborative, nimble, interdisciplinary, flexible and uniquely attentive to student needs. Vertically, we can enhance constructive graduate-undergraduate interaction on both curricular and interpersonal levels; and horizontally, we can promote collaborative relationships with faculty and students inside and outside the disciplines. Such integration should also permit some administrative and instructional efficiencies. And second, the Task Force's principles and practices seek a graduate roster "suitable to the scale, scope, and nature of our small, highly selective, liberal arts, undergraduate women's college environment." Last year's Carnegie reclassification should remind us that we must reassess scale in relation to the proportion of graduate degrees awarded to undergraduate degrees. If most of our graduate and professional programs are indeed "gems," now is the time for shaping and polishing them by establishing concrete objectives and cost controls that make them work both within their own setting and within the overarching—predominantly undergraduate—priorities of the College.

There is clearly a cost to keeping graduate education (about 1.5 million dollars annually, not to mention opportunity costs), and a cost to letting go of it. That second cost involves, I believe, the tarnishing of our national reputation as an academic and scholarly leader, the alienating of a significant subset of loyal alumnae/i, and the demoralization of that almost 50% of our dedicated faculty who are deeply invested in their graduate programs. The wholesale closing of respected programs would further communicate that the College is in financially exigent circumstances, which it is not. We, as a community, clearly need to become more strategic and more accountable builders and stewards of a sustainable financial base, but we are not poised on the brink of financial ruin. Indeed, after many years of skeptical deliberation and now informed by the data so comprehensively assembled by the Task Force, I firmly conclude that an appropriate measure of graduate commitment "done right" is part of what will continue to make Bryn Mawr truly Bryn Mawr.

Three

I therefore write to request your endorsement of the work of the Task Force thus far. We bring forward both a sequence of proposals for addressing Bryn Mawr's projected structural gap (which we have now modeled as moving from an estimated six million dollars to an estimated one million) as well as a related sequence of proposals to advance change in graduate education at the College (which includes some economies and efficiencies). These proposals acknowledge both the great distance we have come and the reality that setting priorities and managing the

> BRYN MAWR'S CENTER IS POSITIONED (AS IT HAS BEEN HISTORICALLY) ON A VITAL, RIGOROUS UNDERGRADUATE MISSION THAT IS BOTH DEMANDING AND EXCITING ENOUGH TO ENGAGE YOUNG WOMEN WHO SHARE THE INTENSE INTELLECTUAL COMMITMENT, THE PURPOSEFUL VISION OF THEIR LIVES, AND THE DESIRE TO MAKE A MEANINGFUL CONTRIBUTION TO THE WORLD THAT ULTIMATELY MAKE THEM "CHARACTERISTIC" BRYN MAWRTERS.

College's fiscal challenges require an ongoing, shared-governance process that is acutely attentive to our ever-changing competitive environment. We therefore propose an initial short-term timeline for task-force work with faculty to articulate specific recommendations for graduate programs that conform to our framework of principles and practices. We propose to work with colleagues from departments both with and without graduate programs, recognizing that, in taking seriously our faculty survey (which showed approximately 75% of faculty to be positively disposed toward Bryn Mawr's graduate commitments), we may have paid too little attention to the concerns of those who remain skeptical about, or opposed to, those commitments. Our final report in April will spell out program specifics and chart a path for future work that will maintain our momentum. In seeking to appoint an Acting Dean of Graduate Studies and an Acting Director of the Graduate School of Social Work and Social Research as of summer 2008, we would place the further modeling and implementation of an integrated graduate agenda in their hands. Their work will, of course, be overseen by the Provost, the President and, ultimately, the Board. However, this arrangement will permit the Provost to focus her leadership on a comprehensive review and revitalization of the undergraduate curriculum (currently being initiated by the appropriate faculty committees) to occur in tandem with our Middle States re-accreditation process, and the President to focus on advancing the substance and the visibility of our core mission. In April (and in consultation with our President-Elect) we also intend to bring forward a proposal for a multi-constituency strategic planning committee that will advise on addressing future projections of structural gaps and on setting institutional priorities with an eye to responding to competitive pressures, including the changing undergraduate financial aid landscape. Though the work ahead will be challenging, the work to date has generated in me a renewed sense of institutional accomplishment and of creative opportunity.

Reprinted from a photocopy of a letter, Nancy Vickers to Members of the Board of Trustees, February 7, 2008.

Above: Bryn Mawr Posse program students, class of 2012, at pre-collegiate training, Boston. Courtesy of The Posse Foundation, 2008

Page 344: Lily Mengesha, class of 2010, English major and founding member of People in Color, a bi-college performance group that addresses controversial social issues through theater, comedy, dance, and music, December 17, 2007. Photograph by Jim Roese

INAUGURATION OF NANCY VICKERS

VICKERS INAUGURATED AS SEVENTH PRESIDENT OF BMC

Preeti Advani and Sarah Wahlberg, both class of 2000

ON DECEMBER 6, 1997, Nancy J. Vickers was inaugurated as the seventh President of Bryn Mawr College. The inauguration was the culmination of a process that involved nearly three years of consideration and five months of introduction. With only six former presidents and only four previous ceremonies (the first two presidents of the College did not have inaugural ceremonies), President Vickers' inauguration was truly a momentous occasion in the history of the College.

The inauguration, held in Goodhart Hall, began with a Prelude performed by the Gabrieli Consort. The participants in the Academic Procession, which consisted of the Grand Marshal, student and staff representatives, alumnae class representatives, faculty and associate administrators, faculty emeriti, delegates from a variety of colleges and universities, Haverford and Bryn Mawr administrators, Haverford College Managers, Bryn Mawr College Trustees, and Platform Party members, all entered the hall cloaked in colorful academic robes. With students, alumna representatives, faculty, and staff, as well as President Vickers' friends, colleagues, and relatives in attendance, it seemed as though the entire academic community had come to see the College present the new president.

Barbara Janney Trimble '60, Chairman of the Board of Trustees, performed the introduction and welcome, recognizing the former presidents or members of their families present at the ceremony. The introduction was followed by a reading by Betsy Zubrow Cohen '63, Vice Chairman of the Board of Trustees and Chairman of the Presidential Search Committee. She selected a passage from the letters of Marianne Moore, describing the College and its wonders.

Next, a multitude of representatives from the community welcomed President Vickers. On behalf of the faculty, Julia H. Gaisser, Secretary of the General Faculty, expressed her assurance that Nancy Vickers would continue in the College's tradition of "dedicated presidents." Valencia Powell, Representative of the Staff Association, offered a bit of advice from her thirty years at Bryn Mawr. Having worked with three past presidents, Ms. Powell stressed that "keeping a healthy sense of humor . . . will help you survive."

Representing the undergraduate student body, Dana Linnell Simpson '98, President of the Self-Government Association, wished the new president "happiness, laughter, and achievement" in her new position. Also wishing President Vickers the best of luck were Sarah J. Kielt, President of the Graduate School of Arts and Sciences Student Association, and Cynthia Christina Chalker, Representative of the Graduate School of Social Work and Social Research Student Association.

On behalf of the alumnae of the College, Susan Webb Hammond, President of the Alumnae

Association, who had, along with the rest of the Alumnae Association, installed President Vickers as an honorary alumna last month, was the last to welcome her, describing her as "a valued colleague and friend."

Among the representatives from other academic institutions, Thomas R. Tritton, President of Haverford College, greeted President Vickers with high hopes for future bi-college cooperation. President Tritton formulated an amusing scenario about a hypothetical Central Casting being burdened with the awesome responsibility of finding someone to play the President of Bryn Mawr College. That someone, Central Casting was told, must be a scholar, a teacher, an administrator, and a leader! President Tritton's amusing scenario described the dilemma of Central Casting as they searched alphabetically through their files for someone who could meet the rigorous qualifications. They labored through the alphabet, with growing frustration, until suddenly, within the V files, appeared: "Vickers, Nancy J." And so, someone was finally found, and as President Tritton put it, "This is our lucky day!" Along with Tritton, Alfred H. Bloom, President of Swarthmore College; Judith Rodin, President of the University of Pennsylvania; and Joanne V. Creighton, President of Mount Holyoke College, welcomed President Vickers into the close brotherhood and sisterhood of the colleges.

After a musical interlude by the Bryn Mawr/Haverford Chamber Singers, Hanna Holborn Gray, Chairman Emeritus of the Board of Trustees, spoke about President Vickers. She advised Vickers that many would soon ask her, "What did you used to be?" And with the reply, "'I was and am a Rena-issance scholar,'" Ms. Gray continued, they will ask "what that has to do with your new role."

Ms. Gray then began to relate to the audience President Vickers' work in the study of Renaissance poetry and the transformation of the lyric genre as a result of changing technology. Comparing Vickers' study of Dante's purgatory to Vickers' current position

at Bryn Mawr's purgatory, Gray pointed out that Vickers' previous work made her "eminently qualified" for the position she now assumed.

Finally, Ms. Trimble presented Nancy J. Vickers with the will and codicil of Joseph Taylor, founder of Bryn Mawr, along with the charter of the College. President Vickers stepped forward to a thundering ovation and the Anassa cheer from students and alumna. President Vickers graciously accepted the position with the usual gleam in her eyes.

Explaining the path which had led her to that moment on the stage, Vickers spoke of her acceptance ten years ago of the position of Dean of Curr-iculum and Instruction at the University of Southern California. She recalled her remark to a colleague then that she did not particularly care for administration and would only want to be President or Provost of a women's liberal arts college.

President Vickers then explained that her appreciation for the importance of this type of institution developed during her undergraduate education at Mount Holyoke, which transformed her from "an ordinary girl . . . from Motown" into a "young woman of substance." Vickers stressed her strong conviction in the importance of liberal arts women's colleges and announced her intention to continue Bryn Mawr's commitment to distinguished academics and boldness. As she starts this new period in her own life, as well as in the history of the College, Vickers encouraged us to take "pride in who we are as we chart our next steps."

At this time, President Emeritus Mary Patterson McPherson read several pieces, including "A Glance behind the Curtain," a poem by James Russell Lowell, who spoke at the inauguration of the College in 1885. She then gave President Vickers a hug before the ceremony concluded with the Bryn Mawr College Hymn.

As the Academic Procession retreated, there was a feeling among those in Goodhart Hall that something incredible had been witnessed. Along with the austere ceremony, the royal colors of the academic robes, and President Vickers' lasting smile, came a feeling of peace as our new president took her place on this memorable day.

Reprinted from the *College News*, December 9, 1997.

Left: President Nancy Vickers (born 1945), 2001

Right: Napkin from the inauguration celebration of Nancy Vickers, December 6, 1997

Opposite: Nancy Vickers, June 2008. Photograph by Enid Bloch, class of 1963. Reproduced by permission of the photographer

NANCY J. VICKERS
INAUGURAL ADDRESS
December 6, 1997

BARBARA TRIMBLE, Betsy Cohen, Hanna Gray, and Pat McPherson; Bryn Mawr alumnae, faculty, staff, students, and trustees; Haverford colleagues and managers; representatives of brother and sister institutions and assembled family and friends: I accept this presidency with great admiration for this institution, for its achievements, for its clear and enduring commitment to its mission, and for the exceptionally talented community of men and women whom I have now begun to know and with whom I look forward to laboring on Bryn Mawr's behalf. It is truly a privilege to join your company.

Three years ago, when I surprised everyone (including myself) by accepting a position as a dean at the University of Southern California, a dear friend asked if I now looked to a future in academic administration. As these stories go, I said no, not really. I was momentarily persuaded, I reported, by the intellectual challenge of thinking through a major revision of the curriculum and by the anticipation of working with a wonderful team of colleagues. But I was sure that once the moment had passed, I would head back to the classroom and to the library. Anyway, if I were to pursue academic administration, I added idly, I would only want to be a President or a Provost of a small liberal arts college . . . preferably a women's college.

At the time, I had no ready answer for my friend's next question. Why a women's college? But I have thought about my offhand remark a great deal since then, particularly this past year. My own undergraduate experience at Mount Holyoke was the heart of my education. It was there that I learned about standards and discipline; there that I felt the exhilarating results that drudgery can yield; there that I have developed so passionate an engagement in my work that I simply had to persist in it. They were life-changing years. I suspect that many of you in this audience know from personal experience, or from close observation, what I mean. I arrived at college a fairly ordinary girl from a very large public high school in the suburbs of a city on the way to becoming "Motown." My energies were focused largely on such issues as my daily selection of Capezio flats and matching headband; I was self-assured in my knowledge that shoes made the woman. I will never forget the mixture of amusement and horror my freshman roommate expressed as she witnessed this soon-to-be-abandoned morning ritual. For over the course of four years I was to become, I like to think, a young woman of substance. "[Should] sweet sixteen at entering be sweet sixteen at graduation?" M. Carey Thomas had asked in her remarks to Bryn Mawr students at the start of the academic year in 1899. Her characteristically subtle answer: "Emphatically no. A college is not a place for arrested development."

This college had indeed never been a place for "arrested development." And in the extended change it now undergoes—that Bryn Mawr rarity, the transition from one president to another—the community has marked development by an appropriate interrogation of mission. The symposium last spring to celebrate Pat McPherson's extraordinary contributions to the College showcased the depth and breadth of Bryn Mawr's commitment to the liberal arts; it testified compellingly to the enduring value of a liberal education. That testimony will need to be given continued and forceful voice not only within, but perhaps more important, well beyond our wall. I envision this inaugural occasion as a sort of companion piece. Beginning with historian Mary Kelley's lecture yesterday on women's education at the turn of the nineteenth century and continuing with a presidential symposium next November on women's education at the turn of the twenty-first century, I would urge us to reflect upon our role as a women's liberal arts college.

From its founding in 1885, Bryn Mawr has sought to make possible the full and equal participation of women with men in a common intellectual, professional, and public life. The College has never been a separate community of women, nor has it conceived of the project of women's education in that way. We owe our foundation to Haverford, though it has been said that we quickly out-flew their well-behaved "barnyard fowl" aspirations for us, to use M. Carey Thomas' language, and metamorphosed into properly feminist "soaring eagles." To their credit and ours, a unique collaboration between two very distinct institutions has evolved over the years, a collaboration that defines and enriches us both. Bryn Mawr's scholarly and pedagogical life has always recognized men and women in an equal footing; the task of running the College has been a shared one. And the long tradition of including men in the College's graduate programs might even lead one to conclude that Bryn Mawr could be termed "coeducational," if the term itself were redefined and qualified along the lines former Bryn Mawr Provost, now President of Barnard, Judith Shapiro sketched in her own inaugural remarks in 1994: "Is [coeducation] being used to describe an institution where men and women are equally likely to study all fields? Where they are equally likely to hold positions of responsibility and authority in extracurricular activities? Is it an institution where men and women are found in similar numbers at all ranks of the faculty and administration? If so, then we might indeed have 'coeducation.' If not, then I believe we have something else." Her wonderful irony, of course, turns on the simple fact that within much of our culture we seem to require an institutional focus on women to produce a "liberated zone" of truly equal opportunity.

At the turn of the twentieth century, in 1899, M. Carey Thomas challenged Harvard President Charles Eliot's assertion that those engaged in the college education of women pursued a highly experimental project of unproven value to society, for which the existing traditions and curricula of higher education for men could not offer any guidance. It was indeed the occasion of a Wellesley inauguration that had somehow inspired him to muse: "It would be a wonder, indeed, if the intellectual capacities of women were not at least as unlike those of men as their bodily capacities are." He might just as well have suggested the creation of "a new Phidias and a new Titian, new Greek tragedies, new Chemistry, new philosophies," Thomas shot back before an audience of Bryn Mawr students a week after hearing Eliot's remarks, "in short, a new intellectual heavens and earth." And a new and separate intellectual heavens and earth were clearly not what Thomas had in mind for her new Bryn Mawr woman.

Thomas returned to this question again in an article for the *Educational Review* in 1901. "Given two bridge-builders, a man and a woman," she wrote, "it is simply inconceivable that the preliminary instruction given to the two should differ in quantity, quality, or method of presentation because while the bridge is building one will wear knickerbockers and the other a rainy-day skirt. You may say you do not think God intended a woman to be a bridge-builder. You have, of course, the right to this prejudice, but you will probably not be able to impose it on women who wish to build bridges." This conviction—that women can and should have access to a full range of choices as they seek to engage the world on their own particular terms—clearly remains as much at the heart of Bryn Mawr's mission as it was a century ago.

But the role of a women's college is no longer in a simple and straightforward way about offering women the education and the access to the world that is denied them elsewhere. There are, fortunately, a great many opportunities and choices open to women at the end of the twentieth century, even if we must admit that the pioneering spirit and determination of Bryn Mawr's alumnae have not yet swept away every shard of a shattered glass ceiling. It is clear, however, that "real" women can study and work at a coeducational college or university, and, as we all know, "real" men can and do study and work at a women's college. But Bryn Mawr's early and abiding commitment to women's education informs not just our decisions about whom we teach but also about what and how we teach. We cannot allow Bryn Mawr to rest on its impressive laurels, to remain only what it has become thus far. We must not become an institutional case of arrested development.

The challenge to us as a community, and to me as a president, is to remain true to the qualities that define the College and yet experience them not only as a justification for the highly laudable status quo but also as an impetus for change. Bryn Mawr is an institution with a remarkable sense of itself and its purpose. I am not likely, in describing it to you, to tell you anything you do not already know. But what I would like to do, from the newcomer's fresh perspective, is invoke three values at the core of Bryn Mawr's character, values which for me not only define its past and present but which speak meaningfully to the directions in which we should be going.

First of all, Bryn Mawr is academic. And I do not mean this in the self-evident sense that we are a place for teaching and learning, but in a deeper, rarer sense. Bryn Mawr's claim for women as people of intellect and ambition has created a rare and precious record of scholarly achievement at this institution. From its early years, the College has embraced the teacher-scholar as the ideal faculty member; graduate study has been an integral component of its educational project. As a result, it has not only replenished the academy with new research and new talent, but inspired its undergraduates to take themselves and their work seriously, no matter what their goals might be. Bryn Mawr's commitment to the active scholarly life continually reaffirms that education is not about mastering a narrowly conceived or static canon, but rather a persistent interrogation of the processes by which we learn and understand. Bryn Mawr cultivates habits of mind which transform its students' relationship to the world and prepare them to do whatever they choose to do with application and success, whether it be geophysical research or international finance, opening a women's health clinic in Africa, founding a production studio, raising a family, or, for that matter, building a bridge. In a society quite skeptical about the worth of the academy, and about the need for such a labor- and cost-intensive project as the acquisition of a liberal arts education, we must remain the strongest of advocates for the value of rigorously and liberally educated women, and men, in this nation and the world.

And second, Bryn Mawr is bold. Its ambitions for women have from the beginning led it to reach beyond the comfortable, the easy and the expected. As the first women's college in the United States to offer graduate degrees to women, the first to offer its students the independence and responsibility of their own Self-Government Association, the first to grant a doctorate in Social Work, the College

Below (left to right): Artist Ying-He Liu, Jane McAuliffe, and Nancy Vickers at the unveiling of Vickers's presidential portrait, Thomas Great Hall, March 18, 2010. Photograph by Jan Trembley, class of 1975

has cultivated a willingness to take risks on behalf of our principles, to experiment, to be different. And it has produced students in its own image—bold, confident, and independent women. It is no accident that we have an independent Alumnae Association or that individualism is something of a cliché here. I hope that we can continue to find new ways to think and act with the boldness which has always characterized the College—to find the next risks worth taking, the new terrain to be explored.

And finally, Bryn Mawr is committed to an engagement with, and a betterment of, the world around it. The College's historic role in providing educational opportunities for women gives us a position of principle from which to pursue even broader concepts of access. Mary Maples Dunn, Bryn Mawr's former Dean, past president of Smith, and director of the Schlesinger Library at Radcliffe, observed with characteristic clarity in her 1985 inaugural that the purpose of women's colleges in their early days was simply "the education of educable people otherwise discriminated against." I think that charge still offers powerful direction to our institutions today. It calls us to build our small community in purposely complex and densely textured ways and to welcome the challenge of generating mutual understanding across the many divides that fracture us nationally and globally. And we must not only conceptualize principles of mutual respect and collaboration; we—as administrators, as faculty members, as staff members, and as students—must live them. Indeed, our commitment to relating to, and working with, one another across our own divides must stand as a model that we carry beyond the confines of the college.

Our very smallness should make it possible for us to confront society's most difficult challenges in constructive ways and to learn from that effort. A proponent of diversity before it had a name, Bryn Mawr's third president, Marion Park, noted in 1922 that "within the small circle of college life, closeness of acquaintance, which in the intelligent person is the foundation for democracy, is especially possible. North and south, professional and artisan, rich and poor, rub unaccustomed elbows, and probably in no other four years of the lifetime of the individual is she open to such complete change in her attitude toward persons and beliefs." Today one in four of the College's undergraduates are American women of color. International students make up twelve percent of the student body. The education we offer is immeasurably enhanced by our socio-economic diversity as by the diversity of age, race, ethnicity, nationality, political perspective, sexual orientation, religious commitment, and physical ability which we manage to achieve. Our history can and should guide us to find more and better ways to make a Bryn Mawr education accessible, and a Bryn Mawr experience amenable, to those who have not always found the doors to American higher education open.

My first task as the new President of Bryn Mawr was to open those doors to the members of the class of 2001, to welcome our freshmen and their parents to the College. It was one of those moments, not unlike this one, in which I felt the full measure of the responsibility I now so gladly and gratefully take up. I stood in awe of the courageous trust of parents "letting go," like so many before them, to the promise of a Bryn Mawr education; I reveled in the eager anticipation of their "millennial" daughters. We, as a community, are charged with the stewardship of nothing less than life-changing years, and the lives that we change will define the century to come. May we, as a community, exercise our high charge with admiration for the extraordinary accomplishments of our predecessors, with pride in who we are, and with a bold and innovative spirit as we chart our next steps.

Reprinted from *A Collection of Readings and Remarks Given on the Occasion of the Inauguration of Nancy J. Vickers as the Seventh President of the College* (n.p., 1997).

BOLD VISIONS FOR TODAY AND TOMORROW: 1997–2010

NANCY VICKERS COUNTS DOWN TO MILLENNIUM

Julia de Hoyos, Class of 2000, and Karla Solheim, Class of 1999

CHANGE IS ON THE HORIZON for Bryn Mawr. And it's been on the horizon for quite a while, it seems. Our new president (is she still "new"?) has enthusiastically supported a whole slew of progressive changes at Bryn Mawr during her year-and-a-half in office.

How close to that horizon have we come so far? That's what we set out to learn in an interview last week with President Vickers. It turns out that behind the scenes, President Vickers is thinking and working hard about Bryn Mawr's new direction. The wheels of progress are slowly beginning to turn. A tradition-bound institution like BMC, though, needs to generate a lot of momentum, and nobody said change is easy.

The Planning Process

Nancy Vickers has plans. Throughout the interview, she spoke of meetings, processes, and reports. She had previously declared her hopes that Bryn Mawr not become an "anachronism." When asked exactly how she'd do that, she replied, "The first thing I've done is to set in place a planning process." Following the well-publicized Middle States Commission accreditation review, President Vickers is compiling "a short list of initiatives that will become the center of my energies in the years to come."

She currently seeks as much input as possible from the Bryn Mawr community. "If you're going to do planning . . . you have to manage to do that planning working through the existent government structure." Otherwise, Vickers argues, the plan becomes the brainchild of only a few individuals, rather than a collective document. So, instead, she is querying SGA, the Committee on Academic Priorities, and the Staff Association about concerns, all of which will eventually report to the Council on Institutional Priorities that reports to Vickers herself. This summer she will finalize a general ten-year plan.

President Vickers also immediately hopes to improve Bryn Mawr as a workplace. "We've got a long way to go there, but we've taken some important first steps." The new College Ombudsperson—an independent mediator of disputes—is a symbol of her commitment. "There was no escape valve for difficult situations as they arose within the workplace," she says of the former situation, one of the first she changed in her time here.

Vickers the Role Model

What was President Vickers's take on her new designation as one of *Vanity Fair's* 200 most influential women? Naturally, she was proud of the attention focused on women's colleges—but she also noted the difference between the "stressed out"–looking women presidents of major research universities and the relaxed photo of the presidents of the Seven Sisters, "institutions that are still a force to be reckoned with." Vickers hopes to use her position to be an advocate for both women's education and liberal arts colleges.

The Great Passion of Nancy Vickers

"What is your great passion?" Julie asked President Vickers point-blank. Vickers responded by describing her "abiding interest in making things right for women." This theme crops up in both her scholarly research and career. "Whether that's making things right for the women of the 1530s in France," she says, "or . . . women at Yale or Dartmouth, that's very much a part of my coming here . . . This college, at its deepest level, is about making things right for women."

New Modes of Learning

Students and faculty . . . have been heartened by President Vickers's vocal support of both interdisciplinary and experiential learning. How has this support manifested so far? According to Vickers, "The concrete steps are that they are both very much on the table and in the planning process." Hesitant to take major steps until she has a strong feel for student and faculty sentiments, she hopes to initiate a "campus-wide conversation" before making any further moves, because, she says, "The only way in which anything happens at an academic institution is if you get the grassroots population—the faculty, the students—standing behind it."

Education in a Multicultural World

Given several recent forums that have brought on-campus issues of diversity and cultural sensitivity to the forefront of public dialogue, Vickers states, "Keeping the college a diverse community that feels supportive to all its students is one of my highest priorities." As for her own role, she says, "It's my responsibility to set the tone for the community around those issues."

In the immediate present, she says she hopes to bring events and occasions to campus to inform and support people, citing the recent Main Line Martin Luther King Day Celebration . . . as an example. A quick fix to years of structural injustice is impossible, though, according to Vickers, and educating people is a long-term process. She says, "Changing culture and modifying human behavior take a very long time." Vickers is hopeful, however, of Bryn Mawr's future: "This is a national issue, not just a Bryn Mawr issue, and I'm hoping that we can be a kind of model institution."

Financial Aid

Those of us who are seniors remember the days when Bryn Mawr was a fully need-blind institution—which it can no longer afford to be. In the wake of the Middle States Review and recommendations for financial stability, how does Vickers see the future of the financial aid process? Will fewer and fewer students who can't pay full tuition end up at Bryn Mawr? In response, President Vickers says, "The question of whether you can remain, in this day and age, need-blind or need-sensitive, has largely to do with how many students who are not of the full means to pay for their college education you have encouraged to apply to your school." Bryn Mawr, according to the interview, recruits at many more lower-income high schools compared with similar colleges. Thus, Vickers says, "If you've encouraged a lot of needy students to apply to your school, you're going to . . . have spent your financial aid budget."

Since demographic studies show the next generation of college-bound students will be relatively needy financially, Vickers hopes that more money can be reallocated to financial aid. At least, she says, "We're certainly not going to move backwards in terms of the amount of the college budget we're devoting to financial aid."

How many college presidents can claim they came of age in Detroit during the heyday of Mo-town? And how many are scholarly experts on MTV? President Vickers is not your typical college president by any stretch of the imagination.

Now is an important time for reflection and change, and these are exactly what President Vickers has in mind. She hopes we will "think back to the Bryn Mawr of 30 years ago and try to project ourselves into thinking about the Bryn Mawr of 30 years from now." This is no easy task; however, our "new" president, and her enthusiasm, have certainly come at the right time.

Reprinted from the *College News,* February 3, 1999.

STRATEGIC PLANNING

THE COLLEGE'S PLAN FOR A NEW CENTURY

THE PLAN FOR A NEW CENTURY was unanimously approved by the Bryn Mawr Board of Trustees at its March 4, 2000, meeting. The Plan sets priorities for Bryn Mawr's energies and resources over the next five to ten years.

"I am deeply pleased by the Board's unanimous endorsement of the Plan for a New Century," says President of the College Nancy J. Vickers. "This is a gratifying vote of confidence in the good work of the entire Bryn Mawr community, since all constituencies—students, staff, faculty, administrators and alumnae/i—participated in developing the Plan. We now move to the exciting work of implementation. We are fortunate to have the generous support of the Pew Charitable Trusts, which has given us a Program Related Investment of $8,500,000. This is a multi-year no-interest loan, from which we will draw spendable income over seven years.

"Thanks to Pew, we will be able to begin fulfilling some of the specific recommendations of the Plan now and to provide seed funding for an array of other initiatives. I have authorized several initial steps towards meeting our goals of improving recruitment and retention and achieving academic innovation. We will be increasing undergraduate internship opportunities, both domestic and international; strengthening our community service and athletics staff; providing modest planning grants to each of the four centers proposed by the faculty; and supporting College-wide planning related to technology and a more robust program of research sabbaticals for faculty."

"I think the process Nancy Vickers used to develop the Plan was quite remarkable," says Wendy Greenfield, Executive Director of the Alumnae Association. "It was truly a collaborative effort born of the Quaker tradition in which she solicited the thoughts and feelings of the entire Bryn Mawr community, including students, alumnae/i, faculty, administration and staff. I think everyone feels heard and feels ownership of the end result. It has taken two and a half years to develop, including the self-study process, and is really a labor of love."

The Executive Board of the Alumnae Association fully supports the Plan, and alumnae/i will be important partners and resources for a number of the initiatives it proposes, including the expansion of internships and international opportunities for students.

President of the Alumnae Association Susan L. MacLaurin '84, an ex-officio member of the College's Board of Trustees, reports that "Board members took very seriously their responsibility to encourage Nancy about the broad concepts of the Plan she had so clearly articulated. At the same time each member wanted to ensure that the Plan would be as complete a picture of Bryn Mawr's future as possible. The conversations about the Plan, of the Board and in more intimate groups, were lively as a consequence. The result is a Plan enhanced by the participation of people wise and vested in Bryn Mawr. Applauding with others on the Board as the adoption vote was taken unanimously was indeed an exciting moment! I will remember it knowing the positive effect it will have for students of the College."

Reprinted from the *Bryn Mawr Alumnae Bulletin*, Summer 2000.

9/11

VOLUNTEERS AT GROUND ZERO GET SATISFACTION OUT OF HELPING OTHER WORKERS CLEAR CITY
Margaret Burton, Lauren Perone, Marot Williamson, and Carl Fleisher (Haverford), all class of 2004

WE FELL SILENT as the altered New York City skyline appeared over a hill of the New Jersey Turnpike. For the first time, we saw with our own eyes the dark smoke that had replaced the proud symbols of American and international prosperity. We left Bryn Mawr and Haverford colleges on the Friday after the attack with a loosely defined objective: to help in any way we could. But the specifics of our trip were still uncertain.

Later that evening, after a few phone calls, we decided to volunteer at Chelsea Piers. In the meantime, we joined the nation in lighting candles to remember all who were lost that Tuesday. We sat together on the rocks in Manor Park, located on Long Island Sound just north of New York City.

Our candles were bright in comparison to the darkened cityscape, and we sat thinking and discussing all we might encounter. We left the candles burning in the Manor but took with us a sense of patriotism and determination.

The next day began early so that we could secure a position at the Piers. The four of us were assigned to work with Chefs with Spirit, an impromptu organization set up to help with the relief effort. Restaurants from all around New York City were donating truckloads of hot food to be given to those working at ground zero.

As the trucks arrived, our job was to unload the food as quickly as possible, then load it onto the ships from Spirit Cruises that would take it to the workers. The many volunteers, who had come from as far as California, worked together by forming chains to get the food moving more efficiently.

In between shipments, we worked to keep the storage areas on board clean and sanitary as the Health Department stood by. While many of us wanted a position on the boat serving food to the workers, they were reserved for employees of Spirit Cruises.

When the shift ended, we felt compelled to stay. So we switched jobs to directing the remaining delivery trucks to the appropriate pier. We split up into pairs and stood at nearby intersections with signs to catch the attention of the drivers. But we caught the attention of military personnel, construction workers, and law enforcement officials as well. While stopped at the lights, many cheered, honked, and thanked us for our work as they carried pieces of the demolished buildings away.

Once the day was done, we felt content in our exhaustion and walked to Grand Central Station. The walk through the city was reassuring in a sense, as the city appeared to be back on its feet. However, the missing-persons signs, the barricaded Empire State Building, and the Humvees rolling down Fifth Avenue were an eerie reminder of all that the nation was trying to work through.

As we left New York City and crossed the George Washington Bridge, we saw the perfect conclusion to an emotionally trying weekend. There, between the two sides of the west end of the bridge, hung the largest American flag any of us had ever seen. In that moment, we felt the spirit and resolve of our great nation.

Reprinted from the News (Bryn Mawr-Haverford), September 25, 2001.

IN WAKE OF TRAGEDIES COMMUNITY COPES BY COMING TOGETHER
Amy Held, Class of 2003

HOURS AFTER news spread around Bryn Mawr's and Haverford's campuses of the terrorist attacks in New York, Washington, DC, and Somerset County, PA, students, staff, and faculty from both schools united in separate campus forums. The goal of the Bryn Mawr and Haverford meetings, called by President Vickers and President Tritton, respectively, was to create a community support network that provided a safe environment for people to voice their outrage and anguish.

Turnout to both forums was testimony of the devastation that the attack wrought and the need for many to attempt to come to terms with their grief. At Bryn Mawr, hundreds of people crowded into the main room of the Campus Center, lining the stairway and hanging over the balcony, until President Vickers announced that the forum would reconvene on the more spacious Merion Green. At Haverford, the bleachers in the Field House couldn't contain all of the community members, who spilled over onto the floor.

Both forums began with a moment of silence. At Bryn Mawr, professors Marc Ross and Marissa Golden of the Political Science Department, Martin Herbert of Peace and Conflict Studies, and Clark McCauley of the Psychology Department sat on a hastily constructed platform along with Nancy Vickers before the Bryn Mawr community. The professors initially led the forum and set the tone by focusing on America's own checkered past as an aggressor, while underscoring the importance of communities coming together in times of strife. However, it was the students who quickly took the reins; for almost two hours, they stood at two microphones facing the stage and made passionate and emotional statements about the terrorist attacks . . .

Perhaps the most poignant testimony in this canon of thought came from Bryn Mawr junior Rabia Qureshi, who was dressed in the traditional Muslim chador, a black loose-fitting garment covering the body and hair. She tearfully related incidents of resentment directed toward her earlier that day. She said that she had been confronted with such questions from students as, "Why don't you go back to where you came from?" and "Why don't you just dig a hole and die?" She concluded by saying, "You may hate the way that I look but I love you as a Muslim and that is the duty of every Muslim." She received loud applause, and most students expressed incredulity that a fellow student would experience such insensitivity and prejudice on their own campus . . .

In accordance with President Bush's declaration that Friday, Sept. 14, be considered a day of national mourning, Bryn Mawr and Haverford cancelled Friday classes between noon and 1 P.M. Quaker-based meetings for worship were held at both schools for further reflection.

At the Tuesday forum, other students commended Bryn Mawr's proactive attitude and caring community that met so quickly after the tragedy and continued to communicate so honestly.

President Vickers said, by e-mail, "In the wake of a national tragedy such as we are experiencing, it is important to find ways to continue to gather as a community; to show support for each other, especially those still waiting for news of loved ones; and to express our sympathies for those who have lost friends and family."

Reprinted from the News (Bryn Mawr-Haverford), September 18, 2001.

RENEWED COMMITMENT TO THE ARTS

November 2004

Dear Friends,

As I continue my series of letters to alumnae/i, parents, and friends of Bryn Mawr, I am delighted to send a missive that celebrates a thoroughly encouraging development: a striking growth in fine and performing arts at Bryn Mawr. Our gains in this sphere have been carefully cultivated over a number of years, and the College must continue to commit time and resources if our arts program is to reach its full vitality and strength.

Ever since M. Carey Thomas was reprimanded by a straitlaced Quaker trustee for introducing a piano to the College's grounds (the outraged trustee referred to it as "the four-footed beast"), the arts have been an integral, if loosely organized, part of campus life. For many years, however, vestiges of that early trustee's reproach survived at the College: while the cultural production of the past was considered a worthy object of study, the actual practice of art was banished to the margins of the curriculum. The College's Plan for a New Century, ratified by the Board of Trustees in 2000, articulated a renewed dedication to Bryn Mawr's leadership in the world of arts and letters, and specifically to strengthening the College's support for the fine arts: "Instead of drawing a line between the arts and the traditional academic programs, it should be possible to take a cue from student practice and explore further ways to connect the two."

The founding of the Arts Program in 1984 had gathered an assortment of dance, theater, printmaking, and creative-writing resources into a coherent curricular structure that complemented Haverford's music and visual-arts curricula, but the program was not financially secure. The College has long drawn a talented faculty from the vibrant artistic community of Philadelphia. While this has allowed Bryn Mawr students to benefit from the tutelage of professional artists of many disciplines, most of these artists taught a course or two intermittently, as time allowed. Only a few made teaching at Bryn Mawr central to their artistic lives. In 2003, the College took an important step towards assuring continuity in arts instruction when we rewarded the superb leadership of the directors of the programs in dance, theater, and creative writing by converting their long-term lectureships to tenure-track positions. In 2004, all are tenured.

The Bryn Mawr-Haverford Theater Company's productions, under the direction of Mark Lord and Technical Director Hiroshi Iwasaki, have become important artistic events not only on campus, but throughout the Philadelphia area, drawing critical praise of a sort rarely accorded to undergraduate productions. Students of dance, led by Director Linda Caruso-Haviland, work with some of the region's most acclaimed performers and choreographers, and alumnae of the program have gone on to find work with highly regarded Philadelphia dance troupes. The Haverford-Bryn Mawr orchestra, chamber music ensemble, chorale, and chamber singers, supervised by

---

> IN THE LAST THREE AND A HALF YEARS I HAVE WITNESSED AN INCREDIBLE INCREASE OF STUDENT INVOLVEMENT IN THE ARTS. THERE ARE AT LEAST 14 PLAYS AND DANCE PROGRAMS BEING REHEARSED ON CAMPUS RIGHT NOW. WE HAVE A GREAT ARTS PROGRAM AND I THINK IT CAN BE BETTER, MUST BE BETTER, SO THAT BRYN MAWR WOMEN CAN PREPARE FOR CAREERS IN THE ARTS—ONE OF THE MANY WAYS THAT WE MIGHT CHOOSE TO CHANGE THE WORLD.
>
> —*Nora Sidoti, class of 2007, theater arts major, reprinted from* Challenging Women: Investing in the Future of Bryn Mawr, *Spring 2007.*

Haverford's music department, typically draw about a hundred student performers from each college annually. And the College's creative writing program has brought national media attention to Bryn Mawr, thanks to the unflagging enthusiasm—and the golden Rolodex—of Director of Creative Writing Karl Kirchwey, who has brought a dazzling series of literary lions to Bryn Mawr's public spaces and classrooms.

The College's curricular commitment to the arts has been accompanied by a parallel growth in students' self-directed artistic activities. This September a group of students illustrated precisely the sort of intellectual independence the college aims to cultivate when they mounted a play in Philadelphia's annual Fringe Festival, an important showcase for avant-garde performance. The student troupe wrote the play, raised the funds necessary to stage it, negotiated its inclusion in the festival, directed it, and created publicity and fundraising materials, including a website to spread the word.

Is Bryn Mawr becoming an art school? No. While there are certainly artistic luminaries among our alumnae/i, relatively few of our students go on to full-time careers as artists. But fine and performing arts have become an exemplary bridge between scholarly and extra-curricular activity at the College—a model of the ideal of balance that can be difficult to achieve in the intensely intellectual environment of Bryn Mawr. As Director of Dance Linda Caruso-Haviland pointed out at this summer's alumnae/i arts weekend in the Berkshires, the "balance" artistic endeavor provides is far deeper than a physical or emotional release from the rigors of study. "The arts," Linda says, "compel students—and faculty—to consider other cognitive modes in which they even more fully experience, embody, articulate, and perform what they have created and what they have come to know. Performance and creation, hallmarks of some of our courses, are also key examples of what Bryn Mawr's Plan for a New Century takes to be a very important skill: adapting to and thriving in the conditions of change."

Our students' enthusiasm for the arts is evident in the perpetual oversubscription of arts courses; students must win spaces by audition or lottery for nearly every one. Our curricular commitment must not falter, and it must be matched by a determination to dedicate resources to arts facilities, an important goal of the Challenging Women campaign. The Boston architectural firm of Finegold Alexander and Associates Inc. is currently consulting with the performing-arts faculty about reconceiving arts spaces across campus. The feasibility study focuses on Goodhart, the anchor space of the arts program, to determine how well the facility supports the arts program and where it falls short. The building is, our projects staff tells me, in dire need of attention.

It is the custom of Bryn Mawr students to aspire to distinction in all their endeavors, and they expect facilities and programs of sufficient quality to support those aspirations. Few of our students aspire to play first violin for the Philadelphia Orchestra, but many nevertheless engage in artistic pursuits with profound passion. We must foster that passion, as we encourage any activity that deepens students' understanding of themselves and their world.

Sincerely,

Nancy Vickers
President

Reprinted from photocopy of a letter, Nancy Vickers to the Bryn Mawr College Community, November 2004, Bryn Mawr College Archives.

Left: Students performing in *The Threepenny Opera* by Bertolt Brecht (1898–1956), Goodhart Theater, April 2003. Photograph by Paola Nogueras, class of 1984

Right: Student dancers in Pembroke studio, c. 2000–2004

REBUILDING THE FABRIC OF CAMPUS

GEOMETRICS OF LIGHT

MAJOR FACILITIES PROJECTS OF THE LAST DECADE have addressed the two overarching goals of academic innovation and of student recruitment and retention; they included [the renovations of] Bettws-y-Coed and Dalton; and the Isabel Benham Gateway Building, Cambrian Row, the Neuberger Campus Center, and several dormitories.

A renovated Colonial Revival house with a new addition, Bettws-y-Coed provides offices, instructional space and state-of-the-art laboratories for the psychology and education departments. Historic Dalton Hall's renovation includes new spaces that are geometries of light. The most technologically advanced building on campus, it houses the departments of anthropology, economics, political science, and sociology as well as two interdisciplinary centers—for International Studies and for Social Sciences.

The Benham Gateway Building, which houses Admissions, Financial Aid and Public Relations, is often the first stop for prospective students, visitors, and the general community. A shingle-style house designed in the mid-1880s by Philadelphia architect Frank Furness, it was extended and renovated in 2000 by the architectural firm of Buell Kratzer Powell, which won an honor award from the Philadelphia chapter of the American Institute of Architects for its work.

Former faculty houses on Roberts Road were renovated to create the Multicultural Center and Cambrian Row. The Multicultural Center includes space for the Office of Intercultural Affairs and for students' socializing, studying, meetings, and activities. Made possible by a gift from Lois Collier '50, and her [late] husband, Reg, the renovated buildings of Cambrian Row house student-activity spaces: SGA offices, the Civic Engagement Office, a center for religious life with kitchens and meeting spaces for many student groups.

The refurbished Campus Center and Uncommon Grounds Café is a wireless hot spot, where students, faculty, and staff gather over coffee, and work on their laptops or catch up on email, hold meetings and show project displays. In the lounges, students play pool, watch the high-definition plasma-screen TV, listen to satellite radio, curl up by the fireplace, and surf the Internet at several computer stations. Career Development is also part of this hub, with offices on the second floor.

"One of our most recent technological innovations is One Card, a campus ID, library, and money account card used to access dorms, the gym, and main buildings after hours," said Director of Facilities Glenn Smith.

Rhoads, the largest dormitory on campus, was completely refurbished in 1999, with new furniture and bedroom spaces, mechanical and electrical systems, updated life-safety features, and a state-of-the-art kitchen and dining facilities. Its leaded glass windows were also conserved and adapted.

Erdman's roof and slate sidings have been replaced. Merion and Radnor received complete exterior restorations. Extensive interior and exterior repairs are being completed on Denbigh, which also received a new slate roof that matches the 1891 original.

Projects completed in Park Science Center include a physical chemistry lab, a biology genetics laboratory/office, a computer and robotics lab, and a synthetic and physical chemistry lab; and the renovation of the green-house. A multi-year project on the biology wing will begin this summer.

"As important as the buildings are, on our beautifully landscaped 136 acres," Smith said, "we maintain a number of gardens and have a tree replacement program underway. The stormwater management pond below Rhoads and the stream restoration at the Graduate School of Social Work and Social Research have received Growing Greener Grants from the commonwealth of Pennsylvania for their environmental contributions.

"It's been a very busy and exciting time to be involved in Facilities Services on this campus over the last 10 years," said Smith, "and we're excited about what the next 10 might hold."

Reprinted from the *Bryn Mawr Alumnae Bulletin*, May 2007.

Top: Cambrian Row, the student-activities "village," completed January 2004

Bottom: Students in the Marie Salant Neuberger Centennial Campus Center, renovated 2004–05

Opposite: Dalton Hall, built in 1893 as a science facility and renovated in 2004–06, now houses twenty-nine faculty offices and eleven classrooms. The glass-enclosed rear staircase, added during the recent renovation, emulates the turrets found throughout the college's campus, and combines traditional materials, such as a slate floor, with glass and brushed stainless steel to create a spectacular rectilinear space.

PEDAGOGICAL INNOVATION

A SERVICE TO THE FUTURE
Jan T. Trembley, Class of 1975

POLITICAL SCIENCE MAJOR Nia Turner, class of 2005, wanted to investigate the role of citizen involvement in policy making by developing an independent study and internship through Praxis, Bryn Mawr's experiential learning program. She had no field site in mind, but Program Coordinator Nell Anderson saw a perfect match, with Aretha Swift of Norristown's Weed and Seed.

This community-based, multi-agency strategy "weeds out" crime in targeted neighborhoods, and "seeds" them with social services and economic revitalization. Citizens themselves identify the community's most pressing needs and decide how best to meet them.

Anderson had first seen Swift, who is Weed and Seed's revitalization coordinator, at a meeting in 2002 to discuss forming connections between Norristown and the College. "Aretha stood up and said, 'I'm a one-woman office, and I would love to have a student intern to help me out,'" Anderson recalled. "When Nia came to me a year later, the opportunities for student learning with Aretha were evident from the relationship we had already developed. What stands out most about Aretha is her involvement at the grassroots and policy levels in the Norristown community. She is represented by individual residents and block captains as well as by agency and government representatives."

Turner is working with residents to explain, in layman's terms, how to apply for grants—communities are expected to tap into the public and private sectors for funding—and comparing their views about Weed and Seed with those of local officials. She is also conducting qualitative research on the collaboration of residents, clergy, law enforcement, and local government agencies and officials to improve the quality of life in Norristown. Turner, who is considering a joint Ph.D./J.D. and a career in social policy and law, is being advised by Marissa Martino Golden, class of 1983, associate professor of political science.

Theoretical Reflection
Bryn Mawr's Praxis Program is characterized by genuine collaboration between students and members of a community in doing what is mutually beneficial, and by the constant movement between theoretical reflection and fieldwork.

"It is the integration of practice and theory that makes the Praxis experience profoundly academic," said Anderson. "In the classroom, Praxis faculty facilitate a dynamic process of reflection, incorporating lessons learned in the field with the curriculum. The development of ongoing partnerships with community organizations—such as social service agencies, government offices, schools, museums—has also been an important element of Praxis. Students work with our partners to address their needs in ways that not only benefit the organizations, but also allow students to integrate their coursework with the field experience. In addition, field supervisors frequently visit the classroom as guest presenters and co-teachers."

The three levels of Praxis courses offered require increasing amounts of fieldwork, but do not need to be taken successively: departmental courses (Level I), interdepartmental seminars (Level II), and independent study (Level III). Since the program began in 2001, Levels I and II courses have been offered through growth and structure of cities, sociology, education, psychology, gender studies, English, arts, biology, and the College Seminar program. "We would love to see more faculty and more departments take advantage of the rich learning potential in combining classroom teaching with fieldwork," said Undergraduate Dean Karen M. Tidmarsh, class of 1971.

Teaching and the Test
A group of undergraduates placed at a Philadelphia area high school for Schools in American Cities, a Praxis I course taught this spring, initially wanted to evaluate the effectiveness of the America Counts tutoring program operated there by Bryn Mawr students. But the school had a more pressing need—prep classes in math for 11th graders taking the Pennsylvania System of School Assessment (PSSA) test in April. Bryn Mawr and Haverford students go to the site three days a week, teaching three classes each morning using a controversial scripted curriculum required by the city school district.

During a weekly planning session, Lecturer in Education Jody Cohen and her site supervisors discussed the tremendous energy students have invested in their project: "They want to know, 'What's our purpose, to increase the scores or make them feel better about taking the test? Are we going to have an impact?'"

Offered through the education program, Schools in American Cities also meets a requirement for cities and sociology majors. "The course is designed for students to investigate the issues, challenges, and possibilities of urban schooling," Cohen said.

"In the first section of the course, we address sociopolitical, cultural, economic, and legal dimensions of contemporary urban life and schooling. The second part focuses on what's going on inside schools, including the perspectives of inner-city students and teachers, theories of curriculum and pedagogy in urban settings, and contested terrains such as language and literacy. In the final stretch, we examine current efforts to restructure urban schools and districts. Throughout we look at cities across the country in terms of culture, demographics, and schooling. Since we are located right outside Philadelphia, the course uses the city as an illustrative 'case'; we pay particular attention to current

events in the city's reform effort."

The 26 students in the course are divided among several high and middle schools, and are doing different research projects . . . In addition to writing papers for their courses, Praxis students keep field logs in which they describe what they observe, and their thoughts and feelings about site experiences. They build on these to reach informed opinions, including knowledge acquired and reasoned conclusions developed through class discussion and readings. In Cohen's course, students from different school placements break into smaller groups to read one another's field notes, pointing out emphases, biases, and omissions, and discussing next steps for research. The course is writing intensive; the final field portfolio includes a 10-page research paper. An analytical paper, a critical review, and a presentation on an investigation of a city are also required . . .

Bridging the Gap

Over pizza and salad in early March at the new Cambrian row home of the Praxis and Community Service offices, eight of the 13 upperclasswomen doing Praxis III projects talked about their progress. Nell Anderson asked each to think about how, as a result of reflecting on her experiences, her focus had changed and her learning circles broadened since first visiting the site.

Classical and Near Eastern Archaeology major Pamela Schwartz, class of 2005, said that on her first visit to the Independence Seaport Museum in Philadelphia, she was introduced "to every single person at the museum. I chitchatted with them about sheep, knitting, and underwater archaeology, something I'm interested in doing.

"Since then, I've been getting all kinds of ideas about careers other than in higher education. I've also been discovering the interconnectedness of the museum world and the importance of knowing what's going on the public school system and in local politics," said Schwartz, who is developing an exhibit on types (and stereotypes) of pirates across time and around the world.

"Before starting my placement, I thought I would go to my field supervisor's office, and she would give me work to do," said Nia Turner. "It turns out that I've been learning the most from going to meetings with her." Some of those are in Harrisburg and Lancaster; the two discuss what happened during the long drives back to Bryn Mawr. Turner recalled a chance for her at a meeting in Harrisburg to review guidelines for the position papers submitted by agencies within Weed and Seed sites to issue monies. "As I was reading along, I noticed places where they could give some examples for the average reader," she said. "People new to the program may not be familiar with the terminology it uses. So I spoke up, and I felt I was not an outsider, not there just to observe, but could contribute to the process."

Political science major Anjali Shenoy, class of 2004, is interning with Philadelphia Assistant District Attorney Gina Smith in the sexual offense unit. Shenoy works with Smith to prepare files for trial, speaks with witnesses, does legal research, sits in on trials, and helps with witness selection. Her research project is to evaluate the effectiveness of Megan's Law, enacted in 1994.

"Beginning data may be returning this year on the policy's effect for communities where sex offenders have relocated," Shenoy said. "I hope to expand my view about the social implications of sex offense laws. For example, does putting the burden on members of the community to avoid the possibility of being victimized place the problem with the community or with the offender?"

Shenoy told the group she was trying to sort out the pull between the need for analysis and strong emotions, both observed and felt. "At one point, I was so absorbed in watching the faces of the jury and defendants as the verdict was handed down, I didn't realize how much I was thinking until I wrote out my journal entries," she recalled.

. . . Support mechanisms for students might include workshops on topics such as grass roots organization and consensus building and facilitation; resource readings; and spaces and regular meeting times for reflection.

"How do we get academic institutions to recognize that experiential and community-based learning programs are academically sound and important in shaping and changing what students perceive as education?" Paula Arboleda, class of 2005, asked. "How can academic institutions support initiatives to forge better relationships with communities and make sense of the challenges that surround us?"

Reprinted from the *Bryn Mawr Alumnae Bulletin*, Summer 2004.

Above: Zanny Alter, class of 2009 (left), in a class facilitated by Alice Lesnick, director of the Bryn Mawr-Haverford education program, as part of the Praxis partnership with Parkway West High School in Philadelphia, fall 2009

Opposite: Colleen Haley, class of 2011, with a YouthBuild Philadelphia Charter School student at the construction site of a day care in Philadelphia. The project was part of the Praxis collaboration in Samuel Olshin's architectural and urban design course, 2008. Photograph by and courtesy of Samuel Olshin

CELEBRATING THE TEACHING AND LEARNING INITIATIVE

STUDENTS, FACULTY, AND STAFF from across the College filled Dalton Hall's largest classroom to capacity at the end of the spring semester in celebration of their experiences in the Teaching and Learning Initiative (TLI).

The event marked the first time participants from all the various TLI programs—Students as Learners and Teachers; Empowering Learners; Student-Mentored Staff Computing Classes; Reading, Writing, and Communication; Continuing Staff Education; and Technology Education Squad—have come together for a year-end celebration. It was also the first celebration conceptualized and facilitated by student participants in the program rather than by faculty coordinators.

The celebration started with presentations from a number of partnerships highlighting the variety of TLI staff-student partnerships.

For their Computing 2 partnership, Ashley Mallon '10 and Public Safety Officer Cat Tavares met at midnight before Tavares started her overnight shift.

"We decided it would be a lot easier than me getting up early," said Mallon, who helped Tavares learn how to use Microsoft PowerPoint.

Public Safety Officer Phil Mairs and Sandra Gandarez '11 overcame competing sports-team allegiances—Mairs is a diehard Phillies fan while Gandarez, a native of northern New Jersey, roots for the Mets—to put together a PowerPoint presentation on a "day in the life" of a Bryn Mawr public safety officer.

During the Empowering Learners partnership presentation, Paul Dolhancryk, Tom Millward, and Mark Watson of Facilities Services talked about how they taught a group of students the basics of home repair and campus physical-plant oversight. The group framed out two walls and added wiring and pipes for plumbing before finishing it off with drywall.

"I now know what all the little valves in my house are for, so if the toilet is overflowing or something I can take care of it. I know what a ground wire is—it's the green one, make sure you remember that," said Julia Vance '11.

"They did very well. They've all still got their fingers," joked Millward. The students, in turn, taught the staff about baking.

"I'm not sure I want my wife to know I can bake," said Dolhancryk.

No matter what the project, what echoed over and over again was praise for the program and the friendships it formed.

"I've been doing this for three years and have had a good time doing it, learned a lot, and made a lot of friends," said Dolhancryk.

"The friendships you make are awesome," said Pen-y-Groes House Manager Lisa Peterman, who led the room in singing "Happy Birthday" to her partner, Maggie Powers '10. Peterman has taught Powers to cook in exchange for instruction in Excel and PowerPoint.

After the presentations, everyone stuck around to talk, to enjoy a bite to eat, and to congratulate one another on the semester's work. Faculty members who hadn't seen their student consultants since the previous semester took advantage of the time to catch up on what has been happening in their classrooms, and conversations among groups who usually work in separate spaces filled the room.

The refreshments included dishes from education-certification student Laura Hummer '10 and Raymond Clark of Dining Services, who teamed up in the Empowering Learners program to create a cooking class. Hummer learned about advanced cooking techniques from Clark, whom she helped explore principles of instruction and plan for his own continuing education. Clark is hoping what he gleaned during the partnership will help him reach his goal of opening a restaurant that will also provide cooking classes.

"Community service is a familiar part of college," said Alice Lesnick, director of the education program and faculty coordinator of the staff-student partnerships. "This program is about community building. When people can share what they know with each other, the community gets stronger."

TLI began in 2006 with the coordination of a number of goals centered on education. With funding from the Andrew W. Mellon Foundation, Associate Professor of Education Alison Cook-Sather started a project in which students served as consultants to faculty on issues of pedagogy. At the same time, Bryn Mawr Chief Administrative Officer Jerry Berenson and Chief Information Officer Elliott Shore were interested in starting a program that would help the College's nonprofessional staff learn basic computer literacy, since the College was moving so much of its operations and communications online. They enlisted Cook-Sather to help create a model for students to become involved in this work to bridge the digital divide on campus.

Cook-Sather, Berenson, and Shore got together with Lesnick, whose course, "Empowering Learners," focuses on theory and practice of tutoring and mentoring. Lesnick agreed to re-envision the course as a think tank for staff-student educational partnerships, including Empowering Learners, a reciprocal learning exchange in which each partnership chooses its focal topics.

To date, 74 faculty members from across all three divisions of the College and several members of the Haverford faculty have participated in one or more TLI forums, including 82 partnerships in which faculty have worked with a total of 38 students in the role of pedagogical consultant. There have been 123 partnerships between staff and students: 48 Empowering Learners partnerships; 72 Computing 1, 2, and 3 partnerships; and four Reading, Writing, and Communication partnerships.

Diane Hoplamazian, a 32-year employee of the College who works in the Erdman dining hall, has been with the program since its start. She's taken several computer-skill classes and is currently working with Lesnick to improve her literacy.

"Now a lot of the other employees come to me with questions. They sent us our summer schedules and someone couldn't open it, so she came to me and said 'Diane, how do you open this,'" Hoplamazian recalled with pride.

"Ultimately, that's what all these programs are about," said Lesnick. "We want to build a community in which everyone is a teacher and everyone a learner."

Reprinted from Bryn Mawr Now, June 2, 2009.

EXPANDING ACCESS: THE POSSE PROGRAM

"IF YOU DON'T KNOW ABOUT POSSE, YOU BETTER ASK SOMEBODY!"
Anka Wilk, Class of 2006

OR SO SAYS LaToiya La Vita of Posse Two.

Posse. It's kind of a funny word, isn't it? In eighties slang, a *posse* was "a group of friends." Well, the idea of a group of friends going to college together is the idea behind the Posse program. The Posse Foundation's goal is to send multicultural and socially diverse groups of urban student leaders to college together. When they get to college, the students already have a support system in an environment radically different than the one of their childhood.

The Bryn Mawr Posses are the result of a three-year-long partnership between the college and Posse Foundation. The Boston office of the Posse Foundation narrows hundreds of applicants into a pool of twenty dynamic student leaders who go through the Early Decision application process. After Representatives from admissions have had a chance to review the applications, they go to the Boston office to meet the applicants in person, in a large group interview.

Afterwards, the administration, with the help from the Posse Foundation staff, narrows the group to 10 or 11 students . . . These student groups will form a Posse. Bryn Mawr currently has two Posses (first-years and sophomores) and will have a Posse in the incoming freshman class.

In order for you to understand the program, you have to understand how Posse students get to Bryn Mawr. The Posse program stresses a whole new take on the college admissions process, with the goal of achieving a "diverse" group of students. While standard college admissions depend on academic preparation, grades, and test scores, Posse has its own method of assessing capable students, called the Dynamic Assessment Process (DAP).

According to the Posse website, "DAP taps into the often unseen qualities of high school students using non-traditional forums to evaluate students. Interactive workshops in which students have the opportunity to work alongside peers to generate and share ideas have proven to be an effective means of identifying an alternative set of qualities that can predict academic success in college. Its primary selection criteria are leadership talent, ability to work in a team with people from different backgrounds, and desire to succeed."

Although Bryn Mawr's student body is more "diverse" than most schools, with about 30% students of color, this does not actually say anything about diversity. For instance, there are many American minority groups which are underrepresented, and students often complain about the homogenous culture. For Posse, diversity is not about skin color or fixed percentages. In fact, Posse's definition of diversity is so broad that according to Sarah, an employee in Posse's Boston office, "We don't really have an official one." This diversity goes beyond inclusion of minority students to embrace students of all social, economic, political, religious, and ethnic backgrounds.

The Posse program has spurred discussions in admissions about what is the meaning of diversity. Sure, it's a word that gets thrown around a lot, especially at a place like Bryn Mawr, where diversity is important and usually cherished—even though there are many different opinions about what diversity is, what it stands for, and how it should be achieved.

The debate over racial diversity will reach the legal arena in an upcoming Supreme Court case on April 1, in which the Bush administration will question the constitutionality of affirmative action. This court case will raise many difficult discussions on our own campus.

In the next few months, it may become harder to talk about issues of diversity, inclusion, exclusion, equality, and race. I hope that in this dialogue, a range of opinions from all ends of the political spectrum will be voiced and that students will be respectful and understand the value in sharing their opinions. I congratulate and thank the student leaders who made Diversity Week happen, and I hope that we as students continue to challenge and explore . . . what diversity means to us.

Reprinted from the *College News*, March 26, 2003.

COLLEGE STUDENTS FIND SUPPORT IN CAMPUS "POSSES"
Campus "Posses" Support College Students Who Might Otherwise Feel Like Fish Out of Water
Kathy Matheson, Associated Press

WHEN SHARHEA WADE ARRIVED at Bryn Mawr College from a big-city high school, it seemed as if every other student on the quiet, leafy campus had graduated from an exclusive private school.

"I felt intimidated by them," recalled Wade. "Bryn Mawr is a different world."

Yet whenever she felt like a fish out of water, Wade could turn to her "posse"—nine other girls who, like her, had been recruited from struggling Boston-area school districts and sent on full merit scholarship to the elite women's college.

Wade's posse is one of dozens sent to top-tier universities each year by the New York-based Posse Foundation. The combination of monetary and social support is a model that experts say could help move the U.S. toward President Barack Obama's goal of having America lead the world in the percentage of college graduates by 2020. Next fall the program hits the Ivy League when it debuts at Penn.

So far, Obama's focus has been on increasing access to higher education—especially for minority and low-income students—through expanded Pell grants and simplified financial aid applications.

But paying for college is only part of the battle. Keeping students in school by supporting their psychological and academic needs is equally important, said Laura Perna, an associate professor in the University of Pennsylvania's Graduate School of Education.

Posse founder Deborah Bial started the organization in 1989 after a once-promising inner-city student told her, "I never would have dropped out of college if I had my posse with me."

Since then, Posse has sent more than 2,600 students to its partner campuses, including Vanderbilt University, Colby College and the University of California at Berkeley.

The program targets students in disadvantaged urban districts who have strong leadership skills but may lack the guidance to wade into what can be an intimidating college admissions process. Posse is not need- or minority-based, though many students fit both categories.

The demand for such help is dramatic, Bial said. Posse, which had been recruiting from six major cities, added Miami as its seventh this fall. The program received more than 12,000 nominations this year for 460 slots nationwide, Bial said.

Posse provides academic support and help with college applications, but admission decisions are made by individual schools, which offer full merit scholarships. A University of Missouri study presented last week links merit aid to increased freshman-year grade-point averages, particularly for minority and low-income students.

Students headed to the same universities are placed in posses of about 10 that begin meeting in high school. The meetings continue weekly at college, creating tight-knit groups where members can find motivation or comfort when they feel lost or frustrated.

"I have this incredible sense that I can succeed and take on whatever I want at school because I have this intensely supportive network behind me who believes in my potential," said Augusta Irele, 21, a member of Wade's posse at Bryn Mawr.

Research shows that integration into a community is important for college retention, Perna said. Having a posse of peers with similar backgrounds creates a bridge to the new institutional climate while helping maintain relationships at home, she said.

Matt Rivera, 20, said his posse helped him and other members through the culture shock of leaving their Chicago-area homes for selective DePauw University, set amid cornfields in Greencastle, Ind.

"Everyone calls it a bubble," said Rivera, a junior. "There's nothing for 45 miles." Some Posse scholars say their presence has spurred some

uncomfortable but needed conversations about race and class on campus. Jenny Rickard, a Bryn Mawr administrator and Posse liaison, said the program has been mutually enriching for the school and the students.

"The scholars have really energized the environment at Bryn Mawr, really creating a culture that is more inclusive," Rickard said.

Both DePauw and Bryn Mawr say Posse students are active campus leaders and have graduation rates on par with or higher than that of the general student body. Overall, Posse officials say their students have a 90 percent graduation rate, compared with a 58 percent rate nationwide for bachelor's degrees within six years.

Bial, whose work with Posse earned her a $500,000 MacArthur Foundation "genius grant" in 2007, said the ultimate goal is for scholars to take their diplomas from the Main Streets of college towns to the boardrooms of Wall Street and beyond.

"We're creating a new kind of leadership network in the United States," said Bial. "It's not a good-old-boys network, it's not the Greek system. You've got young people who represent the real diversity of this country."

Reprinted from http://abcnews.go.com/US/wireStory?id=9087087, November 15, 2009.

Above: Bryn Mawr Posse Students, class of 2014 (left) and class of 2010 (right). Courtesy of The Posse Foundation

Opposite: Posse program students at Bryn Mawr, 2008

Page 363: Posse program students, class of 2010, at graduation, May 16, 2010. Courtesy of The Posse Foundation

ATHLETIC DEVELOPMENTS

"HANDS ON!"
BMC Rowing Community Pulls Together

IN 1999, a group of Bryn Mawr undergraduates with little or no rowing experience dreamed of forming a rowing program and racing for their college. Since then, the Bryn Mawr crew has claimed victories and top-three finishes each year, and is now a recognized NCAA Varsity Rowing program.

The team goes into the spring 2006 racing season fueled by strong fall showings at the Head of the Charles and the Seven Sisters regattas.

Collaborative fundraising efforts for a new shell have also been underway. The program has a group of ambitious parents, alumnae and friends, the kind of supportive network that has taken decades to evolve at other schools.

"When a father of one of our rowers made a significant pledge for a new racing shell, he was joined quickly and enthusiastically by a large number of other parents and recent alums," said Coach Carol Bower. "And in January, Ellen Hooker '70, who has supported the rowing program since its earliest days, issued a challenge to spur us to raise the balance needed to buy the new boat. She will match gifts made through May 31 dollar for dollar up to $7,500.

"Our new shell will be named *The Founders* to commemorate the spirit of the alumnae and of the parents who are 'pulling together' in this vital and supportive community. *The Founders* will be a sister ship to our first quality shell, the *Millie B*, which we were able to purchase through a significant gift from Ellen in 2001."

The shell will be dedicated on March 12, with the group of women who started the program and the new founders present.

"When I first met with the students who started the program, my intent was to work with them for a year or two, and then I was going to finish up my master's degree at Penn and go back to the West Coast or something," Bower said. "But they had a certain kind of spirit that made me think that at some point they were really going to do some amazing things for this world. I wanted to be a part of helping them learn to work as members of a team and as leaders so they would be better prepared to accomplish what they wanted when they left Bryn Mawr."

Bower explained that the rallying call for both the team and its support network is, "Hands on!"

"Our athletes experience a transition when they begin their workout in the morning," she said. "Each person moves independently before she is called to launch the shell. The rowers place their water bottles and oars on to the dock, the coxswains gather their speaker systems and tools. Then, the coxswain issues a command, 'hands on,' and everything happens in unison after this. Each member of the crew lines up alongside the boat as it's sitting in the rack and places her hands on it; they lift it up off the racks, carry it out, place it in the water, and await the command to 'sit in' and 'shove off.' Once on the river, the members of the crew strive to precisely match every motion they make. In so doing, their collective power is unified and they move quickly and gracefully over the surface of the water.

"Historically, boats are a religious form of connection among indigenous peoples. In Polynesia, for example, the community would gather around the big fishing boats. Everyone would place hands on them and carry them down to the water. When the fishermen returned, the community would gather again. It was good luck to have your hands on the boat, carry it out of the water and place it where it needed to be placed. Now we have a Bryn Mawr rowing community, and everyone's placing hands on this new effort.

"Rowing is one of the few sports at Bryn Mawr that you can learn and compete in at a very high level within your first year on the team," Bower explained. "The Bryn Mawr athlete is eager to take on the challenges presented to her, whether she is an experienced oarswoman or just starting out as a novice. We all share the hard work, the good and bad weather, and the rise of the sun each morning. This spirit, combined with our supporting community, is the reason that this proud and ambitious rowing program is off the ground, on the river, and on the rise."

"We couldn't be more fortunate," says former Director of Athletics and Physical Education Amy Campbell, "to have in Carol someone who is bright and creative, who understands Bryn Mawr, who understands rowing, and is passionate not only about the sport but the role athletics play in these students' lives."

Reprinted from the Bryn Mawr Alumnae Bulletin, February 2006.

IN SEASON: A FOCUS ON BRYN MAWR ATHLETICS
Greta Lynn, Class of 2003

YOU'VE SEEN the posters. You've heard the rumors. But how much do you really know about Bryn Mawr sports teams? As a Division III school unable to give athletic scholarships, Bryn Mawr athletes are drawn to the school by academics rather than athletic programs. In many ways, this is a positive thing; no one's education is contingent upon athletic performance. However, as a result, not much is known about the more than thirteen teams on campus, and the more than one hundred women who give their blood, sweat, and tears to them. In an effort to educate readers and to highlight Bryn Mawr's finest, here at the *College News*, we've decided to profile one team in each new issue, to give kudos to the players and let potential fans know what they've been missing.

Since we've already mentioned blood, sweat, and tears, we're going to start with the Horned Toads, Bryn Mawr's rugby team. I know what you're thinking: Women's rugby? Popular images of rugby include men with thick necks in short shorts, a proliferation of battered and broken limbs, and lots and lots of beer. However, Bryn Mawr rugby does not evoke any of these images (with the exception, perhaps, of the short shorts), so we're going to start with some basic facts about the rugby team.

First, it is the biggest team on campus, one that brings an average of forty women together each semester, with a variety of athletic experience and background. With virtually no high school women's rugby teams in existence, nearly everyone comes into the sport a rookie.

A second fact is that for a team of forty or so women, it is incredibly close. Be it the intensity of the sport or the inherently team-oriented nature of the game, the rugby team is a close group of women. Says co-captain Karen Austin '01, "The rugby team is one of the tightest groups of friends on this campus. Everyone on the team is my friend, which I don't think you can say for all the other teams." Her teammate Brown agrees, in considering this closeness on and off the field: "I continue to play because of the team and the bond that we have. When I walk out onto the pitch, I know that there are 14 people out there who would do absolutely anything for me, and

---

EXPANDING OPPORTUNITIES IN ATHLETICS

Women are participating in athletics as never before; they are preparing for lives that will be active physically as well as intellectually. Bryn Mawr's athletics program calls for an increasing commitment from the College. In the wake of Title IX, which requires equal institutional funding for men's and women's athletics, students coming to the College have had far greater opportunities to participate in sports than their predecessors. We will need to meet the expectations these students bring to intercollegiate and club athletics if we are to continue to attract many of our most disciplined and accomplished applicants. The new Director of Athletics has identified several immediate priorities in this regard, including enhanced support for our competitive intercollegiate program, for our physical education and wellness courses, for general recreation, and for outdoor activities. Through its commitment to thoughtful programming, to adequate and talented staffing, and to enhanced facilities (including an improved fitness center), the Department of Athletics and Physical Education will help foster a healthy and balanced extracurricular campus life and support the well-being of the full community.

Reprinted from Bryn Mawr College, *The Plan for a New Century*, March 2000.

Opposite (left): Members of the Horned Toads, the bi-college women's rugby club, c. 2008

Opposite (right): Horned Toads rugby member Natalie Armentrout, class of 2011, who was named the Uncommon Grounds Athlete of the Week on October 30, 2007, for her outstanding rugby play

Page 366 (top): Crew team member Megan Bartley, class of 2003 (right), with teammate, 2000. Photograph by Tommy Leonardi

Page 366 (bottom): Cross-country team members at practice, c. 2005-2009

Page 367: Bryn Mawr crew team competing in a regatta on the Schuylkill River, Philadelphia, 2000, front to back: Elizabeth Beerman, class of 2002; Anna Dunbar-Hester, class of 2002; Megan Bartley, class of 2003; Julia Switzer, class of 2003; Lauren Bloom, class of 2003; Jennifer Koch, class of 2003; Sarah Kim, class of 2002; and Anna Bower, class of 2002. Photograph by Tommy Leonardi

they all know I'd do the same for them. That's pretty powerful, and it's hard to walk away from."

The rugby team is not a varsity sport, it is a club sport. Because of Bryn Mawr College policy, rugby cannot become a varsity sport until the National Collegiate Athletic Association (NCAA) recognizes rugby as such, and though rugby has enjoyed a rise in popularity among college women over the past decade, the NCAA has not yet done so. Maintaining the status of "club sport" has had both positive and negative meanings for the team. "Being a club team gives us more control over what we're doing and when," says Austin.

She continues, "It gives us more responsibility and more 'ownership' of the team." Brown agrees, "Even with the club status, the athletic department can support us. And in some ways they've been very, very helpful. Some other rugby teams don't even have coaches or uniforms, because their schools refuse to support a 'club' team." However, due to the club team status, sometimes ruggers feel less supported by the administration. Both Austin and Brown agree that the lack of a standard-size playing field has hurt the team's performance, given that the Brecon field on which the rugby team plays is about one-third the size of a standard field.

"I don't think it's a coincidence that our level of play decreased when we started having to play on Brecon field," says Brown. Austin agrees, "We're still an amazing team, although I definitely see not having adequate practice facilities taking its toll on our skills." Club team or not, the Horned Toads continue to strive and thrive.

After a difficult first semester, the Toads are back having won two games out of three, beating Ursinus and Franklin and Marshall, but losing to Temple. Indeed, at times the Horned Toads have enjoyed a high degree of success, going to the national tournament in the spring of 1999, and coming in second in the spring of 2000 at the West Chester University Tournament.

Rugby is an incredibly intense, and incredibly fulfilling, experience. Brown says of the sport, "[Rugby] gives me a high that nothing else does. When I play games I feel more engaged and focused than I do at any other time, even if I'm frustrated or angry. It's intense physically, mentally, and emotionally, and it's great." Austin sums it up: "I keep playing because I can't really imagine what Bryn Mawr would be like for me without rugby."

Reprinted from the *College News*, April 11, 2001.

THE HEPBURN CENTER OPENS

SPHERES OF ENGAGEMENT

THE SEPTEMBER 8 AND 9 LAUNCH of the Katharine Houghton Hepburn Center was an "amazing and galvanizing event" for one alumna who attended and who is proud to be nicknamed Kate.

"The two panel discussions, Crafting Policy to Improve Women's Health and Reproduction and the Law, offered us new perspectives and challenges to assumptions, intelligent reasoning and information, and extremely personal stories that brought to life the issues and mission of the Center at Bryn Mawr," emailed Katharine Patterson '75, president of the Alumnae Club of Northern California.

The concluding black-tie gala was "an evening when everyone was beautiful and above average," said another alumna nicknamed Cate. "Everyone seemed to glow, to be enjoying themselves, to be deeply engaged in the celebration," said Catharine Hancock '91, class editor and president-elect of the Club of Philadelphia. "I was very happy that folks from so many classes could come—young, old, you name it." More than 500 alumnae mingled with movie stars and media broadcast figures, undergraduates and their parents, and faculty and staff at Philadelphia's Kimmel Center for the Performing Arts.

The Center honors the spirit and legacy of Katharine [Martha] Houghton Hepburn, class of 1900, a leading social activist for women's suffrage and birth control, and her daughter, actress Katharine Houghton Hepburn, class of 1928, who has long been a symbol of women's independence.

Drawing its focus from the spheres important to its namesakes and to current undergraduates—film and theater, civic engagement, and women's health—the Center challenges Bryn Mawr students and alumnae/i to lead publicly engaged lives and to take on the critical issues that affect women today. The Center will award the Hepburn Medal annually to women whose lives, work, and contributions embody the intelligence, drive, and independence of the four-time Oscar-winning actress. Three Hepburn Fellows, who bridge academics and practice in nontraditional or unconventional ways in any of the Center's three broad areas, will come to campus each academic year to engage students and the College community in their work.

"Not only were the two Katharine Houghton Hepburns wonderful Mawrters, but the Center accomplishes many of the ideas that the student body is looking for at this time," said Self-Government Association (SGA) President Emily McNabb '07. "We are excited not only for this weekend but for what the Center will bring."

Black, White, and Red

The three acts of The Kimmel Center gala—reception, awards program, and dinner—were showstoppers in black, white, and red. Mistress of ceremonies Cynthia McFadden, co-anchor of ABC's *Nightline* and *Primetime*, wove a garland of anecdotes about Katharine Hepburn '28 and repartees throughout the series of presentations, which included the awarding of the Hepburn Medals by President of the College Nancy J. Vickers to stage and screen actresses Blythe Danner and Lauren Bacall, and speeches by six Bryn Mawr seniors on the importance to them of Hepburn's legacy and the role the Center will play in the life of the College.

A video tribute included interviews about Hepburn and clips from her films. (Proceeds of the gala will benefit the Katharine Hepburn Scholarship Fund, established by Hepburn in 1958 to honor her mother.)

Playwright, screenwriter, novelist, and actress Katharine Houghton stressed the opportunities her grandmother and aunt had at Bryn Mawr "to overcome their personal weaknesses." In 1896, "Kit"—an angry young woman who had lost both parents at 16 and "smarted at being bossed around by her tedious relatives"—reveled in her new-found freedom, shocking the neighborhood by riding horseback at night with a friend and smoking a pipe behind the Harriton family cemetery. President M. Carey Thomas asked her to desist as a personal favor, to help counter the prejudice against women going to college. "From that point on, she began to apply herself more vigorously to her studies in the hope that she might prepare herself to be somebody like President Thomas, a force for good in the wicked world, and eventually she succeeded," Houghton said.

The younger Hepburn was put on academic probation in her sophomore year, but her father appealed to the administration and encouraged his daughter to remedy her situation, offering his help at any time. "His complete faith in her . . . helped her overcome her academic impediment enough to graduate two years later and go on, with a confident spirit, to build a successful life in an arena that suited her unique gift," said Houghton.

Hepburn herself said many times that her time at Bryn Mawr showed her she could accomplish whatever she wanted: "I stayed and I studied—I pulled myself up by my bootstraps—got on the road and kept going! . . . Bryn Mawr was my springboard into adult life."

"What a Cool School"

. . . As part of the launch weekend, singer/songwriter Dar Williams performed two packed shows for students and alumnae on Friday night in Goodhart Auditorium, interspersing her songs with commentary on the circumstances that inspired them and taking questions from the audience.

"We could hardly have found an entertainer who illustrates the virtues of the convention-defying Hepburn women more clearly than tonight's performer," stated McBride Scholar Amanda Root '08, in introducing Williams. "In a world where popular music often indoctrinates gender roles, Ms. Williams has called on audiences to examine their assumptions about masculine and feminine identities. Throughout her career, she has used her distinctive voice and her growing celebrity as tools for political and social activism . . . The call to political engagement is strong in Ms. Williams' music, too—nowhere more so than in her latest album, *My Better Self*."

Williams, who gave the May Day concert on Merion Green in 1997, exclaimed as she tuned up, "You guys have been holding out on me. I thought you would set me down on a hay bale again, and here you have this amazing building. It's so austere! What a cool school!"

Reprinted from the *Bryn Mawr Alumnae Bulletin*, November 2006.

The Katharine Houghton Hepburn Center challenges women to lead publicly engaged lives and to take on important and timely issues affecting women. The Center honors four-time Oscar-winning actress Katharine Hepburn and her mother, an early feminist activist, both Bryn Mawr College alumnae who defied conventions. Drawing its focus from the life work of its namesakes—film and theater, civic engagement and women's health—the Center inspires Bryn Mawr students and graduates to make a meaningful impact on the world.

Top left: Mission statement of the Katharine Houghton Hepburn Center, founded in 2006 by Hepburn's family and executors, to commemorate the life and achievements of the actress, who graduated from Bryn Mawr in 1928. In keeping with Ms. Hepburn's wishes, the center also recognizes her mother, Katharine (Martha) Houghton Hepburn, class of 1900, an early suffragist and family-planning advocate.

Top and bottom: Gala for the Katharine Houghton Hepburn Center at the Kimmel Center for the Performing Arts, Philadelphia, September 9, 2006, clockwise from top right: Bryn Mawr students at the gala (photograph by Ed Savaria); gala invitation with Hepburn Center logo, detail; actress Blythe Danner (born 1943) accepting the Hepburn Medal (photograph by Ed Savaria); gala reception in the Kimmel's Perelman Theater

KATHARINE HEPBURN
A Mawrtyr First
Alyson Walkenstein, Class of 2006

SURE, EVERYONE KNOWS who Katharine (Kate) Hepburn was, or at least nearly everyone. She was that tall, slender actress who played opposite Hollywood's finest. She was the one who liked to keep a low profile but who was most unforgettable. She was the one whose quavering voice and high cheekbones were recognized by all. She was a Bryn Mawr graduate.

Kate's mother, Katharine [Martha] Houghton Hepburn, was in the Bryn Mawr class of 1900. Twenty-five years later it was Kate's turn to come to the school. She felt a lot of pressure as her mother began introducing her to the prestigious all-female institution. She was so nervous, in fact, that on the day she and her mother were due to visit the campus, Kate got into a head-on collision.

Kate was accepted to Bryn Mawr College in June 1924. "I came here by the skin of my teeth; I got in and by the skin of my teeth I stayed," Hepburn told the class of 1973. On Monday, September 29, 1924, she moved from her West Hartford home into the most expensive private suite on the first-floor of Pem West, today room 104.

Bryn Mawr College, 1924: Campus activism at this time was highly focused on students' right to smoke. Students argued it was a form of personal expression and liberation. Shortly after Kate's arrival the students were granted the privilege of smoking in their dorm living rooms.

Mawrtyrs also longed for the freedom to travel off-campus. Bryn Mawr's president at the time, Marion Edwards Park, made the women sign out when leaving campus and provide specific information about their destinations for fear of scandalous liaisons with the opposite sex. And, of course, cars were also a no-no, for obvious reasons. Men weren't even allowed to attend school dances, so when Kate arrived at her Freshman Dance in early October, she only had the option of dancing with other girls.

Ali Barbour, who lived in Merion, was Kate's best friend during her first year. Ali, however, soon became smitten with a gentleman in Philadelphia and began to spend many of her weekends in town with him. With her friend off campus most of the time, Kate began to isolate herself.

She wanted desperately to go unnoticed. She went to bed very early in the evening and woke up at four in the morning so as to avoid contact with fellow students in the bathrooms. One evening Kate timidly entered the dining hall, which at the time separated Pem East and West. She was wearing a French blue skirt and an Iceland knit sweater. Upon entering, Kate heard a very sophisticated, confident girl exclaim, "Self-conscious beauty!" Kate was mortified by the remark and rarely entered the dining hall again. Instead, she would either dine off-campus or eat the leftovers from Ali's dinner.

Kate loved athletics and was very good at a wide variety of sports; however, other than swimming for Bryn Mawr's team during her freshman year in order to fulfill a requirement, she once again kept a low profile. To avoid the pressures of trying out for the school's teams, Kate pretended that she had absolutely no athletic ability.

Although Kate spent most hours in her room, she did not study much. She had trouble concentrating, and especially struggled with her basic chemistry class. It became clear that medicine, the field that she had initially planned to pursue, would not be an option. In the spring of 1925, Kate did quite poorly on her exams and was told that she could not participate in the February Freshman Show.

By her second year, Ali had left Bryn Mawr and Kate's grades continued on a downward trend. It was even suggested by the school that she withdraw. This idea sounded just fine to Kate, who had by this time decided that her real dream was to become an actress, but her father insisted that she return for her junior year.

When Kate did return, she befriended Alice Palache, an active intellectual on campus. Alice coached Kate in her studies and inspired her to succeed at Bryn Mawr. The two spent day and night together in the library. As she began to feel more confident in her studies, Kate decided to emerge from her shell. The shy and timid Hepburn underwent a complete metamorphosis. After pulling an all-nighter, Kate ran out of the library just after dawn into the Cloisters, threw off her clothes, and went bathing in M. Carey Thomas' fountain!

By the spring of 1927, with much of Alice's help, Kate's academic standing had improved enough so that she could participate in the college show. She took part in *The Cradle Song* and played Oliver in A. A. Milne's *The Truth about the Blayds*. She even cut off her hair for the role. The show received praise from the *College News*, and to celebrate Kate and Alice went into the city dressed as boys. They were spotted, however, and brought before the SGA. Thankfully, Alice had a very good reputation on campus, and the two were let go with a warning.

During her senior year, Kate's daredevil image flourished. She was spotted climbing up and down drainpipes after dorm hours and was suspended for several days for smoking in her Pem East dorm room.

Kate had caught the theatre bug and starred in a May Day performance her senior year as Pandora in John Lyly's *The Woman in the Moon*. She was also nominated to appear in the beauty contest; however, Kate declined.

Although her time here at Bryn Mawr was precarious at points, Kate told the class of '73 that it was key in defining her as a woman. The professors had a large impact on Kate, for they seemed genuinely interested in helping students succeed. Most important, Kate learned how to think at Bryn Mawr: "I learned here to speak out loud with a certain amount of confidence."

On June 7, 1928, Kate graduated in Goodhart Hall with a major in history and philosophy. She already had a job lined up on stage in Baltimore and was due to start work just four days later. The rest is history. She became a Hollywood actress, a political activist, and a genuine star. But she was a Mawrtyr first.

Reprinted from the *College News*, September 17, 2003.

Author's note: Information from Barbara Leaming, *Katharine Hepburn* (New York: Crown), 1995; and the Bryn Mawr College Archives.

Opposite: The Katharine Hepburn Medal awarded by Bryn Mawr College to women whose lives, work, and contributions embody the intelligence, drive, and independence of the four-time Oscar-winning actress. Recipients include actresses Lauren Bacall and Blythe Danner (2006), and Philadelphia Mural Arts Program Director Jane Golden (2009). Hepburn Medal illustration from the invitation to the medal ceremony and celebration, 2009

A NEW SPACE FOR NEW PERFORMANCE

A VENUE FOR PERFORMANCE

AT ONE POINT last summer, anyone stepping into the 81-year-old Marjorie Goodhart Hall would have met a strange sight. A giant pile of dusty old props, costumes, and scrap material, nearly 15 feet tall, sat on the middle of the stage, and it was still growing. Goodhart Hall is undergoing a major renovation, its first since the building was built in 1928, and it required a massive spring cleaning effort.

"It was quite incredible," says theater director Mark Lord. "We found more old wooden chairs than you could even imagine. Since we're total scavengers, always reusing old stuff, we were pretty excited."

Now that Goodhart's bones are laid bare, it is amazing to consider what Lord and technical director Hiroshi Iwasaki have created over the years. The theater's main stage is quite small by contemporary standards, and its narrow proscenium arch has created design problems. Lord and Iwasaki's signature style of staging performances in unusual, out-of-the-way spaces in the theater and around campus often started in response to Goodhart's limitations. "It's really marked my development as a director," says Lord.

But with growing student interest in the theater program, Goodhart needed to evolve. In the spring of 2007, a $19 million overhaul was approved under the Challenging Women Campaign, and Goodhart is scheduled to reopen in the fall of 2009. A new dance studio and an outdoor theater space were eliminated from preliminary proposals.

"We've been incapable of honoring student demands for theater, and this means we can grow," says Lord. "It's a big, beautiful pamphlet in the middle of campus that says, 'We care about the arts.'"

A look at the history of dance at Bryn Mawr reveals an intriguing interest in new, often revolutionary forms of the art. At the turn of the last century Bryn Mawr taught forms that were out of the mainstream, including the Delsarte Aesthetic Movement, interpretive dancing, and the movement and music improvisation of Dalcroze Eurhythmics.

In 1928, body mechanics and natural dancing were added to the curriculum, inspired by seminal modern dancer Isadora Duncan. At the time, dance courses were offered by the physical education department. The introduction of modern techniques was strongly encouraged by a series of dedicated instructors in the late 1950s. Through their efforts, Dance Composition was offered as the first academic course in dance at Bryn Mawr.

In the first half of the twentieth century, star dancers and choreographers like Ruth St. Denis, Mary Wigman, and Doris Humphrey performed on Goodhart's stage. The Ballet Society, then a neophyte American ballet troupe, chose Goodhart to debut *Serenade*, a new work by their young resident choreographer and director, George Balanchine.

Several alumnae have gone onto notable careers in dance, including Gertrude Kurath '22, M.A. '28, a pioneer in the field of dance ethnology; Anna Kisselgoff '58, former chief dance critic for the *New York Times*; and Senta Driver '64, dancer and choreographer. In 1984 dance found its home within the newly formed Arts Program. The department now instructs hundreds of students each year, and offers both a minor and the opportunity to apply for a major in Dance.

Below: The Bryn Mawr-Haverford Theater Program's fall 2009 production of *Offending the Audience* by Peter Handke (born 1942), the inaugural production in the newly renovated Goodhart Theater

Opposite (left): Bryn Mawr's performing-arts center, Marjorie Walter Goodhart Hall, built 1928 and fully renovated 2009; 2009. Photograph by Eleftherios "Ted" Kostans

Opposite (right): Student dance performance, April 29, 2007

The interior transformation of Marjorie Walter Goodhart Hall, one of the largest capital renovation projects in the College's history, is scheduled to be completed in August. The *Alumnae Bulletin* took a hardhat tour this spring with College Engineer James McGaffin and Assistant Director for Maintenance and Operations Harold Maryea to "see the bones" of two new stages, better music practice rooms, classrooms, offices, and other much-needed support spaces.

The original plumbing, electrical, and heating and ventilation systems from 1928 have been replaced, and the building will be in compliance with fire, safety, and accessibility codes. An elevator will provide wheelchair access to the two lower levels. A movable platform will run from the front of the main auditorium to the right-hand side of the stage, where people can step or roll onto a platform that will take them up to stage level.

A portion of the building between the back of the existing stage and the Common Room wing has been removed to make way for a new, smaller teaching theater.

"We have worked closely with the arts faculty to assess their needs," said Director of Facilities Services Glenn Smith. "For the teaching theater, the arts program decided against a traditional black-box. Instead it will reach out to and embrace the interior and exterior spaces that surround it." A Juliet balcony overlooks the lawn stretching toward Pen-y-Groes, two corner windows at roof level let in natural light, and a glass folding door–partition between the theater and glassed-in lobby faces Thomas and Rhys Carpenter.

This addition will be faced with limestone that is similar in color but not identical to the Wissahickon schist that cloaks the original building.

"This is in keeping with contemporary principles of historic preservation and renovation. The addition will be harmonious with the existing structure, but it won't be disguised as the product of an earlier era," said Joseph Marra, the College architect and assistant director of facilities for planning and projects. "It makes the history of the building visible and ensures that we do justice to our own time."

The main auditorium stage will extend over what are now the first several rows of seats for a 40-feet-wide and 40-feet-deep performance space, pulling it much closer to the audience. "The balcony seats may be the best ones in the house now," said McGaffin. The cast iron seats are being refurbished, seats will replace the church pews in the balcony, and there will be new curtains and rigging. Both stages will have modern catwalks, lighting, and acoustics.

Below the stages will be two full dressing rooms with showers and a flex room for a greenroom or third dressing room, and below those a rehearsal studio. On the two lower levels will be a smart classroom, four music practice rooms, scene and costume workshops, and offices. "The old dressing rooms up the spiral staircase at the top were really nothing more than a couple of closets," McGaffin said. "No one's going to be in a closet any more or sharing space with costumes or instruments."

The Music Room will have new electrical and mechanical systems but no changes will be made in its features other than refurbishing the plaster and refinishing the floor. The organ, which works, will be tested again after construction is completed.

McGaffin said that many of the construction workers regard the project as a once-in-a-lifetime experience. "Most come in for only a short duration of time," he said, "but they're very interested in the use of this building, so we have been taking the time to give them a sense of the whole with old photographs and preliminary renderings."

Reprinted from the *Bryn Mawr Alumnae Bulletin*, May 2009.

INAUGURATION OF JANE McAULIFFE

McAULIFFE INAUGURATED AS EIGHTH BRYN MAWR PRESIDENT
Katherine Bakke, Class of 2011

OCTOBER 3 AND 4 marked the historical celebration of the inauguration of Jane Dammen McAuliffe as the eighth president of Bryn Mawr College.

The inauguration festivities spanned two days, beginning with a community picnic and culminating in the inaugural ceremony. A wide range of faculty, staff, students, alumni, and members of the tri-college community and beyond participated in the memorable event.

The Bryn Mawr community came out in droves on Friday, filling the drive along Taylor Hall and Senior Row with bustling activity at the evening's outdoor picnic and street fair. Vendors hocked their goods, ranging from vintage jewelry to Bryn Mawr Athletics and Traditions apparel, while Dining Services dished out delicious shish kebabs, mini burgers, and miniature pies to hungry patrons. The trees along the drive were festooned with lights, creating a festive atmosphere on the chilly autumn night.

"I think it's gorgeous. All the goodies and things they have are amazing," remarked Erin Glaser, class of 2010.

Magicians, dancers, and Bryn Mawr a cappella groups performed at the end of the street fair on an open stage.

The event was truly a community affair. Many faculty and staff members were present with their spouses and children. Alumni and bi-college students were also welcomed to the event.

"[The best part of the evening was having] a chance to see the college in an informal setting," said Allison Keefe, class of 2011.

When the street fair ended, the celebration moved to Thomas Great Hall, where students and faculty alike learned how to salsa and swing dance under the instruction of professional dancers. A live band supplied music.

Student dancers also taught the crowd basic moves of Indian Bhangra and hip-hop dances like the Wu-Tang, which originated in North Philadelphia.

Students had the opportunity to boogie to the likes of Motown-greats the Supremes with President McAuliffe herself.

The spirit of celebration throughout the night was palpable.

"They should have an inauguration every year!" exclaimed Sophia Abboud, class of 2012.

The following day brought more formality to the weekend's celebrations.

In the morning, a few students joined large groups of visitors and alumnae/i on tours led by graduate students about Bryn Mawr's architecture and the College's special collections holdings. During the architecture tour, two alumni who graduated in the 1950s reminisced about climbing onto the rooftop of Rockefeller via the upper-story windows.

Faculty and students came together in the early afternoon to share their research in three panel discussions. Topics ranged from Professor of Chemistry Bill Malachowski's research on therapeutics, to Emily McGlynn, class of 2009, and her environmental initiatives with the City of Philadelphia, to the work of 100 Projects for Peace grant recipients Adaobi Kamu, class of 2008, and Lucy Edwards, also class of 2008.

At three o'clock on the beautiful, crisp, clear autumn day, the inauguration ceremony began on Merion Green. The Valley Forge Highland Band ushered in the academic procession to the sounds of solemn bagpipes and drums. Members of the procession included faculty in full academic regalia, as well as alumni representatives from every graduating Bryn Mawr class since 1938.

Sally Hoover Zeckhauser, class of 1964, Chair of the Board of Trustees, opened the ceremony. Zeckhauser stated that a presidential inauguration for Bryn Mawr College was indeed a rare event, seeing as President McAuliffe is only the eighth president in the College's 123-year history.

Past College presidents Harris Wofford and Nancy Vickers were in attendance.

Representatives from Bryn Mawr's diverse academic community, including the Graduate School of Arts and Sciences and the Graduate School of Social Work and Social Research, as well as the Alumni Association, offered welcoming remarks. Shelley Gupta, class of 2009, represented the undergraduate college.

"[President McAuliffe] took immediate interest in the student body as we began to arrive on campus. Through a series of campus-wide meetings, dessert receptions at each residence hall, and extensive alumni outreach, she has demonstrated her commitment to know and understand Bryn Mawr's community," said Gupta in her remarks.

Following these welcomes came greetings from the presidents of Bryn Mawr's neighbor institutions, the University of Pennsylvania and Swarthmore and Haverford colleges.

"Dr. McAuliffe is a truly luminary scholar, so highly renowned that she has been elected to the American Philosophical Society, Ben Franklin's creation that represents the absolute pinnacle of intellect in the American academy," said Haverford College President Steve Emerson.

Carol T. Christ, President of Smith College, representing Bryn Mawr's relationship with the six other Seven Sisters colleges, welcomed President McAuliffe to the sisterhood and the "great unfinished agenda of furthering women's education worldwide." After her address, Christ embraced her new sister.

Patricia McGuire, President of Trinity College (Washington DC), where President McAuliffe completed her undergraduate studies, and John DeGioia, President of Georgetown University, where President McAuliffe worked as Dean of the College of Arts and Sciences, also spoke.

I FELT THE SWEEP OF BRYN MAWR HISTORY AND I SAW ITS PROMISE. THIS IS A PLACE TO HONOR AND CHERISH. THIS IS A PLACE WITH A PROUD PAST NOW FACING A FUTURE RICH WITH POSSIBILITY.

—*Jane McAuliffe, Inauguration Speech, 2008*

McGuire quipped that the college president is nothing more than a "high class beggar." DeGioia thanked President McAuliffe for the lasting footprints she left during her time at Georgetown.

A musical interlude ensued with a rendition of the poem "Pied Beauty" by Gerard Manley Hopkins, set to original music composed by Tom Lloyd, Associate Professor of Music at Haverford, and performed by the Haverford and Bryn Mawr Chamber Singers.

Johnnetta Betsch Cole, President Emeritus of Spelman College and Bennett College for Women, offered the ceremony's keynote address, entitled "If You Educate a Woman."

"It feels mighty good to be at Bryn Mawr. A women's college," said Cole in a resonant and resounding voice. "I strongly believe in the promise and the power of educating girls and women."

Cole went on to quote abolitionist and feminist Sojourner Truth, saying that even though "one woman in a garden" turned the world upside down, "women have the power to turn it right back up."

"Sisters, we've got a lot of work to do," said Cole, citing the economic crises and the injustices of the modern world as areas that a new generation of leaders must address.

Cole praised women's colleges, saying that good things happen when women are educated. Not only do graduates of women's colleges study in typically male-dominated subjects, they are also more likely to pursue professional degrees. Also, graduates of women's colleges engage in volunteer activities within their communities.

"Of course we want the graduates of women's colleges to do well, but how much better it is when they do well and do good," said Cole.

Upon finishing her address, Cole shared a hug with President McAuliffe. After a remark from Zeckhauser—describing McAuliffe as emerging from the clouds or from Lake Vickers, as she was such a spectacularly unbelievable candidate for the presidency—President McAuliffe received her official confirmation as president of Bryn Mawr College.

Nancy Vickers, President Emeritus of Bryn Mawr, was the first to offer a standing ovation welcoming President McAuliffe to the Bryn Mawr community. The audience celebrated the confirmation with a resounding Anassa.

"It is a great honor and privilege to stand before you today and dedicate myself to the service of Bryn Mawr College," began President McAuliffe in her address to the audience.

Her address focused on both the past and future directions of Bryn Mawr, and on the four goals she hopes to achieve during her time as president. These include a commitment to maintain and enhance Bryn Mawr's academic excellence; the desire to create and recreate a sense of community within the College; to enrich the student body by increasing diversity and fortifying the tri-college relationship; and to usher Bryn Mawr into modern education in a globalized world.

"One hundred twenty-three years ago Bryn Mawr blew the doors off American higher education, when it answered women's hunger for academic opportunity. Today that hunger is growing in countries where women encounter few options and many obstacles," said President McAuliffe, echoing Cole's remark that there is still work to be done in achieving educational equality.

"Bryn Mawr has the heart to lead the way," said President McAuliffe.

President McAuliffe closed her address with a passage from the Quran, extending the symbolism of the Bryn Mawr lantern into her own personal studies of Islam.

"Despite its challenges the lantern has remained lit for generations," concluded President McAuliffe.

Reprinted from the *Bi-College News*, October 7, 2008.

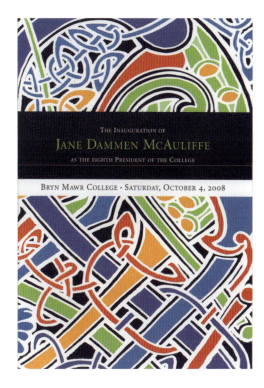

Above: Invitation to the inauguration of Jane McAuliffe, October 4, 2008

Opposite: Jane Dammen McAuliffe (born 1944) at her inauguration, October 4, 2008. Photograph by Paola Nogueras

JANE DAMMEN McAULIFFE
INAUGURAL ADDRESS

October 4, 2008

IT IS A GREAT HONOR AND PRIVILEGE to stand before you today and dedicate myself to the service of Bryn Mawr College.

I am deeply grateful for the confidence of the Board of Trustees. Your devotion to this institution inspires and guides me.

I am humbled by the reception I've received from the Bryn Mawr faculty, colleagues whose wisdom and judgment I will seek at every turn.

The wonderful staff of this College have wrapped me in their good will and also wrapped me in the gift of a gorgeous hand-knit afghan.

I am delighted by the warm welcome I have received from our students. It will be a pleasure to be part of your educational journey.

Alumnae/i of the College have shared with me their recollections of happy and absorbing days on this hilltop. I am thrilled that so many of you could be here today.

And I am especially fortunate to enjoy this extraordinary moment with the distinguished representatives and speakers who share this stage, particularly Dr. Johnnetta Cole, whom I first met when she was president of Spelman College and I was a very junior faculty member at Emory University.

So many family members and friends bless me with their presence today, but my greatest gladness are those seated in the front row: our four children, Jamie, Meg, Katie, and Liz; our four grandchildren, Kevin, Elena, Georgia, and Vivian; and most especially, my lifelong love, Dennis.

Whenever I'm asked, "How do you balance work and family?" I have only one true answer: Marry the right man. My husband, Dennis McAuliffe, is incredibly supportive. He is also an outstanding educator and a selfless scholar. Minus a few fights over the years about who does the dishes, we've managed to figure out the balance that works for both of our professional lives.

Today, family and friends, mentors and colleagues, alumnae/i, faculty, students and staff—we all take part in one of the most beautiful and meaningful academic traditions. We are players in a bit of theater rooted in the universities of the Middle Ages, apparently very drafty universities, which is why we are all robed like monks. Actually, most monks gave up this dress long ago, but we academics do cling to our customs.

The inaugural ceremony recognizes the distinction and continuity of the scholarly life. In its history, Bryn Mawr has staged an event like this for seven of its eight presidents—three of whom are here today!

Eight presidents in 123 years is not a lot of job turnover. My predecessors have clearly treasured—and held on to—this role. I intend to invest my tenure with the same devotion.

Since my arrival at Bryn Mawr on July 1, I've wanted to get to know the College by walking every path and exploring every building on this beautiful campus. What a pleasure these explorations have been!

During one tour, I climbed a splendid circular staircase tucked into a third-floor corner of Taylor Hall. As I ascended its spiraling wrought iron steps, I took turn after turn until finally reaching the very top of Taylor. In every direction, the view was magical. Here were splendid stone buildings, rolling green lawns, and tree-shaded paths, a vibrant campus beloved by generations of students and sustained by devoted alumnae/i. And in the distance, the exciting, challenging, ever-changing city beyond.

From that vantage point, I felt the sweep of Bryn Mawr history and I saw its promise. This is a place to honor and to cherish. This is a place with a proud past now facing a future rich with possibility.

> IN THIS GENERATION, GLOBALIZATION WILL PROFOUNDLY ALTER THE LANDSCAPE OF HIGHER EDUCATION. BRYN MAWR STANDS POISED AND WELL POSITIONED TO LEAD AND TO BENEFIT FROM THIS EVOLUTION.

Today, I'd like to begin a conversation about that future—to contemplate where Bryn Mawr, born in the nineteenth century, developed with distinction in the twentieth, might venture in the twenty-first. Together, I wish us to consider our responsibilities to the liberal arts education of women, to graduate education and productive research, and to civic and global engagement.

Let me be clear: I offer no "to do" list of specific projects. Instead, I'd like to ignite a few sparks that start us thinking about the history we will write together.

It is an honor and a privilege to walk in the footsteps of the powerful, even heroic, women and men of Bryn Mawr. When Joseph Taylor, James Rhoads, and M. Carey Thomas set the college on its bold, historic path, the right of women to an equal—to say nothing of an exceptional—education was a revolutionary concept.

They assembled a stellar faculty fully committed to academic rigor. Florence Bascom came to Bryn Mawr from Johns Hopkins, where she had to sit behind a screen to pursue her own graduate studies. She endured that indignity, became the first woman to hold a PhD in geology, and on this campus educated a generation of geologists.

Then as now, extraordinary faculty attracted exceptional students. Emily Balch, an inveterate organizer and member of the first graduating class, went on to found the Women's International League for Peace and Freedom. She entrusted her Nobel Peace Prize to her alma mater, and recently, as part of my continuing campus exploration, I held that prize in my hands.

In 1889 Umeko Tsuda left her home in Japan for an education at Bryn Mawr. Inspired by her experience here, she returned to Japan to establish that nation's first private college for women, an institution with which we continue to nurture close ties.

Since those earliest days, Bryn Mawr has never wavered from its founding ideals. Despite challenges, its lantern has stayed lit for generations to follow.

Now our hands lift the lantern. With that responsibility, our vision must be equal to the needs and circumstances of the 21st-century world. We are ready for this task.

Medieval scholars divided the liberal arts into two realms: the trivium and the quadrivium. The trivium embraced foundational skills and methods—grammar, dialectic, and rhetoric. Once mastered, they were the scaffolding, the support of a student's future studies. Those further studies were the quadrivium, the four-part curriculum that encompassed advanced learning.

Let me appropriate that structure to frame some thoughts about challenge and opportunity for Bryn Mawr. I'll use trivium to identify the fundamental values that define us as a women's college in the liberal arts tradition, in other words, our core commitments and abiding concerns. These values—excellence, access, and agency—are the foundation for all of our aspirations.

Excellence was at the heart of the animating vision for Bryn Mawr, and it remains so. This is the nation's pre-eminent undergraduate college for women, dedicated to research and scholarship of the highest order and distinguished by its commitment to outstanding graduate education in select fields. Bryn Mawr stands in the top 10 of all colleges and universities in the number of its graduates who earn a PhD. In a recent analysis of names listed in Who's Who, Bryn Mawr ranked 14th of the best 225 universities and colleges in the proportion of graduates listed—the only women's college in the top 20.

Access to excellence was the reason Bryn Mawr was born. From its earliest days, this College has sought to offer the most rigorous education to those who were otherwise excluded from the best undergraduate colleges and the most challenging graduate programs. With each successive generation, the College has expanded this originating mandate as it seeks to enroll the most qualified women from all parts of this country and throughout the world. A recent survey of highly selective liberal arts colleges placed Bryn Mawr among the top 5 in terms of its socioeconomic diversity.

Our third core value is agency. We not only educate our graduates to become engaged citizens of the world but we as an institution act as a force for social justice and social change. With its founding in 1915, the Graduate School for Social Work and Social Research oriented Bryn Mawr toward an ethos of engagement. Subsequent programs reinforced this orientation, as have more recent initiatives that connect us to the people and the needs of our surrounding communities and of the city of Philadelphia.

So with excellence, access, and agency as our core commitments, where can they be effectively deployed to achieve 21st-century goals?

Conjuring up the quadrivium, let me suggest four points of challenge and opportunity.

The first is foremost: We must continually strengthen the educational experience for every Bryn Mawr student. This means recruiting and retaining the best scholar teachers, fostering a culture of intense intellectual activity, and sustaining a community whose connections and friendships will nourish a lifetime.

To this task we bring a legacy of remarkable accomplishment and a willingness to think creatively about how best to teach and learn in the 21st century. Right now faculty members are asking these questions as they tackle an extensive rethinking of our curriculum.

We have a national reputation for science and math education. Our students major in these fields at four times the rate of undergraduates nationwide. We can build on this distinction to create the most innovative science and math programs in the country.

Many prominent scholars and practitioners of the 20th century were alumnae/i of our Graduate School of Arts and Sciences and

Graduate School of Social Work and Social Research. We can honor their impact by exploiting the advantage of our small size. We can encourage close and careful graduate mentoring. And we can enhance our emphasis on undergraduate research through better integration of the strengths of all three schools.

We face a second challenge and opportunity—the creation and re-creation of community, on this campus and beyond. Bryn Mawr is blessed with generations of devoted alumnae/i whose dedication to the College is boundless. We are the proud heirs to a history of deliberative community formation and governance.

Yet we can do more to energize and enhance the connections of students, faculty, parents, and alumnae/i; we can do more to inspire community that spans generations, religions, cultures, and life experiences.

We can do more to assure that our community offers students opportunities for leadership in which they can forge the skills and the spirit needed to live responsibly, ethically, and reflectively in a fast-changing world.

Essential to our commitment to community is our aspiration and obligation to reflect the growing demographic diversity of this country. In the last 15 years, Bryn Mawr has been notably intentional about diversity in its student body and faculty, but more remains to be done to enrich our community and extend the opportunity for a Bryn Mawr education.

One woman in six in this year's freshman class is the first in her family to attend college. Through a foundation partnership we enroll 10 students each year from Boston public schools—students who might otherwise be overlooked in the admissions process of selective colleges.

Such initiatives are part of Bryn Mawr's DNA. But they entail significant cost. To meet student need, we have increased our financial aid budget by 50 percent over the last decade. Today about three quarters of our undergraduates receive some form of financial assistance.

Our third challenge and opportunity centers upon our bi-college and tri-college connections. Bryn Mawr's history has been interwoven with the history of Haverford and Swarthmore from its founding moments. These three Quaker colleges stand at the pinnacle of liberal arts excellence. Together the three are much more than the sum of their parts. Together they make smallness a virtue, not a constraint.

But here, too, we can do more to strengthen existing connections and to forge new ones for our mutual betterment. Close access to the many fine schools in this area, especially the University of Pennsylvania, can further advance this collaboration.

Our fourth challenge and opportunity takes a confident stride into the 21st century. In this generation, globalization will profoundly alter the landscape of higher education. Bryn Mawr stands poised and well positioned to lead and to benefit from this evolution. We have long had an international orientation; our faculty research has a global range; our students come from all parts of the world and study in all parts of the world. We are ready to open our doors wide and to welcome, in the words of one of our greatest leaders, the "world house."

In 1964 Dr. Martin Luther King, Jr., delivered a powerful, prescient Nobel Lecture. Speaking of what he called "the great new problem of mankind," he said, "We have inherited a big house, a great 'world house' in which we have to live together—black and white, Easterners and Westerners, Gentiles and Jews, Catholics and Protestants, Moslem and Hindu, a family unduly separated in ideas, culture, and interests who, because we can never again live without each other, must learn, somehow, in this one big world, to live with each other."

Taking our lead from Dr. King, higher education must seize this threshold moment. We must prepare our students to inhabit this world house, to be genuine world citizens, released from boundaries and barriers that constrain our thinking.

Our student body must itself reflect the world. In the class of 2012, an unprecedented number of international students bring to our community the perspectives and experiences of 37 nations. In this class, we see our future.

Technology is providing us with tools that make distance as irrelevant as distinctions of class or color. Telepresence equipment, collaborative teaching, robust relationships with other institutions around the world, and international campuses are realms for us to explore.

One hundred twenty-three years ago, Bryn Mawr blew the doors off American higher education when it tapped women's hunger for academic opportunity. Today, that hunger is growing in countries around the world where women encounter few options and many obstacles.

About 12 years ago, I took a sabbatical from my faculty position at the University of Toronto and spent a semester as a student in a Muslim university. I did this for several reasons. As a scholar of Islamic studies, I wanted the experience of living for an extended period in a Muslim country; as an Arabist, I wanted prolonged exposure to the language; as a specialist in the Qur'an, I wanted to see how the Qur'an was taught in a graduate school of religion.

What came as a surprise was the reality of being a woman in that environment. I had to sit in the back of the room. I had to huddle with the few other female students and strain to hear the professor conversing almost exclusively with the male students in the front rows.

A few years later I visited another university in the Middle East. At one point, my host proudly showed me the newly renovated and refurbished university library—for men. At my request, he directed me to the women's section of the library. The contrast was stark—and disheartening.

Our world is ill-served by an asymmetry of educational access. We need all our best minds to solve the great needs of this planet: ending poverty, expanding health care, sustaining the environment. Here is where Bryn Mawr has the experience, the enthusiasm, and the heart to lead the way.

As we reaffirm our foundational trivium of excellence, access, and agency, as we embrace the quadrivium challenges of enriching an outstanding educational experience, nurturing a close and caring community, enhancing the advantages of our tri-college consortium, and embracing the adventure of global education, we light a lantern whose glorious glow will radiate far beyond this well-loved hill.

Let me conclude with the image of another lantern, an image drawn from one of the Qur'an's most beautiful verses:

> God is the Light of the heavens and the earth;
> The likeness of His Light is as a niche;
> And within it a lamp: the lamp enclosed in glass;
> The glass as it were a glittering star;
> Lit from a blessed tree;
> An olive, neither of the East nor of the West;
> Whose oil is near luminous, though no fire touched it;
> Light upon Light; God guides to His Light whom He will.

Yes, I am fortunate to arrive at this exciting, important, defining moment for Bryn Mawr. There is much to be done and I relish the chance to work with this extraordinary community.

Reprinted from http://www.brynmawr.edu/president/Inauguration.html.

Above: Presidential inauguration of Jane McAuliffe, October 4, 2008, top to bottom: Arlene Gibson, class of 1965 and trustee (left), and Sally Hoover Zeckhauser, class of 1964 and chair of the board of trustees (right); bagpipers on Merion Green

Page 379: McAuliffe with her granddaughters Elena deGuzman (left) and Georgia McAuliffe (right). Photographs by Paola Nogueras

MEETING MAWRTERS

President of the College Jane McAuliffe has been getting acquainted with alumnae/i and parents across the United States and around the world. In 2009, she visited 11 cities, from Seattle to Istanbul. In January 2010, she traveled to Singapore, Hong Kong, and Tokyo, meeting with alumnae groups and with presidents and other senior leaders at Nanyang Technical University, The Chinese University of Hong Kong, and Tsuda College. She returned to Bryn Mawr by way of Hawaii to attend an alumnae/i and parent event in Honolulu. In the spring and summer she will attend receptions in Philadelphia; Fairfield County, Connecticut; Boulder, Colorado; and St. Louis, Missouri.

Reprinted from the *Bryn Mawr Alumnae Bulletin*, February 2010.

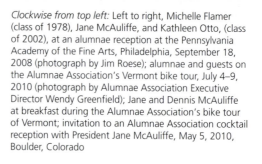

Clockwise from top left: Left to right, Michelle Flamer (class of 1978), Jane McAuliffe, and Kathleen Otto, (class of 2002), at an alumnae reception at the Pennsylvania Academy of the Fine Arts, Philadelphia, September 18, 2008 (photograph by Jim Roese); alumnae and guests on the Alumnae Association's Vermont bike tour, July 4–9, 2010 (photograph by Alumnae Association Executive Director Wendy Greenfield); Jane and Dennis McAuliffe at breakfast during the Alumnae Association's bike tour of Vermont; invitation to an Alumnae Association cocktail reception with President Jane McAuliffe, May 5, 2010, Boulder, Colorado

GLOBAL OUTREACH

BRYN MAWR JOINS DISCUSSIONS OF MULTILATERALISM

TWELVE Bryn Mawr students joined President of the College Jane McAuliffe in March for a special invitation-only panel discussion at New York University featuring British Prime Minister Gordon Brown, former Secretary of State Madeleine Albright, and two-time Federal Reserve Chairman Paul Volcker, chair of President Barack Obama's Economic Recovery Advisory Board.

The invitation to attend the event on multilateralism in the 21st century came about as a result of McAuliffe's participation in the U.K./U.S. Study Group on Higher Education and Collaboration in Global Context, a small group of higher-education leaders from the United States and the United Kingdom formed at the request of Prime Minister Brown, who is deeply interested in the current state and future potential of U.S./U.K. college and university collaboration.

After the forum, McAuliffe, Princeton President Shirley Tilghman, NYU President John Sexton, and the two other U.S. members of the U.S./U.K. Study Group—Association of American Universities President Bob Berdahl and American Council on Education President Molly Corbett Broad—met privately with their U.K. colleagues and Brown, to whom the group had given a final report in January.

"At this point the dissemination and further discussion of our report is in the Prime Minister's hands. I don't know if he will convene the study group again, but I am very grateful for the experience that this endeavor provided," said McAuliffe. "It's been absolutely fascinating to participate in a think tank with colleagues who have given so much thought to the globalization of higher education."

Earlier this year, McAuliffe was elected to the Council on Foreign Relations, the nation's preeminent nongovernmental, nonpartisan think tank on foreign affairs.

Reprinted from the *Bryn Mawr Alumnae Bulletin*, May 2009.

Right: Jane and Dennis McAuliffe (center, right and left) at the Chinese University of Hong Kong, with Lawrence Lau, Vice-Chancellor of the university (third from right); and Sir James Alexander Mirrlees, master of the university's Morningside College and Nobel Laureate in economics (second from right), January 2010

In this century, globalization is going to be one of the most important ways in which we think about higher education, and we need to focus on how Bryn Mawr can contribute to and take advantage of that new direction. Bryn Mawr has long had an international presence and outlook: Many of our students study abroad; we recruit students and faculty from around the world; faculty have research connections with colleagues across the globe. Building on this strong record of international activity, is there more that we can do to establish a Bryn Mawr presence in other parts of the world? Are there forms of sophisticated telecommunications we can adopt to increase our global connectivity?

—Jane McAuliffe, reprinted from "The Inauguration of Jane Dammen McAuliffe as the Eighth President of Bryn Mawr College," *Bryn Mawr Alumnae Bulletin*, November 2008

NICK KRISTOF AT BRYN MAWR: "WOMEN . . . AREN'T THE PROBLEM. THEY'RE THE SOLUTION"

Amanda Kennedy, Class of 2013

TWO-TIME PULITZER PRIZE WINNING *New York Times* journalist Nicholas Kristof closed the Heritage and Hope Conference in Goodhart Auditorium with heartening remarks concerning women's international plight.

Kristof has seen firsthand and written about the injustices faced by women. He shed light upon crimes committed against women across the globe—human trafficking, mistreatment of pregnant women, the denial of education for young girls, to name a few—and while help has been offered through philanthropic efforts, the initiative is far from finished.

"Women and girls aren't the problem," he said. "They're the solution."

Microfinance initiatives, providing funding and resources for the education of girls, and improving health care internationally are steppingstones to a brighter future for women, ways in which they not only can access better care for themselves but also can become leaders, Kristof said.

He and wife Sheryl WuDunn authored the book *Half the Sky*, published in June, to decry injustice against women, and to call for men and women alike to do something about it. Kristof drew inspiration from the Chinese proverb, "Women hold up half the sky," for both the book's title and content.

Kristof told the story of a young woman from Uganda named Beatrice Biira, whom he profiled in a 2008 *New York Times* column. Her parents could not afford schooling for her, but a Connecticut church had purchased six goats through Heifer International, one of which was donated to the family. The goat then gave birth to twins.

Profit from the goats' milk provided the opportunity for Beatrice to attend school in Uganda, Kristof said. The bright young woman continued her education at a prep school in Massachusetts and eventually earned her bachelor's degree from Connecticut College.

"[You] think these issues are depressing, but at the same time you see stories of unbelievable inspiration," Kristof said. "You also see people expressing humanity by at times risking their lives."

Kristof recounted another story in which he bought two girls from their Cambodian brothels in 2004 and took them back to their villages to set up their own small businesses.

"What I think I found most wrenching about that experience was that when I bought them, I got receipts," he said. "I essentially gained title [of human beings]."

Before the journalist set foot in Goodhart to speak to conference attendees, he had lunch with President Jane McAuliffe and several Bryn Mawr students whose experiences—through internships, student organizations, and research opportunities—pertained to global women's issues.

"I sure had a lot to learn from them," Kristof said.

Sara Alcid '11 was selected to have lunch with Kristof. She has experience working in all-female orphanages in Morocco, Costa Rica, and Thailand, where she took care of children and implemented programs that aimed to prevent teenage orphans from becoming sexual slaves.

Alcid was so inspired by Kristof's work that she began Fem-Co., a new club on campus that raises awareness for reproductive rights.

"Due to my great respect for him, I was both excited and nervous to meet him," she said in an e-mail. "He was incredibly personable and sincerely interested in hearing about our work and research concerning maternal mortality, reproductive rights, girls' education, and women's empowerment."

Kristof signed Alcid's copy of *Half the Sky* with the words, "You hold up 2/3 of the sky."

Kristof's own experience studying Arabic abroad in Cairo helped him to gain new insights on cultural perspectives. That experience and many others have shown him a "connection to something larger than ourselves that gives us a sense of meaning in the world and a sense of fulfillment," he said.

The journalist hoped that audience members would walk away from his speech at the end of the Heritage and Hope Conference with the desire to better women's conditions across the globe. Kristof said, "The fact that we are all in this room means that we truly have won the lottery of life, and winning the lottery [means] that we do have responsibility to discharge, as well."

Reprinted from the *Bi-College News* (Bryn Mawr-Haverford), September 28, 2010.

INTERACTIVE MAP SHOWS GLOBAL REACH OF BRYN MAWR FACULTY RESEARCH, WITH MORE TO COME

TODAY, Bryn Mawr College is launching "Bryn Mawr in the World," an interactive map designed to give visitors to the College's website a quickly comprehensible, visual representation of the College's global reach, with links to further information about Bryn Mawr's international connections.

The version of the map being released today focuses on faculty research, highlighting several faculty members' scholarship abroad. The featured faculty members will rotate on a regular basis. Additional information about the international reach of students and alumnae of the College will be added soon.

The information about faculty research was collected by the Provost's Office with help from Associate Professor of Classical and Near Eastern Archaeology Peter Magee, who serves as the special assistant to the president for international educational initiatives. It is being kept in a database administered by the Provost's Office.

"The map represents the true global reach of Bryn Mawr College in terms of faculty research and teaching," says Magee. "Future additions will highlight the locations of alumnae, study-abroad opportunities, international internships, and the origins of our students.

The latter is especially worth celebrating this year, in which over a quarter of our incoming class is international students."

The map is studded with thumbnail photos of seventeen faculty members; each professor is visually linked to the country where he or she has a significant research project or association. Moving the cursor over a photo reveals the name of the professor and the country where she or he has a research connection; clicking on it opens a box with a brief description of the research interest, with a link to the faculty member's webpage. A more comprehensive list of research connections, organized by geographic region, is available in a downloadable PDF.

Reprinted from *Bryn Mawr Now*, September 9, 2010.

Below: Bryn Mawr in the World, an interactive website launched in September 2010 for users who want to explore the college's global outreach, including faculty research abroad. Website design by iFactory (Boston)

Opposite: New York Times reporter Nicholas Kristof with Jane McAuliffe and students, at a luncheon during the Heritage and Hope: Women's Education in a Global Context conference, Pen-y-Groes, September 25, 2010. Kristoff delivered one of the conference's keynote addresses.

RECONNECTIONS

RE-ENGAGE: BLACK ALUMNAE/I CONFERENCE
Jan Trembley, Class of 1975

GATHERING FOR THE FIRST Black alumnae/i conference at the College in more than a decade, 75 alumnae/i from the classes of 1959 to 2007 and from the Graduate School of Social Work and Social Research spent an exuberant weekend reconnecting with the campus community, renewing old bonds, and relating shared experiences.

Alumnae/i attended classes and workshops, held discussions with students and administrators about diversity initiatives, networked, and shared memories over meals. At the plenary session ending the weekend, they resolved to take an agenda to the U.S. president- and vice president-elect and to Congress stating their concerns as Black alumnae/i of Bryn Mawr College. Lobbyist Anita R. Estell, who held a workshop during the conference, will provide training for creating this agenda. Estell represents many organizations, including the Johnnetta B. Cole Global Diversity and Inclusion Institute, the National Women's History Museum, the African American Women's Fund Project, the Congressional Black Caucus Foundation, the Rosa and Raymond Parks Institute, the Mark Twain Museum, and the National Association of Social Workers.

Linda Hill '77, a trustee of the College and co-chair of the conference, told alumnae, "Anita said that the Black community works to get out the vote but doesn't necessarily hold elected officials accountable, and that Black women as a group have not made what matters to them obvious to the candidates of both parties. It is our right as citizens to do this." The group listed possible agenda items and root cause issues. A committee has been formed to prepare a report. "What issues do we need to be educating ourselves about?" asked Hill. "What's the unique proposition about us as Bryn Mawr alumnae?"

Alumnae/i decided to pursue three other initiatives: establishing a national affinity group of Bryn Mawr Black alumnae/i; raising a minimum of $25,000 by May 2010 to fund summer internships for students who are members of Sisterhood or BACaSO (Bryn Mawr African and Caribbean Student Organization); and supporting career and professional development for students and alumnae. Approximately $6,900 has been raised, enough to fund two internships in the summer of 2009.

The weekend began with classroom visits; a tour of the renovated student activities village on Roberts Road; and an hour-long session with students, faculty, and staff about diversity issues on campus. Assistant Professor of Social Work Kevin J. Robinson spoke about his community-based participatory research and partnering with faith-based organizations to effect change. Luvon Roberson '74 conducted a tea sitting and discussion about Anarcha, Betsy, Lucy, and numerous other unnamed slave women who underwent surgery without anesthesia performed by Dr. J. Marion Sims, the father of modern gynecology. Their suffering and pain led to the invention of today's surgical and gynecologic tools and procedures. Roberson is the founder of the High Tea Sisters, whose members study and discuss over signature brews how Black women in history contributed to many advances in this country in the face of slavery and emancipation.

Alumnae/i also met President of the College Jane McAuliffe, who moderated a panel discussion of current students and gave an address at the celebratory dinner. McAuliffe recalled participating in civil rights activities as a college student in Washington, D.C., and attending meetings of the SNCC, the Student Non-violent Coordinating Committee. "I was there on the mall for the March on Washington when Martin Luther King gave his address, which was one of the most formative things that I've heard in my life," McAuliffe recalled.

When she began graduate work in religion a decade later and became interested in the differences and similarities between Islam and Christianity, she saw "another way in which we could begin to achieve some kind of understanding between groups of people that had long been separated.

"I've been impressed at how intentional the efforts at community building are at Bryn Mawr, through the admissions process, diversity leadership, and our students. My work at Georgetown was largely in creating and enhancing the diversity of our faculty. Here I know that I can be involved in much broader conversations."

During panel discussions about diversity at Bryn Mawr as a "work in progress," deans of the undergraduate College and of the Graduate School of Social Work and Social Research, the provost, and members of the College's Diversity Leadership Group talked about recruitment and retention on the undergraduate and graduate levels, faculty, and student life today.

"Back in the 1920s, we had the first Black student at Bryn Mawr," said cochair Willa Seldon '82. "She had a challenging experience. She left after a week and asked that her name be removed from the rolls, so we know very little about her. Our first Black graduate was Enid Cook in 1931, and our second Lillian Russell in 1934. It's appropriate that we begin today with our most important constituents on campus, the students."

Panelists were seniors Teyvonia Thomas, a physics major with a minor in computer science from Montego Bay, Jamaica; Rachel Awkward, a sociology major and education minor from Baltimore, Maryland; Josephine Karanjahi, a growth and structure of cities major with a minor in economics, from Nairobi, Kenya; and Elise Nelson, a growth and structure of cities major from Columbus, Ohio.

Opposite: Chevon Deputy, class of 2005, at the Black Alumnae/i Conference, October 24–26, 2008

They told alumnae why they had chosen to attend Bryn Mawr, how their courses of study had evolved, and about the work of African American, African, and Caribbean students to understand their differences. "Before we arrived, we did not have the identity of 'Black students on campus,'" said Karanjahi. "We were from 'this region or that region.' Especially being international, your attitude is 'I'm just here to study.' When we walk out of the group, we're all Black, but we're at such different levels." Nelson said, "I think one of the differences is how you react to the greater white society. African American women process things differently than women coming from other places, and that's the biggest struggle."

During the weekend, students and administrators referred to the turning point of a racially-charged party invitation that was posted by Bryn Mawr students on Facebook in the spring of 2007. The incident prompted a teach-in organized by faculty, and the town meeting called by students was attended by nearly 300 people despite driving snow and rain. One result was the creation of a successful social justice pilot program, now in its second year. Small groups of students meet on a regular basis to talk about issues; the discussions are facilitated by peers, upperclasswomen, faculty, and staff.

Black Faculty and Staff Honored

Four service awards were given to honor the historical legacy and accomplishments of Black faculty and staff, and special recognition was given to longtime members of the Housekeeping Staff.

Honorees were Florence Goff, the College's associate chief information officer and Equal Opportunity Officer; Ruth Mayden, M.S.S. '70, director of the Program for Families with Young Children at the Annie E. Casey Foundation; Dolores Norton, M.S.S. '60 and Ph.D. '69, trustee emeritus of the College and Samuel Deutsch Professor in the School of Social Service Administration (SSA) at the University of Chicago; and sociology professor Robert Washington.

Beginning in December 2006, gatherings were held for Black alumnae in Washington, Philadelphia, New York, Boston, and San Francisco to gather ideas for the conference. "I am filled with joy that this dream could come true," said Program Chair Nia Turner '05, who attended the gatherings. "Networking is important for all Mawrters, but this weekend we have so many jewels and we each have something valuable to contribute, and the students can benefit from hearing about your work experiences and how you handled situations on campus."

The planning committee included 38 alumnae, Professor of Social Work and Diversity Leadership Group Chair Raymond Albert, and Alumnae Association Assistant Director Cynthia Washington and Executive Director Wendy M. Greenfield.

"I am leaving today feeling very encouraged, empowered, and enlightened," wrote Andrea Roche Fray '05.

Reprinted from the *Bryn Mawr Alumnae Bulletin*, November 2008.

MURAL ARTS FOUNDER HONORED

MURAL ARTS DIRECTOR JANE GOLDEN AWARDED HEPBURN MEDAL

"I'M MIKE NUTTER and I work for Jane Golden," Philadelphia's mayor said on Saturday night.

But it wasn't work that brought Nutter and hundreds of others to the National Constitution Center that evening.

Nutter, Bryn Mawr President Jane McAuliffe, and a host of luminaries were on hand to honor Golden, executive director of the Philadelphia Mural Arts Program, with the 2009 Katharine Hepburn Medal in recognition of her tireless efforts to build community through public art, engage at-risk youth, beautify the city, and work toward social justice.

"Jane exemplifies the type of purposeful life that shapes the Hepburn Center's mission," McAuliffe said in presenting the award. "Where others see walls, graffiti, scribbled words of violence, and the marks of crime, she sees pure potential."

The Katharine Houghton Hepburn Center at Bryn Mawr College is the only organization authorized by the Hepburn estate to commemorate the lives and achievements of iconic screen legend Katharine Hepburn, Bryn Mawr class of 1928, and her mother, Katharine Houghton Hepburn, Bryn Mawr class of 1900, an activist for reproductive rights and women's suffrage.

The Hepburn Medal honors women whose lives and work embody the intelligence, drive, and independence of the four-time Oscar winner. Award recipients are chosen for their commitment and contributions to the Hepburn women's greatest passions—film and theater, civic engagement, and women's health. The award was first given in 2006, in the area of film and theater, to renowned actresses Lauren Bacall and Blythe Danner.

"I am deeply honored to have my work and the work of the Mural Arts Program recognized in the spirit of the great Katharine Hepburn—because Ms. Hepburn was not only a great actor. She was a remarkable woman—years ahead of her time," said Golden in accepting the award.

Lynn Yeakel, director of Drexel University College of Medicine's Institute for Women's Health and Leadership and the Betty A. Cohen Chair of Women's Health, served as master of ceremonies for the event.

Reprinted from Bryn Mawr Now, *February 11, 2009.*

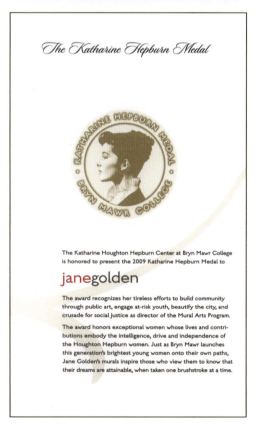

Top (left to right): Philadelphia mayor Michael Nutter; Hepburn medalist Jane Golden, director of the Philadelphia Mural Arts Program; and Jane McAuliffe at the Hepburn Medal award ceremony, National Constitution Center, Philadelphia, February 7, 2009. Photograph by Jim Roese

Bottom: Invitation to the Hepburn Medal ceremony for Jane Golden, February 7, 2009

Opposite: International students from the class of 2013. Photograph by Paola Nogueras

Bryn Mawr Welcomes Its Most Diverse Class Ever

THE 380 INCOMING STUDENTS who arrived on Bryn Mawr's campus on Wednesday, August 26, joined generations of young women who have come from all over the world each year to gather in Goodhart Hall after an arduous morning of hauling and unpacking luggage. But the newly arrived Class of 2013 is "the most international" yet, said President Jane McAuliffe. Twenty-eight foreign countries contributed 21 percent of the incoming class. Dean of Admissions and Financial Aid Jenny Rickard also noted that California, for the first time this year, tied New Jersey as the home of more incoming students than any other state in the Union.

Students of color from the United States make up a record 35 percent of the class. Almost a fifth of the class consists of students who belong to the first generation of their families to attend a four-year college, a figure consistent with Bryn Mawr's top-five ranking in socioeconomic diversity among liberal-arts colleges in the United States.

McAuliffe welcomed the new class, along with 11 transfers, five McBride Scholars (students of nontraditional age), and families and friends of the new students, as the first audience to assemble in the newly renovated Goodhart Hall.

The landmark 1928 building, which serves as the anchor of the College's performing-arts programs, recently underwent a $19 million overhaul that included the replacement of antiquated utility systems, the expansion of the main stage, and the addition of an intimate performance space for teaching and small audiences.

McAuliffe and Rickard were joined on the dais by Dean of the Undergraduate College Karen Tidmarsh; the president was introduced by Rebecca Miller '10. Miller is co-chair of the Customs Committee, which marshals 65 sophomore Customspeople in a five-day, dorm-based welcome and orientation for the new students known as Customs Week. Customspeople continue to serve as mentors and advisers to their first-year hallmates throughout the academic year.

"This is certainly the most international class Bryn Mawr has ever welcomed, and we have long been an international academic institution," McAuliffe said, after reading a list of the 28 countries that contributed students to the new class.

Congratulating both the students and their families on their achievement in being selected to attend Bryn Mawr, McAuliffe noted that in choosing Bryn Mawr, they had "chosen a college with a distinguished history of graduate and undergraduate education and a practice of turning out strong, independent women who have blazed trails in many, many fields.

"Alumnae include the first women presidents of Harvard and the University of Chicago, the founding director of the Congressional Budget Office, a Nobel Peace Prize laureate, seven winners of MacArthur so-called 'genius' awards, pioneers in the treatment of breast cancer and the development of nanotechnology, the woman who is known as the leading screen legend of the 20th century— that'll be on the quiz—founders of banks and founders of rural medical clinics," the president continued.

"And I know that you will follow in these footsteps," McAuliffe predicted, "and a future president of Bryn Mawr will one day be referring to you as she proudly lists alumnae accomplishments."

The president then offered the new scholars some advice: "The greatest gift that you can give yourself in these first months at Bryn Mawr is a spirit of utter openness . . . it's a bit like, I think, the idea of being open to falling in love. You simply cannot predict when a person or an idea or a whole academic field will seize you with the force of a lifelong passion."

Rickard then entertained the crowd with a tongue-in-cheek list of "important facts" about the new class that she claimed were identified by "a very sophisticated software tool." Rickard's list of facts began with "You are all very smart and very impressive women" and ended with the names of two students who celebrated their birthdays on August 26. She led the audience in a rendition of "Happy Birthday" before turning the podium over to Tidmarsh.

"There are only two days in your whole college career in which this many of you and your families are together—this one, the beginning of it all, and commencement," Tidmarsh began. "They are both exciting and happy occasions for Bryn Mawr . . . But while for us these occasions are very pleasant, we know that they are much more complicated for all of you. We, after all, have not been packing and unloading cars for the past several hours, or in some cases, days.

"We are also saying hello, which is much easier than saying good-bye, as you are, even temporarily," she continued. "You are beginning a new phase of your lives—whether as students or parents or siblings or aunts or guardians—and that's exciting but never easy. For one thing, you always leave a lot behind. In your cases, good friends, family, good teachers, faithful dogs, cats, horses, and parrots— all of which we really do hope you've left," she quipped.

She reassured the audience that the new students would soon be more comfortable in their new surroundings—"Not, I hope, too comfortable, though."

Tidmarsh explained that Bryn Mawr's curriculum and system of student self-governance offer students an unusual degree of control over their lives—and a series of sometimes difficult choices. The Dean's Office, she noted, offers students guidance and advice where it is needed, with the aim of fostering independence and allowing students to "run their own lives."

"Making your own decisions is the only way to begin to function independently and confidently in a very complicated world," she averred. "We would like to see you running families and businesses and research centers and countries a few years from now."

Reprinted from Bryn Mawr Now, *August 28, 2009.*

A PLACE TO GROW STRONGER

Top: Architectural rendering of the Schwartz Gymnasium renovation. Courtesy of Buell Kratzer Powell Ltd. (Philadelphia)

Bottom: Jane McAuliffe and students participating in an indoor cycling class during the opening celebration of the renovated Schwartz Gymnasium, September 7, 2010. Photograph by Jay Gorodetzer

Opposite (top): Bryn Mawr lantern alight. Photograph by Amanda Cegielski

Opposite (bottom): McAuliffe and her granddaughters with Bryn Mawr students at the American West–themed Grand May Day, 2010. Photograph by Amanda Cegielski, class of 2009

**SCHWARTZ GYM REOPENING DRAWS CROWD—
AND A PRESIDENTIAL WORKOUT**

BRYN MAWR COLLEGE officially reopened the newly renovated Schwartz Gymnasium Tuesday, September 7, 2010. More than 500 people—students, faculty, and staff—visited the gym to experience the upgrades made possible through the Smart Women Strong Women initiative, which President Jane McAuliffe launched to renew athletic facilities and to highlight the role fitness and wellness play in the daily life of the College community.

"The Smart Women Strong Women project to transform Schwartz Gymnasium was a great success," says Director of Athletics and Physical Education Kathy Tierney. "The innovative layout of the fitness center, with its viewing areas of the pool and gym, supports the many fitness and recreational goals of the College community. The space is filled with natural light, and the energy and spirit in the building is palpable."

To celebrate the re-opening of the gym, the Athletics and Physical Education Department held an open house featuring guided tours of the building and a full schedule of Bryn Mawr Fit Club classes. Students, faculty, and staff enjoyed classes in water aerobics, Zumba, indoor cycling, and yoga.

President Jane McAuliffe took part in the festivities when she joined 15 students, faculty, and staff for an indoor-cycling class. McAuliffe said, "The renovated Schwartz Gymnasium gives Bryn Mawr a state-of-the-art facility for all members of the College community to enjoy. It brings renewed energy to our fitness and athletics programs and makes Schwartz a destination. I encourage everyone to visit and discover the broad range of activities in which one can engage."

Through the Smart Women Strong Women initiative, Schwartz received an exterior face-lift as well as a new roof, state-of-the-art fitness and recreation equipment, and systems updates. Creating more light in the building was a primary goal of the project; spaces are now flooded with natural light and one can see up the hill to Merion Green from the second-floor fitness center. Windows at the rear of the building connect Schwartz to activities happening on Cambrian Row.

Technological improvements to Schwartz include free wireless Internet access, flat-screen televisions, and more than 30 cardiovascular machines designed to accommodate a wide range of personal entertainment devices. The second-floor fitness center boasts three distinct areas: one for cardio and weight machines, a second for classes and group activities, and a third focusing on free weights and functional training.

Reprinted from *Bryn Mawr Now*, September 8, 2010.

TRADITIONS FLOURISH

MAY DAY 2009
Jane McAuliffe

FREQUENTLY during this first year at Bryn Mawr, I've been asked whether I'm having "fun." Usually, I answer with a hearty, "Yes," and enthuse about the students, faculty and staff; the beauty of the campus; the excitement of the intellectual ethos, etc. But today—a day that is definitely devoted to "fun"—I've decided to come clean. The truth is Bryn Mawr College scares the living daylights out of me. This is a truly terrifying place. Let me give you three examples. Within minutes of arriving on campus last summer, a student, calling herself a "Mawrter," walked up to me and asked if I was looking forward to being "helled." Now, it's probably no secret that I'm a religious woman. Words such as *martyr* and *hell* have pretty specific meanings for me, and they are not things I am eager to investigate. So all fall, as Mawrters kept saying they looked forward to "helling" me, I drew only one conclusion—and it wasn't a happy one.

No sooner had I survived that first scare than the second one descended. I was informed, in all seriousness, that previous presidents of this esteemed college mounted horses on May Day. My attitude to large, equine quadrupeds is one of great respect. They have their function and place in the created order of things, and I have mine—and mine is not on top of them. Once, years ago I bowed to the wishes of my husband—just that one time—and stopped at a riding stable for a family outing. After the rest of the family was mounted, they brought out a large beast for me. His name was Storm and, with great trepidation—and awkwardness—I managed to climb on top of him. Storm took one look at the poor pathetic creature he was carrying and promptly walked back into his barn. As the rest of the family merrily trotted off down the trail, I slid off Storm, gingerly backed away from him and then ran for my life. Even getting into a horse-drawn carriage this morning was enough to make me shudder.

After mustering the courage to say, "No, thanks" to the offer of a May Day horse, I was faced with the third serious scare. Each Bryn Mawr president, I was told, traditionally has given a funny speech on May Day. At this point I have to say I reviewed the documentation that was given to me when I accepted the position as President. Throughout my many interviews, my meetings with the search committee and with faculty, students, staff and alumnae, never once were the words *hell*, *horse*, or *funny* mentioned. I suppose these things fall under the heading, "Other duties as assigned." Furthermore, I was to deliver a speech in the spirit of the chosen May Day theme, and this year's theme is the circus. The circus! Could it get any worse?! First and foremost, I am of Norwegian descent and it has been my experience that Norwegians are not funny. In the rhetorical style of Barack Obama, I repeat: "Norwegians are not funny." If you doubt my word, please consult the world's authority on Norwegians, especially Norwegian Americans, Garrison Keillor. Almost weekly on his radio show, *A Prairie Home Companion*, he tells stories about the Minnesota Norwegians. In Keillor's stories they are hardworking and headstrong, cantankerous and crusty, even dour and taciturn but they are never, ever funny. Can you, for example, name one Norwegian comedian—just one? The cause for Norwegian non-funniness has not yet been found, but I have asked the Bryn Mawr Biology Department to investigate this anomaly through intensive research and the sequencing of multiple Norwegian genomes. I expect an answer very soon.

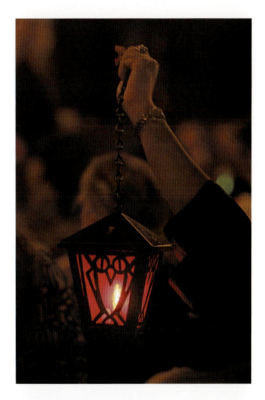

As daunted as I am by the challenge of being funny as I launch this circus, I feel compelled to embrace the tradition. So here's my best effort at a limerick to lead us off:

> Ladies and Gentlemen
> May I have your attention, please!
> As ringmistress of beauteous Bryn Mawr
> In one year I have traveled quite far.
> I know our stone lions are mild, but our
> Mawrters are wild.
> And their triumphs are way above par!

Reprinted from a transcript of the speech given by President Jane McAuliffe, May Day, May 3, 2009.

125th CELEBRATION

BRYN MAWR COLLEGE MARKING 125 YEARS
Kristin E. Holmes

BRYN MAWR College will launch a yearlong celebration of its 125th anniversary this weekend with a reunion of 1,000 alumnae and a renewal of its original mission. Bryn Mawr began "in an era when there were doubts about whether women even had the mental and physical capacity to undertake serious study," said Jane McAuliffe, 66, president of the college.

The school was founded in 1885 with the goal of offering women a more rigorous academic program than had previously been available.

Alumnae include actress Katharine Hepburn; Drew Gilpin Faust, president of Harvard University; and economist Alice Rivlin, former director of the Congressional Budget Office.

Anniversary events began Friday with a reunion, including classes going back to 1940. The highlight will be a women's education conference in September. Also on the bill are lectures, exhibits, and the creation of a mural in West Philadelphia in partnership with the Philadelphia Mural Arts Program.

The anniversary comes at a time when most women's colleges are competing with coeducational institutions, said Leslie Miller-Bernal, coeditor of *Challenged by Co-Education: Women's Colleges Since the 1960s* and a dean at Wells College in Aurora, N.Y., formerly a women's school.

The number of women's colleges in the nation has decreased from about 200 in 1960 to about 50 now. Rosemont College, a Catholic school near Bryn Mawr, began accepting male students last fall in hopes of boosting enrollment and finances.

But the picture is brighter for elite women's schools such as Bryn Mawr, which have long histories, prestigious reputations, and substantial endowments, Miller-Bernal said. Bryn Mawr's incoming class of 378 [students] and the school's current undergraduate enrollment of 1,300 are the largest in its history, McAuliffe said. Undergraduate applications are also setting records, she said.

Reprinted from the *Philadelphia Inquirer*, May 29, 2010.

Above: Jane McAuliffe commencing the 125th festivities, September 23, 2010. Photograph by Peter Tobia

Opposite (top and bottom): Fall convocation community picnic, August 30, 2010. Top (left to right): Sakina Shakur (class of 2013), Naznen Rahme (class of 2013), Caroline Hsu (class of 2013), a visiting Villanova student, and Vanessa Sanchez (class of 2013). Bottom: Bryn Mawr's postbaccalaureate premedical program students. Photographs by Jim Roese

Opposite (center): Bryn Mawr's 125th anniversary logo. Design by GHI Design (Philadelphia)

125 YEARS

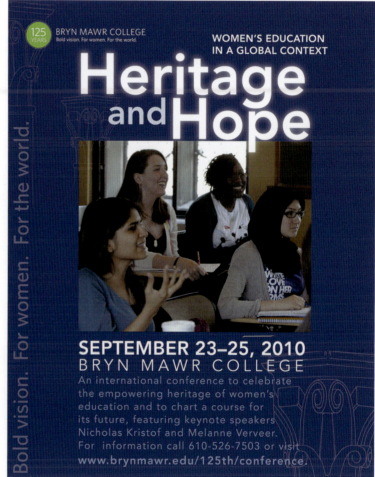

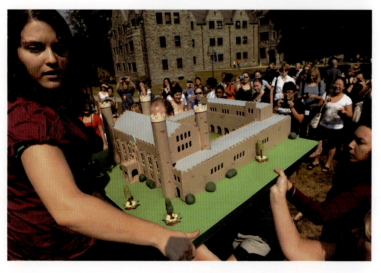

Clockwise from top: Melanie Bowman, class of 2011 (left), and Priyanjali Saxena, class of 2012 (right); poster for Heritage and Hope: Women's Education in a Global Context, an international conference on the past, present, and future of girls' and women's education, Bryn Mawr College, September 23–25, 2010; students Melissa Robinson Schoeller, class of 2012 (left), and Samantha Salazar, class of 2011 (right), carrying the college's 125th anniversary birthday cake in the form of Thomas Library. Photographs by Peter Tobia

Opposite: Catharine Stimpson, class of 1958, addressing Heritage and Hope conference participants during lunch in Thomas Great Hall, September 25, 2010. Photograph by Peter Tobia

HERITAGE AND HOPE
Women's Education in a Global Context

AS PART of Bryn Mawr College's 125th anniversary, the College will host an international conference celebrating the empowering heritage of women's education and charting a course for its future, titled Heritage and Hope: Women's Education in a Global Context.

Happening from September 23–25, 2010, the conference will feature keynote addresses by Nicholas Kristof, Pulitzer Prize-winning *New York Times* reporter and author, with his wife Sheryl WuDunn, of *Half the Sky: Turning Oppression into Opportunity for Women Worldwide*; and Melanne Verveer, United States Ambassador-at-Large for Global Women's Issues.

"As the first women's college to provide graduate and undergraduate education for women, Bryn Mawr is honored to bring together some of the world's brightest and most-respected trailblazers for women's education," says Bryn Mawr President Jane McAuliffe.

During the conference, distinguished international scholars and experts, presidents of women's institutions around the globe, and NGO leaders will examine issues of educational access, equity, and opportunity in secondary schools and universities in the United States and around the world. Conference speakers and participants will also explore how women's colleges, girls' schools, and myriad social and educational initiatives in the U.S. and abroad can advance opportunity for girls and women.

Session topics will include:
Leveling the Academic Playing Field: Strategies for Change; Enhancing Global Networks, a discussion of current and future collaborative connections among women's colleges around the world; and Partnering for Global Justice, an exploration of possible partnerships between schools, colleges, and international NGOs to promote women's rights and educational opportunities.

Reprinted from *Bryn Mawr Now*, April 29, 2010.

BRYN MAWR COLLEGE TO SPONSOR MURAL HIGHLIGHTING ADVANCES IN WOMEN'S EDUCATION AS PART OF ITS 125TH ANNIVERSARY CELEBRATION

AS PART of Bryn Mawr College's 125th anniversary celebration—"Bold Vision. For Women. For the World"—the College is partnering with the Philadelphia Mural Arts Program to create a mural in West Philadelphia highlighting advances in the education of women.

"This project allows us to do two important things in connection with our anniversary," says Bryn Mawr President Jane McAuliffe. "Through our partnership with the City, we're reaching out and contributing to the Greater Philadelphia community in a meaningful way and we're creating a testament to the power of women's education that will last far beyond our year-long celebration."

One of the signature pieces of the 125th Anniversary Celebration, the mural is planned to adorn the Philadelphia District Health Center at 4400 Haverford Avenue and will be painted by Shira Walinsky, with the help of Bryn Mawr students, faculty, staff, and alumnae. Joining the Bryn Mawr community on the project will be members of the surrounding community, including students from nearby Parkway West High School, where Bryn Mawr students serve as classroom assistants to teachers, tutor and mentor individual students, and engage in community-based research projects.

In addition to leading the creation of the mural, Walinsky will join Mural Arts Program Executive Director and 2009 Hepburn Medal recipient Jane Golden to co-teach a course on community mural projects, offered by the Growth and Structure of Cities program.

Members of the College community are meeting with Golden and Walinsky in the next week for "concepting sessions." Painting of the mural is scheduled to begin in the fall. Painting will continue throughout the 125th Anniversary until May 2011, when the mural will be officially unveiled.

As the first U.S. women's college to offer students the chance to pursue a Ph.D., Bryn Mawr College has had since its founding in 1885 a bold vision for women and for the place they should occupy in the world.

Reprinted from *Bryn Mawr Now*, April 23, 2010.

Both pages: Commencement at Bryn Mawr, clockwise from top left: 2008, 1903, 1981, 1985, 1937, 2009, and 1956, center: 1988 (photograph by Lynn Wozniak)

COPYRIGHTS

Page 9: "A Certain Style of 'Quaker Lady' Dress," from *Alma Mater: Design and Experience in the Women's Colleges from Their Nineteenth-Century Beginnings to the 1930s* by Helen Lefkowitz Horowitz © 1984 Helen Lefkowitz Horowitz. Reprinted with permission of the author

Pages 36–38: "Behold They Are Women! Bryn Mawr," from *Alma Mater: Design and Experience in the Women's Colleges from Their Nineteenth-Century Beginnings to the 1930s* by Helen Lefkowitz Horowitz © 1984 Helen Lefkowitz Horowitz. Reprinted with permission of the author

Page 91: "Bryn Mawr Will Allow Students to Smoke, Abolishing 1897 Ban Because Unworkable" © November 24, 1925. The New York Times. All rights reserved. Used by permission and protected by the Copyright Laws of the United States. The printing, copying, redistribution, or retransmission of the Material without express written permission is prohibited.

Page 112: "Women's College Celebrates May Day" used with permission of the Associated Press © 2010. All rights reserved

Page 115: "The Bowling Green: Round the May-Pole" used by permission and protected by the Christopher Morley Estate

Page 123: "New Dean at Bryn Mawr: Eunice Schenck Heads Graduate School, which Gets Own Hall" © March 31, 1929. The New York Times. All rights reserved. Used by permission and protected by the Copyright Laws of the United States. The printing, copying, redistribution, or retransmission of the Material without express written permission is prohibited.

Pages 124–25: "Bryn Mawr Fete Marks 50th Year" © November 2, 1935. The New York Times. All rights reserved. Used by permission and protected by the Copyright Laws of the United States. The printing, copying, redistribution, or retransmission of the Material without express written permission is prohibited.

Pages 127–31: "Bryn Mawr Raises Its Torch: The Gothic Peace of Bryn Mawr's Campus Remains Unshattered by the War" © April 1, 1943. Time, Inc. All rights reserved. Used by permission and protected by the Copyright Laws of the United States. The printing, copying, redistribution, or retransmission of the Material without express written permission is prohibited.

Page 132: "Bryn Mawr Names Dr. McBride Fourth President of the College" © November 29, 1941. The New York Times. All rights reserved. Used by permission and protected by the Copyright Laws of the United States. The printing, copying, redistribution, or retransmission of the Material without express written permission is prohibited.

Page 143: "3 Colleges Share in Unified Program: Bryn Mawr, Swarthmore and Haverford Work Together without Losing Identities" © February 25, 1942. The New York Times. All rights reserved. Used by permission and protected by the Copyright Laws of the United States. The printing, copying, redistribution, or retransmission of the Material without express written permission is prohibited.

Pages 144–47: "Station-Wagon College" © 1949 Saturday Evening Post Society

Pages 163–64: "Higher Education," from *A Life in School: What the Teacher Learned* by Jane Tompkins © 1996 Jane Tompkins. Reprinted with permission from Basic Books, a member of the Perseus Books Group

Page 169: Excerpt from *Where the Girls Are: A Social Guide to Women's Colleges in the East* by Peter Sandman © 1964 The Daily Princetonian. Reprinted with permission of the author

Page 172: "The Renascence of Rugged Individualism" © January 25, 1936 Carl Rose / The New Yorker Collection / www.cartoonbank.com

Page 173: "Have you noticed a very festive table of Bryn Mawr alumnae?" © January 6, 1940 Helen E. Hokinson / The New Yorker Collection / www.cartoonbank.com

Page 174–75: "Call Me Ishmael, or How I Feel about Being Married to a Bryn Mawr Graduate" © 1956 E. B. White. Reprinted with permission of the White Literary LLC

Page 189: "Colleges Oppose U.S. Non-Red Oath" © January 22, 1959. The New York Times. All rights reserved. Used by permission and protected by the Copyright Laws of the United States. The printing, copying, redistribution, or retransmission of the Material without express written permission is prohibited.

Page 210: "Students Fasting over Saigon War" © February 8, 1966. The New York Times. All rights reserved. Used by permission and protected by the Copyright Laws of the United States. The printing, copying, redistribution, or retransmission of the Material without express written permission is prohibited.

Page 234: "Haverford Rejects Coeducation Now; Backs Cooperation" © January 15, 1974. The New York Times. All rights reserved. Used by permission and protected by the Copyright Laws of the United States. The printing, copying, redistribution, or retransmission of the Material without express written permission is prohibited.

Page 239: "Haverford Go Coed? Bryn Mawr Bristles" © October 21, 1976. The New York Times. All rights reserved. Used by permission and protected by the Copyright Laws of the United States. The printing, copying, redistribution, or retransmission of the Material without express written permission is prohibited.

Page 240: "President of Haverford Resigns in Controversy with Bryn Mawr" © January 19, 1977. The New York Times. All rights reserved. Used by permission and protected by the Copyright Laws of the United States. The printing, copying, redistribution, or retransmission of the Material without express written permission is prohibited.

Page 250: "There's No Bryn Mawr Accent" used with permission of Philadelphia Inquirer © 2010. All rights reserved

Page 251: "'Bryn Mawr Walk' Goes Way of High Heels" used with permission of Philadelphia Inquirer © 2010. All rights reserved

Pages 294–95: "Bryn Mawr Puts Women in Their Place: Tradition and Intellect Thrive Together" © September 1986. Newsweek, Inc. All rights reserved. Used by permission and protected by the Copyright Laws of the United States. The printing, copying, redistribution, or retransmission of the Material without express written permission is prohibited.

Page 296: "All-Women Bryn Mawr College Defies Trend" used with permission of the Tennessean, Inc. © 1982. All rights reserved

Page 313: "Bryn Mawr's 'Wellness' Approach to Phys. Ed." © November 30, 1982. Dow Jones & Company, Inc. All rights reserved. Used by permission and protected by the Copyright Laws of the United States. The printing, copying, redistribution, or retransmission of the Material without express written permission is prohibited.

Page 318: "Students Teach a Lesson in Investing" and "Stop-Loss Orders Help Bryn Mawr," from USA Today, a division of Gannett Co., Inc. Reprinted with permission

Page 319: "The Bryn Mawr College Fund Is for Students to Invest" used with permission of Philadelphia Inquirer © 2010. All rights reserved

Page 323: "Goddess Leaves Campus in the Back of a Pickup" © 1996 The Chronicle of Higher Education. Reprinted with permission

Page 325: "Athena or a Rival's President, Bryn Mawr Has Its Lucky Charm" © May 15, 1996. The New York Times. All rights reserved. Used by permission and protected by the Copyright Laws of the United States. The printing, copying, redistribution, or retransmission of the Material without express written permission is prohibited.

Page 325: "Athena Lost Her Head in a Statue Theft Prank" used with permission of Philadelphia Inquirer © 2010. All rights reserved

Page 326: "Disputing the Idea that Women Just Aren't Funny" © April 8, 1990. The New York Times. All rights reserved. Used by permission and protected by the Copyright Laws of the United States. The printing, copying, redistribution, or retransmission of the Material without express written permission is prohibited.

Page 328: "Bryn Mawr College Ends Its Daily Perk" used with permission of Philadelphia Inquirer © 2010. All rights reserved

Page 333: "Pagan Traditions Are Increasing among Students" © December 16, 1990. The New York Times. All rights reserved. Used by permission and protected by the Copyright Laws of the United States. The printing, copying, redistribution, or retransmission of the Material without express written permission is prohibited.

Pages 364–365: "College Students Find Support in Campus 'Posses'" used with permission of the Associated Press © 2010. All rights reserved

Page 392: "Bryn Mawr College Marking 125 Years" used with permission of Philadelphia Inquirer © 2010. All rights reserved